SILENT

CAVALRY

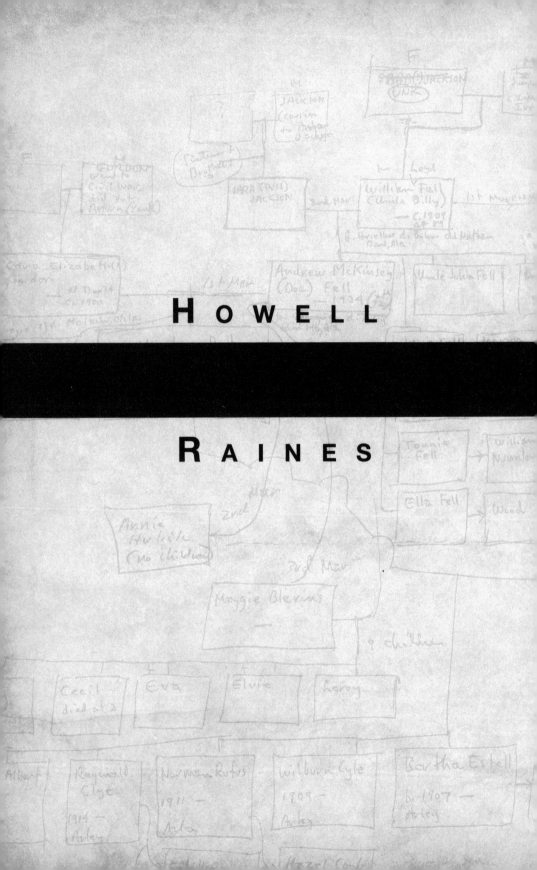

HOWELL

RAINES

How Union Soldiers from Alabama

SILENT

Helped Sherman Burn Atlanta—and Then

CAVALRY

Got Written Out of History

CROWN
NEW YORK

Published in the United States by Crown, an imprint of the Crown
Publishing Group, a division of Penguin Random House LLC, New York.

CROWN and the Crown colophon are registered trademarks
of Penguin Random House LLC.

Library of Congress Cataloging-in-Publication Data
Names: Raines, Howell, author.
Title: Silent cavalry / Howell Raines.
Description: First edition. | New York: Crown, [2023] |
Includes bibliographical references and index.
Identifiers: LCCN 2023021001 (print) | LCCN 2023021002 (ebook) |
ISBN 9780593137758 (hardback) | ISBN 9780593137765 (ebook)
Subjects: LCSH: United States. Army.
Alabama Cavalry Regiment, 1st (1862–1865) |
United States. Army—Southern unionists. | Lost Cause mythology. |
Alabama—History—Civil War, 1861–1865—Regimental histories. |
United States—History—Civil War, 1861–1865—Regimental histories.
Classification: LCC E495.6 1st .R35 2023 (print) | LCC E495.6 1st (ebook) |
DDC 973.7/461—dc23/eng/20230523
LC record available at https://lccn.loc.gov/2023021001
LC ebook record available at https://lccn.loc.gov/2023021002

Printed in the United States of America on acid-free paper

crownpublishing.com

2 4 6 8 9 7 5 3 1

First Edition

Book design by Fritz Metsch
Family tree drawing by Brack Walker

Jacket art: From the Original Painting by Mort Künstler
"War is Hell!" © 2001 Mort Künstler, Inc.

For Krystyna

As many of your readers will perhaps be somewhat surprised to learn that we have Alabama regiments enrolled under the true flag . . . let me say a few words in behalf of the gallant First Alabama, for it has seldom, if ever, received credit for its valuable services . . .

It is needless for me to speak of the intelligence and patriotism of this patriotic body of Alabamians, for their severe denunciation of the rebellion and McClellanism is the best proof of that, but their stainless military record, I deemed worthy of more than passing notice. All honor to the First Alabama Cavalry, and may their lives be spared to reap the rich reward of their unadulterated loyalty.

—*New-York Daily Tribune,*
as reprinted in the Sacramento (CA) *Daily Union,*
December 28, 1864

CONTENTS

CAST OF CHARACTERS

The individuals I've listed below point to the complicated subtexts or mysterious omissions in conventional Civil War histories. Some are familiar names, while others are virtually unknown, their roles surviving in isolated footnotes that give few clues as to the blank or blurry spaces in the war's vast mosaic of unsuspected connections.

THE BATTLEFIELD: UNIONISTS

Charles Christopher Sheats (1839–1904). As Alabama's 1861 secession convention approached, the victory of Chris Sheats—an obscure twenty-one-year-old schoolteacher—in the Winston County delegate election over a Pennsylvania-born slave owner showed the strength of anti-war sentiment in the mountains of north Alabama. Jailed repeatedly for refusing to join the seventy-six-member majority in signing the ordinance of secession, Sheats would become a hero in the Free State of Winston. While on the run, he sparked the clandestine movement that led to the founding of the First Alabama Cavalry, U.S.A.

Probate Judge Tom Pink Curtis (1829–1864). Winston County's most influential Unionist politician. Confederate officials hoped his assassination would end the hill country rebellion. It had the opposite effect.

William Bauch Looney (1829–Disappeared 1870). A leading recruiter for the First Alabama. He owned Looney's Tavern, where Chris Sheats delivered the address that created the "Free State of Winston" slogan.

Major General Don Carlos Buell, U.S.A. (1818–1898). A slave-owning West Pointer, Buell first proposed to Lincoln's War Department the idea of swearing the "Alabama volunteers" into their own regiment.

Major General Grenville M. Dodge, U.S.A. (1831–1916). Dodge was perhaps the most skilled of Lincoln's "political generals." He used First Alabama soldiers on spying missions that earned him the title of "Father of Military Intelligence" in the U.S. Army.

Colonel George E. Spencer, U.S.A. (1836–1893). A New York–born hustler, Spencer left his post as secretary of the Iowa Senate to seek a fortune in contraband cotton in Alabama. As Dodge's adjutant, he shaped the First Alabama into a celebrated force of fighters and guides that caught Sherman's eye.

General William Tecumseh Sherman, U.S.A. (1820–1891) was the charming but ruthless tactician who put the First Alabama out front after convincing Lincoln and Grant that burning Atlanta and capturing Savannah would force the South to surrender.

General Francis P. Blair, U.S.A. (1821–1875). A political sophisticate, Blair originally accused the First Alabama of excessive violence but awarded them the place of honor in the 1864 victory parade in Savannah.

Lt. Colonel Andrew Hickenlooper, U.S.A. (1837–1904). Sherman's mapmaker was escorted by the First Alabama in the dangerous work of probing the Confederate entrenchments in front of Kennesaw Mountain.

Major Henry Hitchcock, U.S.A. (1829–1902). Born in Mobile to the chief justice of the Alabama Supreme Court, he served as Sherman's traveling secretary and in *Marching with Sherman* left an indispensable account of the First Alabama's exploits.

Lieutenant David R. Snelling, U.S.A. (1837–1901) and Lieutenant Francis Tupper, U.S.A. (1839–1899). Raised in Georgia and Illinois respectively, they became Sherman favorites as company commanders of the First Alabama.

Major General Judson "Kill Cavalry" Kilpatrick, U.S.A. (1836–1881). His five thousand cavalrymen shared spear-point duties with the First Alabama, which saved him from humiliation over his infamous "Shirt-tail Skedaddle."

Major General Nathan Bedford Forrest (1821–1877). This butcher of surrendering Black soldiers at the Fort Pillow Massacre was cast as a rebel knight by Lost Cause scholars at Vanderbilt and Sewanee.

Major General Joseph Wheeler (1836–1906). His Alabama Confederate cavalrymen clashed often with their back-home neighbors in the Atlanta campaign. His plantation-owning parents sent "Fighting Joe" to a Connecticut prep school where he became a lifelong friend of J. P. Morgan.

Major General Philip Dale Roddey (1826–1897). Known as the "Defender of North Alabama," Roddey conspired with his Union counterpart, Colonel George E. Spencer of the First Alabama, in selling captured cotton.

Governor John Gill Shorter (1818–1872) and Governor Thomas H. Watts (1819–1892). Under their hard-war policies, these Alabama governors were responsible for, respectively, the jailing of Chris Sheats and the guerilla murder of Tom Pink Curtis.

Andrew Kaeiser (1799–1864). A Pennsylvania-born slave owner, he fingered Winston Unionists for Rebel assassination squads and was, in turn, killed by the surviving brothers of Tom Pink Curtis.

FAMILY

Hiram Howell Raines (1872–1914) and Martha Jane Best Raines (1871–1967). The author's paternal grandparents, this duo kept alive the story of their pro-Confederate neighbors, "those damn Democrats."

Robert Cyle Walker (1881–1972) and Martha Loudella Fell Walker (1888–1990). The author's maternal grandparents, Robert and "Della" were Winston County Republicans who traced their political lineage to a short-lived biracial populist party known as the Jeffersonian Democrats. Later, Robert held appointments as justice of the peace and postmaster in Alabama's only Republican county.

Gradystein Williams Hutchinson (1934-2023). Hutchinson was the Raines family's Black housekeeper who helped the author navigate Alabama's racist culture and educational policies. She was one of the rare Black travelers to Winston County in the 1950s. After moving north in 2017 to live with her daughter, she died in New York City on June 23, 2023.

Wattie Simeon Raines (1907-2002) and Bertha Estelle Walker Raines (1907-2002). The author's parents, who defied the Dixiecrats in 1948 by voting for the Republican nominee, Thomas Dewey, and who would not allow racist language in their home.

Rev. W. S. "Sim" Best (1875-1957). Best led the Raines and Best families out of the segregated Southern Methodist Church into the Church of God of Anderson, Indiana, because of its progressive racial views; he helped build the camp-meeting tabernacle where the families attended integrated revival services during the Bull Connor era.

THE LOST CAUSE HIGHWAY

William Archibald Dunning (1857-1922). The leading historian of his era, his Dunning School established Columbia University as a mecca for Confederate apologists who dominated academia for the first half of the twentieth century.

W. E. B. Du Bois (1868-1963). Coming face-to-face with Dunning at an American Historical Association gathering in 1909, this pioneering Black scholar debunked Dunning School arguments about racial inferiority, only to see his theories effectively banned from American historiography until the 1960s civil rights movement.

Walter Lynwood Fleming (1874-1932). Dunning's star pupil, Fleming ruled the Nashville/Sewanee Axis of Lost Cause scholarship as dean of the Vanderbilt graduate school and guided its conservative Agrarian scholars to a dominant role in southern intellectual life.

Edward A. Pollard (1832-1872). In 1866, his epic Civil War history gave the Lost Cause movement its name and embedded in the public mind the legend of aristocratic suffering later enshrined in *Gone with the Wind.*

William Alexander Percy (1885-1942). As godfather of the Nashville Agrarians, he wrote the urtext of plantation grandiosity, *Lanterns on the Levee,* and trained his adoptive son Walker Percy as a high-toned chronicler of southern gentility.

Ken Burns (1953-). His 1990 public-television documentary, *The Civil War,* was the most influential account of the conflict in modern times. Since criticized as overly kind to the Confederacy, the film gave only fleeting attention to southern Unionists.

Shelby Foote (1916-2005). In hours of interviews, the folksy southern scholar never mentioned to Burns or the documentarian's collaborators, Ric Burns and Geoffrey C. Ward, his detailed knowledge of north Alabama as a Unionist hotbed.

INTRODUCTION

In 1995, an Emory University graduate student, Margaret M. Storey, came to Birmingham to interview my eighty-eight-year-old father. Storey was interested in a Civil War tale my father had heard as a child from a grandfather who fled to the Union lines to avoid the Confederate draft. Storey, a Tennessean, wanted to earn her PhD by exhuming narratives pointedly ignored or distorted by generations of Alabama historians. Over the course of several years, she knit together hundreds of accounts like my father's into a seminal book, *Loyalty and Loss: Alabama's Unionists in the Civil War and Reconstruction.* The book was one of a cluster of revisionist works about the white Alabamians who fought for the Union and were then hidden from history by a cabal of Lost Cause historians founded at Columbia University in New York City. Those books, published between 2004 and 2019, enabled me to complete my seven-decade personal quest for the full story of the First Alabama Cavalry, U.S.A. These soldiers lived what is to me the most amazingly counterintuitive fact in all of Civil War history: White volunteers from the Alabama hills helped Sherman burn Atlanta. They are truly among "the forgotten men of the Civil War," to use the words of the renowned Lincoln biographer Richard Nelson Current. As nearly as my late father and I could reconstruct the information he gave Storey, his grandfather David H. Best (1848–1926) had traveled with the First Alabama Union Cavalry as a horse tender through the Atlanta campaign, then walked home from South Carolina after Appomattox. I had used scraps of that family lore in a novel, *Whiskey Man,* published in 1977, which is how Storey and I came to be in touch. I was working in the Washington bureau of *The New York Times* when Storey contacted me in the course of tracking down clues about the forgotten legacy of Alabama Unionism, and I taped her interview with my father.

The saga of Alabama Unionism had been hard to reconstruct for a good reason. The First Alabama Union Cavalry was overlooked by mainstream historians for a century and a half. It appears, so far as I can tell, in none of the bestselling popular books on the Civil War. The regiment, which ought to be famous for its role in General William Tecumseh Sherman's "March to the Sea," was not even mentioned in Ken Burns's landmark PBS documentary *The Civil War*, broadcast to national acclaim in 1990. I got on the trail of the First Alabama story in 1961, but I did not exhume it from the official archives. That was the work of professional historians, whose work will be credited in full. This book is about *how* the history of these Alabama Unionists was purposely buried by Lost Cause scholars inspired by one of the most famous historians produced by Columbia University in New York City, William Archibald Dunning (1857–1922). His "Dunning School" ruled the world of Civil War scholarship until the revisionist revolt triggered by the 1960s civil rights movement. Not until 2019 did Columbia unveil a website apologizing for the "white supremacist historiography." This book will show how Dunning used the American Historical Association to repress the truthful interpretations of the pioneering Black scholar W. E. B. Du Bois. It will also show how Dunning's star pupil, Alabama-born Walter Lynwood Fleming (1874–1932), and their friends in the Alabama Department of Archives and History (ADAH) conspired to disappear the First Alabama from the historical record. More broadly, this is a book that explores a truism now accepted throughout the scholarly world. History is not what happened. It is what gets written down in an imperfect, often underhanded process dominated by self-interested political, economic, and cultural authorities. That is why government archives, military records, and libraries are so essential to the revisionist process. Mining them is the only sure way to overcome partisan slant in the written accounts. As Dee Brown, a trained librarian who became a bestselling historian, has said: "The librarians know the secrets, not the historians." But Alabama shows us what happens when those official librarians, the archivists, and state university historians are complicit in ignoring or disappearing historical documents, especially in regard to Alabamians without money or status, whatever their skin color. That is the situation that prevailed, almost monolithically, in my native state until the 1970s and has been significantly altered only in the last twenty-five years.

The remarkable success of this academic cover-up cannot be understood without examining what historians have labeled the "Myth of the Lost Cause." During two important epochs of American life—the Gilded Age of 1870 to 1900 and the Southern Renaissance of the 1920s and 1930s—the Lost Cause mythmakers succeeded in a remarkable feat of propaganda. They upended the Civil War narrative and stood it on its head. The war was not a heroic crusade to abolish slavery; instead, it became a tragic story of undeserved suffering inflicted on a noble, if misguided, class of southern aristocrats on their plantations and the dashing knights of the Rebel army. The epic feat of disinformation reached its apex in *Gone with the Wind,* the 1939 film that probably remains the greatest single influence on the national imagination of a conflict that took 620,000 lives. Through powerful agents at universities in Tennessee and Alabama, William Archibald Dunning, a friend of Teddy Roosevelt's and Woodrow Wilson's and a lion of Manhattan society, provided the underpinnings of the Lost Cause movement. But its inventor was a figure of much less exalted pedigree, the curmudgeonly Confederate general whom Robert E. Lee called "my bad old man," Jubal A. Early (1816–1894). This crabbed figure, operating from a man-cave apartment in Lexington, Virginia, accomplished one of the great public-relations triumphs of all time. He transformed Lee from a traitor in danger of being hung into a patriotic hero admitted to the Hall of Fame for Great Americans in the Bronx on an equal footing with Washington, Jefferson, and Lincoln.*

---

*In 2017, the governor of New York ordered the removal of Lee's bust along with that of Major General Stonewall Jackson, C.S.A., who was also aggrandized by pro-Confederate historians.

The principal Alabamians involved in burying the legacy of the First Alabama Cavalry, U.S.A. were Dunning's friend and Alabama host Thomas McAdory Owen (1866–1920) and his widow, Marie Bankhead Owen (1869–1958), who succeeded him as director of the Alabama Department of Archives and History in 1920. I must be one of the few living Alabamians who, as a child, stood before "Miss Marie" in her "Hall of Flags," the exhibition space of the alabaster building she raised in Montgomery using New Deal funds wheedled from her father's political ally, President Franklin D. Roosevelt. It was 1953, during her halcyon days as the doyenne of Confederate nostalgia in the "Cradle of the Confederacy." To my ten-year-old eyes she looked a great deal like Queen Victoria, and I remember her pointing out bullet holes in the flags "our boys" carried in battle. But that was not the event that pointed me toward my quest for the true story of Winston County as the home of the First Alabama Cavalry. My first clue came from Martha Jane Best Raines (1873–1967). She was the daughter of Dave Best, the boy who ran away to join the Yankees.

OVERLEAF: The shaded counties in mountainous north Alabama provided volunteers for an estimated 75 percent of the First Alabama Cavalry, U.S.A. roster of 2,066. With the exception of Winston County, the exact numbers for most counties can't be determined because of variations in military records as to the enlistees' places of birth, residences, and enlistment. However, census reviews by reliable historians demonstrate that the Free State of Winston was the most fertile area for Union recruiters, providing 239 Union soldiers. A similar review of the 1860 census showed that the Union stronghold next door in Walker County provided an estimated 150 volunteers. See the endnote on page 480 for details.

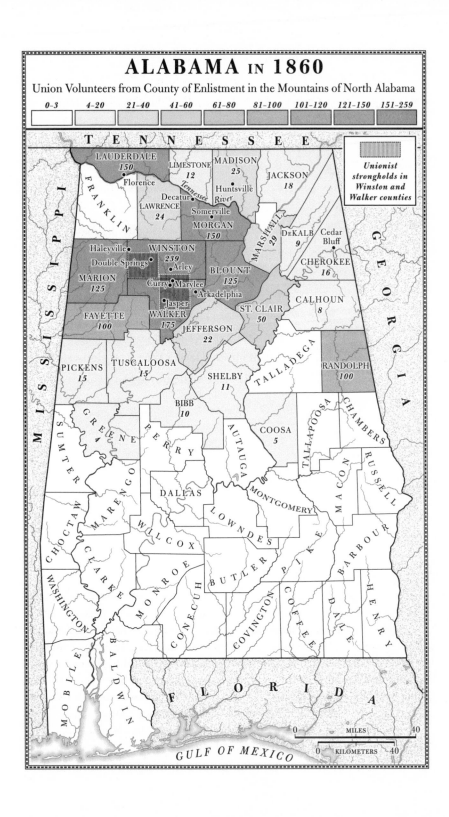

ALABAMA IN 1860

Union Volunteers from County of Enlistment in the Mountains of North Alabama

| 0–3 | 4–20 | 21–40 | 41–60 | 61–80 | 81–100 | 101–120 | 121–150 | 151–259 |

TENNESSEE

MISSISSIPPI

GEORGIA

Unionist strongholds in Winston and Walker counties

LAUDERDALE 150
Florence

FRANKLIN

LIMESTONE 12

MADISON 25
Huntsville

JACKSON 18

Tennessee River

Decatur
LAWRENCE 24
Somerville

MORGAN 150

MARSHALL 29

DeKALB 9
Cedar Bluff

CHEROKEE 16

Haleyville
Double Springs
WINSTON 239
Arley

MARION 125
Curry Marylee
Arkadelphia

BLOUNT 125

CALHOUN 8

Jasper
FAYETTE 100
WALKER 175
JEFFERSON 22

ST. CLAIR 50

RANDOLPH 100

PICKENS 15

TUSCALOOSA 15

SHELBY 11

TALLADEGA

GREENE 4

PERRY

BIBB 10

AUTAUGA

COOSA 5

TALLAPOOSA

CHAMBERS

SUMTER

MARENGO

DALLAS

WILCOX

MONTGOMERY

LOWNDES

MACON

RUSSELL

CHOCTAW

CLARKE

MONROE

CONECUH

BUTLER

PIKE

BARBOUR

WASHINGTON

BALDWIN

COVINGTON

COFFEE

DALE

HENRY

MOBILE

FLORIDA

GULF OF MEXICO

0 MILES 40

0 KILOMETERS 40

Twenty-two counties lying mostly between present-day Birmingham and the Tennessee line had dominant or significant anti-Confederate voting populations that opposed Secession. This was a mountainous region of rough terrain and small farms, whose owners could not afford to buy the slaves needed for large-scale cotton agriculture. Having no economic stake in slavery, they resisted fighting to preserve the "peculiar institution" and sent more than 3,000 residents into the Union army. The flatter lands south of present-day Tuscaloosa and Montgomery contained the vast plantations of the Black Belt and coastal plain, where most of the state's 435,000 slaves lived. This area produced the militant Confederate officials who directed military and guerilla operations against the "disloyal" counties of the north Alabama mountains.

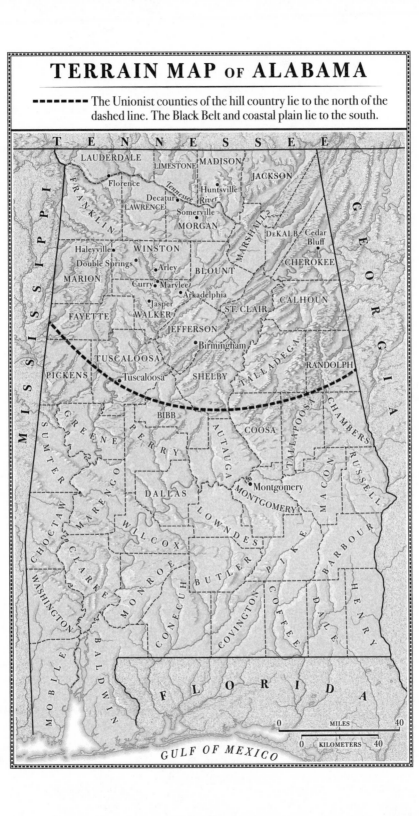

TERRAIN MAP OF ALABAMA

- - - - - - - - The Unionist counties of the hill country lie to the north of the
dashed line. The Black Belt and coastal plain lie to the south.

My grandfather Hiram Howell Raines (1872–1914) seated at a 1912 family reunion. Behind him is his wife, Martha Jane Best Raines (1871–1967). Her memories of their pro-Confederate neighbors were an early clue to our unusual political orientation. The little boy on Hiram's lap is my father, Wattie Simeon Raines (1907–2005), who told me the story of his maternal grandfather, David Houston Best (1848–1926), fleeing the Confederate draft. My aunt Ada Raines, standing behind Martha Jane Best Raines, schooled me as a toddler about life "up in the country."

PART I

Varieties of Racial Education

A FAMILY BEYOND THE REACH OF

CONFEDERATE NOSTALGIA

What Happened to Me at Ma 'n' Ada's

I was born in Birmingham, Alabama, in 1943, when it was America's most segregated city. The process by which I came not to believe what most white children of my era were taught about race and the Civil War was a haphazard affair. As a small child I became fascinated with all things rural and ancient, largely as a consequence of visiting my grandparents' farm in Alabama's poorest county, a throwback redoubt of Appalachian folkways called the "Free State of Winston." It was so nicknamed because anti-Secession farmers in the hill country made a legendary attempt to withdraw from Alabama when the state left the Union in 1861. In 1951, Esther Garrett, a tiny, ferociously flamboyant teacher who called herself "Mama Tadpole," introduced me and the other "Tadpoles" to a glorified version of Alabama history, including the legend of the yellowhammer, our state bird. The black speckles on its tawny breast represented the bullet holes inflicted on Confederate soldiers by the Yankees, Mrs. Garrett explained. The red band on the bird's neck stood for the blood Alabama boys shed for the southern cause, the yellow on its wings for the flashy scarves the soldiers wore on parade. The imagery was intended to school us in that crude, defiant, fatalistic sangfroid much admired in the Heart of Dixie then and now. Paradoxically, she also taught us to affect a high-toned accent for singing the state song. In the chorus, "Alabama, Alabama, we will aye be true to thee," we called our state "ah-la-BAH-ma," the posh enunciation to show we didn't talk like hillbillies.

The next school year, I fell under the tutelage of the more reserved Telulah Rose Love, a stately matron who was in charge of the school library and presided over the reading list on which our report-card marks were based. Miss Love doted on me and my two older siblings as brighter-than-average kids. I was shaken when I laid my list in front of her and she noted with sadness and surprise that I had read only one book in six weeks. It was Mark Twain's difficult miscegenation novel, *Pudd'nhead Wilson,* a didactic condemnation of prejudice based on skin color. To this day I'm amazed that it found its way into a Birmingham public school's library, given that the state and city boards of education strictly policed our reading materials for signs of excessive sympathy for "Negroes," "Communists," or our enemy in the War Between the States. I had plowed through a text that was far beyond my understanding, never quite sure of why one infant was considered Black and another was white. I'm pretty sure Miss Love didn't know what the book was about either. She just wasn't going to give an E for "excellent" to a slacker who could finish only one book a month.

Miss Love's mother was an Owen, and she provided our entrée to the famous woman in Montgomery, the legendary Miss Marie, the widow of Thomas McAdory Owen. Until his untimely death at the age of fifty-three, Tom Owen was a leading figure nationally in higher education. Despite its backwardness in so many fields, Alabama was the first state to establish a state archive to preserve official papers, and as its founder, Dr. Owen hobnobbed with the nation's top scholars at American Historical Association conventions in Manhattan and New Orleans. He had also been the national historian-general of the Sons of Confederate Veterans and an energetic promoter of the Lost Cause school of Civil War scholarship among American historians. Newly widowed in 1920, Miss Marie used her political connections to secure what she called her "meal ticket." Since Marie Bankhead Owen's father was a longtime senator from Alabama, and her brother William B. Bankhead was the

Speaker of the House of Representatives, FDR had given her a New Deal grant to construct the archives building as an imposing alabaster shrine to her late husband. She was named only a week after his death to succeed her husband as director of the Alabama Department of Archives and History.

She reigned there for over three decades as the guardian of his memory and administrator of the gleaming museum of all things touching on the Old South and Confederate glory. Her tigerish reputation among legislators arose from the fact that, in her officerships in the Daughters of the American Revolution, the United Daughters of the Confederacy, the Alabama Library Association, and the Women's Christian Temperance Union, she could flood the halls of the capitol with women supporting any cause she considered sufficiently genteel and conservative. Thanks to the Owen connection, Miss Love was able to lead my fourth-grade class on a field trip to the archives. I remember that Miss Marie radiated the certitude of power and virtue as my classmates and I clustered around her in the high-ceilinged Hall of Flags while she explained the holiness of the bullet holes in the large Rebel battle flag framed on the wall behind her.

Childhood memory is wavery in some spots and crystal clear in others. My mental image of Miss Marie on that long-ago day in Montgomery is of the latter type. She looked to me like pictures I'd seen of Queen Victoria. But I think I must have garbled some of the lore we heard that day about the flag mounted on the wall behind her. For years, I believed Miss Marie had told us this was the flag of truce under which Lee surrendered at Appomattox. But it turned out that the actual fabric surrendered that time was a white dinner napkin carried by Captain Thomas Goode Jones, a Bourbon Democrat and future governor who helped get white supremacy written into Alabama's 1901 constitution. In looking back, I've speculated that Miss Marie may have mentioned that Governor Jones was the father of one of her Montgomery courtiers, a judge and a part-time journalist named Walter B. Jones. The judge, an eccentric who devoted his Sunday newspaper column to Confederate boasting and the defense of segregation, had his fifteen minutes of national fame in 1964. As presiding judge in the landmark libel case *Times v. Sullivan,* he lectured lawyers for my future newspaper on the uses of "white man's justice" in dealing with "racial agitators." Judge Jones also took pen in hand in 1934 to condemn a bestselling book entitled *Stars Fell on Alabama,* whose foreword thanked Marie Bankhead Owen by name.

All these names will recur in my narrative, and I mention them here by way of observing that Alabama is somewhat similar to Flannery O'Connor's Georgia; there everything that rises must converge. The late Alabama folklorist Kathryn Tucker Windham said Alabama is "one big front porch," and life on that porch is more horizontal; everything circles, overlaps, and sooner or later seems to connect. In his 1934 review of *Stars Fell on Alabama,* the book that taught me to see Alabama in its magisterial perversity, the influential *New Yorker* critic Clifton Fadiman dismissively referred to "the native tribes of Alabama," but it was among these presumed primitives that my subversive reflections and my education as a contrarian began. And it's hard to imagine a better family for an inquisitive child to be born to than mine.

Reconstructing my political education at the family hearth is like following a trail of crumbs that can be traced more clearly now than was the case in the beginning, the presidential election year of 1948. On November 2 of that year, I stood at the top of the porch steps of my grandmother's house, a five-year-old watching my parents climb from our maroon Chrysler sedan and start up the sidewalk. They were dressed as if for church or business. My father, a partner with his two brothers in a decade-old business that made store fixtures for the A&P grocery chain, then spreading across Alabama, held aloft two fingers and called out to me and my two sitters, my grandmother and my maiden aunt Ada, "Two for Dewey."

I had no way of knowing how much his words told about Alabama and our family. In political terms, forty-one-year-old Wattie Simeon Raines and his wife, Bertha Estelle Walker Raines, also forty-one, were returning to the family fold by voting for the Republican presidential nominee, Thomas E. Dewey, who would lose to FDR by a landslide. As struggling newlyweds living in small-town Alabama they bolted to the Democrats and voted for FDR in 1932 and in the next two elections. By 1948, with their family of five ensconced in the modern bungalow they built in 1937 in a rising neighborhood in Birmingham, they were city folk who could afford to become Republicans—again. Only a demographer with a good grasp of Alabama's Civil War history could have understood that the Raines and Walker families were, as hereditary white Republicans, *rara avises* in the corrupt Alabama political jungle ruled by yellow dog Democrats.

It was impossible for Alabamians to vote for President Harry S. Truman in Alabama in 1948, because his party's position on the ballot had been assigned to Dixiecrats, the southern Democrats who rebelled against their party's civil rights plank and in a rump convention at the Birmingham Municipal Auditorium in July of that year nominated Governor Strom Thurmond of South Carolina for the presidency. Thurmond won Alabama with almost 80 percent of the vote. Only one of Alabama's sixty-seven counties, the aforementioned Free State of Winston, where my mother was born in 1907, delivered a majority for Dewey, a landslide 64 percent (1,588 votes) to 35 percent (865 votes) for Thurmond. The adjoining county to the south, Walker County, where my father was born in the same year, delivered almost a third of its vote for Dewey.

In both counties, this vestigial Republicanism was a reminder that the Alabama hill country north of Birmingham had been a holdout from the secessionist fever that swept Alabama in 1860. With his shout of "Two for Dewey," my father was assuring his mother that he was returning to the party of her early-dying husband, Hiram Howell Raines (1872–1914), the hero of our family lore for whom I was named, somewhat inexactly as it turned out. Just how inexactly, I was not to discover until my seventy-sixth year, in the research for this book. The mutability of the name I carry—indeed, the byline under which I filed thousands of stories in a thirty-nine-year newspaper career—is a slender thread in the tapestry of life in an up-country South that is far more complex than the monolithic Rebel-crazed South of William Faulkner and Margaret

Mitchell. "Two for Dewey" not only summed up my parents' presidential preference. It also reflected their lifelong practice of always voting against racist white Democrats on the Alabama ballot or—to be more accurate in regard to gubernatorial and congressional races in a one-party state—of always voting for the *least racist* white Democrat.

If the first clue in my political education was delivered in the presence of my parents and my sternly devout grandmother Martha Jane Best Raines (1871–1967), the second was delivered by my grandmother to an audience of one. We were sitting under the elm tree in her backyard on a white porch swing detached from its chains and propped on blocks to make a kind of bench in the small parklike space between her house and the chicken house where I sometimes gathered eggs with my aunt Ada. The two of them had been moved into town by my father and his two brothers, but they had not given up their country ways easily. Ada was a quilter and could still cook, upon demand, squirrel and dumplings or high-domed biscuits of ethereal lightness. My father went to his grave believing that Aunt Ada's biscuit recipe was one of the lost secrets of a vanished world, like the embalming techniques of the pharaohs or the stained-glass formulas at Chartres. For her part, my grandmother still subscribed to the Jasper *Mountain Eagle,* the folksy newspaper that announced her marriage in 1894. Her four worshipful sons and their closely watched wives, the resentful targets of her unsolicited advice on housekeeping and childrearing, all called her "Ma" in recognition of her status as a mountain matriarch. The term seemed countrified to me and my siblings, and we called her "Grandma" unless referring to the little compound where she reigned as part of the reliable babysitting unit of "Ma 'n' Ada." Most of the baby-minding fell to sweet-natured Ada, and Ma Raines kept a kind of regal distance from her eight grandchildren, except for me. A rawboned woman of monumental ugliness and legendary strength, she had embraced widowhood at forty-two and never let it go.

I was the apple of her eye and not just because I was the last born. I was the only one named for her husband. Several others had Howell as the middle name, but only I carried the full patronymic consisting of both my grandfather's given names, Howell and the archaic-sounding Hiram.

My naming illustrated the sociological drama of urbanization as it played out in Birmingham after the founding of the Tennessee Coal, Iron and Railroad Company in 1852 and its takeover by U.S. Steel in 1901. Thousands of white and Black families streamed in from the countryside to meet the manpower needs of the paradigmatic New South industrial city, the "Pittsburgh of the South." As a child, I quickly learned that most of those families placed a high premium on not seeming countrified. Among Black people, Roosevelt was preferable to Willie as a given name. Among whites, frontier names like Israel or Eli fell out of favor. My father told me how he squared the city/country circle when it came to my naming in a family meeting a few weeks before my birth. He quoted himself as saying to my mother, "Y'all are not going to like this, but I want to name him after my father." The trade-off he offered was the reversal of names of the man buried at Curry, Alabama, under the tombstone reading:

H. H. RAINES

1872–1914

ASLEEP IN JESUS

I know exactly what it says because the tombstone has become my albatross. When Grandma Raines died in 1967 and was buried beside her husband, who had died forty-three years earlier, a new tombstone with both their names was installed above the adjoining graves. My father, for reasons never fully discussed between us, put the original grave marker in his basement. When he died, in 2002, I had the tombstone shipped to my garage in Pennsylvania. I found suitable homes for his old tools among the Amish, but I can't figure out how to dispose of the tombstone, an heirloom remarkable only for its oddness. I've thought of sinking it, with appropriate ceremony, in the clear flow of the Delaware River near our house in the Poconos, or in the Gulf of Mexico offshore from our winter retreat in Fairhope, Alabama. But I can't shake the feel-

ing that some kind of a curse might descend on me for severing its connection to the Alabama hills or to me, the last H. H. Raines to exist
(unless some yet unborn great-grandchild gets saddled with both Howell and Hiram). Howell became the name I was known by, on the basis of
my siblings' conviction that it was less countrified than Hiram. It has
made a serviceable byline, although I admit having, under the influence
of F. Scott Fitzgerald, a brief flirtation with writing as H. Hiram Raines.

What I want to convey is that I felt since earliest childhood a kind of
mysterious bond or burden having to do with my name and the man
who had it before me. I don't compare it with the spooky kinship Elvis
allegedly felt with his stillborn twin, Aaron. Rather, the name became
associated in my little-boy mind with a halcyon time that I had missed,
with days of legend when our sprawling tribe lived "up in the country."
We are not, I hasten to add, suspicious mountaineers of the Hollywood
stereotype, yet there was a bit of the "granny woman" about my grandmother. I was shaped, prematurely I think, by her ancient persona (and
by a parallel pioneer narrative, on my mother's side, of whiskey brewed
from the cold, clear-running waters in misty mountain hollows by her
rapscallion grandfather, though I was older when I first heard about the
whiskey). When I was five, I developed warts on one of my hands. Sitting on the propped-up swing under the elm tree, Grandma Raines told
me she could make them disappear.

She directed me to bring her a small stick for each of the two warts.
She rubbed the warts with them. She handed them back to me and told
me to name them and then dig a hole and bury them. "As soon as you
forget where they are buried, the warts will go away," she said. I think I
named them Ned and Ted, but I'm not certain. I am certain, however,
that I could go directly to the place where I scratched out a hole for the
interments. Nonetheless, the warts disappeared, never to return. Her
instructions for animal trapping were less efficacious. Many an hour I
stalked blue jays in her yard, confident that I could catch them if only I
got close enough to "sprinkle salt on their tails." Her formula for squirrel catching was more detailed but equally hopeless. I propped a box on
a stick under her pecan tree, tied fifty feet of string to the stick, baited the

area with nuts, and waited. Our hunting area was marked with small mounds of throwing stones, stacked by her in ragged pyramids of ammunition for throwing at a large, impudent fox terrier that liked to poop on the mowed lawn. Well into her eighties, she would run from the house hoping to get a clean shot at the fleeing beast.

Grandma was a strange old woman, spoiled to a level of queenly pickiness by her adult sons and the long-suffering Ada, who was paid as a live-in minder by the sons' businesses. All families made obligatory Yuletide afternoon pilgrimages to Ma 'n' Ada's house with its tiny table-top Christmas tree. Ada put large cheap thumb-sized chocolates in cut-glass bowls. My father brought Grandma the King Leo candy canes she'd favored when they lived on the farm at the start of the century and the boys counted oranges as fine Christmas gifts. I doubt the Raineses were ever really that poor, but they all stuck to the story of the gift oranges and cedar boughs and holly brought in from the woods for decoration. During this and more routine visitations, Ma sat in lace-collared long-sleeved dresses (which she also wore in every photo ever taken). I have never told anyone of the conversation that passed between us that has made all the difference in my life. This event, my baptism into the mysterious hillbilly rivalries of Civil War days, took place around the time of the burial of Ned and Ted. Grandma Raines was telling stories about life "up in the country" at our spot under the elm. One day, she told me, she and her husband had been walking down the dirt road that ran through their four-forties of farmland. She pronounced his name more like "Hal" than "Howell." Her version, which sounded like "HIGH-el," was another of her ruralisms, like "arn" (iron) or "dreckley" (straightaway). As she recalled, she and her husband spied a neighbor coming toward them on the road. Before the man was in earshot, "High-el" said, "Oh shit, here comes one of those damn Democrats."

Oddly, I do not recall feeling shocked, although I had never heard my parents or any of my grandparents swear or use slang any more forceful than "drot," a mild oath probably descended, like "drat" and "doggone," from "God rot them." Linguistically, such terms are called "minced oaths," meaning words that are altered to make them less objectionable, as in the substitution of "shoot" for "shit." If I was not scandalized by her scatological usage—she did not say "shoot"—I was certainly astonished, or else I would not have remembered the moment for over seventy years. I think my takeaway must have been that Democrats were simply *the other*. Such was my introduction by my saintly grandmother to a profane and violent world of north Alabama partisanship that dated back to the Civil War.

2

THE CENTRALITY OF
GRADYSTEIN WILLIAMS HUTCHINSON

FOR MOST OF my childhood, the clues to our family identity were few, hard to come by, and randomly acquired. For example, my father's affection for Tennessee hams led to car trips across Alabama's northern border to small towns where hickory-smoked, salt-cured, year-old hams could be found in a few specialized grocery and hardware stores. I fell in love with Tennessee because of its abundance of historical markers. They convinced me that little of consequence had happened in Alabama, which had so few. On one foray, we visited the Hermitage, and I came away with a heroic view of Andrew Jackson, an envy of Tennessee as a stage of large romantic dramas, and a budding conviction that life in Birmingham was small and stale. I was on to something, seeing threads that would one day—someday, not far away—braid themselves into a radical view of Alabama's past far different from the version being taught at school.

But my parents were of little help on the details. They were busy citizens of the least nostalgic of major southern cities. While Lost Cause romanticism was a civic neurosis in Atlanta, New Orleans, and Montgomery, Birmingham did not even exist until 1872. It was founded by local iron makers and Yankee speculators who turned an indifferent eye to history and celebrated the Magic City's fortuitous location atop the three materials needed to fire a New South blast furnace: iron ore, coal, and limestone. By the time I was exposed to the propagandistic version of Civil War history mandated by Alabama law, Birmingham was already shaping my political consciousness in a peculiarly irreverent way, a juvenile predisposition no doubt predestined by Grandma Raines's profanity.

I can still picture the primary-grade classroom where around 1950 I first heard the theory that Robert E. Lee was to be admired for choosing loyalty to his native Virginia over his duty to the United States. I distinctly remember thinking that my Alabama, or any single state, seemed a piddling thing compared to the nation that had just defeated Germany and Japan. My reaction to a teacher's comment that Lee's brilliance was such that his military techniques were still studied at West Point was similarly dyspeptic. Why? I asked myself. He lost.

I benefited from Birmingham being a New South island in an Old South state. I never saw in my own home or those of any Alabama relatives a portrait of Lee or Stonewall or Jeff Davis, nor any artwork depicting the Rebel battle flag or other Confederate iconography. Indeed, in addition to Lost Cause propaganda, we were taught at school to honor Lincoln, sing "The Battle Hymn of the Republic," and recite the Gettysburg Address, perhaps a split-the-difference concession to the overweening influence of northern money in the local economy. Yet you must understand that this straddling of modern and antique energy flows existed in a general atmosphere of police-enforced racial brutality, constant segregationist political speech, and a linguistic blizzard, beyond the front door of our home, of derogatory synonyms for African Americans. Given this atmosphere, the noblest thing I can tell you about my parents is that they insisted that we refer to Black people as "colored." If the ubiquitous N-word seeped in, we were reprimanded firmly. We were taught to treat with respect Raines Brothers' Black employees, with whom we had frequent contact. When I was fifteen, the Reverend Louis J. Cunningham, a Black preacher whose main livelihood was hauling away free scrap lumber from the family operation to be resold in his junkyard, told me that my father's color-blind fairness made him a "prophet" of racial kindness in a sinful city.

My parents were not rebellious liberals, but they provided an example of Christian humanism that was not limited to whites. Neither did they try to poison me and my siblings against the racial reckoning that became the constant focus of Alabama's public discourse following the 1954 Supreme Court school decision and the success of the 1955 bus boycott in Montgomery. While my parents were the initial positive influence on my racial attitudes, the most decisive event was my mother's hiring as our weekday housekeeper Gradystein Williams, a sixteen-year-old graduate of all-Black Parker High School, which proved a turning point in my life. I recalled the impact she had on me in a 1991 *New York Times Magazine* article about the "vanished world" of segregation. "Grady showed up one day at our house at 1409 Fifth Avenue West in Birmingham, and by and by she changed the way I saw the world," I wrote. "I was seven when she came to iron and clean and cook for $18 a week, and she stayed for seven years. During that time, everyone in our family came to accept what my father called 'those great long talks' that occupied Grady and me through many a sleepy Alabama afternoon."

Grady told me the Birmingham secrets from which white children were walled off, both the tragic and the trivial. We talked about the teenage boy shot to death in her neighborhood grocery store by the white cop he had sassed. We talked about the tragic truth of Emmett Till; in 1955, she showed me the *Jet* magazine pictures of the boy's battered corpse at his open-casket funeral in Chicago. She also told me about the less gruesome aspects of Black life in Birmingham: the unlicensed neighborhood bars called "blind tigers," the Bobby "Blue" Bland concerts she sneaked into at the Madison Night Spot, the extremely light-skinned Black girl who bought tickets to the whites-only Alabama Theater as a joke on the system, the beautiful classmate who never lived down dumping Willie Mays in high school because he had no future.

Grady's influence on me was magnified by the fact that my siblings had both left for college by the time I was eight. When I asked her years later what was her first impression of me, she said without hesitation,

"You were lonely." My parents gave her the room to fill the open space in my life. I can't think of another household in Birmingham that would have allowed it. Of course, I didn't go around boasting that the two of us had become subversive secret-sharers about the absurdities of segregation. But that permissive atmosphere had something to do with the fact that we were hill people come to town—that we were from north Alabama, with its fealty to the New Deal, the Tennessee Valley Authority, and Yankee landlords, not the Black Belt with its ghostly oligarchy of Rebel worshipers.

The early 1950s were good to all the Raineses, and my father decided in 1951 that it was time to step up from Oldsmobiles. He ordered my mother a 1952 Cadillac Coupe de Ville. She worried constantly about her parents up in Winston County. My grandfather Robert Cyle Walker was a former postmaster and justice of the peace known in the community as "Judge Walker" or "Uncle Bob." He was past eighty and my grandmother Martha Loudella Fell Walker was in her seventies when they were obliged to raise the three children of a divorced son. My mother and Grady set out in the Cadillac for a day trip, during which Grady would clean house and prepare a family lunch for the overworked couple. Of course, Grady knew about the "sunset towns" or "sundown towns" in the hill country, where Black travelers were warned with city-limits signs warning them "not to let the sun set on your head in this town." The stories were often exaggerated through hearsay, but they were accepted as gospel about these segregated municipalities. Cullman, about thirty miles from my grandparents' farm, was Alabama's most infamous sunset town. I can't imagine a Black girl with less gumption agreeing to make the trip—or, for that matter, another white Birmingham matron who would have let Grady ride shotgun in that grand vehicle. (The etiquette of where Black people were allowed to sit in white-owned vehicles was complicated and fraught, to say the least.) It was a road trip that would have challenged the descriptive powers of a Eudora Welty or Flannery O'Connor. Grady liked my Walker grandparents, but in general she viewed country white folks with amused disdain. As Grady approached her eighty-seventh birthday on December

20, 2020, I asked her to tell me yet again about their passage in front of the "liars' bench" outside the only general store in Arley. "Those men would be sitting down on the storefront," she recalled. "Miz Raines has just got that big black Cadillac. They came all the way out in the road to look at it, and I was sitting in the front seat. Oh, they looked at me so bad. I told your mother, 'I'm going to have to get in the back seat when we come home.'"

Their trip was to produce an incident unlike anything I have ever heard in a lifetime of reporting on how white southerners behaved in segregated times. The kitchen in the old country house had a big round table at its center. With the meal on the table, Grady took the chair nearest the stove so she could more easily serve additional portions. At that point a relative entered the room and commented, in rude language, on the sight of a Black person taking lunch at a table with six white people. He refused his seat, and Grady remembered precisely Grandpa Walker's reply.

"She cooked this meal for everyone, and she's going to eat it with us," my grandfather said. "If you don't like that, you take your plate and go eat on the porch." And that's what happened. Many years later, I would decipher what that incident told about my grandfather's politics, and that's what I will relate later in this book. The crucial information I got about his political principles was based on a conversation he and I were to have the next summer. That was in 1953, the momentous year in which I met Miss Marie. I can place it because when I came home from staying with my grandparents for a week of my tenth summer, my father had just installed the first air conditioner at 1409.

The stares that greeted Grady at the Arley general store and the insult she suffered at my grandparents' welcoming table point up an anomalous fact of Appalachian life. Unionists in north Alabama and the rest of the mountain South were not abolitionists. Southern mountaineers harbored intense racist feelings, as did other whites of their time, including Sherman, Grant, and, at least early in life, Lincoln himself. But there is a considerable body of commentary suggesting that the Appalachian people were less vociferous in expressing their racism and that the barriers between races were less adamantine than in south Alabama. No one has dealt with this nuance more brilliantly than Imani Perry in *South Toward History,* winner of the National Book Award in 2022. Sharing citizenship in the nation's poorest region allowed for a "tenderness" of understanding between Black and white people. Perry, a Black Princeton professor born in Birmingham, wrote that "in a rural place, you have intimacies across the color line as well as borders. There are too few people and too much needing of one another to maintain an always strict color line. It falters." Could there be a more perfect description of what took place in my grandparents' kitchen than a "faltering" of segregation?

In general, these upland southerners shared the attitude of President Andrew Jackson that the Union was too important to be dissolved over slavery, and that no state had a right to withdraw unilaterally. This loyalty to the "Old Flag" dated back to the Revolution and the War of 1812, in both of which many of the earliest settlers had served. For this reason, almost all north Alabamians saw themselves as Jacksonian Democrats, with the exception of Judge Walker, which was the key to what happened in his kitchen so long ago.

But as I was to discover in the summer of 1953 in what he called his "law library," Judge Walker began his lifetime journey of political involvement as a different kind of Democrat. Being a Republican was the final destination of that journey, yet it was an earlier way station that made Robert Cyle Walker into the first true populist I ever met, and by "true," I mean he seemed free of the racism that tainted the populism of Tom Watson, George Wallace, and Donald Trump. Most southerners know what the more enlightened among us learned to admit during the civil rights revolution: that racism is learned behavior taught in the bosom of the family. I was not aware, of course, that I was in the midst of what we now call a teachable moment when Judge Walker led me into a windowless, shelf-lined anteroom behind the fireplace to show me his law books. I would be an old man myself before I understood the full portent of a clue he gave me that day, in the sunset of his life, about a fact that cast a long shadow of influence over his life and my own as well. It's a story that illustrates how information fragments are essential to any personal search outside the boundaries of "accepted" history. Cultural leaders and elected officials who want to revise facts to their own tastes do not hide their tricks in plain sight. For me, that meant learning that those fragments of recollection are not illusions just because they lack the authority of hard science or official acceptance. Chance revelations like my grandfather's are specks of reality that reveal their meaning when glued into place in a revisionist mosaic, sometimes far into an unforeseeable future. To say that each state—indeed, each family—has a *subterranean* narrative does not mean that this parallel reality is nonexistent, just that it's been interred by the powers that be. As we stood in front of the shelves that held *The Code of Alabama* and his other treasures, here's what Judge Walker said about his political origins: "I am a Jeffersonian Democrat."

3

SAVED BY UNCLE SIM

THERE WAS, HOWEVER, a form of childhood bigotry from which Grady could not deliver me. When she arrived at 1409, I was in the throes of religious prejudice, and it was only in the writing of this chapter that I have come to grips with it. In the primary grades, I dreaded the day at the start of each semester when we were required to fill in the religion space on our enrollment cards. It embarrassed me profoundly to write "Church of God." Why, I wondered, did the up-and-coming Raines and Best families belong to a sect with a redneck name? By age eleven, I had learned that before his death in 1914, my namesake, H. H. Raines, had been a pillar of the Curry Methodist Church, and I began writing "Methodist" on every form put in front of me for the rest of my life. My religious preference on my U.S. Army dog tags is "METH," and "Methodist" is on every job application I ever submitted. Like a Lost Cause propagandist, I tried to erase the Church of God of Anderson, Indiana, from my own history. Ironically, this high-minded sect, which today numbers only about one million members, did as much to save me from indoctrination into white supremacy as my parents and Grady did, but in a way that was much harder to reconstruct and to acknowledge honestly. This crucial buffering from racist influences occurred in a decade when my Baptist, Methodist, Presbyterian, and Episcopal schoolmates were taught that God was a segregationist and slavery was a benign institution. But the Church of God's influence in the turbulent Birmingham of the fifties and sixties was subtle and unadvertised. By today's standards it was timid, but it made a tremendous difference in my life. It has taken me decades to piece together the backstory of my debt to the pious midwestern denomination of which I was so heartily ashamed. I call it luck that I grew up in benighted Birmingham when I did without being taught that both the Confederacy and segregation had the mandate of heaven. A more spiritual person than I grew up to be might even call it the will of God. All I know is that facts buried in the Church of God archives illuminate an unpublicized chapter of Alabama's conflict that astonished me and the full details of which I did not learn until the final days of this writing.

In regard to these influences on my childhood, it is important that I convey subtle distinctions in what we might call the sociopolitical topography of Dixie apartheid. It was like a blanket of ignorance spread unevenly across the South, thicker in some places than others. All white southern churches failed miserably when challenged on the basis of Scripture by Dr. Martin Luther King. But a few individuals and institutions nibbled at the edges of the blanket or lifted a corner here and there to allow a searing beam of light. That is what happened in 1890 when an Illinois-born evangelist began holding integrated revivals in Mississippi. Daniel S. Warner (1842–1895) was beaten by a white mob there, but not before flooding the Unionist counties of the Alabama hill country with missionaries who established in 1895 a Church of God campground at Hartselle in Morgan County, Alabama. As a site of annual revivals in August and December, it was only about forty miles distant from the Raines and Best farms in Walker County.

Somehow Warner's belief in integrated worship spread to Grandma Raines's younger brother, William Simeon Best (1875–1957), who is recorded as a "radical preacher" in extant Church of God archives about the sermons he preached in brush arbor revivals around Jasper in 1918. My older sister, Mary Jo Raines Dean, was born in 1930 and knew our Best relatives better than I, and so she understood that "radical" clearly referred to his racial views. Those proceeded from the Church of God doctrine of applying an unadulterated and inclusive Christian love in all spheres of life. We both believe that Sim Best's influence accounts for the unusually mild racial attitudes of the people who raised us in the South's most rigidly segregated big city.

Only late in my research have I been able to connect some of the dots in his story. As a reporter, I feel sheepish about my tardy focus on the most important clue. My sister and I have a close bond, and we have discussed our family memories countless times. Yet I never asked her before 2020 if she knew why the Reverend W. S. "Sim" Best led our families out of Methodism. "Grandma Raines always told me it had something to do with the way colored people were treated," she said without hesitation. For all my poring over the design of our family quilt, I had not tugged on that thread. In retrospect, my lack of curiosity about a change in denomination I so abhorred seems almost inexplicable, given my curiosity about other aspects of life "up in the country." But the fact is I had never sought an explanation, as if my inner child accepted that the humiliation of being identified with the Church of God was one of those traumas best ignored and covered up. Once my eyes were opened, it was obvious that I had to have the full story, and to find it, I turned back to the eve of the Civil War as a documentable starting point. In 1860, our patriarchs James Raines (1790–1883) and John Best (1808–1906) each acquired Alabama homesteads of 180 acres and 240 acres, respectively, only two miles apart in the rugged terrain of Walker County near the Sipsey River. When the Confederate Conscription Act was passed in 1862, some of our kinsmen began "lying out" in the woods to dodge the enrolling officers. Others reluctantly showed up to be drafted. John Best was the only red-hot Confederate in the bunch, or at least that's how he wanted to be remembered.

On September 5, 1906, the Jasper *Mountain Eagle* ran a full-length picture of the old man in a slouch hat and black suit, leaning on a thick staff. His mouth was set in a grim, downturned crescent, and his shadowed eyes were downcast, too, almost as if he were slumbering on his feet. The headline was "Uncle John Best 'Passes Over the River.'" The text read:

> John Best, generally called by all who knew him "Uncle John," died at the home of his son, David Best, near Marylee Monday. As we learn it, he was sitting in a chair when death struck him and passed away without a struggle and apparently without the least pain.
>
> He was, perhaps the oldest man in the country and doubtless the oldest ex-Confederate soldier in the country, being passed his ninety-seventh year. Had he lived a little over two years longer, he would have been a centenarian. Up to a short time ago he was remarkably well preserved for one of his extreme age. He cared no more for ten or fifteen mile walk than a man of half his age.
>
> The writer remembers seeing him here in Jasper about a year ago in a wagon driving through the streets. The wagon had a deep bed and "Uncle John" wanted to get out for something. He stopped, put his hand on the side of the wagon bed and hopped out on the ground as nimble as a boy of sixteen.
>
> He was a member of Camp Hutto, United Confederate Veterans, and delighted to attend the Confederate reunions. He did not attend the last, however, as he began to decline a short while before and continued to gradually grow feebler until the end came. Peace to his ashes.

I discovered that this "Uncle John," my great-great-grandfather, was fonder of reunions than of soldiering. The arc of his military career tracks the political feelings of his part of Alabama. On December 24, 1860, Alabama's white male voters elected one hundred delegates—two from each county—to the secession convention scheduled to meet in Montgomery on January 7, 1861. The ordinance they would pass on January 11 over feverish objection from the hill country representatives took Alabama out of the Union. Returns from Walker County showed that about half of John Best's neighbors wanted to secede and about half wanted to stay a part of the United States. Best enlisted in the Rebel army in March 1862, roughly one month before the impending Confederate Conscription Act would force every man in the hill country aged eighteen to thirty-five to choose one side or the other. We don't know whether Best was really an eager soldier. We do know he was a lucky one. Nor does he appear an entirely truthful veteran, given his zeal for Confederate reunions and leaping out of wagons. His 28th Alabama Infantry, C.S.A., was stationed initially at Corinth, Mississippi, but its members were not among the six thousand Alabamians thrown into the horrific Battle of Shiloh, just across the Tennessee line, on April 6, 1862. Falling back on Corinth, General P. G. T. Beauregard ordered the surviving Rebels to dig in, and pension records show that Private Best received one of those nonfatal injuries known to soldiers as a "million-dollar wound." In his 1896 pension application he said he "was hurt while building breast works and has become disabled by old age." When the pension law was updated in 1899, he stated he was "blind in one eye and just can see in the other [and] not able to go without a guide." He also said he served until "surrender 1864," which can be charitably described as an exaggeration.

His service record shows that because of his injury he was fully discharged on July 5, 1862, after only four months in the ranks. He spent the rest of the war on his farm. In applying for his death benefits in 1906, his widow somewhat apologetically assured Alabama officials that while he "became afflicted with disease and was discharged about the middle of war," he had "again re-enlisted and served in the Home Guard." That raises questions that can never be answered about John Best's role in the guerilla war that swept the hills as Confederate fortunes declined. The Home Guard was tasked with hunting men like my great-grandfather Hiram Raines, men who were "lying out" to avoid conscription. Also, it's unknown if Best was in the small force of Home Guards that failed to turn back the First Alabama Union cavalrymen who raided Jasper in the late summer of 1864, burned the courthouse, and freed the Winston County Unionists imprisoned there. We do know with certainty what

John Best told his son David Best (1848–1926) when the boy neared draft age in the last full year of the war: that he should switch sides.

I have the story from my father, Wattie Simeon Raines. I taped the account he gave to Margaret Storey, hoping it would someday fit in my historical jigsaw. David Best was Grandma Raines's father, and my father was nineteen when the old man died. In the summer of David Best's sixteenth birthday, John Best told him to take to the woods and try to reach the Union forces occupying the Tennessee Valley. "Well, the South was losing," my father said, "and he knew his time was short, and he went to walking toward Decatur. He knew that boats came up there, and he might have had the idea to get on down the river. But his idea was to get to the north. He was looking for a bunch of Yankee soldiers, and he was going to run to them with his hands up, and that's what he did."

Luckily, the blue-coated horsemen toward whom he ran had already enlisted older Alabamians from his neighborhood. A man in the ranks called his name: "'Hey, Dave, don't run. Come here.' They waited for him to come on. It was somebody he knew. They didn't need any kids, but he could work. He said they were good to him, had good food. They let him help preparing the meals, work with the horses for the officers." When the war ended in 1865, he walked home from South Carolina, narrowly escaping death in an encounter with disgruntled plantation owners who sicced a big dog on him. He killed the dog with his walking staff and made his escape. (I appropriated the entire episode for my novel *Whiskey Man*.) I had first heard the story years earlier, and it schooled me further in the fact that our family did not view Confederate loyalty as a virtue.

Uncle Sim, one of Dave Best's children, was the eldest of Grandma Raines's four brothers. Only in recent times have I found documentary evidence linking that brother, known professionally as the Reverend William Simeon Best, to the most notorious racial incident in Church of God history. No book on Alabama history known to me even mentions the dramatic attack on a revival meeting, but it has been meticulously documented at the Robert A. Nicholson Library at Anderson University, the denomination's college in Indiana. Church of God historians know it as the Hartselle Incident. It occurred about thirty-five miles as the crow flies from the Best farm at Marylee, in the only part of Alabama that persistently experimented with integrated worship services during Reconstruction. In 1871, a New York–born Methodist missionary, Reverend A. S. Lakin, was preaching equality of the races to congregations in Winston, Walker, and Blount Counties. He was active throughout north Alabama and even served for one day as president of the University of Alabama in 1869 before the Klan chased him out of Tuscaloosa.

After the Church of God founder, Daniel S. Warner, was attacked while preaching to a biracial audience in Mississippi in 1890, Warner picked out the Alabama counties pioneered by Lakin for a renewed missionary effort to promote his vision of a universal church open to worshipers of all races. Warner, who attended Oberlin College and served in the Union army, sent teams of well-educated missionaries to Alabama and established a campground at Hartselle as their Alabama headquarters. Sim Best would have been twenty years old when revivalists tested Alabama's segregation laws, as recounted by Charles Ewing Brown in *When the Trumpet Sounded: A History of the Church of God Reformation Movement*.

"Late in the nineteenth century (1897) the Alabama state camp meeting, held some miles out of Hartselle, was attended by both races, with only a rope stretched down the middle of the tent as a recognition of segregation," Brown wrote. The use of female evangelists was another Church of God innovation, and one of them, Lena Shoffner, called for the rope to be lowered, so that white and Black people could kneel together at the altar. "That night a mob came in wild with fury. They threw dynamite under the boardinghouse and the camp houses and ferreted out the preachers like hounds hunting rabbits. The preachers fled. One man stood in a creek all night. Another preacher put on a woman's clothing and escaped. Next night the mob followed them to the homes where they had fled, in some cases fifteen miles from the campground." Two days later, a guard armed with a shotgun escorted the preachers across the Tennessee River at Huntsville.

It seems implausible to think that Sim Best would not have heard of the attack on the worshipers or that Grandma Raines's recollection of his concern for Black people at church was not somehow connected to that event. By 1920 even the Church of God was establishing segregated congregations in Chicago and Racine, Wisconsin, but against all odds, a tracery of its early idealism persisted in Birmingham, imprinting me from earliest childhood. At the Pinehurst Church of God chapel a few blocks from our home, my mother regularly chatted in the vestibule with a woman who brought Black friends to services in a sanctuary with seating that was not designated by race. As a toddler, I was taken to what were almost certainly the only integrated revival meetings conducted in Alabama in the 1950s. In open defiance of Birmingham law, members of Black Church of God congregations came to the annual statewide camp meetings. My cousin Eudalia Raines Hicks, born in 1935, remembers that they answered the altar calls, mixing with white worshipers in front of the pulpit for final prayers and hymns.

Church of God services were the opposite of Holy Roller meetings. They were somber, as befitted the denomination's roots in Wesleyan Pietism and the Mennonite churches of the Pennsylvania Dutch. That also accounts for the absence of racial doctrine in their services. Sermons dealt with elevated biblical concepts based on Daniel Warner's doctrine that all Christians belong to the same colorblind church. The church's *Gospel Trumpet* magazine relentlessly promoted missionary work in Africa. In the 1920s, Uncle Sim was pastoring churches in Warner's old missionary grounds in Hartselle, Decatur, and Jasper. Newspaper ads touted his high-toned sermons with titles like "The Gospel in the Sixteenth Century." In the 1930s he had moved on to pastorates in Laurel, Mississippi. In 2021, I located his grandson David Best, a successful attorney in Orlando, Florida. He shared my view that race and the Hartselle Incident had been a lingering influence. As a boy, he often visited the old man at Laurel, Mississippi, where the preacher died in 1957, and responded immediately when I speculated there was a racial component to his conversion. "That's consistent with what I know about him," said Best, who was born in 1937. "We lived in Mississippi. Black ministers would come to the back door, and he would make them

go to the front porch and sit on the porch with him. I think he had visited their churches and they would come to visit him at the back door,
and he'd always say, 'No, you're going to sit on the front porch with me,'
and it was right on Highway 11 between Laurel and Ellisville, and it was
a busy highway."

Such a slight bending of racial protocols in public view may seem
mild by today's standards, but it was a significant, even courageous act
in a Mississippi that was then, in the words of the famed civil rights
worker Bob Moses, "the middle of the iceberg" of segregation. Even if I
was introduced to Uncle Sim at some family event, I would not have
understood he was that rarest of southern role models, a white preacher
who believed in brotherhood. I knew his son, whom I called Uncle
Homer, as he and my father were about the same age and remained
friends all their lives. Homer was the family historian, and ironically he
provided my only memorable brush with the Confederate nostalgia industry when we visited his family in Atlanta about 1950. He took us to
that most lugubrious of all Rebel memorials, the carved likenesses of
Robert E. Lee, Stonewall Jackson, and Jefferson Davis at Stone Mountain. The carvings on the sixteen-hundred-foot exfoliation dome were
designed in 1925 by Gutzon Borglum, the Klan sympathizer whose next
project was Mt. Rushmore. At Stone Mountain, the world's largest bas-
relief carving covers 1.57 acres and speaks volumes about the persistence
of the segregationist plague from which the Church of God helped save
me. In a defiant response to the *Brown v. Board of Education* decision
and Atlanta's emergence as capital of the civil rights movement, the
Georgia legislature bought the mountain in 1958 for $1.125 million and
financed the finishing touches on the carvings with state funds. Final
work began as the 1964 Civil Rights Act was passed.

On that 1950 trip, we brought home a chip of granite from the rubble
field at the foot of the towering monument, but its symbolism didn't take
hold of me the way the story of David Best did. I'm convinced that my
early exposure to the humanistic and intellectual tonalities of his son
Sim's distinctively Yankee church, with ministers imported to Birmingham from north of the Mason-Dixon Line, had a profound influence on

me. I was never exposed to sermons touching on southern defensiveness about slavery or the glories of Confederate role models like Robert E. Lee. "I never heard any racial slurs in that church," said my sister, Mary Jo, who also remembered the integrated meetings at the tabernacle on the Birmingham campground. With the help of librarians at the Church of God archives, I discovered to my great surprise that Uncle Sim helped raise the money to build that place of worship. That opened the door to discovering my familial link to an integrationist tradition dating back to the start of the twentieth century—details that are entirely missing from Alabama history and journalism.

In her nineties, Mary Jo recalled a friend of our mother's from the historic Bessemer "white and colored" congregation who regularly brought Black friends to Pinehurst. She also remembered an elderly woman who was greeted by Grandma Raines in the church vestibule on her occasional visits to services at Pinehurst. "She always wore a black dress with a high collar, like many of the older Church of God women. She came by streetcar. I can still see her coming up the sidewalk beside the church from the streetcar stop on Third Avenue," Mary Jo told me. "That was Sister Mitchell."

Her remark stunned me. By now I knew enough Church of God history to connect the dots. As a child carried to church by my parents, I had been under the same church roof with Reverend Elizabeth Longacre Mitchell, the woman who conducted what were probably the first integrated church services in twentieth-century Alabama at Penton, more than 120 years ago. A document in the Church of God archives called "The Townley Report" tracks W. S. Best's development as a Mitchell ally. In 1911, Uncle Sim was ordained, and he allied himself with the Reverend J. Lee Mitchell on a committee that in 1918 purchased six acres for a new campground and open-sided tabernacle near Pinehurst Church in Birmingham; by 1921 the annual camp meeting had been moved there from Hartselle. My cousin Clarence L. Best recorded the transaction in a letter preserved in the Church of God archives at Anderson University in Indiana. I have never found any mention of the Mitchells' integrationist work in any Alabama history book, nor have I found any report of the Hartselle Incident and a similar attack on the Mitchells at Benton, Alabama, in 1901. The simple fact is that race-mixing and virtually all opposition to segregation were simply ignored by Alabama newspapers and the state's professional historians from the time of the Hartselle Incident until the Montgomery bus boycott in 1956.

Sister Mitchell outlived her husband by five years, dying in 1954 in her home near the campground that Uncle Sim and her husband started. So, as an old man, I acknowledge that the church I scorned shielded me from the bullets of racism that maimed millions of white southerners in my generation.

READING THE STARS

IN THE ALABAMA of my growing-up years, the old racial order crumbled faster than any of us comprehended at the time. We had watched in wonder, but without full understanding of the implications, what occurred in Kelly Ingram Park when Eugene "Bull" Connor unleashed dogs and fire hoses on Martin Luther King's Children's Crusade in May 1963. Even those of us who hoped for a new day did not realize that with massive social changes like those wrought in Birmingham by the 1964 Civil Rights Act, "dawn comes up like thunder out of China 'cross the bay," to borrow a phrase from Kipling. Since Rudyard Kipling was the poet of colonialism, perhaps applying his words to Birmingham, with its corporate landlords from the United States Steel in faraway Pittsburgh, is not too great a stretch. In my hometown's case, the metaphor of sudden dawn was apt. Lyndon Johnson signed the bill into law on July 4, 1964. Before the summer was out, Black people were sharing the best restaurants and hotels, and that fall integrated audiences were watching Laurence Olivier in *Othello* at the Alabama Theater. Any hope among white holdouts that Black people would pause before testing local compliance with the new federal law was dashed almost immediately. No one doubted that Black people were ready, but few anticipated how tired middle-class whites were of the public charade of both de jure and de facto segregation. Even conservative whites decided not to behave badly in public places.

For Alabamians, the sixties had two hinge points: the 1964 Civil Rights Act and the Voting Rights Act of 1965. My life had two hinge points as well, but they were spread out over two decades rather than two years. For me those points came in January 1961, when I entered Birmingham-Southern College (BSC), and in March 1978, when I was hired by *The New York Times*.

My father summarized the import of that latter event more crisply than I—and perhaps he understood it more deeply than I did. He spoke with the hard-learned worldliness of a farm boy who was comfortable doing business in the Manhattan offices of the renowned Raymond Loewy, often called the father of industrial design. To him, climbing up to the city signified something grand. "*The New York Times* is kind of like the New York Yankees," he told a family friend. "They keep an eye out for good players in the minor leagues, and every now and then they bring one up to the majors."

But I would never have made it to New York or even out of Alabama but for what befell me at Birmingham-Southern College. To describe little BSC by today's standards seems almost oxymoronic. It was the most liberal school in Alabama, but it was closed to Black applicants by a board of Methodist preachers and laymen determined to keep it segregated even after racial barriers tumbled all across the city. And the college, which urged its students to pursue an intellectual rigor its policies did not embody, became, quite unexpectedly, the next way station in my journey to educate myself about Winston County. My learning process was sporadic precisely because I was able to proceed only by the agency of luck, there being no accessible literature on the subject—at least not unless you knew more about bibliographical searches than I did at eighteen. Southern became my lucky place.

It may seem strange to think of fetching up at such a parochial place on the eve of the civil rights revolution as lucky, but otherwise I would have drifted on down to Tuscaloosa and become part of the University of Alabama's privileged frat-boy culture, where the Kappa Alphas' riotous celebration of Robert E. Lee's birthday stirred envy even among members of Sigma Alpha Epsilon, another deep-dyed, southern-fried frater-

nity co-founded in Tuscaloosa by a Selma preacher named Noble Leslie
DeVotie, allegedly the first Rebel soldier to die in the Civil War. But benign happenstance was on my side. BSC was being frog-marched toward
modernity. The college's board had rather naively hired a courtly Georgian, Henry King Stanford, then forty-two, as president in 1958. He was
a Methodist, to be sure, but he had studied international relations in Hei-
delberg and earned a PhD in political science and government management at New York University, which posted him to run its mission in
Ankara, Turkey. He was a worldly man who served cocktails in the president's mansion, cajoled *Harper's Magazine* into reporting on BSC as an
intellectual oasis in the Deep South, and opened negotiations with the
Ford Foundation about a grant that would replace lost alumni gifts and
church support when the college integrated. The tremors of the civil
rights revolution were being felt strongly on campus, and ministerial students studying Reinhold Niebuhr's political theology of Christian Realism seemed particularly eager to engage the Black community. When Bull
Connor called Dr. Stanford personally to demand expulsion of a ministerial student who was meeting with Student Nonviolent Coordinating
Committee organizers at a nearby Black college, he found himself talking
to a very different kind of cat from the cowed schoolmasters he was ac-
customed to bullying. Stanford defied him, instead hiring Charles
"Chuck" Morgan Jr., later to emerge on the national civil rights stage, to
represent the young man against trumped-up trespass charges. Henry
King Stanford didn't last long, but at a time when Alabama and Auburn
trustees were still arguing over which "integrationist" books should be
stricken from the undergraduate reading lists, Dr. Stanford's intellectual
rigor and the college's well-stocked bookstore put a stamp on me. My interests were more literary than political in those days, and the store carried
the obligatory Faulkner-Hemingway-Fitzgerald canon, along with the regional master spirits, such as Robert Penn Warren, Eudora Welty, and
Caroline Gordon, the burgeoning output of the famous Vanderbilt University conservatives known as the Nashville Agrarians and the Fugitive
Poets, as well as the New Critics, then the regnant masters of southern
literary scholarship. But the store also carried important readings in his-

tory, sociology, and anthropology. There I found what may have been the only copy then for sale in Birmingham of *Stars Fell on Alabama*.

When I brought the green-jacketed paperback home, with its memorable title in bold white letters, my mother spotted it immediately. As I worked my way through an adolescent reading list that included Steinbeck and other left-leaning writers, she had never commented except when I entered my Erskine Caldwell phase as a high school sophomore. *Tobacco Road* presented an insulting picture of the South, she declared, without forbidding me to read it. Her reaction to *Stars Fell on Alabama* was the same; reputedly it said bad things about our state. The book by a New York–born author, Carl Carmer, had been a runaway bestseller when published by Farrar and Rinehart on June 26, 1934, its catchy title drilled into the national idiom by the even greater success of a dance tune from a songwriter who cadged Carmer's title. The song became a hit with the big bands whose singers crooned its dreamy lyrics: "We lived our little drama / We kissed in a field of white / And stars fell on Alabama last night."

My mother would have been twenty-seven when the book and the song of the same title were hits, and her reaction reflected (in a mild form, to be fair) the pervasiveness of what I call the Alabama Inferiority Syndrome (AIS). It is—still—a virulent psychopathology that predates the Civil War. It cuts across all lines of class and educational and social standing, this feeling among white Alabamians of being looked down on. It fills them with rage, which takes a political form in support of KKK-endorsed senators like Hugo Black and "Cotton Tom" Heflin and governors like Wallace—and, since 2016, in a landslide approval of Donald Trump. Under the spell of AIS, white Alabamians are reared to believe that any criticism of the southern way of life is "bad for our image" and, by definition, unfair. Sociological accuracy, as in Caldwell's depiction of poor whites, or journalistic validity, as in Carmer's mild descriptions of racial bigotry, do not matter. AIS embodies the kind of paradox that has drawn cultural anthropologists to the South for decades. Even whites who fully accept integration might, for example, still vote for the most racist available candidates, hence Trump's hold on the state.

For me, *Stars Fell on Alabama* was transformative. Without it, I might never have started my quest for the full facts about southern Unionism. Certainly, I was never again to see Alabama through uncritical eyes or to think of its palpably odd quotidian rituals, regional folkways, and elected leaders as in any way "normal." The book was also life-changing with its dramatic—albeit provocatively incomplete—account of the anti-secessionist heritage of our family's native ground. By the time I entered college I had already figured out the ethical rot at the heart of Alabama politics, meaning that the unfair distribution of government benefits was not limited to the racial sphere. I had already gleaned that the University of Alabama in Tuscaloosa, which called itself the capstone of education, was in fact the keystone of an arc of gubernatorial corruption that touched, for example, the kickback system on roadbuilding and state liquor store contracts perfected by the storied governor James E. "Big Jim" Folsom. As I was to write later in *Whiskey Man,* I had also gleaned that "Montgomery was the place in Alabama where things got done for you or to you." That is to say, legislative conniving was the reason the twenty miles of bad road between Jasper and Arley—with its choking dust in summer and axle-deep mud in winter—was not paved until after the Korean War. In Winston County, where I watched my grandfather plow with mules because no one in Arley yet owned a tractor, I was able to glimpse a last redoubt of unmechanized, nineteenth-century agriculture and village life, as did Carl Carmer.

Stars Fell on Alabama is written as a travelogue, and in that regard it is a forerunner of the kind of reportage later practiced by Bruce Chatwin, Paul Theroux, and Tony Horwitz—books in which an erudite and curious visitor explores an area's culture, history, and politics with the assistance of sympathetic local guides. Carmer's guides in Alabama's Warrior Mountains were one of his students, Knox Ide, who was to go on to Harvard Law School and a successful legal and corporate career in Manhattan, and a character that the book calls Henry, a colorful moon-shiner who has the feel of a composite character, as does his lively, irreverent wife, called Mattie Sue. (In his introduction, Carmer acknowledges blending characters and telescoping time for storytelling purposes.) To some extent, Carmer was a harbinger of the New Journalism, applying novelistic techniques to descriptive narratives, but veering a little further across the wavering border between fact and romance. Notwithstanding an overreliance on what he called "the truth of folk-say," Carmer captured the aura of strangeness surrounding religion and politics in Alabama better than any writer before or since.

The incantatory two-page foreword that I first read at eighteen still enthralls as it did in 1961, by wrapping in a glamorous mist the people and scenes that had seemed routine. It is a fact of maturation that a child growing up in a parochial, brutal, or even abusive environment thinks his or her world is the norm unless there are timely interventions. Carmer's skill in dramatizing the hyperbolic central conceit of his book was such an intervention for me. He argued that Alabama, where he lived for six years in the 1920s while teaching at the University of Alabama in Tuscaloosa, was so unusual, so different from the other forty-seven states, that it had to be viewed as a foreign country. Suddenly, I, who had always felt unhappily marooned in dreary Birmingham, felt energized to be living in such an exotic locale. Charmed from the first lines, I never gave a damn whether it "made Alabama look bad."

> Alabama felt a magic descending, spreading, long ago. Since then it has been a land with a spell on it—not always a good spell. Moons red with the dust of barren hills, thin pine trunks barring horizons, festering swamps, restless yellow rivers—they are all part of a feeling, a strange certainty that above and around these things hovers enchantment, an emanation of malevolence that threatens to destroy men through dark ways of its own.

To say these sentences were eye-opening hardly captures their impact on me, initially by imagery alone. Trees did bar our horizons, and I had never before thought that our rivers could be accurately described as yellow! As for malevolence, it was a lay-down hand when I paused to think about the Alabama of my high school years. In 1957, Klansmen answering to Asa "Ace" Carter, a gubernatorial candidate, had castrated a mentally disabled Black man randomly kidnapped from a roadside north of Birmingham. Not long after, Ace had shot at our neighborhood barbecue king, Jack Cash, at a Klan rally in the neighborhood theater where I watched *Bambi, Snow White,* and Disney's racist fable *Song of the South.* In 1959, a white woman named Viola Hyatt had killed and dismembered two boarders in a trailer on her parents' farm, equidistant from Birmingham and Arley, for forcing her to perform "unnatural acts." She and her father then drove the back roads tossing arms and legs out the car window. When I read about this in *The Birmingham News* I wasn't entirely sure if an unnatural act wasn't some kind of gymnastic contortion. So, yes—dark ways.

I read on as Carmer tried to bridge the credibility gap between two modes of storytelling that seemed to anticipate both the close observation of New Journalism and, on the imaginative side, magical realism. Alabama's "irrationalities," he wrote, dated from "the years the stars fell." He was referring to the Leonid meteor shower of November 12, 1833, when 150,000 streaking "stars" lit up the skies of the Midwest and Deep South. On the plantations, masters and slaves alike saw it as a sign of the Second Coming. The light storm also figured in the legends of the Lakota Sioux and other Plains tribes. Carmer posited that a kind of voodoo "horoscope" descended on Alabama, creating "this state-that-is-another-land." Scientific thinkers and economists might "scorn such irrationalities," he contended, but the contemporary traveler would discover palpable evidence of a spellbound culture that should be viewed as different from that of the United States. Alabama-as-a-foreign-country is the governing conceit of the ensuing collection of folktales, accounts of political and religious gatherings, and reportage on race relations. "The Congo is not more different from Massachusetts or Kansas or California," Carmer concluded. "So, I have chosen to write of Alabama not as a state which is part of a nation, but as a strange country in which I once lived and from which I have returned."

The book's biggest surprise was waiting at the start of the section entitled "In the Red Hills." The name Winston County leapt out at me in a stylized telling of the Free State story. I recognized the rugged road by which Carmer and I, separated by a maintenance-free thirty years, crossed the high, rattling, spidery frame of Duncan Bridge. It had been an engineering marvel in 1900 when it was cast across the Sipsey River at a height of ninety feet. No bridge I've crossed since, including the Golden Gate and the crescent span at Big Sur, impressed me more. North of the bridge, the dirt road was notched into sheer canyon walls, covered with icicles in winter and dripping ferns in the summer. You could see, on the downslope, the skeletons of moonshiners' cars, rusting in the shade of a canyon microenvironment that featured Canadian spruces, deposited far south of their normal range during the last ice age, and the largest of the North American wild magnolias, the cowcumber tree, with its two-foot-long leaves and twelve-inch white blossoms.

The bridge rested atop six tall spindly columns of cast iron. The planks on the floor of the bridge were not nailed down and drummed thunderously against the rusty stringers under the weight of a car. It was one lane, so you had to wait your turn if there was oncoming traffic. Where planks were missing or broken off, you could look down and see the swift green river running among the sunbaked backs of giant tan boulders. The water looked inviting. The passage over the bridge never failed to fill me with dread and awe. In one shabby structure, Duncan Bridge epitomized both the poverty and isolation of Winston County. Carmer described his passage across the bridge with a calmer feeling than I was ever able to muster: "We crossed a clear little stream that hurled itself bravely at boulders in its path. 'Sipsey River,' said Henry. 'Only runnin' water in the county.'"

That's not accurate, of course. With my cousins, I often swam in Brushy Creek, a sizable Sipsey tributary, and hunted arrowheads in the fields and caves along Cutoff Branch, which crossed my grandparents' lower forty. The hills were laced with bold streams of every sort, all flowing into the Sipsey and then into the Warrior River system, which goes all the way to Mobile. But Carmer portrayed accurately the experience of climbing the road as it wound up the northern wall of the canyon, noting that it was steep enough to cause the spirited Mattie Sue to clutch the car door "desperately."

"Winston County road," said Henry. "Never been a good stretch o' pike in it. Folks down at Montgomery ain't through payin' 'em back for stayin' in the Union in the War Between the States."

"Do you mean they didn't secede?"

"I reckon that's what they call it. When they had the war they were some kind o' meetin' down to Montgomery an' Winston sent a man down there name o' Sheets; his folks still live around here. He tol' them they was only three slaves in the whole county and they wasn't worth fightin' over, so he reckoned he and his neighbors would stay out o' the fuss. Well, when the war started the Confederate soldiers come up in here an' shot an' hung a lot o' the men for deserters. That made the rest of 'em mad and a lot went north an' joined the army up there. Some of 'em hid up in the hills though an' kept on makin' their corn liquor same as usual."

This was Carmer's skeletal summary of a story that mainstream historians chose to ignore; the story's blank spots and missing details would occupy me for decades. As a New Yorker in the unpaved backcountry, Carmer was charmed by the whiskey lore attached to a legendary hill country matriarch, Jenny Brooks. According to Winston folklore, Rebel guerillas had killed her moonshiner husband for refusing to join the Confederate army so that he could keep his still operating. I would learn that this cheapening of Unionist motivation was standard procedure for Lost Cause historians who were Carmer's faculty colleagues in Tuscaloosa, and he swallowed the bait whole. Even as a college freshman, I recognized that Carmer was given to exaggeration and favored the romanticized antebellum stories of the plantation class over historical documentation. But there were enough points of contact between what I had heard in Winston County and Carmer's account to convince me I needed to know more about the county's story.

For example, who was this man Sheats? Before I finished college, I would run across his name again.

5

MY ROSETTA STONE

FROM THE VERY first time I saw it, Winston County put a spell on me. My memories of when I got my first glimpse of that high, remote county so unlike the gritty industrial scenes of mundane Birmingham go way back—at least to cotton-picking time in the autumn of 1946. In this case I can pinpoint the time exactly because there is a date-stamped snapshot of me and my country cousins sitting on a mound of hand-pulled cotton on my grandparents' front porch at Arley.

That sunny day I had been wrestling with my first cousin Jerry Walker in the pillowy stuff, and in that photograph I still have the golden Lord Fauntleroy curls that were finally shorn in 1947 by Fred Queen in his barbershop at the Rising Station streetcar stop in west Birmingham to mark my fourth birthday. My fourteen-year-old brother, also named Jerry, walked me five blocks to the barber shop and brought the blond clippings home in a paper bag, as instructed by our mother. She had held out for as long as possible against complaints that I "looked like a girl." She saved those curls for years in a black jewelry box decorated with many-colored pictures of cut diamonds. She was a watchful but remote parent, and I realize now that childhood in the atavistic hill country sixty miles north of Birmingham had put a mark on her too. She longed for pretty things, cleanliness, safety, and health. She told often of burning so with measles that her father roamed the shaded bluffs— "rock houses" in the local idiom—along Cutoff Branch hoping to find the last shards of winter ice to ease her fever. That feckless mission would have been before World War I, when there was not a refrigerator or a yard of pavement or even a septic tank in all of Arley.

Even in my day, much less in hers, Winston County taught caution and limited expectations. It was Alabama's poorest county, punished in each annual budget for sending the only Republican to the state legislature in Montgomery. Usually it was someone named Johnson or Dodd or Weaver, from the more populous west side of the county. For my grandfather Robert Cyle Walker, who was from the hamlet of Arley in the eastern part, rising to justice of the peace (or, under Republican presidents, to postmaster of nearby Old Nathan, Alabama) was as high as a man could go. Judge Walker (the honorific was awarded to Bob after he was named justice of the peace) made the most of his postings and political contacts, amassing the flattest three hundred acres in his part of the Free State. Hence the piles of cotton on which I wrestled. He and his children had plowed and picked those cotton fields themselves.

Both that tussle with my cousin and the haircut a few months later are the kind of poured-in-glass memories (with Kodak evidence) about which there can be no mistake, even in the fungible world of family lore. And I know by the no less definitive method of documentable deduction that, like every Raines or Walker or Best before me, I arrived in Winston by dirt road. The highway from Jasper to Arley was not paved until 1953. In winter or spring, the red clay would be axle deep, the tires of our big Oldsmobile sedan whooshing through deep ruts and its undercarriage scraping against the squeezed-up center ridge of the muddy farm-to-market road. On those Sunday morning trips, I liked the feel of our Rocket 88 fishtailing like the bumper cars at the state fair. On summer days, the dust would choke you. There was constant debate with my parents about whether it was better to keep the windows up and swelter or keep them open and cough. I'm also certain that my parents had not been able to phone ahead to let Grandpa and Grandma Walker know we were coming. Telephone service from Birmingham to Arley was not installed until 1963, when I was a junior in college.

Electric lights had come to Winston County in 1937, courtesy of the Tennessee Valley Authority, and a local history records the frugality of a farmer who had a single light socket installed in each of five rooms and carried a forty-watt bulb from room to room. One Alabama historian observed that Winston remained "a stranded frontier for a full century" after the Civil War. That time frame allowed for the happenstance that as a child I saw the last vestiges of mule-powered frontier agriculture in a world of yeoman farmers far removed from the "Cotton Kingdom" of lowland Alabama and its vast plantations and crystal-ballroom memories. It was one of the luckiest accidents of timing in my life, this chance to glimpse a bygone era.

For Winston County and all I came to learn about it made me a different kind of Alabamian, and much of what I know about the Walkers of Winston County came from a peculiar document created by my late uncle Brack Walker in 1958, while sitting with his parents—my grandparents Bob Walker (1881–1972) and Martha Loudella Fell Walker (1888–1990), known as Della—at the kitchen table of the house where he was born to them in 1929 and where two decades later my cousins and I played in the cotton.

Jimmy Brack Walker, who died in 1994, was one of those restless artistic expatriates who popped up from the Alabama outback with surprising regularity among folks born in the 1920s. Brack, a painter and cartoonist, was less successful in his field than another of this type, the author Harper Lee, born in Monroeville in 1923, was in hers, but not for lack of trying on Brack's part, at least early on. Later, some of the same vices that cut short the career of Hank Williams, another shooting star born in 1923 in yet another sun-stricken Bama hamlet, took their toll on Brack. He was on the downslope of his career when I visited him in Memphis in 1978 and first saw the family tree he had drawn while Bob and Della Walker told all that they could remember of our ancestors.

Alabama had its share of gifted misfits from the early part of the twentieth century, including Zelda Fitzgerald and Tallulah Bankhead. The 1920s and 1930s were the years of the Southern Renaissance, and the influence of this rebirth of southern literature extended beyond novels into the worlds of the visual arts and entertainment. My uncle Brack was of that ilk, and I celebrate him here as the person who converted my budding interest in the First Alabama into a compulsion that would endure throughout my life. He provided the first hint that we might be descended from soldiers who fought to preserve the Union rather than to defend slavery. I can't overstate the attraction for someone born, as I was, in the war zone of the desegregation crusade of the possibility that my ancestors or at least collateral kin might have followed Lincoln rather than Davis and Lee.

Brack Walker was a painter and draftsman of considerable talent, having earned an MFA at the University of Southern California in Los Angeles, where he claimed to have run with the actors Rip Torn and John Cassavetes. Leaving Arley at eighteen for what is now the University of North Alabama at Florence, Brack fashioned himself into a Beat Generation man of the world. Never quite famous, he won his share of museum exhibitions and was plugged in enough to sell a cartoon show to the ABC television network in the mid-sixties. It was entitled *To Build a Catapult* and was a satire on the arms race based on his work as a draftsman at the Boeing plant in Oxnard, California. Visiting the museums of Mexico City and New York, he saw himself as a generational avatar of the somewhat older Jackson Pollock and Mark Rothko. When I was twenty-two, he took me to Cedar Tavern in Greenwich Village, explaining that it was the hangout of the modern artists he admired. We were the only two intellectuals in our family, he said, and he coached me against being overly didactic in my work. Not for us the preacherly Alabama style. "Don't hit the nail on the head," he said. "Just tap it gently to the side." He urged me toward the skeptical worldview he called "Winston County existentialism," which was his way of saluting all that was primal and exceptional about our Appalachian roots. He regarded those roots as formative of a tough-minded creativity and a blessing, an individualized wellspring of material that could be pursued with devotion. He was, in sum, one of those Alabamians who venture into the world in search of something more expansive—in his case Big Art. When I stumbled into newspapering at twenty-one, he told me I had ink in my veins and had to keep writing. He preached ambition and art for art's sake.

But when I saw him for the first time in several years in the fall of 1978 at Memphis University, he had clearly settled into the role of that campus fixture, the divorced hippie art professor with tenure and an airy rental house, clean but sparsely furnished. On the cusp of fifty, he seemed chieftain of the shifting boho cast of wannabe artists and writers, perpetual grad students, and drinking drifters that can be found in any university town. There wasn't much new art in evidence, but he showed me, on a scroll of sketch paper, the document that became my Rosetta Stone. The big drawing, two feet high and over two and a half feet wide, contained a radiating web of spidery lines connecting dozens of rectangles, each representing a relative either dead or still living. From that moment, deciphering it was to become the sporadic, frequently interrupted work of decades.

Some of the boxes contained dates and others were blank, indicating a detail my grandparents couldn't recall. The genealogical chart started with the oldest ancestor they remembered by name, an Irish lad named Fell who jumped ship at seventeen in Savannah during the War of 1812. The second line of boxes contained a Sara "Puss" Jackson, who was allegedly a cousin of Andrew Jackson's. (North Alabama has always been well stocked with purported Jackson kin, legitimate and illegitimate.) The second rank of six boxes contained an entry that leapt out at me: "GORDON Went to Civil War, did not return (Yank)." There was no given name, but this unknown Union soldier's daughter was listed as Cora Elizabeth Gordon. This woman became the first wife of Andrew McKinley "Dock" Fell, the moonshiner who was my great-grandfather. Cora died in 1900 in McClain County, Oklahoma, which adjoined the Indian Territory, where Dock had gone to pursue his trade among the Native American tribes sent there on the Trail of Tears by President Jackson. The whiskey and the Indian Territory were not news to me. But the possibility that I might have a great-great-grandfather named Gordon who fought for the Union thrilled and intrigued me. I had learned that the military gravestones in Winston and Walker cemeteries were of two types; some said "C.S.A." and others said "U.S.A." I'd found none of the latter with any of the ancestral names I knew, but the idea of Gordon kin raised my hopes.

Brack wouldn't give me the document, and it would be another decade before I coaxed a copy from him. Finally, in November 1988 I received a dated photostatic copy of the chart (the document had clearly been reproduced on the art department's large-scale copying machine), with a new explanatory note to me penciled at the bottom of its kinship tree. The note, boldly initialed BW, said: "This information obtained from Della and R. C. Walker, summer 1958." Under his initials, he wrote, "This was done in one session; it was what they remembered at the time. It has not been reviewed by anyone."

I wish I knew the whereabouts of the original drawing, but I suspect my copy may be the only surviving proof of its creation. I had it framed and displayed it for years in my various dwellings, along with the quilted maps of the United States stitched together by Grandma Walker in her nineties. Her artistry as one of the last old-time quilters was celebrated in the Birmingham newspapers before her death in 1990. Brack's drawing would not yield its secrets easily, and I had learned little more by the time he died in 1994. Who was this Gordon, the ancestor with no first name? Brack, through the agency of one of the most casual drawings he ever produced, introduced the possibility that I could disown at least part of the burden of southern history. Close study revealed that one of Grandpa Walker's relatives was a Union cavalry blacksmith. The mountain world that he documented also fit perfectly with the fact that David Best, born less than three miles from my mother and Brack, ran north instead of south when he saw the Union horsemen in 1864. I had never identified with the Confederate heritage or the plantation culture. It did not seem so great a leap from Winston County existentialism to secessionist agnosticism.

The identity knots involving Gordon and the Walkers illustrate the scanty historiographic and genealogical evidence making up what Lincoln called "the short and simple annals of the poor." Whoever he might turn out to be, Great-Great-Grandpa Gordon was not an important player in my search for useful bits of family lore. That distinction belongs to my grandparents on both sides. From Judge Walker I got my passion for politics; from Grandma Raines came a certain flighty orneriness and ingrained hauteur—good qualities, it seems to me now, for a future journalist. As for Grandma Walker, she was a walking history book of the turn-of-the-century Sun Belt. As a young child, Della traveled by horse-drawn wagon from Winston County to the Indian Nations when her father, Dock Fell, migrated there to practice his twin specialties of herbal medicine and distillation. She remembered the isinglass curtains that protected the herb cabinet in the back of the two-mule wagon. Here is the relevance of these old country people for the purpose of explaining the interplay of heredity and racial attitudes passed down to my generation. Neither my sister nor I ever heard any of them use racist language, which reinforced my parents' teaching on this subject. I was ten or eleven when Grandpa Walker, with his statement about being a Jeffersonian Democrat, handed me the essential key to understanding his political education, his lack of the exhibitionistic bigotry so common in the South, and the dining-table incident recalled by Grady. In exiling his relative to the front porch, my grandfather passed a racial test, in the privacy of his own home, that few if any other white Alabamians of his time could have passed. As I would learn later, he had been shaped by a cluster of about twenty loyal Union-sympathizing counties that would be disregarded and ultimately disinherited by his native state.

The lingering evidence of that world, belated as its emergence may be, invites a new look at the canard that all white southerners subscribed to the totems and beliefs of a shared Confederate legacy. The view is as persistent as it is wrong. There were, in fact, *two* white Souths, largely defined by a collision, after Appomattox, of embittered, postbellum nostalgia on the one hand and on the other an explosion of industrial capitalism as theatrical as any other such boom of financial opportunity in imperial Britain or Yankee America. The most authoritative and concise telling of this tale is to be found in *The New South Creed: A Study in Southern Mythmaking,* a landmark work by my fellow Alabamian Paul M. Gaston (1928–2019) of the University of Virginia. Gaston's presence in the book you are holding illustrates what I've found to be a leitmotif: expatriate Alabamians laboring to unearth a more accurate alternative to the standard telling of southern history that has come down to us from across the fifteen-plus decades since the Civil War.

I wrote these words in the coastal retreat of Fairhope, Alabama, which faces westward toward Mobile across the historic bay of the same name. Paul Gaston's grandfather E. B. Gaston, a Christian Socialist during the heyday of American Utopianism, was a leader in a religious group of "Des Moines uplifters" who founded Fairhope in 1894 as a "single tax colony" dedicated to the ideal of "cooperative commonwealth" based on joint-land ownership principles defined by the once-famous political economist Henry G. George (1839–1897). A couple of years before his death in Charlottesville, Virginia, Gaston wrote me upon learning that I had purchased a winter retirement home in Fairhope. He was pleased that an heir to Alabama's small, but energetic progressive political tradition was living on his home ground. Of course, I already knew that the central presence in Gaston's book was Henry W. Grady, the foundational eminence of *The Atlanta Constitution,* where I had worked from 1971 to 1974—an important formative experience in my journey to *The New York Times.* I mention these connections as an example of the one or two degrees of separation among the cadre of professional archivists, historians, and writers who figure in the buried history of Alabama Unionism and the neglected heroes of Winston County.

I don't want to make too much of such synchronistic linkages, but to ignore them is to make way too little of the rootedness and tangential influences that figured in the telling, and mistelling, of the history of Black and white southerners who never marched to the Lost Cause drumbeat. There's another element to this tracery of Alabama-ness, and it extends to the South as a whole when one drills down into the propagandistic history of the Confederacy. Put simply, the characters we encounter at every turn are extraordinarily varied, colorful, eccentric, and obsessed. These days, many Alabamians—especially the wealthy, socially prominent red-state Republicans—hate to admit there is anything unusual about their state, its heritage, and its addiction-like loyalty to political performers such as the secessionist Fire-Eater William Lowndes Yancey in the 1860s, George Wallace in the 1960s and, unto the present day, Donald Trump. Denialism is Alabama's version of exceptionalism. Gainsaying the evidence of our past is an old and familiar task for privileged Alabamians, a bred-in-the-bone analogue to the exertions of the plantation Episcopalians who founded the University of the South in 1857, using slave-trader money, as a citadel for adducing biblical proof that slavery was ordained by God.

In regard to the beloved falsehoods of the Old South delusional system, I think of my childhood visits to Winston County as a kind of reality therapy. No inoculative moment was more important than Grandpa Walker telling me about Jeffersonian Democrats.

Again, it's a poured-in-glass memory that I can date precisely as to season and year. It was high summer and I had been left to spend a sweltering week "up in the country" with my grandparents. I know it was 1953 because that was the year window air conditioners came to Birmingham, and I returned to the city to find my parents had acquired the first one in our neighborhood. Thanks to my father's business acumen, our household was always in the lead when it came to television, refrigerated air, and stereophonic sound.

Why did the term "Jeffersonian Democrat" stick in my memory? In part, it was because I already knew that he was then a registered Republican, even if I didn't fully understand why he had lost his post office job after Wilson won the White House for the Democrats, replacing Taft in 1913. But there was more to the story. Even at that age I knew that the political hero of north Alabama was Andrew Jackson, and the term "Jacksonian Democrat" was already familiar to my ear. According to my research notes, it wouldn't be until January 7, 2020, that I decided to figure out, if I could, why my grandfather had chosen the adjectival form of the earlier president's name. My search started with *Alabama: The History of a Deep South State,* a revisionist work notable as a reliable, spin-free source produced by scholars born or reared in Alabama on the events of the Civil War and the civil rights movement. The fact that it did not appear from the University of Alabama Press until 1994 attests to the long shadow of the Lost Cause on the Tuscaloosa campus. The book is reliable on just about everything except a full accounting of Alabama Unionism.

From this useful book I learned that 1892 was a watershed year in Alabama political history. Stitching together radical elements of the Farmers' Alliance and the populist People's Party, Alabama's secretary of agriculture, Reuben Kolb, ran for governor against the Bourbon Democratic incumbent, Thomas Goode Jones, a Civil War hero of impeccable credentials. Jones attended Virginia Military Institute, marched with Stonewall, and carried Robert E. Lee's flag of surrender before the final ceremony at Appomattox. As a lawyer for the Louisville and Nashville Railroad, he represented a New South capitalist coalition of industrialists and plantation owners that was determined to stamp out the Populist movement that now had chapters in St. Clair, Walker, Winston, and the other "white counties," the usual designation for the Unionist strongholds in the hill country with low slave populations. This conflict, I realized, had shaped my grandfather's political identity. "As 1892 approached, Alabama politics—never strong on calm and rational debate—became a wild three ring circus." The Democrats refused to hold an open primary, using the same tactic that secessionists had used to block the small-farmer majority from defeating the plantation oligarchs. The dissidents then met in a rump convention and nominated Reuben Kolb for governor under the new "Jeffersonian Democrat" banner. His platform called for reforms demanded by the populist movement that was sweeping the agricultural states of the Southeast and Midwest: "better schools and better roads," abolition of the convict-lease system, an "honest count" in elections. In a concession to post-Reconstruction attitudes, statewide party primaries would be restricted to white male voters, but in an important caveat, the new party pledged to protect Black rights in general elections and to sponsor aid programs so that "through the means of kindness, a better understanding and more satisfactory condition may exist between the races."

I was struck immediately by the Jeffersonian Democratic platform as a harbinger of the political values I hold today, especially in regard to race. In the 1892 general election, the Jeffersonian Democrats went into a biracial voting coalition of voters from the newly formed populist movement among white farmers and the already registered Republicans of both races. Their progressive candidate, Reuben Kolb, was defeated by theft. Jones "won" by 11,435 votes from the Black Belt counties in the most famous stolen election in Alabama history. *Alabama Governors: A Political History of the State* put it plainly: "It was generally agreed that Kolb was 'counted' out by Democratic officials who stole the votes of Black men." Jones was reelected, and seven decades later it was his son, circuit judge Walter B. Jones, who was still upholding Lost Cause racial values in the biased 1964 ruling that was overturned by the Supreme Court in the twentieth century's most important libel case, *Times v. Sullivan*. In my Alabama, twigs got bent, north and south, in the Hill Country or in the Black Belt, by the long arm and ghostly reach of history.

So I now understand that my grandfather's use of the term "Jeffersonian Democrat" was conveying something far more profound than I was able to comprehend in his law library that day during my tenth summer. "Jeffersonian Democrat" was a reference to one of the rare promising moments in Alabama politics and, as I later deduced, a telling clue to his careful avoidance all his life of racist language. The Jeffersonian Democratic Party had a short life span during a precisely documented period starting with that 1892 gubernatorial election, which took place when my grandfather was eleven years old. It moved me to learn years later that we were both forging a precocious political identity at the same point in our childhoods. The Jeffersonian Democratic ideal of a biracial voting coalition would not reemerge in Alabama campaigns until after the passage of the 1965 voting rights legislation. Even then, it would not be powerful enough to prevent George Wallace from being reelected in

1970 in the most racist campaign of his career. But such coalitions would eventually bring integrated government to Birmingham, Montgomery, Mobile, and even Selma.

My earliest political writing dates from the following summer, when I was eleven and penning a letter to my brother in the cool comfort of a house that now had *two* air conditioners. Refrigerated air was transforming daily life in the South even as the region plunged into the racial heat wave that would last a full decade. I had forgotten that politics was very much on my mind at that age until I saw the letter from me among the papers left by my older brother when he died in 2008. He was serving in the army in Germany, and the letter, dated May 3, 1954, one day before the Democratic primary, was intended to bring him up to date on the fact that "politics are really hot." As expected, our household was against former governor James E. Folsom in his bid for a second term against the progressive pro-business candidate, a newspaperman from coastal Baldwin County named Jimmy Faulkner. Being for Faulkner fit my parents' pattern of always supporting the most respectable racial moderate in the Democratic primary, where victory was tantamount to election. Folsom was a racial moderate, too, but his drunkenness, womanizing, and financial corruption made him anathema to middle-class voters in prosperous Birmingham. All our Winston County relatives were for Big Jim, whom my parents considered too hillbilly and too crooked. Folsom had taken kickbacks from asphalt and road-building contractors. He was the paving-est governor in Alabama history, and the new road in Arley was understandably more important to our Winston kin than the investigative reporting about asphalt kickbacks in the Birmingham and Montgomery newspapers.

"I guess Folsom will be governor," I wrote with resignation, before noting the emergence in the new medium of televised campaign ads of a figure even more unacceptable in our household than Folsom. "Bull Connor is running for sheriff of Jefferson County. His daughter spoke for him and boy was it sickening." I was confused on one point. Connor was, in fact, running for police commissioner, in which role he would make Birmingham an international code word for racism. I added an update about a school excursion: "We're going to *The Birmingham News.* So we've got to bring in all sorts of stuff on printing."

I read this news flash from my past with a jolt of surprise; the confluence of politics and newspapering seems prophetic. I was fascinated by the typesetting magic of the hot-lead Linotype machines, and in only nine years the machines I saw that day would be setting type on the first stories I wrote as a cub reporter on the *Birmingham Post-Herald,* a Scripps-Howard morning paper that was timidly progressive by the standards of the time and place. In that old-fashioned newsroom equipped with high-fronted manual Underwoods, my political education leapt forward under the tutelage of engaged intellectuals who seethed with disdain for Alabama's primitive politics. I felt I had been plunged into the black-and-white world of the clichéd Hollywood journalism movies. In 1964, the *Post-Herald* newsroom was the nerve center of Birmingham's subterranean population of white liberals, and it reflected the dichotomies of a community being torn asunder by the tension between reaction and revolution. Wallace was our Satan, and we regarded the Republican presidential nominee, Barry Goldwater, as a Lincoln-betraying clown for pursuing the segregationist vote. On the evening shift, I strolled back from dinner with our news editor, Duard LeGrand, an urbane veteran of the New York publishing world. We passed under the Republican campaign sign that had been hung strategically across the street from the building that housed both the *Post-Herald* and *The Birmingham News.* The sign carried the Arizonan's photograph and the slogan "In your heart, you know he's right." In a mild voice, almost as if speaking to himself, Duard said, "In your guts, you know he's nuts." My assignments, covering racist school boards and George Wallace rallies, educated me about the underbelly of segregation. The work also freed me, permanently and invaluably, from any feelings of awe for elected officials of either party. I felt the first whisperings that my life's plan to write novels about Alabama's unembarrassed corruption might be less useful to society than telling the dangerous truth about the state.

As an old man, I find myself flipping back and forth between the twin theaters of my political instruction: "Bad Birmingham," as residents called it with a hint of perverse pride, and the Free State of Winston, the only county in Alabama with an unsullied right to be proud of its Civil War heritage. On that stage, Robert Cyle Walker was the star. In 1953, I thought he was as old as the hills and canyons on the twisting road to his home. But I now realize that he was a backcountry Republican in his prime (he was seventy-two) and that his own political education was more complex than I could have guessed. For the Jeffersonian Democrats were central to the Populist movement, with its radical plan for wealth redistribution, that swept the counties between Birmingham and the Tennessee line starting in 1890. His Republican credentials clearly dated from Winston's loyalty to Abraham Lincoln. But his Populist-tinged boyhood endowed him with a bipartisan tolerance rare in Alabama, as I learned from Congressman Carl Elliott of Jasper shortly before his death in 1999. Since Republicans had no chance of carrying the district, Judge Walker supported Elliott, a New Deal Democrat driven out of office by George Wallace in 1965 because he was Alabama's most liberal member of Congress. "Every election year," Elliott told me, "your grandfather held a watermelon cutting for me under a big hickory tree in his front yard." It was a signal to Arley voters that Elliott was a man of the people they could support as a matter of practical politics.

That hickory was an assembly point that figured prominently in my boyhood. My cousins and I cracked "hiker-nuts" on a boulder beside the trunk, and it was there that I watched Judge Walker's "land court," a holdover from the pioneer days of constant land squabbles. Grandpa Walker presided over property line disputes in this role as a quasi-judicial, avuncular community leader. I watched one morning in that same summer when he convened his land court under the big hickory. Since the Indians left in the 1830s, white settlers had been feuding over land lines. It usually boiled down to a matter of whether a fence line had been fudged to favor one neighbor or another or exactly what big oak tree a grandparent had designated as the corner of his property. Depending on the testiness of the claimants, such disputes could be a casus belli or a source of civic entertainment. The confab I witnessed was of the less tense variety. He advised one party of several men to remain in the shade of the tree, and he directed another group to wait by his barn, a couple of hundred feet away. In those days, a lot of property corners were still marked by piles of rocks in the forest and fields, so family tradition, memory, or restacked rocks were sometimes regarded as more authoritative than the surveyor's transit. A fence line moved ten feet translates into a bit more cotton or corn; a few dollars at harvest time was worth arguing over, but not worth paying court costs. Free of charge, Grandpa Walker scurried—or, rather, ambled—back and forth between the barn and the tree, bearing offers and counterdemands. He chewed tobacco and smoked a pipe as well, so there was a good deal of time devoted to stoking, tamping, and spitting. He was a vigorous old man who plowed using mules into his seventies, but speed was not his style. He liked folksy disputation, and seeing him in his land court made it easy for me, years later, to understand how he would have been drawn to the Populists in 1892. He turned eleven just before the election, and he was the kind of contrarian pre-adolescent that I would become by watching segregationist antics and crimes in Birmingham. For subsistence farmers like him, the "Big Mules" from Birmingham and the Black Belt were inspirational enemies, as disgusting as I found Bull Connor.

How certain can I be in reconstructing my grandfather's political biography? That brings us to the blend of genealogical detection, memory, historical triangulation, and guesswork needed to piece together a story like this one. In a candid biography of a grandfather active in the Louisiana Klan, Edward Ball details a methodology for reconstructing the politics of obscure ancestors. "Archives about unfamous or unrich people are not 'missing,': they are never made," he writes in explaining how he rediscovered his kinship to a violent Reconstruction Klansman who had been blurred out of his family history. "To write a life story from scattered and thin sources is like making a mosaic. A little piece of tile here, a chip of color there, and something from the scrap bin—until you have a picture. Archeologists work a similar process." It is the same process that Ken Burns calls "emotional archaeology," and that is what

I have attempted in investigating this old man's contribution to my civic education.

That 1892 election marked the snuffing out of the last candles of biracial politics lit in Alabama during Reconstruction. It was a reactionary triumph that allowed segregationist Democrats to pass the nation's harshest Jim Crow laws and ratify the 1901 constitution that made it practically impossible for Black people to vote. As the moral archeologist of my family on matters of race, I had an advantage that few diggers into the past possess, even such an expert as Edward Ball. Grady was my living witness to Judge Walker facing a test in his own home that few white Alabamians of his time would have confronted, much less passed. As for the church I grumpily attended when I got home to Birmingham from the hills of Winston, my sister, as noted earlier, remembers seeing Grandma Raines greet Sister Mitchell at Pinehurst in around 1950. Such are the "chips" through which defining traits resonate across generations of families that don't quite buy into the commanding culture. It's a mysterious process, difficult to calibrate, and especially daunting when it comes to rescuing unheralded difference-makers from the scrap bin of history.

6

CHRIS SHEATS: PHANTOM OF THE HILLS

As MY QUEST for buried evidence inched along, I clearly needed to sort out the mystery of Chris Sheats and the arc of his transformation from country schoolteacher to radical organizer. For a man who turned northern Alabama into a fertile recruiting ground for the Union army, Charles Christopher Sheats (1839–1904) left only scattered footprints on the Civil War record. Moreover, later researchers, including Donald B. Dodd, Glenda McWhirter Todd, and the new generation of Unionist scholars on American campuses, would spend hours on a false trail created by a crafty, energetic hill country writer named Wesley S. Thompson. I include myself in the number that rode hell-for-leather after Thompson's compelling yarn about Sheats's role at the secession convention, which convened on January 7, 1861, in Montgomery. The tangled evidence highlights one of the most vexing problems in historiography—what to conclude when a key account appears to conflict with the best evidence otherwise available. In this case the matter is complicated by the fact that Wesley Thompson presented his work trickily, as historical fiction that could be documented as true.

I first heard of Thompson when I was ten years old and my parents and I arrived one Sunday at the Walker farm in Arley to find Winston County abuzz with talk about a locally published book entitled *Tories of the Hills.* My parents brought a copy back to Birmingham to pass around among hill country relatives who had moved to the city. I remember the handoffs involving hushed conversations in which, frankly, I was not all that interested. I didn't fully understand what a "tory" was, but I formed the impression that something disruptive and vaguely scandalous had happened in Winston County during the war. The book finally disappeared from our household, lost to one of the borrowers, I assumed. But when my mother died in 2002, my sister found a copy of *Tories of the Hills* among the books she left, still in its tattered original jacket. Remarkably, it was inscribed to me by none other than Wesley S. Thompson in elegant, flowing penmanship. Old accounts from the Haleyville newspaper show that Thompson, a full-time schoolteacher in Winston County and a part-time minister in Double Springs and other small towns in the area, busily peddled his "historical novel" to women's clubs and church groups of the sort that Grandma Walker attended. Perhaps she bought me a copy at an autograph party. Another possibility is that my mother, knowing my growing fondness for books, picked it up in 1953 for presentation later when, presumably, I was old enough to handle books like *Stars Fell on Alabama* or *Tobacco Road.* It's almost as if one of these women were reaching across the generations to make sure that I would not forget the name I first encountered in 1961 in Carl Carmer's book.

Had I bothered to open *Tories of the Hills* in the fifties, I would have encountered Thompson's references to a flawless, silver-tongued character named Chris Sheats. After imbibing Jacksonian patriotism from his elders' conversation at the general store, Sheats emerges as their leader. They recognize that, at twenty-one, he has a superior grasp of the dangers of secession, and so they deliver him a landslide victory in the December 24, 1861, special election for Winston's two delegates to the secession convention set for January 7, 1861, in Montgomery. In Thompson's account, Sheats's defiant speech in defense of the Union throws the convention into chaos, and he is trundled from the House of Representatives chamber to the Montgomery jail. Despite its clumsy writing, the book has served as an inspiration to the small group of storytellers without whom the Free State saga might have flickered out. Wesley C. Thompson was not the most essential keeper of Free State stories, but he was the shiftiest and, in commercial terms, the most enterprising. Think of him, if you will, as another of the stock types in the Alabama backcountry, the avaricious preacher.

Appreciating the sparse documentation about Charles Christopher Sheats's remarkable career as an anti-Confederate activist requires some context about how Alabama officialdom treats its dissidents. Sheats was not merely an opponent of secession before the war. He was also a "scalawag" after it was over—that is to say, an Alabama-born white man who won political office or accepted federal appointments in the twelve years, from 1865 to 1877, when Republican officials of both races, protected by occupying federal troops and the Freedman's Bureau, dominated Deep South politics at the local, state, and congressional levels. Alabama, for example, sent three former slaves to Congress, and a total of fifteen hundred Black officeholders were elected across the South. But when white-supremacist Democrats took over again after the Compromise of 1877 ended Reconstruction, Republican officeholders were erased from public records, ridiculed or ignored by newspaper reports, and dismissed from public discourse or memory. If mentioned at all by Alabama historians, the actions and motives of these "outsiders" were truncated or misrepresented in a fashion that was comically transparent. For example, the suave congressman James T. Rapier, born to free Black parents in Florence, Alabama, appeared in Alabama histories as a "Canadian," since his prosperous parents sent him to be educated in Toronto. The depiction of Rapier, who was famous throughout Alabama and well known nationally, as a foreigner is telling. Then and now, being imposed upon by outsiders endures as a key trope of the self-pity at the heart of the Alabama Inferiority Syndrome. The scores, perhaps hundreds of native-born white Alabamians elected to office as Republicans during Reconstruction were simply expunged from the official records. As the fair-minded Sarah Woolfolk Wiggins, the leading Reconstruction scholar at the University of Alabama, put it, "Primary sources relative to a majority of Alabama scalawags do not exist, nor does even a satisfactory estimate of the number of scalawags in Alabama." This mirrors the later treatment of hill country Unionists by the Alabama Department of Archives and History. The only biography of Chris Sheats is a children's book with few details about his life. *Chris Sheats: The Man Who Refused to Secede* was published in 2004 by a small Birmingham publisher specializing in religious books. Its author, Martine G. Bates, devoted a chapter to explaining why she hit an informational wall after being intrigued by *Tories of the Hills*. "Instead of finding more documents that I could use to write this book, I was surprised to find almost nothing." She added, "Although the Alabama Department of Archives and History also tried to help, they, too, had almost nothing. . . . I searched the internet, went to the library repeatedly, made numerous telephone calls, and finally accepted that much of the information I was looking for did not exist."

In 2018, I hit the same wall at the archives in Montgomery. At that late date, I found no entry for Chris Sheats or the First Alabama Cavalry, U.S.A. in the newly digitized catalogue. I was in Montgomery on what had become a wearisome mission to cobble together a reliable biography of this brave renegade from scattered nuggets of fact mined from the vast moraine of Civil War documentation and propaganda. Over time, I realized how my work had been complicated by the lively imagination and plagiaristic talents of the scholarly-looking teacher/preacher whose signed book I had inherited. Using a vanity press operation he called Pareil Press, Thompson set up a cottage industry repackaging the Civil War lore collected by the most prominent member of his congregation, Winston County probate judge John Bennett Weaver (1879–1961), who decades earlier had interviewed the last surviving members of the First Alabama Cavalry, U.S.A. In an evasive introduction, Thompson essentially claimed credit for Weaver's life's work as a diligent antiquarian. He wrote of "having seen and talked to more persons who were over 100 years old than any man living." As if to excuse his refusal to credit Weaver, he added, referring to himself in the third person, "It is with regret that the author is not able to give due credit to all those who have given him these stories and in other ways assisted in the confirmation and preparation of the same. But the list would be entirely too long to be practicable."

In fact, Thompson could have used a single attribution to Judge Weaver, who probably knew more Winston County lore than anyone who ever lived. Aside from the anecdotal tales of old Winstonians, Weaver was really Thompson's only source for *Tories of the Hills.* In 1950, the judge had published at his own expense the foundational document about the Free State, an eight-page pamphlet entitled *A Brief History of Winston County, Alabama.* Earlier, in 1948, he provided an overview of Alabama Unionism in a speech I discovered, by luck, at the Birmingham Public Library. In another of those radiating Bama connections, the speech was captured on a wire recording by Professor George V. Irons of Howard College, now known as Samford University. In both its iterations, the Southern Baptist institution was very much under the Lost Cause umbrella. But Irons apparently wanted his students to hear an undiluted account of hill country resistance to the Civil War. Weaver told the Howard College assembly that in 1900, at the age of twenty-one, he had heard the elderly Sheats speak at Haleyville, Alabama, outlining his reasons for opposing secession in 1861 at the secession convention in Montgomery. That means that Weaver was probably the only published Alabamian to see the man in the flesh, a fact that would become relevant almost a century later in a lawsuit involving Thompson's unacknowledged debt to Weaver. On a personal note, Irons's sponsorship of Weaver's visit to the Birmingham campus illustrates the threads linking the small number of Alabamians who have remained interested in this sideshow of the great war. In 1964, working nights at the *Post-Herald* and eager at twenty-one to expand my knowledge of Alabama for journalistic purposes, I took a daytime course in political science from Dr. Irons, then regarded as one of the state's most admired scholars despite his institution's modest academic reputation.

Between them, Judge Weaver and Professor Irons left a provocative if incomplete addition to the historical record. Weaver knew he was addressing young Alabamians raised on tales of southern nobility and textbooks slanted toward the Lost Cause narrative. His soft-soap approach reflects the tentativeness with which southern teachers, preachers, and writers have had to express facts challenging the conventional wisdom that every white person in Alabama favored war against the Yankees. It was true, he conceded, that the northern states had abandoned slavery not because of idealism but because "the business proposition [of owning slaves] didn't pay them." He added, "The Southern people always said that and that's right, and what we want to do is tell the truth just like it is and if it hurts us a little bit that's all right. Let the truth stick."

In the apologetic tone of his language, one can sense the speaker was tiptoeing up to a truth he knew his audience of young Alabamians wouldn't like. The people in the hills "didn't want a war and they loved the Union. They didn't want the Negroes mistreated." Weaver said Winstonians were enraged by a Confederate general who said he'd not only keep his slaves but march them up to Bunker Hill, in Boston, Massachusetts, for a roll call. He also pledged to drink all the southern blood the Yankee cowards could spill. I've been unable to confirm the quote or that this general existed, but Weaver understood he was addressing students who had probably never heard that there were Alabamians who refused to fight for the South. Yet as a seasoned politician, Weaver knew his audience would understand that hot-tempered Alabama backwoodsmen could be provoked by a loudmouthed general from any army. "Well, I don't know if he said it or not, but that was quoted up in our country," Weaver said. "I'm giving you the standpoint of our people. Our people didn't care so much whether he carried his slaves up there but they didn't want to have to go up there and fight the people of Massachusetts to give General Jones that right."

It is noteworthy that even Weaver depicted Free State rebellion as a matter of common sense, not idealistic American patriotism. He began by recalling that in 1860, by order of Alabama governor Andrew B. Moore, each county was to elect two representatives for a secession convention to be held in the New Year. By calling a convention, the governor could avoid having the legislature vote on the secession issue. The elected legislature might have too many small farmers and philosophical opponents of slavery to provide enough votes for secession, whereas the big landowners could more easily dominate a small, one-issue convention. Indeed, seventy-nine of the one hundred delegates convened in the Alabama capital on January 7, 1861, were slave owners. The decision to circumvent the legislature was in keeping with William Lowndes Yancey's strategy of stacking the deck in favor of war. With ferocious oratory and tricky resolutions, Yancey guided the state to secede on January 11, 1861, without putting the matter to a popular vote, which he believed the slave owners would lose.

Weaver reviewed the chronology for the students in a key paragraph that needs to be studied closely.

> [The delegates] were elected on December 24, 1860. Chris Sheats campaigned on the platform if you elect me I will vote against secession first, last and all the time and he was elected and he did. He liked to have gotten in trouble. I think they put him in jail. I think the mistake he made after he refused to sign the secession resolution was that he ought to have come back to Winston instead of trying to go back and try to represent them down there in the Confederacy. Chris was a good man and he made some mistakes. Just like we all make mistakes . . . I heard Chris in 1900 at Haleyville make a speech and it's been a long time and I used to have a good recollection. I can't remember quite as well as I used to but I sort of scan[n]ed [my memory] and tryed [*sic*] to keep up with what he said. He reiterated some of the arguments that he claimed he made down there in the secession convention.

That's where the historiographic quandary arises, requiring me to undertake a detailed search to determine if Sheats really made any remarks in the convention itself, or whether his oratory came later, during his clandestine organizing campaign in the hills and hollows of Winston. An overwhelming weight of evidence supports the latter possibility, as does the fact that Weaver admitted his memory was faltering. None of the many journalistic accounts mention Sheats as a speaker at the convention, although numerous others are named. Most tellingly, the court-like transcripts made by the convention secretary, William Russell Smith, constitute one of the most detailed real-time stenographic accounts in the Civil War canon. Moreover, Smith the notetaker was on Sheats's side in the oratorical battle. He opposed withdrawal from the Union and joined Sheats in the group of twenty-four delegates who refused to sign the ordinance of secession as a matter of principle. Given his detailed accounts of anti-secession speeches, it seems impossible that Smith would have ignored his young ally's being jailed for a speech defying their common foe, William Lowndes Yancey, the overbearing delegate from Montgomery County. No memoirs or diaries have ever emerged that mention Sheats as actually speaking in explanation of his several no votes in every critical head count during the four-day conclave. On the other hand, Judge Weaver did hear Sheats himself, then sixty-one and in failing health, speak about his career in 1900. Were the two aging men confused? Or did something like what Weaver recalled actually happen?

Thompson, in his novel, presented a dramatic account of the moment after the ordinance of secession passed by a vote of sixty-one to thirty-nine. William Lowndes Yancey demanded that those who had voted against secession now sign the ordinance, as a sign of unanimous consent with the majority's decision. Thompson depicted Sheats as responding with a defiant speech, throwing the convention floor into a chaotic battle.

> "Never!" Chris cried firmly, knowing even then what might well happen to him for remaining firm in his convictions. And a moment later action came. He found himself seized by the arms and coat collar and literally being rushed bodily from the hall. In vain did he struggle—there were too many against him. He was thrown into a heavy carriage and the driver lashed the horses—he was rushed off to jail, a prisoner.

Here's where we enter the historiographic tangle. The only tumult in the hall recorded by journalists and participants was celebratory and

involved no physical attacks on Sheats and the other opponents of secession. That fact obliterates Thompson's claim that his book was "definitely more factual than fictional," as does Donald Dodd's painstaking
research in the Alabama archives. Most damaging to Thompson's hyped
account was Dodd's use of Governor John Gill Shorter's "letter boxes"
to reconstruct the first exhaustive chronology of Sheats's activities during 1861 and 1862. In those letters by and to Governor Shorter, Dodd
discovered the astonishing fact that Sheats vacillated between Unionism
and Confederate loyalty before emerging as the guiding spirit of the hillbilly rebellion. That wavering was what Judge Weaver was talking about
in his vague references in 1948 to Sheats's "mistakes." These details
matter, as a historiographic issue, because Wesley Thompson's account
has entered Winston folklore and showed up in accounts by journalists
and some historians. As a novelist rearranging historical events for dramatic effect, he was within his rights to invent a speech. And while
Sheats actually was arrested—in Montgomery, on October 14, 1862, as
we will see—Thompson rearranges the timeline and has the arrest occurring a full twenty-one months earlier.

Sheats, upon returning to Winston County after the convention, was
working both sides of the street, stirring up pro-Union feelings among
his constituents while allowing himself to be elected to the new Rebel
legislature and securing appointment as tax assessor of Winston County
in the spring and summer of 1861. Notwithstanding Sheats's standing as
a state representative and county official, Governor Shorter regarded
him with suspicion, and Sheats was fearful of returning to the capital
and for good reason. Shorter's spies and political allies kept him informed about Sheats's pro-Union speeches and recruiting activities. A
lawyer friend in Huntsville, Joseph R. Bradley, a Unionist who was now
pretending to cooperate with Shorter, convinced Sheats to appeal directly to the skeptical governor to be allowed to operate in Confederate
Montgomery. Sheats hand-delivered to Shorter the lawyer's letter saying Sheats had assured him that "he was loyal to his state and the Confederate states" and that he had been "slandered" as a traitor to the
Confederacy by political foes in the hill country. Shorter not only ig-

nored Bradley's advice, but there is good reason to believe that the governor, along with an Alabama conscription officer named Captain Nelson Fennel who had been chasing Sheats and other Unionist leaders in Winston County, personally arrested Sheats in the capitol. To be sure, Captain Fennel took custody of Sheats as a "prize captive" immediately after the meeting in the governor's office on or about October 4. Shorter rejected a plea for bail that Sheats submitted on October 14 after Shorter had him jailed on the accurate grounds that back home he had been "inducing citizens of the State to enlist, as soldiers, in the Army of the United States." A week later, Sheats was transferred under armed guard to the Confederate prison in Salisbury, North Carolina.

But by then, as it developed, Sheats's great work had been accomplished through a speech at Looney's Tavern near Haleyville, Alabama, that led to the formation of the First Alabama Cavalry, U.S.A. In keeping with the fact that Sheats's real footprints were few and led in at least two directions, Judge Weaver erroneously reported that the Looney's Tavern rally took place on the portentous date of July 4, 1861. In fact, that gathering of up to three thousand country folk unhappy to be Confederate citizens, which can be called the Free State's independence day, did not come until mid-1862, probably in late spring or early summer. The exact date has never been nailed down by state archivists. By that time, in any event, Sheats was on the run from Confederate authorities who had learned of his Looney's Tavern speech.

I was keenly disappointed to learn of Sheats's bargaining for forgiveness with the Fire-Eater governor. Was he another of the war's unprincipled opportunists? The pictures of Sheats drawn by Weaver and Dodd were as different as their methods. Weaver, the amateur, scooped up oral histories unselectively, but even he had discovered Sheats's fallibility. Dodd, an earnest student in the process of becoming a trained historian, had established Sheats's duplicity by meticulously combing through Shorter's letters, and his work left no doubt that Sheats had bargained for a spot in the Rebel legislature.

The next step in my quest to discover the identity of this man called Sheats had me looking back toward the hills. Regardless of his initial irresolution about which side to support, he wound up putting together a popular movement that became a thorn in the flesh of authorities in Montgomery and Richmond. I still had to educate myself about the clandestine community organizing he was doing after returning home to the frozen wilds of north Alabama in mid-January 1861, after the secession convention. It was a double game, to be sure, given Dodd's discovery of Sheats's flirtation with Shorter and his cronies in Huntsville law offices and under the white dome of the capital in Montgomery; there was a certain realpolitik involved. But after his return to Winston County Sheats tirelessly crisscrossed the backroads to set up secret cells of Free Staters. Shorter's letters to military authorities show he was aware of these subversive activities and was keen to stop them. That's why he seized the first chance he had to grab a clumsily calculating Sheats, who, a political novice still only twenty-three years old, may have thought he was more clever than his elders.

I found another important piece of the puzzle in the overall context of what was still only a budding rebellion. It's essential to remember that scrambling was the order of the day across the South for most of 1861. The slave-owning zealots in the Black Belt and Mobile were clamoring for war, but less affluent Alabamians were waiting to see if the new Rebel government would jell. My family tree inquiries convinced me that Sheats was practicing an extreme form of the trickery employed by my defenseless kin in Walker, Winston, and St. Clair Counties, who sometimes feigned Confederate sympathies even as they dodged that government's enlistment officers by "lying out" in caverns and forested hideaways. The historian Michael Fellman, an expert on the vulnerability of civilians in Missouri's guerilla war in the same years, coined a term for what Sheats and the draft evaders were doing. He called it "survival lying," and its workings will require us to take a closer look at conditions in the north Alabama counties whose delegates declined to sign the ordinance of secession.

In any event, without the work of Weaver and Dodd, we could not even begin to draw a portrait of Sheats over the first two years of the conflict. The stories that Judge Weaver preserved were both incomplete and indispensable. In separating fact from fiction in Sheats's life, we find ourselves hopscotching through a gallery of the players and witnesses who endowed Alabama's political culture with its intrinsic strangeness and almost Byzantine intricacy. Two young Free Staters touched by features of that culture (including Weaver's tales and Thompson's pickpocketed version of them) were men I came to know well: the historian Dodd and a federal judge named Frank M. Johnson Jr. Although almost a generation apart in age, Johnson (1918–1999) and Dodd (1940–2021) grew up as princelings in Alabama's only Republican county. Their ties were close. Donald's uncle Pert Dodd, a U.S. deputy marshal, was serving as Johnson's official bodyguard when Klansmen bombed the home of the judge's mother in Montgomery in 1967. In the course of my research, I found a letter to a Haleyville newspaper showing the bonds that formed in the tiny pantheon of Alabama Unionism. Over the years, Weaver, Johnson's father, Frank M. Johnson Sr., and Donald Dodd's father, Ben Dodd (known widely as "Uncle Ben"), had all held Alabama's only Republican legislative seat. Powerless in Montgomery, this tight little triumvirate cooperated in monopolizing political patronage in Winston County. They even withstood an attempt by my grandfather Walker's best friend, a prosperous merchant, to capture the GOP's lone legislative seat for Arley.

So it was only natural that in the early 1930s, Judge John Bennett Weaver took his political ally Frank Sr. on a pilgrimage to visit the grave of Chris Sheats in an adjoining county. The location of the grave was one secret that Weaver did not share with Wesley S. Thompson or, apparently, anyone but the Johnson family, whom he knew to be the direct descendants of First Alabama soldiers. Those kept in the dark included a few other antiquarians who were widely known to be searching for the grave. When the Haleyville newspaper revealed the "discovery" of the grave by other local history buffs in its March 20, 1962, issue, with the headline "Free Stater's Grave Found After Many Years of Frustrating Search," it looked like a coup for a new group of experts. A few days later a letter to the editor from Frank Johnson Sr. appeared, saying that the "late Hon. John B. Weaver showed me one day, [Sheats's] tomb some 30 years ago. Sorry I did not know such effort was being made to locate it, could have saved [the searchers] much time and trouble." By that time, Frank M. Johnson Jr. was becoming famous for his civil rights rulings. Frank Sr. had retired to Montgomery to be near him. No political insider in Winston County could fail to note that the old Johnson-Weaver-Dodd alliance was still intact and that the legend of Chris Sheats still lingered in the hills, even if he was given short shrift in the historical literature.

Other Alabama papers picked up the story of the "long-lost grave," and that marked the second time, after my 1961 reading of Carl Carmer's book, that I saw Sheats's name in print. Meanwhile, Donald Dodd, by now a history student at Auburn, was fact-checking the book that had inflamed his teenage curiosity about the neglected Civil War history of the "Tories" in his home county. He concluded that Thompson was wildly inaccurate and a plagiarist to boot. *Tories of the Hills* depicted Sheats as one of the main orators opposing secession in Montgomery. In an audacious scene, Thompson has Sheats, a political novice, berating the most powerful men in the state and reducing the proceedings to bedlam, saying he'd rather "suffer as a traitor to the Rebels than a traitor to the Union." Yancey had demanded unanimous consent for the ordinance of secession; the two dozen cooperationist holdouts, including Sheats, needed to sign it in support of a united Confederacy or face the gallows.

Perhaps because the description was so grandiose, it would take more than half a century for someone to blow the whistle on his clumsy effort to repackage his phony details in a form that real historians would accept. Indeed, Thompson's version of Sheats's debut at the convention is repeated in one of the best of the new histories, *Alabamians in Blue* (published in 2019), but with a proper note of skepticism and an asterisk. The author, the professional military historian Christopher M. Rein, writes that in 1968 Thompson tried to follow up on the local popularity of *Tories of the Hills* by publishing an allegedly nonfiction account of the same material entitled *The Free State of Winston: A History of Winston County, Alabama.* In what Rein charitably calls this "thinly sourced" work, Thompson presented as straight history the same story of the speech that Sheats never delivered in the Alabama capitol and his alleged beating and incarceration. Rein notes that the only source for this oft-told story is "fictional accounts penned by the [same] author." In other words, the historian Thompson was quoting the novelist Thompson without admitting the details were made up. Rein's exposure of Thompson's circular self-plagiarism was, on balance, a gentle reproof delivered with deadly scholarly reserve.

Donald Dodd had discovered Thompson's deception more than half a century earlier, when he was a graduate student at Auburn in the early 1960s, but kept his feelings to himself for years. He knew that back home in Haleyville and Double Springs, the gregarious Thompson had become a popular figure as a teacher and minister, and *Tories of the Hills* had added to his stature. Dodd also thought he might follow his father, Weaver, and Frank M. Johnson Sr. into leadership of the local Republican machine. So he decided not to take Thompson on publicly, even after he found out that Thompson had secretly secured through a co-religionist in the Auburn library a copy of Dodd's unpublished master's thesis. Dodd told me he thought at the time that Thompson was looking for information he could hijack, repeating the trick he played on Judge Weaver. In one of our last conversations Dodd seemed liberated by the chance to take on the whole business about the speech, telling me that the speech "didn't happen and it didn't come close to happening. [Sheats] was a young Winston County schoolteacher awed by the experience. He didn't say a word. He was jailed later on. He was expelled from the legislature [a year later] because he made a speech recruiting for the Union." I asked Dodd why so many people believed Thompson's version of the convention and why the false account had been picked up in historical and journalistic accounts. "The hardest thing to do is to document something that didn't occur," he told me. "I got mad at him because I spent so much time on false leads."

Chris Rein and Donald Dodd, both trained scholars, treated Wesley Thompson mercifully, but he had not been so lucky in October 1953, when his promotional tour of Alabama newsrooms took him to the

Montgomery Advertiser. It was the lair of a curmudgeonly columnist named J. Fred Thornton. He was a Lost Cause defender every bit as ferocious as Marie Bankhead Owen and her near equal as a local celebrity among Montgomery's keepers of the flame. Thompson was peddling books all over the state for several years and had great success in making *Tories of the Hills* and later self-published books into moneymakers. Surviving documents prove that he may have made the equivalent of $350,000 in 2020 dollars. His energetic salesmanship led him to Thornton's newspaper. As associate editor of Alabama's most important political paper, Thornton was another of those grandiose characters who make prowling Alabama's attic so addictive for me.

J. Fred Thornton was the first critic to pierce the balloon of Thompson's suspect sourcing. Even by Alabama's standards, J. Fred Thornton was an odd duck, odd enough to deserve at least a cameo for sussing out Thompson's grandiosity. A journalist-cum-politico, Thornton knew everyone, and from his perch at the *Advertiser,* he spent the 1950s firing broadsides against "race-mixing in the schools." His column ran with a picture of a beefy man in a Menckenesque pose, necktie, starched shirt, and lots of white cuff shooting from the sleeves of his dark suit coat. He had obviously studied H. L. Mencken's journalism, too. He wrote an easy, conversational prose replete with racism, sexism, and a careful balance of contempt and reverence for the rich and the powerful in politics and religion. The Mencken connection may seem odd, given the Sage of Baltimore's 1918 broadside against southern culture, "The Sahara of the Bozart." But Mencken was revered in southern newsrooms and was entertained handsomely in Montgomery by Fred Thornton's longtime "liberal" boss, Grover C. Hall Sr., whose anti-Klan editorials won a Pulitzer in 1928.

On race, however, Thornton's style was not crimped by his paper's anti-Klan tradition. He invoked Robert E. Lee as the authority for his intuitive distrust of Africans, who he regarded as given to "voodoo" and "loafing in the shade while the women work." Culturally and intellectually, the collision between Thompson and Thornton was a heroic mismatch. Thompson had better academic credentials, including a master's degree from the University of Oklahoma in Norman, a solid regional institution. But in Thornton's eyes, he was a hustling country preacher who wore his hunger like a cheap suit. Thornton had never gone beyond sixth grade in his native Kentucky, but he had soldiered in France during World War I and acquired the dash of a *Front Page*–era newshawk after returning to the *Advertiser*. Under the Halls, his Sunday column had become the voice of mandarin Montgomery. The more I read about Thornton the more my heart sank at a missed opportunity: we had overlapped in Alabama's lively newspaper world but never crossed paths. He had just retired when Grover Hall Jr. interviewed me for a post at the *Advertiser* in 1964, and we probably would have met if I had moved to Montgomery. But Hall and I had mutually rejected each other: I regarded him as a Wallace crony, and he condemned me, thumping his desk, as a "patty liberal," his coinage for "knee jerk."

J. Fred Thornton started at the *Advertiser* as a cub in 1916, and before long he cut a figure in that town of contradictions. He ran to the late hours with "dice-playing" politicians and understood the sexual impact of the ascent of two Montgomery girls, Zelda Fitzgerald and Tallulah Bankhead, to international stardom in the flapper culture. After serving in World War I, Thornton drifted out of journalism and showed up in the public prints as a "bright and husky helper" on the campaign trail with two-term governor Bibb Graves, the Yale-educated Klansman who more than any other twentieth-century politician embodied the conflicting impulses of an Alabama capital forever torn between racism and share-the-wealth progressivism.

In any event, Thornton had the ammunition and the deadly aim to turn on an author manqué like Thompson, who was making his Uriah Heep–like pilgrimage from the hills to peddle his self-published book. *Tories of the Hills* had come out in September 1953, which was the last politically peaceful autumn of my childhood—"Black Monday," the 1954 Supreme Court decision in *Brown v. Board of Education,* was still months away. By Alabama standards all was placid. The Dixiecrat hysteria had died down, and George Wallace was still a racial "moderate" in the mold of that flawed but kindhearted old populist Big Jim Folsom,

"the little man's big friend." The bombings on Dynamite Hill, a changing neighborhood where Black people were buying homes, had slowed
down because Folsom had sent Ben Allen, a rough, old-school lawman
of my acquaintance, up to Birmingham to rein in Robert "Dynamite
Bob" Chambliss, the Klan bomber who operated with Bull Connor's
protection. My YMCA baseball team of eleven-year-olds won the city
championship in August, based on a grand slam I hit to bring us from
behind in the final game of the playoffs. It was the apex of my athletic
career, and a damn good time for Wesley Thompson, on summer break
from his main job as a Winston County schoolteacher. His book sold
well during a tour of the state's civic clubs and newsrooms. Even *The
Birmingham News,* which normally gave scant attention to vanity press
offerings, was kind enough to lower its standards. The *News* had the
state's best Sunday book page, and its editor, J. F. Rothermel, wrote in
the lead review that Thompson's narrative was "more historical than
fictional." He swallowed Thompson's claim to "years of research on the
subject," noting that "he has talked to many of the old residents of the
area, now fading away, gathering first-hand anecdotes and recollections." Not until he got to Montgomery did Thompson face a thorough
frisk about his "facts," and they didn't pass J. Fred Thornton's smell
test. His popular Sunday column opened with a bold, multi-deck, and
typically sarcastic headline: "Confederate Atrocities Finally Revealed."

Tongue in cheek, he ridiculed Thompson's accounts of Confederates committing "butcheries" worse than Hitler's. Better to rely on
"Black Belt brains" than "North Alabama division and ineptitude" for a
true picture of Lost Cause nobility. "Venerated local historical luminar-
ies" had assured him that the first arrest had never happened and the
1862 arrest by Governor Shorter's crew was nowhere near as violent or
dramatic. But, he continued, "I received a visit from Author Thompson
in person. When I raised the point of Sheats's first jailing for refusing to
sign the secession ordinance, Thompson offered to take me to the Capitol and show documentary proof in the Department of Archives & History. On this latter point, he seems to have scored a beat on other
Alabama historians—though I have not read every Alabama history."

When I read that, I thought perhaps Donald Dodd had missed something. But Thompson could not deliver the promised evidence. We know this because on October 21, 1953, the newspaper published a letter from Thompson that made it clear he had not led Thornton on a pilgrimage to the archives to see his "documentary proof." Instead the letter was devoted to an ad hominem attack on Thornton's lack of education under the overly generous headline "Tory Author Answers Rebel Critic." Instead of proof, the preacher was offering gorilla dust, writing, "May I suggest to the reader that after having had training in historical-research and documentary evidences which courses lead to the acquisition of a Master of Arts Degree, and after having made investigations into the incidents and events described in the book, I feel that I am as well prepared to write as my critic, Mr. Thornton, who has had none of these." But on the central charge—that he had imagined a convention-floor assault on Sheats—the letter was silent. To use the Watergate phrase, it was a classic non-denial denial, and it concluded, characteristically, with a sales pitch: "For the benefit of those who would like to read *Tories of the Hills,* for yourselves and form your own opinions about it, it is being sold by the hundreds of copies throughout the state. In less than two months I have sold almost 600 copies myself."

Even if Sheats had delivered the speech invented for him, he would not have been one of the oratorical stars of the four-day convention. It was a showdown of flame-throwing rhetoric dominated by Yancey, generally regarded as the single orator who did more to start the Civil War than any other secessionist ideologue. In 1859 he stunned an abolitionist audience in Boston by joking that he breakfasted on roasted slaves. In the following year, Yancey's incendiary address to the South Carolina convention led that state to become the first to secede. Back in Alabama, however, voters stunned Yancey by choosing for the secession convention delegates who were almost evenly split on the question of immediate secession. A proposal was made to the convention for a public statewide referendum on secession, and while Yancey's Fire-Eaters were able to block it, they prevailed by only nine votes, 54 to 45. Although a majority of the one hundred delegates owned slaves, Yancey believed his side would lose a popular vote, and he worried about the public impact of an unexpectedly close vote when the ordinance of secession passed by an unimpressive vote of 61 to 39. Yancey was intent on "maintaining the fiction of unanimous support for the insurrection," and demanded that "the defeated minority sign the ordinance they had just voted against." Sheats and twenty-three others refused to do so. Almost beside himself, Yancey reminded the delegates that anyone who opposed secession could be hanged, and the threat produced one of the greatest speeches ever delivered in the Alabama capitol—from the real leader of the cooperationist caucus. That was not Sheats, as Thompson alleged, but a wealthy Tuscaloosan named Robert Jemison Jr. Rounding on Yancey, Jemison shouted, "Will the gentleman go into those sections of the state and hang all those who are opposed to Secession? Will he hang them by families, by neighborhoods, by counties, by congressional districts? Who, sir, will give the bloody order? Who will be your executioner? Is this the spirit of Southern Chivalry?"

Sheats had even more reason to keep quiet when his mentor, Jeremiah Clemens, switched sides to support Yancey's demand for unanimous consent. In stentorian terms, Clemens asserted that he was still opposed to secession but would nonetheless sign the ordinance, in order to signal that loyalty to Alabama was every delegate's foremost obligation. It was the same traitorous rationale that would enable Robert E. Lee and hundreds of West Point–trained army officers to betray their oaths to protect and defend the Constitution. With his unexpected surrender, Clemens, a Mexican War hero, ended the debate on the issue, and he salted his remarks with his trademark pomposity. "I believe your Ordinance is wrong," he told Yancey. "If I could defeat it, I would; but I know I cannot," he said. "Acting upon the conviction of a lifetime, calmly and deliberately, I walk with you into revolution." Clemens, an imposing man with a high-domed forehead and a long nose, always had an eye cocked for the main chance. Having already served as a United States senator in his thirties, the forty-six-year-old Clemens envisioned a return to high military office or cabinet rank in the new Confederate government.

If Sheats said anything to protest Yancey's threat of execution or Clemens's duplicity, it was missed by every journalist, government note-taker, and future diarist in the hall; his shining moment was yet to come. Reaching home over difficult, winter-crusted roads after the January 11 adjournment of the convention, Chris Sheats quietly launched a classic campaign of community organizing among constituents still hungry for a way to oppose the war against what they called the "Old Flag." Thompson, in his eagerness to capitalize on Judge Weaver's irreplaceable re-search, had invented a story far less important than Sheats's real-life adventures. That real-life story was the one Judge John Bennett Weaver preserved, but his legal claim to the original scholarship plagiarized in *Tories of the Hills* would be recognized only after many years and in a convoluted way that seems somehow appropriate to Winston County's contrarian ways and Thompson's calling as a teacher, preacher, and lit-erary pickpocket.

A final word on Chris Sheats in the context of Civil War history. Pockets of doubt about the slave owners' Civil War project existed throughout the Appalachian South and as far south as Florida and as far north and west as Arkansas and Texas. We have documentary evidence from a handful of dissidents who either left diaries or received federal pensions for their hazardous opposition to the Confederacy. The most famous was probably Dan Ellis, a Tennessean credited with leading four thousand white mountaineers and escaping slaves to the Kentucky line, where many enlisted in the Union army. But only Chris Sheats inspired a fighting force that helped end the war. That's the story that Alabama refused to celebrate.

7

A Discovery in Atlanta

My CASUAL INTEREST in Alabama Unionism eventually turned into an intellectual quest that, as a result of the rhythm of my journalistic career, would take years to play out. Because of newspapering, it had to remain an intermittent activity, and the two pursuits are braided together in my story. By the start of the 1970s, I had worked for smart editors at three good Alabama papers. They were like professors in my personal graduate journalism school. Then, in 1970, I decided to do something I'd never expected to do in my writing career: leave Alabama. My boss at the time, Vincent Townsend, the testy executive editor of *The Birmingham News,* responded with his usual good grace. "So," he said, dropping by my desk for one of his acid-tongued visits, "we made you a star and now you're abandoning us for Atlanta."

Townsend hated Atlanta for having a bigger airport and better reputation than Birmingham. He had made the *News* into a cozy, prosperous place where it was fun to be a local celebrity, which I had become as the paper's movie critic and resident defender of the avant-garde in Birmingham's stodgy cultural world. Since the *News* could cherry-pick Alabama newsrooms, he was surprised by my departure—and, frankly, so was I. But the overture from Georgia's venerable paper of record disrupted my parochial game plan. I had thought I'd support myself by newspapering or teaching on my native ground while pursuing what I still believed would be my main calling in life: writing thoughtful novels full of local color and piercing social commentary about my favorite subjects, the troubled soul and crazy people of Alabama. But the *Constitution* thought the pay for a Birmingham star ought to be $15,000 a year. I had a young family to support, and the offer from the *Constitution* met my personal criteria for managing my journalistic career: never take a job on the city desk, and move when you're offered a raise.

Besides, I was flattered to get a call from the newspaper of Henry W. Grady (1850–1889). In the 1960s its liberal columnists Ralph McGill and Eugene Patterson won it a place on *Time* magazine's listing of the top ten American papers. It was already famous for creating the New South movement. In the previous century, Grady, as quarter-owner and editor of the *Constitution,* had achieved international fame as an orator with an after-dinner speech in 1886 at Delmonico's restaurant in Manhattan. The plutocratic audience included both J. P. Morgan and General William Tecumseh Sherman, who had burned Grady's hometown in 1864. With his trademark wit, Grady quipped that Sherman was an excellent soldier "but a mite careless about fire." But it was his economic message that attracted Morgan and the other Wall Streeters that evening of December 21, 1886. The South was ripe for Yankee exploitation thanks to cotton crops sufficient for a four-hundred-mile belt of textile mills from Virginia to Georgia and enough Alabama iron and coal to make Birmingham as smoky as Pittsburgh. Grady had lifted the name of this proposed economic/political partnership between northern money and southern natural resources, the New South movement, from the Thanksgiving sermon of his Methodist minister in Atlanta, who was urging a renewal of southern spirit now that the Republicans, by ending Reconstruction, had returned control of the South's destiny to local Democrats and their doctrine of white supremacy. The New South's prosperity would rest on three pillars: loyalty of the Deep South to the restored Union, recognition by all Americans of "the pathos and glory of the Lost Cause," and the right of the South to handle the race issue in its own way. Thus, by adherence to the second principle during the rise of an industrialized New South in the years between 1865 and 1900, the stage was set for the parallel triumph of Lost Cause thinking not only across the former Confederacy but also in popular culture nationally and in the North's leading business and educational centers. In that process, Atlanta supplied the imagery of the Confederate and post-Confederate South, and gritty old Birmingham showed how to mine money from the old fought-over soil.

Vincent Townsend's sour farewell upon my departure for the *Constitution* reflected the fact that he and the city he dominated during a fifty-year career at the *News* had a reverse Midas touch when it came to public relations, as well as a deep antipathy to all things related to Atlanta, particularly its reputation as "The City Too Busy to Hate." The tale-of-two-cities motif has been elaborated in countless articles, with Birmingham always cast as the hard-luck twin. Once the fire hoses and the 1963 bombing of the Sixteenth Street Baptist Church made Birmingham an international target of condemnation, Townsend, another alumnus of Birmingham-Southern, decided that what Birmingham needed, rather than the change of heart urged by Chuck Morgan as a response to the 1963 church bombing, was a better slogan. He was the most deeply corrupt journalist I ever worked for, and he had the advantage of serving as a kind of journalistic plantation manager for the most ethically indifferent national chain, Newhouse Newspapers Inc. Its kingpin, Sam Newhouse, gave him a free hand in Birmingham, and using the front page of the *News*, Townsend shamelessly promoted his invention, Operation New Birmingham, an organization founded in 1962 with himself as its president. Townsend was involved in coming up with a blizzard of slogans that backfired, including "The City of Churches" and "It's Nice to Have You in Birmingham." The former, of course, underscored the brutal irony of the Sixteenth Street Church bombing, and the latter opened the door for Birmingham's firebrand Black leader, the Reverend Fred L. Shuttlesworth, to invite Dr. King's Southern Christian Leadership Conference to begin desegregation marches in the city in early 1963. Operation New Birmingham was a coalition dominated by the department store owners whose refusal to desegregate their lunch counters and restrooms had brought Dr. Martin Luther King Jr. to the city in the first place. Shuttlesworth told me in 1973 about meeting with Operation New Birmingham leaders, including a Townsend favorite, Sidney Smyer, a former Dixiecrat, a realtor, the kingpin of the local Rotary International, and the chair of the Birmingham Chamber of Commerce. Smyer begged Shuttlesworth for help in keeping Dr. King out while Birmingham repaired its reputation. It was the siren song of gradualism, and Shuttlesworth knew exactly how to respond. "I said, 'Well, on your slogan at the airport and elsewhere, 'It's So Nice to Have you in Birmingham' . . . we think that means King, too. We think he's nice enough to come in here. He's nice as anybody else, and there are some things wrong, the mere fact that we have to invite him in.'"

The last time I talked to Vincent Townsend was in 1978 by telephone, about the blowback from another of his schemes. *The Birmingham News*'s longtime lawyer James C. Barton, of Mountain Brook, told me that Townsend, with the help of the FBI, had armed his pet police reporter, Tom Lankford, with the equipment needed to bug the office of Birmingham's segregationist mayor, Art Hanes, a partner with Bull Connor in planned police violence. While Birmingham's reputation twisted slowly in the winds of global condemnation in 1963, Townsend, Barton, and the *News* leadership team laughed at tapes of Hanes setting up an assignation with his mistress. "Why did you wiretap Art Hanes?" I asked the old man more than a decade and a half later. "I don't remember," he said haltingly. "I've had a stroke." It was pointless—not to mention too late—to remind Townsend that Hanes, a former FBI agent, was among several Birmingham mayors handpicked by him to run for the office with the benefit of *News* promotional muscle. The Birmingham-born author Diane McWhorter, winner of the Pulitzer Prize for her history *Carry Me Home: Birmingham, Alabama: The Climactic Battle of the Civil Rights Revolution*, proved that among the things Townsend kept out of the paper was a plan involving Connor's designated liaison to the Ku Klux Klan, a detective named Tom Cook, to hire a Black gunman to kill Shuttlesworth on the steps of his home. Tom Lankford and the *News* had learned about the plot through wiretaps conducted in concert with Birmingham police, the FBI, and the local telephone company.

Despite such skullduggery, Townsend's political meddling was being touted by the end of his life as good civic journalism in carefully sanitized tributes from the Birmingham City Council and the University of Alabama's journalism school, the College of Communications and Information Sciences (C&IS). I almost laughed when I read the C&IS press release from September 23, 2009, marking Townsend's induction into the school's Communications Hall of Fame: "During the turbulent years of the civil rights movement, Townsend worked tirelessly behind the scenes to promote better interracial relations."

I bring this example into sharp relief to make a basic point that intellectual dishonesty of a particularly flagrant sort is a thematic feature, across the decades, of public life in Alabama and, as we shall see, of the Lost Cause campaign. Both injected numerous errors of omission and commission into the historical record. As Yale historian Rollin Osterweis observed, the South had been "surrounded by an intellectual blockade against unwanted ideas after 1831," the year that William Lloyd Garrison founded his abolitionist newspaper, *The Liberator,* in Boston and Nat Turner was hanged in Virginia for leading a slave rebellion that killed fifty-one whites. Together these events presented Alabama with its most nightmarish threats: outside ideas and out-of-control Black men. Certainly, the state was still hunkered behind that intellectual curtain when Alabama's political rulers, the powerful Bankhead machine, permitted the establishment of the nation's first official state archives in Montgomery in 1901, and Alabama remains the most dedicated of all the red states of the Trump era to maintaining, as Osterweis put it, "the tough fiber of the Southern intellectual blockade against progressive crusades."

To be sure, when I arrived in Atlanta in August 1971, the paper, while still waving the progressive banner of Henry W. Grady, had retreated from the overt civil-rights advocacy of its eloquent Pulitzer-winning columnists Ralph McGill and Eugene C. Patterson. Both men had supported the progressive mayors William Hartsfield and Ivan Allen, who guided Atlanta peacefully through the sixties. And the *Constitution* would occasionally beard the establishment rather than play footsie with it behind the scenes. For example, the paper's star investigative reporter, Jeff Nesmith, and I broke the story of how Mills B. Lane Jr., chairman of the Citizens and Southern National Bank, had housebroken Lester Maddox, the incautious segregationist elected governor in 1966, by awarding him ownership of two income-producing properties leased to Burger King in the booming suburb of Marietta. (Nesmith, who died in 2023, would win a Pulitzer in 1997 for exposés about Veterans Administration hospitals.)

To be a young journalist in "Hotlanta" in the 1970s was bracing. I wrote an article for *Harper's Weekly* about how the city had become a magnet for tens of thousands of yuppies from the backwater towns of the South. Novels were coming out from a group of writers including Pat Conroy, Anne Rivers Siddons, and my *Constitution* colleague Celestine Sibley, a venerated columnist and reporter. The Old New York Book Shop, in a ramshackle house off Peachtree Street, also opened the year I got to town, and its alcohol-fueled autograph parties quickly made it what a book-trade website called "the center of the literary community." When Pat Conroy's *The Great Santini* appeared in mid-decade, he and his father, retired Marine colonel Donald Conroy, who was the model for Robert Duvall's title character in the movie, became the presiding mascots there—at least during periods of truce during the decades-long Oedipal warfare that raged between the two hard-drinking Conroys. The owner of the place, and Conroy's closest friend, was a skilled antiquarian book dealer named Cliff Graubart, whose Brooklyn accent and hustle had in no way been softened by Atlanta. Like the city itself in the seventies, the Old New York was one of those hard-rolling places where writers, artists, scenesters, and Atlanta-based correspondents for national news organizations were happy to be. At some point, probably during the autograph party for Celestine Sibley's novel *Jincey* in 1978, I mentioned to Cliff that I had hit a dead end in my search for a book I had seen footnoted in an obscure Civil War anthology. The title

was *Alabama Tories: The First Alabama Cavalry, U.S.A., 1862–1865.*
He tracked it down within days, and we were both a little shocked at the
steep price, over $100. When the book arrived I double-checked the
cover to make sure the footnote had been correct in saying "U.S.A.," not
"C.S.A." Now I was sure that my "Tories of the hills" had somehow
become part of the Federal army.

The book turned out to be a godsend of a perverse sort. For one
thing, I knew the author—or more precisely, knew of him. William Stanley Hoole (1903–1990) was a famously unpopular martinet as chief librarian of the University of Alabama in Tuscaloosa. When I arrived
there as a graduate student in 1967, he was the most despised senior official on campus, hated and ridiculed in equal measure as the classic
small-pond academic shark, an aggrandizer of his own modest accomplishments, and an untiringly jealous hitman in the intramural wars
common to faculty life everywhere. Moreover, as I should have guessed,
he had a typical kind of Alabama connectedness and not just to Winston
County. One of the oddities I discovered was that my career and that of
Hoole, who was forty years my senior, were launched by the same person. He was Professor Richebourg Gaillard McWilliams, my literary
mentor at Birmingham-Southern College and the father of my college
friend Tennant McWilliams.

Before exploring Hoole's strange little book, it's worth examining
the Hoole/McWilliams relationship for the light it casts on the insular
world of Alabama's political and cultural leaders. A wisecrack about
Alabama's power elite—that several million people lived there but only
four thousand mattered—even worked its way into the *Times* as late as
2016. In microcosm, the comment defines the kind of oligarchical networking that I found when I began digging into the catacombs of Lost
Cause scholarship. Professor McWilliams held the Mary Collett Munger
Professorship of English, funded by a millionaire holder of cotton-gin
patents, Robert Sylvester Munger (1854–1923), in honor of his wife,
Mary Collett (1857–1924). The Mungers had presented President Warren G. Harding with a key to the college when they lured him to Birmingham for the installation of their mutual friend Guy Everett Snavely

(1881–1974) as BSC president. Snavely, a worldly man who held a PhD from Johns Hopkins and was later director of the Association of American Colleges and Universities, was drawn to the multilingual McWilliams because of his Harvard credentials, his teaching sojourns in Puerto Rico and Munich, and his Mountain Brook social connections. Snavely cultivated for BSC a diamond-in-the-rough reputation. Before leaving for the national association post in 1937, he expanded McWilliams's authority beyond the chairmanship of the English department and made him acting director of the college library with a mandate to use a $25,000 Carnegie Corporation grant to bring it up to national standards.

Three years earlier, McWilliams had hired Hoole, a freshly minted PhD with a specialty in the antebellum literature of Charleston, South Carolina, as an assistant professor of English. But, in what became a career-long pattern, students found Hoole's personality unpleasant and resisted enrolling in his classes, a significant problem in a school with a small, hard-worked faculty. Suddenly a grant from the Rockefeller Foundation enabled Hoole's appointment as professor of books and director of the library, and he was dispatched to the summer sessions of the University of Chicago Graduate Library School, effectively removing him from the classroom. In later years, McWilliams candidly admitted that was his goal. "Thus in 1935, Dr. Hoole began a challenging and fruitful career in librarianship," as his historian daughter, Martha Dubose Hoole, wrote in a hagiographic monograph about her father that was privately printed in 2001. Through that understandably kind book and Tennant McWilliams's recollections about his father's comments on Hoole, it was clear that Hoole, worshipful grandson of a Confederate colonel killed under Longstreet's command at Chickamauga, and I had a paradoxical connection through Professor McWilliams. My career as a journalist who hoped to untangle the full story of the First Alabama and Hoole's career as a librarian dedicated to Lost Cause disinformation were launched by the same man. Exactly thirty years after he hired Hoole, McWilliams told the managing editor of the *Birmingham Post-Herald* that I was a promising graduate of his creative writing class, thus facilitating my hiring.

Martha Dubose Hoole's survey of her father's long career is nothing if not exhaustive; fifty-seven of its ninety-nine pages are devoted to detailed citations about his lectures, writings, and professional activities starting in 1934. I learned that he addressed the student body of my alma mater, Ensley High School, near the Birmingham steel mills, on March 18, 1936, on the subject of "Books and What They Mean to Me." But, as a literary detective, I couldn't help but notice there was a dog that didn't bark. In her list of Hoole's published books, his daughter does not mention *Alabama Tories: The First Alabama Cavalry,* published in 1960 as part of Hoole's business venture, the Confederate Publishing Company of Tuscaloosa.

With all respect to the late Martha Dubose Hoole, I have to believe it was because it is one of the most embarrassingly inaccurate books of Civil War history ever written, so nearly hysterical in its pro-Confederate bias that his own daughter omitted it from his canon—and not without reason. The 141-page book opens with a seething denunciation of "disloyal" anti-secessionists, who in many counties of the Appalachian South accounted for a majority of the white population, despite their weak position in the plantation-dominated legislatures. His prologue illustrates the Lost Cause historians' hostility to low-caste whites who were sometimes glorified in the press as "Unionists" or "Tories" or "Loyalists" in the Old South. "In the North the Tories were hailed as 'the abused and persecuted' and citizens' meetings were held in their honor, but among their fellow Southerners they were known as 'mountain whites' or, to use a modern term, 'hillbillies,' a poor, often underprivileged people who had long been isolated on their rocky highlands. . . . Blindly hating the affluent slave-holder and his 'nigger' alike, they had first refused to support the cause of Secession and, afterwards, ignored all Confederate civilian and conscription laws." Standing the history of the guerilla war that swept north Alabama on its head, Hoole fumed that the mountaineers formed bands of "Destroying Angels" to raid more affluent folk in the fertile valleys. "By their depredations thousands of Confederate sympathizers were driven from their homes, some to be stripped and whipped by the marauding guerillas and not a few to be murdered or raped." In fact, Hoole was describing the war of terror started by Confederate "Partisan Rangers" who operated with the official sanction of authorities in Richmond and Montgomery. Hoole ridiculed invading Union soldiers for believing "the tales of suffering and misery" told by the victims of Confederate atrocities. He omitted entirely the fact that not until late in the war did bands of Unionist guerillas form to retaliate.

I was struck by Hoole's naked class rage against our state's "mountain whites" and was a little surprised he didn't use the word "trash" instead of the milder "hillbillies." I gave him credit for knowing that "hillbillies" would have been anachronistic as a term used during the Civil War. And whatever his bias, as a Virginian with a Confederate pedigree, he honestly recorded the extent of Hill Country patriotism—or "disloyalty," in his lexicon:

> Altogether, in North Alabama there were thousands of Tories—it is impossible to determine the exact number. Brigadier-General Gideon J. Pillow reported in September, 1862 that at least ten thousand, including some who had deserted from the Confederate Army, were hiding out in the hills. Seven months later General Gustave T. Beauregard received word that in late 1862 they had actually held a large "convention" in the region of Winston, Fayette, and Marian counties at which they had voted, while wildly waving United States flags, to remain "neutral." In the spring of 1863, a similar convention was held in Winston County and in 1864 a Confederate officer wrote Beauregard that in Lawrence, Winston and Blount counties Federal recruiting agents were actively carrying on open correspondence with many disloyal citizens.

The book was a revelation for me in several ways, not least because it proved that the diffuse Union sentiment that I had known about since childhood had a very concrete result: the formation of an entire Union regiment drawn from Winston and seventeen surrounding counties lying between the Tennessee River and present-day Birmingham. So far as I knew then, and as I confirmed as a result of subsequent genealogical inquiry, every root of my family tree rested in the soil of these eighteen jurisdictions of north-central Alabama. Altogether, Hoole wrote, "*only* 2,678 Alabama white men actually enlisted in the United States Army" (my italics). True, that's a small fraction of Alabama's 1860 population of 526,431 white people, but the "only" seemed oddly discordant to me, given the popular notion of monolithic support for the Confederacy among southern whites of all stations. Every person I've ever shared that number with has expressed amazement, usually saying they did not know any southern whites fought for the North, much less those from such a renowned and enduring citadel of racism. Allowing for battlefield enlistments of white Alabamians in Union companies raised in Tennessee and Indiana, the actual number, according to Richard Nelson Current, was probably over three thousand. In any event, the meticulous enlistment records kept in north Alabama fix the exact number of men in the First Alabama at 2,066.

I bristled when I read Hoole's analysis in his prologue of what a worthless lot they were militarily, even though he did want credit for the originality of his scholarship on a neglected subject. He crowed that "so far as this writer has been able to discover, this study is the only one ever undertaken of a *Northern* regiment composed of white *Southerners*" (Hoole's italics). This was preceded by the most magisterial falsehood in the book. "This is not to suggest," he cautioned, "that the day-by-day service record per se of the First Alabama Cavalry, U.S.A., justifies its being singled out for monographic treatment. In fact, a close examination of its chronology reveals otherwise—that by comparison with hundreds of other Union regiments it was *not conspicuous in either accomplishments or attitudes*" (my italics).

In time, over the next four decades of research, this sentence raised two possibilities for me to consider. One was that Hoole's examination of the unit's chronology was not as close as he said. The other, more likely possibility was that he ignored evidence that did not fit into the procrustean framework of Lost Cause delusions of Confederate unity.

Serendipity of a very odd sort brought a new Unionist figure into the crosshairs of my curiosity. Not long after Cliff Graubart located Hoole's book for me, I was in the Birmingham Public Library to research Bull Connor's surveillance files for a story. These reports from detectives assigned to spy on King, Shuttlesworth, and other civil rights leaders had been discovered in a forgotten storage room at the state fairgrounds, and in 1978, Birmingham's newly integrated city government put them on display for journalists and scholars in hopes of cleaning up the city's reputation. There were no smoking guns, but the files made it clear that Klan bombers had operated for years with police protection. While working on my story about Connor's skullduggery, I popped into the library's Southern History Room to ask what they had on the First Alabama Cavalry. I was directed to a casually dressed man at one of the research tables and told he was an expert on Winston County. He was a mechanic of some sort whose hobby was Civil War research. He told me that the key figure in the story was a scoundrel named Colonel George Eliphaz Spencer, and he offered to write me a full report on the man for $350, paid in advance to meet some impending bills. I wrote a check on the spot. I never got the report, he did not respond to follow-up letters or phone calls, and I've long since forgotten the man's name. Still, I've never been fleeced to better effect or, as tips go, gotten more for my money. In the quest for buried history, curiosity and luck make a potent combination.

Union Hero of Alabama: Charles Christopher Sheats (1839–1904), appointed in 1869 as consul to Denmark by President Grant in recognition of his loyalty to the United States. Hill-country voters, clinging to their Unionist allegiance, also elected Sheats to Congress and as mayor of Decatur, Alabama.

PART II

Connecting the Dots

CLUES TO THE EXISTENCE OF DISAPPEARING SOLDIERS

How the First Alabama Almost
Saved Atlanta from Burning

In the 1980s, I took a long break in my First Alabama research. As I climbed the *Times* career pyramid, all the writing I did in my spare time went into a sporting memoir, *Fly Fishing Through the Midlife Crisis*. It became a bestseller in 1993, the only book with "fly fishing" in the title ever to appear on the *Times* list, so far as I can determine. At some point during this hiatus in Civil War research, I did acquire a copy of the *Memoirs of William Tecumseh Sherman*. Buying Civil War books was a habit I'd formed because there was by this time a permanent tickler file in my brain for information related to the First Alabama. That's how quests operate, I suppose, for detectives, reporters, and historians, hence the persistence of "cold cases." But I have to admit that my pursuit of the First Alabama story had stalled because I was fooled by William Stanley Hoole's use of the hoariest trick in the professional writers' tool bag—the "cover-your-ass" paragraph. He had asserted that Alabama's Unionist regiment played only a marginal role in Civil War combat and that only the oddness of its origins could be of interest to serious historians.

The CYA graf is a standard ploy in the political speeches I had been decoding for decades—and, for that matter, in the editorials I was writing for a living. For me to miss it was equivalent to an NFL coach falling for the old Statue of Liberty play. The basic technique involves stating something as unequivocal fact, then following it with modifying statements as a means of preempting rebuttal (or, in my case, curiosity). For a newspaperman or a historian, lack of follow-up is a professional lapse that no mea culpa can cover. That's why, on my cheeriest days, I can tip my hat to Professor Hoole's dexterity. The fact that he was an artist of knowing disinformation doesn't excuse my inattention to the paragraph that began with his flat assertion that on the battlefield the First Alabama Cavalry "was not conspicuous in either accomplishments or attitudes."

It still chagrins me that I, trained as a campaign reporter to look for "weasel words" in every text, ignored the very next sentence. "True enough," Hoole continued, "General William T. Sherman selected the unit as his 'headquarters escort' in the march to the sea, but mostly it was employed in scouting, recruiting, raiding, and guarding the flanks. Only rarely in its three years of existence was it engaged in actual combat with the enemy." That's so outrageous a distortion that it can only be regarded as an intentional lie. In protracted, mobile warfare, most units are indeed rarely involved in firefights. Many more hours are devoted to travel, entrenching, resupply, and camp life. Hoole's statement was a slanderous misrepresentation of men who fought under and against the most renowned generals of the last three years of the war. Long before Atlanta lay in their path, they had participated actively in Union victories at Stone's River, Vicksburg, and Chickamauga, not to mention the war's grand concluding acts, the destruction of Atlanta and the capture of Savannah. If the Civil War were an opera, the First Alabama was center stage in the finale and important members of the chorus supporting its famous soloists. It had faced opposing commanders whose battlefield exploits had won them dashing nicknames: Nathan Bedford Forrest, the bloodthirsty "Wizard of the Saddle"; the resourceful "Fighting Joe" Wheeler; and Philip Dale Roddey, the "Defender of North Alabama." But that's hardly an excuse for the laziness of a reader who spent his working life in a profession that has as its motto "Check it out." In any event, I let the trail grow cold as I rose to the top job in the sixty-person Washington bureau in 1988. If I had been sharper, I would have realized much earlier that the First Alabama deserved inclusion on the roster of such colorful small units as Joshua Chamberlain's Maine infantrymen who turned back the Alabamians' charge at Little Round Top on the second day at Gettysburg. But theirs was a more protracted performance, based not on a single battle but on months of scouting and fighting in the forefront of the March to the Sea. I did not begrudge any group of worthy soldiers their place in the fickle searchlight of history. But once I mastered the facts, I came to see why the absence of the First Alabama from the historical record is so egregious. Sherman's autobiography, published in 1875 to great acclaim, ranks with or slightly behind Grant's memoirs among the best American books of their sort. But once I cracked it, Sherman's account did not yield its secrets easily, thanks to a sketchy index. There was no entry for the First Alabama Cavalry or even for Alabama in my paperback edition. However, its list of southern topics led me to a long, confidential analysis Sherman wrote from a Mississippi encampment for his commander, General Henry Halleck, on September 17, 1863. Sherman wanted his boss, known as "Old Brains," to appreciate the formidable wrongheadedness of an enemy determined to prolong the Civil War beyond all reason. Sherman was a fluent conversationalist and writer, and the memorandum is a brilliant dissection of southern society. The South's leadership caste, "the large planters . . . the ruling class," had tricked the next class down—"the smaller farmers, mechanics, merchants and laborers," comprising three-quarters of the white citizenry—into fighting a futile conflict. "They are essentially tired of the war, and would slink back home if they could." Then he unleashed his acid-dipped pen on a youthful subset of the aristocratic class that had immense military importance as soldiers who embraced combat and were not afraid to die. He wrote Halleck:

> The young bloods of the South: sons of planters, lawyers about towns, good billiard-players and sportsmen, men who never did work and never will. War suits them, and the rascals are brave, fine riders, bold to rashness, and dangerous subjects in every sense. They care not a sou for niggers, land, or anything. They

hate Yankees *per se,* and don't bother their brains about the past, present, or future. As long as they have good horses, plenty of forage, and an open country, they are happy. This is a larger class than most men suppose, and they are the most dangerous set of men that this war has turned loose upon the world. They are splendid riders, first-rate shots, and utterly reckless. [J. E. B.] Stewart, John Morgan, [Nathan Bedford] Forrest and [Stonewall] Jackson are the types and leaders of this class. *These men must all be killed or employed by us before we can hope for peace.* (Italics added)

The italics I added in the preceding sentence are intended to mark this as containing the kernels of the Sherman doctrine, which calls for destruction or reformation of an opponent's civilian infrastructure as the path to victory. He went on to describe these young southerners as "the best horsemen in the world," which invites us to examine his decision to throw the First Alabama riders, untested but mountain-tough, into battle against the South's best cavalry commanders and horsemen. That reliance on Union volunteers from the Alabama hills seems paradoxical given the contempt Sherman expressed in mid-1863 in his memo to Halleck for "the Union men of the South . . . as a political class." He condemned them for "stay[ing] at home, claiming all exemptions of peaceful citizens," and sometimes even allowing their sons to join the Confederate army. "I count them as nothing in this great game of war," Sherman concluded.

But that was because in that era of slow communications among regional commanders, Sherman was probably unaware at that time of the change that swept the hills after Union forces occupied Nashville and entered Alabama's Tennessee Valley in the early spring of 1862. It was the older Unionists in Alabama, like the wavering Jeremiah Clemens, whom Sherman despised. He could not have known that they were being displaced by young firebrands like Chris Sheats who at night took to the roads to recruit peers who didn't want to fight the "rich man's war." Thanks in large measure to Sheats, Bill Looney, and a few other

Winstonians, droves of Alabama Union men were enlisting at Huntsville, which fell to the Union on April 11, 1862. By the end of summer,
groups of a dozen or more men from Winston and the surrounding
counties were walking across the state line to a second enlistment point
at Camp Glendale near Corinth, Mississippi, only a few miles from
where Sherman wrote his lengthy report to Halleck. That report was
prescient as to Rebel persistence but behind the curve in regard to the
clandestine recruitment of hundreds of north Alabamians. Indeed, at
Camp Glendale, the new recruits were being trained into an effective
cavalry force by General Grenville Mellen Dodge, one of Lincoln's "political generals" who turned out to have a natural gift for innovative tactics. In his initial assignment as a junior officer in Missouri, for example,
he had proved that the standard practice of "reconnaissance in force" by
cavalry units did not work as well as sending soldiers in mufti skulking
through the brush. At the start of October, Dodge's chief of staff, Colonel George E. Spencer, led six hundred members of the First deep into
Alabama to strike at Rebel railroads. Sherman would come to admire
the First Alabama as fighters, guides, and spies.

These rustic farmers were far different from the rich layabouts he
had met in his pre-war assignments in the South. His contempt for the
fatalistic knights errant from the plantations was deadly accurate and
prophetic. It was based on his years of army engineering duty in Georgia and Alabama, surveying land he would one day fight over and dancing with the daughters of its slave owners or hunting with their sons. He
was also the founding superintendent of the Baton Rouge military college that became Louisiana State University. He defined with clinical
precision a kind of entitled machismo that still reverberates through
football Saturdays in Tuscaloosa, Baton Rouge, and Oxford and inspir-
its regional publications like *Garden and Gun*. Populist iterations of the
archetype are on display through country music, NASCAR, and red-
state Republicanism (as personified in my poor, hapless Alabama by the
crackpot senatorial candidates Roy Moore and Tommy Tuberville, who
were endorsed by Trump in 2018 and 2020).

With just the title of his 1957 book *The Deep South Says "Never,"*

John Bartlow Martin, then the nation's leading freelance magazine writer, captured the southern gentry's response to the advent of both the Civil War and the civil rights movement. And in his indispensable commentary on Civil War personalities, the leading critic of his time, Edmund Wilson, analyzed Sherman's *Memoirs* as a psychohistory in which a young military engineer who had led survey crews in the South's mountains and frolicked with its belles and swells came to be "constantly sustained by a genuine indignation against the 'disloyalty' of the 'rebels.'" The Confederates' refusal to abandon a rebellion that had clearly failed offended what another biographer called Sherman's "passion for order." Wilson observed, "We are aware, as we read the *Memoirs,* that an appetite for warfare is emerging, and that it grows as it feeds on the South." "War is cruelty and you cannot refine it," Sherman wrote, in a tone of seeming regret to the Atlantans whose city he was about to burn. But in private correspondence, the general wrote about the "grand and beautiful game of war." Although Grant had the reputation of a butcher, he dreaded battle, whereas "there was evidently, for Sherman, a certain relation between the beauty and the cruelty."

I dwell on this language because it invites us to a close study of this complex man whose bristly visage was said by an aide to "look like the face of war itself." There's a mystery here. If he really hated southern Unionists, why would he handpick twenty-one of them from the First Alabama to build his fires and pitch his tent each night? He looked to this group each day for an "orderly at hand with his invariable saddle bags, which contained a change of under clothing, my maps, a flask of whiskey and a bunch of cigars." And why would he pick several companies of them to go in front with his notoriously reckless cavalry commander, General Judson "Kill Cavalry" Kilpatrick, for the campaign that was not only the critical point of his career but also the linchpin of his and Grant's strategy to end the war on Lincoln's terms? I believe it was because he found in these rough, largely illiterate Alabama farm boys the instrument he needed to guide his army against an unyielding foe. He knew the South well enough to understand that his mountain lads were not duelists concerned with the rules of fair fighting. The mountain folk of the South were feudists who thought the most important thing about a quarrel was surviving it. Stung by the insults of their pretentious neighbors on the plantations, they were temperamentally attuned to a Sherman strategy described by one biographer as "a full-court press aimed at killing Southerners until, in essence, they ran out of Southerners."

But Sherman did not underestimate the demonic resolve of the wealthy men who were leading the South's army of shoeless peons. The millionaire slave trader Nathan Bedford Forrest had harassed one of the Union's best generals, Dodge, throughout northern Mississippi, Alabama, and Tennessee in the long Union struggle to occupy Vicksburg and Chattanooga. In 1864, the crafty Rebel commander in Atlanta, Joseph Johnston, and his bloody-minded infantry general, John T. Hood, stood between Sherman and the Georgia capital that was the railroad hub of the dying Confederate government. And after it fell, the Alabama cavalryman "Fighting Joe" Wheeler stood between Sherman and Savannah. Sherman admired Wheeler, a tiny Alabamian who attended a New England prep school with J. P. Morgan, as a hit-and-run artist who artfully deployed his outnumbered cavalry. After Atlanta fell and its defending army was freed to leave the trenches, Sherman wrote Grant, "It will be a physical impossibility to protect the roads, now that Hood, Forrest, Wheeler and the whole batch of devils, are turned loose without home or habitation." That, too, shaped his strategy. Instead of chasing them, Sherman proposed in one of the most memorable martial letters ever written, a journey of "utter destruction" to Savannah. As quoted in the *Memoirs,* he proposed to Grant, "I can make this march, and make Georgia howl!"

I had hoped to find Chris Sheats and the First Alabama Cavalry in Sherman's index, but no. Plowing through the 855 pages, however, I found definitive evidence of their presence in the organizational chart of the three wings of Sherman's invading force: the Army of the Tennessee, the Army of the Ohio, and the Army of Georgia. The modest number of cavalry, only about 5,500 in an army approaching 100,000, reflected Sherman's view that cavalrymen were too given to helling about and striking picturesque attitudes. Sherman listed his "Cavalry Division" as being under the command of the risk-taking Major General Kilpatrick, once described by Sherman as a "hell of a damn fool." The First Alabama fit a plunger like Kilpatrick perfectly. They went into Sherman's three cavalry brigades and operated under Colonel George E. Spencer, whose name I recognized from Hoole's book. Hoole described him with undisguised contempt as a "nefarious" and "corrupt" carpetbagger who served as a U.S. senator from Alabama during Reconstruction. Hoole omits entirely a May 9, 1864, maneuver by Spencer and his Alabamians that led up to the Battle of Resaca and, in Sherman's breathless account, might conceivably have ended the war before Atlanta was burned, which I'll discuss later. Perhaps it was a harbinger of the First Alabama's bad luck at receiving due credit. Even in admitting the importance of this moment, Sherman doesn't mention by name the First Alabama as providing him with what, in retrospect, would come to look like the greatest unrealized opportunity of his career, of the Atlanta campaign, and, perhaps, of the entire war. Indeed, what the First Alabama accomplished outside Resaca, Georgia, on May 9, 1864, seals my case that the First deserves a place in the war's main narrative of the critical events of that decisive year. This was the most dramatic of several shining moments for the regiment on its march with Sherman, and it calls for a look at how they came to be at this pivot point in military history under the command of Dodge and Spencer, Iowa politicians with a genius for self-promotion and timing.

Sherman is almost halfway through his memoir before he introduces the Alabamians as his campmates when he led his army out of Chattanooga on May 5, 1864. They fit his plan to show that his troops would live off the land and move fast. "No wall tents were allowed, only the flies. . . . I wanted to set the example, and gradually to convert all parts of that army into a mobile machine, willing and able to start at a minute's notice, and to subsist on the scantiest food," he wrote. In a pinch, he was willing to leave his supply wagons and "subsist on chance food which the country was known to contain." Indeed, with typical thoroughness, Sherman had studied Georgia's state tax records to determine that crop production was sufficient to sustain his roving army on food taken from the citizenry. No less an authority than the British military historian B. H. Liddell Hart cites this as the beginning of "mechanized warfare," introducing methods studied by Rommel and other German generals in World War II. Edmund Wilson summarized the momentous stakes thusly: "The perpetrator of 'the march to the sea' does seem to have invented the *Blitzkrieg*."

By midsummer, the Alabamians had been riding alongside Sherman as eyewitnesses to his groundbreaking tactics for two months or so. We can date it by Sherman's account: "My general headquarters and official records remained back at Nashville, and I had near me only my personal staff and inspectors-general, with about a half-dozen wagons, and a single company of Ohio sharp-shooters (commanded by Lieutenant McCrory) as headquarters or camp guards. I also had a small company of irregular Alabama cavalry (commanded by Lieutenant Snelling), used mostly as orderlies and couriers."

The use of the term "irregular" probably refers to their enrollment in the zone of battle. The twelve companies of the First Alabama were mounted, armed, on regular payroll, integrated into the command structure, and fully uniformed unless disguised for spy missions. In his official report to Grant, Sherman said he started on the road to Atlanta in late April with 98,797 troops, more than 24,000 of whom were in the Army of the Tennessee under the personal command of his favorite general, James Birdseye McPherson (1828–1864), who'd graduated first in his class at West Point in the celebrated class of 1853. In the course of his meteoric rise to major general, the fresh-faced Ohioan had become perhaps the most popular field commander in the entire army. Above his cavalry on the organizational chart was another favorite of both Sherman's and Lincoln's, General Dodge, who had done more than anyone else to mold the First Alabama into formidable fighters and intelligence gatherers. Their regimental commander was Spencer, who would win Sherman's confidence on the March to the Sea.

As for the singular event of May 9, it took place along the railroad tracks at a mountain pass called Snake Creek Gap, where a charge led by the First Alabama "almost scored a knockout in the first round" for

Sherman. The clash brought the colorful trio of McPherson, Dodge, and Spencer together in a moment that could have made the First Alabama famous and ended the entire campaign seventy miles north of Atlanta and six months early. In that case, Atlanta would never have burned. Sherman's official comment on the incident has the smell of a cover-up. "I was somewhat disappointed at the result," Sherman reported vaguely to Grant after McPherson's cavalry escort, led by Spencer, surprised an unprepared Confederate army under General Joseph Johnston outside the little town of Resaca. Ten years later, in his *Memoirs,* Sherman was able to be more candid, but even then his refusal to identify the First Alabama Union Cavalry in the forefront at this supreme moment of military opportunity underscored the First's hard luck when it came to garnering recognition. Historians have speculated that McPherson did not become the scapegoat of "the affair at Snake Creek Gap" because he was killed soon after in the Battle of Atlanta, when he blundered into a Confederate encampment. Sherman's response to the death made it clear that McPherson, then only thirty-six, was a special favorite. "Sherman's tears rolled through his beard and down on the floor when he viewed the body of his friend upon a door torn from its hinges and improvised as a bier," according to *Generals in Blue: Lives of the Union Commanders.*

Dodge's biographer James Patrick Morgans provided the details about May 9 that the normally blunt Sherman left out:

On May 9, Dodge proceeded to Resaca with his 2nd Division, commanded by General Thomas W. Sweeny. Dodge found that only one brigade of Rebel infantry was in the area, and he quickly pushed them back into the city of Resaca. The First Alabama Union Cavalry also was ready to charge into Resaca with Dodge's troops. However, Major-General James McPherson, head of the Army of the Tennessee, rode up and asked what was going on. Colonel Spencer, leading the First Alabama Union Cavalry, said he could capture Resaca in fifteen minutes. Dodge pointed out to McPherson that they could cut Johnston's rail and supply lines to

Atlanta. Johnston was hemmed in on the west by the mountains, and he would have to retreat to the east off his line of defense. McPherson argued that they were not following Sherman's orders. Some believed that the Battle of Atlanta could have been over by then if McPherson had listened to Dodge and Colonel Spencer of the 1st Alabama Union Cavalry. However, McPherson would not let the town be attacked.

To be sure, not all participants or military historians agree that the war could have ended there. George Spencer, born in 1836 in prosperous circumstances in upstate New York, never wavered in his conviction, nor did Dodge or the reluctant Sherman. Spencer, an opportunist who was appointed at only twenty years of age as secretary of the Iowa state senate, was one of the most extraordinary men in either army. A tireless self-promoter, he wrote a boastful letter saying if he had been allowed to charge with the First Alabama, "which Gen'l Dodge was very anxious should be done, we would have captured Resaca that day, destroyed the railroad bridge there and the railroad, and then and there ended the Atlanta campaign." As a powerful carpetbag senator after the war, Spencer was in charge of Grant administration patronage in Alabama, and Alabama historians have "sealed his historical reputation with terms of derision: he was unscrupulous, unprincipled, vulgar, coarse, cunning, and corrupt, a schemer, manipulator, intriguer, plunderer, spoilsman, freebooter and criminal." These words come from his most sympathetic biographer, Terry L. Seip, whose short monograph is the best source on the life of a man who went into the war to make money and wound up with the admiration of Sherman and Lincoln. His account of Resaca contains what Seip called the usual "Spencer hyperbole," but the historical record fully confirms Spencer's view, even to the satisfaction of Sherman himself.

As a matter of evidence, Dodge's memoirs, read alongside Sherman's, seem to reinforce the case. As Dodge recalled, he and General McPherson breakfasted in a Chattanooga hotel on May 5 before joining Sherman in the field. "I remember that at the breakfast table at the hotel

I was greatly surprised to find the knives and forks chained to the table and concluded that the reputation of Sherman's 'bummers' had preceded us," he wrote in an account that shows the ease of conversation that existed within Sherman's inner circle. But Sherman never strayed far from his goal of scorching Georgia, saying, "Now Dodge, you see what you have to do. Where are your troops?" Dodge replied, "They are unloading." Sherman then said to McPherson, "I think you had better send Dodge to Ship's Gap tonight," and McPherson replied, "Why General, that is thirty miles away." But McPherson obeyed.

The forced march paid rich dividends. Both Ship's Gap and Snake Creek Gap, a few miles to the south, were undefended and opened onto the valley where Johnston's army was encamped near the market town of Resaca. "This enabled us to pass through Snake Creek Gap before the enemy discovered the movement to their rear. To my own surprise and the surprise of everybody else, we pushed through that long narrow gorge before midnight on the 8th, one day ahead of the time fixed." Dodge thought McPherson should have planted himself across the railroad tracks on the Resaca side of the gap, "which would have forced [the enemy] to abandon his trains and fight or make a long detour to the east." After the war, Johnston ridiculed Sherman's claim that his army was slumbering. It was positioned to counteract and overwhelm McPherson's relatively small force. Sherman, he said, had sent too few men to win by surprise. Johnston, however, was miles away, his army facing in the wrong direction, and both Rebel and Union officers on the scene said the gap was "wholly unprotected," to use the words of a participating Confederate colonel. For his part, Dodge recalled that Sherman, up to the time of his death, always claimed that "if the fifteen thousand men we had with us had been planted and entrenched squarely in front of Resaca, it would have broken up Johnston's army." But Dodge, writing fifty years later, said since McPherson was dead, he would not criticize or second-guess him.

Sherman had no such scruples. On the morning of May 10, 1864, he confronted McPherson within the hearing of others and said, "Well, Mac, you have missed the great opportunity of your life." In his *Mem-*

oirs, Sherman said McPherson had a force larger than fifteen thousand, and that McPherson erred in having them dig in rather than attack once they cleared the gap on the morning of May 9: "McPherson had startled Johnston in his fancied security, but had not done the full measure of his work. He had in hand twenty-three thousand of the best men of the army, and could have walked into Resaca. . . . [W]e should have captured half his army and all his artillery and wagons at the very beginning of the campaign." Writing ten years after the incident, Sherman found it hard to unload on the man who at that point had eighty-two days to live. "Such an opportunity does not occur twice in a single lifetime, but at the critical moment McPherson seems to have been a little cautious" (in the first edition of his memoirs, he used the word "timid"). Anyway, he concluded, McPherson acted technically within his orders to use his discretion.

I know of no other example of Sherman pulling his punches as he did for the young general over whom he wept on July 29 during the Battle of Atlanta. His summation is misleading in another way. Having handed Dodge the map of the area, he had to know it was he personally, not McPherson, who had "surprised" the Rebel commander and who would not have let the enemy fall back toward Atlanta with his army intact. And given Sherman's habit of rambling among his soldiers' campfires at night, smoking cigars and talking to his "boys," he had to know that Spencer and the First Alabama were riding point on May 9, as they were to do so often on the long road from Atlanta to Savannah.

9

QUOTH THE GENERAL

THE NEXT IMPORTANT date in my pursuit of the First Alabama story was October 14, 1990, when, as Washington editor of *The New York Times,* I was invited to deliver the annual journalism lecture at Auburn University in Montgomery. Perhaps I was expected to talk about the news of the day or the principles of newspapering, but I turned the event into a traffic jam on my Lost Cause Highway. As I'd hoped, the audience included Winston County's—and perhaps the South's—most important contribution to American jurisprudence: federal judge Frank M. Johnson Jr., whose landmark desegregation rulings propelled Martin Luther King Jr. to leadership of the civil rights movement. It was also the night I met my hillbilly griot, Donald Dodd, the first professional historian to write about the Free State of Winston. And my speech lit up the radar of the leader of Montgomery's formidable Lost Cause establishment, Major General Will Hill Tankersley, a Pentagon official during the Ford and Reagan administrations. As a West Point graduate and former president of both the Montgomery Chamber of Commerce and the Rotary Club, he was cock-of-the-walk in conservative Montgomery.

Tankersley (1928–2015), a decorated infantry lieutenant in the Korean War, earned his rank in the army reserve, but he nonetheless preferred to be called "General," the title that is engraved on his tombstone. He came loaded for bear because I, as a *Times* man, represented a satanic force and was a betrayer of Alabama as well. Although it was my day job to oversee the paper's coverage of Washington, I always looked for opportunities to direct attention back to my home state. My subjects included the colorful, such as the annual Alabama-Auburn football game (the Iron Bowl), and the shameful, such as Klan bombers and political demagogues. In June 1990, I had published a *Times Magazine* article, "Alabama Bound," with a subhead that said: "While neighbors have flourished, weak leadership and excessive perks for business have kept the state in a Wallace-era time warp, dirt-poor and backward. Returning home, the author finds widespread shame and rage." Tankersley, who would go on to a star turn in 1998 in Tony Horwitz's bestselling *Confederates in the Attic,* was enraged, all right, but at me for ridiculing the Republican governor, a crooked bumpkin named Guy Hunt. In his survey of latter-day Confederate sympathizers, Horwitz had praised "Tankersley's balanced approach" to making tourist dollars from what the sixty-two-year-old Montgomerian called "two great cataclysms that started here—the Civil War and the civil rights movement." He presented himself as advocating a classic New South approach based on Henry Grady's formula: accommodating enough racial change to attract Yankee dollars while hewing to hereditary Old South values. Montgomery could reap profits from Confederate monuments and its "Civil Rights Trail," not to mention country singer Hank Williams as well as Zelda and F. Scott Fitzgerald. Such a man was bound to take offense at my speech, which traced Alabama's political corruption to the plantation class and corporate oligarchs from the steel, textile, and timber industries who had maintained the state's intellectual blockade against progressive political thinking.

I was forty-seven at the time of my speech and felt I had learned enough about the First Alabama Cavalry, U.S.A. to assert that the unrecognized heroes of Alabama history were the hill country Unionists and Black civil rights pioneers:

If like me, you carry the genes of poor, uneducated Alabamians . . .
if your parents or grandparents might have been dismissed at one

time with some label of condemnation . . . hillbilly . . . redneck . . . coon . . . sharecropper . . . I address my remarks with special fervor to you. One of the great liberating moments in my life came with the ability to say with pride I am the son of hillbillies, the grandson of hillbillies, the great-grandson of hillbillies and so on back through time until the mind of man and the U.S. Census Bureau remembreth not.

And I called on every Alabamian of humble background "to draw energy from our historical journey to make Alabama what it can be and has never been."

My speech was entitled "Reflections on Alabama: A History of Silence." I could not have written a speech better designed to set on edge the teeth of a Rebel-worshiping Alabamian from a blue-blooded Democratic family who had migrated into Reagan's GOP as the new white man's party. It blamed the myth of the Lost Cause for establishing a silencing of dissent that had crippled Alabama ever since secession. I dwelled on William Lowndes Yancey, as "our first example of that political species we have come to know as the Alabama Blowhard." As you will recall, in *Tories of the Hill* it was Yancey—a lawyer and marginally successful planter who nevertheless became a Montgomery folk hero—who had allegedly jailed Chris Sheats. In Yancey's day, northern newspapers cited his "golden-mouthed" oratory as a prime cause of the Civil War. Yancey had inspired the incendiary stump style adopted by Wallace and the claque of segregationist speechifiers who later used race to divert voters' attention from Alabama's status as a deprived colony of corporations like United States Steel. In my speech, I said of Yancey, "His characteristics were these: He was a charismatic orator. He valued his feelings over ideas or principles. He didn't give a damn for the Constitution or the democratic process unless they served the interests of wealthy plantation owners."

I had provided no advance text of the carefully prepared lecture, but Tankersley had already laid down a preemptive field of fire based on my apostasy. Alabama's creed that only residents are allowed to criticize the state dates to Yancey and, even earlier, to Alabamians' anger over frontier journalists who commented on the state's louse-ridden hotels, riotous religious revivals, and whiskey-at-breakfast menus. Hypersensitivity remains a durable Alabama mindset. Even the sporadically progressive *Birmingham News* had editorialized against my "Alabama Bound" article by saying, "No, we didn't need someone who no longer lives here to tell us what's wrong with Alabama."

Robert Ingram, the Montgomery journalist who was host of the event, gave me a gracious introduction, but not before recognizing the general, as one of its financial sponsors, who proceeded to deliver a querulous speech about the natural inferiority of those who comment on political affairs. He quoted at full length Teddy Roosevelt's denunciation of the sort of "cold and timid souls" who inhabit newspapers. "It is not the critic who counts," he intoned. "The credit belongs to the man who is actually in the arena, whose face is marred by dust and sweat and blood."

I let the insult pass, but that very night Tankersley began a PR counterattack through the local segregationist weekly, the *Montgomery Independent,* getting on the phone to its editor, Tom Johnson, a sour, smart Wallace crony I had met years earlier. Johnson was a master of the tone of world-weary disdain for liberal criticism used by editorialists on Alabama's Confederate newspapers when they railed against abolitionists. In his column, Johnson told of a 10 P.M. phone call from "a Montgomerian of note" in whom my speech had inducted "a state of high dudgeon." Not surprisingly, Tankersley had complained that I had "observed with a casual matter-of-factness, that the greatest Alabamian of all was Dr. Martin Luther King, a slightly unprofessional superlative." Then, while denouncing me as a "Hired Hand" of the liberal establishment, Johnson surprised me by pointing out a new aspect of the Alabama Inferiority Syndrome. He suggested there were holes in the Cotton Curtain with which old Montgomery had protected itself from incoming information. In the arch tone he had once used in writing speeches for Wallace, Johnson chided the audience for applauding my speech:

The Independent finds it all a comical interaction. Something there is about Southerners that impels them to seek out abuse as a form of gratification whether Under the Tent or from the public platform. They adore it when an Evangelistic speaker comes among them, clouds of righteous spittle issuing from his mouth, and Thunders that he, too, was a sinner until he's found salvation at the New York Times. He offers the same sweet deal to his listeners for the price of a speech.

Two months after I left town, Tankersley was still on the attack, lambasting me and Brandt Ayers, the liberal editor of the *Anniston Star* and a frequent *Times* contributor, in a December 9 op-ed in the *Montgomery Advertiser* under the headline "Limousine Liberals Take Unfair Shots at Governor Hunt." "I think both [Ayers and Raines] have an inferiority complex about their Southern origins and feel the need to cleanse themselves of this stain in order to be accepted in Northern liberal circles where they desperately want to be held in high regard," he wrote. "Some Southern expatriates like Mr. Raines and Southern liberal Scalawags use the same technique to appease those who exist in the rarefied atmosphere of Northern liberalism, those whose acceptance and approbation they crave. They explain and interpret for them the outrageous behavior of the strange Neanderthals who inhabit the benighted state of Alabama."

Ayres's offense was a column in the Montgomery paper accurately depicting Governor Hunt (1943–2009), the first twentieth-century Republican elected to his office, as a dishonest rube. His petty offenses included using prison mattresses in his hunting camp and taking "love offerings" when preaching in out-of-state churches. But it was converting $200,000 in inaugural funds to personal use that got him removed from office and sent to prison—an Alabama first—in 1993. His defenders insisted, not without a measure of credibility, that he was held to a higher ethical standard than the many Democratic crooks who had preceded him in the governor's mansion.

For our purposes, Tankersley's writings demonstrate an important theme in the Alabama mindset that figured in the historical shunning of the First Alabama in state archives and textbooks, which effectively removed them from the big screen of American historiography. The Brandeis University historian David Hackett Fischer, in his monumental work *Albion's Seed: Four British Folkways in America,* traces the southern derangement about outsiders to the "stranger-stay-away" tradition of the Scots-Irish settlers who set the tone of Appalachian society and, according to many historians, provided the warrior ethos of the Confederate infantry. This fierce, combative parochialism was especially strong in Alabama because of the role of "the archetypical back country leader," Andrew Jackson, in opening the state to white settlement in both the hills and the Black Belt. "All the world seemed foreign to the backsettlers except their neighbors and kin," Fischer wrote. He quoted an Appalachian woman as describing this legacy to the twentieth century thusly: "We never let go of a belief once fixed in our minds."

These attitudes have had a remarkable cultural persistence among white Alabamians up and down the socioeconomic ladder. Pew Research Center polls usually show Alabama as both the most conservative and most religious state. Not even Will Hill Tankersley's experience at West Point, in Washington, and as a very successful stockbroker could penetrate an aversion to criticism by nonresidents that is virtually impenetrable in both its Montgomery Country Club and Walmart iterations.

But while General Tankersley was hurrying to telephone Tom Johnson to complain about my calling Martin Luther King Jr. "the greatest man to breathe the air of Alabama in this century," another member of the friendly audience was pressing into my hand an autographed copy of his book, *Winston: An Antebellum and Civil War History of a Hill County in North Alabama.* It had been inscribed to thank me for "linking Winstonian/Hill Country individualism with [the] 20th century anti-status Southern movement for civil rights." I recognized Donald Dodd's name from the occasional magazine articles he had written on Alabama history. I was pleased to see that the book had been printed in Birmingham by Grandpa Walker's old political ally, former congress-

man Carl Elliott, who had for years run a money-losing publishing venture for an antiquarian series called Annals of Northwest Alabama. The
book expanded on Dodd's dissertation at the University of Georgia,
where he earned his PhD in 1969. The dissertation, in turn, was based
on the master's thesis Dodd wrote at the main campus of Auburn University in 1966.

Those remain foundational works in what is now an expanding field
of academic study triggered by *Lincoln's Loyalists.* Until 2019, it was the
only scholarly work devoted entirely to the Free State narrative. Completed that year at the University of New Hampshire was Susan Deily-
Swearingen's *Rebel Rebels: Race, Resistance, and Remembrance in "The
Free State of Winston."* Like me and Dodd, she is from a family with
Winston County roots.

Dodd was born in 1940 into the tight inner circle of Winston politics,
a courthouse world that had produced Judge John Bennett Weaver,
Judge Frank M. Johnson, and Dodd's father, Benjamin Dodd (1893–
1962), who had been both Winston's sheriff and its state representative
in the seat usually filled by someone named Weaver, Johnson, or Curtis.
As a youngster he was impressed by *Tories of the Hills,* but his mother
was close kin to the Weavers, and as his interest in local history grew,
Dodd came to resent Wesley S. Thompson's piggybacking on Judge
Weaver's work and the many errors he had written into his Winston
novel. His own budding sense of ownership about Free State history
would, during his collegiate years, bring him into conflict with Wesley
Thompson and with the Lost Cause defenders at the University of Alabama in Tuscaloosa and at the Alabama Department of Archives and
History in Montgomery. Dodd's father was a local character in Haleyville
who used his van as a rolling grocery store to build a grassroots constituency in the hill country. He was a political ally of Big Jim Folsom
and Folsom's successor Gordon Persons, also a formidable road builder.
The triumph of his political career was the paving of the forty-five miles
of dirt road between Jasper and Haleyville. Ben Dodd's political career
ended because his faction of the Winston Republican Party was a rival
of the local GOP political machine run by Judge Johnson's father,

Frank M. Johnson Sr., and Judge Weaver. Hardball politics ruled in the competition for the few scraps of patronage in the impoverished county. Judge Walker's attempt to install his best friend in the lone legislative seat would have been a political coup for neglected Arley over the Haleyville–Double Springs gang. I don't want to lead us too far into the weeds over this local lore, but it's useful to understand the links in the informational chain.

A cause of the tension between Donald Dodd and Wesley Thompson was that the younger writer knew that Thompson lifted the material for *Tories of the Hills* from Judge Weaver without crediting him. In 1968, the friction increased when Dodd saw that Thompson had mined his master's thesis for a new nonfiction history of Winston County he published to cash in on the popularity of *Tories*. In that work, Thompson came up with a new dodge: He identified Dodd as a historian working in the same field but did not mention that he was relying on Dodd's thesis. The details are relevant to something that dawned on me in the course of my research—that the details of Chris Sheats's founding of the Winston County loyalist movement would not have survived without Weaver having interviewed Sheats's elderly followers before they died and, over thirty years later, Donald Dodd becoming the first professionally trained historian to mine the work of Weaver and Hoole, the Alabama archives, and the *Official Records of the War of the Rebellion,* since retitled as *The War of the Rebellion: A Compilation of the Official Records of the Union and Confederate Armies.*

Dodd, who spent his retirement on a Winston County farm called Kudzu Botanical Gardens, was an Alabama type: the clodhopper savant. This kind of academic is also an American type, to be found around such universities as those of Oklahoma and Iowa and among the "cowboy historians" of the Plains and Rocky Mountains. For years, Charles Kuralt made a living interviewing such characters for his popular Sunday morning show on CBS. They are specialists in debunking local folklore, an activity that Dodd plunged into as a graduate student in Auburn University's history department, which in earlier decades was a key factor in Lost Cause historiography. That field, in turn, was strewn with alliances, rivalries, and feuds that still ripple across southern campuses to the present day.

"The late Reverend Thompson is more popular than I am in Winston," Dodd told me one day as we sat beside the still waters of Lewis Smith Lake, the Alabama Power Company reservoir that since 1961 has covered up the historic "rock houses" where mountain Unionists hid from Rebel conscription patrols. "*Tories,*" Dodd added in the tone typical of hill country sarcasm, "is not a bad book for a preacher."

When Dodd was in his twenties, he told me, Thompson was still alive, and his books were energetically promoted by the Haleyville and Jasper newspapers. He was making a tidy living from selling *Tories* and its sequel, *So Turns the Tide,* at churches, civic club meetings, and book signings. But poring over the detailed account of the secession convention left behind by its energetic stenographer in 1861, Dodd could find no trace of the dramatic speech and floor fight related by Thompson.

Sheats neither spoke nor went to jail, according to official records and newspaper accounts of the heavily covered meetings.

In Montgomery, the past still hovers close. Will Hill Tankersley's rant against outsiders descends in a straight line from Yancey's proposal to hang reluctant Rebels. Every March, on the anniversary of the Selma March, King's speeches are still broadcast from speakers outside the Dexter Avenue Baptist Church, well within earshot of the capitol steps where Jeff Davis took the oath of office and George Wallace promised segregation would last forever. Within a golf shot of each is the stately archive building where Wesley Thompson claimed he found proof that no one else can find. But thanks to Judge John Bennett Weaver and Donald Dodd, we can reconstruct what did happen to Chris Sheats, and that's a better yarn than anyone could make up. So, for that matter, is what happened to Don Dodd when he called on Stanley Hoole in Tuscaloosa and also when he tried to get past an austere matron whom Marie Bankhead Owen had put in charge of preventing Confederate records in Montgomery from being touched by unbelievers, as we will soon see.

10

OPEN SEASON IN THE HILL COUNTRY

BY THE TIME Chris Sheats was escorted under guard to the Confederate prison in Salisbury, North Carolina, for recruiting for the enemy, my great-grandfather Hiram Raines (1829–1914) was "lying out." He was hiding from Confederate conscription officers, as he later swore to the Southern Claims Commission (SCC), in the woods near the Walker County farm of his father-in-law, James Hiel Abbott. By night, Hiel and other relatives brought him food. As a stronghold of Alabama Unionism, Walker County was second only to Winston County, contributing an estimated 175 men to the Union army compared to 239 from less populous but more precisely documented Winston County. Both counties were described as "overwhelmingly disloyal" to the Confederate government. That attitude explains why Hiram's son, my namesake H. H. Raines, was cursing the "damn Democrats" for the war several decades after it ended.

The political atmospherics surrounding the hillbilly scramble to escape the draft and otherwise damage the Confederacy have been recorded in a remarkable collection of depositions from southern Unionists collected between 1871 and 1873, then stored in the National Archives and largely ignored by historians for a century. These transcribed statements from 220,000 witnesses amount to an oral history of the war years by Confederate dissidents of all classes. Scholars started bringing them into view in the 1970s, but not until 1994 was a complete index published for the records of the Southern Claims Commission. In another of those paradoxes that seem to cluster around Tuscaloosa, the compiler of that invaluable index, Gary C. Mills (1943–2002), was a history professor at the University of Alabama who wrote often of southerners who had been "forgotten" for political or racial reasons. But his obituary in *The Tuscaloosa News,* another of the papers I worked for, listed him as "commander of the Sons of Confederate Veterans." It struck me as a telling example of the bird's-nest tangle of Civil War history and how long it takes for an arguably balanced version of the facts to surface.

The mandate of the SCC was to test post facto declarations of loyalty and to make cash awards to southerners who could prove they had never supported the Confederacy and suffered financial losses in aiding the Union militarily by, for example, surrendering livestock or crops to official representatives of the federal government. Using strict rules, the commissioners rejected 22,298 claims and approved 7,029 for a total of $4.6 million. Hiel Abbott was approved to receive $178 for a horse and feed he surrendered to the troops of Union general John T. Croxton on April 15 or 16, 1865, when they passed through Abbott's farm on their way to burn the University of Alabama. On January 25, 1872, Abbott's daughter, Acenith Abbott Raines, and her husband, Hiram Raines, appeared at the Jasper courthouse to attest that, among other things, Confederate authorities had threatened to hang Hiel as a "damned old Lincolnite." Of course, the SCC investigators could not prove that everyone they talked to had perfect records of loyalty. For example, Hiram Raines, then forty-five years old, had a secret he didn't share in his deposition, as we shall see later.

The political mood of the area was expressed definitively in one of the few important Unionist documents preserved by the Alabama Department of Archives and History. On April 27, 1861, Winston resident James B. Bell, who acquired a patent to untitled land in Winston County in 1826, wrote a son who had moved to a secessionist hotbed in northeast Mississippi. The date of the letter, only ten weeks after Alabama's vote to secede, is significant because it shows how rapidly pro-Union sentiment spread through the hill country. The timing coincides with Chris Sheats's visits with Union sympathizers and the appearance of pro-Union posters at general stores and gristmills. After expressing perfunctory well-wishes, Bell upbraided his son in a distinctive style:

> *I received a letter from you . . . but it was disgusting to me to think that I had Raised A Child that woud Cecede from under the government that he was bornd and Raised under it is Something Strane to me that people Can forget the grones and crys of our fourfathers in the Revoloutin So quick. Henry just think back to the time when our forefatherse walked over the frozened ground bare foot leaving ther blood on the ground when fighting for the liberties that you have enjoyed ever Since you hav had a being in the world God forbid that I ever Should even be Cald a Cecessionist. I had jest as Soon be Cald a tory, as to Comit treson ganst the government that was Sealed with the blood of my fathers. the Scripture informs us that a House Devided against its Self Cannot stand. The Scriptures informs us that the Isralites divided in to Northism & Souhisn's and She was in bondage in less than ten years. Henry you are out in a Ceceding Country and tha have got you puft up with Cecessionism as tight as a tode. I dont see what you nede to care for you hant got no Slaves. All tha want is to get you puft up and go to fight for their infurnerl negroes and after you do there fighting you may kiss ther hine parts for a tha ceare.*

"Puffed up as tight as a toad" remains as good a metaphor as I've ever encountered for a particular Alabama state of mind—the spoiling-for-a-fight readiness achieved by some citizens when their blood is up. It explains the mood I found among the Trumpites when I visited my grandparents' graves in Arley after Winstonians gave him 90 percent of their votes in 2016. Back in 1861, however, the county was on the right

side of history. The newly installed Confederate authorities were seized
by the kind of whirling anxiety experienced a hundred years later by
Alabama governors John Patterson and George Wallace as they tried to
keep the NAACP and Justice Department lawyers out of Alabama. Initially their anxiety and then their rage were brought on by the low enlistment figures throughout the highlands in 1861. It was a first sign that the
farm boys upstate would not change their contrarian ways. Back home
in Winston, Henry Bell's two brothers and his sister wrote him even
more strenuous denunciations than their father did about going over to
the slaveholders' side. Henry did what he thought was the obligation of
a "puft-up" Rebel. He turned his relatives' letters over to the Confederate postmaster of Lodi, Mississippi, who forwarded them to Governor
Andrew B. Moore in the hope that "Your Excellency . . . may be advised
of the Existence of such sentiments in your state . . . [and] take such
Course . . . as your judgement and duty may dictate." Living only 150
miles from the farm where he was born, Henry had to know that the
condemnation of Tories had already begun back home, and that his letter could become a warrant for arrest or death.

Even so, the initial forced-recruitment efforts by the governor and
county sheriffs in the first year of the war might be parodied as Keystone
Cops–like had they not evolved in so deadly a direction in the war's
middle period. By 1862, anti-war sentiment was sweeping Winston and
the surrounding counties, a development easily tracked in the SCC files.
The hard evidence in those archival records and the publication of
Richard Nelson Current's *Lincoln's Loyalists* in 1992 set off a surge of
revisionist scholarship that greatly aided my research. Doctoral students
hungry for fresh dissertation topics and history professors on the prowl
for articles to write followed, most notably Margaret M. Storey, the
Emory graduate student who arrived in Birmingham in the late 1990s to
interview my father about David Best. Her *Loyalty and Loss: Alabama
Unionists in the Civil War and Reconstruction* (2004) has been rightly
hailed as seminal in illuminating the state's lost legacy of patriotism.
Also, more humble materials—frontier land records and reference to a
"Mr. Raines" in John Martin Dombhart's obscure, self-published 1937

book *History of Walker County: Its Towns and People*—helped me to reconstruct the most salient facts of my family history.

By 1835, James and Robert Rains (to use their spelling) acquired land near the shoaly, cliff-lined Sipsey River in the midst of what was to become a cluster of "disloyal" Alabamians. Through marriage, James and his children and grandchildren—Robert was a bachelor—became linked to the Barton, Best, Abbott, Key, Sides, and Walker families. From the surveyors' grid of their farmsteads I gradually discerned a remarkable political geography. These families were either flagrant Unionists or reluctant Confederates. The only similarly intense concentration I've discovered is defined by the Dodd, Curtis, Weaver, and Johnson families about thirty miles to the northwest around the Winston County dual county seats of Haleyville and Double Springs. Another essential revisionist work, Daniel E. Sutherland's 2009 *A Savage Conflict: The Decisive Role of Guerrillas in the American Civil War*, enabled me to reconstruct what life was like in this hotbed of anti-secessionist sentiment. Taken together, these works and others from the new school of southern Unionist studies demonstrate why an essential element of historiography must always be the study of the biases of earlier writers regarding the mass of fact, myth, and opinion we invoke when we speak of what "history" has to teach us.

In Alabama, the central stereotype of the listless slave has a white counterpart, the vicious hillbilly. Both caricatures are represented in the fulsome works of Walter Lynwood Fleming and William Stanley Hoole. "The Alabama tory was, as a rule, of the lowest class of the population," Fleming wrote. These " 'mountain whites' and the 'sand-mountain people' who were shut off from the world, a century behind times . . . knew scarcely anything of the Union or of the questions at issue." Fleming saw their apparent loyalty to the old flag as motivated by class hatred of the slave owners. "In this feeling the women were more bitter than the men. . . . [W]hen the enrolling officers went after them, they became dangerous. Today [in 1905] these people are represented by the makers of 'moonshine' whiskey and those who shoot revenue officers."

Hoole was even less kind, noting that the lawless "hillbillies" were a criminal class. Forming "themselves into bands of so-called 'Destroying Angels' or 'Prowling Brigades,' they occasionally swept down out of their piney-woods strongholds to raid their more fortunate neighbors in the valleys. Not infrequently, they burned cotton, gin-houses, jails, county court records, public buildings, and dwellings, willy-nilly 'confiscating' food and other properties as they went. . . . Even to the Union commanders, their so-called friends, the Tories were sometimes 'as vicious as copperheads.'"

What is breathtaking by modern standards is that these professional historians knew exactly what they were distorting. Both Fleming and Hoole had closely studied the secession debates, where the pro-Union orators laid out a tightly reasoned constitutional argument, based on Jacksonian principles, for their reluctance—and in some cases outright refusal—to rebel.

11

A Revolving Spy

IMMEDIATELY AFTER SECESSION, Confederate leaders in Montgomery and Richmond faced a conflict between their gentlemanly principles and the political reality that only forced enlistment could give them an army and only racial demagoguery would inspire it. From the future state of West Virginia, along the spine of the Blue Ridge and Smokies all the way down into Alabama's northern counties, the farm boys were refusing to enlist in expected numbers. All across the South, secessionist hotbloods clamored for permission to meet the oncoming Yankees in guerilla warfare, thereby making up for the shortfall in manpower. Confederate secretary of war LeRoy Pope Walker, a native of Huntsville, Alabama, received a letter from "one hundred Gentlemen" from his native Alabama asking to go "Gurillaing" on their "own hook."

Jefferson Davis was tempted to endorse partisan warfare to defend his new nation's mountainous territory. But he and Robert E. Lee regarded guerillas as a threat to the gentlemen's code of civilized warfare they, as West Pointers, preferred. Throughout 1861, the South squeaked by on its high-toned army of men-about-town and plantation scions, and it was slow to give up on its gentlemen's code, resisting all advice to conduct an unorthodox forest war against the invaders. As late as June 1861, Davis wrote a wannabe guerilla captain from Alabama that "his company could not be accepted if 'the term guerilla' implied 'independent operations,'" according to Daniel E. Sutherland.

In the early months of the war, Alabama governor Andrew B. Moore, who was less rabid than his colleague William Lowndes Yancey, also resisted relying on "bandittos," as Rebel vigilantes were sometimes called in Alabama. But he was much closer than Davis to the brushfire insurrection sweeping the hill country and now spreading to a few counties on the Florida border. Moore wanted to operate within the law, sort of. In a letter to a worried Confederate in Jasper, the seething Walker County seat, Moore promised to order county sheriffs to arrest and hold "any citizen declaring himself in favor of the Lincoln government, hoisting the United States flag or declaring a readiness to fight on that side." There was, of course, no mention of habeas corpus, but by the standards of what lay ahead, Moore was a respecter of local authority and reluctant to use military force against the state's outspoken anti-war activists.

But he was succeeded in the governor's mansion on February 4, 1861, by John Gill Shorter, who within a year had switched to a policy of coercive arrests, spying, and military operations. Shorter was even able to secure a Confederate intelligence report written by Confederate captain H. A. M. Henderson, who was assigned to an infantry unit camping at Jasper. Henderson traveled across the Winston County line to a Free State rally convened by Sheats at Looney's Tavern, a rustic hostelry a few miles north of Haleyville; I'm inclined to believe that the well-educated Henderson probably donned civilian clothes and blended into the crowd. We know about Henderson's written report on his spying because a letter referring to it was among the captured Confederate documents preserved starting in 1877 by the extremely efficient *Official Records* archivists in Washington, D.C. Based on Henderson's account of the woodland "convention" addressed by Sheats, an angered Governor Shorter declared that the three resolutions passed that day were treasonable, and he wrote the state militia's adjutant general, George Goldthwaite, that "everyone who participated in the convention is a traitor to the State and to the South and should be, if possible arrested."

He ordered Goldthwaite to dispatch a "Special Aide-de-Camp" to Winston and use whatever force necessary to see that Winston provided its fair share of "volunteers."

The official hand-off of the letter on April 9, 1862, from Governor Moore to Adjutant General Goldthwaite and from him to Colonel Robert Jemison Jr. of Tuscaloosa marks the moment when the Confederacy decided to abandon civilized persuasion and endorse the use of force "even to the death" against dissidents. The exact content of that letter is one of the many mysteries that point us toward an evidentiary Bermuda Triangle comprising the Alabama Department of Archives and History and the University of Alabama Library. The original was mailed to Jemison, and no for-the-record stenographic copy of it exists in the Moore Papers at the ADAH, nor is it listed in the extensive Jemison family papers at the University of Alabama Library in Tuscaloosa.

Only Winston County historian Donald Dodd has written extensively about "the Henderson letter," as he always referred to it, and as far as I can tell he discovered the lone reference to it in the *Official Records*. Dodd believed it was (and still would be, if it exists) the pivotal document in the Free State saga because it would allow us to pinpoint when the Confederate authorities decided to unleash hell on the mountain citizens of Alabama. As a graduate student, Dodd spent an entire summer in Montgomery looking for a copy, and he believed it might yet turn up in some obscure folder or forgotten box. Around the same time, in search of the original mailed to Jemison in Tuscaloosa, he talked his way past a suspicious William Stanley Hoole at the University of Alabama library to go through the Jemison Papers, but he found nothing.

As Dodd had decided and Hoole probably already knew, there is no more important missing document in the communications chain, both because of what it may have said and because of the extraordinary man who wrote it, a turncoat of a different sort from Jemison. At the least, Henderson's report could give us a second source as to the exact date of the rally at Looney's and, more importantly, a means of judging the accuracy of Judge Weaver's reconstruction of Sheats's speech and the critical three resolutions made by the rally's attendees. The first resolution commended Sheats for voting against secession in Montgomery, and the second said that if it was legal for Alabama to leave the Union, then Winston would secede from Alabama. The third resolution declared Winston's neutrality and its wish to be "unmolested" by either side.

There is no lack of documentation for the reign of violence that followed Henderson's report. Looking at this turning point in the persecution of Unionists and the organization of the First Alabama that followed soon after provides me another opportunity to make this point, which I seek to emphasize by taking every opportunity to credit the relevant historians. I am not an original researcher, but as a reporter, I was trained to follow threads of fact and look for patterns in the tapestry that can be woven from those threads. One such pattern is the pivotal role in the persecution of Alabama Unionists played by Confederate officials born and educated in the North. In this light, Henderson and Goldthwaite become two more unlikely players in what remains for me one of the most unusual stories to emerge from the Civil War.

We can intuit a good deal about Henderson's report from Goldthwaite's April 9 letter to Jemison, which amounted to an order to impose martial law and executions. Despite his impassioned oration accusing Yancey of wanting to kill mountain secessionists "by neighborhoods," Jemison, a wealthy Tuscaloosan, had become a special aide-de-camp to Governor Shorter with the rank of colonel. The letter also shows that Shorter, who saw himself as the arch-enforcer of plantation dominance in Alabama politics, had become completely bloody-minded in regard to the Winston County rebellion.

> *Colonel: By the direction of the Governor I herewith inclose to you the original letter from Capt. H. A. M. Henderson. He directs me also to state that he has received evidence from other sources sufficient to satisfy his mind that the facts as detailed by Captain Henderson are substantially correct. . . . Everyone who participated in the convention referred to in the letter by supporting its resolutions is a traitor to the State and to the South*

and should, if possible, be arrested. Lenity and forebearance,
hesitation or faltering would have no other effect than to give
confidence to those engaged in the treason. The infection will
spread and increase unless it is promptly eradicated. . . . [Y]ou
are invested with authority to order out . . . such portion of the
military force of the State as you think necessary; to issue orders in
the name of the Governor . . . to any major or brigadier general,
colonel or any other officer . . . and generally to take such measures
as in the exercise of your discretion you may deem necessary to
effect the arrest of the disloyal leaders and their misguided
followers, unless you are fully satisfied that the last can be brought
back to a true sense of their duty to the State and the South by a
more lenient course.

Goldthwaite, of course, had heard threats at the secession convention that hill country dissidents would shoot invaders from Montgomery, and he warned Jemison not to crack down so hard as to endanger "loyal citizens and their families." Troops would be sent from Montgomery to establish safe havens for loyalists from the Free State radicals. In other words, the state recognized that Winston was ripe for civil war within its own borders. The governor hoped the "extent of the disaffection had been exaggerated" and that "well meaning but loyal but unwise men" could be brought back to the fold by the arrest of their leaders. The governor wanted a "plan of operations for the arrest of the most prominent offenders." Jemison was told he could requisition troops and ammunition. Goldthwaite did not mention Sheats by name, but he did not need to; Henderson's eyewitness report would have identified Sheats as the main speaker at Looney's Tavern. Goldthwaite knew that Jemison would recognize Sheats on sight, since they had caucused together as members of the cooperationist minority in Montgomery in January.

[Governor Shorter] would suggest that, for the purpose of
ascertaining . . . and [to] mature the plan of operations for the

arrest of the most prominent offenders, as well as the course most
expedient to adopt in relation to others, you should take the
earliest opportunity of visiting Winston County upon some
pretext and determining for yourself the course to be pursued. In
conclusion, the Governor directs me to say that he fully
appreciates the difficulty, as well as the delicacy of the disagreeable
but important duty he has devolved upon you. He sees clearly that
the character of the country and the feelings of the people may
render it a work both of toil and danger, and will certainly
require the exercise of great energy, firmness, and prudence, but
he relies on you to adopt and carry out those measures which will
be certain to secure the arrest of the offenders at any risk or cost.
To attempt it and fail would only make matters worse. If
resistance is attempted it must be met even to the death. You will
be sustained in the employment of any means or force you may
think necessary to effect the proposed result. In case of arrest, the
prisoners had better be removed to Tuscaloosa.

It was, by any standard, a remarkable document, and a chilling
one—a license to hunt and, if necessary, kill Chris Sheats and his supporters. The legalistic formality of the "to the death" language meant
that Robert Jemison could not disguise the governor's intention to have
Sheats killed or, at the least, removed from the county where he was
making so much trouble. The order certainly shows that Abraham Lincoln was not alone in believing civil liberties and due process to be legal
niceties that ought to be ignored by chief executives during the Civil
War. Had Sheats seen the letter, surely he would not have gone back to
Montgomery later in 1862 to meet with Shorter. This is another case of
puzzling questions that linger because of gaps in the official record and
the fact that Alabama journalists and historians did not interview Sheats
after the war, even though we will discover that he was readily available.

Unfortunately, Donald Dodd died at eighty-one, just as I was drilling
down on these matters, including the biographies of Goldthwaite and
Henderson. Had he lived longer I would have asked him why he didn't

include their backgrounds in his work. My guess is that it was because he wrestled with the question that confronts every historical writer: how much detail to include. I have little doubt that their stories would have caught his eye. Goldthwaite (1809–1879) was born in Boston, Massachusetts, into a family that came to America as part of the Massachusetts Bay Society. He entered West Point at only fourteen, overlapping there with students such as Jeff Davis, Robert E. Lee, and Joseph E. Johnston, three future Confederate mainstays. He read law with a brother who had moved to Montgomery and rose to chief justice of the Alabama Supreme Court. "Though a staunch Unionist," says the *Encyclopedia of Alabama*, "he was a close friend to many of his notable contemporaries, even the fiery secessionist, William L. Yancey." Accepting Moore's appointment as adjutant general, he spent the war years organizing Alabama's war matériel.

The arc of the life of H. A. M. Henderson, the spy at Looney's Tavern, is even more startling. On May 11, 1893, former president Grant arrived in Jersey City, New Jersey, where his mother had died earlier that day. "To her pastor, the Rev. Dr. Howard A. M. Henderson, Grant entrusted arrangements for the funeral. Grant wanted no mention made of his own success. He asked Henderson simply to eulogize Hannah Grant as a 'pure-minded, simple-hearted, earnest Methodist Christian,'" according to Civil War scholar Peter Cozzens. "The man in who General Grant placed so much trust had served honorably during the Civil War—but on the side of the Confederacy, and as the commandant of a prison camp." The camp in question was at Cahaba, Alabama, between Selma and Montgomery, the least deadly of the notorious Confederate prisons. That fact is in keeping with Henderson's background and education, and it makes me regret all the more keenly that we do not have his doubtlessly literate account of the Free State rally. Happenstance and Google, without which any history-seeker is hobbled, came to my aid in piecing together, in Henderson's case, a portrait of yet another startling personality in this Alabama story. In his own way, Henderson is as colorful and hungry for distinction as others in Alabama history, such as "Old Stars" Mitchel, the spymaster Grenville Dodge, and those ever-calculating adversaries in the battle for control of Bama's mountains, Confederate general Philip Roddey, and Colonel Spencer, the thwarted hero of the march through Snake Creek Gap.

In the case of Henderson, my habit of collecting the kind of books published by small presses catering to genealogists and Civil War hobbyists also played a bank-shot role. Upon learning that John Best, my great-great-grandfather who relished Rebel reunions, was a member of the 28th Alabama Infantry, C.S.A., I ordered a regimental history. In connection with the 28th, I stumbled on a reference to a devout soldier who complained he had heard only one sermon in three months since enlisting. "Isn't that horrid?" Joshua Callaway of Summerfield, Alabama, wrote his wife from camp near Tupelo. "Especially when you consider that we have several able ministers in our own regiment, such as Capt. H. A. M. Henderson."

That meant that somehow a boy like John Best, raised along the cool, ferny, dashing waters of the Sipsey River, was serving with comrades from the historic Summerfield District, in the very heart of the Black Belt, with its steaming heat and sluggish creeks. I knew both areas well, having by coincidence worked as a counselor at a summer camp run by the Selma YMCA only thirteen miles from Summerfield. Since the 28th was founded by two men from another cotton town, Marion, it struck me as odd that Best had been drafted into a flatland outfit started more than a hundred miles south of his village. In an army of units closely identified with their neighborhoods, he would have had little in common with his comrades and commanders in an army. That's where H. A. M. Henderson came into the picture.

To say that this minister who would falsely claim to have been a brigadier general led an exaggerated existence is an understatement and a reminder that Lincoln's war to save the Union was also an arena of opportunism for young hustlers north and south, even men of the cloth who married into the planter elite. Henderson was born in Paris, Bourbon County, Kentucky, in 1836, and his obituary in the *Bourbon News* of January 5, 1912, records a life of accomplishment and no little avidity. His father was a graduate of Exeter and Yale who came to Kentucky to take the presidency of a women's college. Christened as Howard Andrew Millett Henderson, the son graduated from Ohio Wesleyan University and the Cincinnati Law School, but he chose the pulpit over the courtroom and took a church in Demopolis, Alabama. It was a rich cotton-shipping town of fine mansions overlooking the Tombigbee River. Its leading families boasted of Virginia lineages linked to George Washington and ties to exiled French nobles from Napoleon's "Old Guard." The French settlers' effort to plant vineyards and olive groves were spoiled by Demopolis's subtropical humidity and unsuitable soil, but they did succeed in naming the surrounding county for Marengo, one of Napoleon's great victories. From that day to this, Marengo County has remained a focal point of white snobbery and Black poverty. The newcomer Henderson married Susan Watkins Vaughan, daughter of one of the planters who made Marengo the second-biggest cotton producer in the state, its 63,000 bales only a thousand behind Dallas County. About 70 of Marengo's 24,409 slaves belonged to his wife's father, Dr. Alfred G. Vaughan, but according to the generous author of Henderson's obituary, sudden plantation wealth could not have influenced his motives. Said the obituary, "Soon after the Civil War broke out he organized the Twenty Eighth Alabama Regiment, of which he became Colonel. Dr. Henderson's prime object in entering the army of the Confederacy was not to fight for the disruption of the Union nor for the perpetuation of slavery. He was always an advocate for the abolishment of slavery, as was his wife, who inherited from her father much cotton land and slaves. His great aim was to do what he could on the very scene of the war to soften its inevitable horrors and minister to the men."

Then comes a breathtaking assertion that Henderson was "a relative of Jefferson Davis"—whether by blood or marriage is not stated. The genealogical site Ancestry confirms that Henderson was related to Jefferson Davis's wife, Varina Howell Davis, through a Texas family named Stamps. A cynic or anyone with an average knowledge of military string-pulling might think that Henderson's brief service in harm's way was related to kinship-based favoritism, which was common in the Davis administration. The young Reverend Henderson mustered in on February 18, 1862, with praise for his efficiency in recruiting three companies for the 28th Alabama in the northern part of the state. By June he was absent from his company, and in early October he resigned "due to physical disability," diagnosed as chronic bronchitis. After recuperating in Demopolis, he was by the next summer in the first of the "bomb-proof" non-combat assignments, culminating with his appointment as commander of the Cahaba prison and later as a prisoner-exchange official. "During this service he exchanged about 35,000 men," his obituary stated. "Among the most cherished possessions of Dr. Henderson were thousands of letters from Union soldiers expressing gratitude for kindness he had extended to them while he was in charge of them. His headquarters were at Cahaba, Ala. near Selma."

Historian Peter Cozzens credits Henderson's "humanity" with the fact that the mortality rate at Cahaba was 3 percent for its five thousand inmates, notwithstanding rats, lice, and a polluted water supply that Henderson helped improve with enclosed pipelines. By comparison, almost a third of Andersonville's forty-one thousand prisoners died, possibly including Hiram Raines's brother, Allen, another draftee in the 28th. While Henderson was clearly more compassionate than other Confederate prison commanders, there was nothing humane about his spying mission to Winston nor its eventual impact on terrorized hill country families. "Henderson was sent up, attended the convention at the direction of the governor, he sent the letter back and the governor reacted to the neutrality meeting because of the Henderson letter," Dodd told me in a 2019 interview. As a graduate student, Dodd made a six-week search at the ADAH through the papers of all Civil War governors. "I could not find [the letter]. It was not in any government papers, and I don't understand why it would be lost. It was evidence of treason from the standpoint of pro-Confederate types, so I don't think they would destroy evidence that shows treason," he told me.

He was similarly thorough in going through the University of Alabama collection. "You know Hoole was down there [then]. If I had found it I wouldn't have told him." By 2021, I began to question Dodd's conclusion that Henderson was ordered into Winston by Governor

Shorter. I had looked more closely at the chain of command, but Dodd was gone before I could run my findings past him. The outcome would have been the same in any case, but the details add a measure of clarity. Despite the claims in his unsigned 1912 obituary, Henderson neither founded the 28th Alabama nor became its colonel. Those roles were filled by two prominent citizens of Marion, Alabama, about thirty miles from Demopolis, where the twenty-five-year-old Henderson was preaching. They tapped Henderson to conduct recruiting for the new regiment in Walker County, even though most of the enlistees were from well south of there, between present-day Birmingham and Selma. Henderson did become the founding captain of Company E, mustered at Jasper in late February 1862. That would have placed him next door to Winston County and within easy riding distance of Looney's Tavern around the time Sheats was publicizing his rally and Goldthwaite was dispatching Jemison to the county. Moreover, the passage of the Confederate Conscription Act was inspiring turnout for a spring anti-war rally most historians have come to believe took place in the first months of 1862, not on July 4, 1861.

Henderson's presence at the rally bespeaks how he was on his way to becoming the Zelig of the Confederate army. In January 1965, with the Confederacy crumbling, Henderson was ordered to leave Cahaba and take on an unusual assignment within Union-held Vicksburg, Mississippi. He operated under the personal protection of the Union commander, the battle-hardened Brigadier General Napoleon J. T. Dana, who assigned a cavalry battalion as Henderson's personal bodyguard. He was teamed with a Union officer, Colonel A. C. Fisk, to supervise prisoner exchanges that would bring 4,700 newly paroled Union POWs to "Camp Fisk." On orders from this Blue-Gray military odd couple, more than 2,137 men, over half of them from Henderson's Cahaba prison, were loaded aboard the *Sultana,* which had a legal capacity of 376 passengers. The ship's captain, James Cass Mason, bribed the Union quartermaster of Vicksburg to allow him to cram the ship, as he was to receive $2.75 for each Union enlisted man and $8.00 for each officer he carried upriver toward their homes. Both Captain Mason and the corrupt Union officer knew that the *Sultana*'s leaking boilers had been patchily repaired and that the vessel should have stayed at the dock for two or three more days of work. "Early on the morning of April 27, three of the four boilers exploded, and the *Sultana* sank near Memphis. Two-thirds of those on board died," according to Peter Cozzens.

Being a Rebel officer in a Union encampment was dangerous work, especially after the assassination of President Lincoln on April 14. But before Grant relieved him of command a few weeks after the *Sultana* fiasco, General Dana spirited Henderson across the Mississippi and put him in the protective custody of the Texas Rangers. Was there a luckier man in the war than this anti-slavery preacher who went south to inherit a slave-created fortune from his father-in-law? Unlike the commanders of other Confederate prisons, he was never in danger of being tried like the Andersonville commander Henry Wirz, who was executed, and the brutal Lieutenant Colonel Samuel Jones, who succeeded Henderson at Cahaba and vanished while being pursued for over a year by federal prosecutors. Henderson had worked both sides of the street so well that he got a bombproof job from Jeff Davis and had bodyguards provided by a Union general who had been a hero of the critical bluecoat victory at Antietam. If he owed a debt to universal justice for his role in putting vengeful Confederates on the trail of Chris Sheats and undefended mountain families, what better absolution could there be than being picked to preside at the funeral of the mother of the Union's greatest general?

The Tattler of the Hills

Next to H. A. M. Henderson, the Yankee most responsible for unleashing hell on the mountain folk was Andrew J. Kaeiser (1799–1864), a vociferous secessionist from the richest county in the storied Pennsylvania Dutch farming kingdom of the Cumberland Valley. The venerable cliché about converts who become "more Catholic than the Pope" applies to this vindictive owner of twenty slaves, who constantly prodded Alabama's wartime governors to crack down on his Free State neighbors. He was a "Southern Yankee," a type scathingly described by the acerbic Alabama writer D. R. Hundley in his 1860 book *Social Relations in Our Southern States.* Such prosperous newcomers were determined to prove themselves more ardent secessionists than either of the two other groups in Hundley's typology, the "Southern Gentlemen" and the "Cotton Snobs." But Kaeiser is of more than sociological interest. He was a finger man for the murder squads who roamed the Appalachian backcountry in several states but seemed to reach optimal ferocity and efficiency in north Alabama.

Kaeiser's story dramatizes this parallel war that raged while public and official attention was focused on the brand-name battles that earned space on front pages and in the history books that followed. On his way to becoming a key player in sub-rosa operations in Winston County, he was born and grew up in Chambersburg, which Rebel cavalry burned on July 30, 1864, when city fathers failed to meet General Jubal Early's demand for $500,000 in greenbacks or $100,000 in gold. The Pennsylvanian burghers wanted to pay, but they had shipped their money to another town for safekeeping, and after the disaster at nearby Gettysburg, "Ol' Jube" was in no mood to wait since he was still seething about the defeat inflicted on Robert E. Lee's army a year earlier.

Chambersburg, too, was part of an odd symbiosis linking its fertile location, just north of the Mason-Dixon Line, to the mountain South. The town was settled by Scots-Irish immigrants, who arrived before the German Protestants and indulged their preference for rugged terrain by migrating down the Valley of Virginia to become the dominant stock in the range of mountains that finally played out in Alabama. These Ulstermen, who had flooded the port of Philadelphia in Ben Franklin's time, abandoned the best farmland in the colonies to seek the kind of rough living they experienced as Britain's tenants in Northern Ireland. James Carville once quipped that Pennsylvania consists of enlightened Pittsburgh and Philadelphia at each end "with Alabama in between." For me, the duality of Chambersburg has always been symbolized by the fact that it is only fourteen miles north of the Mason-Dixon Line in the same area that produced President James Buchanan, whose sympathy for southern slave owners set the stage for the Civil War. Few people understand that plantation country actually straddled the Mason-Dixon Line, and I've long felt Buchanan was motivated in part by envy for the free labor enjoyed by Marylanders only a few miles away from his own land. That is to say, agriculturally and to some degree culturally, the Mason-Dixon survey line was an artificial boundary drawn in contradictory times. Consider also that Chambersburg was an important stop on the Underground Railroad and that John Brown planned his Harpers Ferry raid during a two-month residency in a rented room in Chambersburg.

Although qualified as a physician, Andrew Kaeiser dreamed of a commercial empire. That is what brought him to Winston County at a time when Lancaster County farmland, widely regarded as the best in the United States, was selling for $68 per acre. In 1852, Kaeiser bought forty acres of good Winston bottomland for only $1.25 an acre, and eventually he would own 360 acres, one of the few holdings in the county flat enough to support a modest, slave-tilled plantation. He had also found his way into one of the most politically contentious spots in Alabama and, indeed, in the entire Confederacy. His eastern land line was just over a mile from the land that James Bell bought three years later, in 1855. In 1861, Bell wrote the letter warning his boy Henry that he was risking death for people who believed he should kiss their "hine parts." (In 1863, death would find Henry at Chattanooga. Only one of Henry's three brothers who went into the First Alabama Cavalry would survive the war.) Kaeiser, who would live a bit longer, was within five miles of the Abbott-Barton-Raines-Best Unionist pod that was developing just over the line in Walker County and the Curtis-Johnson-Brooks pod in north Winston.

Not until 1980 did scholars begin to catch up with what really went on in the hidden war in the southern backcountry. On battlefields and in thousands of tented encampments, officers of each army recorded military events in detail, as they were trained to do at West Point. We'll never know the full truth about the ragamuffin gangs that operated beyond the light of the campfires of organized troops. The prosecutors and victims in what has been called "the South's internal war" had huge consequences for Lincoln's strategy. The president knew, for example, that mountain folk in east Tennessee and adjoining states opposed the war and did their best to hobble the Confederacy's economy, legal system, and military. But he, along with Grant and Sherman, also knew that Confederate irregulars and the plain folk in many plantation communities were working to sabotage Union forces. That led to the momentous decision, executed most dramatically on Sherman's march, to break the will of southern civilians. Only in recent decades has a scholarly consensus emerged that the civilians on both sides suffered greatly, and that the excesses in Alabama, in particular, stemmed from two pivotal acts of the Confederate Congress: the Partisan Ranger Act of April 21, 1861, and the Confederate Conscription Act of April 26, 1862. The former set loose what even Confederate general Henry Heth called "robbers and plunderers . . . notorious thieves and murderers" on the Rebel side in what would today be called a campaign of state-sponsored terrorism. The Conscription Act, America's first compulsory draft law, passed a year after the South attacked Fort Sumter. It was condemned by its opponents in the Confederate Congress because of what it proved: that Dixie's oligarchs had declared a war to which hundreds of thousands of their fellow citizens were unwilling to come.

Based on his surviving letters, Dr. Andrew Kaeiser was one of the first conservative Alabamians to realize the manpower and internal security problems posed by the homely rebellion brewing in Winston. Kaeiser was a reluctant doctor who would treat importunate neighbors and his slaves, but his real interests were farming and running a health spa at a mineral spring in southwestern Winston County. The delegates' election he lost to Chris Sheats on Christmas Eve 1860 was still bothering Kaeiser as the war cranked up. He wrote Governor Shorter that of the 128 secessionists who had voted for him, 70 were already in the Confederate army. Of the 515 who voted for Sheats, however, not a single one had volunteered. He enclosed in his letter a flyer put up around the county the previous July by Sheats and his cronies. It said: "All persons desiring to attach themselves to a union company to form a home guard for protection of our familys and property is earnestly requested to meet us at A. J. Taylor's store on the 14th Inst and at Wm Dodds Store on the 15th. Come one come all good Union men."

Kaeiser's letter reported that he had chaired a group of prosperous Winstonians at his house on November 30, 1861, and perhaps in purposeful imitation of the Looney's Tavern resolutions, this gathering passed three of their own, asking Shorter to take military action "to suppress and strangulate the said spirit of disloyalty and rebellion." They recommended that, if "constitutionally" possible, "a requisition be made upon the county of Winston for at least 250 soldiers for the Confederate Army." That was not to be. During the entire war, Winston sent 121 residents to the Rebel army, as opposed to 239 for the Union. The spirit animating the "disloyal" citizens was illustrated by John R. Phillips (1837–1925), who was forcibly conscripted by Rebel cavalry in the fall of 1862. He deserted and met with several hundred other resisters at Natural Bridge near Haleyville, as described in his 1923 autobiography *The Story of My Life,* one of the most authoritative accounts of life in the First Alabama Cavalry, U.S.A. This group, too, had three propositions, Phillips wrote: "'First, all that want to join the Rebel Army step out!' Not a man stepped out. 'All that want to go to the North and join the Union Army, step out.' There were over a hundred men stepped out. Number three were left to decide for themselves."

Lost Cause historians habitually misrepresented both the political and self-preservation imperatives that motivated Unionists in Alabama and throughout the mountain South. "First, Southerners who opposed the Confederacy formed their own guerilla bands and clashed with rebel neighbors in violent contests for political and economic control of their communities," wrote Daniel E. Sutherland in *A Savage Conflict: The Decisive Role of Guerrillas in the American Civil War,* a rare big-picture look at backcountry conflict that undermined home-front confidence in the new government. "Rebel citizens blamed their government for failing to protect them; winning distant battles became less important than preserving homes. Then the guerilla war bred cancerous mutations. Violent bands of deserters, draft dodgers, and genuine outlaws operated as guerillas to prey on loyal Confederates and defend themselves against Rebel authorities. This broadened the South's internal war, and where deserters and draft dodgers made common cause with armed Unionists and slaves, anarchy prevailed."

In Winston, at least, the anarchists proved to be fiercely motivated and perhaps even to some degree organized by Yankee regulars when Governor Shorter responded to Kaeiser's plea for a punitive invasion of the Tory stronghold. A small but well-armed force was detached from Roddey's command under Captain Nelson Fennel on June 26, 1862. Only two days later, Fennel reported he had been "driven from the Winston mountains by superior numbers of deserters, Union men and Yankees." In what has to be one of the more petulant field reports of the war, Fennel wrote Shorter that he had set three of his men to guard two deserters when "fifteen deserters came down from the hills and fired upon them without giving them any warning." The attackers killed one guard with a shot "under the right nipple" and killed the second by shooting him "six times through the bowels, and once through the nape of the neck." The third guard escaped and reported that he saw Yankee uniforms and heard military drumming. Fennel assured the governor that he was "satisfied that it will take a considerable force to drive them from the fastnesses."

A month later, Brigadier General Gideon J. Pillow, superintendent of the Conscript Bureau in Richmond, was complaining that there were "8,000 to 10,000 deserters and tory conscripts" hiding in the Alabama mountains who were "almost impossible to capture." Tracking dogs, trained to run down escaping slaves, caught a few of the mountain men, but General Leonidas Polk was thinking big. He arranged for a large force to sweep through the mountains "to drive the tories toward a waiting picket line in the fashion of a deer drive." Under orders from Pillow to scout the infested areas "with vigor," General Roddey was to stretch the picket line east from the Mississippi border to intercept the Tories as they fled south toward Tuscaloosa and present-day Birmingham. Many, however, ran the opposite way, into Union lines. As if to underscore the fecklessness of Pillow's plan, Bill Looney, a Union recruiter now known as the "Black Fox," "led fourteen deserters to Union lines during the drive," the Winston historian Donald Dodd wrote happily in 1972.

In Winston County early in the war, Andrew Kaeiser was as active on the Confederate side as Chris Sheats was on the Union side and every bit as passionate or foolhardy. Exactly how he became a physician is unclear, but "doctor" was the title he used as owner of Kaeiser Springs, the health spa he established on his new Alabama holdings not far from the site of Sheats's rallies at Looney's Tavern. He boasted that the bottled blue water he sold had proved an absolute cure for his wife's chronic stomach troubles. After arriving in Alabama, he had served for a time as a deputy sheriff, so he had no doubt learned that the mountain feudists were dangerous men. He proved to be dangerous himself. Throughout 1861, Kaeiser and a friend from Perry County in the Black Belt,

Dr. P. C. Winn, sought to stir up Governor Shorter about skullduggery on the home front. Winn owned forty-nine slaves and served as a surgeon in H. A. M. Henderson's regiment. He and Kaeiser worked Shorter as a team. Kaeiser said "suspicious" strangers had been sighted in Winston, and Winn worried that its Unionists were in communication with the "foul and traitorous" Tennessee Unionists who burned five railroad bridges in East Tennessee in an 1861 guerilla campaign endorsed by President Lincoln.

To betoken his zeal, Winn told the governor he had journeyed into the hills for 125 miles from his plantation to discuss the Tory problem in a November 30, 1861, meeting at Kaeiser's resort. There's every reason to believe he was in the county with H. A. M. Henderson, since it was he who assigned Henderson to canvass Walker County for enlistees in the new 28th Alabama Infantry, C.S.A. Henderson was not, however, included in a list of twenty-two pro-Confederate attendees submitted separately in a letter to the governor by Kaeiser. The list accompanied a resolution designed to convince Shorter that he was moving too slowly to "strangulate . . . disloyalty and rebellion." In his own letter, Winn warned that Winston contained "few loyal citizens" and the majority of its people were ready to fight on the other side. "There are organized companies in the county which drill regularly with the avowed purpose of defending the Union," Winn wrote. "Many men in that county told me proudly, if they had to fight for anybody, they would fight for Lincoln." Kaeiser's resolution actually understated the level of opposition to the new Confederate government. "The half has not been told you," wrote Winn, and he avowed he was ready to use his "sword" against the Free State. Unlike Goldthwaite, Winn did not hesitate to name the troublemaker who needed to be removed.

You will see from Dr. K's letter that the citizens of Winston (the loyal citizens) have no confidence in *Sheets,* [*sic*] their representative, and whatever may be his late protestations of loyalty, they advise that he cannot be *trusted.* When his people change he may change, but so long as they are in a majority, there is no hope of a change in him. I would urge that something be done to strangulate the rebelion & treason in that quarter.

Apparently believing simply removing Sheats would not be enough strangulation, Winn concluded on an even more hawkish note. He was planning to take his Jasper-based 28th Infantry into Winston County in the near future and expected to "have the privilege of drafting about 400 of the Lincoln men of Winston." It was understood by all, of course, that could only be done at the point of a gun.

Winn's meddling in hill country affairs and the war itself may have been a welcome diversion for him, whose history was turbulent. A year earlier, his wife divorced him after he admitted to trying to rape her eleven-year-old daughter from a previous marriage. The court filing said he also "threatened to cut [his wife's] throat" and "placed the blame on his excessive drinking." Things went better for a while. Comrades in the 28th named their first encampment Camp Winn in honor of their surgeon. But by December 1862, he resigned from the service due to "paralysis of the rectum and bowels." After the war, he removed to Texas, where he ran unsuccessfully for office and was involved in disputes over his medical bills.

No doubt wisely, Kaeiser did not follow his friend Winn into the army as a volunteer officer. He was under no requirement to do so because of age and his ownership of 20 of Winston County's 148 slaves. "Anyone who had that number of slaves was exempted from fighting in the Civil War," wrote James Dodd Manasco, descendant of two prominent Tory families and a reliable Winston antiquarian, in his book *Walking Sipsey: The People, Places, and Wildlife.* "So Kaeiser did his civic duty and stayed home serving as an informant for the Home Guard. The guard went into the hills to bring out those who would not fight. Those who did not come out to fight in the rich man's war were killed in many different ways to provide sadistic amusement for the Confederate Home Guard. It was Dr. Kaeiser who was telling the Home Guard who they were and where they were hiding. The number of people who Kaeiser fingered for death is unbelievable but the historic records are correct."

Kaeiser never tired of reminding Governor Shorter that Chris Sheats was unreliable, but he apparently steered clear of Bill Looney, who was credited by the Southern Claims Commission testimony with guiding twenty-five hundred men through the Union lines to enlist. Even if inflated, that number surpassed the several hundred attributed to Sheats before he was jailed. As for Pillow's raid, it stimulated draft dodgers to the extent that a new Union outfit was needed to accommodate them. It also unleashed a continuing effort by renegade Rebels to torture or exterminate Alabama Unionists, and these reprisal killings would continue into the next century. Among the names that would not be forgotten by surviving Unionists was that of Dr. Kaeiser, who became the target of rumors that he led killers to Jenny Brooks's husband and to Thomas Pinckney Curtis, the popular probate judge of Winston County. But before pursuing those leads, we need to take a look at the influential men in blue who greeted the Alabama refugees when they reached the Tennessee River.

13

IN THE UNIONIST POD

I WAS ALWAYS proud of being an iconoclast in regard to glorifying the Confederacy. That was one thing. Proving that I had ties to Alabamians who opposed slavery was another. I'm not sure I could have done so had my father not become obsessed in his late eighties with finding the grave of his mother's brother John Wesley Abbott. My sister drove him on numerous visits to the country cemeteries around Arkadelphia in Cullman County, about forty miles north of his home in Birmingham. At various times in the past, the area had been part of both Winston and Walker Counties. It was familiar territory to my father, being only fifteen miles east of his birthplace in Curry. Blackwater Creek ran between the two hamlets, and he spoke fondly of family fishing trips there before H. H. Raines died in 1914. The boys fished with their father, and Ma 'n' Ada fried the catch right there on the sandy banks at a place called Boldo. It was still a secluded stream with deep pools separated by gentle riffles when I fished and boated there in the sixties. But in searching churchyards around this area during the early 1990s, my father and sister could never find a grave for Wesley Abbott or his parents, James Hiel Abbott (1801–1877) and Jane Mills Key Abbott (1808–1885).

My father said that Wesley Abbott—he was known by his middle name—was a physician in or near Arkadelphia and that his grandmother had died there in his care. Hiram Howell Raines had carried her from Curry to Dr. Abbott's home on a cot in the bed of his wagon, following the same road the family traveled on its outings to Blackwater. Based on our skimpy knowledge of family history, my sister and I dismissed the idea of Wesley Abbott being a doctor. So far as we knew, none of the Raineses nor their old-time relatives had ever been to college. Many of the physicians in north Alabama early in the century attended medical school at Vanderbilt University, and if any of our kin had ever ventured 165 miles north to Nashville, we would surely have heard about it from Grandma Raines or her children. But for the first time I began to inquire seriously into the Abbott line. Following leads from John Martin Dombhart's *History of Walker County, Its Towns and Its People,* I found myself by 1995 in the cemetery of the Sardis Primitive Baptist Church, only a mile or so south of the confluence of Blackwater Creek and the Warrior River. It was country I was coming to know intimately. In the three-decade run-up to the Civil War, virtually every person whose DNA I carry lived nearby. In a shoal near the cemetery, pioneer families had dug coal from the exposed river bottom during the summer droughts. The coal they didn't need was barged downriver to Tuscaloosa on crude flat-boats during the winter floods. The shoal also provided the flat sheets of shale used to build rock enclosures over new graves to protect them from the animals that gave nearby Wolf Creek its name. Inscribed into the slate of one of the oldest graves, there I found an epitaph from 1843 that unlocked the world of the families that occupied my ancestors' Unionist pod. I rubbed chalk into lines scratched in the slate and found that an amateur stone carver had carved the name of the "disseid" person as "Millia Rains."

In Dombhart's history, I found a "Milley Barton, who married a Mr. Raines." Other sources show that while her name was pronounced as "Milly," the more common spelling was "Millia." Dombhart also helped me identify the woman who had died at Dr. Abbott's. She was John Wesley Abbott's sister Aseneth Adeline Abbott. "Aseneth Adeline married Hiram Raines," Dombhart reported, he being the son of James Rains. The two spellings of my surname (Raines and Rains) frequently alternated in nineteenth-century records. I don't want to tax the readers' patience with too much genealogical detail, but a closer look at John Martin Dombhart, who died in 1952, illustrates the slender threads of information by which family histories are preserved.

Dombhart was a Washingtonian sent by the Southern Railway Company as an auditor for its Alabama operations in 1929. Locally, he was remembered as a loner who was tight with a dime. His wife, who was from an established Jasper family, knew lots of local lore and was a diligent comber of land and cemetery records. With her assistance, he wrote over a thousand local biographies and in 1937 compiled them into a volume of which he published five hundred copies at his own expense and priced at five dollars apiece. He personally retrieved a review copy sent to *The Birmingham News* to enforce his no-free-books rule. When the Queen's Library in London wrote for a copy for its Americana collection, Dombhart responded that he would accept Her Majesty's check. Former congressman Carl Elliott brought out his version in 1987, and without it I would know little about the history of my extended family.

From it I gleaned that my direct ancestors Thomas Barton and Susan Keys Barton arrived in Alabama Territory from Virginia in 1817, "the first white settler[s] north of the Tallapoosa River." The Bartons provide my only link to elevated ancestry. The first David Barton arrived in Virginia in 1672, and from him descended the David Barton who went with Daniel Boone into wild Kentucky and was killed by a combined force of Shawnee, Cherokee, Delaware, Wyandot, and Tawa warriors at Harrodsburg in 1782. Five of the original David's sons served in the Revolution, and one of them, also David, was a colonel who served with Washington at Valley Forge. From that line came Moses Barton, who in 1822 entered land on Blackwater Creek. He built the first gristmill on the creek, and his daughter's husband, James Raines, would build the second. With the start of the Civil War, the Bartons rallied to Chris Sheats's call in droves, and six of them served in the First Alabama Cavalry. All survived except the unlucky Private William H. Barton, who was taken prisoner only thirty-one days after enlisting and died a year later at Andersonville prison.

Families within the Unionist pod—Bartons, Raineses, Abbotts, Keyses—lived close together and intermarried energetically. The kinship patterns among landholding families underscore a pattern that prevailed in the Black Belt and the Warrior Mountains. Whether on vast holdings in plantation country or the patch farms in the hills, land ownership was the key to a prosperous or at least bearable lifestyle. The difference was in scale. Even a yeoman farmer like James Raines, who acquired more than three hundred acres, did not identify with the flatland gentry, but small cotton patches like his produced income enough to buy former tribal land at bargain prices through the Huntsville Land Office. The Raines brothers and cousins shared land lines with Bartons and Abbotts, and the romantic fallout predictably kept land titles within a small cluster of families. Moses Barton's grandson Hiram Barton owned farmland next to forty acres acquired by James Hiel Abbott in 1838. Hiel and his wife, Jane (known as "Cricket"), had a daughter named Aseneth Adeline, born in 1832, whose marriage to Hiram Raines took place in 1864, a few years after Hiram finished "lying out" to avoid the Confederate conscription officers, who had learned to stay out of the woods of Walker and Winston Counties once it became obvious the war was ending. Aseneth's brother William Washington Abbott married Hiram's sister Peggy Ann.

Being within the Unionist pod was not an absolute protection from the Confederate draft, however. Hiram's older brother, Allen Raines, was mustered into the 28th Alabama Infantry in 1863 by one of the area's most ardent Confederates, Captain Francis A. Musgrove. Allen died in the Confederate hospital at Macon, Georgia, after fighting against Sherman's forces pushing south from Atlanta, which included the Barton boys from back home. The juxtaposition reminds me of the strange intimacy behind the cliché of "the brothers' war," which was also a cousins' and neighbors' war. Here at the start of the third decade of the twenty-first century, it seems eerie to me that my father knew both Hiram, who died in 1914, and his wife, Aseneth, as she started her death journey a few years later. The Abbotts no doubt played with Allen or attended Sardis church or saw him at the weddings of their kin. The time seems somehow compacted yet almost inexpressibly distant, like the measure in time and miles between the Sardis cemetery and the old *New York Times* building in Manhattan.

I hope I've made their world live in your mind without taking too many creative liberties with the life stories of people who were often illiterate, who left no writings, who exist now only as ghosts in odd scraps of family lore or as skeletal entries in courthouse, cemetery, or enlistment records. That is why the Southern Claims Commission records were such a trove for me once Mills and Storey made them accessible. They were to show me old man Hiel Abbott strutting along the same dirt roads where Hiram Howell Raines cursed the "damn Democrats." Hiel's story seems a part of me now, like his name. As I said, it's a tracery of slender threads. I know about Hiel only because my father thought he remembered an Abbott who was a doctor.

It would turn out that my father, "Mr. Wattie," was right. But Wesley Abbott wasn't among the state's doctors who studied at Vanderbilt, nor at the medical school that operated at Dadeville, Alabama, from 1852 to 1961, nor at the Birmingham Medical College that opened in 1894. I learned that small-town Alabama acquired doctors the same way it acquired many of its lawyers—by apprenticeship. Wesley Abbott had, in fact, read law and served as Cullman County tax assessor, collector, and surveyor, "having secured sufficient education, mostly at home, to fill these positions credibly," according to the *Cullman Democrat* report after he died on October 7, 1915. "At the age of forty he began the study of medicine and was a practicing physician until a year or two ago when he retired from active practice." A cynic might take the headline on the article as dodging the question of his professional expertise: "Cullman County Loses an Old Citizen." Reading between the lines, one can see a changeable, even contentious man. He left both the Methodist and Baptist churches because of "disagreeing with some of his brethren on certain doctrinal points." He became a member of the Holiness faith—that is to say, a Holy Roller. But he never lacked for energy, having owned a gristmill, a cotton gin, and a general store after buying land in 1875 a few miles east of the Raines and Best farms. In 1890, he passed the examination required of self-taught doctors by the Medical Association of the State of Alabama, meeting the more rigorous standards adopted by the state in 1877. He was a good enough doctor to get insurance for the private hospital he opened at Bug Tussle, a crossroads near his home in Bremen.

My online genealogical sleuthing led me to Dr. Abbott's parents, and *The Abbott Newsletter,* published by a distant cousin in Texas, enabled me to establish, for the first time, my blood ties to the Unionist Alabamians I had long admired. The story of Hiel and Jane's marriage illustrated the contradictory aspects of frontier life in Alabama and the turmoil that swept the hills in the first two years after secession. Hiel and Jane had fifteen children, the first born when she was sixteen and the last when she was forty-five. Their portraits on the front page of every newsletter showed a woman whose fine features suggested why she was called "Cricket" within the family. The picture of Hiel, with his narrow, straight nose and cleanly defined brow, struck me immediately for a very specific reason. In that photo he looked remarkably like his grandson and my grandfather, Hiram Howell (originally Hiel) Raines, in the only surviving picture of him. Most of his sons, including my father, were big beefy fellows with broad features and noses that hooked as they aged.

Two main themes emerged in Hiel's life. One had to do with craftmanship and a spirit of enterprise. When his father died in North Carolina, both Hiel and a slightly older brother were apprenticed to a cabinetmaker, and that became their trade as they migrated, Hiel to Alabama and the brother to Indiana. A great-grandson wrote of Hiel's cabinetry skills: "He built fine cabinets, furniture, wagons, machinery such as looms, reels, wheels, etc. Very well do I remember some of the furniture: a bureau, bedstead, and chairs which he made and were in my grandfather's house." Thus originated the woodworking skills that eventually issued in the founding of the Raines Brothers enterprises.

The other side of the Abbott legacy had to do with a particular brand of violence identified with the Scots-Irish frontier. My older brother remembered hearing that Hiel's sons were fierce knife-fighters who sometimes held bloody, ritualized slashing contests at a place called Abbott's

Bottom. It is unclear if the bottom was on the forty acres acquired in 1858 only a quarter mile from property owned by James Raines. But there's no doubt that at least two of Hiel's boys, Ira Abbott (1851–1936) and Hiel Copeland Abbott (1833–1892), became notorious cutters. Their brother Sheran Abbott (1852–1924) spun stories for my father about Abbott fighting rules. Sometimes men would tie their wrists together and slash away until one cried uncle. Inflicting a mortal wound by stabbing was forbidden. Sheran Abbott told his descendants about the time "Ira and Cope were fighting in Bremen with some King boys and that the person who sewed Cope up was Dr. John Wesley. It was told that all the time John Wesley was sewing up Cope, Cope was saying, 'Doc, your needle is too dull.'" Family rivalries often played a role, and Ira was once described as the last man standing in a cutting brawl with five rivals that broke out at a general store near Bug Tussle.

Ira's own grandson passed along the tale of the time Ira and Cope got drunk in Jasper and turned over a wagonload of cotton on the way to the gin. Ira blamed Cope for the mishap, and "he pulled his knife out and cut Uncle Cope's guts out." Cope apparently survived the attack, and we don't have to rely entirely on family legend for an account of his death. On another cotton-hauling mission, he stopped over at a tavern owned by a white woman who had two Black sons born during a period of the biracial community life during the first decade of Reconstruction. One version of the story is that Cope told the sons that he was a Republican, all right, but not a Black Republican, enraging the sons. In a series of cryptic stories in 1893, the Jasper *Mountain Eagle* identified "the Negroes charged with the foul murder of Polk [*sic;* Cope] Abbott" as Bob and Charley Williams. Bob Williams was convicted and sentenced to sixty years, but Charley Williams may have died before he could be tried.

The incident makes it clear that white mountaineers were not free of racial prejudice, but the *Official Records* firmly document that Alabama's Unionist soldiers were less brutal than Confederate regulars and guerillas toward former slaves and in a few cases served in minimally integrated units. But the main thing I learned about Hiel Abbott was his role in helping neighborhood men evade the Confederate draft. The hill country of Alabama was crisscrossed with a network of dirt roads and hard-packed trails used for centuries by the Creeks and Cherokees, and by the second year of the war hundreds of men were heading north along these routes. This was the "best underground railroad," described in exaggerated terms by the Union officer quoted in a volume titled *Anecdotes, Poetry and Incidents of the War*. But there were links between the two operations of little or no interest to Alabama's Lost Cause historians. For example, few have noted that John Henry Kagi, an abolitionist lawyer and John Brown's top aide, had scouted the state for possible future Underground Railroad efforts before he died with Brown at Harpers Ferry. The much smaller Unionist operation depended on caves rather than safe houses, but it also used "guides" like Sheats and Looney to take groups, from a handful to more than a hundred, by night or along hidden pathways. Indeed, the Union officer quoted above was one of the first outsiders to take note of Sheats's talents as an organizer and speaker.

Hiel Abbott's involvement in smuggling would-be soldiers was sporadic and peripheral but nonetheless courageous, which is why his testimony wound up before the Southern Claims Commission. A deposition taken by his attorney in 1871 testified to his political loyalty and asked for $220.50 for a horse and fodder supplied to the Union cavalry.

The commission report records Hiel Abbott's statement as taken down by his attorney:

> Claimant says that from the first beginning of hostilities against the United States to the end he was always opposed to secession and Rebellion, and done all he could against it and was sorry that he could not do more against it and was as much in favor of the Union cause. Claimant says that he did not vote in the Presidential election in 1860 because there was no Lincoln ticket and that he could not vote for him, so he would not vote at all. Was as strong a Lincoln man as he knew how to be.
>
> That in 1860 he also voted for Sheats for delegate to secession

convention as the Union candidate from Winston County Ala and used all his influence in the election of said Sheats, and that he continued to advocate the Union cause as much as he knew how until the end of the Rebellion.

Claimant says that he encouraged men in deserting the Rebel army and done all he could for them and advised them to go to the Union army. Claimant says that he lived near the Sipsey River during the war and that he was the owner of a canoe that he has many a time took men across said River that were getting out of the way of Rebel authorities and Union men who belonged to the Federal army and that he always done so free of charge.

Claimant says he was often threatened to be arrested by the Rebel authorities in consequence of his Union sentiments and at one time was threatened to be killed because he had said that he was in favor of Lincoln's administration.

Claimant says the Rebel authorities took from him one yoke of oxen and that they did not take much forage but came and destroyed it as much as they could in consequence of his Union sentiments.

Claimant says that as old a man as he was he was compelled to lie and part of the time to keep out of the way of Rebel authorities to keep from being arrested and threatened. Never was arrested by United States authorities. Never was connected with either the civil or military service of the so called Confederate states, that he never owned any confederate bonds or did anything to sustain the credit of the so called Confederate states and claimant solemnly declares that from the beginning of the hostilities against the United States to the end his sympathies were constantly with the cause of the United States that he never of his own free will did anything or offered or sought or attempted to do anything by word or deed to injure said cause, or retard its success and that he was at all times ready and willing when called upon to aid and assist the cause of the Union so far as his means and power and the circumstances of the case permitted and that after the war closed he was in favor of reconstruction and in the year 1868 voted for U.S. Grant for president.

Two nearby landowners, Jeremiah O'Rear (1818–1890) and Hiel's son-in-law Hiram Raines, swore statements supporting Hiel's Unionist bona fides. My great-grandfather Hiram stated in regard to "keeping the canoe in the Sipsey River, that he has seen claimant ferrying Union men across said river and has seen him ferry Union soldiers across said river, who were dressed in their United States uniform." Hiram added that "he was kept lying out a large portion of the time during the Rebellion, keeping from being arrested and conscripted in the Union army." He added that he "heard Rebel authorities [were seeking] to go and hang [Hiel] because as they would say, he was a 'damned old Lincolnite.'" O'Rear also testified as to Hiel's ferrying and "secreting" potential Union enlistees.

But not everyone made it to the Union lines. Three of O'Rear's kinsmen, including his eldest son, had to join the Rebel army. By September 1863, Hiram Raines could no longer hide, and he went into the 10th Alabama Infantry. This was the secret he omitted from his testimony to the Southern Claims Commission in support of Hiel Abbott's claim. In 1864, when the time came for Hiel's youngest son, Israel Pickens Abbott, to cross the Sipsey for the other side, the old Lincolnite was able to help him enlist in the First Alabama—though, as it turned out, that would not end happily.

Contrary to Lincoln's dictum, the "annals of the poor" are not always so simple when it comes to the task of reconstruction. If they are short, it is because preliterate families could not write down stories of their lineage. For all that, my patchwork history of relatives in the Unionist pod around Jasper, Alabama, brought me to the threshold of the March to the Sea, which changed southern history forever.

Molders of the First Alabama Cavalry, U.S.A.: Major General Grenville M. Dodge (seated, left end) and Colonel George E. Spencer (seated, right end) in the regiment's camp at Corinth, Mississippi, 1863. They impressed on General Sherman the value of the Tory volunteers from the Alabama mountains as spies and fighters.

PART III

Marching to Savannah

THE FIRST ALABAMA'S REMARKABLE

BOND WITH UNCLE BILLY

14

Cotton Thieves and Draft Dodgers

In the daily life of north Alabama, April 1862 was the month everything changed. It was as if the cannons at the Battle of Shiloh in Tennessee on April 7 were sounding an overture for momentous times ahead across the state line. Their roar could be heard deep into Alabama, a full fifty miles away at the Forks of Cypress, the nationally known Thoroughbred stud farm near Florence. Events of the next eight days had two repercussions that shaped the future of Alabama's hill country and, indeed, the entire war in the west. On April 11, the critical river town of Huntsville fell to a surprise invasion by the Yankees, triggering a cotton-selling craze that would sweep the officer corps of both armies. Then the passage of the Confederate Conscription Act on April 16 inspired a wave of resistance among thousands of young men in the hill counties. Amid this swarming of cotton pirates and draft dodgers, the First Alabama Union Cavalry was born. Its emergence proved the unpredictability of the fortunes of war. Not even the erratic genius who captured Huntsville, Major General Ormsby M. Mitchel, known as "Ol' Stars," could have predicted that the farm boys sneaking through the lines to evade the enlistment officers from Montgomery would become stars of a very specialized sort in Sherman's army.

Shiloh's combined twenty-four thousand casualties convinced the nation's citizens that the war would be long and bloody. The battle was also a wake-up call for Confederate officials like Governor John Gill Shorter, who had been predicting that the cowardly Yankees would soon march home. Instead, their occupation of Huntsville, with its controlling position astride the Tennessee Valley's rail and river traffic, would be a wound to the heart from which the Confederacy never fully recovered. Governor Shorter was one of the first southern officials to realize that by signing the first conscription law in American history, Jefferson Davis had kicked a hornets' nest. True, the "young bloods" of the plantations were rushing to enlist in Montgomery and Mobile. But the low level of voluntary enlistments in Winston and Walker Counties infuriated Governor Shorter. He sent in conscription agents, and soon a new term, "lying-out," would enter the vocabularies of the draft-age men hiding in "rock houses," the shallow caves under overhanging bluffs in the Sipsey River watershed. Returning from Montgomery, Chris Sheats worked secretly to organize Unionist rallies, but he also stood for election to the House of Representatives of the new government in Montgomery. Without disguising his opposition to secession, Winston County probate judge Thomas Pinckney Curtis continued to run things at the courthouse while urging local men to resist the Confederate draft. Sheriffs throughout north Alabama reacted with varying degrees of enthusiasm or downright reluctance to directives from Shorter that they should make arrests under the new Conscription Act. Suddenly, in this fraught time, Ol' Stars, an astronomer few in the state had heard of, fell on north Alabama's most important cotton port.

Ormsby M. Mitchel (1809–1862) was one of the most unlikely warriors in either army. Just past fifty years of age, he had a West Point degree but had chosen life as a college professor of astronomy, hence his nickname. His appointment as resident commander of the captured city of Nashville seemed to vindicate his decision to return to the army in 1861 with the rank of brigadier general. He thus became associated with General Grant, the new leader who emerged from Lincoln's search for generals who would fight. Grant's dramatic, largely unexpected victories at Fort Henry and Fort Donelson in February had opened the back door to Nashville, which became the first Confederate capital to fall, on February 25. Mitchel was put in command there when the city's captor, General Don Carlos Buell, left for Shiloh, where his arrival turned the tide of battle in favor of the emerging team of Grant and Sherman. In overview, Shiloh marked the point at which Confederate spirits began to flag and Union victory began to seem inevitable. In regard to Alabama, Mitchel's occupation of north Alabama's legal and commercial center meant that Montgomery and Richmond would never again have solid control of the upper half of their states, and the fires of patriotism that Sheats helped light in Montgomery would burn throughout the war and become a factor in its finale.

Once in charge as caretaker in Nashville, Ol' Stars Mitchel recognized one of those facts on the ground that control military destinies. Realizing that the road due south to Huntsville, Alabama, was open, Mitchel, on his own initiative, marched 110 miles and took the city on April 11 without firing a shot. His eight thousand men woke up the city's residents with the regimental band playing "Yankee Doodle." It was a strategic coup that brought Mitchel instant fame, enabling the Union to block traffic on both the Tennessee River and the Memphis & Charleston Railroad, the major links between the eastern and western halves of the Confederacy. The fall of Huntsville also set the stage for the formation of the First Alabama Cavalry, U.S.A., and for Mitchel's reign as a kind of viceroy over what a Lost Cause historian called a corrupt and "almost unrestricted intercourse" in contraband cotton between the warring competitors. But within a year the general would be dead. To call him star-crossed is more than just a bad pun.

Before the war, Mitchel had been considered the nation's leading astronomer. He founded the U.S. Naval Observatory in Washington, D.C. He also established acclaimed observatories at Harvard and the University of Cincinnati, where he taught math and astronomy and helped found the law school. A polymath, Mitchel knew a bit about soldiering, having entered West Point just before his sixteenth birthday. He graduated with the class of 1829 along with Robert E. Lee and Joseph E. Johnston. So great was his fame after taking Huntsville that Secretary of War

Edwin Stanton "told him that he would rather see him commander-in-chief than any other man." That line is from a hagiographic biography by Mitchel's son, but it does not conflict with the conclusion of no less an authority than historian Bruce Catton. In his 1956 Civil War masterwork, *This Hallowed Ground,* Catton recognized the magnitude of Mitchel's achievement by reaching into the Confederacy's inmost state scarcely a year into the conflict. A few days earlier, Grant, Sherman, and Buell had triumphed at Shiloh, killing the South's best general, Albert Sidney Johnston, on the first day and driving back its next best infantry commander, P. G. T. Beauregard, on the second. Now, with Mitchel in control of over a hundred miles of both the Memphis & Charleston tracks and the Tennessee River itself, Buell's Army of the Ohio needed only to march east on the railroad, combine with Mitchel, and pounce on lightly defended Chattanooga. As Catton noted: "Mitchel was a voice crying in the wilderness. . . . He kept pestering headquarters with urgent messages, asserting that from where he was he could see the end of the war. If Buell came over fast, he said, he could get into Chattanooga without trouble; after that he could capture Atlanta, and from Atlanta he could March all the way north to Richmond, because all of that part of the Confederacy was 'comparatively unprotected and very much alarmed.'" Catton concluded, "Mitchel may very well have been right."

Indeed, the quick-witted but excitable Mitchel had outlined precisely the strategy upon which, a bit later, Grant and Sherman settled to win the war: Follow the Tennessee River and the M & C tracks to Chattanooga, then turn south and follow the Georgia railroads to Atlanta. Before going to bed for the first time in the captured city of Huntsville, Mitchel dispatched Russian-born colonel John Basil Turchin and a small force by overnight train to Decatur, Alabama, twenty-five miles to the west. At dawn, they took the town with very few shots and thwarted an attempt by fleeing defenders to burn a river bridge. Thus, the two most important market towns for the Union sympathizers who lived south of the river were now in Union hands. This happened just as the new Confederate draft act was beginning to pinch the hill country's farmers, drovers, and tradesmen. Everyone in those hills knew how to reach Huntsville and Decatur by road or by a network of centuries-old Native American trails that crisscrossed the mountains or followed north-flowing creeks emptying into the Tennessee. Alabama newspapers scared readers by reporting on three "conventions" calling for a Union uprising in Winston and two adjoining counties. The ever-hawkish *Montgomery Advertiser* warned "the astronomical General Mitchel" that "star gazing" in the North was easier than fighting the Confederate troops, undisciplined Partisan Rangers, and bushwhackers being dispatched to recapture the Tennessee Valley. The *Mobile Advertiser and Register* said the "guerilla way" would drive the Yankees out and, presumably, stop the rebellion being fomented by Chris Sheats and Jeremiah Clemens. Ever adaptable, Mark Twain's cousin Jere had resigned his generalship in the Alabama militia and secretly sworn loyalty to the Union in occupied Huntsville.

The taking of Huntsville was enough to make Ol' Stars an instant celebrity and hero. Had successive events not proved him a crackpot, Mitchel might have been as acclaimed as other key difference-makers such as George Thomas, the "Rock of Chickamauga," or Joshua Chamberlain, the defender of Little Round Top. Today, if Mitchel is mentioned at all, it is in connection with the Great Locomotive Chase, the feckless spy mission in northern Georgia that led to the execution of Union spy James Andrews and five foolhardy volunteers from Mitchel's command. As Bruce Catton noted, Mitchel, who had dreamed—not without reason—of commanding an entire army, instead provided comical fodder "for novelists, dramatists and feature writers ever since." The Great Chase started on April 12, the morning after Huntsville fell. But Mitchel's triumph in Alabama overshadowed the debacle in Georgia, in part because the fate of the raiders took weeks to play out and because Buell also had his fingerprints on the hapless plan to send railroad hijackers to Big Shanty, Georgia, a stop on the crucial supply line between Atlanta and Chattanooga. Most of those raiders were caught and hanged after failing in their plan to drive the stolen train north to Chattanooga and destroy tracks as they went.

But as it turned out, the Great Locomotive Chase was not the greatest of his misfortunes. Happenings in Huntsville are another evocative part of the stage-setting events in how the hillbilly revolt produced the First Alabama. While serving as the military governor of north Alabama, Mitchel opened the trade in captured cotton that corrupted the officer corps of both armies, thus raising the curtain on an era of legalized larceny in the cotton empire, an orgy of capitalism run amok that took place among and around the deaths of 600,000 men in combat. In this regard, Ormsby Mitchel's story illustrates how the war became a kind of chemist's retort, condensing the best and the worst vapors of the nineteenth-century American character—courage and creativity, vaulting ambition and greed.

For their part, Halleck and Buell hated Mitchel because he had a powerful sponsor in Treasury Secretary Salmon P. Chase and a private channel to Secretary of War Edwin M. Stanton, which he did not hesitate to use. On one occasion, Mitchel got Stanton to reverse Buell's order that fugitive slaves could not be welcomed in Union camps. That's because Mitchel had hired slaves to serve as an effective grapevine for tracking Rebel crossings on a hundred-mile stretch of the Tennessee River. Such an endeavor was typical of Mitchel's almost bipolar swings between inspiration and self-defeat.

After Huntsville, Lincoln promoted Mitchel to major general, retroactive to the day he took the city. Stanton sent the former professor a letter stating: "Your spirited operations afford great satisfaction to the President." Lincoln, thinking he had at last found a leader with dash, penciled Mitchel in for a vital command to seize control of the Mississippi River around Vicksburg. A northern newspaper said Mitchel's ascent marked "a new era of generalship in his war." Buell's biographer noted that Mitchel fit perfectly into Lincoln's wish "to eliminate conservative commanders from the army." Lincoln was growing into a master of military strategy, and he was in the process of shifting the entire army from the original approach of limited conflict in the rebellious states to the "hard war" philosophy of Grant and Sherman. There was, for a few months in 1862, every prospect Mitchel would rise as high as those generals.

But there were problems. The historian Stephen D. Engle picked him as "the army's second most [long-]winded, conceited, and vainglorious commander" after Stephen "Bull" Nelson. Not surprisingly, Mitchel and Nelson hated each other, but their feud was cut short when Nelson was shot to death in 1862 by another general he had slapped in the face. Then there was the issue Buell would use to destroy him— Mitchel's selling of cotton seized on Alabama plantations to favored brokers in the North. The trade in contraband cotton compromised hundreds of field-grade and commanding officers in both armies, but it is inaccurate to label that trade as unlawful. Rather, it was a form of legalized larceny endorsed by both Lincoln and Jefferson Davis, and in many ways it resembled the remorseless grasping for profit by corporations, Wall Street, and high-tech billionaires in our own era. Its true scope will never be known because of the lack of documentation, but we know about Mitchel's greed, ironically enough, because of an honest southern scholar trained at Vanderbilt University during its heyday as the citadel of Lost Cause apologetics. Robert Frank Futrell (1917–1999), born in Mississippi and buried in Montgomery, Alabama, wrote important histories of the air force's role in World War II and Korea, but as a student he focused initially on the illicit trade in Union salt in Tennessee when future vice president Andrew Johnson was installed as military governor in Nashville.

"Such petty smuggling, however, was dwarfed by the scandals arising from cotton purchases and seizures in central Tennessee and northern Alabama," Futrell wrote, singling out Mitchel as "the chief of the offenders." His enemy Buell may have set him up by authorizing him to facilitate the marketing of captured cotton, which was legal under the U.S. policy of military-assisted trading. But Mitchel brought to bear his unique hurry-up blend of bad judgment and bad luck in regard to ten thousand bales stashed near Huntsville. He wrote his son-in-law E. B. Hook to rush down from Tennessee to join New York brokers invited to Alabama for the bonanza. The letter, discovered by Futrell, deserves study as a gemlike expression of the grasping spirit of the war years and the chumminess among opposing officers.

W. B. Hook, Esq., Nashville, Tenn.:

I fear you are again losing a most favorable opportunity to commence the purchase of cotton. [Confederate colonel] John Morgan's raid has brought down the price and gives to buyers a chance which will not probably return again soon. Purchasers are here in advance of you and are making contracts this very day, and to them I offer the same facilities that I have offered to you, and will do so until you arrive.

The cotton first purchased will be first transported by me on the Government trains, and it is the bold man who wins. I have no personal interest in this matter, as you very well know, and had you come forward promptly on reaching Nashville this whole matter would have been in your own hands.

[Your captured brother] Ned will be exchanged for Lieutenant Morgan, the brother of the colonel

> *Very Truly and affectionately,*
> *O. M. Mitchel*

As for bad luck, consider how the Hook letter fell into the hands of investigators. It was seized from Mitchel's courier by troops under Confederate major general Kirby E. Smith. The result was a possibly unprecedented instance of a Confederate commander general turning in a Union general for financial corruption. Smith sent the incriminating letter under a flag of truce to General Buell with the recommendation that he report Mitchel to the authorities in Washington. Senate investigators there estimated the scale of the north Alabama cotton trade at $2 million, but that is probably conservative. Throughout the war, there were two kinds of crooks, the caught and the uncaught, the prosecuted and the unprosecuted, some of the latter having friends named Lincoln, Stanton, and Seward.

Had Ol' Stars been as lucky in his personal life as, say, Sherman and Grant, he might have survived the cotton scandal. Julia Dent Grant accompanied her husband on his major campaigns and helped curb his drinking. Eleanor Ewing Sherman saved her husband's career by meeting with Lincoln in the White House to counter newspaper reports that the general had gone "crazy." Louisa Clark Trask Mitchel was known in Cincinnati for her efforts to "temper her husband's vanity" and for "providing structure to an erratic, energetic and flighty Ormsby." She stuck with him when he failed as a lawyer and helped him establish the nation's first observatory for the University of Cincinnati. Arriving to dedicate the facility, former president John Quincy Adams found her charming and Ormsby irritatingly discourteous. She managed their ascent in Cincinnati society as intimates of the famous abolitionist preacher Lyman Beecher. But Louisa died on August 20, 1861, two days after Ormsby left for Washington to accept his commission as a brigadier general. In his biography of his father, F. A. Mitchel said that if his mother had lived to join her husband in Huntsville, she might have restrained him. The son's biography, entitled *Ormsby MacKnight Mitchel, Astronomer and General; a Biographical Narrative,* while intended to be exculpatory, presents a portrait of pathology, a man with "an unusually reckless nature" and a "singularly sensitive disposition." Without Louisa to apply the brakes, he set himself up in a Huntsville mansion as a kind of Federal viceroy, "determined to make all understand that he was the greatest of living generals."

As his son, who also served as an aide-de-camp, watched helplessly, Mitchel plunged into the "sale and transportation of cotton" with his customary headlong style. "General Mitchel relied upon the purity of his intentions, and upon reporting beforehand all he proposed to do to the Secretary of War and the Secretary of the Treasury. But in his desire to accomplish results he showed a trait that had been with him all his life—a want of foresight in laying himself open to attack. There had been one who had made it a constant study to remedy this defect. But that one was not with him now."

Perhaps not even Louisa could have protected Mitchel from the wrath of his duplicitous provost marshal, one Colonel Jesse Norton. Born in Toledo in 1825, Norton appears in Ohio's Civil War narratives as "a gallant little fellow . . . with a penchant for controversy." He was a tricky little fellow, too, cultivating friends in the press and using them in

1861 to discredit his then-commander in the Battle of Scary Creek in Virginia. In the next year, he targeted Mitchel after the general condemned him for attending a fish fry held by slave owners in Confederate territory, an incident that points up Norton's taste for working both sides of the street in north Alabama, which was surprisingly relaxed at this early stage of the war. "Col. Norton was a great favorite here, always acting the gentleman," wrote Mary Jane Chadick, who started her diary the day Huntsville fell and whose insights compare favorably with the more famous diary of Mary Chestnut. Chadick noted that when Colonel Norton and his wife moved to Athens, "officers and citizens met on friendly terms, chatted, drank together and were merry." Such relaxed, prolonged fraternizing even extended to romance—along proper class lines, of course. The daughters of Huntsville's leading Unionist officeholders—federal judge George Washington Lane and U.S. congressman Nicholas Davis—married a Union colonel and a Union general, respectively.

Notwithstanding Colonel Norton's popularity with the plantation class, he at the same time cast himself as a defender of Union enlisted men. When General Mitchel arrested twenty-four members of the 21st Ohio for vandalism carried out during the incident known as the Sack of Athens, Colonel Norton threatened to resign and take the imprisoned men home with him. Norton's insubordination peaked when General Mitchel was recalled to Washington after General Don Carlos Buell relieved him in Huntsville on July 2, 1862. Expecting cover from his friends Stanton and Chase, Mitchel was still counting on the prestigious Vicksburg assignment and thought of himself as a contender for command of the entire Union army. Norton left Huntsville at the same time, armed with reports that Mitchel was speculating in cotton and converting the funds to his personal use. The disaffected colonel "first stopped at Louisville," F. A. Mitchel reported in his book, "where he visited a newspaper office and published his first report; then Cincinnati, and other cities by the way, till by the time he reached the capital, General Mitchel had been defamed a pillager and a cotton-stealer from one end of the land to another."

With Lincoln's approval, General Halleck refused to sign off on the Vicksburg assignment for Mitchel and sent him to swampy Hilton Head Island as head of the Department of South Carolina. He marked his arrival with long, tendentious lectures to his troops and an assembly of freed slaves—"you colored people," as he put it—on the duties of citizenship. "Your lives are not your own," he told the soldiers, nor did his life belong to him for long.

Mitchel died of yellow fever on October 31, 1862, probably still believing that Stanton had once wanted to give him the supreme command that went to Grant. Perhaps on his deathbed, he was comforted by the wonderful prescience of the Cincinnati *Daily Gazette* correspondent who wrote on the day he entered Huntsville, "We have achieved a victory . . . [that] can hardly be overestimated. The main line, and for all practical military purposes the only line of communication between the eastern and western armies of the enemy, is in our hands." He added, "General Mitchel's division is making history faster than I can write it."

For a century and a half, Alabama historians found it impossible to deal with what the diminutive, cocky astronomer accomplished at Huntsville. His geographic penetration of the two innermost states of the Confederacy made it impossible for Jefferson Davis and his generals to control the war in the west, and he opened the way to federal recruiting in Alabama. But recently there have been two breakthroughs in Alabama scholarship, *Civil War Alabama* by Christopher Lyle McIlwain Sr. and *Alabamians in Blue: Freedmen, Unionists, and the Civil War in the Cotton State* by Christopher M. Rein, published in 2016 and 2019, respectively. Rein, a former Air Force Academy faculty member who is currently the managing editor of Air University Press at Maxwell Air Force Base in Montgomery, put it plainly: "Marching south from Nashville, Mitchel's troops entered the Tennessee Valley, initiating a chain of events that led directly to both Black and white Alabamians serving in the Union Army."

In some respects, historians and journalists operate under a common handicap. The most important narrative facts—those bearing on causation, credit, or blame—usually emerge in retrospect. Often the reporter's excuse for abandoning the search for defining details is being called away by the need to keep up with "breaking news." With historical omission, we must look for other reasons. In retrospect, Alabama's historians have entirely missed both the importance of events in the Tennessee Valley and the scale of the First Alabama's war operations because of the ideological lens through which they viewed the conflict. Alabama historian Charles Summersell, for example, does not mention the occupation of Huntsville in April, but he gave exaggerated importance to the sack of another valley town, Athens, on June 14 by the Russian-born Union colonel John Basil Turchin, saying that the one-day attack "added bitterness to the war." Although of no long-term consequence, it was a spectacular event in which Turchin, hewing to a path typical of czarist military education, gave his conquering troops two hours to run amok in a captured town. While Turchin consumed a leisurely lunch at a local hotel, his Illinois troops looted private homes, terrorized the women, and in at least one case assaulted and possibly raped a female slave. As Walter Lynwood Fleming noted in his breathless account of the same incident, "His Russian ideas of the rules of war were probably responsible for his conduct." Turchin was convicted of "a case of undisputed atrocity" in a court-martial that illustrated how lightly Washington weighed the rough treatment of southern civilians. Turchin's energetic and attractive wife, who had been sharing his quarters at the front, traveled to Washington to appeal personally to Lincoln, who reinstated Turchin as a brigadier general. In terms of Lost Cause bias, Summersell and Fleming made the same error. They misunderstood Huntsville as a watershed event and dwelled on the Sack of Athens and even more fulsomely on Forrest's victory the following year in Streight's Raid. The latter they depicted as the war's major event on Alabama soil, though in fact neither incident figured in the war's outcome. Consistently misrepresenting Alabama's role and importance was a leitmotif of Lost Cause writers. After bemoaning the fate of Athens, Fleming resorts to one of his boldest lies: "The Confederate and state governments strictly repressed the tendency of Confederate troops to pillage the 'Union' communities of north Alabama."

In fact, the Montgomery authorities and guerillas under the command of Philip Roddey, a former hill country sheriff and Tennessee River flatboat captain, preyed relentlessly on Alabama Unionists throughout 1861, driving them first into the forests, then legitimizing the army-coordinated terrorism by sheltering it behind the Partisan Ranger Act of April 21, 1862. That act, along with the new Rebel conscription law, took full effect just as Mitchel was passing from the scene. Among those replacing him in the cotton trade started by Mitchel were Roddey, who became an effective regular cavalry general under Forrest, and the future commander of the First Alabama, Colonel Spencer. As General Buell took command in Huntsville on June 29, the trickle of refugees into Huntsville and Decatur from Winston and the surrounding counties became a flooding tide, and by summer's end, the recruiting of the "hillbillies" despised by Hoole began in earnest. Union field operations changed, too, in one striking respect. Where Mitchel had sheltered runaway slaves and used them as paid informers, Buell drove them out of the federal encampments and ordered his troops to return them to their former masters. That was one reason he always moved slowly, except, paradoxically, when it came to organizing the First Alabama.

15

THE SLAVE OWNERS' FRIEND

DON CARLOS BUELL (1818–1898) was one of those dilatory Union commanders who drove Lincoln crazy during the first year and a half of the war. He was the opposite of the frenetic Mitchel, always finding reasons to slow-walk his army. Both men would see their careers destroyed in north Alabama, but not before playing key roles in the formation of the First Alabama. The other slow-walkers who would feel Lincoln's wrath were George B. McClellan and William S. Rosecrans, sacked for lethargy in Virginia and Tennessee, respectively. As for Buell, this highly regarded general with the flamboyant name simply ignored repeated urgings from the president and Secretary of War Stanton to march into east Tennessee from Nashville to unite with its resident Unionist majority. The president believed that all or part of the state could be pulled back into the Union. Major General Buell's fifty thousand troops occupied Nashville on February 25, 1862, capping Grant's game-changing victories at Fort Henry and Fort Donelson earlier that month. With the Tennessee capital in hand, Lincoln was obsessed with the opportunity to expand his army by enlisting the tens of thousands of known Unionists stranded in the Smoky Mountains counties, about two hundred miles east of Nashville. But like Major General George McClellan, his close friend and fellow delay artist, Don Carlos Buell simply did not want to risk his shiny new army in frontal assaults on an enemy with whom Buell shared family ties.

The forty-nine-year-old general and his Georgia-born wife owned eight slaves at the start of the war, and kept one of them in their household when he served in Washington, D.C., early in the war. As commander of the Army of the Mississippi, Buell specialized in returning runaway slaves to plantation masters in Tennessee, Georgia, and Alabama. Both he and McClellan, who was simultaneously frustrating Lincoln with his dawdling advance on Richmond, were conservative Democrats who wanted to preserve the Union but were not eager to abolish slavery in the process. They believed that protecting southern civilians and preserving chattel slavery would make it easier to reunite the country after a period of brief and mannerly warfare. The paying of slaves from Tennessee Valley plantations as anti-Confederate spies was one of two issues that made Buell determined to remove Ormsby Mitchel, despite the capture of Huntsville by Ol' Stars. The other was Mitchel's insubordinate (and prescient) complaints to Lincoln and Stanton about Buell's refusal to make a speedy march on Chattanooga. So what Buell did immediately upon relieving Mitchel at Huntsville on July 2, 1862, seems all the more remarkable. He welcomed the Winston County Tories who were trying to reach nearby Decatur on the south bank of the Tennessee River, and he would soon become the founder of the First Alabama Cavalry, U.S.A. His mention of the Winston County refugees, who were traveling by night, singly or in small groups, to reach the Union lines, in his reports may be the first official mention of the county in Union army archives. Buell's outreach to disenchanted Alabama civilians came as both armies initiated changes in strategy and positioning that would play out in the second phase of the war as a shocked public was realizing, after the combined total of five thousand deaths at Shiloh, that the conflict would be longer and bloodier than anyone had predicted.

A frustrated Lincoln decided at the end of 1861 to take over management of the war, ending a freshman presidential year in which he had naively believed that his West Point–trained professionals would cooperate in a zealous effort to defeat the South. But officers like Ormsby Mitchel, a fervent abolitionist and reckless grasper after military advantage, were rare at the top. When war came, 294 West Pointers became Union generals and 151 opted to fight for the South, and these men were bound by a common culture and undergraduate friendships. In response, Lincoln set out to purge conservatives from the officer corps. Under Lincoln's hardening gaze, nothing marked a man like being soft on slavery, a sign of sympathy for the southern Democrats who had sundered the Union. By modern standards of institutional analysis, both Buell, fired in October 1862, and McClellan, fired the following month, look like dunderheads for thinking their commander could be defied with impunity. But each man had his shining moment, Buell by coming to Grant's aid on April 7, 1862, the decisive second day of Shiloh, though Buell and Grant bickered for years about the importance of Buell's role. McClellan's costly and debatable "victory" at Antietam on September 17, 1862, nonetheless turned back Lee's first invasion of the North and so strengthened Lincoln politically that he could issue the Emancipation Proclamation.

That's the big picture, but the origins of Alabama's blue-coated regiment are not to be found in the classic references like *Generals in Blue: Lives of the Union Commanders* or the "Index to Special Studies" in E. B. Long's exhaustive and indispensable *The Civil War Day by Day: An Almanac 1861–1865*. I think it's fair to say that prior to 2000, even a motivated researcher had to dig for details in places that lay beyond the reach of card catalogues and popular titles. For our purposes, then, Buell's decisive action in regard to Winston County is of paramount relevance and all the more intriguing because its decisiveness was out of character. It may be unfair to say Buell was a plodder; rather, he was a proceduralist, addicted to strict rules and resistant to the constitutional fact that civilians got to pass judgment on military decisions. Early in the war, he exhibited military acumen, as in seeing that Grant's back-door advance up the smallish Cumberland River would make Nashville the first Confederate capital to fall. Still, Mitchel rightly savaged him in letters and press accounts for not immediately marching from his base in

Corinth and following the M & C Railroad into Chattanooga, as Lincoln wished. After dithering, Buell did recognize what was afoot when the Confederacy in the early summer of 1862 abandoned the cordon strategy that had pinned Braxton Bragg's army in place at Tupelo, Mississippi. For over a year, Bragg's assignment had been to conduct shielding actions in defense of Mobile, Memphis, Vicksburg, and New Orleans. But after Shiloh, protecting Chattanooga and the railroad link to Atlanta became a higher priority for Jefferson Davis. With Buell in the way and Mitchel at Huntsville, Bragg could not take his main force across north Alabama. He had to move his army circuitously, by rail across lower Alabama, up to Atlanta, and then north to occupy Chattanooga and strategic Lookout Mountain. Buell also sussed out what Bragg was up to in a diversionary move to send a smaller force to Moulton, Alabama, where the level floor of the Tennessee Valley rises up to meet the Unionist strongholds in the hill country. In Civil War storytelling there's a constant tension between the macro narrative about large troop movements and the micro narrative about sideshows like the civilian unrest beyond the soldiers' campfires.

Generals had to have a sense of balance. As he arrived in Huntsville on July 29, 1862, Buell received a panicky message from Brigadier General James Dada Morgan at Union-occupied Tuscumbia on the north side of the Tennessee. He reported that his four isolated companies holding Decatur on the south side were about to be overrun by the Rebels investing Moulton, only twenty miles away. Buell responded that the real Confederate goal was Chattanooga, and Bragg could probably not spare the troops to overrun Decatur. Instead Bragg was likely feinting toward Decatur with a small force. His "object would be to stop our communication with the Union men of Winston and surrounding counties, who have recently been joining our ranks." Morgan had best move to thwart Bragg if he could, Buell wrote; then he softened the message by saying he would try to send some infantry and artillery.

The message shows that whatever Buell's sympathy for the slaveholding class, he recognized the recruiting potential of the yeoman farmer insurrectionists as a majority of the white population in Winston and the dozen contiguous counties that were to provide the core of the First Alabama. As early as July 12, he had noted the "volunteers from Alabama" who had slipped into Huntsville and Tuscumbia in groups numbering up to eighty, but Decatur, the principal trading town for the hill country folk, was more accessible to draft evaders slipping north by night along the roadways and old Indian trading routes. Even for men on foot, it was a manageable journey to Decatur from the southernmost recruiting ground for First Alabama volunteers, Shelby County, now part of the prosperous Birmingham suburbs that sprawl toward Montgomery. At this point, Buell's interest in Alabama volunteers may have been stimulated by widespread grumbling in his army that if Ohio soldiers were going to risk their lives, they wanted to do it in order to free slaves, not to carry them back to their masters.

The tactical games in north Alabama have received relatively little attention in history books because they are sandwiched between two major events, Shiloh in April and Chickamauga in September. But even earlier, the future "Rock of Chickamauga," Major General George H. Thomas, serving under Buell, commented in dispatches on the promise of Confederate "desertions . . . from the Alabama, Mississippi, and Tennessee regiments," which were bringing in "many barefooted" prospects. Thomas may have felt a kinship with the loyalist mountaineers, as he was a Virginian who would himself be defamed by several generations of that state's historians for holding to the soldier's oath he had sworn at West Point. Lost Cause historians were not a forgiving lot. My guess is that Walter L. Fleming, who combed the *Official Records* pretty thoroughly in the early 1900s while at Columbia, must have found the reference to Winston County that surprised me many decades later during my Buell research. But for all his cuddling up to the plantation caste, Buell does not even rate an index entry in Fleming's *Civil War and Reconstruction in Alabama,* meaning that Fleming was likely in denial that the ripple effect of the birth of the First Alabama would continue until the end of the war.

The unit's birth is presaged by Buell's Special Orders No. 100, issued on July 12, 1862, in which he refers to "volunteers from Alabama."

The day before, his subordinate, Major General George H. Thomas, had written about ninety Alabama refugees trying to "enlist in our army" near the Tennessee River town of Tuscumbia. That led to Buell's Order No. 106 of August 8, 1862:

> The volunteers from Alabama will be organized into companies, under the direction of Capt. H. C. Bankhead, who will enroll and muster them into the United States service in accordance with the laws and orders on the subject. Company officers will be selected from among the men and appointed by the general commanding condition upon the confirmation of the President of the United States. The provost-marshal in Huntsville will give Captain Bankhead such assistance as he may require in this duty. All Alabama men now traveling with any of the regiments of this command will be sent or left at this place.

Why did Buell move so speedily in forming the First Alabama when he had been so recalcitrant about going to east Tennessee to enlist from the more populous Unionist enclaves there? At Nashville and later at Corinth, which fell to the Union on May 30, 1862, he had ideal excuses to stay in place to guard these prizes. Corinth, where the Mobile & Ohio Railroad crossed the Memphis and Charleston, had been called the "vertebrae of the Confederacy" by Davis's first secretary of war, the incompetent LeRoy Pope Walker of Huntsville. Still, I was impressed that Buell had absorbed the fact that Winston County was as intense in its Unionism as east Tennessee. Perhaps he had begun to understand—and fear—the impatience of the man he worked for. Assistant Secretary of War Charles Dana said that Lincoln's military expertise—and his confidence in his own instincts—progressed steadily throughout the war. Indeed, Lincoln had seemed apologetic in a letter of January 6, 1862, timidly prodding Buell to move on Knoxville. Saying he was "not competent to criticize your views" to the contrary, he added, "My distress is that our friends in East Tennessee are being hanged and driven to despair, and even now I fear are thinking of taking rebel arms for the sake of self-protection." By August, Buell had ample reason to fear being sacked, and perhaps that helped him overcome his officer-class preference for helping plantation owners rather than their piddling neighbors who could not afford slaves to work their small, rocky farms. Whatever energized him, the selection of Captain Bankhead as recruiting officer showed that Buell was serious about enlisting southern Yankees.

H. C. Bankhead, West Point class of 1850, was recalled in 1860 from frontier posts for an important task in preparing the army for war. A thirty-two-year-old captain, he became a mustering officer in the essential Union recruiting office in New York City. New York's newly elected mayor, Fernando Wood, was a "Copperhead"—slang for Confederate sympathizer—because Dixie cotton provided half of the city's transatlantic exports. Even so, expert army recruiters in New York City had signed up thirty thousand volunteers by the end of May 1861 for Lincoln's initial call-up. Over the course of the war, 150,000 soldiers and up to 50,000 sailors would pass through the city's enlistment centers. In terms of army politics, Buell had put an ace organizer in charge of the new regiment he envisioned. Serving with Buell at Shiloh and with Hancock at Gettysburg, Bankhead would go on to important assignments as an inspecting officer, specializing in readiness and command structure. After the war, he won praise from Sherman for "commendable energy" in fighting Plains Indians and commanded Fort Wallace, Kansas, when Custer passed through on his way to Little Big Horn. In other words, organizing the First Alabama was not a make-work job; it was a serious assignment for a respected senior staff officer, an assignment likely to—and perhaps designed to—curry favor with a president who was learning to be his own chief personnel officer.

Throughout the summer and fall of 1862, Buell's position as senior general in charge of north Alabama became increasingly important as Bragg massed his army to defend Chattanooga. Grant's letters show that he had been thinking for some time of taking the city and putting one of his best fighting generals—either Sherman or McPherson—in place to use it as the stepping-off place for Atlanta, the last remaining spinal connection in the Confederate railway system. Looking back, Davis's faith in a grandiose poseur like Bragg at this point in the war seems almost touching in comparison to Grant's methodical strategic thinking as it was developing even before he became general-in-chief in March 1864. On a micro level, we can also see the stage being set during late 1862 for the fledgling outfit of Alabama volunteers to play a dramatic role in the concluding chapters of the war. The coming months would prepare them for big events with glamorous martial titles: the Battle of Chickamauga on September 18–20, 1863, the Battle of Lookout Mountain on November 24, 1863, and the Battle of Missionary Ridge on November 25, 1863. These were ferocious, legend-making conflicts. The improbable ascent of 1,800-foot Lookout Mountain on November 24 was glamorized in Union lore as the "Battle Above the Clouds." Another vertical assault the next day at Missionary Ridge produced a Medal of Honor for the nineteen-year-old "Boy Colonel," Arthur MacArthur Jr., father of Douglas MacArthur, the insubordinate World War II general lionized for his "old soldiers never die" farewell to Congress in 1951.

Hill country partisan that I am, I take the First Alabama's lack of legendary status as proof of the suppressive power of Lost Cause historiography. Not even Chris Sheats earned a snazzy sobriquet like those given to the commanders the First Alabama encountered, including Forrest, Wheeler, and the First's regular adversary in their home state, Roddey. Even Roddey, a tricky, cotton-trading politician from the same hills, got a grandiose title as the "defender" of Confederate homesteads in the Unionist counties. He was a cruel fighter, although never as notorious as Forrest became for slaughtering three hundred freed Alabama slaves and a smaller number of white Tennessee Union soldiers at the Fort Pillow Massacre on April 12, 1864. In a masterwork of Lost Cause hagiography, *Bedford Forrest and His Critter Company,* Andrew Lytle justified the murders because a formal "surrender was never made." But Forrest's own words undermined Lytle's clumsy apology. A month earlier, Forrest had instructed his troops on how to treat defenseless opponents. "Now, boys," he said, "war means fight and fight means kill. What's the use of taking prisoners to eat up your rations?" Recent scholarship has suggested that the presence of the "Tories" from Tennessee may have "provoked" Forrest's men into being even more vicious toward the integrated force that surrendered. Measured against Forrest's, Roddey's record looks more avaricious than pathologically malicious.

Roddey had the kind of scattered career highlighted in many supporting-cast biographies of the Civil War. Born in Moulton in 1826, Roddey had been variously a tailor, the elected sheriff of Lawrence County, Alabama, and a steamboat owner. Along with most of his neighbors and constituents, he initially opposed secession. But when Union gunboats reached Muscle Shoals in February 1862, Roddey burned his freight boat to prevent its capture. After Mitchel took Huntsville, Roddey emerged as a terrorizer of Unionist households and pesterer of the occupying army in his role as "captain" of the Tishomingo Regulars, one of the many Partisan Ranger outfits that the Richmond government employed for dirty work in the back country. As a soldier, he proved to be a natural. His men participated in the Battle of Shiloh and the ensuing struggle to hold Corinth. On May 4, 1862, the *Official Records* show Bragg writing, "Roddey is invaluable." Bragg used Roddey to keep Buell busy while he relocated his main force to Chattanooga, and in October he regularized his troops and promoted Roddey to colonel. Roddey soon rose to brigadier general under Forrest and Wheeler, and enters the next chapter of the First Alabama story as a gifted player in the officers' bilateral game of cotton theft.

This seems an appropriate point to underline the kinship of social class that united many, if far from all, colonels and generals in the two armies. The aforementioned bonds of West Point friendships, the cooperative cotton trade, and the northern upper-class tendency to view southern leaders as worthy citizens trapped into defending a bad cause were important precursors of the boom in Lost Cause literature and history writing that emerged in the decades following Reconstruction. Both Roddey and the leading officers of the First Alabama would become players in the boom times of the Gilded Age and the concordant romanticization of the Confederacy and the plantation grandees.

In 1862 Lincoln finally sacked Buell along with his protector McClellan for moving too slowly against the southerners they were believed to admire. In an act of misguided if understandable optimism, Lincoln and his general-in-chief picked Major General William S. Rosecrans. "Old Rosey" was one of the top engineering students in the "brilliant class of 1842," which produced eighteen Union generals and eleven who served under the Confederate flag. A Methodist, he was, like so many cadets, prepared to enter America's governing class via the academy's official religion of Episcopalianism. "Rosecrans' sociability and high spirits is everywhere to be found throughout his correspondence with Academy friends," according to his biographer. "He thought dueling stupid, yet risked dismissal by consenting to fight a duel in a fracas over a lady." The opponent backed out based on Rosecrans's reputation as a marksman. He was, in sum, one of the army's golden "old boys," and the appointment should have worked out brilliantly. And in a way it did for the Alabamians he inherited from Buell.

CHRIS SHEATS IN THE WILDERNESS

THE PRINCIPAL REASON Chris Sheats is unknown to most students of the Civil War and is missing from the master narratives of its leading scholars has to do with the way the relatively new field of academic historiography operates. Professionals in the field rely on the histories of individual states, such as those cranked out beginning in the early 1900s by university history departments and state archives. The authors of the main texts on Alabama, written between 1880 and 1960, either ignored Chris Sheats's speeches or misrepresented and downplayed his organizing efforts as the Cotton South's most passionate anti-war activist. In fact, Sheats was well known during the war in both Confederate and Union circles. His obscurity, therefore, is a challenge to any researcher, especially since in his cameo appearances in Alabama textbooks, he is invariably cast as a villain or, at best, an eccentric without a popular constituency.

The most reliable accounts of his wartime activities appear in small sprinkles in the 138,579 pages of the seventy volumes of the *Official Records of the Union and Confederate Armies during the War of the Rebellion*, published between 1881 and 1901. He is also mentioned favorably in the long-ignored chronicle of patriotism compiled by a federal agency, the Southern Claims Commission, during Reconstruction. Before the era of digitized searches, combing for mentions of this talkative Alabama schoolteacher required diligence and resources greater than those of all but the most ardent scholars and curious amateurs. The diaries of witnesses and the casual writings of local antiquarians take generations to surface. Indeed, the content of the Sheats speech that inspired the nicknaming of "the Free State of Winston" would have been lost forever but for the fact that Probate Judge John Bennett Weaver interviewed three surviving Union soldiers who heard Sheats speak at Looney's Tavern after his return to Winston County from Montgomery following the 1861 secession convention. That speech was the pivotal event in Sheats's career and sparked the founding of the First Alabama Cavalry, U.S.A., but neither the exact date of Sheats's return to the hill country nor the date of the Looney's Tavern rally can be nailed down with certainty. Rather than drag the reader through a wilderness of footnotes, I choose to offer his story as I have pieced it together as a predicate to the wartime story of the First Alabama and how its legacy got buried.

Given his bad luck with historians, it is not surprising that Sheats is missing from the index of the exhaustive, four-volume *Encyclopedia of the Confederacy* brought out by Simon & Schuster in 1993. He was similarly ignored in the bestselling trilogy by Shelby Foote that Random House published between 1958 and 1976. The same was true of landmark works by top historians like Bruce Catton and James M. McPherson. However, Winston County itself did figure in a key paragraph in the *Encyclopedia of the Confederacy,* and it pretty well summed up what an exceptionally well-read Civil War buff might have gleaned about southern Unionism and anti-Confederate Alabamians in the period when Sheats, having refused to sign the ordinance of secession, stepped onto the main stage of Civil War history in 1861 and 1862. Indeed, by 1863, his name would have been familiar to every Union and Confederate commander operating in Alabama—and newspaper readers as far away as New York—illustrating that flash-in-the-pan celebrity was not a modern invention. *The Encyclopedia of the Confederacy* sets the stage for us:

> Although most Southerners had welcomed secession, many slaveless farmers in the uplands of Alabama and Mississippi, in

the rural parishes of Louisiana, and in the German settlements of
northern Texas had quietly opposed it. After passage of the Confederate Conscription Act [April 26, 1862], however, simple indifference to the Confederate cause in those regions often erupted
into anti-government violence. Secret societies sprang up, loyalist
neighbors were threatened, and when enrollment officers tried to
enforce the draft, they were chased, beaten, and sometimes killed.
In Winston County, Alabama, Unionists worked to form their
own Free State, and other Tories in the northwest corner of the
state considered merging with the mountain regions of Tennessee
and Georgia to create the nonslave commonwealth of Nickajack.
When Col. A. D. Streight led a Federal cavalry raid through Alabama and Georgia, companies of local Unionists eagerly served as
guides.

It's probably unfair to expect a Confederate reference book to note
that without Sheats's clandestine recruiting activities, those several
"companies" of Alabama Unionists would not have been present at the
fabled 1863 clash known as Streight's Raid. The episode is still celebrated by Lost Causers as the supreme proof of what Shelby Foote
described as Nathan Bedford Forrest's military "genius." As for historiography, Forrest's eventual victory in a fourteen-day running cavalry
battle is significant in another way. It illustrates perfectly the most prominent scholarly "tell" as to the bias of Alabama's pro-Confederate historians: the celebration of Confederate victories that had no impact on the
outcome of the war so long as they depict the southern soldiers as superior to their foes in courage, dash, and cunning. We'll return for a closer
look at Streight's Raid after exploring what can be learned about Chris
Sheats.

His father, William Wiley Sheats (1809–1895), was among the estimated 95 percent of whites in the seceding states who owned not even a
single slave. But that did not mean Chris Sheats did not enjoy certain
advantages. The elder Sheats, a Georgian, patented forty acres of Winston County land in 1835, only one year after Andrew Jackson "re-

moved" the Creek owners to Oklahoma. (His place was about thirty-five miles north of the eighty acres my great-great-grandfather James Rains acquired in 1857. There's no evidence they ever met, although James's nearby Barton, Abbott, and Key cousins answered Sheats's call to join the Union army.) The elder Sheats prospered more as a local official—county commissioner, census taker, tax assessor—than as a farmer. He was able to send Chris to board at Somerville Academy, over forty miles away. Despite its remote location, the school was said to provide "a good English education." Some years earlier the future Confederate general James Longstreet had prepped there for West Point. By the age of eighteen, Chris Sheats was back home in Houston, Alabama, a Unionist hotbed, as a schoolteacher.

An anonymous obituary writer remembered William Sheats, the father, as "a Republican and a strong partisan." That probably accounted for Chris Sheats's speedy emergence as a candidate in local politics. Sheats's biographer Martine Bates, without attribution, says that young Chris quickly became a star in the fireside debates at the Houston general store. That makes sense, since he announced himself as a candidate for the election on December 24, 1860, of the one hundred delegates who would decide whether Alabama left the Union. Judge John Bennett Weaver said his platform was a simple one: He would "vote against Secession first, last and always." Surviving photographs from around the time when he became a schoolteacher back home in Winston County at the age of twenty reveal a handsome man with a strong jaw and closely trimmed beard. He was said to walk with a distinct limp from a childhood illness. His fierce anti-secession views were shaped by the fact that Winston County ranked fifty-second of the state's fifty-two counties in two categories, cotton production and slave ownership. It produced only 352 of the 1 million cotton bales grown in Alabama in 1860, and its residents owned 122 of the state's 435,080 slaves that year. He is believed to have sharpened his verbal skills in arguments at the Houston general store and to have studied the oratory used by Jeremiah Clemens (who had yet to go wobbly) in his debates with William Lowndes Yancey. Details are scarce before he leapt from political obscurity into being elected as a convention delegate with a landslide victory over Dr. Andrew J. Kaeiser, the zealous Pennsylvania-born slave holder.

A contemporary spoke of Sheats's emergence as "a great stump speaker" who debated "political questions in every county of the state," another piece of evidence that he was later shortchanged in annals of the state's public men. The best depiction of Sheats is to be found in the writings of Judge Weaver and Colonel Streight, the latter one of the first senior officers to recognize the military potential of the Alabama mountaineers. Sometime in the spring of 1861, Sheats and a tavern owner named Bill Looney had emerged as Winston County's leaders. In late spring, Unionist elders associated with them convened a meeting in the county seat. They recruited six men "to quit their crops and each one ride a week, giving publicity to the mass meeting to be held at the said Looney's Tavern, on July 4, 1861," Weaver wrote. The canvass produced what may have been the largest anti-war rally ever held in the Confederacy, "about 2,500 people from Lawrence County, Morgan County, Blount County, Marshall County, Fayette County, Marion County, Franklin County, as well as Winston." If accurate, that number exceeds the estimated one thousand or so participants in the various "bread riots" in Richmond, Atlanta, Mobile, and other Confederate cities during the war.

"Charles C. Sheats was the principal speaker," Judge Weaver wrote based on his interviews with participants, who said the group passed three resolutions by voice vote. When I first read the resolutions I was struck by their untutored eloquence. They seemed to bespeak honest country folk proceeding on their rough idea of parliamentary niceties. As we have seen, the first commended Sheats for "fidelity to the people." The second invoked Andrew Jackson as the authority that a state cannot unilaterally depart from the Union. "But," it added modestly, "if we are mistaken in this, and a state can lawfully or legally secede or withdraw, being only a part of the Union, then a county, any county, being a part of the state, by the same process of reasoning, could cease to be a part of the state." A third resolution declared neutrality, pledging that Winstonians would not shoot at their neighbors to the south or at the "Flag . . . [of] Washington, Jefferson and Jackson! Therefore we ask the Confederacy on the one hand, and the Union on the other, to leave us alone, unmolested, that we may work out our political and financial destiny here in the hills and mountains of Northwest Alabama."

As it turned out, the eloquence was Judge Weaver's. His surviving article gives the misleading impression that he had the document in hand. P. J. Gossett, a Haleyville, Alabama, newspaperman who collects First Alabama lore, told me that Weaver's summary was not based on surviving documents, but represented his polished version of what the old men told him. Weaver was also the source for the fact that there were Confederate sympathizers in the crowd. One of them, Richard Elliott "Uncle Dick" Payne, was a celebrated raconteur and finagler who may have been affiliated with a counterfeiting gang that operated for a time in a Winston County cave. Payne's reactions to Sheats's proposals were in keeping with his reputation as a wag, Weaver wrote. "On the reading of the Second Resolution," Weaver wrote, "Uncle Dick Payne, sitting back in the audience, made the following remark: 'Oh, oh—Winston secedes!! The Free State of Winston.'" The acerbic comment provided the county's enduring sobriquet. Weaver's sources were three participants who later enlisted in the First Alabama Cavalry, one of whom died in 1909 and two of whom died in 1928. There has been no dispute, however, about the accuracy of the eyewitness accounts that Weaver merged into one narrative.

Payne, who served under Stonewall Jackson and Longstreet, is another of those Civil War bit players too irresistibly colorful to pass with a bare mention. He became one of the best-known privates in either army, serving his comrades in arms as a banker. "'Payne money' has been in circulation in this part of the army for several months," wrote a fellow soldier in the 27th Alabama Infantry in his diary. "'R. E. Payne the Banker' is known all over this part of the army and is not half as green as he looks or as one would suppose a man to be who has lived 40 years or more in the Sand Mountains of North Alabama. He is a great forager

and trader; buys and sells anything a soldier can use, from a pint of lou-
isianna rum to a blanket or suit of clothes." Payne printed several thousand dollars in "money" stamped "Redeemable in Confederate money
when presented in sums of $20 and upwards. Signed R. E. Payne."
"When he buys or sells he makes change with his own money. . . . He
has turned the bulk of what he has accumulated into Confederate, and is
now rolling in wealth. When we leave here, he will be compelled to buy
a pack mule to carry his money." Despite his support of the Confederacy, "Payne money" was also used by Winston County Unionists when
Payne left the army in 1863 and returned home as informal "governor"
of the county.

There is even more direct documentation for Sheats's next shining
moment as a recruiter and orator. It came after he had been on the run
for months and came into contact with Colonel Abel Streight (1828–
1892). Streight's 51st Indiana Infantry was based along the Tennessee
River to fend off lightning strikes from Forrest and another skilled area
commander, Brigadier General George Roddey, the aforementioned
"Defender of North Alabama." They were trying, with little success, to
stop Sheats, Looney, and "guides" from leading volunteers into the
Union lines. With his regiment on occupation duty in Decatur, Streight
received a courier on July 10 who reported "that there was a party of
about 40 men some 5 or 6 miles towards the mountains trying to come
to us." They were in a cat-and-mouse game with an equal number of
Confederate cavalry trying to block them from reaching the river.
Streight's report provides one of our most vivid pictures of conditions
in the hills.

> I wish to say a word relative to the condition of these people.
> They are mostly poor, though many of them are, or rather were, in
> comfortable circumstances. They outnumber nearly three to one
> the secessionists in portions of Morgan, Blount, Winston, Mar-
> ion, Walker, Fayette and Jefferson Counties; but situated as they
> are; surrounded by a most relentless foe, mostly unarmed and
> destitute of ammunition, they are persecuted in every conceivable

way, yet up to this time most of them have kept out of the way sufficiently to avoid being dragged off by the gangs that infest the country for the purpose of plunder and enforcing the provisions of the rebel conscription act. Their horses and cattle are driven off in vast numbers. Every public road is patrolled by guerilla bands, and the Union men have been compelled to seek protection in the vastness of the mountain wilderness. They cannot hold out much longer. This state of things here has so disturbed them that but very little attention has been paid to farming, consequently many of them are now destitute of food of their own and are living off their more fortunate neighbors.

Streight swore forty of the hill county refugees into his regiment before leading a column on a sixty-mile march along Sand Mountain, a commanding elevation that knifes into the heart of the Alabama uplands about fifty miles southwest of Lookout Mountain in Tennessee. They set up a recruiting camp at Davis Gap, deep in Confederate territory. Streight reported that twenty recruits were delivered there by Anna Campbell, "not in good health and fifty-five years old [who] had ridden a poor old horse over the mountains, tracing the mountain pathways through the gorges and around the precipices, sixty four miles, counting the distance to and from her friends, and had made the trip in thirty hours." Then, appearing dramatically from the forested slopes, Chris Sheats came limping into camp. A regimental chaplain of the 51st Indiana left an account of almost cinematic clarity in an 1880 anthology called *The Civil War in Song and Story*. The author described an ingathering of Alabamians who were the opposite of "highfalutin aristocracy," humble citizens "deprived of culture" who "think for themselves." To a striking degree, the caste distinctions of white Alabama were key facts in the sociology of war. These "plain, candid, industrious people" "came to us all day Monday like doves to the windows." That evening Sheats appeared with "a strange tune coming from an Alabamian." He told the roughly dressed crowd gathered in the twilight not to help a Confederate "cause they hated" when they were welcome in the U.S. Army.

Sheets [*sic*] is a young man of fine promise and makes a splendid speech . . . He advised them to join that [Union] army and be men, and fight the Southern Confederacy to hell and back again. Said he, "To-morrow morning I am going to the Union army. I am going to expose this fiendish villainy before the world. They shall hear from me. I have slept in the mountains, in caves and caverns, till I am become musty; my health and manhood are failing me. I will stay here no longer till I am enabled to dwell in quiet at home."

It was perhaps the best speech of his lifetime, and certainly the most carefully documented one. But not until Reconstruction, after adventures considered unworthy of truthful memorializing by Alabama archivists and historians, would Chris Sheats dwell quietly at home. He did not make good on his promise to join the Union army, probably because of his bad leg, which he tried to ignore and which was the second thing most people noticed about him, after the oratory. Back in Walker and Winston Counties, on my kinfolks' farms in and around the Abbott homestead on the Sipsey River hamlet of Garrison's Point, words like those spoken in the light of campfires and pine torches at Davis Gap were having an effect. As the chaplain told it, men inspired by Sheats had "left their homes and fled to the mountains. Some made for the Union army, coming through the mountain pathways for twenty, forty, sixty, and some even ninety miles, having a complete line of friends to help them extending from Decatur to near Montgomery—the best underground railroad ever heard of or ever established."

That's exaggeration, of course, even if well intended. The actual Underground Railroad used by escaping slaves had a network of way stations stretching from Florida to Canada and was used by an estimated 30,000 to 100,000 African Americans starting in the late 1700s. Yet there were similarities, and Christopher M. Rein, the leading authority on Union soldiers from Alabama, said the Alabama version, while shorter in length and briefer in duration, did carry both white and Black people into the Federal lines. Altogether, woodland guides like Chris Sheats, Bill Looney, and Anna Campbell would help enlist more than three thousand white Alabamians in the Federal army, where they joined seven thousand former slaves to become Alabamians in blue. It would take me even longer to identify relatives of mine who donned that uniform because of Chris Sheats's words and work than it did to find out about Sheats himself.

17

A Murderous Conspiracy
in the Whirling Hills

THE SECRET TO understanding any conspiracy is connecting dots of evidence across time. So it was with the semi-official Confederate murder plot against the family of Winston County's Unionist patriarch Solomon Curtis (1797–1860). It took me a long time to discern the pattern of this plan to eradicate Winston's most prominent Unionist family with this operation that used both uniformed and civilian enactors. I use the term "semi-official" for this chain of killings because it involves Alabama's governor, a senior ranking Confederate general, and a cluster of nominally independent informants and hit men who had been given the go-ahead from Montgomery. I use the term "conspiracy" because the operational links among the players can be documented right up to the final finger-pointing by Governor Shorter when the publicity became too ugly to ignore. This neglected aspect of Civil War history is important because it gives the lie to the Lost Cause narrative that attacks on southern nonconformists were spontaneous, disorganized, and dismaying to Confederate officialdom. In the main, they were state actions performed under cover of the Partisan Ranger Act, the conscription and confiscation laws, or the non-enforcement of assault, murder, and arson laws.

Solomon Curtis was on his deathbed at the family enclave, called

Curtis Bottom, in 1860 when he pledged his nine sons to fight against the coming rebellion. He was one of the last living links to the Unionist legacy of Andrew Jackson. As a fourteen-year-old "Tennessee Volunteer," the boy soldier had been with Old Hickory when the general signed the Fort Jackson Treaty of 1814, opening twenty-two million acres of Creek Indian land in Georgia and Alabama. Solomon stayed on to patent 280 of those acres near Double Springs, Alabama. He was worth $20,000, signaling his primacy in the non-slaveholder community, when he swore his sons to the oaths that would see at least six of them oppose the Confederacy and three of them die as a result.

Several months after Solomon's death, six of his neighbors signed the document that began the killing season in the hills. It was a poster calling for "all good patriotic men" to rally on June 15, 1861, at the store of William Dodd, the great-great-grandfather of my hillbilly griot, Donald Dodd. (The signers included W. B. Manasco, ancestor of a Haleyville attorney named Hobson Manasco who was a classmate of mine from BSC and with whom I stayed while researching these events.) That set off a series of dueling meetings. Andrew Kaeiser, the Fire-Eating Pennsylvania-born slaveholder, wrote Governor Shorter that Sheats and other "avowed Unionists" were drilling to fight the Confederacy. On May 24, 1862, at a "secret" meeting of the Unionist elders, Probate Judge Thomas Pinckney Curtis (known as Tom Pink) gave the speech that probably sealed his fate with its bellicose tone and his unblinking refutation that secession was about states' rights. "The chief corner stone of the Confederacy is perpetuation of slavery," Curtis said, boldly endorsing armed opposition to Stokely "Old Stoke" Roberts, the guerilla leader sponsored by Governor Shorter to forcibly enlist local men and chase down draft dodgers. He listed nine rules of survival for evading "the threat of Stoke Roberts." If unable to escape Roberts and his equally violent Partisan Ranger running mate, Captain Daniel H. Whatley, Curtis announced, Free Staters should desert from the Rebel army, then return home to lead others to Union enlistment posts. In no time, Kaeiser and spies such as Captain H. A. M. Henderson informed Governor

Shorter of what was going on in Winston against the backdrop of the all-out guerilla war sweeping north Alabama.

So desperate were Shorter and General Gideon Pillow (the Richmond government's chief enlistment officer) to catch evaders that they organized new "independent" local outfits, the "conscript cavalry," to patrol the hills. Initially, the plan backfired because secessionist citizens signed up "to circumvent the very thing they were trying to enforce—conscription," according to a Cherokee County Unionist. Supposedly, this ragtag cavalry was "to gather up conscripts and deserters . . . but their main business was to keep from going to the front themselves and to do as little as possible and stay home." The captured Union men were "arrested, put in the county jail, others sent to military prisons, some hung and others shot." Escapees fled to the Union lines to enlist, while entire families converged on the garrisoned cities. Indeed, when the Union retook Corinth, refugee family groups numbering more than thirteen hundred civilians flocked to the Union camp there. By 1863, violence on the home front had long since become "atrocious and systematic" throughout Alabama and in much of the southern interior, according to historian Daniel E. Sutherland. "Unionists believed that Confederate conscription, confiscation, impressment, and similarly oppressive measures were extralegal actions taken by an illegitimate government. They responded by enlisting in Union service and forming guerilla bands to oppose the usurpers. As a result, whirl became king, anarchy threatened, and both sides engaged in a brutal internal war to bring the other side to heel."

Which side was more brutal in the whirling hills of Alabama? That tireless Confederate apologist William Stanley Hoole had no doubt. He described a one-sided conflict in which Unionist hooligans preyed on the patriot families of Alabama men who were off fighting for southern honor. His tales of "Destroying Angels" was Lost Cause exaggeration run amok. There were depredations on both sides in Alabama's bushwhacker war, especially by Indiana bluecoats stationed near Huntsville in the last year of the war. But there is hardly any parallel in Civil War annals to match the assassination campaign carried out by Alabama of-

ficials, Confederate troops, and black-flag irregulars against the sons of
Solomon Curtis. But the outspoken judge Tom Pink was not the first to
go when the black-flag captains, Stokely Roberts and Daniel H. Whatley, took over Winston County roads.

Surviving documents leave no doubt that the extermination campaign aimed at the Curtis family and similar atrocities proceeded with
the blessings of Governor Shorter and his successor, Thomas Hill
Watts, who defeated him in the 1863 election. Both governors worked
closely with the brutally efficient General Gideon Pillow, superintendent of the Conscript Bureau in Alabama and Tennessee in 1863–1864.
Pillow and General Roddey coordinated the movements of regular
troops with the freelance operations of the helter-skelter team of Whatley and Roberts. The latter, a sociopathic torturer who lived just across
the state line in Itawamba, Mississippi, may have become a Mississippi
police officer after the war or been murdered in the manner described
below—another sign of the "whirl" that descended on the Alabama
backcountry. One of Roberts's specialties was driving slivers of heart
pine into the organs of bound victims and lighting the highly flammable
wood. According to Wesley Thompson, Roberts had his men hang Private Henry Tucker, captured on home leave from the First Alabama,
upside down like a slain deer, castrated the man, cut out his tongue,
gouged out his eyes, then ordered him skinned so as to create an epider-
mal sack for his internal organs. Tucker's service record and death were
convincingly confirmed by a history-minded descendant and author,
Joel S. Mize, in a privately published history of First Alabama soldiers.
A narrative version of the events was also provided to a history blog by
a woman descended from both Stoke Roberts and a Union gang leader
named John or George Stout (he answered to both), who specialized in
revenge slayings. By her account, Stout kidnapped Stoke Roberts from
a primitive prison where he held Unionist youths and took him to a killing ground in Winston County called the "Wolf Pit." "A long iron spike
was driven completely through Stokely's mouth, nailing him to the root
of a huge oak tree." But newspaper accounts have Old Stoke being murdered three years after the war in his barnyard by an unknown person

who was probably Stout. That fits with Judge John Bennett Weaver's claim that he had as a source a man who said he hunted down and killed Roberts in his Lawrence County barnyard in 1868.

The first Curtis to die was the eldest son, William Washington "Wash" Curtis. Only two weeks after his defiant speech about the nine rules of draft dodging, Tom Pink received word that his brother Wash, who lived on a neighboring farm, had been targeted by Stoke Roberts. The brother realized "that the invaders would be happy to capture any one and especially a brother of the Probate Judge," according to Judge Weaver's reconstruction of the messy event. In its pitiable domestic details and clumsy execution, the event was typical of the off-the-books war authorized for the Alabama backcountry by Confederate officials. Wash had slipped home from "lying out" for his first visit with a new-born granddaughter. Wash's daughter was married to a Confederate sympathizer who may have betrayed his father-in-law. Wash's wife told him that suspicious strangers had been lurking about. Wash's mother had come over to see her son off. The women were imploring him to hurry his getaway, making for a wartime tableau of crushing banality as Wash resisted their advice.

> "I will have to hug and kiss my grandbaby this morning, for I may never see it again." Just as Wash was making the foregoing reply . . . Wash's wife screamed out: "Wash, yonder they come! . . . It looks like an Army . . . Hurry Wash, or it will be too late." . . . Just as he got balanced in his saddle, he applied his heel spurs to his horse a little too hard. This excited the horse, and caused him to stand on his rear feet. Just as the horse's front feet reached the ground, he refused to go forward. Wash, again, applied his spurs to the horse's sides . . . which caused the horse to whirl to the left in a circle almost half around to face the invaders. . . . They were within sixty to seventy-five yards up the road, the old Cheatham Road, and they were still getting nearer every second. Without any orders to halt, or any warning whatever to the victim, Wash Curtis was shot by several of the invaders led by Stoke Roberts.

Wash died in less than a minute. When Roberts saw that Wash Curtis was dead, he immediately turned and fled up the road, down which they came. They fled in great haste. . . . As [neighbors] viewed the tragic scene, Wash's body on the ground drenched in blood, and witnesses grief-stricken, sobbing mother and daughter, Wash's mother fainted.

The second child of Solomon Curtis to die during the Civil War was Joel Jackson Curtis, who was captured in December 1863 by a Confederate unit that had established a much-feared execution spot near the Jasper jail house. According to Charles E. Wilson, "He was given five days to sign up with the Confederate Army. Joel refused and they carried him to what they called the Slaughter Pen and shot him in the back. He was buried in a shallow grave," from which his wife exhumed his decaying body and took him home to be buried next to Solomon and Wash. "On her way back some of the people along the way tried to get her to spend the night with them. She refused due to the condition of Joel's body as he was stinking."

Such garish tales are commonplace in Free State lore and, more reliably, as sworn testimony in the hundreds of pages of victims' depositions and witness statements collected about Winston County outrages by the Southern Claims Commission. The testimony shows Captain Daniel H. Whatley to be a more businesslike terrorist than Stoke Roberts, preferring threats to torture. He led a larger band of one hundred to two hundred men, and his dedication caught the eye of Roddey and Pillow, the latter Richmond's senior on-site official in Alabama during the last two years of the war. As a result, Whatley became a commissioned captain under Roddey and Forrest, and as such provided an essential evidentiary link about higher-ups' knowledge of the Curtis conspiracy saga.

About a month after Joel's funeral, Captain Whatley and a force of two hundred Confederate cavalry came for Tom Pink in a manner that illustrated how regular Confederate units used their bloodthirsty civilian accomplices. At the jail in Houston, Whatley's men threatened Tom

Pink's wife into turning over salt that had been set aside for the county's poor. Then they handed Tom over to a death squad of about six men. They mounted him on his mule and took him home on a frigid night. He seemed for a moment to have bought his freedom with $2,000 in hidden cash. But under torture with a hot poker that severed his spine, Judge Curtis coughed up another thousand dollars he had been suspected of holding back. Convinced they had it all, the executioners took him to a remote bluff, shot him twice in the right eye, and tossed him into a nearby branch. He was found the next morning, his body frozen into the iced-over shoreline.

Solomon's six remaining sons survived because they were hiding out or away in the Union army. At this point, the conscript cavalry and their main local ally, Dr. Andrew J. Kaeiser, may have thought they were rid of the pesky Curtis family. But one of the younger boys, James G. Curtis (1837–1896), came home on a furlough from his service as a Union hospital orderly and was jailed in Jasper after being captured by the Home Guard. From jailmates he learned the names of the men who had killed his brother and Jenny Brooks's husband, Henry (of *Stars Fell on Alabama* fame). That meant the war would not end in the hill country for a long time. It had become what the military historian Sean Michael O'Brien calls the "civil war within the Civil War."

The assassination of Tom Pink Curtis turned out to be a public relations disaster for Governor Watts. Even though he was an outspoken Unionist, Curtis was also serving as the duly elected top official of a sitting governor, Watts, who was supposed to guarantee civic order in Alabama. Surviving letters indicate that Unionist associates of the late judge and Chris Sheats banded together against Governor Watts in a political squeeze play. On January 27, with Curtis newly in his grave, one of the most prominent citizens of Lawrence County, Thomas Minot Peters, wrote Watts on behalf of nineteen Winston County notables demanding appointment of an immediate successor to the late probate judge. It was, by any standard, a meddlesome letter, loaded with political spin. Peters was a nationally known botanist who had been corresponding with President Buchanan about the need to keep Alabama in the Union.

Watts, of course, knew from the Alabama newspapers that Peters had been every bit as outspoken as Chris Sheats as an opponent of secession. Lost Cause historians would later denounce Peters as a "notorious Scalawag" when he rose to be a Reconstruction chief justice of Alabama. At this remove in time, it's hard to know whether he was pranking Watts, or alternatively, asserting that he was too influential for a newly seated governor to ignore. That's because Watts had defeated Shorter, a Confederate hard-liner, by appealing to an Alabama electorate that was turning against the war because of battlefield losses, draft inequality, and partisan violence at home. In any event, two of the nineteen names on Peters's list of prominent Winstonians must have leapt out at Watts. One was Tom Pink's brother William V. Curtis, who had just been elected sheriff on the Unionist vote. The second name was another brother, James G. Curtis, who was away serving with the First Alabama Cavalry. Winston dissidents had become so bold that a dozen men had attended Tom Pink's funeral in their Union uniforms. This clearly was a tide Watts didn't want to swim against. Only seven days after hearing from Peters, Watts acted to get to the bottom of what he now saw as a troublesome murder. And he knew where to write in an official request for information: to the staff of General Pillow, the ranking Confederate commander in the Alabama department.

Lieutenant Colonel Harrison Claiborne Lockhart was commander of the "conscript rendezvous" in Talladega, Alabama, where General Pillow sent captured draft evaders to be held for induction. It was not a piddling operation. Military historians later credit the "always aggressive" Pillow with replenishing the army of General Joseph E. Johnston sufficiently enough to allow his credible resistance to Sherman's March. Governor Watts wrote Lockhart, who was Pillow's assistant adjutant general, a fiery letter.

*Dear Sir; I have received information, that a Capt. Whatley
(who, I believe, is under your command) with a portion of his
command, sometime about the 20th of January, went to Houston,
the county-site of Winston Co. Ala, and arrested the Judge of*

*Probate of that County, T. P. Curtis and carried him off, in the
direction of Jasper, Walker Co. and murdered him . . . It is
further said that, after having arrested Judge Curtis, they forced
his wife to give up the keys of the Jail, in which the salt sent there,
by the State to be distributed among indigent families, was stored,
that this salt was taken—and sold—and the proceeds,
appropriated to the use of the men in Capt. Whatley's command.
If these things are true, no punishment is too great for such men.
Such conduct will do more injury to our cause, than a Yankee
Raid. I write you this, believing that you will have the matter
properly investigated, and, if the facts justify it, have the proper
punishment inflicted for such conduct.*

But Lockhart, an experienced Tennessee politician who had raised
his own company to oppose Grant at Fort Donelson, was not about to
be intimidated by a mere Alabama governor or take the fall for a renegade captain or a commanding general he wanted to undermine. Lockhart also knew that Pillow, Governor Watts, and General Philip Roddey
worked as a team in directing conscript chasers like Whatley. "Capt
Whatley is not, nor ever has been under my command. I know nothing
of him or his men. Perhaps he may have been acting under orders from
some Rendezvous commander assigned to duty by Brig Genl Pillow
whilst sequestering conscription," Lockhart wrote. "I will forward a
copy of your letter to my immediate supervisor, (who has a list of the
Rendezvous and the Cavalry on duty at and account each,) and request
him to aid in a vigorous and thorough investigation of the matter, that
appropriate punishment may be inflicted." The letter was also a shot
across the bow of Pillow, with whom Lockhart had been feuding over
how to allot the conscripted Alabamians. He wrote their superiors that
Pillow had stripped the defense force in Talledega and thrown operations into a "chaotic state."

Students of bureaucratic communication might read Lockhart's letter as a masterpiece. It let Watts know that his political ally General Pillow would have records as to where unit officers like Whatley were

supposed to be on duty at a given time. If Pillow wanted to alibi the murderous underling, that was his business.

Then Lockhart concluded with a bombshell postscript: "P.S. Since writing the above I learn from Mr. R. B. Crowe of Marion Perry County Ala that Whatley claims to belong to Genl Roddey's command." In other words, if the governor needed to know more about the treatment of the most recently buried Curtis he should contact his close friend, the "Defender of North Alabama." Lockhart was signaling that he knew what was common knowledge in Montgomery and north Alabama: Although nominally assigned to Roddey's 10th Alabama Cavalry, C.S.A., Whatley had gone "rogue" and, as historian Christopher Rein put it, "operated with increasing autonomy" beyond Confederate or state control. It was a tricky time for Watts. He had much to worry about, including two of the remaining Curtis brothers still living and wearing their defiance on their sleeves.

Natural-Born Spies
of the First Alabama

IF THERE'S EVER been any doubt about the efficiency of the hill country grapevine, the birth of a distant Raines family cousin with the unlikely name of General Buel Barton near the Sardis Primitive Baptist Church on the Black Warrior River in Walker County, Alabama, ought to clear it up. His parents, Nancy Hanes Barton and her husband, Gilford M. Barton, a future private in the First Alabama Cavalry, U.S.A., welcomed him on July 12, 1862. On that same day, ninety miles to the north in Huntsville, General Don Carlos Buell issued Special Orders No. 100, the first document noting the "volunteers from Alabama" who would within a few days be sworn into the new Union regiment. Aside from dropping the second *l* in the general's surname, the new parents had clearly been following closely the news from occupied Huntsville. Ol' Stars Mitchel had just been recalled, and Buell, a cautious, slave-owning general from Ohio, was in charge.

I had studied these matters for most of my life before discovering the coincidental events of July 12, 1862. The Barton family tree is a testament to steadfast Unionism. The infant Buel's father and four of his brothers from nearby farms would become mainstays of the First Alabama, although General Buell would be gone by the time most of them enlisted. As for Buel Barton, he would live until 1951, when he was buried in the Sardis church cemetery near my great-great-grandmother Millia Barton Raines (1802–1843). That's the little picture.

As for the big picture, General Buell's ascent at Huntsville marks the beginning of the First Alabama's essential role in the most effective Union spy operation of the entire war. The importance of this espionage network in General Grant's conquest of Vicksburg is well known to military historians, but it is treated as a sideshow and source of colorful anecdotes by popular historians. Of course, Lost Cause historians ignored completely the dozens of operatives supplied by First Alabama soldiers and their families, and until recent years, the same applied to modern scholars who specialize in Alabama war stories.

At the risk of getting too cute on the role of omissions in historical inquiry, I have to mention that 159 years after Buell issued Special Orders No. 100 about the Alabama volunteers, I found an article in *The New York Times* headlined "Overlooked No More: 'Skipped History' Explores Forgotten Events." The article detailed how Ben Tumin, a comedian identified as a "historical satirist," started a Web series during the COVID-19 shutdown about events that had been misrepresented or ignored in the teaching of the conventional versions of the American narrative. I wished immediately that I had coined the term "skipped history" because it so perfectly summed up what I was facing in reconstructing the military career of the First Alabama. As we've seen, it had been dismissed as "not conspicuous" and simply ignored when the Alabama Department of Archives and History compiled histories of every Confederate regiment from the state. This politically motivated selectivity typified what the historian Tiya Miles termed "the conundrum of the archives." Tumin drew inspiration from Miles's explanation of "how the historical record tends to relate what people in power want it to relate." Miles argues that "archives tend to skew toward power, which is to say white and male, making them especially fraught guides to the history of the antebellum South." Miles wrote, "It is a madness, if not an irony, that unlocking the history of unfree people depends on the materials of their legal owners." A similar paradox exists when Walter L. Fleming and William Stanley Hoole write about their political nemesis, "the Sand

Mountain people." The label reflects their class-based denigration of yeoman farmers whose acreage was productive enough to support families but did not yield enough income for the purchase of slaves. I do not equate the suffering of a few thousand white Alabamians with the tragedy afflicting the 435,080 slaves living in the state when the Civil War began. But the analogy points to what the writer Hilary Mantel learned in researching her brilliant series of novels about Elizabethan England: "History is not the past—it is the method we have evolved of organizing our ignorance of the past. It's the record of what's left on the record. . . . It is no more 'the past' than a birth certificate is a birth, or a script is a performance, or a map is a journey."

In this context, the First Alabama Cavalry, U.S.A. illustrates the fallibility of the historiographic process in the century or so since the talented amateurs of the Victorian era were driven out of the field by opinionated "professionals" with an exaggerated faith in a "scientific" approach modeled on that pursued in German universities. In that time, American historians of all ideological inclinations have read deeply into the *Official Records of the War of the Rebellion,* but I've found no twentieth-century historian of national reputation who assembled from these millions of words an account of how within months of the start of the war these Alabama agriculturists served, successively and with success, under the three difference-making generals of the Civil War in the west: Grant, Sherman, and the less-renowned but accomplished Dodge, who welcomed hundreds of Alabama recruits and their families into occupied Corinth and a fortified camp in nearby Glendale. Virtually unnoticed, the First Alabama contributed notably to two key events in the strangulation of the Confederacy, the fall of Vicksburg and the destruction of Atlanta. These facts alone give the lie to Hoole's snobbish declaration that nothing in its record "justifies its being singled out for monographic treatment." Doubling down on error, Hoole added, "Only rarely in its three years of existence was it engaged in actual combat with the enemy." That is simply not true, as the First Alabama fought early and often in 1863, its first full year of existence. Hoole claimed to be a close student of the *Official Records,* but by ignoring or not reading key elements of it, he stumbled into two easily debunked generalizations intended to villainize the unit: "[A] close examination of its chronology reveals . . . that by comparison with hundreds of other Union regiments it was not conspicuous in either accomplishments or attitudes." "It had altogether proved itself a liability rather than an asset," he wrote of the lively war calendar of 1863. "Surely, the First Alabama had thus far added no prestige or glory to the United States Cavalry," he continued. Hoole even argued that the group's early performance did not enhance the career of Colonel George E. Spencer, when in fact, based on his leadership of the First Alabama, he was temporarily sent to Nashville to solidify the Union's hold on that critical city.

An accounting of the full measure of the First Alabama's accomplishments in espionage had to wait for the appearance in 2002 of William B. Feis's exhaustive *Grant's Secret Service: The Intelligence War from Belmont to Appomattox*. It contains statistical information I've encountered nowhere else about the First Alabama and the Iowan sent to Mississippi by Grant to lead them and the 6th Tennessee. "Dodge began constructing an intelligence organization that would eventually stretch from Corinth to Atlanta and into the interiors of Mississippi, Alabama and Tennessee," reaching over 130 operatives by late 1863. Scouts covered the Tennessee Valley and penetrated into enemy lines. There were resident spies in Vicksburg, Meridian, Selma, Mobile, Chattanooga, and Atlanta, who sent reports to Corinth by secret messenger. "The First Alabama Cavalry (U.S.), formed by Dodge in the fall of 1862 from Unionists in northern Alabama and commanded by his chief of staff, Col. George E. Spencer, became a source of operatives, producing at least twenty-two secret service recruits," Feis wrote, quoting Dodge as to their skills: "These mountain men were fearless and would take all chances," something that Dodge believed perfectly equipped them for espionage. Plus their relatives in Confederate territory fed them information by letters and while visiting. "From November 1862 through July 1863, Dodge's men completed over two hundred missions and logged thousands of miles," Feis found.

These facts tickled the contrarian streak I developed coming of age

in Bull Connor's town and George Wallace's state. One element of Alabama's multifaceted inferiority complex is regret that nothing of military
consequence took place on its soil. (I'm counting Farragut's capture of
Mobile as a marine occurrence.) Surely providing close to 20 percent of
the best spy network in the South could count as something of import if
the state's thinkers hadn't, in effect, revoked the citizenship of its hillbilly patriots. Despite all this, I've come to feel a measure of sympathy
for Hoole in one regard that goes beyond his being blinded by a Lost
Cause orthodoxy crafted from threads spun in his native Virginia and
woven into a fact-obliterating lattice in New York. Even without a crip-
pling bias, assessing the role of a single company, battalion, or brigade is
difficult because a long war is such an oceanic event. Only rarely, as in
the case of the 20th Maine at Little Round Top, is a unit's contribution
obvious. Yet the information is there for the digging. Who knows how
many gems remain to be mined from the *Official Records*? It was not
until 1959 that Edwin C. Fishel, a National Security Agency historian,
discovered a "half-roomful" of operational files in the National Archives
that contained the untold story of how Union intelligence operations
were managed from Washington. His definitive book on the subject did
not appear until 1996. Not until the final weeks of research on this book
on August 5, 2021, did I get lucky on a smaller scale, though what I found
was directly pertinent to the neglected question of what exactly was
noteworthy about the First Alabama other than their hill country origins.

In reviewing an unpublished master's thesis submitted at Iowa State
University in 1976, I stumbled upon the name of E. D. Coe, who had
corresponded after the war with Major General Dodge about their adventures together in Mississippi. On a hunch, I checked Hoole's book
for the roster of the First Alabama. (I do credit Hoole with being the first
scholar to make it available in book form.) I found that an Edwin D. Coe
had enlisted on November 1, 1863, and mustered out on February 6,
1864. The first hit on my next Google search proved they were one and
the same man. That dot-connecting moment illuminated the role that
Alabama Unionists played in Dodge becoming known as the U.S. Ar-

my's "Father of Military Intelligence" and how Grant prevailed at Vicksburg using information from a clandestine network in which Alabamians were founding members. It also showed how Dodge cherry-picked his command to find talent for the war's best battlefield spying operation. Dodge, at the age of thirty-one, had become a managerial genius with an unerring eye for talent and a parental protectiveness toward his agents. By arriving in Corinth in late fall of 1862, the First Alabama fit smoothly into the spy "network that . . . Dodge was then slowly extending through the whole Confederacy," according to John Bakeless, an Army intelligence officer and Harvard-trained historian who specialized in Civil War espionage. Dodge also admired the bravery of soldiers willing to go through enemy lines disguised as civilians.

It took a good eye, one supposes, to see that the slender Coe had the right stuff. He arrived in Corinth in a safe post as a bass horn player in the regimental band of the 17th Illinois Infantry. They were assigned to the XVI Army command and billeted with the First Alabama, new volunteers being drilled rigorously by Dodge. General Stephen A. Hurlbut decided he needed riflemen more than musicians and disbanded Coe's band. The very next day, November 1, 1963, Coe joined the First Alabama as a second lieutenant. Coe's story also illustrates how completely and quickly the First Alabama was integrated into the Union command structure and readied to participate in Dodge's main assignment, which was to protect Grant's rear as he assembled an army of forty thousand to capture Vicksburg. The crucial Mississippi River port was defended by an equal number of Confederates under General John Pemberton. In March 1863, Grant wrote Dodge to "send a spy to Meridian." He was worried about rumors that large trains were being organized to carry thousands of troops on the 175-mile journey to Vicksburg. If that was the case, Grant would have to alter his developing plan to close in on Vicksburg and engage Pemberton. He might even have to split his army, holding Pemberton in place while wheeling twenty thousand or so of his men around to face the arrivals from Meridian.

The job of getting Grant the information he needed required preternatural nerve from an amateur like Coe, and his mission came to be a pivot point of the Vicksburg campaign. We can surmise that Dodge believed his Illinois accent would be a plus in selling the cover story—or "legend," in modern parlance—on which his life would depend. Coe's accent figured in the story he told when surrendering himself at a farm near Meridian. He said he was a Yankee soldier eager to desert. A Confederate cavalry unit came to question him. Dodge had equipped him with two letters addressed to friends supposedly serving with Bragg. After two days of confinement in Meridian, Coe talked his way to a parole and bought a horse with the money—$300 Confederate and $120 gold—Dodge had given him. Without breaking cover, Coe found Dodge's pickets and convinced them to take him to see Dodge. Coe reported to Dodge that the Rebels had no intention of moving troops out of Meridian to threaten Grant. Coe's report was critical to the vast southern chess game brilliantly described in Brent H. Ponsford's thesis at Iowa State. Four more of Dodge's spies reported about Rebel movements in Mississippi and Alabama. Those reports triggered Dodge's mission to ravage the Tennessee River Valley, thereby keeping Roddey tied up in the valley and sending Forrest haring off in pursuit of Streight's Raid in April.

"The month of May, 1863, saw Dodge's intelligence operation reach its pinnacle," Ponsford wrote. Thanks to dawdling by the Confederacy's duet of blunderers, Jeff Davis in Richmond and Braxton Bragg in the field, the Confederacy's best general in the Deep South, Joseph Johnston, had been pulled out of Tennessee far too late to close Grant's window of opportunity. By the time Pemberton surprised Davis by reporting on May 1 that Grant was right on top of him, an urgent wire from Richmond to Johnston on May 9 to "proceed at once to Mississippi and take command of the forces there" did not matter. Jackson fell on May 14. The next day, in the pivotal battle of the Vicksburg campaign at Champion Hill, Grant drove Pemberton's army back to Vicksburg, twenty miles away, and the Siege of Vicksburg began. Pemberton surrendered the city on July 4, just as Lee was being whipped at Gettysburg. The Confederacy was dying but would need two more years to expire. To my way of thinking, this cascade of events was started by the mission to Meridian by the horn-playing lieutenant from the First Alabama.

This is the kind of detailed backstory often missing from broad-brush popular histories. Dodge's network of spies was an eclectic group that carried out its activities in ten states between 1861 and 1865, including Georgia, Alabama, Mississippi, Tennessee, Missouri, Illinois, Iowa, and Minnesota. "With his raids and secret service work, Dodge clearly made up in shrewdness and zeal what he lacked in military brilliance," Ponsford concluded. For much of that time, the First Alabama was at the center of the orchestral surge of espionage that swirled around the diminutive general. As soon as he met the Alabamians, he began utilizing men in the ranks and their relatives back home, as with the Berry brothers of Blount County. James Berry enlisted at nineteen, fought at Chickamauga, and died in a Confederate prison. By that time, his older brother Isaac identified himself as Dodge's "Chief Scout" in north Alabama, and after the war he organized an anti-Klan gang that raided the homes of KKK members at night.

Another unenlisted Alabamian who came to be regarded as a shape-shifting wizard was Philip Henson. He worked closely with the First Alabama and before the war was associated with Chris Sheats in a group romanticized as the "Mossbacks of Nickajack." At the time of the Battle of Shiloh, he was a thirty-five-year-old overseer dodging the Confederate draft on a plantation near Corinth under the twenty-slave exemption. A Zelig-like character with a round, bland face and a high-domed forehead, he met Grant even before he met Dodge. By one unverified but plausible account, it was Henson who first brought the Alabama Unionists to Grant's attention. Dodge awarded him the title of colonel, but Henson never officially enrolled in the Union army. He worked closely with one of the regiment's colonels, William H. Smith, a future Reconstruction governor of Alabama, in tricking none other than Nathan Bedford Forrest. That episode was part of a dangerous, long-running cat-and-mouse game Henson carried on with his constant antagonist Dale Roddey and a surprisingly gullible Forrest. Another southern gen-

eral, Samuel J. Gholson, had assured Forrest that Henson was a true
Rebel for the very good reason that Gholson thought he had hired Henson away from Dodge and converted him into a paid spy for the South.
The still-suspicious Forrest was swayed when Henson admitted he'd
been in Dodge's camp and tricked the leaders of the First Alabama into
entrusting him with a packet of fifty letters to be taken through the lines
to the soldiers' families in the Alabama hill country. "They were turned
over to General Forrest, who read every one of them," reported Henson's biographer. Then Henson gave Forrest operational documents allegedly stolen from Dodge's desk and told him that Dodge had just sent
a wave of spies into Joe Johnston's army. He described them in detail,
knowing they were already safely back home. "General Forrest was
completely won and the main point was gained. He gave the scout a pass
good for sixty days and to be used at his pleasure."

Even allowing for the self-aggrandizement of an "as told to" biography, Henson's tale illustrates the efficacy of the tactic of selective truth-
telling that Dodge taught his minions. In fact, it had something in
common with what the Winston Unionists called "survival lying" when
their farms were invaded by Confederate soldiers or guerillas. Eventually General Roddey, who had twice arrested Henson, finally convinced
Forrest that the garrulous fellow was indeed their enemy, and at their
next meeting Forrest had Henson manacled and sent to brutally hot Mobile, where he was kept in an unventilated "sweat box." Almost unbelievably, Henson bribed his way out of the timbered cage and in 1865
escaped for good when a sympathetic Confederate colonel taking him
from Alabama to Castle Thunder in Richmond looked the other way as
they passed through Selma. As the war wound down, he walked into the
hotel housing Dodge, who said, "Well, Phil, the rope has not been made
yet to hang you."

Dodge had a hustler's admiration for members of the hustling tribe.
His total expenditures for his spy network—in official reports, at least—
would top $17,000 in cotton money, a pittance compared to what awaited
in the black market trade that would soon attract Dodge's famous rail-

road associate Thomas P. Durant, Colonel Spencer, and the "Defender of North Alabama," as well as the horde of speculators that descended on Memphis after Grant made it his headquarters.

Part of the fascination of the First Alabama story for me is the way fate kept throwing them among the shapers of glorious events and high-rolling deals. Henson, for his part, claimed to have handled over $60,000 in his missions for Dodge. In any event, Dodge's success at espionage could not have been predicted when, in 1861, as a lawyer and political insider of some prominence in Des Moines, he unsuccessfully lobbied Iowa governor Samuel J. Kirkwood for an appointment as an officer in the Iowa militia as a means of joining the Union army at a rank commensurate with his ambition. We know from his correspondence that Dodge saw the coming war as an opportunity for fame and wealth to be garnered through his Republican political connections. Rejected for a colonelcy by Kirkwood because of his lack of military training, Dodge journeyed to Washington to lobby Secretary of War Stanton and Lincoln himself. They overruled Kirkwood.

Dodge had previously met the future president during a campaign visit Lincoln made to Council Bluffs, Iowa, in August 1859, to make an anti-slavery speech and look over property that had been pledged to help finance his presidential campaign. That event was to have considerable import for the war effort and the future of transportation in America. As an Illinois legislator, Lincoln became convinced that the nation needed a transcontinental railroad to achieve its Manifest Destiny, and Dodge, with his early training in a two-dollar-a-day surveying job for an Illinois rail line, assured Lincoln he knew the best route. It lay along the 42nd parallel, not a more northern route from St. Paul to Oregon. After the speech, Lincoln found Dodge on the porch of his hotel, where Dodge told him that "nothing was more important than the transcontinental railroad" connecting Iowa and the Midwest to the Pacific coast. Lincoln was taken with Dodge, who "jabbered incessantly about a railroad to the sea." That is almost certainly why Lincoln later overruled the governor about commissioning Dodge, then only twenty-eight years

old. Dodge was to become one of Lincoln's favorite generals. No one
could have predicted his success in the army, although military science
was an element of his engineering studies at Norwich University in Vermont. Suspended from Norwich for misbehavior, he spent a penitential
three months at Vermont's Thetford College in open rebellion against
its cadet uniforms and in brawls to sharpen his boxing and fencing skills.
But something must have rubbed off. Like Grant and Sherman, he could
fight and think. However, unlike them, he was not a one-dimensional
product of the warrior factory at West Point. He became more a Renaissance man like Lincoln, and they shared a trait hardly in keeping with
the historic halo with which Carl Sandburg and other hagiographers
wreathed the sixteenth president. Like the leader he courted and admired, Dodge's eye carried the steady gleam of ambition and always focused on the main chance. His biographer depicts him as a man of his
age—"greedy, ambitious, brave, adventurous and forceful" and, one
might add, unguilty about using any position of public trust for personal
gain.

Adaptability was a cardinal trait of these characters who won the war,
reconstructed the South, and tamed the Midwest and West, and that
explains, to the degree that anything can, how Dodge became a genius
in clandestine intelligence gathering. Serving in 1861 under the flighty
General John C. Frémont on Missouri's chaotic battlefields, the newly
minted colonel wore out his cavalry trying to satisfy Frémont's appetite
for fresh information on Rebel deployments. He quickly recognized that
reconnaissance in force was a mug's game and adopted a subordinate's
suggestion that he send soldiers in civilian clothes to ramble around in
enemy territory. In preparing men for these dangerous—indeed, often
fatal—missions, Dodge virtually invented spycraft as it would be practiced for the next hundred years in the collection of "humint," which has
entered the language as a term of art for covert collection of an enemy's
military or political information.

Dodge did not start out as a particularly kind or sensitive man. At
Thetford, he had thrown a plate of stewed oysters in the face of a "Nig-
gar" waiter he believed to have insulted him. As a commander, he would

order several executions of cowards or spies. But his concern for and instruction of his agents was exquisite, and that extended to agents for the other side. In a celebrated incident that made national headlines, Dodge tried repeatedly to talk Sam Davis, a twenty-one-year-old spy for Braxton Bragg, into avoiding the death sentence by telling what he knew about Bragg's spying operations in Tennessee. By going to the gallows atop his own coffin on November 27, 1863, Davis became a figure in southern folklore, poems, and novels as "The Boy Hero of the Confederacy."

That November was also the month when Dodge received a reward from a grateful president for the successes of 1863. Chattanooga fell on November 25 largely because Dodge had rebuilt the Memphis & Charleston Railroad that Union troops followed into the city. Earlier in the year, Dodge had left the battlefield to protest to Lincoln that Congress was making it impossible for him, Thomas P. Durant, and their investors in the transcontinental railroad to sell securities they needed to finance their ownership. Lincoln agreed to reverse Congress's decision so as to, in effect, subsidize the construction costs of the railroad to the benefit of Dodge's group, and on November 17, 1863, Lincoln announced that the tracks would pass through Council Bluffs on the route surveyed by Dodge.

This payoff was part of the spoils system with which Lincoln was fully comfortable, and it capped a year of espionage-centered accomplishments for Dodge and his military creation, the First Alabama. Their intelligence gathering had been crucial to Grant's success at Vicksburg, the biggest prize for the Union in the Deep South in 1863. But if spying was the theme of their contribution in the year just ending, fighting in the war's defining campaign would be the main business of their next chapter.

The First Fights
of the Fighting First

It took more than a century for the First Alabama's fighting ability to achieve anything approaching official recognition in their home state. *Alabama: The History of a Deep South State,* mentioned earlier, was the first rigorously professional history of the state. Its authors were Leah Rawls Atkins and Wayne Flynt, both professors at Auburn University, and two Alabama-born scholars, William Warren Rogers of Florida State University and Robert David Ward of Georgia Southern University. The book came out in 1994 from the University of Alabama Press, which had done yeoman's work over the years in ignoring or defaming Alabama Unionists. It contained four references to the First Alabama and a fair, if scanty, summary of its record in a single passage: "The regiment fought well in several engagements and its knowledge of the terrain and roads in North Alabama proved invaluable." The passage also noted the service of up to ten thousand former slaves in "Northern regiments," while failing to note that Dodge recruited many of these "Colored Troops" at Corinth while organizing the First Alabama. The work does show fulsome Alabama-ness in treating Streight's Raid as a major event that created a "heroine and a hero" in Emma Sansom and Forrest, the "Wizard of the Saddle." But there are no cheap shots at the Tories. By some standards, a few lines in a 735-page book might seem cursory, but in terms of Alabama scholars reckoning with the facts rather than the legends of its history, the work represented a great leap forward.

I'm proud to say, too, that an alumna of my college, Professor Virginia Van der Veer Hamilton, broke new ground in her concise *Alabama: A History,* perhaps the first book concentrating on the state's history to be published by a house of national reputation since Carmer's *Stars Fell on Alabama.* Noting the revisionist studies of slavery published in the 1960s, she wrote: "Yet in Alabama, where intellectual exchange is not common sport, black and white alike have had little exposure to recent scholarship about the subject which haunts their history most persistently." She devoted 6 of her 189 pages to summing up the impact of Lost Cause doctrine on the emergence of Tory pride in north Alabama during Reconstruction. "Yet as the Confederate legend bloomed with time, that of Alabama Unionists faded from memory and schoolroom history lessons. United Daughters of the Confederacy saw to it that almost every courthouse square in Alabama had its statue of Johnny Reb, rifle in hand, a symbol of which helped convince later generations that the Southern cause went unquestioned in their state." Hamilton called for a revision in the Alabama idiom to mark the nation's two-hundredth birthday so that "it might not seem so heretical to recall this minority of the 1860s as loyalists to the United States rather than as traitors to the South."

Hamilton was writing during the blossoming of biracial progressivism in Alabama and neighboring states in the 1970s. The twin blows of the Reagan Revolution and Trump mania put a stop to the influence of academics, intellectuals, and minority leaders in the state. The current demography-driven Democratic resurgence in Texas and Georgia is at least a generation away in Alabama—two to three generations seem more likely. Today, Alabamians who would agree with Hamilton are in full retreat and have as little influence in Montgomery as progressives did in 1860 and 1960. That said, the Chamber of Commerce and corporate spokesmen, like my critic Will Hill Tankersley, discourage public expressions of racism so as not to damage civil rights tourism in Selma, Birmingham, and Montgomery. In any event, it is too late for conservatives to stop the revisionist tide that has exhumed the military records and reputation of Alabama's "Lincoln loyalists."

The fact that the First received praise in national newspapers even before joining Sherman makes it doubly shocking that no Alabama historian seemed to notice its appearance in the war's leading pro-Lincoln paper, *The New York Times,* in its war digest of August 15, 1863. The paper used boldface type and all caps to highlight its account.

FIRST ALABAMA CAVALRY—Col. George E. Spencer, the commander of the First regiment of Alabama cavalry, is in this City, on a brief leave of absence. The regiment, which is composed entirely of Alabamians and Mississippians, is one of the finest in the Southwest, and has done an extraordinary amount of hard service since its organization. It is now stationed near Corinth, Miss. and is one of the regiments in the command of the late Brig. Gen. CORWYN [*sic*]. There are clergymen, members of the legislature and Southern planters serving as privates in Col. SPENCER's regiment—men who know by experience what the rebel tyranny is, and are willing to spend their life in exterminating it. They are a noble body of soldiers, and have a most accomplished and gallant leader.

The headline on any fair regimental history of the First Alabama would say that it was plunged into hard combat within a few months of its founding and acquitted itself with military efficiency in view of the fact that it received only such training as camp life afforded. As for courage, it obeyed the order to make a charge with unloaded weapons, as will be explained later in this chapter. This jarring tidbit merits a brief aside about the cultural roots of the inherited ferocity of these Alabamians. Two essential works, *Albion's Seed: Four British Folkways in America* by David Hackett Fischer and the less-known *Westering Man: The Life of Joseph Walker* by Bil Gilbert—explore the Scots-Irish tradition that was a dominant strain of the hill country settlers of Alabama. They were part of the great migration of settlers from Britain's "Ulster plantation" in

Northern Ireland that spread from Pennsylvania starting in 1720 down to Alabama and across into Texas by secession. Its hallmarks are Andrew Jackson's deadly temper and fetishistic devotion to honor, on the one hand, and, on the other, the woodland cunning and warrior ethos typified by boundary-pushers like Joseph Walker, a massive six-foot-four-inch Tennessean who became a prototype of the "Mountain Men" of the Rockies and discovered the Yosemite Valley. Forebears like Walker, from the "sprawling Scotch-Irish clans that dominated the American frontier" after arriving in pre-Revolutionary Philadelphia, were hardened for battle by decades of "forest wars" with the Shawnees, Cherokees, and Creeks. Ben Franklin and the peaceful Quakers denounced them as "white savages" upon their arrival and urged them to migrate south through Virginia's Great Valley. Within a few generations, fighting and carving farmsteads from the wilderness produced a raw white tribe with the traits that would be needed for "lying out" in gorges and caves. Gilbert says "they starved, froze, drowned, were burned out . . . stung, poisoned . . . tortured by Indians; went mad, became suicides and drunks, chopped each other up in bloody intramural feuds . . . Toward the beginning of the nineteenth century they got the hang of it"—"it" being living rough to fight hard. They also had a seething Celtic peasant contempt for the Anglophilic gentry of the southern plantation class.

Many historians and works such as W. J. Cash's *The Mind of the South* assert that this cohort provided the obstinate core of southern character and, when war came in 1861, the bellicose spirit of the Rebel infantry. The same traits fitted their cousins, who became Tories of the hills, for Federal service, and the correspondence of Union generals showed they were quick to recognize the value of these unusual volunteers. The First had been in the ranks for only a year when Major General Stephen A. Hurlbut, Dodge's commander, explained in an official dispatch why he was picking this force of 650 men for an extraordinarily daring mission. They were to ride 250 miles through enemy territory to the Alabama capital and destroy the vital railroad linking it to Atlanta, a mission that would not be accomplished for another two years. In the context of the war as it stood in 1862, it would have been a strategic long shot but at the least a stunning symbolic coup. In a report to the War Department, Hurlbut wrote glowingly of the prospects: "Colonel Spencer's regiment is wholly composed of refugees from Alabama. They have been in several engagements and behaved well. They are thoroughly acquainted with the country, well mounted and armed . . . Spencer is certain that he can get through the outer cordon without observation and if he does so, I am satisfied he will make his way to Montgomery."

Another aspect of the mission has eluded most historians. It signified the willingness of Spencer, invariably identified as a scoundrel by southern scholars, to push his Alabamians toward the main stages of the war. Con artist that he may have been, the New Yorker was brave and excelled in bringing his obscure regiment into the orbit of big occasions and important generals. In the event, the First had gone only about forty miles when they stumbled into an unexpected force of two thousand seasoned Confederates, who killed twenty of them and chased the rest back to their encampment near Corinth. The Rebel force was part of an uptick in Confederate activity that threatened Grant's plan to advance on Vicksburg, Mississippi's most important port for troop movement and cotton transport. That threat and Dodge's background as a railroad man prompted Grant to summon him from the field to Corinth so hastily that he reported in his work clothes. He was relieved to see that Grant, typically, was dressed in a similar rough way. Grant offered him command of the Second Division of the Army of the Tennessee. "And I want you to understand that you are not going to command a Division of cowards," Grant said, reflecting the long-standing strain between Grant and the slow-moving Rosecrans. The latter had accused the Second, which was organized by Grant, of "cowardly stampeding" at the Battle of Corinth a few weeks earlier.

In his new command, Dodge quickly added a thousand men in five companies to the two companies originally mustered at Huntsville in July 1862. As for those two companies, they had followed Buell when he shifted his base from Huntsville to Nashville in a move to block Bragg from reaching Chattanooga on his way south from Kentucky. Originally assigned to the First Middle Tennessee Cavalry, these two units kept their Alabama identity and proved to be the most battle-tested units of the emerging First Alabama. The lengths to which William Stanley Hoole, Walter Lynwood Fleming, and Alabama's state-approved textbook went to deny the units' baptism of fire can seem comical, malicious, or a matter of simple ignorance of the pertinent battle records. Hoole resorted to what appears to be sleight-of-hand, saying the units do not appear in "the earliest official" field reports until March 1863. This ignores the fact that the Alabamians, who had been officially designated an independent Alabama unit the previous year, went almost directly into the bloody Battle of Stone's River, which raged from December 31 to January 2, 1862, near Murfreesboro, Tennessee. As the first Alabama Unionists to see combat, they "were actively engaged" against the "powerful raiding force" of Confederates led, ably and furiously, by their Alabama neighbor, General Wheeler.

With armies totaling seventy-six thousand men engaged, the three-day affair had the highest casualty rate—31.5 percent killed, wounded, and missing—of any big Civil War battle other than Gettysburg. It was bloodier than Shiloh or Antietam. This was the Alabamians' first taste of victory, as Bragg was expelled from Murfreesboro and cut off from Chattanooga's back door. A half year later, he'd try the front door at Chickamauga, and the enlarged regiment of Alabama Unionists fought him there, too. Those engagements alone give the lie to characterizations of the hill country volunteers as laggards who shunned combat. There are no libel statutes for history books, but if there were, the depiction of the First Alabama's combat record would meet the newspaper standard defined in the key First Amendment case of *Times v. Sullivan*. That is to say, the First Alabama was depicted with reckless disregard for the truth by writers who knew they were conveying a version of reality that was "false and defamatory."

After Stone's River, the Alabama cavalry was split. The two companies that served with the Tennesseeans were renamed as companies I and K of the First Alabama Cavalry and were assigned as guides to Colonel Abel Streight of the 51st Indiana Infantry in preparation for his raid that summer. The rest of the force was sent to Dodge in the Department of Corinth. It's worth following the two groups separately, if for no other reason than to disprove Hoole's theory that they don't deserve the kind of regimental history accorded virtually every other unit that participated in major battles. Rosecrans's expensive "victory" at Stone's River stalled Lincoln's plan to replace him. So he would remain in command until his career-ending collapse at Chickamauga eight months later. Under intense pressure from Lincoln to move toward Chattanooga, Rosecrans ordered Dodge and Colonel Streight to rendezvous their forces, numbering eight thousand and fifteen hundred effectives respectively, at Tuscumbia, with Dodge to provide mounts for Streight's men. There being a shortage of horses in the theater, Dodge turned over several hundred mules, creating a force that Confederate nostalgists ridicule to this day as the "Jackass Cavalry." Rosecrans's chief of staff, Brigadier General James A. Garfield, the future president, conveyed the daring order that Streight's small force was to speed diagonally across Alabama "to cut the railroads which supply the Rebel army by way of Chattanooga. To accomplish this is the chief object of your expedition." Streight's 51st Indiana would follow its two companies of Alabama guides deep into the legend-haunted and guerilla-infested Sand Mountain country of north central Alabama, the roughest terrain in the state for military operations. Dodge's mission, meanwhile, was to provide diversion so that Streight's raiders could give the slip to General Roddey's small force in the Tennessee Valley and to Forrest's larger command at Spring Hill, Tennessee. Dodge's force included the main body of the First Alabama, the five companies assigned to Florence Cornyn. They were feeling their way eastward along the Tennessee River and the M & C Railroad to lure Forrest away from Streight.

Forrest was not fooled. On April 28, he left Roddey to deal with the Yankees in front of them and took after Streight, whose lot of unhealthy or untrained mules were collapsing under their riders. Forrest had only six hundred men, but they were hard riders mounted on seasoned horses. Forrest caught Streight at Hog Mountain on April 30 for the first of a series of running fights that covered 150 miles and scotched the

Union plan to reach the Western & Atlantic Railroad at Rome, Georgia. With Streight's battered force hunkered down in an Alabama hamlet only twenty-five miles short of Rome, Forrest tricked the foe into thinking he had a superior force by marching his men in a circle past a fixed point within view of the Union position. Streight's staff convinced their reluctant colonel that he had no choice but to surrender on May 3 to save his men from mass execution. No one on either side doubted Forrest was capable of executing a defenseless force, as he would subsequently prove at Fort Pillow in 1864.

Ever since, the story of Streight's surrender has appealed to the Lost Cause appetite for bootless victories. Dr. John Allan Wyeth, a Confederate veteran who in 1881 went on to found the nation's first postgraduate school of medicine in New York, where he trained the Mayo brothers, set the tone of false consequence: "In the brilliant tactics of retreat and stubbornness in defense on the one side, and the desperate bravery and relentlessness in pursuit upon the other," this event "has no analogue in military history." The military grading scale of Lost Cause writers reflected Dr. Wyeth's estimate with ever more fulsome and gleeful accounts of Forrest's victory. For example, in his official state-financed textbook, the ever-reliable glorifier of Rebels, Charles Summersell, devoted three pages and a map to the subject while failing to mention General Mitchel's tide-turning capture of Huntsville. Colonel Streight did one thing right in his surrender negotiations with Forrest. He made the Confederate general promise to treat the First Alabama cavalry as prisoners of war rather than executing them on the spot as traitors.

Militarily, with Forrest tied up with his passel of Union prisoners, Dodge was conducting business of far greater consequence on the other side of Alabama, another indication that big-picture analysis was never a strength of pro-Confederate writers. After launching Streight's mission, Dodge undertook his own Alabama "expedition" from April 15 to May 2, as ordered by Rosecrans. His infantry marched for two hundred miles and his cavalry, the First Alabama, covered four hundred miles; they "fought six successful engagements, driving the enemy, 3,000 strong, from Bear Creek to Decatur taking the towns of Tuscumbia and

Florence, with a loss not to exceed 100, including 3 officers. Destroyed 1,500,000 bushels of corn, besides large quantities of oats, rye, and fodder, and 500,000 pounds of bacon." His men captured 150 prisoners, 1,000 head of horses and mules and 100 bales of cotton, destroyed miles of railroad and 60 transport boats, followed by a few days of mop-up operations in Mississippi. In a letter to his commander, Major General Hurlbut, he concluded that he and his men "rendered useless the garden spot of Alabama for at least one year."

For decades, Alabama historians did not bother to dig out—or, at least, repeat—a key line from Dodge's report about his multi-state force: "The fighting of the cavalry was excellent. The Tenth Missouri, Seventh Kansas, Fifteenth Illinois, and First Alabama all did themselves credit, they invariably drove the enemy, no matter what their force." That set a pattern of the First getting high grades from generals. Early the next year, a commander from Ohio praised them for fighting against Forrest's troops near Memphis. Another detachment of Alabamians serving under General Morgan L. Smith caught the New Yorker's eye: "The loyal Alabamians are invaluable and exceed in number and are equal in zeal to anything we discovered [among Unionists] in Tennessee." As for courage, Smith knew whereof he spoke. General Sherman said of him, "He was one of the bravest men in action I ever knew."

William Stanley Hoole had to look hard for evidence that these Alabamians were "half-hearted comrades" to the Yankees they served among, and he was able to find a solid speck of it in the battle report filed by Colonel Cornyn on May 16, contradicting Dodge's report of the same action that was filed on May 5. I've been unable to find evidence that the two men discussed the matter, although it is known that Dodge admired his colleague and was upset when Cornyn died under most peculiar circumstances. On the second day of Dodge's movement toward Alabama, the aggressive "Defender of North Alabama," Roddey, invaded Mississippi and wedged his force between Dodge's infantry and Cornyn's cavalry. In his official report on the engagement, Dodge wrote, "Colonel Cornyn, hearing firing in the rear, immediately fell back, and with the First Alabama Cavalry, charged the rebels and retook the [just-captured] artillery and caissons . . . The charge of the Alabamians with muskets only, and those not loaded, is credible, especially as they are all new recruits and poorly drilled. In this charge, Captain Cameron, the commanding officer of the Alabama Cavalry, a deserving and much-lamented officer, was killed." Dodge's infantry, arriving on the scene, "opened a heavy and destructive fire, which caused the rebels to fall back in confusion, utterly routed."

Cornyn put things differently in a report designed to cover up a serious blunder on his part. After leading his force out of Corinth, he had let his artillery caissons fall two miles behind his horsemen, creating the gap into which Roddey's "flying rebels" charged. Cornyn had stopped to rest the horses when the sounds of battle and a messenger alerted him that his guns had been captured. "I immediately ordered the First Alabama Cavalry, Captain Cameron, to move down the road to our rear and attack the rebels, and recapture, if possible, the guns." Dispatching additional cavalry from Missouri and Illinois to follow the First Alabama, Cornyn himself "moved out on the road, and soon came in sight of the enemy, with the two guns, when I ordered a charge by the First Alabama Cavalry, which I am sorry to say, was not obeyed with the alacrity it should have been. After charging to within short musket-range of the enemy, they halted for some cause I cannot account for." The enemy then wheeled around, killing Cameron and inflicting losses that happened because the First Alabama "had desisted from the charge." Cornyn's report fit the timeless pattern of line officers dodging blame, but if Dodge's report was correct, the Alabamians probably "desisted from the charge" when they came within "short musket-range," as Cornyn put it, for the very good reason that their guns were not loaded. By his own admission, Cornyn had already let some of his artillerymen run out of ammunition that day, which was a factor in creating the disastrous gap in his column.

Writing of these events almost a century later, Hoole used Cornyn's report of the "first brief but inglorious foray of the First Alabama" as the cornerstone of his argument that theirs was a record of generalized incompetence with shaming episodes of outright cowardice. He cited a

Confederate report that for several days stragglers were "still being caught over the countryside—all from the First Alabama Tory Regiment." Clearly the two companies of cavalry of the First, with their unloaded guns, had taken a licking early in a two-hour engagement in which their Union comrades arrived on the scene and eventually forced Roddey to withdraw. Word of Cornyn's accusation filtered up the chain of command. Commenting from nearby Iuka, Mississippi, Sherman grumbled that the "erratic Alabama regiment of ours, which had gone off on some recruiting or other errand" had been "worsted." But Sherman commented without knowing Dodge's overall plan or the eventual outcome of Dodge's seventeen-day Alabama expedition.

For his part, Dodge never lost faith in the Alabamians or departed from his habit of defending them. Both he and Spencer liked the fact that they were motivated by vengeance and wanted to "extract more than the usual toll" from the enemy. "All of this and more made the First Alabama distinctively useful to Dodge and Spencer," according to Spencer's biographer, Stanford historian Terry L. Seip. "Their chief value was that they knew the country and the mentalities of the enemy, a good rationale, of course, for using them on the more dangerous incursions into Confederate territory and to put them out front as was later the case with William Tecumseh Sherman's march through Georgia." Dodge never wavered from his view that "these mountain men were fearless and would take all chances." That probably prompted General Hurlbut to select Colonel Spencer and his men for a mission toward Montgomery that was even more audacious than Streight's Raid. With only 650 men, they were to head for Montgomery, 250 miles away, to destroy the West Point Railroad, which connected the Alabama capital with Columbus, Georgia. This would disrupt the roundabout way by which Bragg had finally succeeded in moving his troops to Chattanooga and by which he was supplying them for another showdown with Rosecrans. Only forty miles outside Corinth, the Alabamians ran into two thousand Confederates under Brigadier General Samuel Ferguson on October 26. "I have succeeded in effectually destroying the First Alabama Tory Regiment," Ferguson exulted after the Alabamians broke ranks and fled into the woods they knew well. This forced Ferguson to dial back his report a bit. "The chase was kept up for some 10 miles through dense woods and over a mountainous country until dark. Their perfect knowledge of the [terrain] enabled most of them, however, to escape by separating into small squads and leaving the road."

The rout, in which the five companies lost only eight men, served as a kind of rite of passage for those who had missed the vicious fighting at Stone's River. In order to separate the Alabama troops from the large number of refugees encamped near them at Glendale, they were moved to a new camp in Corinth proper. "It looked more like an immigrant train than a regiment of soldiers," Ohio-born Sergeant Major Francis Wayland Dunn said of the move. Nonetheless, a regimental order insisted that "all women must leave this camp at once; a man cannot do his duty as a soldier and keep house at the same time." Other orders called for instruction in dismounted fighting, increased drilling, and tighter military order for mountain men who never became amenable to being bossed. But the clampdown worked to the extent that it toughened them for campaigning with Sherman. The war-loving general who had called them "erratic" would in less than two years defend them from criticism that they were too ferocious in pursuing his plan to "make Georgia howl."

A clue to what Dodge thought of Cornyn's leadership in the battle of April 17 may be found in the fact that two days later, the First was removed from Cornyn's brigade and transferred to that of Colonel Moses M. Bane, whose Illinois infantry had saved Cornyn's cavalry on that day. As for Cornyn, his fate, like that of so many soldiers in this war, provides a bundle of fascinating loose ends. In August 1863, he and a fellow officer, Lieutenant Colonel William D. Bowen, were being jointly court-martialed at Corinth over charges each filed against the other during an earlier feud over promotions. Just outside the courtroom, Cornyn slapped Bowen in the face, and Bowen pulled his pistol and shot Cornyn dead. Bowen was kicked out of the army, but after the war he became a St. Louis police commissioner and arrested one of Missouri's most ferocious bushwhackers. After Cornyn's death, Lieutenant Colonel Frederick Benteen became the commander of the 10th Missouri Cavalry. Like many Union officers, he accepted a reduced rank to stay on duty as a captain in the famed 7th Cavalry's war against the Sioux and Cheyenne. If his name is familiar, it is because he was accused of moving too slowly to rescue General George Armstrong Custer at the Battle of Little Big Horn. The charges were debatable and his identification of Custer's corpse provided a memorable punctuation to Custer's hubristic blunder. Sighting the general among the 7th Cavalry corpses at Little Big Horn, Benteen blurted, "By God, that is him."

The Civil War was not just a matter of brother against brother. It was also a conflict in which Alabama neighbors found themselves facing one another, first in places like Red Bay, Alabama, and Stone's River, Tennessee, and then in more famous battles to come. It was also a war in which improbable friendships stretched across the political divide, sometimes in poignant ways. For example, "Fighting Joe" Wheeler's Connecticut-born father sent him to the Episcopal Academy in Cheshire, Connecticut, a prep school where one of his classmates was J. P. Morgan. After the war, Morgan advised Wheeler on his industrial investments in rapidly developing Birmingham. When Wheeler died in New York City in 1906, Morgan was an honorary pallbearer, as was John Jacob Astor. It's a reminder that whether we're talking wartime cotton stealing in the Old South or smokestacks in the New South, the business of America was always business.

20

Partners: A Meeting of the Minds

In the years I've spent uncovering operational details about the First Alabama, Colonel George Eliphaz Spencer, U.S.A., and Brigadier General Philip Dale Roddey, C.S.A., have become my two favorite supporting characters in the entire war. They are grand rascals on the scale of Union general Dan Sickles, the self-promoting New Yorker who after his leg was severed at Gettysburg had the limb delivered to the Smithsonian. He waved, cigar in hand, as stretcher-bearers carried him from the battlefield. The more I learned about the odd couple of Spencer and Roddey, the more fascinated I became about a partnership that lasted from 1863, when Spencer talked his way into Roddey's enemy encampment, until 1893, when Spencer died in reduced circumstances (Roddey would die four years later in London after a bizarre final act). George Spencer, born in 1836, was younger by ten years than Roddey. Hailing from vastly different social backgrounds, they were perfectly cast for an era not unlike our own, a fermenting time offering occasional glimpses of heroic purpose but replete with every kind of masculine folly, political malice, and dollar-driven venality.

I have to think that when Spencer "charmed" Confederate pickets on April 11, 1863, and rode into Roddey's headquarters camp at Tuscumbia, Alabama, that Roddey must have recognized a rising talent in the international brotherhood of brazen con artists. I like to think of them sizing each other up as they stood outside Roddey's tent that spring day on the greening southern bank of the Tennessee, fellow voyagers on that universal river of tireless ambition and opportunistic self-interest. I picture them, two bulky men in their prime, as they must have appeared to each other, Spencer with his round, boyish face ending in a straggly goatee and Roddey with narrowed, appraising eyes under a hard, bushy brow that in surviving photographs looks almost simian.

Before moving on with their fascinating story—and any attempt to solve the multiple mysteries it entails—I invite the reader to meditate with me on the differences in reportage about living persons and rescuing the lives of public figures from the deadening touch of surviving documents. One of the first things I learned about political reporting was that the best stories the statehouse reporters knew never made it into the paper—"best" being defined as most illuminating, most entertaining, most humorous, and most revealing as to the character of the people who made our laws. Those stories were shared in saloons and in that vast archive of newsroom stories regarded as "too good to check out" or as insider jokes considered too frivolous for a serious newspaper. With the simple goal of sharing with my readers the political intel I found most interesting in covering Alabama and Georgia politics early in my career, I developed a backfilling technique, whereby I would take grapevine buzz and check it out for facts that were fit to print. There usually was a hard kernel of truth behind most rumors, gossip, folklore, and bar stories told for laughs wherever candidates, campaign operatives, and reporters got together. Making such information publishable under standard newspaper rules usually involved a sifting of circumstantial evidence, and that is where talking to people rather than reading about them shines a light on the defining difference between riveting journalism and even very good history writing: the kind of illuminating detail that drops out of the latter.

For example, consider an often-reported fact that has made its way into many books on Alabama's twentieth-century political history—that the Ku Klux Klan supported John Patterson's winning campaign for

Alabama governor in 1954 but switched in 1962, making George Wallace the victor and ending Patterson's elective career. That's true, as far as it goes, but some details won't be found in the polling results or in any single newspaper account. For example, Patterson told me what the Klan endorsement meant to a campaign in practical terms: an additional five thousand people to distribute bumper stickers. Wallace got them to switch by promising Imperial Wizard Robert Shelton the franchise to sell Goodyear tires to the Alabama state troopers. According to Robert Chambliss, mastermind of the Sixteenth Street Church bombing, Wallace also promised to pay for a deep-sea fishing trip for Chambliss and his bumper-sticker crew from the 1962 campaign. Chambliss claimed Wallace reneged on the fishing trip after the old Klansman surfaced as a bombing suspect. We know that by that time both Shelton and Wallace's highway patrol chief, Colonel Al Lingo, had assured the governor that Chambliss led the four-man crew that bombed the church on September 15, 1963, killing four Black girls. Bombing investigators told me fifteen years later that Chambliss had come to hate Wallace for snubbing him when Chambliss tried to introduce his wife to the governor at a conservative political rally at Birmingham's Redmont Hotel. Yet when I interviewed Chambliss at Kilby Prison in 1982, Chambliss was certain that the newly reelected Wallace would pardon him for murdering eleven-year-old Denise McNair, one of the four girls who died at Sixteenth Street. From Chambliss's point of view, it was not a totally irrational hope. He remembered that one of Wallace's first acts as governor was to pardon the Klansmen who kidnapped and castrated Judge Aaron, a randomly selected Black man.

I know about this web of connectivity through a lifetime of personal experience and journalistic investigation. This kind of vivifying detail is not readily available in historical accounts, but I felt this was one of those occasions when my newspapering skills of cross-analysis and reading between the lines were an asset. They gave me a feel as to how Spencer and Roddey, these brothers under the skin, found each other across the blue/gray divide. There is little eyewitness evidence about the illicit cotton trade that Lincoln expected to amount to $50 million with

England alone. But the fact that Roddey and Spencer each ended the war with enough capital to start investment careers bespeaks a battlefield arrangement that seemed highly commercial and even slightly treasonous. The *Official Records* documented that they often met under flags of truce as their respective regiments tracked each other across northern Mississippi and Alabama and southwestern Tennessee, skirmishing often. And there are enough mentions of captured cotton in the *Official Records* to make one suspect a commerce-based coordination between who captured, or bypassed, baled cotton on any given day. Then I found what one needs as a keystone of any dot-connecting reconstruction: a hard fact of indisputable authority.

In the first three months of 1862, General Dodge, settling into this new command, sent the First Alabama under Spencer on a series of scouting missions involving up to 150 men on ride-abouts of three to five days in length. He was preparing for a military excursion into the breadbasket of Alabama, the vast grain fields along the Tennessee River. In 1911, Dodge published a memoir of his campaign up the Tennessee Valley that is remarkable for its candor. "To ascertain what enemy I would have to meet, I sent my chief of staff, [then] Captain George E. Spencer, a very competent officer who was a genius in getting inside of the enemy's lines, with a communication to General P. D. Roddey, who had returned to Tuscumbia and was in command of the rebel forces south of the Tennessee River. I told Captain Spencer that the communication was an important one and he must not deliver it to anyone except General Roddey; that he must impress upon the officer on the enemy's picket line that he must take him to General Roddey and in that way he would be able to determine very closely what forces I would have to meet. Captain Spencer went prepared to do this. He met the picket officer; they became very chummy, and the officer took Captain Spencer right through all of the enemy's forces between Bear [Creek] and Tuscumbia, and he delivered the message to General Roddey, who was in great anger at this officer; but they made the best of it. After the war, Captain Spencer and General Roddey were great friends and I believe partners in some business."

Dodge's comment that they "made the best of it" is another of the war's great understatements. Whether through instinct or luck, he had brought about a melding of like minds. Spencer and Roddey were the kind of thrusting men who, upon learning that the powers that be are going to have a war, were determined to be part of it, and not just for patriotic purposes. In that respect, they remind me of a pair of nineteenth-century Milo Minderbinders, to invoke the name of Joseph Heller's GI entrepreneur in *Catch-22*. Milo, of course, seemed little interested in military outcomes, whereas both Spencer and Roddey were determined to sharpen their military and spying talents. These traits they had in common despite their very different backgrounds. Roddey had come from nowhere, born poor in Moulton, a town that marked the dividing point between the peons of the hardscrabble hill counties like Winston and the Virginia-connected masters of the lush river-bordering plantations that spanned upper Alabama from border to border. He found work as a tailor, gained a foothold as a sheriff, then made money with a riverboat he burned, bitterly, when Yankee gunboats arrived in Muscle Shoals in 1862. He had been a solid Unionist until he lost his business. Switching sides, he soon proved himself as a pirate on horseback, a "captain" of guerillas tormenting Unionist homesteads. Confederate officials recognized an untutored but ruthless talent, made him a real captain, and gave him first a company, then several companies, then a regimental colonelcy under Forrest. He became a cavalryman general every bit as formidable as "Fighting Joe" Wheeler, the West Pointer also born in 1836 a few miles east of Moulton. The hard-to-please Forrest relied on him, and Braxton Bragg regarded him as "invaluable."

By comparison, Spencer had an easy life, though never lacked fire in the belly. He was born in upstate New York to a surgeon father who sent him to Montreal for college and to Watertown, Iowa, for the legal education that enabled his swift rise in Iowa's patronage politics. He was always hungry for money and even took a fling at gold mining in Colorado before the war. General Dodge, a political crony from Des Moines, recognized his gift for infiltration. True to form, Dodge did not want to undertake his Alabama expedition without adequate intelligence. Next

to gold, baled cotton was the most valuable medium of international exchange available to both presidents. "Generally, Confederate president
Jefferson Davis looked the other way out of necessity, whereas Lincoln
looked the other way out of policy," wrote historian Philip Leigh in
2014's *Trading with the Enemy.* "Unfortunately, the lucrative profits
available in cotton trade inevitably subjected the permitting process to
influences of political favoritism that invited bribery and other forms of
corruption. Lincoln would later complain that if an intelligent angel
were to observe White House conversations, 'I think he would come to
the conclusion that this war is being prosecuted for obtaining cotton
from the South for Northern cotton mills.'"

Fastidious men like Grant, Sherman, and Stanton raged against the
legalized larceny throughout the war, but Lincoln personally assigned
permits for forty people, including some openly corrupt cronies. As
with any wartime black market, precise figures and conclusive evidence
are hard to come by. Suffice it to say that up to two million 400-pound
bales went from southern battle zones to northern and European buyers
at prices up to $1.90 per pound. It is known reliably that Major General
Ben Butler, the ringmaster of the New Orleans cotton syndicates, increased his net worth from $150,000 in 1862 to $3 million in 1868. Indeed, every general officer except Sherman who commanded the First
was touched, if not tainted, by the cotton trade. It was important to
Dodge because he used cotton sales to finance his spy ring and because
his notoriously crooked partner in developing the Union Pacific railroad, Thomas C. Durant, used cotton profits to capture control of the
railroad's stock. Researchers for a PBS documentary on Durant concluded flatly that "he had made a fortune smuggling contraband cotton
from the Confederate states with the aid of Grenville Dodge." Dodge
tried to create an impression of purity by claiming to Grant that he had
turned down a $200,000 bribe to move cotton through his lines for the
Jewish brokers Grant was trying to run out of Memphis.

Neither the trickle-down nor the trickle-up would have worked without men like George Spencer and Philip Roddey. They came into the
war willing to risk being killed in order to make a killing, and they merit

our attention because the First Alabama was so central to their connection. In 1861 and 1862, Spencer moved around the war like a man circling a Monopoly board. At the time of Fort Sumter he was working in Dodge's banking and real estate firm, but "I am d——d tired of it I would like some active service of some kind, and would not object to a guerilla warfare anything for excitement or that would pay." A patronage appointment as a supply-selling sutler for a new Nebraska regiment got him to Memphis; there, facing the draft, he applied for a staff position with Dodge, now a brigadier general in Corinth. "I have got over being ambitious and only want to situate myself pleasantly and would serve your interests with fidelity," he wrote in August 1862, and Dodge, in a pattern that would last the rest of their lives, responded helpfully, with an important post as his assistant adjutant general with the rank of captain. What Seip called his "never-abated ambition, now to win reputation and glory" kicked in.

Most assistant adjutant generals settled into desk jobs as the corresponding secretaries of their commanders. Spencer pushed for field assignments, studied cavalry tactics, and began leading his corps of Alabamians on intelligence-gathering forays into Confederate territory. Meanwhile, Alabama's politicians and nervous Tennessee River planters had blocked Richmond's effort to transfer Roddey to Virginia. He and his force of twelve hundred to two thousand men roamed the valley, headquartering as far east as Huntsville or Decatur when they were periodically pulled out by the Union for tactical reasons. Dodge and Roddey began meeting under truce flags in places like Glendale, Mississippi, allegedly to discuss prisoner exchanges. "The relationship, which seems to have taken on a 'respected adversary' tone, continued into the immediate postwar period when Roddey apparently assisted Spencer in his cotton-buying operations in Alabama and even extended into Nevada mining operations in the 1880s," Seip found.

The fact that both men had significant money to invest at the end of the war suggests they had been splitting cotton proceeds during their meetings. Records of troop movements show there were ample opportunities for them to leave cotton bales about for capture by the chosen partner. For a while, Spencer was conveniently based in Athens, Alabama, allowing for "skirmishes" with Roddey in his role as northern Alabama's roving "defender." On at least one occasion, Spencer spent the night in Roddey's quarters at Decatur when the town was briefly back under Confederate control. It's hard to find examples of two senior officers on opposing armies having a more congenial time enjoying what the British call "a good war." And for Spencer, there was plenty of time for romance and politics. Late in 1862, Spencer went to Washington to get General-in-Chief Henry Halleck to approve payments owed him during his sutler days by dead soldiers from Nebraska. "Halleck runs the machine here now, and has everything his own way," Spencer wrote Dodge in their familiar way. He lobbied Halleck to promote Dodge to major general. Spencer "took special pains to give him extra good opinion of you." He added that the top general "is a peculiar man & I know how to handle him." Spencer's self-confidence often veered into grandiosity, and sometimes it's hard to blame him. He spent Christmas in the East, acquiring a wife in twenty-two-year-old Bella Zilfa of Philadelphia, a lively, accomplished novelist born in England. The newlyweds spent the winter of 1863 with General and Mrs. Dodge in Corinth. Spencer liked literary women; Zilfa died young, and in 1877 Spencer made a glamorous marriage to a well-known actress, "May" Nunez, who wrote novels under the name William Loring Nunez. She was named after her uncle, Confederate general William Loring, renowned for colorful postwar service as military adviser to the Khedive of Egypt. Spencer was never one to let political labels spoil an opportunity for a flashy connection.

I cannot find a document that categorically proves that Spencer and Roddey were splitting cotton proceeds during their truce-flag and spend-the-night meetings. However, there is no lack of documentation for the commercial climate in which those meetings occurred. Spencer had to know that Dodge was enabling his Union Pacific partner Thomas P. Durant in his epic cotton deals. Moreover, immediately after the war ended, Spencer boasted of his partnership with an even more audacious cotton thief, Rhode Island governor (later senator) William Sprague, a principal in the Matamoros Cotton Ring. Sprague's ownership of a blockade-running ship operating out of the Mexican port eventually resulted in nine treason charges, but his political connections and those of his father-in-law, former treasury secretary Salmon P. Chase, protected him from prosecution. Indeed, Chase in his role in Lincoln's cabinet had been a major booster of the "belligerent cotton trade." Spencer's First Alabama connection came into play with the new Andrew Johnson administration. He promoted William Hugh Smith to be Reconstruction governor of Alabama. As a resident of Russell County, on the southern fringe of the hill country, Smith was a main recruiter for the First Alabama and as a colonel joined it on Sherman's March. "If we can get Smith [appointed] we can control the state without trouble," Spencer wrote Dodge, who was still awaiting his discharge. "When you get out of the army I wish you would come south and operate. We are bound to succeed ultimately and if we can't any other way we can by 'Negro Suffrage.' I have been figuring with the radicals and I think I am in the ring. As I am in business with Gov. Sprague I can get his and the [Salmon P.] Chase influence & expect when Congress meet to knock this Provisional Governor system higher than a kite."

These sentences are easy to unpack if you know the political context. Spencer would succeed in organizing the vote of ex-slaves to make Smith Alabama's first elected governor during Reconstruction when the period of "provisional governments" ended in 1868. Whenever Spencer and Roddey began their cotton business, it was fully matured in the first months after Appomattox, and cotton was the text and subtext of his letters to Dodge as he reported that Tuscaloosa, having been protected by Roddey up until the very end of the war, was now their hub. "I have bought a lot of cotton there and now return with money to finish paying for it. I ought to make at least fifty thousand dollars but shall be satisfied with half that amount." Helped by Roddey and financed by Sprague, Spencer had a quarter share in a thousand bales at 28 cents a pound that would pass through Mobile and sell in New York at 60 cents a pound.

The final price is not known, but Bella Spencer wrote General Dodge's wife, Anna, in January 1866 that her husband was "well satisfied with his venture."

As for the progress of the war, 1863 proved a stepping-off point for further adventures for the duo of Spencer and Roddey. In that year, the attention of their respective armies shifted east, to Chattanooga and Atlanta. The first phase of the war in the Deep South states had revolved around Vicksburg and the M & C Railroad. In its final phase, they would be widely separated. Wheeler, not Roddey, would be the Confederate cavalryman most frequently in front of Sherman in Georgia. After the fall of Atlanta, Roddey and Forrest would fail together, disastrously, in front of Nashville and the last Confederate arsenal at Selma. Later in this book, we will return to their roles in the war's last act and how they achieved notoriety in later years through political and financial scandals. Indeed, given Spencer's powerful role in the Grant administration and spectacular newspaper coverage of Roddey's Manhattan divorce, it seems odd that their novelistic adventures faded quickly from public awareness. On the other hand, the stories of the Alabama mountaineers they either led or fought in battle would have disappeared altogether but for the meticulous pick-and-shovel research of the obscure historians who stayed on the trail of the First Alabama.

In Praise of Amateur Historians

I WAS LATE all the way round when it came to *First Alabama Cavalry, U.S.A.: Homage to Patriotism*. Glenda McWhirter Todd published it in 1999. Even though it was footnoted here and there, I did not get around to ordering it from Amazon until 2017. Then the author died on September 3, 2017, before I could contact her. I was slow in acquiring the book for another reason. By the time it came out, I had gathered a lot of information about the First Alabama to feed my imagination, and I was still fixated on the idea of writing a novel about it as a sequel to *Whiskey Man*. That first novel had been good to me. The substantial sale of paperback rights was the first real money I ever saw. By 2017, the movie option I had signed with an accomplished Hollywood producer had lapsed, but I still saw the Winston County story in novelistic and cinematic terms. I would portray my protagonist in the new novel as the grandfather and namesake of the Depression-era narrator in *Whiskey Man*, Brant Laster. I saw the name as evocative, in that outlasting adversity seemed to me the essence of the mountain Unionist experience. Then I went through a period of thinking I would footnote the novel with extensive notations about the real events that inspired the story. Luckily, my bright agent, Rob McQuilken, nixed this as the bad idea that it was, and we shifted our efforts to this book.

Digging into Glenda McWhirter Todd's book, I soon recognized what this tireless amateur historian and genealogist had accomplished. In my day at *The New York Times*, we were forbidden to refer to any news event as "unprecedented" for the good reason that one might have forgotten something or missed something or, in any event, lacked the divine omniscience to declare any human event a "first." So I'm not saying no one else has ever given the *Official Records of the War of the Rebellion* such a thorough plowing.

I'll just say *Homage* was an eye-opener for me, and I take its inclusion in the bibliographies of the most significant works to emerge in the twenty-first century as part of the renewed scholarship on southern Unionism as a sign that it has been useful to other modern trackers of the First Alabama. The book begins charmingly and speaks for thousands of southerners disfranchised by Alabama's state-sponsored policy of disowning these veterans who did not fall for slave owners' propaganda and joined the Yankee army.

> Several years ago, a friend asked me to join the United Daughters of the Confederacy. My response to her was something like this, "Sure, no problem, my great, great grandfather, Andrew Ferrier McWhirter, from Marion County, Alabama was in the Civil War," thus inaugurating the quest for my heritage. Much to my surprise (and dismay, I might add), I found him buried in the Nashville National Cemetery along with one of his sons, nineteen-year-old George Washington McWhirter. A few months later, I was able to discover the fact that another son, Thomas A. McWhirter, also joined the First Alabama Cavalry Volunteer Union army, was captured and held prisoner several times but lived to return home to north Alabama where he faced the wrath and persecution of his southern neighbors. . . .
>
> The few books that had been written about the First Regiment, Alabama Volunteer Cavalry, U.S. were written by Confederate sympathizers and were not very kind to the Union cause and had portrayed these Unionists as "hill people," "poor, often un-

derprivileged people who had been isolated on their rocky high-lands," etc.

The more I studied these men and their cause, the more deter-mined I became to "tell their story" to the world and it is a story that is long overdue. Rather than being the cowards that some had portrayed them, they were brave men who stated their grand-fathers fought too hard and suffered too much during the Revolu-tionary War for them to turn against their country and they refused to fire on "Old Glory," the flag of their forefathers.

With her first sentences as a writer, Todd destroyed William Stanley Hoole's thesis that the First Alabama lacked military significance. If her prose lacks professional polish, the book's 161 pages of text deliver a previously unavailable company-by-company chronology and impor-tant battlefield diaries and profiles. The survey of company postings shows that, far from being a lethargic unit, the regiment was split among important Union generals posted across three states—the Alabama river towns; Union garrisons in Memphis, Nashville, and Rome, Georgia; and all along Sherman's route of march in Georgia and the Carolinas. Todd also compiled a 243-page roster with original biographical nota-tions to be found nowhere else.

Every time I read her modest obituary in the *Tullahoma News*, I rep-rimand myself for not interviewing her. She provides a classic example of a dedicated amateur outdoing professional academics in the basic work of historiographic digging. No doubt her long career at the State of Tennessee Department of Employment Security Office gave her both the research skills and patience needed for her avocational career. The obituary states that she was born in Knoxville and "moved to Tullahoma in her young-adult years and immediately called it home. She worked at the State of Tennessee Department of Employment Security Office in Tullahoma for 30-plus years, where she could do what she loved in help-ing other people find meaningful employment . . . She was also an avid historian and genealogist, and she is best known for her research and her published works regarding the 1st Alabama Cavalry, U.S.A. Her research and books have touched thousands of people over the last two decades."

Her combing of enlistment records showed that sixteen members of the First Alabama were listed as "colored" and served in the ranks rather than being restricted to menial tasks. The website she helped maintain noted that "at least one [Black] man was wounded in action and another was killed while enlisted as troopers in the 1st Alabama Cavalry." Todd provided information to the U.S. Department of Veterans Affairs that led in 2009 to a regulation army stone marker being put on the grave in Decatur, Alabama, of Amos McKinney, an ex-slave who served in the First Alabama.

In her interpretive passages, Glenda McWhirter Todd celebrated the contrarian heritage of the family's Scots-Irish settlers and the Jacksonian patriotism of the hill counties. To a marked degree, these are general traits of the rural white southerners who were not among the slave-owning class, which was estimated to include ten thousand families in eleven states. As commentators like W. J. Cash, C. Vann Woodward, and David Hackett Fischer have observed, this yeoman class of farmers who worked their own fields had a natural insolence, a resistance to discipline coupled with an anti-aristocratic insouciance. As Cash noted, Confederate soldiers said "Cap'n" and "Gin-ral" with an ironic sneer and were as likely to jeer the fastidious Stonewall as to salute him. These excellent fighting men had to be cajoled, not commanded, and that was the colossal political stupidity embodied by the Confederate Conscription Act, which essentially said, "You are commanded to fight for a class of men who think they are better than you."

By 1863, these hill country qualities had begun to erode, on a broad regional scale, the initial enthusiasm for secession. The almost simultaneous defeat of Lee at Gettysburg and Grant's victory at Vicksburg in July 1863 marked the beginning of the end of what historians call "Confederate nationalism" and majority public support for the war among southern whites. For the rest of the war Davis's government and the southern press would have to battle the viral spread of defeatism among civilians as fiercely as the overmatched southern armies were battling the invaders. Throughout 1863, Alabama would remain a sideshow, but a much more vigorous one than might be imagined from reading the main popular histories of the war.

For one thing, all of northern Alabama and the cluster of counties bordering Florida were caught up on a vicious and virtually unremitting "war within the war" involving a motley mix of regular forces, freelancing partisan guerillas and, as 1863 gave way to 1864, ferocious bands of apolitical pirates on horseback. Lost Cause historians who had played down the systematic atrocities against Unionist homesteads throughout 1862 would never forgive the successful retaliatory violence inflicted by Unionist troops and the mixed bands of blue-coated troops, the deserters, and draft dodgers that emerged across the Appalachian South. Christopher Lyle McIlwain Sr., a full-time attorney in Tuscaloosa, summed up this horrific period in his revisionist masterwork *Civil War Alabama,* published in 2016, with chapter titles like "The Hard War" and "Horrors of the Black Flag." McIlwain has published so vigorously over the past twenty-five years that it seems a misnomer to list him as an amateur, but his deep research, like that of Glenda Todd McWhirter, testifies to how much research the PhDs have left undone. McIlwain set out specifically to rebut the "deeply engrained myth" promulgated by Walter L. Fleming, and his 435 pages amount to a root-and-branch dismantling of Fleming's 1905 classic *Civil War and Reconstruction.* Amazingly, *Civil War Alabama* is the first book ever to take on Fleming's falsifications, which McIlwain charitably dismisses as "spurious logic." He blows the whistle on how Fleming purposely "downplayed the extent and quality of Unionist sentiment" so as to create the "deeply engrained myth" of monolithic Confederate loyalty in Alabama. McIlwain documents that the First Alabama was so much the focus of opposition that in early 1864 General Dodge could report that Union troops and Unionist residents "hold the mountain district in spite of all efforts of the rebels to catch them. I know of several companies of at least 100 men, each led by our scouts and members of the First Alabama Cavalry." McIlwain deals with the contention of other Alabama-connected historians that the regiment was peripheral to the main events of the war by his initial reference to it as "a unit that conducted numerous military operations for the Union during the war."

"Hard war" is an appropriate term for the blue-coat Alabamians' introduction to the more rigorous training and harsher discipline they experienced under Dodge and Spencer starting in 1863, events totally ignored by Fleming and his acolytes at the University of Alabama. The Alabamians turned up frequently in dispatches to and from Grant and Sherman. Although Lincoln had fully endorsed the more forceful tactics of this rising generation of commanders in the West in ending the "soft war" regime of Buell and Rosecrans, even he bridled at Dodge's brutal handling of a pitiable First Alabama private named Alex J. Johnson. He enlisted on June 1, 1863, was assigned to guard duty around the Glendale encampment, and deserted in less than three weeks. Shortly thereafter, some of Dodge's pickets were mysteriously killed, causing him to suspect that someone had told the enemy about their routines. On July 18, Johnson was apprehended with a band of Rebels near the camp. Dodge ordered an immediate "drumhead court martial" with intention, according to a subordinate officer, that "the wretch should die before the President should have time to pardon or commute." It sometimes happened that hill country Unionists, captured while visiting their homes, were enlisted into the Confederate army at gunpoint, but Johnson did not get the benefit of such doubts, nor apparently did any of his fellow troops think he deserved it.

Dodge wanted an elaborate show, assembling five thousand men in an open-sided square. An ambulance rolled into the arena with Johnson seated on his coffin. Then, with four men carrying the coffin, he was paraded around inside of the square on foot, followed by a brass band playing dirges and a twelve-man firing squad chosen from the First Alabama. Glenda McWhirter Todd discovered that the local newspaper covered the event. "At precisely 23 minutes past nine," the *Daily Corinthian* reported, "the band sounded the funeral dirge . . . The chaplain offered prayer and the order of execution was read as ordered by Brigadier General G. M. Dodge. At four minutes past ten o'clock, the order to fire was given after which the troops were marched past the corpse so

that troops might have the opportunity of seeing the doom of a deserter."
Aside from having to endure an agonizing thirty-seven minutes of con-
certizing, prayer, and proclamations, Private Johnson was submitted to
one final disappointment. "His last request was to see his photograph
which had been taken the morning of the execution. This was denied
but he was told that the picture would be sent to his wife." Perhaps the
widow was spared from looking at another photograph taken that day. It
shows Johnson in repose beside his coffin.

In the background, a formation of the First Alabama Cavalry can be
seen sitting on their horses, the rumps of which are turned to the dead
man, whose hat has been carefully placed atop his coffin. It is the only
known photograph of the First Alabama in the field. The speed of the
execution peeved Lincoln. When Dodge came up for promotion to
major general, Lincoln snapped, "Do you mean a man who shoots a
deserter and then sends the proceedings to the president for approval
should be promoted?" But Dodge got the promotion and other more
important favors from Lincoln, and the spirits of the First were un-
daunted. The diary of Lieutenant Francis Wayland Dunn, preserved at
the University of Michigan, Ann Arbor, provided an eyewitness appraisal: "The scene was solemn but it did not seem to affect the soldiers
that witnessed it. They are a careless set."

Careless and caring more about revenge applies to the attitude that
took hold among First Alabama troops and Unionists back home.
Throughout 1863, hill country farmsteads and towns were savaged by
Roddey's 4th Alabama Cavalry and their paramilitary partners answering to Governor John Gill Shorter, who did not discourage summary
executions. The Brooks family and Bill Looney, the Black Fox, were already on the revenge trail. Guerilla bands with colorful names like the
Buggers, led by Bugger-in-Chief "Mountain Tom" Clark of Florence,
operated in Lauderdale County on the border with Tennessee. Clark's
story illustrates the collapse of order that peaked in 1863 and the wavering line between military action and pure criminality. Clark was already
an accused murderer when he was forcibly conscripted into Roddey's
Confederate calvary. He deserted for life as a pro-Union bushwhacker,

and as he was being lynched in 1872 he boasted that he had killed "a score and ten more" pro-Confederate neighbors during the war. At the gallows, he repented of only one murder, the bayoneting of an infant whose parents he had just killed. According to Bugger legend, the lynch mob buried Mountain Tom under the street leading to the city cemetery to mock his claim that "no one ever ran over me."

Local historians in Florence note with rueful pride—and with some degree of plausibility—that the brutality in their area influenced Sherman's tactics on the March to the Sea. Their insight provides another example of how avocational historians spot themes that trained scholars overlook. There is no doubt that the authors of the Atlanta campaign, Grant and Sherman, kept close tabs on developments in Alabama's brushfire war, as did Sherman's favorite field commander, General James B. McPherson, who was based at Huntsville. Dodge had made his own punitive raid that spring to destroy the "garden spot of Alabama" along the river. And most searingly for Confederate residents, General Florence Cornyn—called "Carcajou," another term for wolverine, by local antiquarian Wade Pruitt—brought his original Destroying Angels, cavalrymen from Missouri and Illinois, to ravage the area from April to June. He did a thorough job because his guide, Tennessee Union cavalry captain Rid Deford, grew up in Florence. He knew the area's roads intimately as the son of the local Methodist circuit rider, a Unionist preacher from Pennsylvania, and pointed out to Cornyn which houses to burn and which to spare. For months north Alabama and neighboring parts of Tennessee were a seething pit of partisanship run amok. It was the one time during the war when killings by Unionist gangs may have matched those of Rebel bushwhackers. For his part, Cornyn burned LaGrange College, the self-styled "West Point of the South" and alma mater of Jeremiah Clemens, near Moulton. He destroyed seven cotton-fabric factories in the area, including one that employed two thousand workers. "The loss to the Confederacy in this respect alone amounted to several millions of dollars," Cornyn boasted to Dodge in a report written two months before Cornyn was murdered.

The above-referenced amateur, Dr. Maurice "Wade" Pruitt (1910–

1976), was a physician in Florence, Alabama, and an avid collector of oral histories and folk tales. His posthumous book, *The Bugger Saga,* though self-published, has been "very influential" as a source mined by scholars for vintage newspaper clippings and as a guide to colorful characters and violent incidents. Although she regarded Pruitt's accounts as "sensationalized," the historian Margaret Storey used it as a tip sheet for two authoritative works, *Loyalty and Loss: Alabama's Unionists in the Civil War and Reconstruction* and *Tried Men and True or Union Life in Dixie,* a diary by Tennessee Unionist Thomas Jefferson Cypert (1827–1901), which she edited and annotated. To the extent that Civil War diarists can be regarded as amateur historians, Cypert to my way of thinking stands with Todd and Pruitt as examples of the value to be drawn from works that lack professional rigor but are indispensable to a full understanding of what Storey called the "guerilla surge" in the southern mountains. "One of the challenges of excavating the history of . . . any of the partisan cavalries in the Civil War," she noted, "is that people on each side of the conflict were almost always reluctant to confess their own misdeeds but eager to condemn their enemies for similar transgressions. Moreover, their wartime conflict became the stuff of legend throughout the South." *The Bugger Saga* is "essentially an edited compilation of legends, familiar stories, and reminiscences about the Civil War in the Tennessee Valley of Alabama and Tennessee." But one of the things I've learned from the Todd-Pruitt-Cypert trio is that these words can be studied not just for incidents but also for analytical insights that would do credit to any trained historian.

For example, Cypert opens his reminiscences with a long meditation on the "rich-man's-war-poor-man's-fight" conundrum that has confounded generations of scholars as to what held together such socioeconomically different groups during the period of secession mania. "Perhaps the most wonderfully strange circumstance of the whole movement," Cypert wrote, "was the fact that so many of the most indigent men of the country, who never owned or expected to own a single slave, could be induced to abandon their houses and leave their families, to engage in a war upon what they knew to be the best government on the face of the earth. And that merely to gratify a party of corrupt, designing, and disappointed politicians, newspaper publishers, and preachers; for such alone were the classes that got up the rebellion."

To return to Pruitt, the doctor did not let siding with the Rebels stop him from delivering a telling psychobiographical cameo about the almost demonic behavior that Florence M. Cornyn exhibited as the war progressed. Perhaps he understood the man because both had medical experience. Pruitt suggests that Cornyn, a surgeon, became seized by a growing *rage de guerre* in his treatment of his own soldiers and Alabama civilians. Before joining Dodge, Cornyn, in his initial role as a regimental doctor, had witnessed the atrocities committed along the Missouri-Kansas border.

For the most part, Pruitt wrote, "Invading armies did not make war on civilian property. Cornyn's Raid changed all that, in fact, it was designed to destroy the civilian property in the area and put out of action, once and for all, its industrial potential. Thus started a trend in warfare which was to reach its apogee in Sherman's March to the Sea." The claim is not entirely accurate. Dodge's destructive Alabama expedition preceded Cornyn's excesses by a few days. But, allowing for hyperbole (to which amateur historians, possibly including this writer, may be prone), Pruitt points up a parallel worth noting. The events by which the armies of Sherman and Grant converged on Chattanooga—destroying factories and food crops, capturing cattle and horses, tearing up and rebuilding railroads and bridges—presage exactly what would happen in late 1864 and into 1865. I suspect there's merit to Pruitt's linking the two. Indeed, it's an intuitive leap I've seen nowhere else.

22

DR. KAEISER VERSUS THE FEUDISTS

THE LAST TIME I visited Donald Dodd in the Free State, at his whimsically named ancestral farm, the Kudzu Botanical Gardens, he took me on our second visit to the grave of Tom Pink Curtis. It's in the Union Grove Missionary Baptist Cemetery in the area a few miles north of Double Springs called Curtis Gulf. Curtis's sons used its under-bluff caves, or "rock houses," for lying out from the Conscript Bureau, the feared operation commanded, with considerable efficiency in Alabama and Mississippi, by General Pillow and Lieutenant Colonel Lockhart. The defiant inscription on the stark granite slab marking Tom Pink's grave had been clearly legible when Dodd took my late brother and me to the spot years before. Now it was so blackened with age as to be illegible, and on this summer day in 2020, I regretted my decision not to bring chalk to bring out the lettering for a photograph. Not that I needed that for up-close inspection. The inscription was carved with a professional precision so unlike the wobbly scrawl on Millia Barton Raines's tombstone at the Sardis cemetery. His said:

TO THE MEMORY OF T. P. CURTIS

WAS BORN NOVEMBER

27, 1829 WAS KILLED BY

A CONFEDERATE RAID

ING PARTY JAN 19 1864

AGE 34 YEARS 1 MO 22 DS.

The lachrymose epitaph seemed to fit with the bittersweet nature of
our pilgrimage. Don's health was failing. He knew this might mark his
farewell stopover at this shrine to the quintessential Tory martyr. I felt a
reverence for the life's work of this rustic historian who had dedicated
his life to the Free State. Almost alone, he had constructed the armature
of fact that supported our hill country legend. It was his paper trail,
painstakingly unearthed at the Alabama Department of Archives and
History, that preserved the story of Tom Pink's death and the identity of
the vindictive Yankee slave master who caused it. Had there ever been a
more clear-cut case of symmetrical feudist justice? Only 227 days after
Tom Pink's death, the Curtis boys sent Dr. Andrew J. Kaeiser to his
grave. His slaves helped bury him in the regalia of a Royal Arch Mason.
Tom Pink was a Mason, too.

At the time of our graveyard visit, we were then in the waning days of
the Trump presidency, and it saddened both of us to think how far the
Free State had fallen on the scale of independent political thinking.
Donald Trump was running for reelection, and 90 percent of Winston's
residents had voted for him in 2016. Their gullibility shamed ancestors
who had not been afraid to carve their lasting enmity to the Confederacy
into hard rock. The grave of Tom Pink Curtis is adorned with the best-
known Masonic symbol—the intersecting compass and square—and a
coded message about his standing in the fraternal order that erected the
marker a few years after his death. Those are unmistakable clues to a
part of the state's history that Walter L. Fleming got right—the emergence in 1864 of what he called a "semi-treasonable secret order—the
'Peace Society.'" He added, "In 1864 the 'tories' and the Peace Society
began to work together." The gravestone reflects a link between Unionism and Masonic practice that was real and important, although again
little noted by historians. From the Freemasons, the society borrowed
ritualistic tools such as handshakes, passwords, and closed-door meet-

ings of its illuminati. Its strength across the top of Alabama and the state's southeastern counties near Florida was such for the last two years of the war Governor Shorter could enforce the law—any law, not just the Conscription Act—in only half the state. The Peace Society operated mainly through a Huntsville activist, J. J. Giers, whose personal diplomacy extended all the way to Grant himself and included George S. Houston, who three years earlier had served as then governor Moore's anti-Union informant and propagandist in the hill country. Although murderers still roamed the hills, many were switching sides. Indeed, Fleming could easily have dropped the "semi-treasonable" qualifier from his description of the Peace Society. Its aim was to encourage treason against the Confederacy. Even with the war still raging, the Peace Society had the active cooperation of the "Defender of North Alabama," General Roddey. So well-known were his Peace sympathies that at one point the Confederate authorities assigned his unit to Mississippi to stop the leakage of information and loyalties to the other side. At this late date, however, Richmond was too hard-pressed to lose Roddey's fighters or to consider sacking—or hanging—him, and he and the 4th Alabama Confederate Cavalry, C.S.A. were allowed to return to Alabama to be watched over by the supposedly more reliable Forrest.

When I arrived at the Kudzu Botanical Gardens in 2020, Dodd had recently been hospitalized for heart trouble. Although it was high summer, there was an unmistakably autumnal feel to this tour of the old "debatable ground," as one hill country diarist called the area. The historian wanted to show me the unmarked site where Looney's Tavern had stood. He wanted to tell me about locating it by old land records and hiking the forests that had taken over since the Civil War. We parked on a dirt road near a small cemetery. My grandson Jasper Raines videotaped the interview. With his usual precision, Dodd told me of debunking the local legend that the person buried under a Jackson gravestone in the cemetery was a relative of Old Hickory. Dodd delighted in showing these spots to witnesses who shared his Winston roots. He knew that I knew what he meant when he said he had to "go hillbilly" to get access to some of the records in Montgomery. And I appreciated how much digging he had done to disprove William Stanley Hoole's contention that the bush war in north Alabama was driven by Unionist outrages. Dodd was ingenious in sorting out the body count. For example, there had long been talk that Captain Whatley's run-amok company or the Home Guards had killed all six sons of a family named Hyde that lived about ten miles from my grandparents' farm in Arley. Local legend had it that the men were tortured and hanged, then buried in a common grave by their family. Dodd's circumstantial method of explaining the truth behind the legend seemed beyond convincing. "All six [victims] appeared on the 1860 census, yet none on the 1870 census, although their father, William Hyde, appears on both," he wrote.

Jefferson Davis's War Department hired 2,443 Conscription Bureau agents to chase men like the Hyde brothers and the Curtis brothers. (The Confederacy employed only five hundred more tax collectors, a measure of its desperate need for manpower.) The authoritative *Encyclopedia of the Confederacy* says the conscription agents were the "least successful" of the department's seventy thousand employees. Certainly they were the most hated by the men they consigned to "conscript rendezvous" camps like the one administered by Colonel Lockhart in Talladega. Even southern governors disliked the bureau for infringing on their ability to raise troops for state militias. The murder of Tom Pink Curtis on January 19, 1864, can be seen as introducing the most intense year of the conscription war. It also marked the emergence of the surviving brothers as avengers. The events of the year also bring into focus one of the most puzzling characters in Winston history, Andrew Kaeiser. It was almost as if this southernized Yankee didn't understand the difference in sensibility between his Alabama neighbors and the mild-mannered religious folk of his boyhood in Pennsylvania Dutch country. Friendly persuasion may have settled disputes there. He may have even absorbed the ethos of the plantation world, in which duels of honor might be required to finish some disputes. But in the feudist world, nothing is ever settled, nothing is ever finished so long as the people in the wrong or the people who believed themselves wronged are breathing.

Andrew Kaeiser conducted himself as if he were bulletproof when it came to flaunting his Confederate bona fides. He was a confidante of both Governors Shorter and Watts in their pursuit of "layouts." He was known as a finger man for Stoke Roberts and Captain Whatley. Wesley S. Thompson, although unreliable on some details, summed up the consensus view in Winston histories and family traditions. Andrew Kaeiser led a group of about a half dozen secessionists who "served as informers and advisers, to tell the impressment men the names and home locations of the 'Tories' who were laying out . . . [or] joined the Yankees in Decatur." That put him crossways with two of the most powerful Unionist clans in the county, the whiskey-making Brookses and the highly political Curtises. His sense of impunity took no account of their colorful histories, which bespoke a certain willfulness in regard to grudges and the taking of child brides. As a member of Andrew Jackson's Tennessee volunteers in 1814, Solomon Curtis rescued an eight-year-old girl who had been scalped and left for dead in a Creek massacre. When she was eleven and he was twenty-two they married, and their eldest son was born when she was fourteen. She wore a lace cap all her life to cover her scars. Jenny Bates was a fourteen-year-old half-Cherokee girl when she married Willis Brooks Sr., who was twenty years older. Her boys had watched their father hanged and riddled with bullets by eight Home Guards. Jenny and Willis ran a roadside inn, and the family believed Willis's murderers had been sent by Kaeiser. He was subsequently linked to all three Curtis killings, making him that family's "number one target for an avenger," according to Donald Dodd.

Accounts vary as to who was killed by which Brooks and which Curtis, but a credible timetable emerges from the evidence preserved by Dodd, Judge Weaver, the *Official Records,* and the Southern Claims Commission. By 1863, Alabama authorities had declared open season on hill country dissidents. A Black Belt newspaper assured its readers that the deserters and draft evaders there were "idiots of the lowest type." These "Yahoos of North Alabama" needed only be whipped into line as "their instinct was always to fly from danger." If that was ever true it changed with the completion of the state-endorsed Curtis murder cycle with Tom Pink's death in January 1864. It took until August for thirty-two-year-old Jim Curtis, now the eldest surviving son, to arrange a furlough from his assignment as an enlisted nurse in a Union army hospital in Nashville. Partisan guerillas arrested him near the home place in Curtis Gulf and carried him to Jasper to await death in the Slaughter Pen that one of Whatley's associates had established there. The next-eldest brother, thirty-year-old Benjamin Franklin Curtis, known as Frank, smuggled a saw into the jail and Jim escaped. With a gang of seven associates, he made his way back to Winston County by way of Andrew Kaeiser's plantation. That part of the story was related to Judge Weaver in 1910 by Frank Curtis (1835–1927), and it meshes with the autobiographical account of Andrew Kaeiser's daughter, Mattie Kaeiser Moody, who dictated a memoir shortly before she died in 1946 at the age of ninety-three. As an eleven-year-old, she was living with her parents on the 360-acre Kaeiser plantation.

"September 2 was a miserable day for all of us," Mattie recalled. She had called her mother's attention to two men lurking near her late sister's grave in the cemetery across the road. "About that time my father walked out into the front yard. The men . . . at the grave must have given a signal, for immediately six men came riding down the road to the front gate . . . the man in front who had his gun raised and cocked, asked, 'Who are you?' Pa answered, 'Dr. Kaeiser.' He took aim and shot him through the heart. The bullet went through his body and buried deep in a plank of the house. Pa fell and Mother sprang to him and took his head in her lap. He opened his eyes once and that was the last. . . . The men who killed him met some of the Negroes coming home from the field and said to them, 'We have killed your old master. So dig a hole and put him in it.'" She added, "The man who fired the shot was Jim Curtis."

Mattie Kaeiser Moody's memoir provides evidence of prescient observation for an eleven-year-old in traumatic circumstances. She understood that the death of the first son, Wash Curtis, motivated "the 8 brothers who were all bad, wicked men, [and] swore they would have a gallon of blood for every drop of his. Dr. Kaeiser was the first victim, but he was not the only one." Nor were the Unionists through with the

Kaeiser family, even after sixty mounted southern soldiers escorted the family to a new rental home in Jasper. Mrs. Moody, who as an adult married into a prominent Tuscaloosa family, recalled with impressive accuracy the January day when a Tory raiding party galloped into Jasper, "released the prisoners, burned the jail and courthouse, burned our house and left town." The date was January 10, 1865, and the young girl had witnessed "one of the most spectacular Unionist raids of the war." It was in large measure the work of Bill Looney, the legendary "Black Fox" inspired by Chris Sheats's speech at Looney's Tavern. His instruments were members of the First Alabama Cavalry, U.S.A., who had been granted leave to come home from their base in Huntsville to free five Unionist prisoners awaiting execution in the Slaughter Pen.

Looney had talked the Union commander in Huntsville into allowing Anderson Ward, a battle-hardened sergeant in the First Alabama, to take a dozen uniformed cavalrymen to Winston County on a rescue mission. The group included a celebrated fighter from the Curtis Gulf area named Storex "Dock" Spain. He was known in the Free State as inventor of the guerilla tactic called the "Spain method." It amounted to turning Union conscription officers back at the county line by shooting a warning shot into the rumps of their horses. The next shots would be for the riders. Fourteen Free State civilians volunteered for the raiding party.

On a hill outside Jasper, Sergeant Ward arranged his uniformed men in a V, arming them with rifles. The rest of the men clustered behind them, armed with shotguns and pistols, and the group dashed on foot the final 150 yards into the town. Their shouts frightened everyone away from the square, including thirty-five uniformed Confederates, and the raiders battered down the jailhouse door. Jim Curtis ordered the jailer to open the cells and then made the man set fire to the building. The jailer is identified as Gilbert Sides, who was either killed by Jim Curtis or allowed to run away toward Curry, where the Sides family had farms near the Raines and Best homesteads. (There is no Gilbert among the Sides graves in the Curry cemetery, and my genealogical researchers have not been able to resolve the question of his exact identity or fate.) We do know that the successful raiders, after burning the Kaeisers' rental house, confronted his widow with a charge that seemed to have more to do with her husband than her. One of the mounted men said, "Mrs. Kaeiser, you are the supreme judge of Alabama. Every [Unionist] prisoner that is taken is brought to you to be judged." In Mattie's account, her mother heatedly denied being involved in her husband's finger-pointing, saying she had been asked to identify only one man.

What else happened in the yard of that smoldering house will never be known, but in one critical respect, Mattie's memory of her mother being threatened jibes with an unsourced anecdote preserved by Wesley S. Thompson. He says there was a William Brooks in the raiding party, and this man held a cocked pistol to Mrs. Kaeiser's head, demanding to know the names of the eight men who hanged Willis in 1863. The man, apparently a Brooks cousin, said, "Woman, if you will talk you can live—if you fail to do it, you can go into eternity with your husband." As usual, Thompson's sloppy sourcing raises problems, but the daughter's account that her mother was threatened and the subsequent history of what came to be known as the Brooks Gang make it plausible that some member of the extended family was part of the Jasper raid.

The Brooks saga is more encrusted with legend, but it is worth examining as a window on the feudist mythology that blossomed in Appalachia and on film in Hollywood after the war. The most famous postbellum feud, which began in 1865 between the Hatfields and McCoys on the West Virginia–Kentucky border, was less political and produced a far lower body count than the partisan violence in the Alabama mountains or in the highlands of Tennessee, Georgia, and the Carolinas. The Hatfield-McCoy conflict started when a Confederate gang associated with "Devil Anse" Hatfield killed a single Unionist veteran, Asa McCoy, on January 7, 1865, seven days after his discharge. In Alabama lore, the Brookses occupy a place similar to that of the Hatfields and McCoys and their notoriety endures on their home ground. The twice-married Jenny Bates Brooks Johnson is buried in a remote section of Winston County's scenic Bankhead National Forest near the house where she died in 1924. Hikers still leave coins on her gravestone in the Pine Torch Cemetery. In a 1920 interview in *The Birmingham News*, Jenny Brooks Johnson at ninety-seven told how eight raiders had hanged Willis Sr. and killed a fifteen-year-old son who tried to rescue his father. "But seven uv 'em been got," she told the interviewer. That began the legend-making picked up by Carl Carmer when he arrived in the Free State shortly after the old woman died. He told of "Aunt Jenny" swearing her young boys to revenge on their father's body and how she boiled the skull of one of her husband's killers and turned it into a dish for hand soap. The most flamboyant iteration of the skull story holds that Aunt Jenny's last request to the preacher at her bedside was, "I'd like to wash my hands."

There is ample documentation that some of the surviving sons became deadly gunfighters in Texas and the Indian Territory of Oklahoma, but it is less than certain that all their victims helped kill Willis Sr. Willis Brooks Jr. was shot to death while pursuing a vendetta of some sort in Spokogee, Oklahoma, in 1902. Aunt Jenny's only surviving child, Henry, was killed in 1920 in Lawrence County, while tending a still not far from his mother's home. "He was my last bit of flesh and blood," Aunt Jenny told *The Birmingham News* reporter, adding that her five sons all died "with their boots on." Donald Dodd told me that some of his relatives were members of the revenuers posse that got Willis Jr. in 1920. All of Winston County, it seems, would have resonated to another of Aunt Jenny's recorded maxims: "I hate a coward."

On the Curtis side, the killer-tracking motif is clearer and, to my mind, more credibly linked to Civil War events through Frank Curtis's brother's 1910 account and the family lore. Therein we find that Jim married a sister of "Dock" Spain, who begged him to abandon his crusade to find his brothers' killers. Instead, he shot two Walker County men in the dogtrots of their homes. Two other men fled to Texas, and "Jim hunted them down and killed them. Two others fled to Mississippi, and they met the same fate." Fearing for his own life, Jim moved to Tennessee and established himself as a farmer and, improbably, as a doctor. The man known to neighbors as "Dr. Jim" died while picking cotton in his own field and is buried in the Whitten's Cross Roads

Methodist Church Cemetery at Cypress Inn, Tennessee, about eighty miles from his old home in Curtis Gulf. He is buried under a Union army marker that shows he joined a Kentucky infantry regiment instead of the First Alabama. Information associated with the cemetery identifies him unmistakably as a son of Solomon Curtis, the patriarch of Curtis Gulf, and Charlotte Heaton Curtis, the little girl who was scalped. Buried near him is Priscilla Spain Curtis (1831–1907), the wife who asked him not to chase the killers from Winston County.

Such verifications underscore a pattern that emerges with unmistakable, almost spooky consistency in the First Alabama story. Even sensational-sounding details often have a sound basis in fact, and these facts are usually ignored or glossed over in conventional accounts. The details in the Brooks family lore are in some sense spongier than those in the Curtis records. But as Dr. Kaeiser found, feudists were efficient and persistent pursuers of revenge. Not every *i* can be dotted and *t* crossed, but it seems clear that even so dangerous a character as Old Stoke Roberts had to account for his sins after the Civil War. It seems unlikely to me that he died with a spike through the roof of his mouth or was shot by person or persons unknown several years later as he fed his horses near Moulton, Alabama, in the 1870s. The historical society in Itawamba, Mississippi, where Roberts became a deputy U.S. marshal after the war, probably got the details of his death at least partly right. In 1899 Roberts abandoned his Civil War haunts and his blood-soaked career as a lawman and bought a ranch in Coryell County, Texas. (Thousands of Alabamians migrated to Texas both before and after the war, hence the state's prominence in tracking stories.) On January 25, 1904, Roberts's body was found in the Leon River near Gatesville, Texas. "The evening before he had left home to go across the river to check on some cows and hadn't returned," according to the *Itawamba History Review*. "It was thought he had fallen in the river and drowned."

What is striking in so many of these revenge tales is their mordant tone and unmitigated finality. In that regard, Bill Looney sets the Winston paradigm. Donald Dodd collected the tale of a group of Home Guards who got the drop on Looney, telling him, "We are from Hell."

He asked if they had seen a mutual acquaintance who ran with them. "I just sent him there last night," Looney said before opening fire. There was even less preliminary conversation in an account written by First Alabama Cavalry veteran John R. Phillips in his autobiography, *The Story of My Life*. Phillips told of riding with Looney on a country road when Looney drew his pistol and shot a passing civilian without saying a word. Asked why, Looney said the man was a member of a group that had tried to hang him in Decatur, and he had promised to kill the man if they ever met again.

23

Meanwhile, Back at the War

IN ANY OVERVIEW of the climactic year of the Civil War, a striking paradox emerges in regard to the historical obscurity of the First Alabama Cavalry, U.S.A. General Sherman pushed them to the forefront of the Union army for the two defining victories of 1864, the Atlanta campaign in the springtime and the March to the Sea in the fall. As a result, the regiment was more famous to the men who crushed the Confederacy than it would ever be in the national memory or to the people of its home state. We discover this through the *Official Records,* the memoirs of key players, the whereabouts of the generals to whom they reported, and the regimental calendar reconstructed by the tireless Glenda McWhirter Todd. These provide a telling snapshot of the official awareness of Alabama's Unionist troops.

Official communications show that Grant was informed about them as the linchpins of the spy network created by General Grenville Dodge on his orders and as cavalry fighters who helped keep Nathan Bedford Forrest off his rear throughout 1863 at Vicksburg. It seems safe to assume that Lincoln knew about them through his White House meetings with their commander, General Dodge, and as a result of George E. Spencer's meetings at the War Department with General-in-Chief Henry W. Halleck. Spencer was there twice in 1862 specifically to lobby for the colonelcy of the First Alabama. He may have met with Lincoln as well. Around the same time, Lincoln's favorite editor and 1864 campaign manager, Henry Raymond of *The New York Times,* had praised Spencer and the Alabama regiment in his paper. They were in the extensive war coverage of the *Cincinnati Daily Gazette* as well.

Sherman brought them to his side in Rome, Georgia, in May 1864 because in less than two years they had become seasoned troops. In particular, Companies I and L had "cut their teeth on Sherman's hard war tactics and honed their notorious reputation in the Confederate press." That language is from one of the most incisive works in the burgeoning field of Unionist studies, a dissertation submitted at the University of Virginia in 2020 by Clayton J. Butler. The First Alabama had been in the town of Rome, Georgia, a year earlier—as captives imprisoned there after being captured by Nathan Bedford Forrest on May 3, 1863, at the unsuccessful end of Streight's Raid. The conventional wisdom among University of Alabama historians like William Stanley Hoole, A. B. Moore, and Charles Summersell that the outfit lacked military potency would have been surprising to Rome citizens and local journalists, who no doubt spotted familiar faces among the POWs returning as an occupying force. The *Rome Courier* had described them then as "villainous whelps" and "thieves and murderers" and hoped that the authorities would "bring the traitorous wretches to a punishment befitting their crimes."

Their presence in the Georgia mountain town illuminates another of those deliciously symmetrical ironies frequently neglected in panoramic histories of this war among neighbors. Most wars—and perhaps this one most of all—reveal their essence in the close-ups. The rough-riding Alabamians had been freed in a prisoner exchange. They knew they were lucky to be alive; Forrest had wanted to execute them on the spot as traitors after Streight surrendered to him about thirty miles from Rome on May 3, 1863. The victorious Forrest acceded reluctantly to Streight's insistence, in the terms of surrender, that these renegade Alabamians be sent to Richmond as regular prisoners of war. Within a month, this made them eligible for the routine exchanges of POWs that both sides needed to replenish their armies. Sherman, of course, knew the histories of the men who were returning to his ranks. As a result of his engineering work in north Georgia as a young lieutenant, Sherman knew the social hierarchy of the area. With his fondness for thumb-in-the-eye gestures, he arranged for the First Alabama to erect their tents on the lawn of the grandest dwelling in Rome: the Shorter mansion, owned by one Colonel Alfred Shorter, Rome's richest citizen and a first cousin of that nemesis of his state's Unionists, Alabama governor John Gill Shorter. Once again, we are reminded of the tight circle of wealth in the Old South, a circle closed in by land deeds and marriage licenses. The Shorters owned some Georgia plantations, but their real prominence was as the keystone family of the "Eufaula Regency" of Barbour County, Alabama, the snootiest caste of Black Belt slave masters.

However, the Alabamians pitching their tents in Rome had neither the need nor inclination to kowtow to anyone. They were having a high time on their scouting and skirmishing forays out from Rome. Sergeant Major Francis W. Dunn noted in his diary that "Boys got to Jayhawking. One man in Company L stole a watch the colonel made him give up." But Colonel Spencer otherwise did little to soften the introduction of Georgians to the realities of being invaded by Sherman. When a plantation mistress complained about the capture of her cotton, "Spencer told her we were the children of Israel bringing the plague on them." The term "jayhawking" got into the vocabulary and, perhaps, the habits of the Alabamians when they were assigned for a time in Alabama to ride with the notorious Union cavalry from Kansas. Sergeant Major Dunn's diary, preserved in the University of Michigan library, was one of Glenda McWhirter Todd's great discoveries, and it gives us an insight into how Sherman put together his personal team for the march.

He would use some of the Alabamians as personal aides to ride by his side and pitch his tents and use others as mounted point men to guide his infantry toward Atlanta. Most units in both armies were geographically based, but casualties, recruiting, and assignments gradually made them more diverse. Hoole found that birthplaces were recorded for 1,432 of the 2,066 volunteers in the First Alabama, and based on that, he estimated that fully 72 percent of the men came from Alabama. Of those with recorded birthplaces, 712 of the men were native-born Alabamians, with 271 from Georgia and 150 from Tennessee. Replacements even included five New Yorkers, three from Pennsylvania, one from New Jersey, and eight men born abroad. Since few north Alabamians had military educations, the Union high command clearly turned to other states for commissioned and noncommissioned officers for structural discipline while still relying on the core of Alabama mountaineers for fighting and spying. The Alabamians came mainly from the two dozen hilly counties lying north of present-day Birmingham and Tuscaloosa. Walker County, home of the Bartons and their Raines, Abbott, and Best cousins, provided the largest number of volunteers after Winston. Their joint total was over four hundred, while seven other mountainous counties clustered closely around Walker and Winston provided more than three hundred volunteers.

We can see Sherman's team coming together from afar. What is remarkable about them is their youth and diversity of experience. As a twenty-year-old graduate of Hillsdale College in Michigan, Dunn was ideally suited for his assignment of "office work" and the logistics of moving the regiment across Alabama, through Chattanooga, and down to the aforementioned Snake Creek Gap in early May 1863. There he would be joining a budding leadership team enlisted during the summer of 1862 in the first wave of recruits directed into Huntsville in the summer of 1862 by Chris Sheats and Bill Looney. Mustered in on the same day, August 13, 1862, were Anderson Looney, a future first sergeant who was the son of the Black Fox himself, and a future lieutenant named David R. Snelling, who had defied his plantation-owning Georgia family to fight with Sherman and who was destined to become one of the general's favorite junior officers. During the meticulous research for his historical novel *The Unionist: A Novel of the Civil War,* Georgia author W. Steven Harrell showed that Snelling and Sheats actually met in 1864 and Sheats told the Georgian of his thwarted ambition to become a

Union officer. As a general who camped in the field with his troops and jawed with them constantly, "Uncle Billy" assuredly knew the capabilities of his command.

For the purpose of riding point for his infantry generals, he put together an advance guard of two dozen First Alabama horsemen under Lieutenant J. H. Day. This twenty-three-year-old Alabama farmer had enlisted at Huntsville three weeks before Snelling and Looney; he could have had no idea what Sherman would throw at him in Georgia. Sherman's most striking move in regard to the First had to do with a second detachment of twenty-one men. Of them, Sherman said, "I also had a small company of irregular Alabama cavalry (commanded by Lieutenant Snelling), used mainly as orderlies and couriers."

Generations of Alabama scholars would overlook these men hidden in plain sight on page 406 of Sherman's *Memoirs*. If camp duties had been the whole story, perhaps the regiment could have been ignored by scholars, as William Stanley Hoole recommended. But once at Rome, the regiment was "almost constantly engaged" in prolonged scouting and "severe skirmishes" as part of the Army of the Tennessee under General James B. McPherson, the Sherman favorite. That army's XVI Corps was commanded by Grenville Dodge with Colonels Spencer and George L. Godfrey leading the "escort" cavalry from Alabama. In a typical action, Spencer led the entire regiment on a two-hundred-mile swing into Alabama. Its big test came when General Joseph Johnston entrenched his sixty-thousand-strong Rebel army behind Rocky Face Ridge, a ten-mile-long stone massif that lay athwart the route to Atlanta. While Sherman's main force demonstrated in front of the eight-hundred-foot-high ridge, General Dodge and Colonel Spencer led a force of four thousand men on a diversionary move to Snake Creek Gap, the southernmost of three cuts through the mountain. Coming behind them were another twenty thousand men led by General McPherson. Francis Dunn's diary suggests a romp-like attitude among the men approaching the gap "up a cliff so steep that it was not walking but simply climbing. It hardly seems possible that such a place could be taken."

Snake Creek Gap was eight miles long and very narrow, pierced by the stream and a railroad. As related earlier, a force of four thousand led by the First Alabama was to follow the stream and railroad on a surprise march through the narrow gap. Once they emerged near the market town of Resaca, they would be in the rear of Johnston's entire army, which would be facing in the other direction. We have heard the contention of Colonel Spencer, who led a detachment of First Alabama Cavalry through the gap, that the war would have ended then and there had McPherson not panicked and called them back. In Sherman's plan, McPherson's remaining twenty thousand troops would have flooded through behind the initial force. A more neutral statement than Spencer's put the situation this way in E. B. Long's day-by-day Civil War almanac. "Sherman was disappointed in McPherson's failure to cut in behind Johnston and it has been a source of dispute ever since."

One does not have to be a First Alabama partisan like Spencer to see that as massive understatement. Johnston had expected a frontal assault on Rocky Face there and had put only a token force at the Resaca end of the gap. As Robert L. O'Connell reconstructed the scene in his even-handed biography, *Fierce Patriot: The Tangled Lives of William Tecumseh Sherman*, "Sherman almost scored a knockout in the first round. On May 9, McPherson and the Army of the Tennessee poured through Snake Creek Gap and got within a mile of Resaca when they encountered some earthen fortifications manned by a rear guard that turned out to be about 4,000 strong. Had McPherson attacked promptly, Johnston would have been trapped. Yet he hesitated and dug in instead. 'Well, Mac, you have missed the great opportunity of your life,' Sherman told him later."

Sherman's cutting remark, verified in his own writing, was not delivered until May 12, when he encountered McPherson in person after the Battle of Resaca. He had obviously been saving the words, and they must have cut the proud and popular McPherson so deeply as to be almost unbearable. Death at the Battle of Atlanta two and a half months later relieved McPherson of the shaming burden, but it was inscribed on his permanent record. Not even the postwar debate inspired by the equally embarrassed Joe Johnston could change that record and its fallout. Johnston's retreats after Snake Creek Gap, Resaca, and Kennesaw Mountain caused Jefferson Davis to sack him on July 12 and replace him with that devotee of the suicidal charge, John Bell Hood. Two decades later, Johnston was still seething from the double insults of being surprised in battle and then removed in favor of an inferior general, insisting that he had not been caught napping at Snake Creek Gap. Writing in *Battles and Leaders of the Civil War,* he took aim at Sherman, even though the two became fast friends after the war. But there are no revisionists so diligent as defeated generals.

"General Sherman claims to have surprised us by McPherson's appearance in Snake Creek Gap on [May] 9th, forgetting that we discovered his march on the 8th. He blames McPherson for not seizing the place. That officer tried the works and found them too strong to be seized," Johnston contended. He challenged Sherman's belief that "all Johnston's army" could not have stopped McPherson. "Had he done so, 'all of Johnston's army' would have been upon him at the dawn of the next day, the cannon giving General Sherman intelligence of the movement of that army. About twice his force in front and three thousand men in his immediate rear would have overwhelmed him, making a most auspicious beginning of the campaign." However, Johnston's case was demolished in that same volume by his subordinate Colonel W. P. C. Breckinridge, who commanded the 9th Kentucky Confederate Cavalry at Snake Creek Gap. He said flatly that Snake Creek and other nearby gaps "were not guarded" sufficiently. Echoing Sherman and Spencer, Breckinridge said, "One serious attack by McPherson, and Resaca must have been captured" on May 9.

Christopher Rein, the professor of military history who wrote *Alabamians in Blue,* is not so sure that Johnston's glaring "tactical error" would have had the strategic consequences predicted by Sherman and others. Such a dispute is "great fodder for the 'mem-wars' and gives old generals something to argue about in retirement!" he wrote me in an email. "It was so incredibly difficult to win a 'decisive' victory in the Civil War." For my part as a studious amateur, I find it hard to argue outcomes with the general who understood that the war would be over if Lincoln and Grant had turned him loose on Atlanta, the "Gate City of the South." I think the preponderance of eyewitness evidence supports the judgment that he bungled an unrepeatable opportunity at the gap, but with Dodge and the First Alabama as official parts of his command, he performed well in the two-day Battle of Resaca. The First became a familiar part of the advance on Atlanta. With alternating flanking movements of his superior force, Sherman drove Johnston steadily back toward Atlanta, which lay on the south bank of the Chattahoochee River. Finally, in mid-June, Johnston entrenched his army on Kennesaw Mountain, the last topographic barrier before the river. Their forward positioning brought important situational opportunities for the First Alabama. Way back at Corinth, twenty-seven-year-old Major George L. Godfrey and his scouts from the intrepid Company L had become known for their audacity in probing enemy positions. One afternoon, "General Dodge sent for the best company that Godfrey had to report to Captain Hickenlooper as a permanent reconnoitering party" to "accompany him as he rides around" in front of Rebel trenches and gun emplacements at Kennesaw Mountain. "I suppose," Wayland Dunn noted in his diary, "that there will be more danger connected with it than guarding [the] wagon train but more pleasant in other respects."

The assignment probably put members of the First Alabama within earshot of one of Sherman's most deadly spontaneous orders. He kept Hickenlooper, a trusted mapmaker, and the young captain's boss, Colonel Orlando M. Poe, chief engineer, close to him at all times. Riding with his entourage on June 14, Sherman spied a cluster of Confederate officers in an exposed position near Kennesaw Mountain. He ordered General Howard to have his Ohio cannoneers fire on the distant target. Lieutenant Snelling and the escort were almost certainly watching, and General Howard was using First Alabama scouts as well. Soon after Howard issued the order to fire, the third round struck General Leonidas Polk. He had recently arrived to bolster Johnston's army with fifteen thousand conscripts forced into Confederate service in Alabama by the efficient strong-arming of Governor Shorter and General Pillow. The three-inch projectile tore Polk in half, thereby killing the Episcopal bishop who had been among those who founded the University of the South as a finishing school to instruct young plantation owners in the humane treatment of slaves. The Battle of Kennesaw Mountain, which commenced on June 27, was instructive as a matter of military tactics and southern sociology. In a rare mistake, Sherman abandoned his flanking strategy in favor of a frontal assault that cost him three thousand casualties to only one thousand for Johnston's dug-in troops. As for the sociology of the battle, only four hundred yards separated the two sides, which means that the north Alabamians serving under General Howard at the Union center were facing Rebels conscripted from their home ground. Alabamians from the two armies were within shouting and shooting distance of one another, but if there are any colorful anecdotes about battlefield contacts, I haven't found them.

In late June, the First Alabama and other regiments were posted back to Rome to operate from there in protecting the right side of Sherman's army as he closed on Atlanta. There was skirmishing aplenty, but Spencer fretted about being so far from Atlanta and was sidelined for several weeks by dysentery. In July, a frustrated Jefferson Davis foolishly sent General Braxton Bragg, his military adviser and worst battlefield strategist, to Atlanta to reprimand Johnston for his effective post-Kennesaw strategy of protecting Atlanta by fighting on the defensive. Davis sacked Johnston on July 17, replacing him with General John Bell Hood, a laudanum-addled amputee who was devoted to suicidal frontal assaults against larger armies. This enabled the Union victory at the Battle of Peachtree Creek on July 22. On that day, General McPherson, of Snake Creek fame, rode accidentally into Confederate lines and was killed. General Dodge was there, but it's unclear if the entire First Alabama was back in Rome by this time. I have to believe that Lieutenant Snelling's men must have witnessed a distraught Sherman kneeling beside McPherson's body, which was brought to him on a wooden door used as a makeshift litter.

That day's victory broke Hood's hold on the Georgia capital, and on September 2, Sherman occupied Atlanta for good. For the next two months, Sherman chased Hood around the area, fretting that holding the roads against Wheeler and his mobile cavalrymen would damage his army, especially if Forrest was sent in to help. During this confusing period, the First Alabama lost the leader who had positioned it in the heart of Sherman's war machine. On August 19, a sharpshooter aimed at a peephole General Dodge was using and put a Minié ball through it, furrowing his scalp with what appeared to be a mortal wound. As was his habit, Sherman went to the hospital tent to visit his wounded subordinate. The Iowan awakened to hear Sherman tell the surgeon, "See, Dodge isn't going to die. He is coming to." Sent to Indiana to recuperate, Dodge would never return to Georgia, depriving Spencer of a sponsor who had Sherman's ear. By mid-autumn Spencer had recovered from his illness and returned to duty; he almost immediately began plotting against his new commander, Brigadier General William Vandever, another Iowa politician with ties to Dodge.

In a letter to Dodge, Spencer was raging against Vandever, calling him "a granny besides being only half witted" for keeping his regiment away from the main action closer to Atlanta. "I have a good Regiment the best I ever saw & if I could get Carte Blanche to go where I [wanted] to for about two months I could make for myself & Regiment a name and reputation," he told Dodge—prophetically, as it turned out. On October 5, Hood's army pinned down General John M. Corse and a Union force of two thousand near Allatoona, where the railroad from Atlanta went through a mountain pass. Sherman, with downtown Atlanta safely occupied, was observing Hood's advance ambling from ten miles away atop Kennesaw Mountain. To rescue Corse, he sent the First Alabama Cavalry and his own 9th Illinois Mounted Infantry to Allatoona. By messenger, he told Corse to refuse a surrender demand as help was on the way. The well-publicized incident inspired an evangelical hymn that became instantly popular in northern camp meetings, using a quotation that the fastidious Sherman complained was an imprecise rendition of his actual message. Even so, his alleged words, "Hold the Fort, for We Are Coming," still survive in some hymnals.

Based on the Allatoona operation, Spencer's stock soared. In official correspondence, Sherman praised "Spencer's First Alabama Cavalry" by name. He credited the unit and their Illinois partners for their "skill and bravery" in protecting the railroad from Hood's wreckers. He felt the Alabama and Illinois troops "together furnished an excellent mounted brigade for offensive operations and reconnaissances." With uncharacteristic clumsiness, the frantic Spencer picked this period to overplay his hand with Sherman, who had ordered the burning of Rome as a hotbed of enemy mischief. Spencer, in his role as godfather to his troops, wanted to preserve some houses there that were being used to billet families who had come in from Alabama and Georgia with his new enlistees. By assiduous recruiting, Spencer had built the regiment up to 868 effectives, but he blundered seriously in appealing to Sherman to cancel his burn order as a favor to the refugees. "You have known for ten days that Rome was to be evacuated, and have no right to appeal to my humanity," Sherman wrote him in a blistering rebuke. "You have neglected to care for these families and I am not going to regulate the movements of an army by your neglect and want of foresight."

There was more bad news for Spencer. Up until now what his biographer called his "never-abated ambition" had served him well as a young wheeler-dealer in the Iowa capital. But he was now on his own amid the court intrigue at Sherman's headquarters as General Francis P. Blair, the brother of Lincoln's postmaster general, Montgomery Blair, was plotting to absorb the absent Dodge's XVI Corps into his own XVII Corps. Soon, as Dodge's biographer put it, "the sick and helpless Dodge was a general without a command," and Spencer, in lobbying unsuccessfully for his absent friend, had made a powerful enemy in Blair, who became his new boss. In a way, the forty-three-year-old Blair and the twenty-eight-year-old Spencer were cut from the same self-promoting fabric. Both were "hard to tolerate," as Dodge's biographer, Stanley Hirshson, said of Blair. "Everywhere he took with him a corps of reporters whose primary function was to glorify and preserve for posterity his every move." Blair and Dodge hardly spoke, and Spencer believed he would get full title to Blair's antipathy.

Spencer could console himself that Sherman and General Howard had made him "some good promises" in regard to rescuing General

Corse, and he was optimistic that he could work his way into Sherman's favor based on the fallout from the events there. Virtually everyone who has observed Sherman or studied him has commented on his acute observational skills, his eye for detail, and the clinical rationality of his mind. All those qualities display in the decision he reached on October 9 as a consequence of seeing that it was futile to chase after Hood's cavalry and infantry in the hilly terrain or to try to guess where the erratic Confederate commander would hit the railroad next. Better to let him march his men into Tennessee and send the reliable General George Thomas to finish him off there. Hence the telegram he sent to Grant from Allatoona after arriving there to survey the after-battle scene:

> It will be a physical impossibility to protect the roads, now that Hood, Forrest, Wheeler, and the whole batch of devils, are turned loose without home or habitation. I think Hood's movements indicate a diversion to the end of the Selma & Talladega road, at Blue Mountain, about sixty miles southwest of Rome, from which he will threaten Kingston, Bridgeport, and Decatur, Alabama. I propose that we break up the railroad from Chattanooga forward, and that we strike out with our wagons for Milledgeville, Millen, and Savannah. Until we can repopulate Georgia, it is useless for us to occupy it; but the utter destruction of its roads, houses, and people, will cripple their military resources. By attempting to hold the roads, we will lose a thousand men each month, and will gain no result. I can make this march, and make Georgia howl! We have on hand over eight thousand head of cattle and three million rations of bread, but no corn. We can find plenty of forage in the interior of the State.

There is hardly a more prescient or portentous paragraph in the *Official Records*. With it, Sherman began the Savannah Campaign, popularly known as the March to the Sea. But first he wanted to destroy everything of potential military value in Atlanta, and that would take a few days. I had hoped at one point to find evidence that Alabama soldiers lit the matches that burned the city, but that honor fell to Colonel Poe's 1st Michigan Engineers and Mechanics. Again the First Alabama was close at hand, as Sherman attached the Michiganders directly to his headquarters' entourage, and the regiments traveled together for the rest of the campaign. Sherman described the decimation of the city and his departure in a manner that was at once vivid and matter-of-fact: "I reached Atlanta during the afternoon of the 14th, and found that . . . Colonel Poe, United States Engineers, of my staff, had been busy in his special task of destruction. He had a large force at work, had leveled the great depot, round house, and the machine-shops of the Georgia Railroad, and had applied fire to the wreck." A Rebel arsenal exploded during the fire, dropping shells and shot on the residence where Sherman and his staff were dining. Sherman's messmates that night included two newcomers whose memoirs would become important documents in reconstructing the activities of the First Alabama. One was Major George Ward Nichols, author of *The Story of the Great March.* After the war, as a newspaperman, he wrote the sensational stories that made Wild Bill Hickok a national hero. The other was Major Henry Hitchcock, who had used family connections to secure a position as Sherman's traveling secretary. He became a zealous promoter of Lieutenant David Snelling and, by extension, a trumpeter of the exploits of his Alabamians and Colonel Spencer. The main force marched out of Atlanta on November 15. Sherman lingered to oversee a final leveling of buildings and "on the morning of the 16th started with my personal staff, a company of Alabama cavalry, commanded by Lieutenant Snelling, and an infantry company, commanded by Lieutenant McCrory, which guarded our small train of wagons."

Colonel Poe's eulogy for the city he had destroyed was sparse and simple: "For military purposes, the city of Atlanta has ceased to exist." Sherman biographer Burke Davis was one of the few popular historians who paid attention to Uncle Billy's interaction with his riding companions. "Sherman left Atlanta at seven in the morning of November 16, riding his favorite mount, a blaze-faced little horse whose 'horribly fast' walk was the dismay of his staff. The general was erect and vigorous in the saddle, like a gamecock, some of his men thought. His face was drawn with fatigue and half-concealed by a broad-brimmed hat jammed down over his ears, a formless black worn without braid or tassels. The sunlight revealed streaks of gray in the cinnamon beard. Sherman's cigar rolled constantly across his mouth, even as he talked with staff officers and his bodyguard of Alabama cavalry, waving and gesturing with his slender, feminine hands. His nose twitched as if the general were snuffling out the trail ahead."

To my surprise, I discovered that Chris Sheats may have been a witness to this scene, according to testimony he gave the Bureau of Pensions in 1903 on behalf of Snelling's widow. W. Steven Harrell, an attorney in Perry, Georgia, found the document in researching *The Unionist: A Novel of the Civil War*, a lightly fictionalized biography of Lieutenant Snelling's adventures with the First Alabama. In several interviews, I found Harrell an expert on all aspects of their role in the March to the Sea. In archives now held by the Veterans Administration, he found a document that, so far as I know, has eluded historians. "I saw [Snelling] once at Atlanta with Sherman's Army in November 1864," Sheats told pension officials for the Department of the Interior, then in charge of payments to Civil War veterans and their survivors. I believe that Sheats, having been freed from prison late in the war, traveled to Atlanta to join his political ally, William Hugh Smith, who as a prolific civilian recruiter had accompanied the First Alabama on its travels with Sherman. "I knew David R. Snelling very well," the aging Sheats told pension officials who traveled to Decatur to depose him. "He commanded General Sherman's escort on the Georgia campaign. He was selected by Sherman because he knew all that Georgia country, and is complimented by General Sherman in his memoirs. I first met Snelling at Atlanta and after the surrender I got to know him very well."

For a few years after the war, the two men lived as friendly neighbors in Decatur, where Sheats practiced law and Snelling worked for a newspaper. Sheats confessed that he had hoped to become a colonel of the First Alabama, his crippled leg notwithstanding, but imprisonment prevented his enlistment.

24

PATHS OF GLORY AND OBSCURITY

FROM ITS INCEPTION, the March to the Sea was a masterpiece of counter-intuitive thinking. After the Union army occupied Atlanta permanently on September 2, 1864, strategists on both sides had expected Sherman to chase Hood's wounded army into Tennessee to protect the railroad that was his supply line for the troops in Atlanta. But Sherman headed the main body of his army in the opposite direction and left it to the competent Major General George H. Thomas, with a force of twenty-five thousand, to pursue Hood beyond Chattanooga. "Let him go north," Sherman said of Hood to an initially dubious Lincoln and Grant. The march for him became a path to glory, but for the Alabama cavalry who rode at his side every mile of the way it became a pathway to obscurity. It did not start out that way. Sherman assigned a place of prominence for his Alabama Unionists.

To fully understand their role, it is useful to undertake a quick anatomy of Sherman's purpose-built military machine of 110,000 soldiers. The words "magnificent army" appear repeatedly in accounts of what was officially known as the "Military Division of the Mississippi in the Field."

As a manager, Sherman combined a mastery of detail with a comprehensive strategic vision. In World War II history, FDR and Dwight

Eisenhower come to mind as comparable executives. Sherman had assembled an army of role players chosen for both predictable and surprising talents. He was drawn to men like Dodge and Spencer, intuitive spymasters who, as field commanders, also thwarted Nathan Bedford Forrest's ferocious efforts to defend Vicksburg and the train tracks between Memphis and Chattanooga. There were trained officers like Poe and Hickenlooper, geniuses at, respectively, bridge repair and mapmaking, who rode alongside Sherman and his First Alabama Cavalry escort. At the junior level, there was another talented pair of amateurs doted upon by Sherman: Snelling, the plantation lad from Georgia, and Francis W. Tupper, an enlistee from Illinois. This "magnificent" machine was also "a team of rivals," to use Doris Kearns Goodwin's term for Lincoln's cabinet. Dodge, one of Lincoln's favorite civilian generals, detested his fellow corps commander, Major General Francis P. "Frank" Blair Jr., who was famed for his bravery under fire and for the potency of his family connections. Lincoln called the Blairs of Missouri a "closed corporation" of political influence. In both Dodge and Blair, driving ambition produced many feuds. During the crucial Battle of Atlanta at Peachtree Creek, Dodge got into a fistfight with Brigadier General Thomas W. Sweeny, a dilatory subordinate who was with him at the First Alabama's moment of near-triumph at Snake Creek Gap. Sweeny, a West Pointer, bloodied the nose of the much smaller Dodge, and Sweeny shouted out a highly inaccurate insult as he was dragged away under arrest for striking a senior officer: "Go, you God-damned inefficient political general, with your God-damned cowardly inefficient staff." Dodge was neither of those things, but while he was away on convalescent leave, Sherman allowed Blair to absorb Dodge's command. When Spencer protested, Sherman admitted he was afraid to cross Blair politically because of Lincoln's reliance on Postmaster General Montgomery Blair, Frank Blair's brother.

This infighting had two amazing results, both underscoring the full integration of the First Alabama in the Union command structure. Spencer was kept informed of the rival generals' plot against Dodge by orderlies in their headquarters who had served under Dodge and Spencer as members of the First Alabama Cavalry and were now eavesdroppers for Spencer. Then Blair, despite his distaste for Spencer and his awareness of Spencer's intrigues, picked the First Alabama to lead his corps, a development noted by the entire army that followed them, yet largely overlooked by historians.

The oversight amazes me every time I review the paper trail of the First Alabama Cavalry. Yet not until 2020 did I find a comprehensive analysis of this scholarly lacuna in the dissertation of Clayton J. Butler. I was pleased to see that Butler drew inspiration from the same paradoxes and sources, including avocational scholars like Glenda McWhirter Todd, that motivated my quest. "During the Civil War era," he observed, "Unionists took on a symbolic importance out of proportion to their limited numbers. But, as the case of Glenda Todd illustrates, the intervening years extinguished almost all awareness of their existence. These particular Unionists, long unacknowledged and still understudied, can teach contemporary scholars much about the Civil War and Reconstruction."

They emerged into full view just as Sherman divided his army into a left wing comprising the XIV and XX Corps and a right wing comprising the XV and General Blair's XVII Corps. "A common refrain of Blair's orders placed 'the First Alabama in advance,' and the regiment consistently led the 17th Corps en route to Savannah," wrote Clayton Butler. "Making up the vanguard, the First Alabama Cavalry most often received orders to secure towns, ferries, bridges, and railroads in advance of the main host. . . . The men often seemed to take special glee in the destruction and seizure to vent their frustration toward their late countrymen, they sometimes overindulged their desire for retribution."

The final sentence would have delighted William Stanley Hoole, for it revived a favorite canard he discovered when mining the First Alabama record for defamatory documents. A letter of reprimand delivered to Spencer only five days into the march showed that General Blair had bided his time in regard to the insults aimed at him by Dodge and Spencer. It also provided a window into Sherman's own feelings about suffering inflicted on southern civilians by the troops he had ordered to "forage liberally" across Georgia's farms. On November 20, Blair's adjutant wrote:

Col. George E. Spencer,
Commanding, First Alabama Cavalry

Colonel: The major-general commanding directs me to say to you
that the outrages committed by your command during the march
are becoming so common, and are of such an aggravated nature,
that they call for some severe and instant mode of correction.
Unless the pillaging of houses and wanton destruction of property
by your regiment ceases at once, he will place every officer in it
under arrest, and recommend them to the department commander
for dishonorable dismissal from the service.

The best measure of Sherman's attitude toward the depredations of the First Alabama is the fact that he did nothing in response to Blair's outburst. The crisp analysis by Spencer's biographer has a long-story-short ring of truth: "The fact is, Spencer and his men were pretty much doing what Sherman wanted done, he knew Spencer and the Alabamians were capable of doing it, and the regiment remained in the vanguard," he wrote.

There were other factors known to Sherman in his role as maestro of a complex orchestra, and most accounts of Union excesses, influenced by Lost Cause horror stories, lack sophistication as to context and political spin. The skillful Blair was almost certainly managing up, knowing that his immediate boss, Major General O. O. Howard, was both a prig and chronic bumbler. This stern, deeply religious New Englander, known as the "Christian General," could not have had less in common with Spencer's southern plowboys.

When Colonel Cornyn had accused them of cowardice in their first battle, Dodge stepped in as their protector. Sherman assumed that role on the March to the Sea. The even-handed author of *The March to the Sea and Beyond: Sherman's Troops in the Savannah and Carolinas Cam-*

paigns, Joseph T. Glatthaar, noted that Howard "went so far as to organize a detective force" to search for takers of "watches, jewelry, money."
A balanced reading is that the Alabamians and some Illinois regiments
were ravenous eaters and wreckers of parlors who carried away little due
to Sherman's strict one-backpack limit.

Even so, as the right wing neared Milledgeville there was an escalat-
ing boisterous tone to its conduct. Consider this eyewitness account
from a Georgia teenager who saw Sherman's army encamped on an
Oconoee River plantation. "Captured wagons, drawn by captured
teams, driven by captured teamsters, and lade with captured grain and
other stores, rumbled incessantly along toward the camps," said the
boy's account in the *Philadelphia Weekly Times.* "Groups of rollicking
cavalrymen, nearly hidden beneath great panniers of hay or fodder
strapped on before and behind their saddles, passed every moment,
singing and laughing as they went. Others with masses of cackling geese
or squealing chickens dangling at their saddle flaps filled up the inter-
vals or accompanied the wagons by way of needless escort."

At this point, Sherman was not immune to the triumphal mood.
There are abundant accounts of Sherman's manic conduct in the field
and of his flippant witticisms, as when Major Henry Hitchcock, his ob-
servant adjutant, wondered aloud about the burning earlier of houses in
Marietta, Georgia. "I never ordered the burning of any dwelling . . . but
can't be helped. *I say Jeff. Davis burnt them.*" Those are Hitchcock's
italics, and they capture a constant theme in Sherman's conversation
and writings: that the South had earned its suffering and could end it by
behaving as orderly citizens of the Republic. As Hitchcock reported of
a later point in his essential *Marching with Sherman,* it was also not
strictly true that he would not order a house burned, as long as it had an
important-enough master.

Before we leave the subject of atrocities, it's important to consider
the psychology of Union soldiers whose absence left exposed their families back in the Alabama high country. Confederate regulars and Home
Guards clung to murder as an instrument of policy. Important Black
Belt newspapers called for instant execution of traitors. As Glatthaar

saw it, "Members of the First Alabama (Union) Cavalry, notorious in Sherman's army for their plundering antics, felt that they had a right to retaliate for the way pro-Confederate southerners had pillaged their family homes, imprisoned family members and drove them from their communities."

Hitchcock's writings (not published until 1927) and Burke Davis in *Sherman's March* provide a good depiction of what life on the road with Sherman must have been like for the orderlies who carried his whiskey, lit his cigars, and spread his blankets beneath the longleaf pines of central Georgia and the live oaks of its coastal plain. "Sherman's headquarters would have done justice to a bandit chief," Davis wrote. "It traveled in a single wagon, including baggage for all clerks, aides and orderlies. 'I think it's as low down as we can get,' he said." As the Atlanta victory brought him a flood of letters, he turned his correspondence over to Hitchcock, a young lawyer he barely knew. "Just tell 'em something sweet, Hitchcock—you know, honey and molasses." One of Grant's staff officers, Horace Porter, sent on a visit to Sherman, captured this portrait: "With his large frame, tall, gaunt form, restless hazel eyes, aquiline nose, bronzed face, and crisp beard, he looked like the picture of 'grim-visaged war.'"

His usual seat in camp was a cracker box, and whether telling a joke or barking orders, he talked incessantly. "He talked of the enemy, of Southern women, of U.S. Grant and President Lincoln, heedlessly gulping his food, then returning to the smoldering cigar, still talking and laughing, giving orders . . . 'bright and chipper,' one of his generals noted." A war correspondent, allowed a visit despite Sherman's hatred of the "free press," reported, "He walked, talked or laughed all over. He perspired thought at every pore . . . pleasant and affable . . . engaging with a mood that shifted like a barometer." He loved strolling among soldiers at their campfires. "No better body of soldiers in America," he told Grant. And he never wavered from the plan he and Grant had devised when Lincoln, weary of dilatory West Pointers and beribboned strutters, gave them control of the war. But when Sherman pulled this small cluster of southern mountaineers into his inner circle, it was not

because they were murderers or beyond discipline. Even as pro-
Confederate a historian as Shelby Foote attested in an interview that
"it's absolutely incredible" that the Union invaders army committed "so
few atrocities. Sherman marched with 60,000 men slap across Georgia,
then straight up through the Carolinas, burning, looting, doing everything in the world—but I don't know of a single case of rape. That's
amazing because hatreds run higher in civil wars."

So this was the role the First Alabama had carved for itself as the
Union legions neared the temporary state capital at Milledgeville. In
slightly over two years in the ranks, through the roughest kind of on-the-
job training, the First Alabama Cavalry had become fearless probers
of new terrain and ready to fight the enemy when it made a stand. A
sleepily prosperous cotton-trading and college town, Milledgeville lay
80 miles from Atlanta and 140 miles from Savannah. Many of the Alabama Unionists were now about 250 miles southeast of the tavern where
they had heard Chris Sheats's "Free State of Winston" speech, almost
certainly farther from their embattled families than most of them had
ever been. If they were ferocious, it was worry that made them so. They
were approaching the peak of their military careers and a burst of national recognition and fame that would quickly disappear. Thanks to the
letters, diaries, and memoirs of Sherman and his officers, we have a remarkably clear picture of this period.

The riotous behavior of what Sherman biographer John E. Marszalek called this "lean, hard army" was peaking as Sherman moved into
the governor's mansion in Milledgeville on November 23, 1864. The army's approach had been marked by the constant shooting of chicken
and pigs in an impromptu hunt so manic that two Union soldiers were
killed and three wounded by their own comrades. Sherman calmly
blamed the chaos on irritating but irrelevant "stragglers . . . [who] are
harder to control than the enemy." General Judson "Kill Cavalry" Kilpatrick, flush with a victory en route over "Fighting Joe" Wheeler's
good cavalry, presided at a drunken mock assembly in the Georgia legislative hall in which Yankee officers "voted" to repeal secession. Major
Hitchcock primly claimed that he was too busy with paperwork to serve

as recording secretary of the rowdy charade. In his *Memoirs,* Sherman noted, "I was not present at these frolics, but heard of them at the time, and enjoyed the joke." Here lies a key to understanding Sherman's tolerance for the tactics that have gone into Lost Cause legend as war crimes against southern property and non-combatants. Marszalek says Sherman was driven by "a passion for order," and he viewed total war as a necessary tool for restoring it. "Sherman's march across Georgia was the successful implementation of the use of destruction to produce order," Marszalek wrote in *Sherman: A Soldier's Passion for Order.* Sherman's view of war was clinical, supremely rational, and icily unforgiving of Confederate emotionalism. He summed up his Georgia campaign and subsequent move into South Carolina as a victory "won with minimal human casualties though substantial property loss." He wanted to convince "chastened" southerners they must rejoin the Union. "If they refused, he was ready to inflict further lessons in the Carolinas."

I should acknowledge a debt to Steven Harrell, a lawyer and sometime novelist born in Milledgeville, for teasing out the fascinating background of the two references to Lieutenant David R. Snelling in the *Memoirs.* Harrell's novel *The Unionist* is based on an accurate chronology of the march and, using a variety of sources, dramatizes the fact that Snelling became a significantly popular figure in Sherman's campfire circle. In evaluating Snelling's personal qualities, I came to see him as a counterpart to Chris Sheats of Alabama. As Clayton J. Butler put it, "C. C. Sheats was an unusually strident figure who represented an unusually outspoken constituency" of Unionists who nonetheless had to suppress their opinions to avoid persecution. The same was true of Snelling, who had attended a good private preparatory school and, unlike Sheats, even managed a year or two of college. His education served him well in dealings with senior officers and with Sheats himself.

Placing Snelling in context as a founding spirit of the First Alabama, worthy of standing alongside Chris Sheats, is illuminating as a matter of frontier South sociology. Snelling, born in 1836, was three years younger than Sheats. They had in common an antipathy toward slavery that, while more political and geographic for Sheats, was more spiritual for

Snelling. Together, they covered the gamut of motivations that led the majority of white common folk in the South to regard slavery more as an inconvenient accident of history than as an unalloyed blessing. As descendants of the Anglo-Celtic migration that swept from Pennsylvania, down the valley of Virginia, through the Carolinas, and across Georgia and on into Alabama, both men were heirs to the brand of independence of spirit indigenous to the upland South via Daniel Boone and Andrew Jackson. This fractious heritage made a truly monolithic South the stuff of Confederate dreams rather than a reality that could sustain a national identity and loyalty. Snelling's Virginia-born father and his mother, born to slave-owning families in South Carolina, were a notch higher on the social scale than the Sheatses, who came into Alabama from Georgia and established themselves as self-sufficient landowners and petty officeholders.

Once the Atlanta campaign began, Snelling's military awareness and his ease with Sherman seemed to blossom. The contrast between his background and position with that of Sherman made him stand out to officers like Lieutenant Colonel George Ward Nichols, a peacetime journalist with a good eye for a story with legs. In 1865, on assignment from *Harper's New Monthly Magazine,* he traveled to Springfield, Missouri, and wrote the sensationally exaggerated article that created the legend of Wild Bill Hickok. He seemed to sense that Snelling, too, had the star quality needed in a bootstrap hero.

> The lieutenant commanding the escort of General Sherman was born and had always lived in Milledgeville, is an officer of the first Alabama cavalry regiment, and tells me that he never saw a copy of the New York Tribune until he joined our army. His history, by the way, is a most interesting one, and will one day be worth the telling. His adherence to the Union grew out of his natural abhorrence of slavery, whose horrors he had witnessed from childhood. His name is Snelling—a young man of good education, of high integrity, simple-hearted, and brave, who has been most useful to

the cause of this country. It surprised no one when Snelling told Sherman he wanted to confront the uncle who raised him after his own father died. This man, David Lester, had sent his own sons to a good college while sending David to a lesser school and then dispatching him to the cottonfields as an overseer. The matter came up when Sherman, as was his habit, was interviewing an elderly slave who had crept up to murmur "Dey say you is Massa Sherman." Sherman recalled, "He only wanted to look at me, and kept muttering, 'Dis nigger can't sleep tonight.'"

Like Grant, Sherman considered Black people inferior, but his conduct, while patronizing, was often solicitous. He prided himself on being approachable and had his staff give the old man a strong drink that loosened his tongue. This passage from the *Memoirs* captures the mood.

Lieutenant Snelling, who commanded my escort, was a Georgian, and recognized in this old slave a favorite slave of his uncle, who resided about six miles off; but the old slave did not at first recognize his young master in our uniform. One of my staff officers asked him what had become of his young master, George. He did not know, only that he had gone off to war, and he supposed him killed, as a matter of course. His attention was then drawn to Snelling's face, when he fell on his knees and thanked God that he had found his young master alive and along with the Yankees. Snelling inquired all about his uncle and the family, asked my permission to go and pay his uncle a visit, which I granted, of course, and the next morning he described to me his visit. The uncle was not cordial, by any means, to find his nephew in the ranks of the host that was desolating the land, and Snelling came back, having exchanged his tired horse for a fresher one out of his uncle's stables, explaining that surely some of the "bummers" would have got the horse had he not.

Aside from the writings of his supervising officers, much of what we know about Snelling comes from a biased source that illuminates a distinctive feature of a post-Confederate culture that varies subtly from state to state. In the Alabama Black Belt, willful, sullen defiance became the dominant postbellum mood, as reflected in Alabama politics up to the present day. In Georgia's cotton country, the legacy of the march was an enduring but fatalistic self-pity, a factor that may figure in Georgia's more nuanced response to racial change. It's revealing that Georgia's emphasis on undeserved suffering resulted in Lieutenant Snelling, who was, after all, a fairly obscure figure, meriting his very own Dunningite biographer with links to the Lost Cause mother church at Columbia. The scholarly article "David R. Snelling: A Story of Desertion and Defection in the Civil War" appeared in the *Georgia Review* from the University of Georgia in 1956, when the university's history department reflected the magnolia-scented nostalgia of E. Merton Coulter. Coulter's masterwork, *The South During Reconstruction,* is regarded as the last important contribution to the Dunning School canon. The author of the article, Professor J. C. Bonner (1904–1984), got a double dose of Dunning doctrine. He earned his PhD at the University of North Carolina (UNC) in 1943 during the heyday of J. G. de Roulhac Hamilton, one of the six original doctoral students Dunning dispatched to the South as disciples of the plantation gentry. This was the same influential group that included Walter L. Fleming. I will expand on this kind of historians' incest as a Lost Cause motif in the final section of this book. For now, it's worth observing that Bonner's determination to defame Snelling stemmed from a family grudge. From 1944 to 1969, J. C. Bonner was the history chair at what was then Georgia State College for Women in Milledgeville. Professor Bonner was related to Captain Richard Bonner, the Confederate officer who recruited a reluctant Snelling into the 57th Georgia Infantry, C.S.A. while Snelling was unhappily employed on the plantation of his wealthy uncle, David Lester. Captain Bonner would marry one of the Lester daughters after the war and no doubt felt doubly aggrieved by Snelling's defection to the Union army, which had burned the nearby Bonner plantation a few months before the march began.

Snelling's visit to his uncle, which Sherman endorsed, preceded the burning of the Lester cotton gin on November 22, 1864.

Even so, the historian Bonner conceded that Snelling's knowledge of Georgia roads and his "constant association" with Sherman "made him an extraordinary figure in an army of 65,000 men who were now swarming over the Georgia countryside." But from the point of view of Bonner, Snelling had a fatal flaw for a Georgia native. "Snelling was temperamentally unequipped for the job of supervising Negro slaves." He speculated that this "abhorrence of slavery as an institution" may have been conditioned by "the circumstances of poverty and his status as a poor relation to the affluent Lester family." But with his Sherman alliance, Snelling appeared headed for great things after as he sought to make his mark in journalism and politics in Alabama and Arkansas during Reconstruction. By 1882, Snelling had moved on to establish the *Ozark Echo,* a weekly newspaper in Arkansas. Bonner reported that a lawyer there remembered him as "the smartest man I ever knew" and a person of extraordinary generosity. But nothing could erase the stain on his military record represented by his association with the First Alabama and a general who promised to turn all of Georgia into a single military target. "It is significant to note that this Tory regiment achieved the reputation of having wrought more unnecessary destruction to civilian property than any other unit which participated in the Georgia campaign," Bonner concluded in fidelity to the Lost Cause principle of restricting war to military targets.

Major Henry Hitchcock's memoir, *Marching with Sherman,* published by Yale University Press in 1927, has come to be regarded as definitive in regard to Sherman's inner circle. On key points, Hitchcock, a member of a sophisticated political family, dilates upon Sherman's observations about the value of Snelling's advice about the roadways and sociology of middle Georgia.

> All through this pine country there are better farms than we expected, and large stores of corn, fodder and potatoes (sweet), but Lieut. Snelling tells me that this is true only along the main roads

and that off these, there are either no farms or mere patches cultivated by the poorer whites, whom he described as a very inferior class. S. is the lieutenant commanding our Headquarters escort (cavalry) and was assigned to that duty for this trip by Col. Spencer of "1st Alabama Regiment" because he is a native Georgian, "raised" near Milledgeville. People whom he speaks of as very ignorant, etc., certainly cannot be very high in point of culture or education—"poor white trash." But he is cool, quiet and certainly brave. He has repeatedly run great risk on this trip, going off on scouting and foraging parties, after horses, etc. with five and ten men. Yesterday morning we thought he was "gone up."

But instead of being killed or captured, Snelling had led his men on a fifty-mile end run around Rebel cavalry and rejoined the main column as it moved into Milledgeville on the way to greater dangers. This anecdote about Snelling's roundabout rides leads me to a quibble I have with Hoole and even the solid Clayton Butler, who contend that the First's exposure to danger was sporadic by virtue of the episodic nature of actual combat. It seems to me, rather, that the First existed in an atmosphere of constant threat, leavened by moments of ease and even amusement. Such moments were used by Sherman to cement his bond with his subordinates and ridicule his enemies.

One "unusually raw and cold" afternoon, Snelling led the way to a house he knew for a rest stop. "My orderly was at hand with his invariable saddle-bags, which contained a change of underclothing, my maps, a flask of whiskey, and a bunch of cigars," Sherman wrote. "Taking a drink and lighting a cigar, I walked to a row of negro-huts close by, entered one and I found a soldier or two warming themselves by a wood fire. I took their place by the fire intending to wait till our wagons had got up, and a camp made for the night."

An elderly female slave told the general he could find a more gracious house down the road. There, upon entering a comfortable room, "I saw a small box, like a candle-box, marked 'Howell Cobb,' and, on inquiring of a Negro, found that we were at the plantation of General Howell

Cobb, of Georgia, one of the leading rebels of the South," Sherman re-called, noting that Cobb had served President Buchanan as secretary of the treasury, igniting his special animus toward public figures who had grown prosperous in government service, only to become disloyal. "Of course, we confiscated his property, and found it rich in corn, beans, pea-nuts, and sorghum-molasses. . . . I sent word back to General Davis to explain whose plantation it was, and instructed him to spare nothing. That night huge bonfires consumed the fence-rails, kept our soldiers warm, and the teamsters and men, as well as the slaves, carried off an immense quantity of corn and provisions of all sorts."

If there's a note of glee in Sherman's summary, it probably had to do with the fact that the self-satisfied Cobb was just the kind of lofty, pomp-ous turncoat he detested, laboring to destroy a government he had also served as Speaker of the U.S. House of Representatives. Without show-ing a smidgen of regret, Cobb emerged in 1861 in Montgomery as main architect of the Confederacy's provisional government and promoted the building of the prison at Andersonville. Burning out Cobb under-scored the clarity of Sherman's political vision. If southerners wanted to preserve their property, every white person, gentry and common folk alike, must end their support for an army in rebellion. It's a waste-laying version of Martin Luther King Jr.'s message of nonviolence to places like Birmingham: If the white majority wanted calm streets and a flourishing economy, they had to abandon an entire cultural mindset. Once back in the town where he was educated and benefited from the largesse of his plantation-owning uncles, Snelling seemed to be steeped in the Sher-man doctrine.

Notwithstanding the slight divergences in background, both the Sheats and Snelling families produced sons who were nonconforming political thinkers who partook of the political ethos that spawned the notion of the "Free State of Nickajack" where the Appalachian sections of Alabama, Tennessee, and Georgia come together in a dogleg intersec-tion. This region, close to mountainous parts of the Carolinas as well, was defined not only because of its topography; its egalitarian personal-ity and corn-based agriculture made it culturally distinctive from the layered social world of the cotton-growing southern flatlands. "The First Alabama Cavalry drew its men from the politically marginalized corners of the Deep South, where the Union army's presence provided an outlet for their collective frustration," wrote Clayton Butler. Even though an estimated three-quarters of its men came from Alabama, others arrived from other states with the same difficult saw-toothed terrain and contentious spirit: 271 from Georgia, 150 from Tennessee, 76 from North Carolina, and 65 from Mississippi. Even South Carolina, the place that invented the political impulse to break apart America, contributed 98 native-born sons to the outfit. This supports Richard Nelson Current's groundbreaking discovery that loyalty to the Union was a significant pan-southern bond. Paul D. Escott's definitional scholarship on "the failure of Confederate nationalism" argues that Confederate leaders' inability to instill a sense of united purpose was the fundamental reason that the South lost the war. Of course, no one had more to do with the final collapse of Rebel will than Sherman. Yet the impression that Alabamians had little to do with the Union's culminating campaign was planted with such success that even Wesley S. Thompson, who had been tutored by John Bennett Weaver, came away convinced that the Free Staters didn't really matter. His 1968 nonfiction book *The Free State of Winston* turned out to be more erroneous than *Tories of the Hill,* with an odd passage seemingly designed to assure Alabamians not to worry about official Alabama's erasure of the First Alabama from its history:

> The fact that the First Alabama Cavalry made very little contribution toward the Union winning the war may be explained on the basis of that many, if not most of these men, preferred to be neutral on the conflict and that they joined the Union forces—not so much as a means of becoming outstanding soldiers as to provide a means of safety for themselves during the war. This principle was well understood and sanctioned by some of the Federal officials in order to prevent their joining up with the Confederate armies.

If the First Alabama was a safe haven, it wasn't much of one. Out of the 2,000-plus enlistees, 345 were killed in action or died of other causes. That's about 2.5 percent lower than the overall death rate in both armies, which lost 620,000. The most dangerous part of the march lay ahead. If the First Alabama "made very little contribution" to Union victory, that would have been news to Sherman and Blair, the generals who followed them down sandy roads to the sea. Indeed, these men from the hills seemed to have a gift for coastal warfare. It was, by comparison to north Alabama, an easeful environment for fighting, a place that allowed fast riding on level ground, a place with open forests of pine and oak, a terrain of good sight lines with few gullies, caves, and boulders to hide the people who were shooting at you. Sherman had a gift for finding men with the skills he needed at any given phase of a campaign, and it was as if Spencer and his freckle-bellied country boys were made for the business of closing in on Savannah. Each night, dozens of them slept just outside the circle of light from the campfire their comrades under Lieutenant Snelling had built for Sherman. At this point, only a few hundred people back home on their mountain land in Alabama knew, through letter and the grapevine, that the young men from Alabama's insular hill country were center stage in the final act of the war to save the Republic, as directed by their worldly commander. Thanks to the way history was written, generations of Alabamians would remain ignorant of that fact, even unto the present day. What, one wonders, did they make of this man Sherman, who shared many of the prejudices of the self-styled aristocrats they were trying to defeat?

25

UNCLE BILLY AND HIS BOYS

ON SOME NIGHTS en route to the coast, George Spencer visited Sherman's tent to discuss the next thrusts against the ten thousand entrenched infantrymen with which General William J. Hardee was trying to defend Savannah. Hardee's nickname was "Old Reliable," a tribute to the fact that he had better judgment than the two Rebel superiors he hated, Braxton Bragg and John Bell Hood. At this point, Hardee's military aim was modest. He wanted to do what Bragg and Hood had failed to do at Atlanta, which was to prevent Savannah from being bombed flat and burned by Sherman. Sherman's "aim . . . was to whip the rebels, to humble their pride, to follow them to their inmost recesses, and make them fear and dread us." On the surface, then, the stakes looked simple, but much intrigue was afoot, some aspects of which would bring into play two of Sherman's weaknesses: his temper and his distaste for African Americans.

Now that he had the South by its throat, Sherman's grandiosity and his "soldier's passion for order" were on full display. It's fair to say of his escort that few ordinary Alabamians have ever had such prolonged exposure to so towering an American figure, and he was a man who wanted to be observed at his peak. "I wish my friends and enemies to understand me," Sherman wrote in an argumentative preface to his *Memoirs*.

His allies and foes should view him not as a scholar but as "a witness on the stand of the great tribunal of history." By that standard, the subject of race marks one of the few areas in which Sherman's own testimony does not serve him well.

The white volunteers in his escort were not the only Alabamians in his army of conquest. It included three companies of "Pioneers" of the 110th United States Colored Infantry assigned to build corduroy roads in the boggy lowlands between Milledgeville and Savannah. Reflecting prejudices that were widespread in the Union officer corps, Sherman resisted assigning freed slaves to front-line duty, although the combat records of outfits like the 54th Massachusetts showed that Black soldiers fought bravely when given the chance. But Sherman and Grant were both men of their times. Both blamed "the Jews" for the feverish cotton trading practiced by gentile commanders and endorsed by Lincoln and Davis. As for freed slaves, Grant's views were hardly less biased, but less pungently expressed than Sherman's. As Sherman told Dodge of his reluctance to use his U.S. Colored Troops as combat soldiers, "I do not propose in this campaign that the rebels shall say it was necessary for me to whip them, to take part of their [slaves] to do it." As was his habit, he used the most pungent epithet to describe the freed Black people.

Understanding Sherman's attitudes as to race and class challenges the skills of would-be psychobiographers. His life, like that of so many nineteenth-century icons, illustrates that professional brilliance does not fence off a formidable intellect from the dominant stereotypes of a given era. As to caste, he wanted Confederate officials and especially the South's landed "chivalry" to understand that they had been crushed by a superior army of white commoners. He bonded ferociously with the men close to him, whether they were officers who shared his elite background or mud soldiers with Dixie pedigrees. After Milledgeville, the vision of Savannah lured him on, like a ripe peach trembling on its limb, begging to be plucked. He fretted about the twenty thousand freed slaves who left Georgia plantations to follow his army and, in his jaundiced view, soak up its resources. He failed to reprimand General Jeff C. Davis, a Kentuckian suspected of Copperhead tendencies, for allowing several hundred slaves to drown when he removed a pontoon bridge at a deep creek. Yet Sherman relished his role as liberator. He often interviewed slaves encountered in the field, and once installed in Savannah he greeted with ceremonial courtesy the delegations of ex-slaves who begged to meet him. In this last stage of the march, soldiers, too, wrestled with the paradoxical "American dilemma" of race, to borrow Gunnar Myrdal's term.

Joseph T. Glatthaars's incisive 1985 study, *The March to the Sea and Beyond,* documented a change in attitude around Union campfires between the army's departure from Milledgeville on November 25 and its arrival outside Savannah on December 11, 1864. Even those who had been lukewarm about the Emancipation Proclamation now saw the elimination of slavery as a worthy moral goal that was also essential to restoration of American nationhood. "Campfire discussions no longer centered on whether or not slaves should be free," Glatthaar concluded. "That was a willingly accepted fact. Instead they revolved around what rights freed men should have in peacetime." And up and down the chain of command the scent of victory seemed to override the constant fear of annihilation that is a fact of wartime life. "I wouldn't miss going on this expedition for 6 months pay," a Union officer confided to his diary when departing for Savannah. The First Alabama Cavalry, as part of Blair's forward element and, increasingly, as part of "Kill Cavalry" Kilpatrick's merged cavalry division, had ringside seats to the lying competition that developed between Kilpatrick and his constant adversary, "Fighting Joe" Wheeler, who persisted with his mosquito-like attacks. "As reported by Kilpatrick and Wheeler, the intensity of the fights between the Union and Confederate cavalry on the march was in the same class as the battles of Shiloh, Antietam, Gettysburg, and Chickamauga," Glatthaar concluded with sarcasm. Wheeler's falsehoods about stampeding his fearful adversaries made it into newspaper accounts that irritated Sherman, who had settled into his persona as the grand conqueror. Lost Cause historians ignored one salient fact about this phase of the war. A variety of diaries by march veterans make a strong case that Wheeler's Alabama cavalrymen were more feared as plunderers by Georgia civilians than their First Alabama neighbors from back home. In the ranks, the daily experience at this point in the campaign was very much like that recorded by war-lovers from Napoleon to Teddy Roosevelt and Winston Churchill: Combat is the supreme adventure for young men who survive it. An Illinois officer, after observing a clash between the commands of Wheeler and Kilpatrick, observed that "a cavalry fight is just about as much fun as a fox hunt; but, of course, in the midst of the fun somebody is getting hurt all the time."

Sherman's infantrymen reflected another of Uncle Billy's biases, that the cavalry avoided the hard fighting, but that was not the case for the First Alabama, in part because of their proximity to the commander. Also, danger increased for the First Alabama because of a tactic devised by Sherman's mapmaker, Captain Andrew Hickenlooper, who had bonded with the Alabamians at Kennesaw Mountain and now camped with them as part of the headquarters staff. Although Dodge was no longer available, at this point Colonel Spencer came into his own, using private talks with Sherman to denigrate the generals—Blair, John A. Logan, and O. O. Howard—who had replaced his mentor. When Sherman confessed to him that Blair had "political power that is useless to fight," Spencer boldly accused him of being unfair to Dodge. "I have found out the secret of managing him," Spencer wrote the recuperating Blair. "It is to complain of bad treatment and injustice on his part. He can stand anything but that." In letters and field reports, Spencer emerges as a tireless conniver who was proving increasingly valuable and brave as a leader of the marchers. Subservience was not part of his nature. He called Blair, now his direct superior, "an unmitigated nuisance," even though a strange chemistry had developed between the patrician Blair and his southern cavalrymen.

One reason was that as leaders of Blair's XVII Corps of 13,164 men, the First knew how to push back that familiar foe from back home, "Fighting Joe" Wheeler. With his fondness for narrative detail, Burke Davis noted that Wheeler was, at twenty-eight, the youngest and probably the smallest major general in either army. He was five feet five inches tall and weighed 120 pounds "with a rock in each pocket." He had in common with Sherman a personality "as restless as a disembodied spirit and as active as a cat . . . frank, fearless, outspoken to the verge of bluntness." In contrast to Sherman, he favored snappy dress, sometimes including a red sash and a black plumed hat. A comrade described him as "game as a pebble," and indeed, he had about as much judgment as a rock. Nonetheless, Sherman respected Wheeler for his "hard and persistent fighting ever since the beginning of the Atlanta campaign."

Contrary to Hoole's depiction of them as cowards, the First Alabama was crucial to the mission of Kilpatrick's cavalry division, which was double the size of Wheeler's reduced force of twenty-five hundred. Their job was to bump back Wheeler's raiders. As guides, the First Alabama repeatedly probed Wheeler's skirmish lines and pickets. "Skirmishing" is a catchall term used dismissively by Civil War writers who've never been shot at. But it's extremely dangerous work that cost a number of First Alabama troopers their lives. At this stage of the war, skirmishes meant encountering potshot artists armed with fast-loading carbines who would unleash a volley and then dash back to their own lines. Andrew Hickenlooper, who had risen to lieutenant colonel in his role as Blair's adjutant, devised a method of inviting such contacts that must have seemed exhilarating to survivors. He closely supervised the leaders of his advance cavalry, including Lieutenant Francis Tupper of the First Alabama and Lieutenant David F. Day, Blair's daring chief scout, who had won the Congressional Medal of Honor at Vicksburg. The probing technique designed by Hickenlooper required the cavalry units to ride at a gallop toward the enemy, under orders not to stop at a single shot, but to deploy skirmishers only when they received a volley. "Close up!" Hickenlooper would shout, meaning the lead battalion would send out a skirmish line. "He would only call a halt if a large hostile force developed behind breastworks" or a natural barrier like a river, according to the historian Michael David Kaplan. "On those occasions the men would dismount, leave their mounts in the care of designated horse holders and advance on the enemy. Usually, these tactics dislodged the Rebels and the infantry would not have to be called upon to supply reinforcements." This "cavalry screen," as it was called, was "largely responsible for preventing the short-handed Confederates from delaying the progress of Blair's corps."

But sometimes these run-ins led to the kind of set battles that awaited Blair's division at the Oconee River on November 25. Howard, a bumbler, and the more able Blair both thought they could take their wing of the army across the Oconee at Ball's Ferry. Not surprisingly, the State of Georgia has been more generous than Alabama officialdom in recognizing the First Alabama through a highway marker, erected in 1957, that says: "On Nov. 24, 1864, the 1st Alabama Cavalry [US] reached Ball's Ferry (1/4 mile N) to secure it for the passage of the Left Wing (15th and 17th Corps) of Gen. Sherman's army [US], which had left Atlanta on Nov. 15th on its destructive March to the Sea. Finding the boat on the east bank, guarded by Confederate pickets, the cavalrymen moved upstream, crossed on rafts, and dislodged the pickets, but developed a larger force [CS] approaching the ferry and were forced to recross the river under fire." Pontoon builders from Michigan arrived, allowing the XV and XVII Corps to cross on November 27 after Union infantry dislodged dug-in Confederates on the south bank. In his monograph on Spencer's career, Professor Seip was one of the few mainstream historians to address the disparity between the First Alabama's accomplishments and its lack of recognition. "The regiment's advancework for Blair, Howard, and Sherman was constant for nearly a month, and one wonders, if the unit had been of Northern origin if it would been put so consistently out front or whether it would have received better press and historical coverage. But again, the men of the regiment were Southerners who understood the native population and the lay of the land, and it seemed that they belonged in front."

Major Hitchcock's diary, with its usual italics, recorded both the sporadic nature of the fighting to date and the increasing prominence of the First Alabama's commander. "I learned today from Col. Spencer of our 1st Alabama Cavalry, that the only fight at all with our cavalry about here was with fifty of his men who crossed Oconee at Ball's Ferry in the morning of the 25th—held the position all day—were two or three times attacked, repulsed Rebs having lost six killed and fifteen wounded."

Soon Hitchcock also noted that Sherman was fuming about baseless claims that found their way into northern newspapers from Wheeler and General William J. Hardee, who was in charge of defending Savannah, that they had " 'whipped Kilpatrick's cavalry division' at Oconee!!" Thus northern readers were completely misinformed about "our first week's uninterrupted march" and actually believed that Sherman was about to retreat. Sherman "was very angry at these publications and said last night he had a great mind to resign as soon as this campaign ended— 'it's impossible to carry on war with a free press.' That's talk and only means how provoked he is. No wonder."

That burst of anger from Sherman was mild compared to what happened the next time the First Alabama took casualties. This towering rage was rooted in the close bond Sherman formed with officers of all ranks and in his contempt for the tactics embraced by a panicked Jefferson Davis. Responding to increasingly desperate messages from Howell Cobb to send more troops to stop Sherman, Davis sought to placate Cobb. On November 18, only four days before Cobb's plantation was to burn, Davis wrote the Georgian that he would have the Confederacy's ace bombmaker, General Gabriel Rains, put "torpedoes"— land mines—from his munitions factory at Macon in front of Sherman's army. As Hickenlooper led cavalrymen from a camp about fifteen miles outside Savannah on December 7, Lieutenant Day's horse was shot dead. Sent sprawling on the ground, Day saw signs that mines had been placed in the road ahead. "A squad of First Alabama Cavalry galloped to his rescue, and he was unable to warn them in time." A dozen more horses and several men were injured as Hickenlooper and Tupper rushed to brush the dirt away from one of the torpedoes, apparently to get a closer look at the device. It detonated, the fragments missing Hickenlooper, but "literally blowing off all of the flesh from one of [Tupper's] legs," Sherman wrote later. "This was not war, but murder, and it made me very angry," Sherman said. Day covered Tupper with a blanket to await the surgeons and amputation. Sherman's next steps became one of the March's most famous episodes.

I immediately ordered a lot of rebel prisoners to be brought from the provost-guard, armed with picks and spades, and made them march in close order along the road, so as to explode their own torpedoes, or so to discover and dig them up. They begged hard, but I reiterated the order, and could hardly help laughing at their stepping so gingerly along the road, where it was supposed sunken torpedoes might explode at each step, but they found no other torpedoes till near Ft. McAllister.

Sherman's mood was not lightened when he saw a puff of smoke from an accurate cannon, called the Whitworth Rifle, aimed at him from the parapets outside Savannah. Stepping aside, he saw the thirty-two-pound missile carry away the head of a Black civilian standing near him. Perhaps these incidents made Sherman ever more solicitous for his own men over the next two days as he pondered how to approach the ten thousand troops Hardee put in trenches in front of Savannah. Now the men of the First Alabama seemed to be everywhere as Sherman formed his plan to negate Fort McAllister as the city's last guardian outpost. By this time the First Alabama had been formally transferred to Kilpatrick, becoming a third division of his cavalry force. Sherman knew that Kilpatrick, whom he had once called "a hell of a damn fool," would seal the seaward side of the fort even though it bristled with heavy artillery. Judging from the tone of his writing, this was a time of heavy nostalgia for Sherman. From his days around Vicksburg, Sherman knew swamp warfare better than any general in either army, with the possible exception of Grant. He vetoed a plan by O. O. Howard to take his command across the Ogeechee River and approach Savannah through the riverine marshes.

On the night of December 12, he called a trusted West Pointer from Vermont, Major General William Babcock Hazen, to his quarters in a plantation house five miles from Savannah. He gave the hawk-faced forty-five-year-old orders to march his XV Corps down the right bank of the river and "carry Fort McAllister by storm." Sherman knew the man and the troops he was picking to remove this last redoubt. Uncle Billy also realized he had the Confederacy by the throat, and there was nothing avuncular about the cold deliberation with which he moved. "I explained to General Hazen, fully, that on his action depended the safety of the whole army, and the success of the campaign. Kilpatrick had already felt the fort, and gone further down the coast to Kilkenny Bluff, or St. Catherine's Sound, where, on the same day, he had communication with a vessel belonging to the blockading fleet. . . . I was not aware of this fact, and trusted entirely to General Hazen and his division of infantry, the Second of the Fifteenth Corps, the same old division which I had commanded at Shiloh and Vicksburg, in which I felt a special pride and confidence."

With the fort squeezed between two generals he trusted, Sherman moved ten miles down the Ogeechee to a rice plantation. An observation platform had been put up there for his staff officers and escort. The parochialist in me is compelled to observe that at this decisive moment Alabamians were on both sides of the fort as a Union steamer came up the river. "Is Fort McAllister taken?" they signaled. Sherman signaled back, "Not yet, but it will be in a minute." Sherman watched across the salt marsh as Hazen led his men out of the woods, and the fort fell within minutes, with a loss of twenty-four Union men killed and sixteen Confederates. Sherman, this hater of slavery who was ever in the grip of the reflexive racism of his time and profession, "exclaimed, in the language of the poor Negro at Cobb's plantation, 'This nigger will have no sleep this night!'"

I think it's fair to say that Alabama scholars expended thousands of hours in denial about the weighty, indeed eerie symbolism at this apex moment that so excited Uncle Billy. Several companies of the "mountain whites" most despised by our state's political leaders and its social elite were with Sherman when his fist closed on the Rebel windpipe. Years later, Grenville Dodge would tell of Sherman's rage on the day of Tupper's injury, although he had not witnessed this attack on Sherman's Alabama outfit. Dodge's purpose was political. He was defending his close friend, President Theodore Roosevelt, in a 1902 speech ridiculing

American newspaper journalists calling for Roosevelt to punish U.S. troops using cruel tactics in the American-Philippine War. Dodge noted that no one had called for Sherman to be demoted or shot for the way he responded to Confederate tactics. "In one case torpedoes were placed under a road over which our troops were marching, and several soldiers were killed. Sherman happened to come along just at that time, and said to the Colonel of the First Alabama Cavalry, which was his escort, 'Burn the country within fifteen miles surrounding this spot.' You all know what that meant; it was a license under which other things besides burning was done. An eye-witness describes Sherman's march to the sea and through the Carolinas as a 'cloud of smoke by day and a pillar of fire by night.'" For purposes of entertaining a twentieth-century political audience, Dodge had bought into the scorched-earth exaggerations then being vigorously promoted by the Dunning School and the Lost Cause movement. In reality, at this point in the war Sherman had been moving too methodically to mess with pillars of fire, and besides, Savannah was much too valuable to torch.

On December 18, General Hardee sent a letter to Sherman declining to surrender, and Sherman waited, perhaps too patiently, as Hardee slipped one of the last functioning Confederate armies across the Savannah River and into South Carolina. On December 22, Sherman sent his famous cable to Lincoln saying, "I beg to present you a Christmas present the city of Savannah, with one hundred and fifty heavy guns and plenty of ammunition, also about twenty-five thousand bales of cotton."

The ever-calculating Sherman was smart to mention the cotton. Soon Secretary of War Stanton would arrive to take possession of it on behalf of his political cronies and to accuse Sherman of treating cruelly the freed slaves who followed his army into town. Only a week after his troops invested Savannah, Sherman's commander and defender, Henry Halleck, wrote from Washington that Stanton and others around Lincoln were accusing Sherman of an "*almost criminal dislike to the negro*" (Halleck's italics). But that sniping did not dim the luster of the parade of review that took place when Generals Logan and Blair led their troops down Savannah's main street. Whatever his past differences with Dodge and Spencer, Blair gave the place of honor to the First Alabama in the front right column "in recognition of its role and service throughout the brief campaign," as Christopher Rein put it in 2019. To my knowledge, no history of Alabama published earlier mentions the fact that the First Alabama was selected for this signal proof of its contribution to the Union war effort. The long and short of this neglected fact of southern history is that Alabama Unionists led the victory parade that culminated the March to the Sea. One has to wonder if Alabama's traditional reputation for political backwardness would have been altered if its educated class had embraced that fact rather than buried it. Could the Alabama Inferiority Syndrome have survived praise for the First Alabama's patriotism?

For Spencer, an annunciatory moment of praise occurred as the march reached Savannah. For the past fifteen days Blair and Sherman had ridden behind the First Alabama and been their campmates. In a letter written on December 16 to the recuperating Dodge, he reported on a summing-up conversation with Sherman: "He took occasion yesterday to say to me that I had the best Cavalry Regiment he ever saw & has taken his escort from the regiment." Even allowing for Spencer's boastfulness, it puts paid to the allegation that the First Alabama was never close to the front.

As for the men who marched to the coast with Georgia's nemesis, they went into camp at a place called Thunderbolt to await Sherman's next campaign. It was a march through the Carolinas, anticlimactic in some ways, yet notable because it brought into the forefront of glory and public embarrassment two of the irrepressible rascals of the war, Judson "Kill Cavalry" Kilpatrick and George Eliphaz Spencer of the First Alabama.

26

SKEDADDLING HOME

As 1865 BEGAN, Grant and Sherman knew they were in the endgame of the war Lincoln had entrusted to them, but they were at odds as to how to play it. As they had planned, Grant had Lee at bay outside Richmond. Grant wanted to put Sherman's army on ships, bring them to Virginia, and crush Lee's Army of Northern Virginia between them. Sherman insisted on taking his troops into the Carolinas in order to prevent the Confederacy's best remaining general, Joseph Johnston, from taking a dwindling but still viable force of perhaps twenty thousand into Virginia to rescue Lee. Grant backed down because he couldn't find enough ships, although Sherman did move Howard's wing by water to Beaufort, South Carolina. The stage was set for Kilpatrick and Spencer to take their star turns, traveling by land under General Henry W. Slocum, commander of what was now called the Army of Georgia. They were chasing Hardee, and all were to rendezvous with Sherman in the unscarred city of Columbia, South Carolina. In all likelihood, somewhere in the train of the First Alabama, seventeen-year-old David Best, carrying DNA essential for my creation, was tending horses. Back home, on the Winston-Walker county line, Hiel Abbott was keeping his youngest son, Israel, out of the Confederate army by sending him to Stevenson,

Alabama, on the Tennessee River, to enlist in the First Alabama companies remaining behind in north Alabama.

On the march from Savannah, there was fighting aplenty for Kilpatrick's cavalry division and its Alabama brigade, now down to 18 officers
and 292 men, who left Thunderbolt on January 28. They defeated the
tenacious Joe Wheeler outside Barnwell, South Carolina, and burned
the town on February 5. In his report, Kilpatrick claimed to have tried to
prevent the arson, but he did not stint on praise for Spencer: "Colonel
Spencer alone conducted the fight, displaying much skill and great gal-
lantry. Several hundred stand of arms were abandoned by the enemy
and left scattered along the road. One officer and many men were killed
and many wounded. Colonel Spencer pressed the enemy so close for a
distance of seven or eight miles that he was finally forced to leave the
roads and scatter through the woods and swamps in order to escape."

For his part, Spencer described his treatment of five whittled-down
regiments of Wheeler's Alabama cavalry as "one of the most thorough
and complete routs I ever witnessed," noting the taking of "five battle-
flags . . . including the brigade and four regimental flags, and a large
number of horses and over thirty prisoners."

Later, Kilpatrick got a laugh out of Sherman by calling the town
"Burnwell." Although he had spared Savannah because of its beauty
and future value as a Federal port, Sherman continued to want his men
to be "careless with fire." When Kirkpatrick asked how their traveling
columns should keep in touch, Sherman joked in the presence of Howard, "Oh, just burn a barn or something. Make a smoke like the Indians
do." It's hard to assess how much more suffering Sherman thought the
South needed to endure to appreciate the hopelessness of its situation.
On February 16, he ordered General Howard to destroy the public
buildings, railroads, and factories of the South Carolina capital, but to
"spare libraries, asylums and private dwellings."

But even that plan seemed not in the forefront of Sherman's thinking
when the solicitous mayor, Dr. Thomas Jefferson Goodwyn, secured
him a room in the best hotel and then strolled with him to call on a society matron whom Sherman had courted in 1845 when she was the artis-

tically inclined daughter of the elegant Poyas family on their Cooper River plantation. Sherman was charmed when she showed him a water-coloring book he had inscribed for her as a first lieutenant. Taking his leave, Sherman was visiting at another fine townhouse when he noticed a "bright light" dancing on the walls of the room where he was resting. He went outside and discovered that a "boisterous wind" had fanned a smoldering pile of cotton bales into a general conflagration. As the fire waxed into the night, things got badly out of hand as the Union soldiers drank and gambled with "an immense quantity of money" that was blowing through the streets. Sherman conceded that the right wing of his army had "utterly ruined Columbia," but he blamed the retreating troops of a hard-line Rebel general he hated, the pompous Wade Hampton, for lighting the cotton bales as they fled the city.

By March 10, Kilpatrick and Spencer had pushed on to Monroe's Crossroads near Fayetteville, North Carolina, for a storied, seriocomic episode that has gone into Civil War lore as "Kilpatrick's Shirt-tail Skedaddle." It almost cost Kill Cavalry the major generalship for which he had been brevetted by Sherman for his good showing on the march and at Fort McAllister. The deadly clash also marked the apex of Spencer's career and serves as a classic example of how campfire gossip can be transmuted into historical "fact." Judson Kilpatrick was a tireless womanizer but so ugly that his troops were amazed by reports that he had been in bed with Columbia's most beautiful belle in a house at Monroe's Crossing when a cavalry charge led personally by Wade Hampton and Joe Wheeler surprised his encampment. By one scholar's account, at least twenty-five Civil War histories have identified nineteen-year-old Marie Boozer, a popular young socialite, as the paramour abandoned by Kilpatrick when he dashed from their cabin in his nightclothes, leapt onto a horse, and galloped into the foggy twilight. The panting, sexist description of Marie by Columbia's leading secessionist, General John S. Preston, has been quoted repeatedly by scholars. Preston, a brother-in-law of Wade Hampton and a social lion, said, "Marie Boozer was the most beautiful piece of flesh and blood my eyes ever beheld."

Boozer was an adventurous woman with many lovers, escaping the

South by briefly marrying a Yankee officer and later establishing herself in fast European circles as the wife of a French count. But recent scholarship has established that she and her Union-sympathizing mother were traveling under the decorous protection of General O. O. Howard when she was accused of being with Kilpatrick. A long-neglected eyewitness identified the woman chased from Kilpatrick's cabin as a considerably older Vermont schoolteacher who had been stranded in South Carolina. Who, then, promoted the tale of Kilpatrick "dressed only in his shirt and drawers" and Marie "caught in her chemise," as repeated in 1911 by an ex-Confederate private? Once again, some threads of fictionalized history lead back to the Alabama Department of Archives and History. The original director, Thomas McAdory Owen, had hired John Witherspoon DuBose, the worshipful biographer of William Lowndes Yancey, to help the ADAH compile (and concoct) tales of Confederate glory. DuBose also worked closely with Walter Lynwood Fleming on the history of the Civil War and Reconstruction in Alabama. Writing in the periodical *Confederate Veteran* in 1912, DuBose reported a richly imagined scene in which the young woman and the "Brevet Major General's staff . . . were virtual prisoners" in the house at Monroe's Crossroads.

The story of the hunched, long-nosed Kilpatrick and his beautiful concubine was so enticing that E. L. Doctorow put it into his historical novel *Sherman's March*. A true account can be found in Deborah C. Pollack's aptly titled 2016 biography, *Bad Scarlett: The Extraordinary Life of the Notorious Southern Beauty Marie Boozer*. And it was another notable scholar, Mark L. Bradley, a historian for the U.S. Army Center of Military History, who identified Kilpatrick's house guest as a northern schoolteacher. Even so, most available histories on the campaign parrot the version wholesaled by DuBose during his tenure at the Alabama archives.

By way of contrast, all sources seem to agree on Spencer's role at the Battle of Monroe Crossroads as Wheeler's men dashed back and forth through the camp and prostrate Unionists, some still wrapped in blankets, tried to surrender. Then came the moment for the audacious colonel from New York to shine. "In the cavalry camp," he wrote in his report, with his usual modesty, "the firing became very severe, and for a time the enemy gained and held nearly two thirds of the camp, when, by desperate fighting behind trees, the men succeeded in driving the enemy entirely out of camp and partially away from the headquarters." At this point, a Lieutenant Stetson crept to a cannon and opened fire on the invaders, rallying the Unionists to withstand three charges by Wheeler's men. "About 7:30 the enemy retreated in confusion. . . . One hundred and three of the enemy's dead were left on the field . . . Our men were too much exhausted and fatigued to follow the enemy, and nearly all were out of ammunition. For two hours and a half three small regiments, numbering in the aggregate less than 800 men, had successfully resisted the oft-repeated charges of three entire divisions numbering not less than 5,000 men. We remained on the field till 3 P.M., burying the dead . . . Our loss at the battle of Monroe Cross-roads was 18 killed—including eight officers of the First Alabama—70 wounded and 105 missing." For once Spencer was willing to share credit. Stetson, "unaided and alone," had unlimbered the gun that routed the enemy. "To this fact, more than any other," Spencer wrote, "I ascribe a terrible disaster turned into a brilliant victory."

Reviewing this vigorous account takes me back into dead-horse-whipping in regard to William Stanley Hoole. He transcribed Spencer's lengthy account verbatim, too, yet it did not alter his judgment that the First Alabama "was not conspicuous in either accomplishments or attitudes" and that "mostly it was employed in scouting, recruiting, raiding, and guarding the flanks." That judgment, now digitally memorialized by Wikipedia, runs counter to the multiple instances in the *Official Records* of the battalion searching for the enemy, shooting at them and being shot at by them—the primal combat activity of war. Hoole concluded with a demonstrably false sentence: "Only rarely in its three years of existence was it engaged in actual combat with the enemy." Is there a distinction to be drawn between Alabama's traditional mode of political discourse— both substantive and recreational lying—and outright dishonesty in scholarship? Are old-timers like Yancey and DuBose and latter-day

practitioners like Wallace and Trump simply inheritors and beneficia-
ries of that bred-in-the-bone mendacity that hovers over my poor Alabama like a spell? A less biased analyst than I am would probably see
them in a more kindly light—perhaps, like Spencer and Kilpatrick, as
just the sort of tainted situationalists produced by politics and war alike,
in any place or time.

In any case, Sherman's march through the Carolinas ended on
April 17, three days after Lincoln's assassination, when Johnston surrendered his army at Raleigh. Sherman ordered the First Alabama back
to its home state to restore order in the hill counties, which were still
seething with guerilla warfare and random criminality. Men who had
forded creeks and hidden in caves to sneak into the Union army returned as victors who were to be hated and defamed for generations.
From May 4 until June 14, the First Alabama was on the march from
Hillsboro, North Carolina, to Huntsville through very rocky and mountainous terrain that wore out its horses and forced their abandonment.
Spencer rejoined them in Huntsville. He had been on leave since April,
having written Kilpatrick and Sherman that he needed time to attend to
an "important private business involving the loss of a large sum of
money." This, of course, was the $50,000 in cotton that he had ware-
housed in Tuscaloosa back when he and Roddey were meeting under
white flags to discuss their deals.

Based on the timing, I know this also had to be the period when
David Best was making his way home—on foot, as he told my father. It's
unclear whether he was on his own or with the cavalrymen he had
served. It's also unknown exactly where and when he encountered the
dog in the road and killed it with his staff while its owners watched im-
passively from a nearby field they were hoeing. Such specifics are forever missing because my father, Wattie Simeon Raines, died in 2002,
and he was the last living Alabamian to hear the story of that homeward
journey from David Best's lips. I have a picture of my father as a tow-
headed boy sitting on his father's lap on the front porch of David Best's
home at Marylee in 1912. A photographer had been hired from Jasper to
photograph this reunion of sixty of my relatives arranged in three rows

across the wide porch of the patriarch's farmhouse. Seated three chairs to the right of Howell and five-year-old Wattie is David Best. At sixty-four, he looks relaxed despite holding still for the camera, hands folded atop the top knee of his crossed legs, a churchly kind of pose. Resting on each of his shoulders is a hand of one of the grown daughters standing behind him, one pretty and one plain—though not heroically plain in that ruggedly gothic pioneer way of some hill country women. For that quality you need to study another of the Best daughters in the picture.

The tall woman standing behind my seated grandfather, H. H. Raines, is his wife, Martha Jane Best Raines, the mother of the little boy in his lap. It is her face that connects me to the scene through inescapable memory. Her hair is gathered in a high bun, but not yet gray with age. The straight-on camera angle does nothing to minimize the noble dimensions of her wide, long nose, a promontory bisecting a face that narrows abruptly into a sharp chin. This is the face I was looking into the day she told me about the "damn Democrats." Within a year of the day this picture was taken, H. H. Raines was dead. David Best would last until 1926. These are the mountain folk of Alabama, descendants on the same soil of the men and boys who wanted to see the Union preserved. For the rest of my years, I will guard their story. It, unlike so much of what happened around them across the Deep South in the 1860s, does not deserve to be gone with the wind.

Censors of the past: Thomas McAdory Owen (1866–1920), founder of the Alabama Department of Archives and History, and Marie Bankhead Owen (1869–1958), its director for over three decades. He found an ally in William Archibald Dunning of Columbia University. She greeted the author and his classmates in her Lost Cause shrine in 1953.

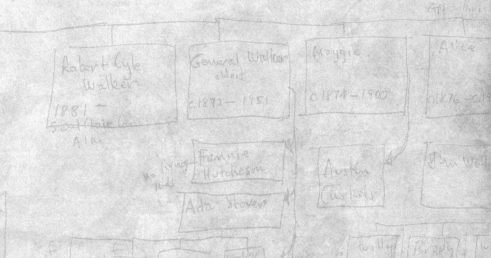

PART IV

Hiding the Evidence

THE SCHOLARLY CABAL THAT DISAPPEARED THE FIRST ALABAMA

Ryland Randolph's famous—or infamous—pro-Klan cartoon
in the Tuscaloosa *Independent Monitor.*
(Alabama Department of Archives and History)

Viral Tuscaloosa
and the Aristocratic Fallacy

THERE WAS NOTHING spontaneous or self-generating about the myth of the Lost Cause. It was a "civil religion" manufactured and codified during the Gilded Age by revanchist thinkers in Virginia and at Columbia University. Its origin story begins with embittered Confederate veterans in Richmond and Lexington in the Old South and, improbably, on a midtown Manhattan campus, with the nation's first generation of academically credentialed historians. My skepticism about the myth's mock-heroic version of the Civil War and Reconstruction shaped my quest for a true history of Alabama and was a catalyst for this book. But before we look at the myth's ties to those places outside Alabama, I want to introduce a case study of how it operated in a Rebel-steeped city in my home state.

My time in Tuscaloosa exerted on me a more powerful instructive influence than anything other than my early visits to the Free State of Winston and the anecdotal scraps of oral history dangling from my family tree. On the leafy streets of Alabama's self-styled "City of Oaks," I encountered the legacy of Ryland Randolph, another largely forgotten figure who probably had more to do with founding new chapters of the Ku Klux Klan and establishing murder as its principal tool than did the order's legendary Grand Wizard, Nathan Bedford Forrest. In perpetuating the aristocratic fallacy at the center of the Lost Cause faith, Alabama historians have consistently ignored the fact that Randolph had a loftier colonial pedigree than any of the state's Confederate leaders. I use "fallacy" here in the same sense that literary critics speak of the "pathetic fallacy" as an intellectual delusion that assigns human qualities to inanimate objects, as in "weeping skies" or "dancing leaves." In my idiom, the aristocratic fallacy is that plantation-owning oligarchs exhibited moral and intellectual qualities superior to those of the common folk, particularly in the military, political, and cultural spheres.

As his surname indicates, Ryland Randolph was born in 1835 into perhaps the most foundational of the First Families of Virginia. By the time he died in 1903, shortly after being shot in the throat by the mayor of Birmingham, he had lived a life that fully merited a Lost Cause cover-up. That cover-up was needed to ensure that his criminality did not detract from the lofty self-image of the plantation class. He was a man who boasted of the murders he committed or encouraged as editor of the nation's most virulent Klan newspapers. After a privileged upbringing among the Randolphs' Alabama kin, the hot-tempered dandy purchased the weekly Tuscaloosa *Independent Monitor* with $1,500 in family money in 1867. He immediately began a stabbing and shooting spree that made him kingpin of a Klan-like terrorist group meeting in the gloomy Sipsey Swamp a few miles north of Tuscaloosa.

When I moved to Tuscaloosa in 1967, exactly a century after Randolph took over the *Monitor*, it was nothing like the hip, energetic city on display most autumn Saturdays on ESPN. The sleek, gentrified downtown Tuscaloosa of today features a "strip" of Vegas-like clubs, and the University of Alabama's central quadrangle is surrounded by high-rise condominiums where fashionably dressed students frolic courtesy of their parents' money. The fact that it's now a show-business town is obvious every time the network sports broadcast crews arrive to document the ritual destruction of another Crimson Tide opponent in high-tech Denny Stadium, in front of Nick Saban's four-hundred-foot video screens with their 2.3 million LED bulbs and the smoke-belching light shows that prompt the "Roll Tide" bellow from a hundred thousand throats. More than 60 percent of the undergraduates are from "away," arriving by hundreds in fancy cars from the suburbs of Dallas–Fort Worth and Atlanta for parties wilder than what's on offer these days in Austin or Athens. The out-of-state tuition of about $32,000 looks like a bargain to affluent parents, making it an attractive landing zone for rich kids turned down by more competitive home-state universities or the Ivys. Columned Greek-letter mansions still dot University Boulevard and Fraternity Row, but while the visual effect is Old South, the ambiance is much more entitled brat than good old boy. Roiling in its festival of conspicuous consumption, modern Tuscaloosa has no sense of the irony of the university's new television slogan, "The Place Where Legends Are Made."

In the 1960s, it was still a drowsy, rustic place where family-owned retail stores had yet to recognize the threat of the new shopping mall rising out of the red clay on the southern bypass. Two tin-roofed shacks in Black neighborhoods, Dreamland and Archibald's, vied for the privilege of providing take-out barbecue for a pair of leading citizens: Bear Bryant, the fabled football coach, and Jack Warner, a self-parodying equestrian who used the slick magazine of his Gulf States Paper Company to celebrate his adventures in the U.S. Army's last horse cavalry. Taken together, the strutting big shots epitomized the state's enduring cultural affinity for rich or charismatic narcissists. Neither interfered with the secret, rearguard actions by the Tuscaloosa City Commission and the administrators of the University of Alabama to dodge the integration mandates of the 1964 Civil Rights Act.

The sleepy-college-town overlay of white Tuscaloosa rested on a tripartite socioeconomic structure. It was prosperous enough to support two country clubs—a new one, favored by the Bear, and the old Tuscaloosa Country Club, where the racist police commissioner held court in the bar. One of his causes was preventing patrons of the "colored pool halls" from hogging the limited downtown parking spaces. (The older club appears in *Stars Fell on Alabama* as the place where Carl Carmer peered through the hedges of a golf fairway to spy on an erotic voodoo ceremony conducted by a chanting Black priestess and entranced dancers shouting, "Satisfy! Satisfy!")

One odd sociological fact struck me as soon as I began to learn my way around the posh neighborhoods. The wealthy Chamber of Commerce crowd still favored Early Times, the rough, authoritative bourbon they learned to drink as fraternity and sorority kids in the ersatz plantation houses along University Boulevard. (Coach Bryant, a Sigma Nu, liked Smirnov and orange juice, which became a staple in the bars of boosters who hoped to entertain him on their private planes.) Bryant's crowd of bankers, contractors, businessmen, and landowners provided one leg of the three-legged scene. They overlapped somewhat with the university officials, faculty members, physicians, and string-pulling Democratic lawyers who made up another leg, in a wary but respectful version of the traditional town-and-gown game of campus towns everywhere.

The third group represented Tuscaloosa's gritty, industrial side— unionized workers at Mr. Warner's reeking Gulf States paper mill, the Goodyear Tire plant on the two-lane highway toward the Black Belt, and the riverfront foundries at nearby Holt. That's where the Ku Klux Klan came in. Like most southern industrial cities, Tuscaloosa became a recruiting ground for the Klan resurgence triggered by the Supreme Court's 1954 school desegregation decision. But in Tuscaloosa the Klan enjoyed a historical rootedness and social tolerance that made it an enduring presence. Even the local society folk took a perverse pride in Tuscaloosa's primacy in the Invisible Empire during Reconstruction and during its two major "revivals" in the 1920s and 1960s. Klan-led riots blocked integration of the University of Alabama in 1956, and Klansmen with guns and shortwave radios caravanned around the city at the time of George Wallace's "Stand in the Schoolhouse Door" incident in 1965. Thus, across the decades, Tuscaloosa had been a hothouse where the KKK virus slept in the soil, ready to break out whenever the ruling class needed the uncouth guerilla warriors it shunned in normal times.

The cartoon at the start of this chapter is from the Tuscaloosa *Independent Monitor* of September 1, 1869, and it is the "most notorious image from post–Civil War America" in the well-documented analysis of the historian G. Ward Hubbs. The woodcut has become the standard illustration of Klan terrorism in countless books on Reconstruction history. Before that, it was reproduced more than half a million times in 1868 by Ohio's Republican newspapers to rally support of voters for Ulysses S. Grant's presidential campaign. It has been credited with helping Grant carry Ohio by 41,000 votes. The caption from the *Encyclopedia of Alabama* gives the basics: "The lynched images represent two educators: Arad S. Lakin, right, a Methodist minister and 'carpetbagger' from Ohio who had just been named president of the University of Alabama, and Noah B. Cloud, a southern-born Republican, or 'scalawag,' politician serving as Superintendent of Public Instruction of Alabama. The mule is marked with the initials of the Ku Klux Klan, and the image serves as a threat to enemies of the Klan." The date of March 4, 1869, appears atop the drawing because that was Randolph's deadline for Lakin and Cloud to leave Tuscaloosa. The two educators beat it by several months.

We know that the striking woodcut was carved in Ryland Randolph's *Independent Monitor* office, because he was interviewed about the "famous hanging picture" before his death by Walter Lynwood Fleming for *Civil War and Reconstruction in Alabama*. In a typical passage, Fleming condemned the closing of the *Monitor* by a Union general as one of the many undeserved sufferings inflicted on the white people of Alabama. To me, the cartoon signifies the intimate connection between Alabama and its university and the national Lost Cause movement, with its technique of willful distortion of historical facts. Indeed, Fleming's selective, slanted use of the primary source material Randolph gave him stands as a paradigm of Walter Archibald Dunning's technique of ignoring facts that did not support his thesis. As with the First Alabama narrative, the principal tool was withholding of information readers and later historians would need to make a balanced judgment about what really happened. In Fleming's preface, Ryland Randolph is thanked as one of several Alabamians who "materially assisted" the author, and that understates his importance as a source. In Fleming's introductory comments the newspaper editor is listed on an equal footing with the revered Lost Cause guardians Thomas McAdory Owen and Marie Bankhead Owen, the directors of the Alabama Department of Archives and History, and their chief legend-maker, John W. DuBose. All are key names in the Lost Cause cabal that eradicated the fungus of Unionism from Alabama history.

Randolph, an embittered Civil War veteran, made the *Monitor* into a national presence when he "turned it into the South's most virulent pro-Klan and anti-Republican mouthpiece," as Hubbs put it. It was the Klan's most important organizing tool in Alabama and a major promoter of the violence that led Congress to showcase Alabama in its 1871 Klan hearings. Yet for decades, Randolph was relegated to walk-on roles in Alabama histories. A. B. Moore, author of a key Lost Cause history of Alabama appearing in 1934, gave him a single sentence in 834 pages, and it did not mention the Klan. Walter L. Fleming interviewed Randolph extensively about the murders he supervised as Grand Giant of the Tuscaloosa Klan and about the officials and students he chased out of the university. Also, Randolph gave Fleming his extensive self-incriminating writings and an irreplaceable original copy of the sixteen-page Klan "Precept" written during Forrest's brief tenure as Grand Wizard. Yet nowhere is there any explanation or judgmental analysis of Randolph's activities. His misdeeds are described in Fleming's footnotes with a blandness that few, if any, contemporary readers or newspaper reviewers in 1905 could have decoded. Nor does Fleming reveal that Ryland, a man who described himself as having an "ungovernable temper," was connected to the Randolphs of Virginia and through them to Thomas Jefferson, John Marshall, and Robert E. Lee. To do so would have given the lie to the entire theory of the superior moral character and cultivation of the plantation class as model citizens in comparison to Union leaders, the "poor white trash" in both armies, slaves, and free Black people. We can be sure that Fleming knew the facts he never shared because we can cross-check the timing and content of his research. In

1904 he wrote his archival adviser Thomas McAdory Owen that he was finalizing his big book for publication and was now seeking additional correspondence by Ryland Randolph because he was "thinking of writing him up as a Reconstruction editor" as his next project. He asked Owen, "What do you think of it? I have some of his letters on the Klan." My informed guess is that the ambitious Fleming backed off on the project because he realized that while Randolph was an important witness to the founding of the Confederacy and the Klan, he was a reprehensible criminal who would have shamed his forebears and detracted from the supposed nobility of the Lost Cause. We don't have to guess about Randolph's renegade past. As in so many cases in my research, the essential biographical data about Randolph came to me when I happened on an avocational historian whose work on Alabama's buried Civil War history was ignored at the local level and escaped the notice of most mainstream scholars.

Finding Gladys J. Ward's master's thesis at the University of Alabama was almost as exciting as discovering the works of Glenda McWhirter Todd on the First Alabama Cavalry. Although Randolph rubbed shoulders as a social equal with the Confederacy's founders, key details of his story might have been lost but for the sixty-four-page thesis of this obscure graduate student. Interestingly, both women earned their living as minor bureaucrats, Todd in Tennessee and Ward in the Alabama Department of Revenue in Montgomery. Ward became well known in writing clubs in Montgomery as a writer of inspirational verse, and in retirement she performed locally in a senior citizens' dance group called the Rocking Chair Mamas. For undiluted Alabama-ness, it's hard to beat the fact that this genteel lady became the biographer of a Klan sociopath every bit as violent as Forrest. To be sure, Ward's "Life of Ryland Randolph," submitted in 1932, hews to the pro-Confederate orthodoxy of the University of Alabama history department in her time on campus. "No one was truer to the white man's cause than he," she wrote of Ryland Randolph. "For a period, conservative people of the Democratic party fairly idolized him." Ward's "for a period" caveat provides an essential clue as to how a pro-Confederate version of political correctness worked in southern higher education. As a field of scholarly inquiry, the deconstructing of Lost Cause bias was almost virgin territory before the 1960s. So there is still a kind of shocking newness to figuring out why Ryland Randolph, who had mixed socially with the founders of the Confederate nation, remains almost as elusive a historical presence as Christopher Sheats. They were close contemporaries, born a hundred miles and five years apart, and reduced to walk-on roles by Fleming for what he saw as their obvious shortcomings. Sheats's sin was political apostasy, and that made him easy to ignore. But the contrast between Randolph's elevated background and his lead role in the reign of terror that led to a hundred Klan murders in Alabama between 1868 and 1871 put Fleming in a scholarly bind. Randolph's information was central to his research. At the same time, as Columbia's missionary to southern academia, Fleming was obliged to defend Dunning's wholehearted adoption of the aristocratic fallacy. But how could he hold up Randolph as a sterling example of Old South gentility? The famous cartoon would not go away, and there was no hint of noblesse oblige from the First Families of Virginia (FFV) in Ryland's story. Indeed, in 1868 he accomplished something that was almost impossible, then and now. Randolph was kicked out of the Alabama House of Representatives for bad behavior. He called its fifteen Black members "the colored monkeys" and suggested they fight out their differences with "a few coconuts placed in their paws."

So Fleming compromised. He listed Randolph among the dignitaries who gave him "special favors" in his research, but he disguised his essential role by mentioning him only four times in his index. Aside from the "monkeys" episode, none of these entries dealt substantively with the horrendous incidents recorded by Gladys Ward. Fleming used a kind of sleight-of-hand to deal with the inside information gleaned from the Randolph letters in his possession. Fourteen references in his footnotes labeled simply "Randolph" are used to convey gamier episodes, such as his acquittal by a military tribunal in 1868 for assaulting a Black man. The verdict, which was puzzling in light of the evidence, earned Randolph his only mention in *The New York Times,* a three-line notice with a Selma dateline. In quoting Randolph's letters, Fleming let the old terrorist get away with exculpatory statements he knew to be untrue. "Unfortunately, the Klan began to degenerate into a vile means of wreaking vengeance for personal dislikes or personal animosities," Randolph observed, forgetting that was exactly the policy he imposed after leading his roughneck militia, the "Sipsey Swampers," into the official Klan. Fleming even tolerated Randolph's crocodile tears. "Many outrages were committed in the name of Ku Klux that really were done by irresponsible parties who never belonged to the Klan," he lamented, inventing an excuse that was to play a lasting role in KKK public relations.

Like Alabama itself, the university in Tuscaloosa always had a big front porch where everyone was acquainted. But it seemed crowded to Randolph in 1868 when William H. Smith, a recruiter for the First Alabama who had made the March to the Sea with Sherman, was elected Republican governor of Alabama's integrated Reconstruction government. He was a close friend of Colonel George Spencer's and an ally of Chris Sheats. In his footnotes, Fleming had let Randolph claim that KKK activity tailed off in 1870, but in fact his rascality was peaking, and he was clearly the most influential disrupter in Tuscaloosa. Thanks largely to his editorials and threatening KKK letters to faculty and students, the University of Alabama was reorganized eight times between 1865 and 1871. In April 1871, the university effectively closed down when the last four students ran away from the whites-only institution after getting warnings pinned to their doors with daggers "by order of the KKK." Meanwhile, Governor Smith emerged as Randolph's nemesis. Already, investigators from his biracial administration came to Tuscaloosa and reported that Randolph was "the head devil of all the lawlessness that has afflicted and brought disgrace on the County and City of Tuscaloosa."

One result was that Randolph got into a running pistol-and-knife fight with a student, William Smith, a nephew of Governor Smith who had also been a Union soldier. A thick address book blocked what would have been a killing shot to Randolph's heart, but another round hit him above the knee, requiring an amputation. His stump was too short for the fitting of a prosthesis and as a result Randolph acquired a crutch, a walking stick, and a morphine habit for his chronic pain. By that time, Randolph and his "Swampers" had already achieved their crowning campaign. In 1869, he led a gang of eighty "extemporized cavalry" through Northport and Tuscaloosa in a rampage that left one white and three Black men shot or hung. That incident Fleming omitted entirely. It is simply impossible to reconstruct the full story of Alabama's most important Klan leader from Fleming's massive book, for which he was the most important eyewitness source.

As noted above, the protocols of Lost Cause propaganda required disguising Randolph's lineage. Fleming's writings contain nary a word about Randolph's Tidewater bona fides. Gladys Ward, who had the cooperation of Randolph's only surviving son, documents that he was a direct descendant of the "Adam and Eve of Virginia," Colonel William Randolph and his wife, Mary Isham Randolph, of Turkey Creek Plantation. The colonel was Ryland's great-great-great-grandfather. William and Mary Randolph's son Isham Randolph (1651–1711) had a daughter named Jane Randolph (1720–1776), who was the mother of Thomas Jefferson. It must have pained Fleming to pass on these potent proofs linking Alabama to aristocratic pretensions. To me, these calculated omissions about a man Fleming knew well demonstrated the intellectual dishonesty at the heart of the Lost Cause narratives. Facts always gave way to the desire to cover up the seedier aspects of Confederate lives. There's an almost Byronic flavor to the entry into the highest levels of Confederate society of this privileged brat of ungovernable temper. Young Ryland was raised amid what he recalled as "luxurious wealth" on the plantations of relatives west of Tuscaloosa. His mother, August Granberry Randolph, had come home to Clinton, Alabama, in 1835 to give birth while her husband, career navy officer Captain Victor Moreau Randolph, was at sea. The career naval officer was a cousin of Thomas Jefferson's wife and seventh in a line of descent from Pocahontas.

As an FFV scion of such lofty blood, young Ryland was slated to become a man of the world. By the time he entered the University of

Alabama in 1852, Ryland had been around the globe three times as an aide on his father's ships. He first went to sea with his father at seven, and when he was about fifteen, they visited the court of revolutionary Haiti's Black ruler, Emperor Faustin I. Randolph's early exposure to what he called "the rule of Negrodom," installed as a result of a slave rebellion in 1804, confirmed his racism. "The court officials have some ludicrous titles, such as the Lord of Lemonade, Duke of Marmalade," he wrote years later in autobiographical notes called "Scribbles." (He was unaware those were actual place names in Haiti.) Some of his father's officers danced with Black "countesses" and "a big buck Negro officer waltzed with a daughter of the American consul." Gladys Ward felt the seething temper suggested by these remarks pointed up the core problem of Randolph's roustabout childhood: "Ryland had all the material things he needed, but lacked the restraining influence of his parents." Ward's 1932 narrative was brilliantly expanded upon by Professor Hubbs in *Searching for Freedom After the Civil War: Klansman, Carpetbagger, Scalawag, and Freedman,* published in 2015 as a signal addition to the new Alabama revisionism.

Both Randolph's elitist contempt for Black people and his temper fit well with the next stage of his education as a southern gentleman, which brought him into the home of the Fire-Eating orator most directly responsible for the Civil War, William Lowndes Yancey. On the eve of secession, Captain Randolph retired from the navy and bought an impressive house in Montgomery's best neighborhood. After an unsuccessful try at planting cotton on his own, Ryland moved in with his father in 1858. That, in turn, allowed him, at twenty-three, to mix with the new nation's founders, including Jefferson Davis, Alexander Stephens, and even Howell Cobb, whose plantation was to be burned by Sherman. He was often invited for tea at the home of the theatrical Yancey, having befriended the son of the nationally renowned secessionist speechmaker at the university. Gladys Ward wrote, "He greatly admired Mr. Yanc[e]y's ability and silvery voice but thought his manner domineering and unsympathetic." Even so, he found Yancey's call to battle at the Montgomery opera house in the fall of 1860 the "grandest oration" ever. He recalled that Yancey told the "wild" crowd that "the South had nothing to hope for from the North, and must rely on the god of battles."

I try to be understanding that Fleming's failure to put this wonderful material into his book was not simply a matter of his abundant prejudice. I have had the benefit of journalistic training and over a century of scholarship that was not available to Fleming. In his use of newspapers and his in-person interviewing of authorities like General Wager Swayne, the Union overseer of Alabama during Reconstruction, he was ahead of his time. But there were fewer models for sophisticated historical narration when he wrote his dissertation under Dunning, who shepherded its 1905 publication by Macmillan. Even so, Fleming's lack of curiosity about what Ryland Randolph heard and saw in the salons of Montgomery is striking, and it follows the Dunning model of ignoring colorful detail and conflicting information. There's no evidence in Fleming's published writings or papers that he even asked Randolph what these important men said in private about their disastrous undertaking. This indifference to exploiting first-person witnesses to the fullest would surface again, dramatically, as I tracked Fleming through the Alabama Department of Archives and History. The Confederate history that has come down to us, manifestly, is not just what scholars have cared to write about but what they chose not to ask about.

By the early 1960s, thanks to *Stars Fell on Alabama* and Birmingham-Southern College, I became a chronic asker of questions about Alabama. Then, a few weeks after passage of the 1964 Public Accommodations Act, I became a professional one when I was hired at twenty-one by the *Birmingham Post-Herald*. The old racial patterns still persisted in Alabama politics and some newspapers despite the new civil rights law, and at the newspaper, covering the implementation of the law was like living in a random, ill-managed, and dangerous sociological study. Being young was no disadvantage; it was all hands on deck for a breaking-news hurricane. Within months, I was covering important stories like the desegregation of Birmingham schools, unhinged speeches by George Wallace, and the death watch at a Birmingham hospital for the Reverend

James Reeb, a Unitarian minister mortally clubbed by Klansmen after the Selma March. As a gesture of civic responsibility, the *Post-Herald* raised money to offset the Reeb family's medical expenses. I gave $50 to the fund, and my name was published on the front page of the paper along with those of other contributors. It was a clear breach of journalistic ethics that I never repeated, but it also marked my personal coming out at a time when Wallace's slogan was "Stand up for Alabama." I had been too fearful to march with Dr. King in 1963, but now I was ready to stand for a different Alabama. I rationalized my activism as fulfilling the *Post-Herald*'s masthead slogan, "Give the people light and they will find the way."

By 1967, I was still toying with the idea of becoming an English professor, so I enrolled in graduate school and took a full-time job at *The Tuscaloosa News* to support myself. I was proud to be working for Buford Boone, the most courageous anti-Klan and anti-Wallace editor in the state. My time in his newsroom enabled me to assemble for this book an overview of Klan connectivity that I've never seen anywhere else. It draws on linkages I might have missed but for my obsession with Alabama's ignored past and experiences on my native ground.

Buford Boone (1909–1983) was a gentle, upright grower of prize camellias who had a stainless steel backbone. He won the 1956 Pulitzer Prize for editorials supporting integration of the University of Alabama. He made sure to let the local Klan leader, Imperial Wizard Bobby Shelton, know that he slept with a shotgun under his bed. I admired the muzzle velocity of editorials like the one calling Shelton a "jackal," a none-too-subtle reference to the lank-jawed, vulpine appearance of George Wallace's favorite Klansman. Anthropologists use a tool called a "reflexive journal" to record field notes that, cumulatively, may capture a pattern of cultural persistence. Over time I realized that Klan events during the careers of Carl Carmer and Buford Boone demonstrated just that kind of ingrained reflexively antisocial behavior issuing from a common source. The timeline below attempts to show that the malady Ryland Randolph implanted in the "City of Oaks" was a recurring virus.

Without it, the city and state would have had a cleaner racial reputation. Here's the evidentiary timeline of this enduring Alabama pathogen.

1921: The initial pages of *Stars Fell on Alabama* read like a reflexive-journal entry about Carmer's discovery that the Klan remained as ubiquitous a presence as it had been in Ryland Randolph's day. "Tuscaloosa Nights" is the title of the book's first section, and it is illustrated with a drawing of masked Klansmen encircling a burning cross. These pages are so richly evocative that I read them periodically when I'm tempted to expect normative public behavior from Alabama's elite. The state's newspapers protested that Carmer exaggerated the Klan's strength, when, in fact, his X-ray cultural vision had detected immediately that the order's influence was braided through every aspect of community life in an otherwise sophisticated university town. During a bibulous joyride on the night of his arrival, his upper-class hosts warned that KKK morality police might invade their secluded destination, a riverside trysting spot for lovers and drinkers. The next day at a Klan parade Carmer spotted a businessman's fine brogans peeping from the robes of a masked figure. The sight gave the lie to the comment by Carmer's snooty host that only "the poor white trash are wearing the sheets now." Although a romanticist, Carmer had a clear-eyed gift for penetrating the facades constructed by protective southerners. He had picked up immediately on Tuscaloosa's continuing reality. At any moment, "virulent . . . germs of violence" left over from plantation days could disrupt a college town that "prides itself on its culture."

1934: In a coda to *Stars Fell on Alabama* written eight years after he returned to New York, Carmer reported the germs' continued potency. He cited news reports that a machine gun had been set up on the steps of the Tuscaloosa courthouse to prevent a mob of a thousand men from lynching a Black prisoner. The Klan's "old irresistible urge is upon the shifting crowd," Carmer wrote. "The spell cast in the 'year the stars fell' is not yet broken."

1947: Buford Boone became editor and publisher of *The Tuscaloosa News* and published his first exposés of the continuing Klan violence.

1949: A caravan of 129 Klansmen arrived from Birmingham to encircle Boone's paper in a show of support for Randolph's original Klavern. It was a historic alliance, resulting eventually in a partnership of Imperial Wizard Bobby Shelton and the "action squad" of Birmingham's Eastview Klavern 13, the most violent urban Klan unit in twentieth-century America.

1956: Klan-led rioters drove graduate student Autherine Lucy, the University of Alabama's first Black enrollee, from the campus. Buford Boone won the Pulitzer for editorials condemning university officials for failing to protect her and accomplish peaceful integration.

August 1963: Armed members of Eastview Klavern 13 were arrested outside Tuscaloosa to prevent them from attending Governor Wallace's "Stand in the School House Door," a political stunt that failed to stop U.S. deputy attorney general Nicholas Katzenbach from successfully enrolling the university's first Black undergraduates.

September 15, 1963: Four members of Eastview 13 planted the bomb that killed four Black children at Sixteenth Street Baptist Church in Birmingham. Bobby Shelton denied KKK responsibility, but in secret meetings with Wallace and his investigators, he provided the names of "Dynamite Bob" Chambliss and three accomplices as the murderers. Wallace, who had attended anti-integration rallies with Chambliss, sabotaged the state and FBI investigations by revealing their identities prematurely.

March 25, 1965: Four members of Eastview Klavern 13 shot to death Viola Gregg Luizzo, a Detroit woman attending the Selma March. Bobby Shelton hired an attorney, Imperial Klonsel Matt Murphy of Birmingham, to defend them in a murder trial.

By 1969, Ryland Randolph's nickname for Tuscaloosa, the "City of Oaks," had been changed to one preferred by the Chamber of Commerce. The towering trees still lined University Boulevard, but Tuscaloosa was now known as the "Druid City." One day in March, my newsroom telephone rang, and it was the arch-Druid himself, Hudson Strode, one of the last living champions of pro-Confederate historiography and the most famous retired professor on the shaded campus. I could not have been waved onto the Lost Cause Highway by a more appropriate guide. At twenty-five, I was an innocent in the intricacies of historical deception, having never even heard of Strode's bête noire, Edward A. Pollard, the newspaperman who gave the Lost Cause movement its name.

28

Bad Boys of Richmond

IN SINGLING OUT Edward Alfred Pollard as Jefferson Davis's prime journalistic tormentor, Hudson Strode was on to a more salient idea than he appreciated in regard to the blazing of the Lost Cause Highway. That's how I think about the pathway of disinformation that wended its influential way through the campuses and capitals of Georgia, Alabama, Tennessee, Mississippi, Louisiana, the Carolinas, and Virginia for over a century and a half. Strode's nominees as the "disloyal" journalists who had most grievously misserved his hero Davis and the South as a whole were Jonathan Moncure Daniels, wartime publisher of the *Richmond Examiner;* his editorial page editor, H. Rives Pollard; and the paper's lead opinion writer, Edward A. Pollard, Rives's brother. Although less well-known at the outset of his career, Edward surpassed both his boss and brother by embodying the spirit of pro-slavery Confederate nationalism and by casting Jefferson Davis as its idiot king.

Pollard was plagued throughout his life with emotional instability, and his crusade to destroy Davis's reputation had a distinct bipolar edge. "His hostility to Davis had grown out of his Southern nationalism," a mindset Pollard advocated in his newspaper as essential to Confederate victory. Davis's administration was marked by "'imbecility of purpose' and making war by 'half way measures.'" The only way to victory was to invade the North and execute Unionists, dissenters, and draft dodgers at home. Yet Pollard was capable of wild swings of opinion. In *Echoes from the South* in 1867, he suppressed his hatred enough to praise Davis's oratory and speculated that he might lead a Confederate comeback. But by 1869, he'd penned a monumental bashing of the southern president in *Life of Jefferson Davis, with a Secret History of the Southern Confederacy: Gathered Behind the Scenes at Richmond.* Davis's bungling had caused southerners to lose faith in the Cause, in slavery, and even in their cultural superiority to the money-grubbing North. By 1871, Pollard had swung again, praising Yankee capitalism and voting rights for Black people. His ideological evolution first emerged in *The Lost Cause Regained,* an 1868 book that surfaced an idea that later occurred to many mainstream historians about the failure of Reconstruction to curb white supremacy in Dixie. That is, by using the national Democratic Party as the instrument of its racism, the Old South actually "won" the war by achieving its main goal of keeping Black people in servitude.

Pollard's biographer Jack P. Maddex advanced what seems to me the best explanation for Pollard's largely successful attempts to destroy Davis's reputation: He had an economic motivation. He wrote for a living, and he moved to seize the "early lead among those who were founding a cult of veneration for 'the Lost Cause.'" If Davis remained an honored leader, his credentials would have trumped Pollard's for "solidifying the South around the Confederacy's memory." Dismantling Davis was "necessary" for his postbellum "propaganda work for the continuing Southern nationalist cause."

As the end of the war neared, Edward Pollard wrote: "If the cause was to be lost, it was to be so by weak despair, by the cowardice of suicide, by the distress of weak minds." In Pollard's worldview, Davis fit the bill as the prime betrayer of the slavocracy for one overriding reason: He was not a Virginian. So Pollard's masterwork, *The Lost Cause,* appearing with almost magical speed only fifteen months after Appomattox, not only established the name of the school of southern apologetics but would warp American historiography for a century and a half and taint popular culture to this day. Its Virginia chauvinism cemented the aristocratic fallacy as an enduring feature of American literature.

Public appetite for plantation novels sharpened in the Gilded Age with Thomas Nelson Page's crushingly sentimental *Marse Chan* in 1884 and extended to *Gone with the Wind* and beyond through spinoffs in cinema and journalism. It would be a mistake to devote too much space to this train wreck of a person, but it would be an even bigger mistake to dodge the question of whether a more erratic individual has ever exercised more damaging influence as a public intellectual.

Pollard (1832–1872) was born into the velvet-lined catbird seat of Ol' Virginny through connection to not one but two leading plantations controlled by the potent Cabell-Rives family, Oakridge and Altavista. He epitomized the dangerous class of "young bloods" defined by Sherman in every way except one: He had no intention of jumping on a cavalry horse and risking his life in the war he so ardently cheered. Like his near contemporary Mark Twain, he took shelter from the Minié balls by entering the newspaper business in the West. Like Sherman, the general whose "zigzagging" March to the Sea Pollard ridiculed, he fetched up in California for the Gold Rush.

In sharp contrast to his present obscurity, Edward A. Pollard became famous in every southern mansion and the New York newspapers in 1859 by publishing a bestseller to answer *Uncle Tom's Cabin*, entitled *Black Diamonds Gathered in the Darkey Homes of the South.* "Mr. Pollard," *The New York Times* declared in 1869, "was about as well known, to any one at all familiar with the origin and history of the rebellion, as Jeff. Davis or Lee." By 1870, both Edward and his brother Rives had been shot by persons unhappy with their journalism, the latter fatally. By 1872, Edward was dead of kidney disease, leaving leadership of the movement he started to a non-aristocratic Virginian he disdained, General Jubal Anderson Early. Clearly Pollard was a man to whom attention must be paid, but as is often the case with the war's supporting cast, one has to cast the net broadly and into obscure waters.

The best early scholarship I found on Pollard was from the University of New Mexico, not exactly a hotbed of Civil War studies, in a 1952 master's thesis by a teaching nun of the Sisters of Charity named Maria Theresa Darcy. "Almost nothing has been written about Pollard," Sister Darcy wrote in her preface to "Edward Alfred Pollard, The Richmond Examiner, and The Confederacy"; "one must learn about the man from his works." Sister Darcy did a workmanlike job of just that, although her thesis seems to have been checked out of her university's library only once, in 1991, before it was digitized in 2016. Since then it was downloaded only forty-one times, several times by me—another illustration of the pattern in which obscure, unpublished scholars keep turning up as the most persistent Civil War detectives.

Through the magic of Google, we have Sister Darcy's slightly breathless but not unsupported assessment of the man: "He was undoubtedly the ablest journalist of the Confederacy. His writings did bear weight. In spite of the fact that he was a skillful, capable writer, he was bitterly opinionated and unfair where his prejudices were concerned. The bulk of that censure and criticism, both in his books and in his editorials in the *Richmond Examiner,* fell upon Jefferson Davis, the President of the Confederacy, his cabinet of 'dummies,' and the inarticulate and inert Confederate Congress." Today, we might replace the sister's noun "journalist" with "polemicist" or "commentator," but the aspersions cast on Davis, his cabinet, and his Congress are beyond argument. Indeed, the entire Lost Cause project, as we shall see, was invented to disguise how bad they really were—a risible irony in view of the fact that the man who named this vast school of apologetics was himself a character of ungovernable instability, if not a kind of "imbecility," to use one of Pollard's favorite terms for the Davis team.

Sister Darcy's curiosity about Pollard has never been widely shared in the academic world. Only one fully credentialed historian, Jack P. Maddex, a Chapel Hill–trained professor at the University of Oregon, attempted a detailed biography. Its 110 pages open with a mannerly indictment of Civil War scholars: "Edward A. Pollard and his intellectual

biography have remained curiously unknown to historians quite familiar with his name" despite his one-time "prominence as a Southern controversial writer." Maddex sketched to my satisfaction how this rapid
transit from household name to forgotten scribe is related to the man's
bipolarity, although that is my term, not his. Pollard's philandering and
taste for street fights and gunplay meant that incriminating details would
be "necessarily obscure," concluded Maddex, adding, "He pursued a
turbulent lifestyle, marred by episodes of sex and violence." In the newspaper world of wartime Richmond, he was very much a man of his time
and place.

For all the violent restlessness of his personal life and *Examiner* career, Pollard marked the end of the Civil War with an unmatched burst
of writerly productivity, finishing *The Lost Cause* in June 1866. The
timetable was possible because the volume collected the annual round-
ups of the war that Pollard published in the *Examiner* and a ranting
conclusion that urged southerners not to accept defeat as final. Then
came *The Lost Cause Regained* in 1868 and *The Life of Jefferson Davis,
with a Secret History of the Southern Confederacy* in 1869. These books
established three main tropes of Civil War thought. The first, of course,
provided the title for Lost Cause orthodoxy and its main theme that
the culturally superior, racially homogenous white South had not really
"lost" but rather had been ground down by capitalist industrial might
and the multiethnic "mongrel" North. *The Lost Cause Regained* provided a template for winning the war after the war by maintaining white
dominance through recalcitrance, legal trickery, and political deals. Finally, as Hudson Strode conceded, the Jefferson Davis biography established the stereotype of the Confederate president as an incompetent
administrator whose dabbling in strategy doomed his generals to defeat
and wasted the lives of a quarter-million southerners.

"Conceit" was an important term in Pollard's *Lost Cause,* both as a
condemnatory adjective applied to the northern personality and, in the
conceptual sense, to the Yankees' fetishistic devotion to a Union that
had been seen as binding, indissoluble, and divinely ordained. Pollard

scathingly attributed this political-science position to Yankee Fourth of July orators. In Pollard's view, the United States was really "two nations of opposite civilizations" that had been artificially conjoined, in opposition to John C. Calhoun's insistence that the time had come for the superior southern realm to go its own way. The very idea that the Union was permanent was an ideological "afflatus," Pollard scolded.

He maintained that the material benefits of slavery had provided the means for a genteel way of life that could never be achieved under wage capitalism. The social mechanics of southern superiority were defined in three paragraphs that deserve to be read in full because they so perfectly express the attitudinal parameters of the Lost Cause thinking as it first sprang to life, already bristling with its cementing claims of racial and class superiority. Today they read like caricatures of southern myopia, but by the start of the twentieth century Pollard's ideas would harden into nationally embraced stereotypes accepted in the parlors and campuses of high-caste northerners. "In the ante-revolutionary period," he wrote,

> the differences between the populations of the Northern and Southern colonies had already been strongly developed. The early colonists did not bear with them from the mother-country to the shores of the New World any greater degree of congeniality than existed among them at home. They had come not only from different stocks of population, but from different feuds in religion and politics. There could be no congeniality between the Puritan exiles who established themselves upon the cold and rugged and cheerless soil of New England, and the Cavaliers who sought the brighter climate of the South, and drank in their baronial halls in Virginia to confusion to roundheads and regicides.
>
> Slavery established in the South a peculiar and noble type of civilization. It was not without attendant vices; but the virtues which followed in its train were numerous and peculiar, and asserted the general good effect of the institution on the ideas and manners of the South. If habits of command sometimes degener-

ated into cruelty and insolence; yet, in the greater number of instances, they inculcated notions of chivalry, polished the manners
and produced many noble and generous virtues. If the relief of a
large class of whites from the demands of physical labour gave
occasion in some instances for idle and dissolute lives, yet at the
same time it afforded opportunity for extraordinary culture, elevated the standards of scholarship in the South, enlarged and
emancipated social intercourse, and established schools of individual refinement. The South had an element in its society—
a landed gentry—which the North envied, and for which its sub-
stitute was a coarse ostentatious aristocracy that smelt of the
trade, and that, however it cleansed itself and aped the elegance of
the South, and packed its houses with fine furniture, could never
entirely subdue a sneaking sense of its inferiority. There is a singularly bitter hate which is inseparable from a sense of inferiority;
and every close observer of Northern society has discovered how
there lurked in every form of hostility to the South the conviction
that the Northern man, however disguised with ostentation, was
coarse and inferiour in comparison with the aristocracy and chivalry of the South.

The civilization of the North was coarse and materialistic.
That of the South was scant of shows, but highly refined and sentimental. The South was a vast agricultural country; waste lands,
forest and swamps often gave to the eye a dreary picture; there
were no thick and intricate nets of internal improvements to as-
tonish and bewilder the traveler, no country picturesque with
towns and villages to please his vision. Northern men ridiculed
this apparent scantiness of the South, and took it as an evidence
of inferiority. But this was the coarse judgment of the surface of
things. The agricultural pursuits of the South fixed its features;
and however it might decline in the scale of gross prosperity, its
people were trained in the highest civilization, were models of
manners for the whole country, rivalled the sentimentalism of the
oldest countries of Europe, established the only schools of hon-

our in America, and presented a striking contrast in their well-
balanced character to the conceit and giddiness of the Northern
people.

With such passages, Pollard crystallized one of our country's most enduring regional stereotypes—that of the mechanistic, unsoulful North
versus a white South of superior sensibility and pastoral pursuits. While
The Lost Cause swept the field of postbellum apologetics, Pollard was already famous in the South and Northeast for providing slave owners with
a public relations weapon to deploy against Harriet Beecher Stowe,
whose *Uncle Tom's Cabin* came out in 1852. As a retort to Stowe's exposure of the cruelties of slavery, Pollard published *Black Diamonds Gathered in the Darkey Homes of the South* in 1859, and it made him an instant
celebrity. Repeated attacks in Horace Greeley's nationally circulated
New-York Tribune, the most influential paper of its time, probably backfired and contributed to *The Lost Cause*'s sales of more than fifty thousand copies in its first year. Based on Pollard's wanderings in three
continents while he was a young man, the book argued for a hemispheric
expansion of slavery and a reopening of the slave trade based on the cultural and biological superiority of whites and the furthering of their economic interests. But it is most important today as the apex expression
of yet another enduring exculpatory theme of southern thought and
literature—that of paternalism. Where Stowe had argued that the nation
would destroy its soul by failing to free Black people from bondage, Pollard insisted that slavery was a moral issue only for Stowe and "a few
thousand persons of disordered conscience." He added, "It was significant only of a contest for political power, and afforded nothing more than
a convenient ground of dispute between two parties, who represented not
two moral theories, but hostile sections and opposite civilizations." The
southern slave master, he argued in an article written in 1870, had a superior concern for Africans as human beings, offering himself as an example.

My regard for the negro has a basis infinitely broader than political party. I owe him many happy hours in that early home of my

childhood, where not less than five hundred slaves constituted the ancestral estate. The humor, the tenderness, the real virtues of his race had impressed my heart, even when he had no opportunities of showing these qualities but in the hard and narrow fortune of the slave. I believe I was the first to invent for these then despised creatures a poetic name. I wrote the book *Black Diamonds* more than ten years ago. I risked my life, even in the days of slavery, to defend a poor, nameless negro on the fortifications of Richmond from the brutality of a white overseer whose fierce bullyism had hitherto been the terror of the cowardly city. . . . I fought him to the point of bloodshed; and I rescued from his savage lash the poor, cringing slave, whose only claim to my protection was that he was wronged and stricken in my sight. My battle . . . I am ready to renew with whatever lawless man dares to abuse a negro, or any other unprotected human creature in my view. I intend to stand by the negro in the South, and before Southern men, and that despite the weapons of the Ku-Klux-Klans, or the more cowardly stings of libel and abuse. Of the male members of a family greatly ravaged by death there only remain myself and a brother in Lynchburg, Virginia, and I dare to say that there is not a negro who has ever lived in the home of either of us, or knows either of us, but would stand by us in any difficulty or peril. For myself, I here, solemnly touched by the spirit of many recollections of what has passed in my life, remembering many loved ones among a humble and despised people, speaking in the disposition of egotism, and with many possible accents of boastfulness, declare and pledge myself that on every occasion and in every presence I shall protect and defend the negro to the last extremity that Justice and humanity shall ever demand of me.

Pollard was only twenty-seven when *Black Diamonds* was published, and the ferocity with which he was attacked in an unsigned article in the *New-York Tribune* of April 9, 1860, attests to its impact. It also suggests that Greeley, the *Tribune*'s canny, pro-Union editor, recognized that his northern readers might be susceptible to elegantly expressed sentimentality about southern intentions. "Perhaps we have taken more notice of this silly book than it merits," the newspaper said. "But endorsed as it is by Southern statesmen, or, more accurately speaking, by Southern Members of Congress, we have a right to regard it as the best literary defense which the South has to offer." And the skill of that defense clearly worried Greeley, who was initially more interested in destroying slavery than in preserving the Union. He had once advocated letting the South go, as a means to encapsulating the infection in a few states. Switching to outright Unionism, he spent the first years of the war criticizing Lincoln as moving too slowly in issuing the Emancipation Proclamation. The *Tribune* writer seemed aware of how Pollard's worldly posturing and ornate language might contrast with Stowe's somber persona and close-up focus on plantation life:

> In his initial chapter, he informs us, that like Ulyssess, he has wandered from his native "soil to other parts of the world"; that he has seen "English colliere" and "costermongers," and Chinese "coolies" and "Siamese slaves"; and that he found the sight upon his return to his home, of an "unadulterated negro" in the highest degree "refreshing." It hurt his sensitive nature, that negroes should be caricatured by Mrs. Beecher Stowe and by other artists. Prompted by affection, Mr. Pollard determined to conscientiously draw his humble friends; and the result of his pious fidelity in this book of "Black Diamonds."

Patronizing as Pollard's expressions of love for African Americans may sound, he nonetheless defined an enduring racial delusion of Dixie's highborn white supremacists, a self-pardoning mental gymnastics that was driven underground during the civil rights movement. The main idea was that expressions of protective concern for individual African Americans and a generalized benignity toward the minority population as a whole somehow canceled what was done legislatively and economically to hold them down. This form of soft-core racism had a second flowering in the old Confederacy among suburban Republicans and newly converted Democrats following Ronald Reagan's election in 1980. It spread like kudzu after 2016 with Donald Trump's embrace of Confederate iconology. The main idea is that a person is motivated by a bootstrap ideology, not racism, if he or she supports policies that, say, suppress minority voting, or opposes compensation to Black people or Native Americans for sins against their ancestors. But Edward Pollard exemplified and codified a racial animosity so outrageous and a narcissism so vaulting as to deserve the adjectives "Wallaceite" and "Trumpian."

Even so, he wrong-footed many of his followers with *The Lost Cause Regained,* which accepted a reunited nation and cooperation with northern financial interests as a necessary tactic to achieve prosperity and a semblance of states' rights autonomy. In those respects, he presaged Henry Grady's New South movement, while making it clear that operating within the Union must be tolerated as a means of subordinating freed slaves. On its surface, this pragmatic acceptance of Unionism, set forth in wild sweeps of contradictory prose, was a sign of the documented mental and physical deterioration that set in when Pollard was in his mid- to late thirties. It also reflected a kind of desperation he must have felt as control of the revanchist movement inspired by the Lost Cause was being taken over by former Confederate officers and Virginia's potent ladies' memorial associations, or LMAs.

For me, there's an irresistible irony in contrasting Pollard's far-reaching influence and his rakehell personal history. In a life span of only forty years, he embodied all the most easily satirized elements of Old South masculinity. Before reaching twenty, Pollard outdid even the Tarleton twins in *Gone with the Wind* in collegiate misbehavior. Scarlett O'Hara described the Tarletons as so wild they were even thrown out of the University of Alabama, where they'd landed after being booted from the more mannerly universities of Virginia and Georgia. Edward blasted his way though UVA and three other Virginia colleges, including William and Mary, where his law studies were terminated by unanimous vote of the faculty. Not even a cadre of uncles that included four members of Congress and the U.S. ambassador to France could save him.

Perhaps the connections accounted for the gentle language of the expulsion order: Because of "'improper conduct,'" he was given "leave to withdraw." Dating back to the exile of Robert E. Lee's bankrupt father, "Lighthorse Harry," to Nassau and the Turks, the FFV had been gentle with their renegades.

In the first of his several nervous collapses, Pollard even presaged what became a fad among well-educated southern bankers and lawyers in my own time. Nearing thirty, he fled into the Episcopal priesthood when his first wife, the well-born Sarah James, died in 1860, and the bishop of Richmond sponsored him for holy orders. The fit passed, and by 1861 he was a newspaperman. The first was the happiest of Pollard's three known marriages; he actually underwent four wedding ceremonies to erase an issue of bigamy between numbers two and three. In good times or bad, whether married or single, Edward didn't lack for ambition or energy or entrée into influential circles. He joined the Forty-Niners in the California Gold Rush, and while there fell in with William Walker, the notorious "filibusterer" who took over Nicaragua in 1856. In that same year Pollard addressed a pro-Walker rally in New York City in support of their shared vision of a vast slave empire throughout the Caribbean basin. He claimed that travels to Nicaragua, Mexico, China, Japan, Siam, and Georgia went into research for *Diamonds,* although the formidable Lost Cause historian J. G. de Roulhac Hamilton questioned whether ship schedules of the day would have allowed him so many ports of call. Pollard practiced law for a bit in Baltimore and New York and was on the federal payroll as clerk of the U.S. House of Representatives Judiciary Committee throughout the Buchanan administration. Like many Virginians, he had doubts about secession, but P. G. T. Beauregard's victory in the Battle of Bull Run seemed to convince him that he was still for the enslavement of the people of color he professed to love. His younger brother, Rives, gave up his job as news editor of the Baltimore *Sun,* and the two of them joined Daniels's *Examiner* in Richmond. As Edward's denunciations of the "imbecilities" of the Davis administration gained traction with the southern people, his personal life spun ever more out of control, providing fodder for the *Tribune* and other northern papers. By 1866, after a brief stint at the *Memphis Avalanche,* he deserted his second wife to marry a sophisticated divorcee, Marie Antoinette Nathalie Granier Dowell. She had divorced her first husband and the father of her children in 1865 because her Unionist views conflicted with his Confederate sympathies. Apparently Edward's modified views on slavery in *The Lost Cause Regained* sufficed to allow their bigamous first union and a fail-safe second ceremony in 1867.

In 1864, Pollard fled Richmond to board a blockade runner heading for England. It was captured, leading to eight months of comfortable incarceration in a New York prison. That produced another book, and after Lee's surrender, Pollard wrangled permission to return to Richmond as a journalist. He put up with the Yankee correspondents and Union officers at the city's best hotel and, almost unbelievably, wound up at a dinner party with Assistant Secretary of War Charles A. Dana, who had been sent by Lincoln to oversee the occupation of the former Confederate capital. Undeterred by his company, Pollard penned violent denunciations of the victors, leading to his arrest and another prison term. Very late in my research, in November 2021, I was helped in analyzing Pollard's career and his sad last days by my grandson Jasper Raines's discovery of yet another master's thesis from an unlikely author. On February 11, 2021, the history faculty of Eastern Michigan University approved the thesis of an Ann Arbor dentist named Justin F. Krasnoff entitled "The Contributions of Edward A. Pollard's 'The Lost Cause' to the Myth of the Lost Cause." Like Sister Darcy, Dr. Krasnoff felt there was an inconsistency between Pollard's relative obscurity and his authorship of "a historiographical landmark" that "established most of the basic tenets of the Myth of the Lost Cause except the Lee mythology or 'Leeolatry.'" As best I can tell, "Leeolatry" is an original coinage, and other aspects of the seventy-four-year-old author's research are, to the best of my knowledge, found nowhere else. Krasnoff demolishes a theory that Horace Greeley's reference to a "lost cause" in his newspaper or the popularity of Sir Walter Scott's novels in the South may have injected the term into the historical vocabulary. Krasnoff points out that the phrase popped up here and there in postwar writings and speeches, but the popularity of Pollard's book indisputably contributed to "grafting the phrase . . . onto the public imagination." This happened because Pollard and his New York publisher undertook an advertising and publicity campaign starting in December 1865 that led to first-year sales of fifty-three thousand.

Krasnoff and Maddex both document how bad luck and bad health combined to cost Pollard control of the movement he'd created. In the South, criticism of *The Lost Cause* focused on its key features of hostility toward Davis and its unremitting Virginia chauvinism. By blaming General Jubal Early of Lynchburg for losing the Shenandoah Valley campaign of 1864 to Union general Phil Sheridan, Pollard offended an even more energetic Virginia cheerleader in the person of Early. In an 1869 article entitled "Popular Errors in Regard to the Battles of the War," Early wrote, "Of all the writers on the war, none have perpetrated greater blunders as to facts, or delivered more presumptuous and erroneous judgments on military operations, than Mr. Edward A. Pollard, author of a book which he styles 'The Lost Cause.'" He then goes on to reproduce part of an advertisement from E. B. Treat, the publisher, in which Treat did indeed make the false claim that Lee and other generals had endorsed it.

By that time, Early was whipping an ailing horse. (Pollard was soon to withdraw to the home of a brother in hopes of recovering from the kidney disease that would kill him in 1872.) His spirit had been substantially broken on November 24, 1868, when his brother Rives, now editor of a Richmond paper called the *Southern Opinion,* was shot to death by the socially prominent brother of a Richmond socialite who had eloped with a "gay young" Texan of dubious reputation. The Richmond correspondent of *The New York Times* feasted on the society killing. Rives Pollard had spent the previous day in his office "well armed as was the custom with him, for he was always a sort of walking arsenal." On the fatal day he arrived by carriage "from his country residence, known as The Cottage." As he alighted, a twenty-four-year-old sniper killed him with buckshot fired from the second floor of a nearby building. "He was the very man to do the job," the *Times* said of the assassin in its mordant way. "He had been in the Confederate Army, on the staff of JEB STUART, and was thought to be brave and chivalrous." The assassination provoked Edward Pollard's last burst of advocacy journalism. He covered the trial that acquitted his brother's murderer in *Memoir of the Assassination of Henry Rives Pollard*.

The Pollards were not strangers to unhappy armed readers, and, as the *Times* implied, regarded them with cool composure. In 1867, almost exactly a year before Rives died, two sons of Virginia governor Henry A. Wise tracked Edward and his wife to the Maltby Hotel in Baltimore to punish him for repeating in a lesser work, *Lee and His Lieutenants*, the widely held opinion that the senior Wise was an incompetent general who lost West Virginia to the Union side. The *Harrisburg Telegraph* reported the confrontation as occurring on November 14, 1867. The coverage of the event in regional papers shows that Pollard's fame outlasted the war, as does the fact that both *The Lost Cause* and *Lee and His Lieutenants* were mentioned in the lede. Hearing that the Wises were hunting him, Pollard went to the hotel lobby with his wife. Eyewitnesses told the newspaper that "one of the Wises (there are conflicting reports as to which) asked him, 'Are you Mr. Pollard?' Pollard replied that he was, and the shot was immediately fired, without a word further being said by the assailants. Pollard had his arms folded over his breast, and the ball penetrated his right arm about an inch below the elbow." Pollard drew a revolver and fired inaccurately. "Pollard's wound is not dangerous, no bones being broken, and the ball having been immediately extracted. He, however, suffers intensely."

Pollard's wife, Marie, was holding her husband's arm protectively when the bullet struck her husband. She was not much afraid of guns, as the *Baltimore Gazette* reported on July 2, 1869, by which time the Pollards were estranged during what the newspaper termed "one of their not unfrequent matrimonial difficulties." She was accused of having shot a Dr. G. A. Moore "through the left wrist with a single barreled pistol, at his apothecary store" for refusing to disclose the whereabouts of her husband, a friend of the druggist. Mrs. Pollard was stylishly dressed for her trial. She advanced to the witness stand, and throwing back her veil, disclosed a very pretty, clever face, and made a most pathetic appeal to his honor recounting the story of the woes and ill-treatment she had received from Mr. Pollard, and implicating Dr. Moore, his intimate friend, as one of the sources of her troubles. She had only shot after being assaulted by Dr. Moore's clerks, she said. Expecting a small fine for throwing herself on the mercy of the court, she "moaned and sobbed unceasingly" until taken to the jail to serve thirty days.

She was back in the headlines of a West Virginia newspaper at the start of December 1870. The *Daily Intelligencer* stated that Marie Pollard had secured her release from the Government Insane Asylum in Wheeling and planned to sue the owner of the hotel she had leased for allegedly administering drugs to her as a basis for getting her out of the property. Again *The Lost Cause* got the publicity due a national best-seller. "Her husband, the well-known historian of the 'Lost Cause,' Edward A. Pollard from whom she has been separated for two or three years is now in New York. She has written him with a view to reconciliation, and to secure his aid in the intended suit."

The paper was wrong about Edward's whereabouts. By that time he was at death's door, bedridden at the Lynchburg home of a surviving brother.

According to Pollard's biographer Dr. Krasnoff, "neither he nor his work has enjoyed anything close to the reputation that it deserves as a landmark in American history and historiography." Indeed, even as he declined, Pollard was "being officially shunned" by leaders of the movement he had named. As for Jubal Early, he was just getting started in the Lost Cause business.

LEE'S BAD OLD MAN

TO BOLSTER ESPRIT de corps, Robert E. Lee liked to nickname certain generals. James Longstreet was "My Old Warhorse," and Jubal Early was "My Bad Old Man." Longstreet was his best division commander and Early one of the most unreliable, so erratic that Lee finally sacked him for losing the Shenandoah Valley in the massive, prolonged defeat over the summer and into the fall of 1864 that has gone into Virginia lore as "The Burning." Yet Longstreet and Lee are linked in a way that, based on the facts of their lives, is counterintuitive and illustrates the unintentional accuracy of Lee's sobriquet for Early. Getting fired by Lee on March 30, 1865, was, in some ways, just a beginning for Early. Through his propaganda efforts after the war, the crabby old Virginian turned his rival Longstreet, the highest-ranking Alabamian in the Confederate army, into the scapegoat of Gettysburg. Early, who himself had committed a disastrous tactical delay on the first day of that momentous battle, not only blighted Longstreet's image for all time but also crafted one of the most successful public-relations campaigns in American communications history. He changed the reputation of Lee from that of a traitor into a universally admired American hero. More broadly, Early took Edward Pollard's catchy title, *The Lost Cause,* and turned it into a scholarly and literary movement that still cripples the ability of many Americans to think straight about the Civil War. I would submit he is one of the most influential—and one of the most unlikely—public intellectuals in the entire national narrative. Aside from John Wilkes Booth and the other presidential assassins, few Americans have exceeded him in energetic perversity. Yet to most Americans, he is little known, especially in comparison to his impact on our Civil War sensibility.

Even though Rollin Osterweis's 1973 *Myth of the Lost Cause* introduced me to a rich vein of scholarship, it took me a long while to understand the centrality of Jubal Anderson Early to the story it tells. Amazingly, there is no index entry in *Myth of the Lost Cause* for Early, who is remembered these days mainly for his hammy given name, borrowed frequently over the years by romance novelists and Hollywood screenwriters. It seems an odd oversight for a scholar of Osterweis's accomplishment. His masterwork, 1949's *Romanticism and Nationalism in the Old South,* demonstrated that the "Old South rested on a tripod"— cotton plantations, slavery, and the "cult of chivalry" as part of a general romantic movement that swept America in the first half of the nineteenth century. Perhaps he missed "Old Jubilee," as his soldiers called him, because Osterweis did not grow up in the South. He was reared in New Haven, Connecticut, the Yalie son of a wealthy cigar maker. Had he grown up south of the Mason-Dixon Line, he would have heard the name in that tier of formidable generals just behind Lee and Stonewall. In any event, once I started digging, I found "Ol' Jube," as he was also called, was more responsible than any single Civil War figure man for the modern South's wicked political delusions and, indeed, for many of the tropes that drive Trumpian-style neo-Confederate fantasies today.

Despite shortchanging Early a bit, Osterweis provided two other key concepts for understanding the enduring irrationality of conservative white political conviction in the South. The region's leaders set up an "intellectual blockade" to see that Dixie romanticism did not develop along the egalitarian, humanistic lines of English, European, or New England romanticism. On the sparsely settled, violent frontiers of the Old Southwest, the individualistic, honor-bound code of Sir Walter Scott had greater appeal for a defeated region undergoing a religious conversion that could more aptly be called a convulsion. Scott's glorification of Celtic sangfroid also resonated with the region's Scots-Irish frontier settlers.

Another factor in the rise of Dixie's brand of a narrow, vengeful romanticism was a religious shift that began two or three decades before the war and extended into Reconstruction. The dominant pre-war religions were losing their popular appeal, Episcopalianism because of its class snobbery and Presbyterianism because of its bothersome belief that everything—including Appomattox—was predestined. These denominations of the frontier elite were identified with defeat rather than the exuberant salvation on offer from circuit-riding Methodists and foot-washing Baptists. Thomas P. Abernathy, an influential historian of the frontier South, pointed out the paradox: "It was probably Grant who helped the evangelicals conquer the South." He saw the high-church austerity of the old brands being replaced by a new "romantic Christianity" that emphasized communal solidarity and unrestrained emotion. Sensing their marketing opportunity, the Methodists and Baptists both trimmed their sails on issues such as slavery, whiskey, gambling, and dancing, giving the term "Holy Roller" a religious aptness that fit with recreational customs and produced the persistent evangelical sleeper hold on Alabama politics. There is, of course, no better sensibility for a defeated people than romanticism, which provides fertile ground for feelings of self-pity and undeserved suffering. Thus, the regional ethos called out for a new kind of leader with alchemical manipulative and organizational skill. One does not have to pull too hard on the threads on the enduring hold of reactionary, theocratic impulses in the politics of the modern South to pull to the surface the lively corpse of Jubal Anderson Early.

Southern historiography has lagged in documenting the triumph of this seedy, unappetizing character. For my part, the process of learning about Early's importance to reactionary politics and cultural stagnation could have been shortened by twenty years if I had followed a lead that appeared practically in my front yard in 1978 when I arrived in Atlanta as a newly hired national correspondent in the *Times* bureau there. I moved my family into a center-hall colonial across the street from the city park with its historical markers designating the center of the Battle of Peachtree Creek on July 20, 1864. The neighborhood and nearby Buckhead were favorite haunts of Atlanta's large community of relic-hunting hobbyists, including the poet James Dickey. Sometimes operating at night to avoid National Park Rangers, they prowled the golf courses and memorial sites with metal detectors. My little boys found Minié balls on the creek bank. They fished for rock bass along shorelines where the Confederacy lost at least 2,500 men in a defeat that made the fall of Atlanta inevitable.

My genial across-the-street neighbor in this subdivided battleground was a familiar type of southern yuppie, a Washington-and-Lee man given to tasseled loafers, madras shorts, and deep devotion to Robert E. Lee. The latter quality emerged because the summer we met, in 1978, was a troubled time for him, marked by the publication of *The Marble Man* by Thomas L. Connelly, a revisionist historian born in the insufficiently reverent state of Tennessee. Perhaps because of my connection to Yankee media, my neighbor insisted that the scandalous attack on his college's namesake hero was essential reading if I was to have any chance to understanding my new beat.

Not until more than two decades later did I finally turn my full attention to Connelly's offending analysis, discovering a writer who understood both Lee's feet of clay and Early's preeminent role in shaping what generations of American students had been taught about the Civil War.

Connelly noted that a number of former Confederate officers had lionized Lee, aided and abetted by the emergence in Richmond and other Confederate capitals of ladies' memorial associations, which were quickly recognized as a political force. An outgrowth of the soldiers'-aid societies organized by Confederate women during the war, the LMAs enrolled many widows and surviving female relatives to raise funds for statues that popped up across the South between 1865 and 1900. They demanded monuments recognizing Lee as a national, not just southern, hero. The LMAs and Confederate veterans' groups engendered a kind of hysterical hagiography that swept the southern press and cropped up in northern newspapers as well. "But the driving force behind the first Lee cult," Connelly concluded, "was Jubal Early, *perhaps the most influential figure in nineteenth-century Civil War writing, North and South.*" Those are my italics, and they denote my admiration for Connelly having the guts to state explicitly what other scholars had soft-pedaled. I would quibble only with Connelly's use of the word "perhaps" in describing this odd, cranky fellow's lasting influence on American history writing, literature, and popular culture. Indeed, it came as a shock to me to realize that the reign of political error and racial terrorism into which I was born in the Heart of Dixie must all be traced to the "civil religion" evangelized from Early's relic-filled apartment in Lexington, Virginia. Later, I will trace how Early's legacy, flowing through Tuscaloosa and into Birmingham, made my hometown the murder center of the civil rights movement.

Connelly nailed Early's essential role in institutionalizing the Lost Cause sensibility in American letters, and his work spurred me to look more deeply into the long shadow Early cast over southern race relations and American popular culture by fostering an overly sympathetic view of a "noble" if misguided South. In 2014 came another book that at last provided a balanced look into the military record of a general who finished the Civil War as one of the most hated of all Confederate officials. Early fled the South for Mexico and Canada immediately after surrender for two reasons: to escape blame for failing Lee and to avoid prosecution as a war criminal. It seems an odd fate for a soldier who came very close to ending the Civil War on southern terms, as described in *Jubal Early: Robert E. Lee's Bad Old Man* by Benjamin Franklin Cooling III. Cooling briskly sums up Early's paradoxical war record. In mid-July 1864, his surprise cavalry invasion of the suburbs of an unprepared Washington, D.C., caused panic in the North and threatened the safety of Abraham Lincoln, "perchance changing the course of American history." But within two months Early's military errors in the Shenandoah Valley led to the fall of Richmond and "essentially lost the war for the South."

In appearance and behavior, Early seemed preternaturally cast for his malevolent role in American culture. An attack of rheumatism during the Mexican War in the 1840s left him with a permanent stoop that emphasized what biographers have called his "crabbed" personality. Descriptions in numerous books are salted with words like "acerbic," "embittered," "profane," and "drunken." He had "dark, piercing eyes," a frowning countenance, a "bald pate." His Ichabod Crane–like appearance played into the American stereotypes exploited by Dickens, Twain, and the Yankee travel writers who rattled around the antebellum South. He dressed in custom suits of Confederate gray for his entire life, and when in the company of journalists and military visitors to Lexington always found occasion to shoot his cuffs, revealing colorful enameled links replicating the Confederate battle flag.

In a typical act of self-promotion to appeal to northern audiences, he published a lengthy account of his "raid on Washington" on August 6, 1881, at the peak of his run as the Confederate survivor best known and most influential among Yankee readers. At that point, he had another thirteen years to go in the PR campaign that fed a credulous national audience, and press, tales of Rebel grandeur and plantation romance. He was a tireless promoter of the idea that Virginians were the best generals on either side, and that the war was decided in the famous battles in and around their state, where the "butcher" Grant prevailed only by dint of overwhelming numbers. But his Virginia-centric explication overlooked certain key facts. The surrender ceremony at Appomattox was a formality. The spine of the Confederacy was really severed by the "War in the West" with the fall of Vicksburg in 1863 and Atlanta and Savannah in 1864. And Early himself was not the "quick and generally sound tactician" lauded by friendly historians like Frank Vandiver (1925–2005), the prolific Texas scholar who wrote *Jubal's Raid: General Early's Famous Attack on Washington in 1864* and *Mighty Stonewall*. Although he exhibited "cold courage" in battle, Early's hesitancy and lack of follow-through caused him to snatch defeat from the jaws of victory in all his critical battles. The tendency toward fatal pauses burst into view dramatically on July 1, 1863, the first of three days in the Battle of Gettysburg, and his well-publicized failure there forced him into a campaign of character assassination that stands as an ignoble bookend to his rehabilitation of Lee's reputation. Early led the campaign of Virginia veterans of Lee's staff to lumber the competent Alabamian, James Longstreet, with the blame that rightly belonged to Early, Richard Ewell, and, especially, "Massa Robert" himself.

Put simply, soldiers led by Early and Richard Ewell initially whipped an inattentive Federal force led by General O. O. Howard in sleepy Gettysburg, chasing them from the downtown streets, but their failure to pursue farther allowed the Federals to settle on Cemetery Ridge, a saddleback of commanding high ground between Cemetery Hill and Culp's Hill. After hours of indecisive discussion, Early and Ewell called off the attack around 4 P.M. Lee was dismayed when he arrived to find they had carried the day but surrendered the best terrain to a shattered enemy. This hesitation by Lee's trusted division commanders—overly trusted, as it turned out—was the original sin that led to Confederate defeat at the war's defining engagement. Early doubled down on the side of caution by convincing Lee not to attack Cemetery Ridge at daybreak on July 2, before the Federals had time to solidify their hold on the strategic position. Over the next two days, Lee ignored Longstreet's advice to forget about the ridge and move around General George Meade's army, flanking his entire force to threaten Washington. Instead, Lee destroyed his army with assaults culminating in Pickett's Charge on July 3. The suicidal charge was aptly called the "High Tide of the Confederacy"; thereafter, Rebel fortunes slowly ebbed except for two plausible opportunities handed to Early to redeem himself in Lee's overly forgiving eyes.

In these episodes, Early would blink again: once at the gates of Washington on July 12, 1864, and again at the decisive Battle of Cedar Creek in the Shenandoah Valley on October 19, 1864. These were complicated situations with cloudy outcomes that historians still debate. But for our purposes here, the point is that in both cases Lee had bet on Early, rather than the more competent Longstreet of Alabama or the more decisive General George Gordon of Georgia, and was betrayed again by his incurable favoritism toward sons of Virginia. In the spring of 1864, Lee had settled on a risky but plausible strategy to send perhaps the South's best remaining fighters, fifteen to twenty thousand veterans of Stonewall's famous "Foot Cavalry," into the Shenandoah Valley to distract Grant from his grinding assault on Richmond. While Lee's force delayed Grant, Early was to defend the vital wheat crops in the valley and, if possible, march stealthily to the north, slip into Maryland, and get into position to pounce by surprise on poorly manned Fort Stevens in Silver Spring, Maryland. Grant had even opened the door to Washington by withdrawing heavy cannons and seasoned troops from Fort Stevens. Approaching the Federal capital from the north seemed possible.

Initially Early's hesitancy was not a problem. On July 1, the first anniversary of his unfortunate pause at Gettysburg, he set out from Winchester, Virginia. By marching Stonewall's speedy veterans up to 25 miles a day, he was in front of Fort Stevens on July 11. Sitting astride his horse near the District line, he could see only a few Union troops atop the barricades; looking toward the south, he could see the new dome of the Capitol, only six miles away. Civilian Washington was in a panic, and Lincoln rode down to the docks to greet the first troops arriving by steamer from Richmond and see them off for a fast march on Fort Stevens. Soon Early saw blue-clad columns approaching the fort, and he believed his men were too exhausted to attack immediately. He decided to bivouac them overnight and take the place in the morning, then march on the White House, where he might kill or capture the president. His troops, although exhausted, were disgruntled by the delay.

But Ol' Jube felt his staff officers needed a rest, too, and he dipped into the wine cellar of a mansion he had captured, the Silver Spring home of Francis P. Blair Sr. (1791–1876), an influential adviser to presidents dating back to Andrew Jackson; continuing family tradition, Blair's two sons were playing significant roles in the war, with Montgomery Blair as Lincoln's politically astute postmaster general and Francis P. Blair Jr., as we have seen, a major general commanding one of Sherman's Georgia divisions that included the First Alabama Cavalry, U.S.A.

As drinks went round the polished table in the elder Blair's dining room, one of Early's senior advisers, Major General John Cabell Breckinridge, regaled the group with tales of how much fun Washington had been between 1856 and 1860, when he served as Buchanan's vice president. Then, according to Shelby Foote's reconstruction of the scene, someone commented that Breckinridge would be able to visit his old haunts at the White House and on Capitol Hill. "This brought up the question Early had called his lieutenants together to consider: Was an attack on Washington tomorrow worth the risk? Time was short and getting shorter. . . . Early considered with the help of his four division commanders and decided that it was. He would launch an attack at dawn, he told them, 'unless some information should be received before that time showing its impracticability.'"

The danger to Lincoln was captured brilliantly by Foote in the third volume of his Civil War history. After meeting with his cabinet at a White House that was still in denial on the morning of July 12, the president decided to take a look at the war, hoping that seeing himself and Secretary of State William Seward at the forts around Washington would calm public hysteria and hearten the ragtag militia and the late-arriving regular troops dispatched by Grant. Upon arriving at Fort Stevens, Lincoln bumped into its surprised commander, General Horatio Wright, who had just ordered a sortie by some troops in an effort to figure out why Early hadn't attacked at dawn.

> Informed of what was about to be done, [Lincoln] expressed approval, and when the general asked, rather casually, whether he would care to take a look at the field—"without for a moment supposing he would accept," Wright later explained—Lincoln replied that he would indeed. Six feet four, conspicuous in his frock coat and a stovepipe hat that added another eight inches to his height, he presently stood on the parapet, gazing intently at puffs of smoke from the rifles of snipers across the way. Horrified, wishing fervently that he could revoke his thoughtless invitation, Wright tried to persuade the President to retire; but Lincoln

seemed not to hear him amid the twittering bullets, one of which struck and dropped an officer within three feet of him. From down below, a young staff captain—twenty-three-year-old Oliver Wendell Holmes, Junior, whose combat experience had long since taught him to take shelter whenever possible under fire— looked up at the lanky top-hatted civilian and called out to him, without recognition, "Get down, you damn fool, before you get shot!" This got through. Lincoln not only heard and reacted with amusement to the irreverent admonition, he also obeyed it by climbing down and taking a seat in the shade, his back to the parapet, safe at last from the bullets that continued to twang and nicker overhead.

Foote, a none-too-closeted Lost Causer, believed "Early had won the admiration of his fellow countrymen, whose spirits were lifted by the raid, but also of foreign observers, who still might somehow determine the outcome of this apparently otherwise endless conflict. 'The Confederacy is more formidable than ever,' the London *Times* remarked when news of this latest rebel exploit crossed the ocean the following week."

It's unknown whether Early spotted Lincoln on the ramparts. But the sight of Federal troops atop the once-deserted walls of the fortress caused him to back down, even though his "frustrated" troops were convinced they could defeat the smaller Federal force, and for years afterward, officers and enlisted men wrote memoirs regretting not being allowed to camp on the White House lawn on July 12. Early spent the rest of his life arguing that he made the prudent decision to avoid a position that would have been hard to defend against a Union counteroffensive. But what he called prudence, the Richmond chattering class and probably Jeff Davis and Lee saw as hesitancy, possibly aggravated by a hangover from Blair's wine cellar.

To my mind, both Bruce Catton and James M. McPherson skip too readily over the might-have-beens in concluding in their *American Heritage* history of the war that "Early's march had given the government a case of nerves, but it had been barren of accomplishment." Others, including Cooling and Shelby Foote, believe the public relations impact of Early's foray could have been milked for concessions from a war-weary North. Plus there was the possibility of Lincoln being captured, kidnapped from, or killed at 1600 Pennsylvania Avenue by Rebels assaulting a lightly defended mansion. If Early had pinned down the Federal troops inside Fort Stevens, a raiding party detached from his main force of fifteen thousand would have been on Lincoln's front yard in a little over an hour at the "forced march" pace of four miles per hour.

But for our purposes, it's more important to note that no famous Rebel general had more to do with the Lost Cause being lost on the battlefield than Early. Consider the outcomes of his actions in the fateful Julys of 1863 and 1864. On July 1, 1863, he and Ewell captured downtown Gettysburg. But, as previously mentioned, they blundered so severely that not even Pickett's Charge of July 2 could reverse their error.

Early's hesitancy at Fort Stevens is more understandable, given that Grant could have moved his entire army up the Potomac. But by not even thrusting toward the White House with one of the few viable Confederate forces still in the field, Early proved that his personal bravery under fire, which no one questioned, could not make up for his hesitancy as a commander. He withdrew his army from the Washington suburbs under cover of darkness on July 12, with the Union braced for the attack that never came. Even so, Lee remained doggedly loyal to his "old man" and let him resume his guardianship of the Shenandoah Valley grain harvest, which was needed to sustain Richmond in the coming winter.

Over War Department objections, Lincoln and Grant sent tiny (five-foot-four), young (thirty-three) General Philip Sheridan to chase Early. He bested Early in a series of summer battles, raising public and official alarm in Richmond, but Early charged into a sleeping Union encampment at Cedar Creek on October 19, 1864, and Sheridan's men skedaddled in confusion. Early's men fell to looting the tents, and Early halted the drive. Sheridan, ten miles away, heard the gunfire and, mounting his famous Mississippi-bred horse, Rienzi, he raced to the scene and led a successful counterattack. A poem lionizing the diminutive general, entitled "Sheridan's Ride," became a national sensation and is credited with contributing to Lincoln's reelection.

This time Early's dawdling did not go unforgiven. Lee removed him from command by a letter so mild as to seem disingenuous, a kind of ceremonial last dance between Virginia gentlemen. Despite Lee's kindness, Early's career ended in a firestorm of condemnation that focused renewed attention on his dilatory performances at Gettysburg and Fort Stevens and his role in delivering the Shenandoah to Sheridan for "The Burning," which presaged Sherman's total-war tactics in Georgia. But Lee's solicitude for his fellow Virginian never wavered, even at the end. His letter of dismissal to Early expressed "confidence in your ability, zeal and devotion to the cause." The document that ended Early's military career was so gently worded that Early clung to it as a keepsake for the rest of his life. And its invocation of "the cause" proved to be prophetic, as it freed Early for the great work of his retirement: the promotion of the myth and the lumbering of Longstreet, Lee's most reliable fighter, with the blame for Confederate defeat. In a fearsome act of psychological displacement, Early would convict Longstreet in the tribunal of history with the very failing that had destroyed his own usefulness to the Confederacy, that of delay. So began the dual campaign of military scapegoating and reputational resurrection that has yet to end.

30

HAIL COLUMBIA

JUBAL EARLY, WHO died in 1894, did not live to see the apex moment of his campaign to rehabilitate Robert E. Lee. That came on May 30, 1901, with the dedication of the United States' first "Hall of Fame," the grand edifice in the Bronx that set the pattern for Cooperstown and all the "halls" to follow. The sprawling pavilion encircled the library of the University Heights campus of New York University, on a bluff across the East River from Manhattan. Architecturally, the Hall of Fame for Great Americans remains a triumph of Beaux Arts architecture executed by its definitive American practitioner, Stanford White. Selection for the first class of citizens enshrined in its 630-foot ring of statues was intended to be "the ultimate accolade for an American," as *American Heritage* put it, and it "remains the very embodiment of the old-fashioned great-man view of history." Lee was included along with Washington, Jefferson, Adams, Franklin, Jackson, Lincoln, and Grant, probably marking the first time that an empire had honored a traitor in so forgiving a fashion. To be sure, Lee's inclusion was a triumphant recognition of all that Old Jubilee could have hoped to accomplish with the Lost Cause crusade.

The dedication was a spectacular milestone of literary and academic acceptance for Confederate values. It was a journey to respectability marked by two epic films, *Birth of a Nation* and *Gone with the Wind,* and enduring as a sociopolitical force beyond the civil rights movement of the 1960s and unto the present day. Twenty-first-century public opinion polls by CNN and the Pew Research Center show that almost six in ten Americans believe the war was about states' rights, not slavery, and almost half see the Confederate flag as a symbol of southern pride, not racism. CNN found in 2015 that 43 percent oppose removing the Confederate battle flag from government property, and Pew reported four years earlier that 45 percent of African Americans had no negative reaction to the flag.

How had public opinion been so swayed toward sympathy for traitors?

By 1901, with Early seven years dead, the task of converting his public relations victory into a regnant intellectual movement on American campuses had passed into Yankee hands, specifically those of William Archibald Dunning, born in Plainfield, New Jersey, in 1857 into a family that honored its Union army veterans. Young Willie Dunning heard his first war stories at the knee of an uncle who had fought with the Union army in Virginia. But the greater influence would be the boy's father, John H. Dunning, who was "a carriage manufacture, amateur painter and art critic." He built a stately home in Plainfield, New Jersey, which became a Gilded Age enclave when a new railroad connected it to Wall Street. By all indications, John Dunning identified with southern plantation owners as his class peers, and in the dedication of his first book, William Dunning credited him with inspiring his conservative views on Reconstruction as a time of undeserved white suffering.

I first came across the name William Archibald Dunning on page 90 of Rollin Osterweis's *The Myth of the Lost Cause: 1865–1900.* As eye-opening as the book was for me, its author understated Dunning's foundational role in America's first generation of professionally trained historians. Even more curiously, given Osterweis's scholarly rigor, his book's index contained no reference to the Dunning School, the most potent name in Civil War historiography for much of the twentieth century. Digging into the scant genealogical material on Dunning, I quickly discovered he was another of those charismatic personalities whose biographies serve both as connective tissue in the story of Alabama Unionism and as missing links in any useful exegesis of the impact of Lost Cause concepts on American thought. As Jubal Early dominated the first wave of the Lost Cause movement, in the 1870s and 1880s, Dunning, known as the "Old Chief" to his cultish academic groupies, turned the southern nostalgia industry into a scholarly movement. It shaped the Civil War canon and continues to influence the American imagination with romantic fictions about paternalistic planters and servile slaves. The astonishing home truth about the Lost Cause's second wave, an academic tsunami that flooded collegiate history departments until the 1960s, was that it was set in motion by this quintessential grandee of the eastern establishment. So while the Lost Cause was a Virginia invention, named by Edward Pollard and forged into a publicity instrument by Early, it was transformed into a national cultural and academic movement by Ivy Leaguers and a colorful set of enablers in Alabama and adjoining states.

A footnote to Dunning's resume is that he was not the first prominent Yankee writer to whistle Dixie's tune, and this tidbit, too, points up to the centrality of Columbia University in the bowdlerization of the Civil War and Reconstruction narratives. Dunning often praised the work of a slightly older Ohio millionaire who was the most important amateur Civil War historian of the late nineteenth century, James Ford Rhodes (1848–1927). Rhodes's father, a Cleveland industrialist, was a prominent Copperhead who criticized Lincoln throughout the war and pressed him to let the South go its own way. Retiring on his inherited coal-and-steel fortune to write full-time, the younger Rhodes penned a series of histories arguing that the ex-Confederate states were victimized by freed Black people and carpetbaggers, and in 1918 Columbia's trustees awarded him the second Pulitzer Prize for history, adding another layer to the university's reputation as a hotbed of Rebel sympathy by elevating a writer who believed that Black people were "one of the most inferior races of mankind." He wrote, "No large policy in our country, has ever been so conspicuous a failure as that of forcing universal

Negro suffrage upon the South." In the masterly *Race and Reunion: The Civil War in American Memory*, David W. Blight credits Rhodes with "open[ing] the door of national imagination wide to the admiration of beleaguered Southern leaders, especially Robert E. Lee. He reinforced the idea that exemplary men can choose the wrong, or doomed, side in a great war, a notion the Lost Cause promoters had tried to teach Americans." Blight pointed out the crucial turning point that lay ahead for the Dunning School: "With his stellar reputation for fairness, Rhodes had set the stage for William A. Dunning and his many students who, as professional historians, were to plant so deep the tragic legend of Reconstruction that it simply became an article of faith in American historical understanding." Blight described an astonishing turnaround in which the disloyal, sinful South had been replaced in the public mind by a "victimized South" that had been unfairly saddled with blame for "the race question" and now deserved a place of honor for redeeming itself despite the excesses of congressional radicals and corrupt Black officeholders. "The victors of Southern redemption over Yankee carpetbaggery and treachery held as high a place in national memory as the victors at Gettysburg or Appomattox."

Dunning had the academic bona fides that Rhodes lacked, earning his PhD from Columbia in 1885 under the tutelage of John W. Burgess (1844–1931), who established political science as a separate discipline in U.S. universities. After supervising Dunning's dissertation on the Constitution, Burgess boosted his younger protegé into editorship of the *Political Science Quarterly* in 1894 and recommended him for a full professorship in 1903. Dunning may have had rivals on the Columbia faculty, but the campus seemed to yield willingly to his "intense desire for worldly success and a penchant for self-promotion," according to his biographer James S. Humphreys, writing in *The Dunning School: Historians, Race, and the Meaning of Reconstruction*. Humphreys cited the "pervasive racism" of his era for what seems an amazing fact: "Few challenges to the Dunning view, from either scholars or non-specialists, arose during Dunning's lifetime." One timid critic at the University of Nebraska noted Dunning's "one-sided and 'northern' approach" but went on to praise the victory of "Southern Saxondom" over Black "barbarism."

Dunning's mentor, Burgess, had absorbed the "Teutonic germ" philosophy of racial superiority during the two years he spent at universities in Gottingen, Leipzig, and Berlin. Although a member of a Unionist family from middle Tennessee and himself a Union soldier, he exhibited such an unbending Confederate bias that he has come to be remembered as the "godfather of the Dunning School." Although Dunning himself was to die before the two men who taught him to worship at Confederate shrines, he outshone both of them in force of personality. He would be remembered long after his death for attracting zealous, talented, and like-minded graduate students from the Old Confederacy to his seminars at Columbia's Manhattan campus, then located in midtown at Madison Avenue and 49th Street. The shaping influence of Dunning acolytes on American academia was such that in 1957, for example, William M. Brewer, editor of the *Journal of Negro History*, complained that the field of Civil War scholarship was being ruled by scholars "trained under Burgess and Dunning in the nostalgic mecca which those historians developed at Columbia University for Southern historical students."

Brewer's comment underscores the fact that this geographic warping of the Civil War scholarship was common knowledge in the emerging field of professionalized history. In his definitive introduction to *The Dunning School,* John David Smith describes how Dunning campaigned from his Manhattan mecca with near-military precision to colonize southern campuses. He directed eight dissertations on Reconstruction in individual states by handpicked students who would become his intellectual ambassadors to the Deep South. The most influential members of the Dunning School (and their state studies) were William W. Davis (Florida), Walter Lynwood Fleming (Alabama), James W. Garner (Mississippi), J. G. de Roulhac Hamilton (North Carolina), Charles W. Ramsdell (Texas), and C. Mildred Thompson (Georgia). Ulrich B. Phillips, the historian most identified with the Dunning School's defense of plantation masters, studied with its founder at Columbia but wrote his dissertation on pre–Civil War Georgia politics. All those names, especially that of Fleming, are important to the long reign of Lost Cause doctrine in southern universities; they established a regional pattern in which southern graduate students ground out theses and dissertations excusing southern military incompetence and the violent disfranchisement of Black people.

Academia as a whole—and the Ivy League in particular—have been slow to acknowledge Columbia's paralyzing precedent. Significantly, the most important book on the subject, cited above, was not published until 2013, and its editors, John David Smith and J. Vincent Lowery, were from regional universities, in Charlotte, North Carolina, and Green Bay, Wisconsin. (It's an odd fact that the wave of revisionist scholarship inspired by Current and becoming a force in the first two decades of the twenty-first century has involved few brand-name universities.) The first line of the book, in a foreword by Eric Foner, is apt. "It is a peculiarity of the historical profession that it displays remarkably little interest in its own history. For this reason alone, a volume on the Dunning School— the first generation of university-trained historians to study the Reconstruction era—is extremely welcome." It was, Foner commented, a "sad reminder of the price paid when racial prejudice shapes historical judgment."

Foner's authority in the field is unquestioned. As the DeWitt Clinton Professor of American History, he has succeeded Dunning and Phillips as the reigning eminence of the Columbia history department and is primarily responsible for the university's effort, after more or less a century, to own up to its legacy. Among his honors was his selection in 1982 to deliver one of his profession's most important annual addresses, the Walter Lynwood Fleming Lecture at Louisiana State University. Publication of Foner's monumental *Reconstruction: 1863–1877* in 1988 put a kind of official stamp on his replacing Dunning and Phillips as the most important Reconstruction specialist of the century and joining C. Vann Woodward and John Hope Franklin among the towering figures of southern history during that time.

Foner taught a research course in the spring of 2015 that spawned a series of similar courses and ongoing research carried on under a project called "Columbia University and Slavery." The tone of that effort was captured in a 2017 video featuring a sophomore history student named Tommy Song. The title of his paper, "William Archibald Dunning: Father of Historiographic Racism Columbia's Legacy of Academic Jim Crow," makes up in punch what it lacked in punctuation. "Dunning was perhaps the most influential figure in twentieth-century historiography of the American Reconstruction," Song said. "His graduate students and his colleagues . . . helped create a narrative that is essentially false and extremely white supremacist." A reckoning is particularly important at this time, Song added with notable restraint, because of the "uncertainty and hostility surrounding the nation's racial past."

The tone reflects that of Foner in his foreword to the Dunning essay collection: "The writings of the Dunning School did more than reflect prevailing prejudices—they strengthened and helped perpetuate them. They offered scholarly legitimacy to the disenfranchisement of southern blacks and to the Jim Crow system that was becoming entrenched as they were writing." The exaggerated depictions of "the alleged horrors of Reconstruction helped freeze the mind of the white South in bitter opposition to any change in the region's racial system." These analytical conclusions, however, tell us little about how Lost Cause fabrications infiltrated southern institutions and through them the paranoid mindset of many of the region's citizens. Activities of the Alabama Department of Archives and History offer a prime example, and once again long-neglected files provide evidence of how the warped scholarship at Columbia trickled down among like-minded believers in a suffering plantation class. It was a matter of getting everyone on the same page, and a signal event was the triumphant entry of William Archibald Dunning into the Cradle of the Confederacy just as Thomas and Marie Bankhead Owen were perfecting their censorious hold on the Unionist story from the Alabama hills.

My discovery in 2018 of letters detailing the collaboration between Dunning and Owen to southernize the American Historical Association was a decisive moment in my quest to show the connection between two signal events in American historiography. These were the expansion of Lost Cause thinking into a dominant national mood and the establishment of the Alabama archives as a Rebel shrine. The Mississippi historian Charles Reagan Wilson has referred to the Lost Cause as a "civil religion" that was "baptized in [the] blood" of Confederate defeat. In that religion's gospel, the meeting in Montgomery in 1903 of Dunning and Owen amounted to a kind of apostolic succession. Its St. Peter was none other than Walter L. Fleming, who had been jointly mentored by the two new friends. "Collusion" might be a better word than collaboration for the joint effort described in a letter to Owen by Fleming dated December 1, 1902. Fleming had brokered the meeting in service of Dunning's mission to bring new southern members into the AHA to strengthen its pro-Confederate caucus during Dunning's upcoming presidency of the association. For some time Dunning had wanted the American Historical Society to meet in a southern city, and his passage through Montgomery on the way to New Orleans in 1903 had the feel of a royal progress.

Dunning was a handsome, theatrical man who moved in the highest social and political circles in New York and Washington. He was a spellbinding conversationalist and a famous wit, once remarking that a tumor that was slowly killing him would, if allowed to speak, make a pompous "noise like Woodrow Wilson." More important for our purposes, he was a tireless academic politician who used the American Historical Association as a vehicle for his vision of creating a zone of forgiveness around the Old South. He identified with the leaders of the Confederate South as part of an American upper class, whose solidarity overleapt whatever political and economic rivalries occasionally separated the rich people north and south of the Mason-Dixon Line.

The celebration of Dunning's arrival certified Thomas McAdory Owen's full emergence as a national leader in his field and in retrospect it guaranteed that the Owen stranglehold on the Alabama archives would last until my elementary school class reached Montgomery five decades later to meet Owen's widow, the redoubtable Miss Marie. In

1902, Walter L. Fleming was still studying with Dunning in Manhattan, and the correspondence between Fleming and Thomas McAdory Owen reflects the bonding at Columbia that would, in time, produce the Dunning School as a defining force within the American Historical Society and set up Fleming as the chief Dunning disciple in the South. As a graduate student, the combative Fleming, fresh up from Alabama's "cow college" at Auburn, must have reminded Dunning of the British stereotype of the "wild colonial boy." At any event, Fleming quickly became a campus star, dropping into his letters home the names of new acquaintances like the aforementioned Rhodes; Charles Francis Adams Jr., a dynamo who served both as president of the Union Pacific Railroad in the 1880s and as president of the American Historical Association in 1901; and Alfred Thayer Mahan, the internationally famous naval historian who became AHA president in 1902.

In his letter to Owen on December 1, 1902, Fleming reported Dunning's coup within the ruling council of the AHA, which at his urging would for the first time hold an annual convention outside the North. "It was a hard fight" in which Dunning's lobbying and some "whooping" from former AHA president Charles Francis Adams Jr. defeated western scholars who wanted the meeting on their turf. "Prof. Dunning has worked hard for it to go South and told me to tell you that they would expect you to stir up Ala" so as to lure more southerners into the society. Fleming asked to be remembered to Colonel John Witherspoon DuBose, an impoverished veteran whom Owen had hired for a pittance to make sure the archive's growing collection reflected Confederate glory. He added some chatter about writing about plans to write unfavorably about "Tories, Deserters and the Peace Movement in Ala." He wanted to expose the "treasonable practices" of north Alabamians late in the war, indicating that even before his career-making book came out in 1905, Fleming had Alabama Unionists in his crosshairs.

The letter illustrates the clubby bond among the group of men and women who would put a heavy, pro-Confederate thumb on the scales of Alabama's history and that of the larger South. The "treasonable practices in 64 and 65" to which Fleming refers were political maneuvers by

Lewis E. Parsons, Confederate colonel John J. Seibels, and Confederate general Philip Roddey. As opinion leaders who understood the Confederacy was defeated, they were proposing reasonable accommodations with the victors. Parsons was a level-headed lawyer and former Confederate lieutenant who, as provisional governor in the second half of 1865, oversaw the repeal of the ordinance of secession, thereby allowing Alabama to reenter the nation. Seibels, a former newspaper publisher, greeted the Yankee general who had just burned Selma at the Montgomery city limit and persuaded him to spare Alabama's capital. Roddey, who had fought doggedly alongside Nathan Bedford Forrest and against the First Alabama Union Cavalry as the Confederacy's "Defender of North Alabama," met Grant's battlefield representatives to effect the peaceful surrender of north Alabama when the time came. In the hardline history that Fleming was writing, all were traitors.

Fleming's warm reference to "Colonel" John Witherspoon DuBose is telling as to the archival practices at Owen's ADAH. It also shows how tidbits of information are important in any kind of reconstructive inquiry, whether in investigative journalism or historical research. I have developed what prosecutors call a "theory of the case" about the quixotic DuBose. He may have been a lieutenant colonel as quartermaster of the fashionable "Canebrake Guards" militia in Demopolis, Alabama, at the start of the war, but he got out of combat duty in the regular Confederate forces on the basis of a surgeon's letter about his deafness. After Reconstruction he gave up growing cotton on his inherited plantation and moved to Birmingham to work on his hagiographic biography of William Lowndes Yancey and a propagandistic tome on Reconstruction, *Alabama's Tragic Decade*. Based on circumstantial evidence and timing, I believe that he was Thomas and Marie Owen's agent in winnowing the Unionist materials from the river of documents that flowed into the ADAH after Thomas Owen issued in the early 1900s a public appeal for all surviving records. We do know that, based on his pro-Confederate writings, Owen hired him to plow through the material. We know he is thanked in Fleming's foreword, on an equal basis with Owen and Ryland Randolph, for his research assistance. One account places him as Randolph's colleague in the Ku Klux Klan, but other sources say DuBose belonged to the better-pedigreed secret order favored by Black Belt plantation owners, the Knights of the White Camellia. We also know that no less a Lost Cause partisan than William Stanley Hoole hailed DuBose as a neglected southern historian in having his Confederate Publishing Company print his essays posthumously.

These, then, are the credentials of the man put in charge of Alabama's Civil War documents from 1901 to 1915. At the least, DuBose has to be regarded as a suspect in the archive's tainted provenance and the gaps in its subject matter. I thought of him in regard to Donald Dodd's unsuccessful summer-long search for a missing document that we know existed—the 1862 spy report about the large, patriotic crowd at Chris Sheats's first rally in Winston County. In journalistic and historiographic speculations, there are actually few smoking guns. (Even so, I was to find in the Owen correspondence a letter that comes close to smoking-gun status about Sheats being denied a prominent role in Fleming's book and all the subsequent books that cited it as their main source on events in Alabama. We'll get to that in due course.)

Right now, the more important point regarding the Dunning School is that there was plenty of heroic Confederate memorabilia for Thomas and Marie Owen to use in a dramatic nighttime presentation for the distinguished visitors who arrived at the Montgomery depot on the evening of December 27 with Columbia's "flawed colossus," to use the title of one scholarly monograph about Dunning. Another of Thomas Owen's influential New York friends, Edward R. H. Seligman, president of the American Economic Association, had written Owen in advance to ensure a reception befitting Dunning's status. He advised Owen that when the guests arrived, they should find the whitewashed capitol awash with floodlights and lights sparkling from every window. Although no pictures survive, it must have been a dazzling holiday display. The *Montgomery Advertiser* reported the event under an imposing three-deck headline: "Montgomery's Guests / Party of Historians En Route to New Orleans / Mr. Owen and Local Committee Showed Them over Capitol."

The fawning unsigned article reported that 150 "distinguished and famous men and women of the American Historical Association stopped over in Montgomery Sunday night," having traveled on a "special train" from New York. The breathless author made it clear that Dunning and Owen were the stars of the affair. Owen led the travelers up the long slope of Goat Hill to the glowing capitol, where they visited Jeff Davis's "Little White House of the Confederacy" and the chamber in which William Lowndes Yancey gaveled through the ordinance of secession. "He kept the attention of the party with his ready wit and graceful command of his subject, and his audience was highly entertained with the stories of Yancey and Emma Sansom," the *Advertiser* said. I found it almost touching that Owen had to trot out Emma Sansom's horse ride with Bedford Forrest to flesh out Alabama's paltry history of Civil War battlefield action. The gift pack for the visitors included a copy of the newly passed state constitution that disfranchised Black people and, for some reason, an article on the beef cattle industry in the South. But the reporter got the key point: that the occasion marked Owen's coming-out as something of a national figure in the nostalgia racket. At a monument to the Rebel dead, Owen recounted the "heroic conduct of those Alabamians who gave their life's blood for their country," the newspaper reported. "Here just before breaking up and starting back to their train, Dr. W. A. Dunning proposed a vote of thanks to Mr. Owen for his kind attention, and it was given with a will and enthusiasm."

Self-congratulatory letters about the success of the event flew back and forth among the participants and absent friends. Their excitement is palpable. These men and women were inventing a profession together, and its ethos was to be friendship toward the glamorous South that Owen showed them. In that respect, their enthusiasm reminds me of what reporters of my generation felt in the 1960s and 1970s when the rules of southern journalism began to change, liberating us to be change agents rather than the passive stenographers of a dying order. We hoped to glorify the new, while Dunning's crew sought to legitimize a failed past. But their zeal resonates across the years.

After returning to New York, Dunning wrote to his acolyte Fleming, who had not attended, that "your enterprising friend, Owen, at Montgomery, made a particularly good impression for himself; he treated us royally well. When the train stopped there at 9:30 in the evening, the historic old state house was very impressively and entertainingly exhibited by him, and his whole spirit, both there and at New Orleans, won him a host of friends in the Association and at the same time, I think won for the association a very earnest friend in him."

There was a natural affinity between Dunning and Owen. They had corresponded but never met until that spangled night in Montgomery. Later that evening, they would ride the train to New Orleans together through the Alabama night, crossing the storied cotton prairies of the Black Belt, and arriving around daylight at the showplace city of New Orleans. The Owens were a family of college-educated doctors and planters whose holdings lay between Birmingham and Tuscaloosa. Thomas Owen's marriage to Marie Bankhead gave him permanent status in the mighty Bankhead political machine based in Jasper, guaranteeing social entrée and cushy jobs in Washington and Montgomery. Owen was almost Dunning's equal in grabbing the opportunities for self-promotion that came with access. Addressing the AHA in New Orleans, he pointed out that Alabama, at his instigation, was the first state in the Union to establish an official archive. Using his legislation as its model, Mississippi quickly followed suit.

"Scarcely any states in the Union are doing as much as Alabama and Mississippi, where the state governments have established departments charged with the task of collecting, preserving, and publishing historical records," he said. It was not a time, obviously, to point out that some records were being destroyed or diverted by DuBose into the vast personal collection in the Owens' Montgomery mansion. But few in the audience of academics and archivists could have missed the point that Alabama, an educational backwater, was now a national leader in archival affairs.

Both Dunning and Owen hovered pridefully over Fleming's budding career. They conferred about the forthcoming publication of his dissertation in book form as *Civil War and Reconstruction in Alabama* in 1905, during which year the American Historical Association met, in dismal January weather, in Chicago, and Owen was now part of Dunning's entourage. "I am very sorry that you were not able to be at Chicago," Owen wrote in a letter to "My dear Mr. Fleming." "I dined with Dr. Dunning on the evening of the 30th ult., and he had many good things to say of you and your work. I told him of having read your manuscript in part, and how gratified I was at its fullness and thoroughness. He says you are one of the very best men that ever attended Columbia University."

Owen was no stranger to acclaim. The New Orleans papers always covered his arrival there in his role as historian-general at conventions of the Sons of Confederate Veterans. But Dunning was in a different league. He was hardly out of his forties before worshipful colleagues at Columbia began calling him the Old Chief. As an "elite mugwump northern intellectual," he moved with ease in Ivy League, Manhattan, and Washington society. With his piercing gaze and precise beard, he was a strikingly handsome man and a famously caustic raconteur. His lectures were performances, and his former students and faculty colleagues obsessively stockpiled and traded stories about him. One such student, Milledge L. Bonham of Louisiana State University, wrote Dunning a letter about a reunion dinner in Baton Rouge in 1916 with two other Columbia PhDs—Fleming, then teaching at LSU, and the flamboyant J. G. de Roulhac Hamilton of the University of North Carolina, who was on his way to becoming the South's most successful collector of plantation documents.

"Hamilton delivered a lecture here recently, after which Fleming and I accompanied him to the Hotel, where we sat talking until nearly midnight. At first we conversed about Dunning, then we discussed Dunning, after which we talked about Dunning," Bonham wrote to Dunning. Dunning wrote back, "Judging from the topic of conversation, there were no ladies present at the recent meeting of Hamilton, Fleming and yourself." Dunning's "rare gifts of whimsicality and repartee" made him a popular drinking companion at New York's exclusive Century Club, but his joviality and fondness for practical jokes masked a razor-edged flair for academic politics, exercised by dispatching his students to influential teaching jobs and by derailing challenges to the Dunning School's pro-southern interpretation of slavery, plantation owners, states' rights, the Confederacy, and especially Reconstruction. Between his arrival at Columbia as an undergraduate and his death in 1923 as America's leading historian, only one serious challenge to his whiteman's-burden view of Reconstruction was to arise. It would take the master stroke of Dunning's career as an academic hit man to sideline his towering rival, W. E. B. Du Bois.

Tom and Marie

It was in the early summer of 1952, about a year before I, as a fourth-grader, would meet Marie Bankhead Owen in the Hall of Flags, that an aspiring historian named Allen Jones met her under more formal circumstances. Freshly graduated from Auburn University, he arrived at the Alabama Department of Archives and History at 5 A.M., so as not to be late for his summer job. He was admitted by another habitual early bird, one Mr. Miller, the building supervisor, and the two were to become fast friends over their morning coffees. Miller introduced Jones to several secrets of the place, including the fact (or rumor, or legend) that the light-skinned African American woman who had a lifetime sinecure as the elevator operator was the love child of a former Alabama governor.

The ADAH was a monument to sinecures, patronage, and nepotism. Soon young Jones was to become friendly with the four stately matrons who ran the main departments under the relaxed administrative oversight of Marie Bankhead Owen. One of them rented him a room in her nearby home in the fashionable neighborhood that spread south from Goat Hill to Cloverdale, where the newlyweds Zelda and Scott Fitzgerald rented their honeymoon cottage after they married on April 3, 1920. As it happened, Marie had become director of the archives only two days earlier, on April 1, following the untimely death of its founding director, Thomas McAdory Owen, in late March. Her late husband had written the legislation creating the department in 1901, giving Alabama the distinction of having the first publicly funded state archive in the nation. After he died, Marie and her family decided its leadership should stay in their powerful family, as it would for the next thirty-five years. Word of her appointment by the board of trustees came from her brother, John H. Bankhead II, who was a member of that board. Marie, who was chronically strapped for cash despite family help, thanked him for the "meal ticket," as she called the $4,000 annual salary.

The Bankheads were used to a comfortable life on the public purse, but 1920 had been an unsettling year. Their father, John Hollis Bankhead Sr., potentate of the eponymous political machine that was a power in Montgomery and Washington, had died at seventy-seven on March 1. A loan from J. P. Morgan had allowed the Bankheads to expand their coal mines. Family holdings also included a hotel and a dairy farm on Blackwater Creek, the same stream where, as it happened, my great-great-grandfather James Raines had built a gristmill in frontier times. But the Raineses were not in the Bankheads' league. In Jasper, Washington, and Montgomery, the Bankheads' lives seemed preserved within an aspic of glowing coincidence. Thanks to the senatorial careers of the elder John H. Bankhead and, later, his son, jobs appeared as needed—at the U.S. Post Office when newly married Tom and Marie lived briefly in Washington, by legislative fiat when they decided to move back to Alabama. It was an existence that seemed charmed, but also a little creepy. At one point, Marie moved to the Algonquin Hotel in New York to chaperone her niece Tallulah, a fifteen-year-old ingenue of the Broadway stage. The attention Marie garnered from the *New Yorker*'s "Roundtable Writers" made for a glittery artistic debut in Manhattan.

Back home in Alabama, Marie became famous first as the "Dragon Lady," who presided over the *Montgomery Advertiser*'s society pages, and then, upon receiving her "meal ticket" at the ADAH, as "Miss Marie." She reigned there until 1956, always strapped for cash and applying at various times for better-paying jobs, whether as her now-

famous niece Tallulah Bankhead's press agent or as a writer for
Paramount Pictures, NBC, a Hollywood-based radio syndicate, and the
New York advertising firm of Batten, Barton, Durstine and Osborn. Her
restless ambitions for the fast life in Hollywood and Manhattan did not
prevent her from churning out a stream of propagandistic textbooks,
plays, and histories about the glories of the Lost Cause. Between them,
as their lifetime achievements, Tom and Marie made the Alabama archives into an institution that was the lengthened shadow of their elitist
prejudices about Confederate virtue and the incompetence of African
Americans and poor whites. Alabama's politicians and newspapers
feared and glorified the square-jawed matron who came to resemble either Queen Victoria or J. Edgar Hoover in a black dress. Consequently,
Alabamians were never vouchsafed a glimpse of what greeted young
Allen Jones on the day Mr. Miller invited him up to the top floor of the
179,000-square-foot building. Even after seven decades, the sight left
him struggling for words as he recounted it to me.

"He took me into the attic, and the attic! You wouldn't believe the
attic," he told me by telephone in 2020. "You go up a long back stairway
and the whole floor—the attic was a whole room—just one big room of
the whole building, the top. And there was stuff—Howell, I'm not lying
to you now. This is—the first time I saw it I almost fainted. We got to the
top of the stairs and we walked in and there was a little walk space, and
I looked down that building and there were records and books and papers and all kind of stuff. They were over knee deep, both from knee
deep until waist high. You hear what I'm saying?"

I asked if the records were randomly stacked, as opposed to being in
labeled files. "Just stacked," said Jones, who retired as an Auburn University history professor after founding the school's innovative graduate
courses in archival preservation. "Just stacked. I mean you had to walk
on top of the records. There was no place to walk. It was just like an
open field, everything, and I said, 'My God, Mr. Miller!'" He added,
"Nobody touched it until Ed Bridges got here and cleaned it out."

Edwin C. Bridges, the first ADAH director with an earned doctorate,
succeeded Milo Howard, a Montgomery socialite and longtime Owen

apparatchik, in 1982. He found that his curators referred to the vast inherited collection in the attic as "the sea." He had the documents as-
sessed and found mostly commonplace periodicals. There was little of
value to Confederate history and certainly no original material about
Alabama's white Unionists. In this respect it reflected the policy shift
that occurred when Marie took over in 1921. Although he shared the racist and pro-Confederate biases of the Dunning School, Thomas Owen
had been respected nationally for creating the "Alabama Model" for the
legislative establishment of archives as an independent agency with its
own governing board. Owen's reputation received a tremendous boost
when the American Historical Association, with prodding from Dunning, recommended the "Alabama Model" over the more political "Wisconsin Model" of funding preservation by giving state grants to existing
historical and civic organizations. While Tom Owen collected documents, Marie changed the museum into "a veritable attic of the gentry"
that emphasized the heritage of the white elite. As Alabama historian
Virginia Van der Veer Hamilton observed, the collection even included
the wooden leg of Wilcox County's largest slave owner. A scathing 1932
report by the Brookings Institution concluded that since taking over for
her husband, Miss Marie had turned his orderly if narrowly focused collection into "store-rooms rather than a library." It recommended the department be abolished and replaced by a new "Bureau of Records."

Ed Bridges does not share my suspicion that the Owens purposely
destroyed documents, but the first scholarly biography of Thomas
McAdory Owen, fully available only since 2021, makes it clear they
didn't need to. The biased screening process Tom used from 1901 until
his death achieved a dual purpose. Not only did it block out from local
and national awareness the story of Alabama's mountain Unionism and
the First Alabama Cavalry, but its ripple effect had a previously underemphasized role in establishing Lost Cause dogma as a major force in
American scholarship and popular culture. Daniel Eric Cone has described the fallout that occurred when "Owen made it clear he was looking to acquire Confederate records first and foremost" for the nation's
first, trend-setting archive. That decision in the first decade of the twen-

tieth century coincided exactly with the emergence at Johns Hopkins and Columbia of history as a profession based on "scientific" procedures taught in graduate-school seminars like those conducted at German universities. The timing multiplied Owen's national impact, which Cone documents with precision.

Without Owen's example of drafting legislation to create a state-funded department committed to the collection of historical and contemporary papers, it is debatable how successful other pioneers could have been in fostering an American archival tradition. Without Owen employing pen, press, and personal connections to fill that department with basic records from Alabama's Confederate era, our present scholarly understanding of the tumultuous 1860s would be poorer, but substantially more accurate and inclusive. Perhaps most significantly, without Owen collecting primarily pro-Confederate materials and promoting a pro-Confederate view through the archives and its public partners, the Lost Cause memory might not have become such a part of America's academic as well as popular vernacular for over a century.

We now know, of course, that Owen was not as objective as he pretended to be. He made his goal sound innocuous: to let the records "speak in defense of the Southern Confederacy." In practice, Owen, casting himself as a polite proponent of white southern "heritage," had a specific view of what historical records mattered, and he focused his efforts on acquiring records favorable to his worldview while ignoring others.

As Alabamians come of age, we are encouraged to believe that what happens in our long-running, comical sideshow in Montgomery doesn't harm the nation. As a political journalist, of course, I learned to hope that voters in more conventional venues would beware of us as a pesthouse of dangerously mutating governmental germs. In a manner of thinking, the Bankheads begat Folsom begat Wallace begat Reagan begat Trump. The arc, like that of our current political scene, follows a slow curve from progressive economics to budgetary self-immolation. Racially, the curve moves from insensitive paternalism to cosmeticized bigotry. So shouldn't it seem less strange to see Alabama as more central to the way we think about the Civil War—and what we don't know about it—than has been customary? "In the past several decades," Cone noted, "there has been a greater scholarly appreciation of the Lost Cause as the primary lens through which many Americans—in particular white Southerners—remember the war and its aftermath." Cone quotes Chief Justice John Marshall as saying the power to document is the power to control. "Archives in this sense," he writes, "determine what people are allowed to remember." While Owen gave lip service to "letting the records speak," he expected that they would "speak in defense of the Southern Confederacy," Cone wrote. "The result was that the Alabama archives, while on paper a disinterested organization, became a partisan collecting institution."

The point about what people are "allowed" to remember certainly applies to descendants of Alabama's hill country Unionists. I thought about that when I visited my Walker grandparents' graves in 2017 during the special Senate election in Alabama in which Trump endorsed a Republican accused of child molesting against a Democrat with a strong civil rights record. Trump had put a spell on the hills. In delivering a landslide for Trump in 2016, voters in the modern Free State had no way to find out they were violating their tradition of independent political thought in support of a unified nation. In the sense of being threatened by twisted history, we are all Alabamians now.

Few Alabamians know about the odd role of Auburn University in the development of the Lost Cause establishment. We'll deal more fully with that when we again turn our attention to the career of Walter L. Fleming, the Dunning disciple who graduated from the Alabama Polytechnic Institute (now Auburn) in 1896. Meanwhile, I don't want my praise for Daniel Cone's interpretations to be taken as special pleading on behalf of another Alabamian. Cone's groundbreaking work illustrates the precision with which Tom and Marie Owen installed Rebel worship as official state policy, and it is an example of the enlivened scholarship about southern Unionism that has emerged nationally in the last thirty years.

Much of the best work has not come from the usual suspects among the famous historians of the Northeast. Another case in point was the publication in late 2021 of *Deep South Dynasty: The Bankheads of Alabama* by Kari Frederickson as the latest modernizing work from the University of Alabama Press. I have drawn heavily on both Cone and Frederickson in puzzling out the tactics of Tom Owen in inflicting systemic Rebel-worship on Alabama and the trickery of Miss Marie in establishing herself as the sociological arbiter of white Alabama between 1920 and 1956. Neither author, however, mentioned the formidable ADAH operative known as "Miz Pate," who exercised a Gorgon-like guardianship over all Civil War military records. In Greek mythology, there were three Gorgons, described by Ovid as women who guarded the entrance to the underworld and could kill unwanted visitors with a glance. The heart of the Neoclassical archives building in Montgomery required only two fierce wardens, Miss Marie and Alma Hall Pate. Allen Jones and Don Dodd helped me re-create their world, the command center of the institution as it existed in the 1950s and 1960s. Neither had snakes in her hair, like Medusa, but they were formidable in their differing ways. By the time I arrived with Miss Love's class, Miss Marie had an imposing, even monumental presence. Mrs. Alma Hall Pate was her physical opposite, a tall, slender woman with cropped hair who lived at Ellerslie, the oldest house in nearby Millbrook. She matched Mrs. Owen in iron will and Old South pedigree. Ellerslie, built in 1816 by her Virginia-born grandfather, was reputed to be the first house in the Montgomery area with glass windows. But transparency was not the rule at her place of employment.

On one wing of the first floor was Miss Marie's lair, a grandly decorated space with period furnishings and a lordly portrait of her departed Tom. Across the hall, a friendly woman named Miss Cobb and her staff clipped articles about Alabama from newspapers and periodicals. "They were nice ladies. What they did was cut articles out of the newspaper and paste them on paper and did that all day long," Allen Jones recalled. "She had a couple of helpers so they just gossiped and cut newspapers. That was their job in the library." The detail is important because it demonstrates the ADAH's shift of focus from Tom Owen's mission of collecting governmental records to Miss Marie's obsession with monitoring Alabama's public image. Miss Marie was renowned for marching into the room, scissors in hand, and cutting away paragraphs that were insufficiently positive—that is to say, overly factual—about life in Alabama.

On the floor above her office and the library were the Hall of Flags and the storage area for Confederate military records, Jones told me. His precise description of the floor plan confirmed my childhood memory of the lofty, well-lit space that greeted me and my classmates on our field trip. "That's the part I'm sure y'all went into," he said of my class visit. "That's where Miz Pate was. She was kind of really possessive of those records and she didn't want anybody else to use them, particularly just to go through them and see what they could find," Jones told me. That activity—poring over primary documents—is exactly how historical discoveries are made. At the ADAH, a hundred years after the start of the war, the records were still stored in poorly labeled boxes. There were no finding aids or alphabetization. The organizational process had ended with Tom Owen's death in 1920.

Allen Jones remembered his shock at Pate's response to a request from someone who was, after all, a member of the staff. "She wouldn't let me in. I said there was some stuff I would really like to check on, and she said, 'No, those records are not available.' And I said, 'What do you mean they're not available?' [She said,] 'Well, they're just not available.'" Jones appealed the case to Miss Marie, who was sometimes absent for weeks due to failing health and outside speaking engagements. Before she could rule, absenteeism of another sort intervened. "I caught Miz Pate gone. We were working on this map . . . of all the skirmishes that the Confederates had with the Yankees in the state. It's a very extensive thing and shows where all they engaged. And so this was the record I wanted to see and she wouldn't let me see it. She was out sick and I found out about it, the door was unlocked, just closed, and so I just went in there."

For three decades, trickery seemed the only sure way to get unregulated access to Civil War archives. Although he was interested only in

Confederate records, Tom Owen was at least a meticulous collector of those. His death liberated Marie to unleash her existing powers as the leader of Alabama's women's clubs, school librarians, the United Daughters of the Confederacy, and resident enforcer for the Bankhead political machine, whose leadership passed, upon the death of her father, to her brothers, U.S. House Speaker Will Bankhead and United States senator John H. Bankhead II. Tallulah's success on the stage and in Hollywood added to the ubiquity of the family name in Alabama. With her added power as director of the state's premier cultural agency, Marie devoted herself to promotion of "a particular historical narrative that romanticized the antebellum era . . . legitimized secession, heralded the heroism of the Confederate soldier, *minimized the contributions of poor white citizens, and all but erased African Americans entirely.*" Those are my italics in Kari Frederickson's comprehensive summary of her career. My intention is to emphasize that this campaign to bury the history of the two largest population groups required limiting access to an already distorted historical trove.

Informational barriers in schools, libraries, historic shrines, and courthouses are a fact of life familiar to every Alabamian of my generation. Even as a child, I understood I was being led into the presence of a personage that day in the Hall of Flags, but I had no context for understanding her ferocity. It's not just another only-in-Alabama story, but one of the best. Everyone in Montgomery knew the role of the "Tiger Woman" in the showdown between Klan-friendly but otherwise progressive Bibb Graves, governor from 1926 to 1930, and his successor, Benjamin M. Miller, a scholarly foe of the Invisible Empire. The Bankheads and Graveses had conspired to help Marie's brother John reclaim their late father's Senate seat from the strenuously anti-Black, anti-Catholic "Cotton Tom" Heflin in the 1930 Senate race. With Graves's blessing, Marie had used "time that could have been spent organizing records" to delivering civic-club speeches to promote her rarefied version of state history, a campaign that included putting her doted-upon son, Thomas McAdory Owen Jr., on the ADAH payroll for a weekly radio program, *Romantic Passages in Alabama History*. Using

Depression-driven budget cuts as an excuse, Governor Miller fur-
loughed four archival clerks, including Tom Jr., accused Marie of nepotism at a public ADAH board meeting, and cut her salary from $4,000 to
$2,700. She was now "spoiling for a fight" with Miller and stunned by
the accusation that putting a Bankhead on the public payroll was wrong.
"I hope that I conducted myself as a lady," she wrote her brother John,
"but also with the courage that our father would have expected [of] one
who had sprung from his loins. If I would follow my instincts at the
present moment, I would cut his G D throat."

Elected to a second term in 1934, Graves set things right with the
Bankhead machine in a spectacular way that has been repeated countless times in Goat Hill bull sessions and in every modern political history of Alabama. This time, Marie's target was far more powerful than
the hapless Governor Miller. Graves took her to the White House to
meet with Harry Hopkins, delegated by FDR to distribute New Deal aid
to the states. Miss Marie presented her case that the archives needed
more space and that help should be delivered in the form of a building
dedicated to the memory of her husband. Alabama's political historians
have embellished the tale into a number of amusing iterations depicting
Hopkins as a shape-shifting groveler. Most accounts quote Hopkins as
scoffing initially to Graves that he "did not have the money to construct
a building for every little old lady who wanted an archive." Some say she
marched out of the White House and had to be chased down by Hopkins once he found out she was one of those Bankheads.

The *Alabama Historical Quarterly* says the critical exchange took
place over the telephone with Roosevelt's powerful aide saying,
"Madam, we can't just go around building buildings. We've got to have
a reason."

"Well," shot back Mrs. Owen, "my brothers are John Bankhead and
Will Bankhead." To which Mr. Hopkins replied, "Those are two of the
best reasons I ever heard."

Another version of the story, which strikes me as more plausible, was
shared with me by Steve Murray, the current director of the Alabama
archives, who responded to the Black Lives Matter movement by issu-

ing a formal apology for the ADAH's failures in regard to Black history. Murray, a modernizer, has also assigned staff to go through the long-neglected Owen papers. I had hoped they might find a desk calendar or diary that would nail down the date of my class field trip to the Hall of Flags. So far nothing of that kind has been found. He confirmed my view that Marie effectively junked her husband's more professional approach to archival science and doubled down on his racism. "She was just thoroughly un-Reconstructed. She was a national leader in opposition to the Nineteenth Amendment," he said, explaining her bank-shot racial reasoning for opposing suffrage. "The idea was that if the federal government guaranteed the right to vote to women, there would be calls to go back and enforce rights for African Americans."

According to ADAH folklore, Murray said, Marie did go to the White House to speak directly with Hopkins and "felt quite dismissed" when he gave her the high-handed treatment she routinely dealt out to Alabama's common folk. "[She] just asked if he wouldn't mind calling her brother's office to send a car around to pick her up, and he said certainly. . . . [She said,] 'Well, just call the Speaker's office and he'll send somebody right over.'" That's when the lightbulb went on, "and Hopkins changed his tune and said, 'Well, let's sit here and talk about this a little more.'" Miss Marie was ferocious and mean, and although Hopkins awarded her a construction grant for her building, she was by no means through with his Works Progress Administration. In 1938, she sicced Governor Graves on the well-credentialed Birmingham-born newspaperwoman who was appointed editor of the WPA-published *Alabama: A Guide to the Deep South*. Under the Federal Writers' Project, each state was to have its own guide produced by large staffs of unemployed writers, artists, and journalists. Myrtle Miles had been city editor of the *Alabama Journal* in Montgomery and an editor and feature writer at the *Cincinnati Times*, and she worked in New York in public relations for the New York Central Railroad. Miles said she wanted to use her staff of a hundred in Alabama to focus on folk culture, unique collections, and handicrafts. According to an investigation by the Alabama historian Hardy Jackson, Miles cited as an example of the guide's contents an article about a "Negro living near Birmingham who is making remarkable attractive original ornaments out of coconut shells." Under pressure from white politicians, Miles hired only three Black people for her staff, but that did not appease Miss Marie. She was working on her own racist, pro-Confederate *History of Alabama for Junior High Schools* at the time. Professor Jackson, my classmate at Birmingham-Southern and a lifelong student of Alabamiana, speculates that she feared the *Guide* would compete with her book for purchase by the state education department. Moreover, WPA editors in Washington saw to it that the Alabama guide "gave readers a look at black life that was far more positive and candid than one might expect."

When chapters of the book began appearing in 1937, Miss Marie denounced the manuscript as "full of errors" and attacked Miles as an amateur. The newspaperwoman responded with a list of errors in Owen's own work and condemned her for writing her "in the scolding manner of a person punishing an unruly or perhaps an idiot child." Owen was not used to people hitting back. She persuaded Governor Graves to withdraw state aid, and by 1940 Miles had resigned and her operation had lapsed into chaos. By that time, Owen had won two major concessions. When the finished *WPA Guide* came out in 1940, it included praise for the new building Hopkins had financed and it referred throughout to the "War Between the States" rather than the "Civil War." The point here is not that Marie Bankhead Owen had sharp elbows but that she knew how to make systemic the alterations and omissions of history that she and Tom achieved. Had he lived longer or she been more disciplined a manager, their suppression of the First Alabama story might have continued indefinitely. Their information dike was finally breached when Donald Dodd introduced himself to Miz Pate.

"Well, I very quickly got the impression that I was not doing a popular subject. Why would I have an interest in these traitors to the South?" he said. "Unless you could prove that you had a Confederate ancestor, she would try to keep you out of that room." Dodd clearly failed that test, having had two grandfathers in the First Alabama.

Dodd's family farm had been renamed the Kudzu Botanical Gardens by his cousin James Dodd Manasco (1933–2018), an environmentalist who saved the old-growth hardwoods in the nearby Sipsey Wilderness from logging during the Reagan administration. The Manascos were another old Unionist family in Winston. Carter Manasco had been private secretary for Miss Marie's brother and Tallulah's father, House Speaker Will Bankhead, and he inherited the old man's congressional seat during World War II. The Sipsey Wilderness trees were part of the Bankhead National Forest, of course. During a visit there in 2018 I stayed the night at the sylvan estate of Hobson Manasco, my BSC classmate who was now attorney for the Winston County Commission. He introduced me to Roger Wade, the County Commission chairman, who grew up with "lots of Abbotts" a few miles from the now inundated farm of Hiel, the patriarch. (It presently lies under Lewis Smith Lake, which has made Winston County a popular stop on the professional bass-fishing circuit.) "They were good people, but they were rough as cobs. You didn't mess with an Abbott," he said, noting the alleged family fondness for knives.

This digression is necessary to telling the story in something close to Alabama-style—that is to say, with at least a sprinkling of tie-ins from a seemingly endless skein of connections. I could go on in that vein, but I won't, except for this: The first Manasco to arrive in Winston, General John Manasco, was by some accounts born at Nickajack Cave when it was the headquarters of Cherokee pirates preying on Tennessee River flatboats near Chattanooga. Manascos were reputed to be the only white people allowed at Nickajack, which lent its name to the Free State of Nickajack, the failed Unionist entity that proposed to secede from the Confederacy. It should be clear by now that the family threads of the hill people run every which way. Perhaps that was in the back of my mind when I decided to try out my grandson Jasper, a history student at the University of South Alabama in Mobile, as a paid researcher for this book. It proved more than fortuitous when he traveled to Montgomery in 2018 to start work in the same building where I heard Miss Marie tell about the bullet holes in the battle flags of "our boys."

As for the Dodds, Donald told me that when he failed Alma Hall

Pate's Confederate kinship test, he realized that he would "have to go a little hillbilly" to gain access to the records, for an obvious reason: "Those were her records." So he threw a tantrum, and the raised voices drew from the director's office Peter A. Brannon, the mild-mannered pharmacist who had succeeded Miss Marie. Perhaps because he and Dodd were both Auburn men, he intervened by allowing Dodd an uninterrupted week to spool through microfilm in Pate's space. Dodd was told by the staff that he should wait until Friday to print out all his work at one time. As he went along, he inserted slips of paper in the reels to mark images he wanted for his records. Pate struck when he left for the day at close of business on Thursday. "She's seen what I was trying to do, and she pulled all my slips out. She didn't approve of my topic. But I'm paranoid and have a natural distrust of most people, so I had recorded all those [reference numbers on the film frames] before I did it. So I exploded on her, and Peter Brannon, the archives director, came in and said, 'What's going on?' I said I'm not that interested in politics, but I'm gonna run for governor of Alabama [or] I'm gonna work for free for whoever's gonna win and the one thing I'm gonna do is fire that lady over there!

"Peter Brannon at that point said, 'Have you got your stuff over there? Put it together, and we'll microfilm it for free.' I got friends in the archives as a result of that conversation. People in there didn't like the way she ran the room. Some of them in there were trained as a librarian . . . to serve the public and stuff like that."

I assumed whatever Dodd found on the microfilm was covered in his book, so in our own visits to the archives, Jasper and I concentrated on the paper records that had been under the care of Miss Marie and Miz Pate. Who knew what else we might discover? The files were sometimes labeled by name, but more often jacketed in clumps that required page-by-page inspection. Almost nothing was digitized except for the modern computer catalogue of all subjects and materials in the archive. Searching in alphabetical order, we saw there were no listings for the First Alabama Cavalry, U.S.A., Christopher Sheats, or Colonel George E. Spencer. I don't want to be overdramatic, but a researcher landing from

Mars or New York would have no way of knowing they ever existed. To penetrate the storage system, one had to get a box number from the computer listing, fill out a form, and in due course the box would be brought out on a cart. The cardboard containers were the size of the long filing boxes used by banks. The workspace was clean and well-lit, but the atmosphere was strangely Dickensian.

In a series of library stacks at one end of the room, there was a single catchall folder about Winston County, which consisted mainly of newspaper clippings, many yellow with age and the sharp edges created by Miss Marie's scissors, crumbling or torn. Still, I believed, there might be treasures in there, and indeed, there was at least one. A clipping from the Haleyville newspaper showed that Marie Bankhead Owen had accompanied Governor "Big Jim" Folsom to a Winston County centennial celebration in 1951. There had been speeches and a parade. She had also been to a similar event in 1958 in the company of Congressman Carl Elliott, the amateur historian and energetic spreader of Free State lore. On that occasion there were remarks by Probate Judge John Bennett Weaver, author of the short historical pamphlet that told the entire story of the Looney's Tavern meeting, including Chris Sheats's speech, the antisecession petition passed by voice vote, and the satirical shout from Uncle Dick Payne that created the "Free State of Winston" slogan. The speeches from that day in 1958 have not survived, but a 1948 wire recording by Samford University professor George Irons (mentioned earlier) gives us an idea of the detailed Free State historical overview that Weaver is known to have given in many similar settings at historical gatherings. Did he communicate some of that information when he and Miss Marie were together on the dais? In any event, these clippings convinced me that Marie Bankhead Owen, who had grown up in a house only a few blocks from the courthouse that the First Alabama burned in 1864 and who had toured Winston in her official capacity, had to have known at least the basics of the story the ADAH was ignoring.

As a manipulator of historical facts, she was as tricky as Walter L. Fleming and Tom Owen. Like them, she was an artist of omission. She would admit to knowing just enough about Alabama Unionism to minimize its importance, misstate the military identity of the First Alabama, and if possible, refuse to mention its name. Updating her late husband's multivolume history of Alabama in 1947, she noted that Winston failed to secede but "did raise 5 companies of infantry for the Union Army." I found no record that she ever knew or acknowledged that the Free State troops were, in fact, cavalrymen who rode with Sherman. Their county, she noted in a perfunctory 462-word entry in an alphabetical listing of counties, was known for mining, timber, and "fruit, especially apples." While I am pleased to prove that she knew at least some of the history she was covering up, there is nothing to indicate she experienced this awareness as guilty knowledge. Her distortions were done in unblushing devotion to the Lost Cause and what she called "the great struggle for white supremacy" that ran through her life like a taut string of barbed wire.

But the boxes would have even more to tell, as Jasper soon discovered. Before getting to that, I want to revisit my own education in historiographic interpretation. In 1974 and 1975, I took an eighteen-month leave from newspapering when I secured an advance from the publisher G. P. Putnam's Sons to compile an oral history of the southern civil rights movements from the Montgomery bus boycott of 1956 to Dr. King's death in 1968. I learned a great deal about how to interweave the historical information from documents with the more anecdotal accounts that emerge during tape-recorded interviews. The latter are often more vivid (and sometimes less accurate) than the surviving documents, but oral history turns up facts that are omitted or underemphasized in conventional accounts. For example, the book I produced during that period, *My Soul Is Rested,* provided a detailed account of the dispute among Dr. King, the Reverend Fred L. Shuttlesworth, and Attorney General Robert F. Kennedy over calling off the 1963 demonstrations in Birmingham. In effect, the fiery Shuttlesworth stiffened the spines of the two more famous men. In the same book, my interview with a law enforcement official was among the first accounts to single out Klansman Robert Chambliss as the prime suspect in the Sixteenth Street Church bombing.

Similarly, by using the new scholarship about southern Unionism and my own interviews, I was able to envision a schematic to explain how the First Alabama escaped widespread notice for so long. The words that we commonly apply to neglected pieces of history that are no longer part of our operating reality—words like "lost," "buried," or "forgotten"—are not literally true. If no evidence whatsover had survived in my area of interest, there'd be nothing to tell. But we can reconstruct the process of how those pieces of history fell out of our ken. In this case, it involved combining the authoritative new books published in the past thirty years and the testimony of witnesses to the daily operations of the Lost Cause temple the Bankheads constructed. And that is what is important about re-creating the world of Alma Hall Pate.

She ruled a tiny fiefdom within a small, eccentric empire created through political manipulation that, for all its flaws, accomplished a massive task of public disinformation. We can now see that this disinformation was made possible by a four-part process. First was Tom Owen's decision to collect only Confederate records and memorabilia. Second was his wife's decision to ignore the Alabamians she wanted the public to forget—all African Americans and the "trash" portion of the white population—and focus on an underappreciated Alabama oligarchy composed of Black Belt landowners and Birmingham-area industrialists. The third stage of the process was the ban on professional archival practices that prevailed from her husband's death in 1920 until the appointment in 1982 of the first trained historian to lead the ADAH. The fourth stage was the policy epitomized by Pate to use sloppy preservation tactics and denial of scholarly access to prevent the basic pick-and-shovel work of historical scholarship. By observing that organizational backdrop, we can see that only a slipup here and there allowed for survival of the vestigial evidence that illuminates, at least partially, the outlines of a cover-up.

Yet even in the era of segregation, Tom and Marie had a canny sense of public relations. When distinguished Black historians came to the ADAH for their early research, they were received cordially—up to a point. "They had a special room they put them in," Allen Jones told me. "We're talking 1951 and 1952. I would go get the materials for them."

Smoking Letters

ALL ALONG THE way, I hoped to find a smoking gun, a single document that nailed down the precise moment when a scholarly cabal decided to write the First Alabama Cavalry out of history. If such a weapon existed, I supposed it would be found in letters, and there were plenty of those from around the time Miss Marie accompanied Big Jim Folsom to the centennial celebration in Haleyville in 1951. Although Marie Bankhead Owen probably felt contempt for Folsom's popularity among the great unwashed, she also understood that he needed solid support among the mountain counties ruled by the Bankhead machine to offset his lack of popularity with Black Belt segregationists and U.S. Steel workers and their Big Mule industrial overseers in Birmingham.

In Alabama's largest city in 1954, my parents' preferred candidate for governor, Jimmy Faulkner, a polished (by Alabama standards), pro-business newspaper owner, outpolled Folsom handily. But Folsom's margins in the old Unionist counties reached as high as 75 percent, and my Winston relatives applauded his pledge to pave every dirt road in Alabama. Miss Marie catered to Folsom's ego, announcing that the archives would house the "suds bucket" and "corn shuck mop" he lugged in the 1946 campaign to symbolize his determination to clean up Montgomery. That year he won his first term with a base among the rural whites in the Bankhead-machine counties of north Alabama.

As we scoured the archives, my grandson Jasper found a letter Marie Bankhead Owen wrote to make sure that Folsom understood the political geography that should influence his decision when the issue of textbook purchases came to his desk. She was never one to beat around the bush.

> *I am the author of "Alabama, a Social and Economic History of the State," a copy of which I presented to you recently.*
> *. . . It is the book that should be used for the eleventh-twelfth grade. In saying that, I am doing so without any financial expectations to myself. I have planned to give all my royalties in case the books are put in the public schools, to the University of Alabama for a scholarship in memory of my husband, an honor graduate of that institution in the academic and legal departments. I feel therefore that my motive in urging the adoption cannot be criticized on the basis of any financial gain to myself.*

The letter was classic Marie in several respects. She claimed she had spent $1,000 of her money to have it fact-checked by a schoolteacher who lived near Folsom in north Alabama. This reflected a favorite assertion: that she and Tom, as young marrieds, had nearly bankrupted themselves buying history books that would eventually be given to the archives. The overall tone was a familiar one, too—*I am only leading you to water that I'm sure you'll be smart enough to drink.* The rival publication under consideration by the textbook committee was written by a non-Alabamian trained at the University of North Carolina, already a stronghold of leftist sociological teachings. In addition, Marie's letter reminded Folsom that the United Daughters of the Confederacy, whose ten thousand members followed her voting advice, were presenting a bill to make the teaching of state history a mandatory part of the public school curriculum, something that was already required in other ex-Confederate states.

In an earlier book for junior-high students, Miss Marie gave a remarkably even-handed paragraph to "Unionists," but it also contained an important clue about how she and Tom would shape the archives. "There were large numbers who felt that the state should not leave the Union," and in the election of delegates to the secession convention "about half as many voted not to secede as voted for Secession." She even noted that "the vote for the ordinance was only 61, with 39 against." Then came a key mendacious sentence after which the question of dissent is dropped: "After the majority voted for the movement, however, almost everyone supported the movement to the best of his ability."

This sentence jumped out at me, especially because it was penned by one raised in a county that provided so many white citizens to the Union army. No mention is made of Governor John Gill Shorter, whose letter box in the archives documented his use of military force, state-approved terrorism, and threat of execution against Alabamians who refused to support the Confederacy to the best of their ability. The most effective grassroots leader of the Unionists, Chris Sheats, is omitted entirely from the book. Jeremiah Clemens, who defied Yancey in public debates and in the secession convention, is mentioned only as an author of an obscure novel about the feud between Hamilton and Burr. There is no mention of Clemens's *Tobias Wilson: A Tale of the Great Rebellion,* a more important work about an Alabama mountaineer persecuted for his pro-Union politics. Miss Marie's description of Reconstruction is pure Lost Cause doctrine as handed down by Dunning et alia: "After some years, the better people of the North and some good citizens among the carpetbaggers realized that the plan of Reconstruction was all wrong. Gradually the native white man was able to exercise some influence in the state," she wrote. "The bitterness that was stirred up between the negroes and the Southern white man . . . was caused almost entirely by the influence of Reconstruction. The bitterness toward the North that lived for years was caused a great deal more by Reconstruction than by war."

George E. Spencer, the commander of the First Alabama and arguably the most important politician in Alabama during the Grant administration, is left out of the 1938 book and the 1947 update. As a Reconstruction senator, he oversaw Grant administration patronage in Alabama, and his controversial power plays were the object of prolonged hearings in the state capitol, adjacent to the site of the archives. The point, of course, is that both Tom and Marie Owen knew the real history of Alabama and knew exactly what they were leaving out. And it was a matter not just of omission, but of willful misrepresentation and refusal to follow up on leads that would have carried the archivists outside the procrustean mold of Lost Cause doctrine.

About two years before he died, Winston historian Donald Dodd and I were discussing the lax security at the archives and long-standing rumors of document theft by conservative Alabama scholars for ideological reasons. "Sometimes it's hard to distinguish between malicious behavior and incompetence, and they cross lines a lot in our area," he remarked. I was asking him about a cryptic footnote in his book about a letter from John Bennett Weaver to Marie Bankhead Owen. Since Weaver was the fountainhead of Free State history, I desperately wanted to see the letter, which spoke of eyewitness accounts of the Looney's Tavern meeting. Dodd was seventy-nine at the time, and his energy was beginning to fade. He told me there were twenty-two boxes of files in his garage. The letter might be there, and my grandson and I were welcome to search for it. We spent a long, hot day in the little building looking for the document, without success. I sent Jasper to Montgomery, where he was told there was no record of correspondence between Owen and Weaver. As I later recounted to Dodd, "Finally, out of frustration, Jasper says, 'Bring me all the Winston County boxes.' They bring him three boxes, and by chance he looked at the bottom of one and that letter was lying at the bottom, unfiled."

It was a letter written on January 6, 1941, to Marie Bankhead Owen by Probate Judge John Bennett Weaver of Winston County, and it proved beyond doubt that the old gatekeeper had to have known the details of the Free State when she visited Double Springs ten years later with Governor Folsom. The tone was businesslike.

"Dear Mrs. Owen," the judge started. "In reply to yours of December 31, 1940, relative to an article in 'Birmingham News,' in which I was quoted as to certain historical facts, permit me to thank you for your inquiry." The article in question was by Leroy Simms, the Associated Press correspondent who operated out of the Birmingham newspaper building that housed the newsrooms of the Newhouse-owned *News*, the *Post-Herald*, owned by Scripps-Howard, and the cubbyhole offices and ceaselessly clattering teletypes of both the Associated Press and United Press International. I knew that Leroy Simms was an important figure in that world. He had left the managing editorship of the *News* about a year before I entered that building as a cub for the *Post-Herald*. He was also a noted Civil War buff, and in spotting the article in which Simms had quoted Judge Weaver, Marie Owen's newspaper clippers had served her well. The thousand-word article on an inside page of the *News-Age Herald* on April 7, 1940, was the most complete journalistic account of Unionist history to appear in Alabama up to that time. It included virtually all the details that Fleming had omitted in his trend-setting *Civil War and Reconstruction in Alabama*, published thirty-five years earlier. Simms, an energetic roamer of the state who was promoted to publisher of the Newhouse-owned *Huntsville Times* in 1963, quoted Weaver at length as to information not then available, in one compact telling, in any Alabama history book or public school textbook. The article may have reminded Marie Owen that newspapermen had been sniffing after the Free State story for some time. In 1931, Robert L. Ripley had written her wanting information on Alabama Unionists for his popular national newspaper feature, "Ripley's Believe It or Not."

Simms didn't miss much in his remarkably comprehensive article. He devoted packed paragraphs to Chris Sheats, the murder of Tom Pink Curtis, and the State of Alabama's terrorism-enforced enlistment campaign:

Winston, deep inside the Confederate lines, was safe from moles-
tation by Union troops, but Confederate recruiting officers soon
made their appearance and the county's red hills became a battleground for four bitter years. Many men of military age were taken
to Confederate prisons or forced into the army. Those who resisted were shot, and those who left the army and returned to
their homes were condemned as deserters when they could be
caught. . . . Winston became a union stronghold in the midst of
the Confederacy. It furnished five companies of infantry for the
union forces before the end of 1863.

Simms even named the obscure Winston bluecoat Anderson Ward
as leading the burning of the Jasper courthouse and the assassination of
an unarmed Andrew Kaeiser, the chief informer against Union sympathizers. He quoted Judge John Bennett Weaver on the importance of the
slaying of Tom Pink Curtis and the ties to Andrew Jackson: "Men believed responsible for the death of Judge Curtis, Judge Weaver said,
were 'hunted down and shot to the last man. Winston was now in the
hands of its own people and the Confederacy was too far spent to do
anything about it,' the judge said. 'We have remained free ever since.
And when you hear a Winston County Republican talking about Gen.
Jackson, he doesn't mean Stonewall.'"

Details omitted in the *News* version of Simms's article, possibly for
reasons of space, were the name of the First Alabama Cavalry, U.S.A.
and its role in burning Atlanta and the March to the Sea. Perhaps Miss
Marie, given her strong belief in the power of newspaper publicity, was
relieved by that. The article was clearly a threat to her policy of ignoring
Unionist leaders and defaming "traitors" to the Cause. But we can infer
by Weaver's response to her that she wanted to know more about what
Weaver knew. "No," he wrote her,

> *I have not the original resolution adopted by the mass meeting on*
> *July 4th 1861. However, a mass meeting was held, having been*
> *widely advertised. It was composed of several citizens of Blount, a*

*large group from South East Franklin, south Lawrence, East
Marion, North Walker, and citizens from all parts of Winston
County. It was held at "Looney's Tavern," about three miles north
of present day Addison. The resolutions commended "Mr. C. C.
Sheets [sic] for his loyalty to his campaign pledges in voting
against secession first, last, and all the time," agreed "with
Jackson, not Lincoln, that no state could get out of the union, but
if a state could secede from the Union, then, by the same process of
reasoning, a county, any county, could cease to be part of that
state."*

*When the above was read, uncle "Dick" Payne, who was
present, exclaimed: "Oho! Winston secedes! The Free State of
Winston," and it has been called, "The Free State of Winston"
until this day.*

*This concluding part of the resolution said: "We think our
neighbors in the South made a mistake when they bolted the
democratic ticket; which resulted in Lincoln's election. However,
we do not wish to see them mistreated, and will not take up arms
against them. On the other hand, we will not shoot at 'old glory,'
the flag of our fathers, of Washington, Jefferson and Jackson.*

*"Therefore, we ask the Confederacy on the one hand, and the
Union on the other to leave us alone, as we desire to remain
neutral, that we may work out our own political and financial
destiny."*

*I got this information about 35 years ago from at least three
competent, dependable persons who were present at the meeting.*

Again, thanking you for your interest in this matter, I am,

Very truly yours,
John B. Weaver

Who, I wondered, were the three competent witnesses interviewed
by Judge Weaver? Donald Dodd didn't remember, and we couldn't find
the names in his files. After some casting about, I turned up a single

sentence in one of the foundation documents I had read years before, John Bennett Weaver's own eight-page pamphlet from the 1930s, *A Brief History of Winston County*. After quoting his reconstruction of the Looney's Tavern resolution, Bennett wrote, "The above information came from B. F. Curtis, Gooder Walker, and Tom Lay." I felt a surge of optimism; perhaps Weaver had sent Marie Bankhead Owen additional information about his informants.

Benjamin Franklin Curtis was from the prominent political family that had left a fair amount of genealogical material. A Thomas H. Lay turned up in Hoole's regimental roster as enlisting on April 1, 1863, perhaps six months after he heard Chris Sheats speak at the original Free State rally. Most provocatively, could Gooder Walker be one of my Walker relatives from St. Clair County who had served in the First Alabama? The proper archivist's response would have been to ask Bennett for any notes he made while interviewing the men circa 1905 or to ask him to write a fuller narrative of what they had told him. Such material would have a value exceeded only by what Dodd called the "Henderson letter" (H. A. M. Henderson's report of the meeting, which he attended, likely in civilian clothes), which at some point was presumably in the possession of the ADAH as part of Governor Shorter's papers.

My hopes of finding more Weaver-Bankhead correspondence rose when I learned that a doctoral dissertation by Susan Neely Deily-Swearingen had been approved in April 2019 at the University of New Hampshire under the title "Rebel Rebels: Race, Resistance and Remembrance in the Free State of Winston." I learned from her that John Bennett Weaver's last surviving son, Sam Weaver of Double Springs, had promised her his father's papers. She arrived to claim them only to find that Sam had died the day before, but the family honored his wishes to turn over the records, and Dr. Deily-Swearingen, now at Harvard, agreed to share them with me. I felt I was on a hot trail. Alas, the interviews were not among the valuable materials in this trove, most of which the industrious Weaver had long ago mined in his own writings.

Still, approval of the Deily-Swearingen dissertation in April 2019 signaled a new wave of acceptance in academia of the burgeoning field of southern Unionist studies. As noted, Richard Nelson Current's *Lincoln's Loyalists,* appearing three decades earlier, had been the breakthrough work. In 2020, the University of Virginia history department accepted "True Blue: White Unionists in the Deep South During the Civil War and Reconstruction, 1860–1880," the PhD dissertation by Clayton J. Butler, who also authored a lively article entitled "Union Troopers with a Southern Twang" about the First Alabama's role in the March to the Sea. In August 2020, the Auburn University history faculty accepted a dissertation by Daniel Eric Cone entitled "The Lost Cause Archived: Thomas Owen, the Alabama Archives and the Shaping of Civil War History and Memory," which "examines the specific ways that Owen tailored the archives' acquisitions, public services, research assistance, and publications policies to further the Lost Cause."

The roles of both Virginia and Auburn are noteworthy. "Mr. Jefferson's University" at Charlottesville had long been a citadel of cultural conservatism, but the current director of its Civil War studies program, Caroline E. Janney, has emerged as a leading critic of Trump's revival of Old South apologetics. Cone's adviser, Professor Kenneth W. Noe, edited *The Yellowhammer War: The Civil War and Reconstruction in Alabama,* published by the University of Alabama Press in 2013 as a pointed rebuttal to Fleming's 1905 masterwork. In my opinion as an expat Alabamian, liberal white southerners of my generation sometimes expect excessive commendation for corrective political acts and scholarship admitting past mistakes by southern governments, educational institutions, and churches. After all, the "mistakes of the past" were conscious actions embedded in law and institutional policies and committed in the face of—indeed, most often in defiance of—enlightened criticism from other regions. Even so, the penetration of new thinking about the Civil War into southern intellectual life is noteworthy for its depth, its candor, and its root system in institutions of higher learning that once fostered false history.

The case of Auburn is particularly interesting, as its history department was once known as the "Auburn Oasis" because its chairman (and first football coach), George Petrie (1866–1947), took his PhD at Johns

Hopkins in 1891, when it had yet to be succeeded by Columbia and Dunning as the favorites of southern scholars intent on preserving Rebel legends. A lot of Confederate jasmine blossomed in Auburn's isolated oasis in the wiregrass plains of southwest Alabama. A 1916 graduate, Frank Lawrence Owsley Sr. (1870–1956), was a leading member of the Southern Agrarians, who were based at Vanderbilt University; Owsley would leave the faculty there to establish the Lost Cause regency in the University of Alabama history department. And Fleming, an 1886 Auburn graduate, would, with the aid of Thomas McAdory Owen and William A. Dunning, bestride southern academia as the primary architect of a powerful Confederate shadow empire anchored by Vanderbilt University in Nashville and the University of the South in Sewanee. As always in Dixieland, the connections tell the tale.

And in the case of Winston County, so do the missing connections. Surviving tidbits provide a provocative glimpse of what B. F. Curtis, Gooder Walker, and Tom Lay told Judge Weaver. As we've seen, Benjamin Franklin Curtis was one of the nine sons of Solomon Curtis (1797–1860); Solomon had marched into Alabama with Andrew Jackson's Tennessee Volunteers in 1814, and "on his death bed in 1860 he called all of his children to his bedside and asked them to remain loyal to the Union," according to a family document. As we know, three of the boys, including Tom Pink Curtis, were killed by Rebel home guards. Four others fought for the Union, and Benjamin Franklin, who was probably Weaver's most important source, was crippled by war wounds.

The lack of follow-up on Thomas H. Lay probably represents the greatest loss to First Alabama lore. His Union service record shows that he was one of the twenty-two First Alabama cavalrymen chosen for spy duty by Dodge and Spencer in what students of military intelligence regard as the best espionage network in Grant's army. Lay's service record in the *Official Records* has two notations in addition to the routine entries about enlistment and mustering out: "On detached service" and "On secret service," entries made on November 22, 1863. William Stanley Hoole, with his usual eagerness to depict the First as lazy and cowardly, said the unit was "inactive" in its Corinth encampment in late 1863 and that "after more than a year's service, the 'erratic regiment' had done nothing of which really to be proud. . . . It had altogether proved a liability rather than an asset."

Glenda McWhirter Todd, with her closer reading of the *Official Records,* established that General Dodge and Colonel Spencer would have disagreed with Hoole. Thirty-six-year-old Tom Lay's assignment to "secret service" on November 23 was almost certainly to provide scouting about a large operation launched by Lay's Company E a few days later. Their mission was to keep tabs on the Rebel calvary threat to Grant's operations against Vicksburg. Todd found this in the regimental returns for Company E: "Nov 26th Co. went on Scout toward Tupelo, Miss, had several skirmishes with enemy. Returned Nov 29/63, distance marched 120 miles. Dec. 20 Co. went on Scout towards Jackson, Tenn. to attack Gen. Forest (Rebel)." Private Lay was soon assigned as a nurse in the Union hospital at Memphis in January and did not move out with the company when it left at the end of February to join Union forces massing at Mooresville, Alabama, for the coming assaults in 1864 on Chattanooga and Atlanta.

No Gooder appears among the eighteen Walkers on Todd's version of the First Alabama roster or among the thirteen Walkers in Hoole's compilation. Such disparities are common for wartime personnel listings, which existed—or, more to the point, survived—in multiple versions. Initially I wondered if Gooder might be a nickname, but the ever-reliable P. J. Gossett found an obituary for William Gooder Walker in the *Haleyville Advertiser* of February 2, 1928. That meant he was the last survivor among Weaver's eyewitnesses, Lay having died in 1909 and Curtis in 1927. The rosters put together by both Todd and Hoole contain a listing for William F. Walker, who in the spring of 1864 joined a First Alabama company that made the March to the Sea with Sherman. I believe he is one of my Walkers based on the information my grandparents gave Uncle Brack. Brack's entry reads "William (?) Felix Walker," meaning that my grandparents were unsure of the first name of that great-great-grandfather of mine known to them as Felix. Brack Walker's notation added that this man was a "blacksmith during Civil War." His enlistment date coincides with the period when Sherman was enrolling Alabama Unionists for camp duties, including getting his horses ready for the Atlanta campaign.

These are the thin reeds of supposition, partial documentation, and hearsay on which the genealogy of uneducated rural families must often rest. As my paid researcher, my grandson Jasper had become a sharp-eyed student of Brack Walker's family tree. He noted that "William (?) Felix Walker" was married to a Flannagan. A prominent ancestry website lists William Gooder Walker as related to a Flannagan family that lived in the same neighborhood as my Walkers. If—and only if—the Felix mentioned by Grandpa Walker is the "William (?) Felix Walker" in Brack's drawing, then I am related, no matter how tenuously, to that Gooder Walker, one of the three men without whom the whole Free State narrative might have been lost.

How certain can one ever be? Lincoln's phrase about the "short and simple annals of the poor" has always haunted me as an indicator of how little we know about the comings and goings of frontier folk. As noted, Edward Ball wrote insightfully in *Life of a Klansman: A Family History in White Supremacy* about the mutability of generational knowledge. So I have to confess a jarring discovery about Corporal William F. Walker of M Company, First Alabama Cavalry, U.S.A., who was born in St. Clair County in 1832 or 1833. The website maintained by First Alabama descendants displays next to Walker's service record a photograph of a gravestone inscribed "WILLIAM F. WALKER, CO K, 16 ALA. INF. C.S.A."

It was fairly common for reluctant Confederate draftees to desert and then to reenlist with (or unofficially fall in with, as David Best apparently did) the Yankees who captured them. It was also common for even so careful a researcher as Glenda McWhirter Todd to be mistaken about which army one's ancestor served. In that regard, did some conservative survivor of the William F. Walker buried north of Jasper secure a Confederate gravestone to remove from the family escutcheon any taint of Unionism? The opposite impulse—to preserve every scrap of Union sympathy in my family tree—was the raison d'être for this book.

So I was not in any way prepared for the email I received late in 2021 from Melissa Folsom Boyen of Honolulu. She and I were both born in 1943 and had several Alabama friends in common, although we had never met. Through these friends, we became email correspondents, and Melissa agreed to use her expert genealogical skills to help run down some First Alabama leads and information about my Winston County grandparents. As a young girl she greeted visitors who came to see her father, Big Jim, in the governor's mansion after his election in 1947. We had also shared memories of Miss Marie. Writing from her retirement home in Hawaii, Melissa sent me one of the most surprising messages I had ever received about my mother, née Bertha Estelle Walker in Winston County in 1907, and our family tree: "I thought I would put your mother's name in and see how far I might go. You and Marie Bankhead Owen are 4th cousins 3 times removed. You share John Brockman II as a common ancestor. He is your 6th GGGrandfather and her 3rd GGGrandfather."

I soon discovered that Brockman was a Revolutionary War colonel born in Tidewater Virginia into a Kentish family that might have been driven from England by Cromwell's Roundheads. He died at his plantation on the Enoree River in South Carolina in 1831 as the owner of nineteen slaves. Had I done all this digging only to discover that my Unionist heritage had been diluted by Cavalier blood from the FFV?

33

A SCHOLARLY LYNCHING

THE WAY I look at history was shaped by the way that *New York Times* colleagues like James Reston, Tom Wicker, David R. Jones, Bill Kovach, and Max Frankel looked at politics. These journalists watched for decisive points of conflict and divergence, for the motives of the actors and the down-the-road impact of what they did. Applying such a lens to the Dunning School, it becomes clear that there was a fork in the road at which American historians could have gotten off the Lost Cause Highway. It occurred on December 30, 1909, at the Waldorf Astoria Hotel in Manhattan. Over the years, there's been precious little interpretative writing about this twenty-fifth annual meeting of the American Historical Association. Once I put this story together, I realized it was a pivotal moment—a scholarly lynching that had never been fully accounted for. The target was William Edward Burghardt Du Bois, and the perpetrator was William Archibald Dunning himself.

It was probably the only time these two giants of Reconstruction history were in the same room, and it was a setup. Du Bois was the first African American to earn a PhD at Harvard and the first to be invited to speak to the AHA. He came prepared to throw down the gauntlet in front of Dunning and his almost equally famous colleague Ulrich B.

Phillips. The title of his paper, "Reconstruction and Its Benefits," was intended as a direct rebuttal to the Dunning-Phillips idea that after the war, suffering white plantation owners had been unfairly tormented by corrupt Black Republican officeholders and their carpetbagger and scalawag allies in a "tragic decade" of political corruption. If Du Bois had been able to get away with his evidence-based attack on white supremacy, the entire Lost Cause project could have been strangled in its cradle. The uppity professor from Atlanta University had to be dealt with, but how?

The New York Times had touted the event as the premier attraction of the AHA's weeklong convocation in Manhattan. But the best way to approach this complicated tale of academic intrigue is through the account that ran in the *Times*'s more sensational rival, the *New-York Tribune,* on New Year's Eve of 1909. When I first found it online, the story hit me with a jolt of recognition. Here on display, in an august setting and over a thousand miles from its home base, was dear old Alabama's peculiar brand of rube exhibitionism—that immemorial impulse to look as benighted as possible on a national stage. Somehow a garrulous Birmingham lawyer known mainly as a promoter of grandiose Confederate reunions had wormed his way into the second paragraph of a news report on the new century's most distinguished practitioners of the new academic specialty of professionalized history.

TALK OF NEGROES
Southern Race Problems Discussed by Historians

The discussion of Southern History before the American Historical Association in the Astor Gallery at the Waldorf last night turned largely to the negro problem and the part that the reconstruction period played in the development of that section of the country.

After Professor W. E. B. Du Bois, of Atlanta University, one of the best known negroes in the South, had endeavored to point out the benefits of reconstruction and had denied many of the attacks made upon those engaged in that work, Robert Chisholm, of Birmingham, Ala. [d]rew a sad picture of reconstruction days.

"For nearly ten years satan took the saddle," he said. "It was a plague greater than all the plagues that infested Egypt. The Anglo-Saxon was brought to bay, and he became dangerous, as he always does under such circumstances. He shook the incubus off.

When we do a thing in this country it is right because we do it. The negro lost his vote. His getting it back will never be left to hazard. He will get it only when he proves worthy of it."

Mr. Chisholm speaking to the north said with much feeling: "Without loving the negro any less, cannot you love the South a little more?"

Distracted by the inexplicable presence of Chisholm, a lawyer without academic credentials, the *Tribune* reporter entirely missed the importance of the scene before him. More charitably, I should say a general-assignment reporter would have had no way of knowing he was witnessing a decisive academic showdown that had been brewing in ivied halls out of public view. Du Bois was addressing a body of white men who had been schooled in the "scientific history" of Teutonic/Anglo-Saxon racial superiority. To them, it was self-evident that blame for a political cataclysm like Reconstruction should be ascribed to a lesser race. Du Bois had traveled to Manhattan determined to challenge those he called "the Columbia crowd." The title of his presentation, "Reconstruction and Its Benefits," was a radical affront to their racial elitism. "To suggest that there had been benefits to Reconstruction was equivalent to descrying benefits in the aftermath of plague," wrote Du Bois's biographer David Levering Lewis, who has left the best account I've read of the AHA session at the Waldorf.

The setting for this gathering of grand old white folks could hardly have been grander—the hundred-foot-long Astor Gallery with its seven French windows stretching twenty-seven feet from floor to ceiling and looking out over 34th Street. Nor could the cultural distance between them and the nation's leading Black scholar have been greater. At forty-one, he spearheaded the founding of the National Association for the Advancement of Colored People. Lewis described how the slender, balding professor—a handsome man with skin the color of light cocoa—made his way across a parquet floor. The soaring hall was draped in gold, blue, and gray, a color scheme borrowed from a grand Parisian hotel. He was addressing the Ivy-dominated AHA as Columbia, Johns Hopkins, and Harvard were competing for dominance in the fields of history and political science. Three decades would pass before another dark-skinned speaker would be invited. "Only a few feet away from the lectern on which Du Bois arranged his speech sat Columbia University's William Archibald Dunning, high priest of the regnant dogma in Reconstruction writing—the Dunning School, whose successive generations of historians deplored the decade of federal intervention in the South as a 'tragic era' of Negro misrule."

Du Bois's attack on their central thesis was direct, and it was dangerous. The benefits of Reconstruction consisted of the South's first public schools, fairer taxation, and advances in public transportation and economic development. "Seldom in the history of the world has an almost totally illiterate population been given the means of self-education in so short a time," Du Bois said. Establishment educators should support the main agencies of this progress, Black churches and schools. They should cease their attacks on the Freedman's Bureau. Dunning School scholars focused on the corruption of inexperienced Black legislators while ignoring giant wrongs like the $50 million Crédit Mobilier scandal in Washington and "less distinguished thieves like [New York's Boss] Tweed." With a nod to Henry Grady's New South industrial theory, Du Bois said, "Virtually the whole new growth of the South has been accomplished under laws which Black men helped to frame thirty years ago." With a remarkable lack of confrontational rhetoric, Du Bois was calling on the history profession to abandon the doctrine being taught at Columbia. They would have to dismantle its racial prejudices root and branch and admit that to blame the abuses of Reconstruction on "negro suffrage is unfair."

Dunning had already decided on a strategy for responding to the speech. They would ignore it; they would deny it the oxygen of debate. No one addressed the substantive points Du Bois raised. To the newspapers, Dunning issued a mild statement of praise for Du Bois's research methods. In his remarks, Phillips ignored the speech entirely. To extend the charade of fairness, Dunning saw to it that the paper was reprinted in full in the July 1910 issue of the AHA's journal, the *American Historical Review,* although its editor would not allow Du Bois to follow the new fashion of capitalizing the word "Negro." In other respects, too, Du Bois's ideas were twisting slowly in the wind. He was not rebutted in scholarly publications. Indeed, as David Levering Lewis wrote, "virtually nothing more was ever said among white professional historians about its heterodox interpretation. . . . Du Bois's cogently reasoned paper failed to have virtually any impact upon the mainstream scholarship of the day." John David Smith observed that Du Bois's explanation of Reconstruction disappeared from most university classrooms despite "all its brilliance and methodological and interpretative prescience."

On balance, we are lucky to have even the sketchy newspaper accounts of what went on that day. In the New York of 1909, only a tirelessly networking Ivy League insider could have figured out that what they were reading about was a carefully prearranged showdown between academic titans. It would lead to a half century of isolation for Du Bois, the most clearheaded thinker in American academia on the racial legacy of slavery. Decades later, an unbiased historian would conclude that the main speakers—including Du Bois and Ulrich B. Phillips—were "propagandists" for their rival historical schools. But within this conclave of polemicists, Du Bois had hold of a kernel of truth. His short address putting a positive spin on biracial southern state legislatures of the 1870s would blossom into the paradigm-shifting book *Black Reconstruction in America,* published in 1947.

As valuable as it is, Lewis's re-creation does not exploit the backstory of the meeting, which also involved the reigning eminence of the Harvard history department, Albert Bushnell Hart. He was the only figure grand enough to block Dunning's emergence as the leading historian of the Civil War and Reconstruction in American universities. They were near contemporaries—Hart being only three years older—and friends of an edgy, calculating sort. So daring was the act of inviting Du Bois into this den of Reconstruction mythologizers that even Du Bois's Harvard classmate and a co-founder of the NAACP, Oswald Garrison Villard, warned Hart that Du Bois "was rather unsafe on the question" of the issues surrounding Reconstruction. It is unclear from the surviving correspondence if Villard, a grandson of the famous abolitionist William Lloyd Garrison, fully understood what the wily Hart was up to. Villard was a lifelong crusader for racial justice. For him to say that Du Bois's ideas were dangerous attests to their transgressive power and their potential to disrupt the Dunning/Phillips vision of a mannered South of julep-scented verandas and coddled slaves. Clearly, in his last act as AHA president, Hart, later eulogized in the *Times* as the "grand old man of American history," understood that he was setting up Dunning for a battle over the governing theme of Civil War scholarship. He was as fierce on the evils of slavery and slaveholders as Dunning was forgiving. Within three years Dunning would succeed Hart as president of the AHA, cementing the hegemony of pro-Confederate interpretations of the "tragic era."

Did the historians at the Waldorf Astoria that day realize what was playing out while the Birmingham attorney Chisholm blathered about Satan? It was a Miltonian struggle between the titans of a new profession, Dunning and Harvard's more liberal Albert Bushnell Hart, for the racial psyche of their craft. The two men were friends on the surface, but wary. Each had come with his most brilliant disciple, Ulrich B. Phillips of Columbia and Du Bois, who had earned his Harvard doctorate under Hart's tutelage. The essential clue for understanding the conflicting aims of two parties was Hart's keynote address, entitled "Imagination in History," as he concluded his tenure as president of the association. Even though the *Tribune*'s un-bylined correspondent did not explain the clash, he seemed to sense it, quoting the fifty-five-year-old Hart targeting Dunning.

"American history, on its controversial side, has been enriched by several distinct attempts to manufacture myths to order," Hart said, noting that the first such myth, concerning the piety of the Pilgrims, concerned his own Massachusetts ancestor. "A similar myth," he added, "causes the exaltation of the Southern cavalier, who was a personage about as infrequent in Virginia as in New York; it is at least remarkable that few of the great Virginia families of the nineteenth century can show a cavalier lineage; neither the Jeffersons, nor Madisons, Monroes, Marshalls, Carters, Carys nor Bryans trace undoubted descent from the bearers of the love-locks."

An academic politician of Dunning's sophistication must have recognized that Hart's speech seemed designed to parody his gullibility about the aristocratic pretensions of southern slaveholders. Both men understood that 1910 capped a fraught period in the battle of theoretical dominance in their field, a conflict that had been building since Dunning got his Columbia doctorate in 1885 and Hart got his two years earlier at the more liberal University of Freiberg in Germany. John David Smith summarized the competing forces in his indispensable essay collection focusing on the Dunning School.

> Hart, who directed Du Bois's doctoral dissertation [at Harvard], took pride in the fact that he was "a son and grandson of abolitionists." Hart interpreted slavery as a force undermining southern prosperity and morality. It was, in his judgment, responsible for the bloody Civil War. These sentiments no doubt helped fuel Du Bois's hostility to the slave system. Dunning, on the other hand, established his reputation by interpreting slavery and the Civil War and Reconstruction from a decidedly pro-southern perspective. Southern graduate students like Phillips found Dunning's seminar congenial to their social philosophies and racial attitudes . . . Phillips appealed for new approaches in historical scholarship, he said, because "The history of the United States has been written by Boston and largely written wrong."

Through field work far from the ivied halls of Harvard, Phillips claimed, the Columbia team had found the "absolute truth" about southern history. It was a view that would not be cautiously challenged in academic writings until the 1930s and not overturned until the 1960s. In their valuable accounts, David Levering Lewis and John David Smith describe that moment with admirable scholarly discipline. But they do not fully capture, in my view, its import, as measured by the way the nation's leading historians reacted to Du Bois's message.

Dunning was more strategic than Hart in evangelizing his view of a sunnier South. Between 1900 and 1923, he sponsored thirteen dissertations that dealt with the Civil War and Reconstruction. They were his force multipliers. Dunning famously recruited seven graduate students from former Confederate states who earned doctorates in the 1900s and dominated Deep South campuses for decades to come. They saw themselves as cultural warriors in defense of a noble South inflicted with undeserved humiliation. The North Carolinian among Dunning's recruits, J. G. de Roulhac Hamilton (1878–1961), once leapt across a seminar table to "spike the cannons" of another student by throttling him. Dunning's pet Walter L. Fleming came to blows with another student he regarded as unsympathetic to the South. In a letter to Thomas McAdory Owen he denounced George Bancroft (1800–1891), the revered historian who founded the U.S. Naval Academy, as "too much of a . . . negrophile." He defended Dunning's mentor, John W. Burgess, against attacks that he was "too aggressively Southern" in his comments on Black inferiority. Fleming's rise to the peak of southern academics at Vanderbilt reminds us that it's hard to keep white Alabama's knights-errant out of any national fight over race and tradition.

The same was true, on the opposite side, of Du Bois. But what ended at the Waldorf Astoria was any chance of heading off the reign of Jim Crow scholarship within the lifetimes of every educator in that room. It was truly the defining moment in Civil War scholarship. Neither Hart nor Du Bois had counted on the cleverness of Dunning's faction. Their response to Du Bois was subdued and calculated, and it worked. Even

Hart seemed to be taken in. He congratulated Du Bois on showing his "ability to handle complicated material" and wrote the younger man that "Professor Dunning also had spoken . . . of the paper in high terms." To use a pugilistic term, they were rope-a-doping Du Bois, letting him punch himself out while they pulled their punches. And it seemed to have worked on Du Bois, at least up to a point. Thirty years later, he was still thinking about that day. He wrote that his paper "greatly exercised Ulrich Phillips, protagonist of the slave South, but brought praise from Dunning of Columbia, Hart of Harvard and others." Without doubt Du Bois was the most innovative thinker and courageous speaker in the room that day, but had the Old Chief tricked even him with his honeyed insincerity?

BIRMINGHAM MONEY:
THE HOUSES OF CHISHOLM AND PERCY

FROM CHILDHOOD I collected the minutiae of Birmingham history. And so perhaps I should not have been surprised that an unreconstructed crank like Colonel Robert Chisholm wormed his way into the Dunning–Du Bois showdown, a watershed moment in Lost Cause scholarship. The plain fact, however, is that I had never heard of Chisholm until I saw the 1909 newspaper account from the Waldorf Astoria. In time, though, the fall of the house of Chisholm led me to an even more important tragedy: the fall of the house of John Walker Percy, who was born in Greenville, Mississippi, in 1864 and died in Birmingham in 1917 as the most admired citizen in that bustling industrial city.

This chapter is necessary for understanding the unexplored story of how Alabama money helped fund the Lost Cause industry that ruled southern academia during my formative years. The star-crossed Percy family is the connecting link in the process that turned Birmingham into the New South's most condemned city and Greenville, Mississippi, into its most preciously "aristocratic" town. The two places became opposites in their signature traits, shame for the Magic City and self-congratulation for the Paris of the Mississippi Delta. I hope you'll take my word for this oversimplified but compelling gestalt. Historians and journalists have for too long left the southern narrative to novelists because its truths are so improbable. My South is a land of big themes, but you'll never fully appreciate them unless you dig out the details few bother to explore. Take, for example, the decline of Robert Chisholm and the nervous collapse of the two Percys who brought the family name to Birmingham, made their fortunes representing the steel industry and shot themselves to death there. They were John Walker Percy (1864–1917) and LeRoy Pratt Percy (1889–1927). They were the grandfather and father, respectively, of the novelist Walker Percy (1916–1990), a literary giant born in the gilded suburbs established by Birmingham's financial barons.

How does this come round to the First Alabama Cavalry? Because the second Walker Percy, the famous novelist, was one-half of the most celebrated Deep South literary friendship of the mid-twentieth century—that between Percy and Shelby Foote, the Civil War historian who was Ken Burns's muse for the most influential Civil War film since *Gone with the Wind*, the PBS documentary *The Civil War*. Because this is a southern yarn, the truth, like the devil, is in the details. And the details have to do with incremental blossomings, with reverberations and atmospherics—in a word, with connectivity.

For my purposes, the many biographers of the accomplished Percy family make too little of the Birmingham connection. I understand this. Greenville and New Orleans, the cities most closely identified with the novelist Walker Percy and his gifted cousin and adoptive father, William Alexander Percy (1885–1942), are more romantic and magnolia-scented. But the fact remains that the first Walker Percy founded the Birmingham Country Club, brought in United States Steel as the city's duplicitous absentee landlord, and, as noted, became the grandfather of the most gifted of the post-Faulknerian novelists who explored the malaise of Dixie's declining aristocrats and privileged suburbanites, his namesake Walker Percy. This youngest of the three Birmingham Percys won the 1962 National Book Award in a stunning literary debut with *The Moviegoer*. Although set in New Orleans, it contained multiple references to Alabama. Later, I was somewhat surprised to learn that the novelist was born in Birmingham. I say surprised because the Birmingham papers, which I read religiously from an early age, always relentlessly promoted any writer, from Harper Lee to Fannie Flagg, with Alabama connections. The exceptions, it seemed, were almost always Carl Carmer and, mystifyingly, the author of *The Moviegoer*. Walker Percy lived in Birmingham and its hubristic white suburb, Mountain Brook, until he was thirteen, spending the last five years in a mansion his troubled father, Leroy Pratt Percy, built across the street from the Birmingham Country Club, where the first Walker Percy's portrait still hangs in the vestibule.

His early background puzzled me because Birmingham's civic boosters, always eager for some cultural tidbit to offset their city's "bad image," never laid much of a claim to Percy or noted the obvious references in his work to Mountain Brook, still one of the Deep South's most gilded enclaves. I think that was because Percy's six novels limned the snobbish self-indulgence long attributed to Mountain Brook by less fortunate white citizens who lived "over the mountain" in Birmingham, with bad air and with Black neighbors. My sense that there was a great deal more to learn about the Greenville-Birmingham connection was confirmed by Jay Tolson's 1992 biography of the novelist, *Pilgrim in the Ruins: A Life of Walker Percy*, and by Bertram Wyatt-Brown's compelling 1994 biography of the entire family, *The House of Percy: Honor, Melancholy, and Imagination in a Southern Family*. The Percy family's experience in Birmingham represents, among other things, a charged symbolic encounter between an archetypal "Old South" family and a prototypical "New South" city, and this encounter played a crucial role in shaping the character and imagination of Walker Percy.

For my investigative purposes, this pairing played a key role in understanding how the Lost Cause cultural edifice came to be constructed in the period between, say, 1917, when John Walker Percy killed himself, and 1961, when Knopf published his grandson's first novel, a surprise bestseller that carried off the nation's grandest literary prize with its polished writing and existential seriousness. In my analysis, the two foundation stones of that sentimental edifice to bygone glory are Birmingham money and Greenville's plantation pretensions. Through the influence of another Percy literary personage famous in the 1930s, the abovemen-tioned William Alexander Percy, the edifice blossomed into a post-Confederate dream world based at Vanderbilt University in Nashville and the University of the South, ninety miles away in Sewanee, Tennessee.

My trail of understanding the puzzling obscurity of the First Alabama Cavalry, U.S.A. led through this charmed world in the Tennessee mountains, a redoubt of connectivity and causation. It was at a mountaintop retreat near Sewanee that two aspiring novelists from Greenville High School, Walker Percy and his closest friend Shelby Foote, were ushered by William Alexander Percy into the rarefied mysteries of selective ancestor worship and Old South literary salons. In mystery-story terms, Foote was to become the dog that didn't bark. The rich complexity of the story merits our circling back to poor Robert Chisholm, who would be dead only three months after he encountered Du Bois and Dunning at their showdown over the future of southern history in Manhattan.

Initially, the Zone of Exemption from blame for families of good Confederate pedigree operated strongly in Robert Chisholm's favor at the darkest period of his life. All was well on May 22, 1906, when *The Birmingham News* reported that his son Alex R. Chisholm, who "holds the responsible position of paying teller of the First National Bank," was hailed as one of four principals of the city's first advertising firm. Alas, less than three months later, the rival *Birmingham Times* reported that the twenty-four-year-old Chisholm had been arrested for stealing $100,000 from the bank. But with exquisite sympathy, the paper kept the Chisholm name out of the headline and seemed focused more on the grandeur of Alex's family than the impressive size of the theft (the equivalent of over $3 million—and, in later accounts, perhaps as much as $7 million—in 2022 dollars):

> He is the son of Col. Robert Chisholm, formerly of Charleston, but for many years a prominent and honored citizen of Birmingham. No family in the South stands higher. Nor did any young man in Birmingham possess more thoroughly the confidence of

his associates and employees. It was simply the old story—first of dabbling in cotton and stocks on small margins . . . and finally using the bank's money in hope of evening up. The calls for margins were incessant. First, he took from the bank's cash a few hundred, then a few thousand and so on until the $100,000 mark was reached and with it the climax.

The *Jones Valley Times* said, "We are sorry, inexpressibly sorry for all those whose hearts bleed at the awful stain on a good name." Sympathetic coverage extended to the national press. The August 1907 issue of the *Literary Digest,* an influential weekly, noted the "tragic circumstances" of young Chisholm's downfall. He had been caught up in a national disgrace of "gamblers" ruling the stock market. In Birmingham alone, the *Digest* said, several "young men . . . had gone to ruin due to speculation in bucket shops," those shady establishments that allowed long-shot bets on the rise and fall of stocks that never actually changed hands.

At first, the Chisholms' neighbors in Birmingham's elite Highland Avenue enclave of turreted Victorian townhouses and ersatz plantation mansions rallied around to protect them. John Walker Percy, known to all by his middle name, was a First National director and counsel for his father-in-law's mighty Tennessee Coal, Iron and Railroad Company, now known as TCI. This paramount leader of Birmingham society told Alex's older brother John that he'd help bond the young banker out of jail. Given Percy's role as "an almost unbeatable champion of big business interests in Birmingham," the gesture showed, as much as the low-key coverage did, that the Zone of Exemption for fine families was holding. But the offer was withdrawn when John responded that Alex, a maniacal plunger, was surely guilty. Instead of arranging bail for the accused, Percy secured the confession that was used against Alex in two trials.

The humiliations were only beginning for the elder Chisholm. The "temporary insanity defense" had just come into fashion because earlier that year, the drug-addicted millionaire Harry K. Thaw had used it to avoid prison for murdering New York's leading architect, Stanford White, in what was billed as "The Trial of the Century." What the *News* called the "Famous Chisholm Case" had some of the same legal elements, but it never made the front page in the protective Birmingham press. Only two months after testifying to a New York City court that Thaw was insane, the nation's most famous "alienist," or psychiatrist, Dr. William A. White, turned up in Birmingham. By that time, Alex had sheltered in the state insane asylum at Tuscaloosa, and the prosecutor had hired Dr. White to determine if he qualified for the defense that had kept Thaw out of prison for murdering his wife's lover. White's arrival showed that the reporters at the Birmingham papers were wearing kid gloves when they went to their new typewriters. Dr. White was front-page news in *The New York Times,* but his presence in Birmingham was relegated to page eight. The *News* noted that White's "expert" testimony had figured in the "notorious Thaw case" and reported that he would testify after examining Chisholm.

Walker Percy testified for two hours to the effect that he thought the accused was sane. Then the director of the Alabama insane asylum testified that he saw symptoms of "delusions of grandeur." After that, Alex's parents offered humiliating details about insane relatives. His trembling mother said she was descended from a former Supreme Court justice who had gone crazy. Robert Chisholm told of "a grandson who imagined himself a clock and stood in a corner and ticked"; at other times he thought he was a grain of corn and "people were chickens after him."

The desperation of Alex Chisholm's parents fairly radiates from the detached reportorial prose. What this public display of ancestral laundry must have cost them! The colonel operated on a high rung of the rapidly professionalizing bar in a city that had become the financial center of Alabama in the thirty-four-year boom sparked by its founding in 1871. It was also the gem of the expanding New South industrial empire that exploited mineral wealth and cotton in new ways. The cotton was picked now by sharecroppers of both races and spun into thread in sweatshop mills manned by a white underclass of "lintheads," female workers, and child laborers. The white working class was an emerging political force, feared and ridiculed by high-caste Alabamians. Unless Colonel Chisholm could come up with something, his son would suffer the humiliation of being exiled to the federal pen in Atlanta, infamous throughout the hill country as the place where revenuers sent Winston County moonshiners and other hillbilly whiskey makers. He began lugging his law books into court and finally shoved aside the high-priced defense lawyers he had hired and presented the closing argument himself.

In an impassioned sixty-minute address he asked, in effect, for expansion of the Zone of Exemption into a zone of outright forgiveness based on social position. It was a daring bet on Brahmin arrogance in the state that had birthed the Populist Party in the 1890s and whose coal fields had quickly become a battleground between armed company thugs and coal diggers newly organized by the United Mineworkers of America. True, only white men would serve on the jury judging Alex Chisholm, but the federal panel was drawn not from Birmingham's elite but from the small towns scattered across the Mineral District. Yankee capital and labor practices were changing the social and political chemistry. Neighboring Ensley, where I grew up, was the site of the giant blast furnaces owned by Walker Percy's father-in-law, Henry Fairchild DeBardeleben. The *News* reported that even in Ensley, aka "The Steel City," thousands of steelworkers and miners rallied for the Bryan Club, organized by corporate capitalism's fiercest critic, William Jennings Bryan.

In an address that had Chisholm family members openly weeping, the colonel bet everything on noblesse oblige. He told the jury that people of his son's stature should be judged not by the written law but by the "higher law" of whether they really intended to do harm. It was the same time-honored argument used to defend well-intentioned slave owners. How could they have sinned against the Africans they purchased if their religion told them the "peculiar institution" was sanctioned by the Bible? What did it matter if Alex had violated "an act of Congress," the father asked, since "he was not guilty of a violation of the law of God in that no intent to defraud had been shown"? Otherwise,

Chisholm said, his son would not have come back—presumably from the asylum in Tuscaloosa—"putting his neck in the halter, as it were," unless he deserved acquittal under "the higher law" governing people of character. Colonel Chisholm avoided the question of whether betting other people's money in a bucket shop proved intent. Rather, he insisted that human law can rise no higher "than the law of God on which it was based." He invoked the biblical King David and Robert E. Lee to support his view that there were no perfect men. Many in the room grew misty-eyed as he argued, in effect, that Alex's social standing, youth, and promise obliged the jurors to "spare his son the ignominy of a sentence of imprisonment."

It was a double-barreled plea for forgiveness from the letter of the law, based on craziness and social rank. He almost lost control of his temper when he portrayed Alex as betrayed by elders he had taken as his equals in social status—Dr. White and family friend Walker Percy.

Colonel Chisholm attacked the Thaw trial expert as "that big, bloated doctor from Washington." He commented on the fact that Dr. White owned two automobiles and said he had rather be a rogue than such a doctor. Chisholm referred sarcastically to the friendship of Walker Percy, saying a hug Percy had given the young man after his confession "could hardly be called an act of friendship." Percy's testimony about the confession should be disallowed because it had been obtained under "compulsion" in Percy's office, where both the interrogation and the hugging had occurred. Despite the drama of the account, the *News* kept to its decision to keep the story off the front page. The one Chisholm family member who was never seen to tear up or weep was Alex himself. His tidy wardrobe and "air of nonchalance" were commented upon. When prosecutors or witnesses described his alleged criminal acts, including his belief he possessed some supernatural gift for predicting markets, he "preserved a fixed stare into vacancy." In that respect the luck of privilege prevailed, and the summation worked up to a point in another regard.

Alabama's two leading "alienists" from the Tuscaloosa asylum— Dr. James T. Searcy and Dr. David Partlow, social equals of the

Chisholms—obligingly testified that Alex's belief in his predictive powers proved he was deranged. By this time the Zone of Exemption was looking a bit tattered. The prosecutor said Alex was not crazy but was possessed of a generational "curse of every young man at some point in his life—the 'get-rich-quick fever.'" Its kindly, inside-pages news play notwithstanding, the paper did not spare the scandalous details.

The exemption defense worked—up to a point. "Birmingham Bank Embezzler Gets Off with Light Sentence," proclaimed a Black Belt newspaper. The judge cited the mitigating factors of youth and background in giving Alex only six of a possible ten years in prison. But the affair virtually destroyed the family. Mrs. Chisholm died before Christmas, earning an obituary that cited her link to "some of the most illustrious families of the nation" and listing her surviving children, including Alex, without any details as to their whereabouts. Her pallbearers included the millionaire cotton ginner Robert Sylvester Munger (1864–1923), the chief benefactor of Birmingham-Southern College. He patented the automated gin that accomplished what economists called "the second revolution" after that achieved by Eli Whitney. Connections do not prove causation, of course, but it does say something about the role of Birmingham money in the New South and the speed with which the wheel of fortune was spinning in Birmingham those days. Walker Percy was at the top of the rotation in 1907, but Colonel Chisholm would be dead by 1910 and Percy would be carried low in events that had tremendous ramifications for his troubled family and the Confederate nostalgia industry.

The good, the bad and ugly of Birmingham's bloody racial and union history all stem from the massive financial deal that Walker Percy put together later in 1907 for his father-in-law, Henry F. DeBardeleben, the founder of Birmingham's steel industry. DeBardeleben was the foster son of Daniel Pratt (1799–1873), a visionary New Hampshire businessman who established the world's largest cotton-gin factory in 1836 a few miles north of Montgomery in a new town he built to house his employees and named for himself. In 1856, he took as his ward Henry Fairchild DeBardeleben (1840–1910), the son of a neighboring plantation owner who died in 1850. While serving in the Prattville Dragoons, C.S.A., Henry married Pratt's only daughter, Ellen, in 1863. The farsighted Pratt sent the young couple to Jefferson County to oversee the coal and iron-ore lands he had been buying around present-day Birmingham. Expanding the holdings of his late father-in-law, DeBardeleben by 1887 owned 150,000 acres of mines and iron furnaces worth $13 million. In 1891, the DeBardeleben Coal and Iron Company merged with the Tennessee Coal and Iron Company. TCI had been founded at Sewanee, Tennessee, in 1852 by investors from Nashville, details that are important to remember as we connect the geographic dots in this Gilded Age corporate saga. DeBardeleben became vice president of TCI and, of course, a founder of First National Bank of Birmingham. Walker Percy, who had helped destroy the Chisholms, came into the picture in 1886, when he settled in Birmingham rather than his native Greenville, Mississippi, after graduating from Sewanee and the University of Virginia Law School. As Jay Tolson noted, Percy quickly worked his way into the Birmingham establishment and punctuated his arrival with his marriage in 1888 to Mary Pratt DeBardeleben, the handsome, strong-willed daughter of Henry and Ellen DeBardeleben. Daniel Pratt's name would live on in the name of Pratt City, the Birmingham suburb that sat atop TCI's biggest coal seam, which fed the giant Ensley furnaces that in my day still lit up the nighttime skies over Birmingham-Southern. A tripod with three-mile legs would connect the locations, so it always puzzled me that the story of what befell the first Walker Percy washed out of Birmingham lore so quickly, if a half century can be called quick.

Financial success, depression, and suicide marked the story of the Percys wherever they went. The family's founder in America, Charles "Don Carlos" Percy (1740–1794), made a fortune in slave-raised indigo on a six-thousand-acre plantation near Natchez, then under Spanish control. In 1780, at age forty, he married sixteen-year-old Susanna Collins, with whom he had four children who survived to adulthood. Despite his financial success as the titled *alcalde* of Spanish Natchez, his sanity began to crumble when a woman named Margaret, a former lover or wife, showed up with the two children he had fathered in Ireland while serving in the British army. That is a vastly simplified version of the account in William Wyatt-Brown's *The House of Percy: Honor, Melancholy, and Imagination in a Southern Family.* There were ongoing problems for Don Carlos with Spanish authorities in New Orleans and feuding neighbors, and on the night of January 30, 1794, Percy tied a kettle to his neck and drowned himself in a bayou now known as Percy Creek. But he had established a family pattern that would persist, that of lordly pretensions leading to self-destruction. He claimed without evidence to be related to the Percys of Northumberland and to Sir Henry Percy, the Hotspur of Shakespeare's *Henry IV, Part I.* When Spanish authorities in New Orleans appointed him a magistrate in the Natchez militia, he was entitled to call himself "Don Carlos." That name, as we shall see, became a point of pride in *Lanterns on the Levee,* the family history penned by William Alexander Percy, a gifted poet and nephew of John Walker Percy, the TCI attorney who testified in 1907 in the "famous Chisholm case."

Does the case and the gothic tale of family collapse deserve the detail I've lavished on them? Let me argue that it does beause of its place in historiography and southern literature. The greater importance of the trial was that it showed the first Walker Percy at the apex of his status and power. What happened in the next few decades shaped the emergence of the Lost Cause academic ethos at the University of the South at Sewanee, Tennessee. An adoptive link to Birmingham had been established when TCI bought the Sewanee Mining Company, which in the 1850s donated ten thousand acres as the site for a new college. The literary ambitions of future novelist Walker Percy and his closest friend, Shelby Foote, flourished during teenage summers at the Percy retreat near the sprawling, sylvan campus. Rubbing shoulders with the southern intellectuals and writers drawn each summer to Sewanee's cool mountain air would help shape the literary future of Walker Percy and also that of Foote, who became a novelist and historian and, eventually, Ken Burns's confidant and enabler in the neglect of the First Alabama

Infantry, U.S.A. Did Foote intend to throw the last shovelful on the grave on purpose? I can't quite prove it. All I can do is lay out the chain of events that played out over the course of a half century.

The first big development was that the curse of Don Carlos Percy descended on Walker Percy of TCI a few months after the Chisholm trial in 1907. That fall J. Pierpont Morgan, Elbert H. Gary, and Henry C. Frick made President Theodore Roosevelt an offer he couldn't refuse. They wanted to purchase TCI, the nation's number-two producer of steel, for their Pittsburgh-based U.S. Steel. An ailing New York bank under their control owned $35 million in TCI stock. Unless Roosevelt exempted them from his antitrust laws, they would let the bank fail, triggering a nationwide panic. Henry DeBardeleben had already lost control of TCI in a failed Wall Street raid on the other stockholders, but Walker Percy was still TCI's chief counsel. In that role he went to Washington, D.C., to help draw up the documents enabling U.S. Steel and the Roosevelt administration to circumvent the antitrust laws. Four years later, the government tried to reverse the sale, but by that time Walker Percy had already been sent to the Shepherd-Pratt psychiatric institute near Baltimore for hospitalization after multiple depressive episodes. The consensus of Percy family biographers is that his decline was triggered by shame and guilt from turning over the Alabama steel industry, then conservatively valued at a billion dollars, for the piddling amount J. P. Morgan had paid to keep the New York bank afloat. "He belonged to the class of people who finally failed to hold together the old system and so were now working (often with the Yankees they had once bitterly opposed) to replace it with something else, something more closely resembling the northern model of capital and industrial relations," Jay Tolson wrote. "So Walker Percy's class was faced with trying to arrange an honorable compromise, a difficult task since honor is always inimical to compromise."

John Walker Percy was haunted by the compromise he had engineered. While Henry F. DeBardeleben had lost control of TCI in a Wall Street proxy battle, at least he had gone down fighting for home ownership of Alabama's premier industry. "Perhaps Henry DeBardeleben had not won his struggle, but at least he had not betrayed it. If Walker chose to adopt the perspective, he had grounds to call himself a Judas of sorts in that he had helped to surrender the T.C.I. Company to the United States Steel Company Corporation in Pittsburgh and New York" and made it into a "captive company," Tolson continued. The shift from home ownership to managers residing temporarily in Birmingham did incalculable civic damage to the "Pittsburgh of the South." Whereas Coca-Cola helped its hometown, Atlanta, navigate the racial crises that lay ahead for the New South, U.S. Steel supported the election as police commissioner in 1931 of political novice Eugene "Bull" Connor, a racist baseball announcer known for his roaring voice and violent temper. Connor still had U.S. Steel's support when he unleashed firehoses and police dogs on Dr. King's marchers in 1963.

The Percy suicides all sound mundane, almost routinized, in the re-telling, like Don Carlos using a metal kettle to pull his head underwater in the shallows of Percy Creek. In January 1917, Walker Percy and his son, Leroy Pratt Percy—grandfather and father, respectively, of the novelist—were planning to visit their Greenville cousins for a duck hunt. They lunched in the elder Percy's gloomy Victorian mansion off fash-ionable Highland Avenue. Afterward, Walker was cleaning shotguns in his gun room. Leroy was in the library reading when he heard the gun-shot. The old man had killed himself with a blast to the heart. The Zone of Exemption held briefly, as the *Birmingham Age-Herald* reported it as a gun-cleaning accident. The coroner ruled otherwise, and *The Bir-mingham News* reported the scene correctly: "LeRoy Percy heard a faint report and thought nothing about it, but later went to his father's room and found the body in a trunk room adjoining where he had been ac-customed to keeping his sporting implements."

Leroy inherited both the mansion and the recurrent depression that the Percy family called the "crouching beast." In 1924 he moved his wife and three boys over Red Mountain to Mountain Brook, which to this day remains a gemlike suburb of Olmsted-inspired landscaping and Tudor mansions like the one Leroy and his wife, Mattie Sue Phinizy Walker, raised on Country Club Road. Leroy became president of the

Birmingham Country Club and supervised the building of two courses that introduced the national golfing craze to the city's industrial executives, doctors, and lawyers. The Percys had none of the financial troubles that led two local bankers to kill themselves in the summer of 1929. The two older boys—Walker, thirteen, and LeRoy, twelve—were away at summer camp. The youngest, eight-year-old Phinizy, was at home with the housekeeper. Leroy's wife was shopping in downtown Birmingham when she heard a newsboy shout, "Prominent Birmingham lawyer takes his life!" Mattie Sue turned to the woman shopping with her and said, "It's Leroy."

After sheltering for a year with her wealthy kin in Georgia, Mattie Sue and her three boys moved to Greenville at the invitation of Leroy's first cousin, William Alexander Percy, who had succeeded his father, former senator LeRoy Percy, as Greenville's leading citizen and local lawyer for out-of-state clients like the Illinois Central Railroad. They were direct descendants of the first William Alexander Percy (1834–1888), a Confederate hero known as the "Gray Eagle of the Delta." In his dual role as Speaker of the Mississippi House of Representatives and lawyer of choice for northern investors in the Delta, the "Gray Eagle" had invented and passed to his sons a Mississippi version of the DeBardeleben/Percy plan that worked so well in Birmingham. Among Deep South families, the Percys probably best demonstrated the efficacy of clinging to plantation grandiosity while profiting from inherited land and northern industrial money. The arrival of the three Percy boys in Greenville was transformative for Will Percy. Already the cultural leader of Greenville, he abandoned both his career as a poet and the glamorous Italian vacations he had enjoyed with like-minded men from New York, Boston, and England. For the last thirteen years of his life he became "Uncle Will," an exemplary father to his adoptive sons and— even more influential for our purposes here—the literary mentor of their best friend, his surrogate son, Shelby Foote.

For a number of reasons, Greenville is one of the only places where this particular southern connection could have occurred. It happens to be one of the rare southern towns where, for economic reasons, Jews were allowed to join the country club. As in Selma, another cotton town, the club needed every person with a white skin who could afford the dues in order to maintain its pool and golf course. In this and other aspects of its civic life, Greenville prided itself as being more tolerant than most southern towns. Foote, whose mother was Jewish, was fifteen when Will Percy recruited him at the country club to take "under his wing" the arriving Percy boys. Foote was a year older than Leroy, a year younger than Walker. Phinizy, the youngest, was ten when the boys and their mother took up residence. Initially, Leroy and Shelby bonded over their shared interest in girls and socializing, but soon Walker and Shelby were sharing Uncle Will's ample library and extensive collection of classical music. The two young aspiring writers were introduced to a series of house guests who knew Will by his reputation as a poet and cosmopolitan host for northern intellectuals in search of a Delta immersion. Before they were out of high school, Walker and Shelby had met Dorothy Parker, Vachel Lindsay, Stephen Vincent Benét, and Stark Young. Foote was frustrated by the fact that his personal idol, William Faulkner, had been banned for showing up drunk for a tennis match on Uncle Will's court. Will Percy saw to it that Shelby read *Ulysses, The Magic Mountain,* and *Remembrance of Things Past,* whose authors became his heroes and career models.

Shelby Foote published his first novel in 1949, twelve years before Walker came out with his breakthrough work, *The Moviegoer.* But not until Shelby's Civil War trilogy began appearing in 1958 and Ken Burns put him on television would Foote become anywhere near as famous as Walker Percy. He was never as good a novelist as his friend, but that did not stop him from condescending to Percy's work, just as he had condescended to Robert Penn Warren's. Iron self-confidence seemed to have been groomed into Shelby by Greenville and Will Percy, and it would pay off when Burns's documentary made him a millionaire through book sales. Money was never a problem for Walker, with his Birmingham and Greenville inheritances. But there is another inheritance that concerns us here.

As Tony Horwitz reported in his Pulitzer-winning *Confederates in the Attic,* he was surprised by "Foote's retroactive allegiance to the Confederacy. 'It was the honor-bound code of the Old South. One's people before one's principles.' Foote explained, 'It's a bunch of shit really. But all Southerners subscribe to this code to some degree, at least male Southerners of my generation.'" In his view, "It's what kept them going through Appomattox, that attitude of 'I won't give up, I will not be insulted.'"

Foote's scatological reference reminded me of what Jimmy Carter's White House press secretary Jody Powell told me around 2005 about inviting Foote to tour the Gettysburg Battlefield as a guide for President Carter and a group of political supporters and Civil War scholars. Foote was surprisingly reticent as they visited the classic scenes of Pickett's Charge and Little Round Top. Foote finally suggested that the National Park Service guide fill in the gaps—a fact confirmed to me by Bob Prosperi, the career NPS employee involved. Powell told me that he arranged to drive Foote back to the White House and urged him to be more forthcoming in his remarks at the East Room dinner for the entire party that evening. "Jody, you don't understand," Foote told Powell. "The minute I finished that book I forgot all that shit."

I've often wondered if Foote had found forgetfulness a useful tool for editing his memory. That could explain why, even though he lived less than ninety miles from Corinth, Mississippi, where the first three companies of the First Alabama Cavalry were sworn in and then plunged almost immediately into battle with Foote's hero, Nathan Bedford Forrest, Foote kept the existence of the Alabamians secret from Ken Burns's scriptwriters. Maybe he forgot about them, which at first blush seems unlikely given the exhaustive nature of his own Civil War research and the fact that he lived his entire life within a 275-mile radius of Looney's Tavern. On the other hand, it took me a lifetime to understand the First Alabama and my blood ties to Winston County and its patriots. What is fair to say is that Foote never exhibited an awareness of the First Alabama to match the attention he gave to the Free State of Jones in the PBS documentary.

That leads us to the deep-dyed acculturation that Walker Percy and

SILENT CAVALRY

417

Shelby Foote experienced in Uncle Will's distinctive brand of Dixie Brahmin prejudices against lower-caste whites and Black people. Foote saw a Union monument for the first time in 1946 when he and Walker Percy, then both about thirty, made a road trip to Sante Fe. "We immediately made plans to blow it up," he told Tony Horwitz.

They did not, but the incident lingered on in Walker Percy's memory as an emblem of their struggle to overcome Uncle Will's indoctrination. In his Mountain Brook novel, *The Last Gentleman,* Will Barrett, the protagonist, admits: "When I was at Princeton, I blew up a Union monument. It was only a plaque hidden in the grass behind the chemistry building, presented by the class of 1885 in memory of those who made the supreme sacrifice to suppress the infamous rebellion, or something like that. It offended me. I synthesized a liter of trinitrotoluene in the chemistry lab and blew it up one Saturday afternoon. But no one ever knew about it. It seemed like I was the only one who knew the monument was there. It was thought to be a Harvard prank."

With the two Delta boys enrolled at the University of North Carolina by 1936, Foote was the first to express doubts about the southern gentry's belief that segregation would endure as a way of life. Integration "would probably not be a bad thing," Foote told Walker during a spring break trip to New York City in 1936. The incident was recorded in Jay Tolson's biography of Walker Percy. "Shocked, Percy replied, 'I cannot believe you, a southerner, would say that.'"

Foote would make his final break with segregation as a kind of class protest against the coarseness of Arkansas governor Orval Faubus, Alabama governor George Wallace, and Mississippi governor Ross Barnett, whom he denounced in a letter to Percy as "pussy-faced politicians." By 1963, Foote was ready to pen this disclaimer in a biographical note to the second volume of his Civil War trilogy: "I am obligated also to the governors of my native state and the adjoining states of Arkansas and Alabama for helping to lessen my sectional bias by reproducing, in their actions during several of the years that went into the writing of this volume, much that was least admirable in the position my forebears occupied when they stood up to Lincoln."

The biographers of both writers have struggled with the fact that neither ever fully escaped the shadow of Uncle Will's version of what Tolson called "the southern romance—the idealized picture of the southern gentry, the happy submissiveness of blacks, the codes of honor and chivalric heroism." That's not to say they didn't accept integration once it came to their respective homes in Louisiana and Tennessee. Foote even canceled a plan to build a beach home in Gulf Shores, Alabama, because of what he perceived as persistent Klan sympathies there. But he was already a national television celebrity when Tony Horwitz's book on lingering Lost Cause fallacies came out in 1998. "What has dismayed me so much is the behavior of blacks," Foote said. "They are fulfilling every dire prophecy the Ku Klux Klan made. It's no longer safe to be on the streets in black neighborhoods. They are acting as if the utter lie about blacks being somewhere between ape and man were true." As Horwitz concluded, there "was a side of Shelby Foote that hadn't come through in Burns' documentary." But then, neither had the First Alabama Cavalry.

35

THREE KINGDOMS

WHEN I ROAMED the South as a newspaper reporter covering the new biracial politics triggered by the 1965 Voting Rights Act, a more worldly Birmingham was emerging, with an integrated political leadership that looked more to Martin Luther King Jr.'s Atlanta than to George Wallace's Montgomery as an aspirational model. Mountain Brook was still lily white, but fashionable couples of my age who were dabbling in liberalism had taken to calling their cosseted world the "tiny kingdom." The phrase—which was both prideful and self-mocking—immediately leapt to mind when I began researching the decision by the widowed Mattie Sue Phinizy Percy to move her three sons to Greenville. I recognized that Greenville, too, was a tiny kingdom of earlier vintage where a kind of hip modernism could be experienced in an environment protected from the pushy egalitarianism of militant Black people and the New Rich tackiness of declassé whites in the newer suburbs.

The tiny-kingdom concept is a useful tool in understanding the sociology of the modern South. As a sociohistorical construct, it reminded me of the viral analogy applied to Tuscaloosa and the industrial side of Birmingham, but the tiny kingdoms fit into a larger frame of southern intellectual history. I soon discerned that Greenville and Mountain Brook were hardwired to a kindred realm that was more expansive and influential in the institutionalization of scrubbed-up Old South attitudes. The tiny kingdoms of Alabama and Mississippi were seminal influences on the syndrome's third iteration, which I refer to as the Nashville/Sewanee Axis. This is the high-gloss academic world anchored by Vanderbilt University in the Tennessee capital and by the University of the South in Sewanee, perhaps the most precious corner in the world of tiny kingdoms. Along the Nashville/Sewanee Axis, the Dunningite fallacy of an unjustly put-upon Confederacy reached its most potent expression under the direction of Alabama native Walter Lynwood Fleming. Under his leadership flourished the twin pillars of the South's most important conservative intellectual movements: the Southern Agrarians and the Fugitive Poets. The Percys are a connective, indeed causative force in these tiny kingdoms. Their essential literary expressions are *Lanterns on the Levee* by William Alexander Percy and *The Last Gentleman* by his adoptive son Walker Percy. They are such enticing targets for psychobiography and literary analysis that they could lead us far afield from our main interest in examining their world, which is how their mentorship of and friendship with Shelby Foote fed into the continued obscurity of the First Alabama Cavalry, U.S.A.

I'll try to unpack the story of all three without taking my gaze too far from the main prize. Foote is our link to Ken Burns and his iconic documentary and the First Alabama's last chance for fame. As a Percy acolyte, Foote proved an apt advocate for Greenville's special brand of hubris, based in large part on a literary tradition that had produced more than thirty published writers. "I don't know how to explain it," Foote said late in his life. "I guess the hand of God reached out and touched Greenville. Or the hand of whatever." He also echoed the Greenville elite's favorite canard about poor upland whites—that the Delta folk, and by extension the plantation gentry, are "more sophisticated" and "more liberal than the hills." It's a small but resonant point. If the hill people, be they Mississippian or Alabamian, are of lesser importance, what's the harm of leaving them out of the greatest southern story?

Certainly, William Alexander Percy had no problem with omitting from his 1941 memoir his inextricable links to two Alabama centers of wealth. Although his unswerving disdain for Black people and low-caste whites is contemptible, this bestselling homage to Mississippi snobbery is in one respect a very brave book. While Percy was officially closeted, few gay writers of his era have written so boldly of the sexual awakening that he experienced in revels of "Dionysian abandon" among the centaurs and satyrs of "Arcady," his term for the forested glens of the University of the South campus at Sewanee. Only the most blinkered reader could miss what was written between the lines. It seems hard to reconcile the boldness of his defiance of the nation's endemic homophobia with the way he salted his lyrical prose with the ugliest expressions of defiant misogyny and racist paternalism. For the most part, Percy was spared the sexual demagoguery visited on Tennessee Williams and Truman Capote, perhaps because of his association with Yale University. From 1925 to 1932, Percy edited the Yale Younger Poets series, the first of its kind in the country. He also published four volumes of poetry with Yale University Press. Percy cultivated and promoted many fellow writers, southern, northern and European, including William Faulkner. He welcomed Langston Hughes to his home and knew other figures associated with the Harlem Renaissance. He has been described as "godfather" to the Fugitives at Vanderbilt, a group that included John Crowe Ransom, Allen Tate, and Robert Penn Warren.

The "godfather" reference touches on what concerns us here: the linkage among Birmingham and Greenville and the two young writers who would be schooled in post-Confederate exceptionalism in the idyllic, Rebel-worshiping groves of Tennessee's academic Arcadia. Will Percy spent many summers with his three adoptive sons and Shelby Foote at his summer home, Brinkwood, which he owned with his longtime partner, Huger Jervey, dean of Columbia Law School. The handsome clifftop retreat near Sewanee is a notable place on the southern literary map. It was a rich scene, with Greenville's leading propagandist for an alleged aristocracy mentoring two aspiring novelists: Walker, in whose novels fictional versions of Mountain Brook would assume more relevance than Greenville, and Foote, whose Faulknerian novels would be surpassed by the Civil War trilogy that made him a millionaire and led to his starring role in Ken Burns's documentary.

For Will Percy, the idea that his inherited Trail Lake plantation near Greenville owed its existence to Alabama money was too sordid to mention in *Lanterns*, but too well documented to be forever covered up. The Alabama thread in the Percy tapestry dates back to 1803 at Princeton University, the Ivy League school of choice for striving southern Presbyterians able to afford it. There Thomas George Percy (1786–1841), the eldest son of Don Carlos Percy of Natchez, formed a blood-brother bond with his classmate John Williams Walker (1783–1823), the future U.S. senator from Alabama. (Genealogists have found no link between him and my Walkers, who lived within 150 miles of the Walker estate near Huntsville.) These Walkers were part of the Broad River Group, old Virginia families who bought the best Tennessee Valley cotton lands and controlled Alabama's antebellum politics as the "Royal party." Abandoning the family seat at Natchez, Thomas George Percy bought a five-thousand-acre plantation, Belfield, next door to Walker's prosperous Oakland Plantation. In 1819, the "Royal" faction in the Alabama legislature saw to the election of John Williams Walker as the first senator from the new state of Alabama. Percy ran both plantations while Walker was in the nation's capital. "Thomas G.," as he was called, was the first dreamy, artistic Percy; he preferred gardening, reading, and travel to producing cotton with his own seventy-six slaves and the additional slaves on the Walker plantation. Nonetheless, he successfully navigated the Panic of 1819 and piled up fortunes for both men during the cotton boom that followed. The men married daughters of John Pope, a Huntsville lawyer who claimed blood ties to the English poet Alexander Pope. John Pope's grandson LeRoy Pope Walker became the first secretary of war of the Confederacy.

So there were reasons aplenty for Alabama's brand of Old South snobbery, but that version was not to the poetic Will Percy's taste. Around 1829, Thomas G. used his Alabama earnings to buy wild lands in the Mississippi Delta's Washington County near Greenville, which had been founded only five years earlier. At his death in 1843, his sons took over the plantations he started in the surrounding county. Thereafter the Percys would be identified as a Greenville family, and you have to scratch pretty hard to find out that Alabama money was behind their arrival and their identification with the new town of Greenville, rather than more glamourous Natchez. It's also hard to discover that Thomas George Percy, who established the Greenville beachhead, is identified in some histories as an "Alabama settler." You have to scratch even harder to understand that the name Walker enters the Percy lineage as an homage to an Alabamian, when Thomas G. named his firstborn son John Walker Percy (1817–1864) after his closest friend. John Walker Percy left no heirs. The Greenville Percys descend from his eldest brother, the very first William Alexander Percy, born on May 10, 1834, in—you guessed it—Alabama.

That means that the William Alexander Percy who was born two generations later and wrote *Lanterns on the Levee* as an homage to the Mississippi Delta was directly descended from a line of the family that started in the Alabama highlands. He became lord of Greenville's tiny kingdom upon the death of his father, U.S. senator LeRoy Percy, in 1929. As such, he provides a case study in a matter that surprisingly few southern intellectuals have addressed directly: the pure snobbery and falsified history inherent in the Old South narrative's account of white common folk. Witness the diatribe directed at southerners who lacked his own Delta pedigree.

"I may seem to have implied that all Delta citizens were aristocrats," Percy wrote to start the second chapter of *Lanterns,* which is an overview of his homeland's caste system. "If so, I have misrepresented my country. The aristocrats were always numerically in the minority; with the years they have not increased." He sprinkles praise on "the other and very different children of God who took up their abode beside the waters of the great river," including shanty-boat "river rats," Jews, Italians, Chinese, Irish, and Syrians. Percy then elaborated the eugenic doctrine enshrined in literary portraits like Erskine Caldwell's *Tobacco Road* and Faulkner's depiction of the barn-burning Snopes family, as well as in twenty-first-century reality television shows like *Duck Dynasty, Swamp People,* and *My Big Redneck Wedding:*

> But the basic fiber, the cloth of the Delta population—as of the whole South—is built of three dissimilar threads and only three. First were the old slave-holders. . . . Second were the poor whites, who owned no slaves [and] worked their small unproductive holdings ignored by the gentry, despised by the slaves. Third were the Negroes.

The reader can feel this white supremacist working himself up to a crowning insult. The poor whites of the South were lower than Negroes. Their ancestors scattered the genes of English convicts through Georgia before settling in the clay hills of Alabama and Georgia. They were "pure English stock" on whom the "virus of poverty, malnutrition, and interbreeding has done its degenerative work." With this frothing malediction, Percy seemed to have written himself into a corner that required a snobbish row-back:

> I know they are responsible for the only American ballads, for camp meetings, for a whole new and excellent school of Southern literature. I can forgive them as the Lord God forgives, but admire them, trust them, love them—never. Intellectually and spiritually they are inferior to the Negro, whom they hate. Suspecting secretly they are inferior to him, they must do something to him to prove to themselves their superiority. At their door must be laid the disgraceful riots and lynchings gloated over and exaggerated by Negrophiles the world over.
>
> The Delta was not settled by these people; its pioneers were slave-owners and slaves.

In Percy's distorted taxonomy, the noble flatlanders were not responsible for the violence against slaves and freed Black people that offended the international community of bleeding hearts. Delta slave masters were a cultivated subset of the white population that must not be confused with the degraded upland whites from other southern states, particularly the hill people along the Alabama-Mississippi line. Those folks made up the backbone of the First Alabama Cavalry, U.S.A. The First stood up ably to Nathan Bedford Forrest's assaults on Grant's rear in the Vicksburg campaign, buying him time for his successful siege of the river city. The accomplishments of these Alabama Unionists so near Greenville does not show up in Will Percy's writings nor in those of his protegé Shelby Foote. I'm inclined to doubt that Percy shared that bit of redneck lore with Foote, who was coached from the age of fourteen by the older man in literature, music, politics, and Civil War history. After all, Will Percy's prejudice against white highlanders was so strong that he could not bring himself to admit, for example, that the quintessential Appalachian states, North Carolina and Tennessee, contributed 129,000 and 115,000 troops, respectively, to the Rebel army as compared to Mississippi's 70,000. Clearly these mountain folk could be helpful in war if only they understood their place in the postbellum pecking order and did not trample the sacred soil and lofty folkways of the Delta. The fact that they eventually entered Mississippi politics offended him. When "the poor whites—'hill-billies,' 'red-necks,'" he wrote, "shall have supplanted the Negro, ours will be a sadder country, and not a wiser one."

It makes a "nice study," to use Percy's term, to ponder how little Percy revealed of his Alabama roots and how his relatives profited, in fame and dollars, when John Walker Percy won the hand of Mary Pratt DeBardeleben, known as Pratt, heiress to the Pratt-DeBardeleben industrial fortune. The elder Walker made his way in Birmingham after his older brother, under Delta primogeniture, inherited the Percys' Twin Lakes plantation outside Greenville, a modest operation in comparison to TCI. The political and economic import of the wedding was described by the novelist's authorized biographer, Patrick Samway, S.J., in a *Mississippi Quarterly* article that gave second billing to the Mississippi family. It was entitled "The Union of the DeBardeleben and Percy Families."

In the quietly exquisite Episcopal Church of the Advent in downtown Birmingham, Walker Percy married Mary Pratt DeBardeleben on April 17, 1888. . . . The merger of these two families solidified the positions of both Pratt and Walker in Birmingham society; it also meant that the accumulation of wealth and power could expand. And who could imagine how far it would go? Other families in Birmingham could only stand in awe of the potential of this new branch of the Percy family. . . . After the wedding, the young couple visited the Percys in Greenville. Henry ("Harry") Ball was not initially impressed with the new Mrs. Walker Percy: "Mrs. Pratt DeBardeleben Walker Percy—the great Birmingham heiress. Verily I think she must be very rich. I think Walker has sold his birthright for a mess of pottage." Six years later, Ball had a change of heart: "I remember setting down my impressions of Mrs. Walker Percy as unfavorable. I take it back. She is a very good natured, bright, and pleasant young woman. Not pretty, nor particularly refined or elegant, but nice. I like her."

Thus began a foundational link in the emerging oligarchical formula of the New South: the combining of antebellum landholdings with Yankee capital. The subtext that flowed through *Lanterns* and into the Lost Cause orthodoxy that would emerge along the Nashville/Sewanee Axis was fundamentally eugenic and very much to William Alexander Percy's taste and mode of historical analysis. The elegance came from the old landed families, and the money came from the necessary toil of those two great inferior tribes of the South with their shallow gene pools, the African Americans and the rednecks. At the point where skinny, effeminate William Alexander Percy, at fifteen, rode a choo-choo called the Mountain Goat into the mountains to enroll at a military school attached to the University of the South, great figures begin to enter the events of his life, characters without whom we cannot fully appreciate the long march of the First Alabama into obscurity. The weight of family history lay heavily on the shoulders of young Will. He understood that his dead brother was the favorite of a father who half loved him but to whom he was almost pathetically devoted. He was a devout Roman Catholic who knew he was most comfortable in the society of men but rebelled instinctively against Rome's view that sex between men was deviant. Paradoxically, one of the reasons his mother wanted him to go to a military school was to toughen his masculine side and thus save him from the priesthood in her own church. Percy men were soldiers, not priests or poets. At Sewanee, he lost his faith and adopted "Greek bisexuality" as his ideal.

There, too, he absorbed the pastoral conceits and chivalric imagery that would lead generations of aspiring southern writers to identify with the graceful legends of antebellum Georgia, Mississippi, and Louisiana rather than the raw energy of industrial Alabama. Artists as different as William Faulkner and Margaret Mitchell would plow those plantation fields to a fare-thee-well, leaving Birmingham and Mountain Brook as virgin novelistic territory for the talented adoptive son growing up under Will Percy's tutelage in his Greenville mansion and mountain retreat. In the sociologically astute *The Last Gentleman,* Walker Percy explores the difference between Greenville and Birmingham by having his engineer protagonist, Will Barrett, host a party for visiting Mississippi collegians at the Mountain Brook mansion where Walker lived as a boy.

> His guests were Deltan, from the engineer's country, though he did not know them. But he knew their sort and it made him uneasy to see how little he was like them, how easy they were in their ways and how solitary and Yankeefied he was—though they seemed to take him immediately as one of them and easy, too. The young men were Sewanee Episcopal types, good soft-spoken hard-drinking youths, gentle with women and very much themselves with themselves, set, that is, for the next fifty years in the actuality of themselves and their good names. They knew what they were, how things were and how things should be. As for the engineer, he didn't know. I'm from the Delta, too, thought he, sticking his hand down through his pocket, and I'm Episcopal; why ain't I like them, easy and actual: Oh, to be like Rooney Lee.

I quote this passage at length because it crystallizes the difference between Will Percy and Walker Percy as thinkers and writers. The former was comfortable in every aspect of who he was, including his prejudices. So was Rooney Lee, the favored second son of Robert E. Lee, who studied at Harvard and, after fighting for the Confederacy, settled happily into the plantation he inherited from George Washington's foster son, George Washington Parke Custis. Walker's novels explored the new kind of suburban southerner, still rich and privileged but haunted by existential dread and guilt about the South's "infinitely dreary amalgam of Fundamentalism and racism." Walker Percy's first novel, *The Moviegoer,* has been more heavily praised than *The Last Gentleman,* which I regard as his masterwork when it comes to dramatizing the time-warped sensibility of the late twentieth-century southern "aristocrats" and the tiny kingdoms that shaped them.

Everyone who knew Will Percy, man or boy, remembered his beauty, his wonderful hair, and, most of all, his haunting blue-gray eyes. "They were terrible and beautiful eyes, eyes to be careful around," Walker Percy recalled years later. "I cannot see them otherwise than shadowed by sadness." Part of that sadness may have stemmed from the fact that he gave up poetry and homosexual cruising, the latter at least when it could be observed by his boys. He operated flawlessly *in loco parentis* for the Percy boys and Walker's closest friend, Shelby Foote—flawlessly, that is, if you exempt snobbery and racism from the calculation. As an Alabamian, I couldn't help noticing how the snobbery manifested itself in *Lanterns on the Levee* in the detailed history of Twin Lakes Plantation, the profitable 3,300-acre holding that Will Percy inherited. It is presented as entirely a Mississippi project, descended from Don Carlos and his son Thomas G. There is no mention that this taming of the Delta had to await the arrival of Thomas G.'s widow and their young Alabama-born son, the first William Alexander Percy, from the more mature Alabama plantation culture that the families of the Broad River Group established along the Tennessee River while Washington County was still a jungle that the un-diked Mississippi flooded annually. Also missing from Will's truncated version of family financial history is the name of Belfield, the

Bama plantation where Thomas G. stuffed his pockets with the cash he invested in a Greenville jungle that had yet to be cleared for cotton. The first William Alexander Percy inherited Thomas G.'s first plantation, Percy Place, in 1841, and returned to it after the Civil War as the colonel known as the "Gray Eagle of the Delta."

The description of him by his grandson in *Lanterns* gives a good idea of the values that Will Percy brought to his leading role in the literary world of the Nashville/Sewanee Axis during the Southern Literary Renaissance, which lasted from 1920 to 1940:

> [The Gray Eagle's] life work became the re-establishment of white supremacy. That work required courage, tact, intelligence, patience; it also required vote-buying, the stuffing of ballot-boxes, chicanery, intimidation. Heart-breaking business and degrading, but in the end successful. At terrific cost white supremacy was re-established. Some of us still remember what we were told of those times, and what we were told inclines us to guard the ballot as something precious, something to be withheld unless the fitness of the recipient be patent. We are the ones I suppose who doubt despairingly the fitness of Negroes and (under our breath be it said) of women.

To understand how the author of such words could be glowingly reviewed in *The New York Times*, we need to look more closely at the Southern Renaissance, a two-decade period when a new generation of literary stars—Robert Penn Warren, Allen Tate, Donald Davidson, John Crowe Ransom, and Andrew Nelson Lytle—were flocking to study under Dunning's star pupil and Thomas Owen's soulmate, Walter Lynwood Fleming, at Vanderbilt. Between 1920 and 1940, the hills were alive with literary and sexual exploration and literary log-rolling that brought many famous names into play. *Lanterns on the Levee* represented a triumph for Alfred A. Knopf and his most celebrated author, H. L. Mencken, editor of the *American Mercury*, in their campaign to introduce a new generation of southern writers.

Faulkner, of course, was already famous for fiction haunted by Confederate ghosts. Erskine Caldwell novels such as *Tobacco Road,* a 1932 bestseller, offered a jaundiced view of a scratch-ankle South. In 1934, Carl Carmer's *Stars Fell on Alabama* tried, in a sense, to split the difference between stereotypes of violent corn-pone southerners on the "bottom rail" and the fading grandees of the decaying plantation world of the Black Belt. Carmer even tipped his hat to the minstrel tradition by introducing Antimo, a joke-telling barbecue chef so gifted he could even sass the rich clientele at the exclusive Dollarhide Hunting Club between Tuscaloosa and Eutaw. For all the commercial success of Caldwell, Carmer, and formidable female writers like Katherine Ann Porter and her discovery, Eudora Welty, it was Alfred Knopf and his wife, Blanche, who put an exclamation point to the peak years of the Southern Renaissance with twin triumphs in 1941. On February 10, they brought out an enduring dissection of southern attitudes from W. J. Cash, a North Carolina newspaperman who had been groomed in the skills of acerbic commentary for over a decade by Mencken himself. No one had ever seen anything quite like *Mind of the South,* which stressed the continuity of white southerners as a brave but difficult people driven by obdurate folkways, a distinctive language, and abiding racism.

Then on March 10, 1941, came *Lanterns on the Levee,* which Alfred Knopf had nursed to completion despite its author's failing health and doubts about the reception of his reactionary celebration of inflated, largely imaginary glories. Some see the books as opposites, given Cash's populist, sociological emphasis, reflecting the influence of Walter L. Fleming's most formidable academic rival, Howard Odum of the University of North Carolina. Odum's Chapel Hill Regionalists would go into academic history as the natural rivals of the Agrarians, the former favoring social science and the latter tending the coals of legend. As professor and founder of the University of North Carolina Press, Odum had made UNC the citadel of social sciences in the South, while Fleming was making Vandy a literary powerhouse. To add spice to this clash of scholarly visions, Odum had commissioned an economic study of the sharecropper practices at Percy's Trail Lake plantation.

As Percy grumbled in his book, "One of Doctor Odum's boys showed up in the summer of 1936." The scholar found that 124 families made a net average income of $437.90. Percy countered that the families worked only 150 days a year and received garden plots, free houses, and loans for medical care. "The Negroes who received this cash and these benefits are simple unskilled laborers," he wrote. "I wonder what other unskilled labor for so little receives so much." He added, "I watch the limber-jointed, oily-black, well-fed, decently clothed peasants on Trail Lake and feel sorry for the telephone girls, the clerks in chain stores, the office help . . . not only for their poor and fixed wage but for their slave routines, their joyless habits of work, and their insecurity." Complaining about FDR's attack on the practice and other critics in "the sainted East," he concluded, "Share-cropping is one of the best systems ever devised to give security and a chance for profit to the simple and un-skilled." Sharecropping was simply a case of "a stronger race carrying on its shoulders a weaker race."

Prior to publication, friends tried to persuade him to remove racial commentaries from his manuscript. Huger Jervey, dean at Columbia Law School, and his partner in ownership of Brinkwood, was among those advising caution, according to Bertram Wyatt-Brown's introduction to a 2005 reprint of *Lanterns*. "On the other hand, Alfred Knopf, highly pleased with the manuscript, advised him not to change a word. Unfortunately, he took his publisher's counsel," concluded Wyatt-Brown. But in fact Knopf, a celebrated New York sophisticate, had a better feel for the national literary audience. He also had a practiced feel for the Zone of Exemption on which Percy could count. He wrote the nervous author that his views were "so strong . . . and beautifully written" that readers would be carried along. That appeared to be the case despite what Wyatt-Brown called the author's "racial blindness and self-deluding romanticism."

The long *New York Times* review was astonishing both for what it said and for what it did not say. The *Times*'s naive tribute to plantation values was penned by Herschel Brickell (1889–1952), the respected book editor of the *New York Post* and a Senatobia, Mississippi, native.

The *Times* ignored flagrant conflicts of interest in publishing the rave review. Brickell was a friend of the Percy family who had edited the Jackson *Daily News* and idealized Will's father, the old senator, whose war with the Klan was the narrative spine of the book. As for who was responsible for the bad reputation of sharecropping, Brickell agreed with the author as to whom to blame: "The best of the Delta planters, like Mr. Percy, dealt fairly with their laborers, but the get-rich-quick invaders from the hills, called by Delta people 'peckerwoods,' are less bound by principle." Brickell was using the oldest dodge in the Lost Cause trick bag. The no-account hillbillies were useful only as cannon fodder. Moreover, southern shortcomings could not be blamed on the noble likes of Lee and General Leonidas Polk (1806–1864), the founder of the University of the South and a figure not to be overlooked in the history of Confederate propaganda and military failure. Polk's legacy permeated the Sewanee that welcomed Will Percy when he arrived "in short trousers, small, weakly, self-reliant, and ignorant as an egg."

Polk, an Episcopal bishop, operated from his mansion on the vast "Rattle and Snap" tract between Nashville and Sewanee, and he owned between four hundred and a thousand slaves. He became alarmed when the Church of England, long complicit in the slave trade, renounced it in 1833. Polk blamed abolitionist propaganda about the brutality of plantation life for turning English political opinion. He convinced his fellow bishops in the American Episcopal Church that, as a matter of preemptive public relations, it needed a college to train the rising generation of slave owners to avoid the disciplinary practices described by Harriet Beecher Stowe in *Uncle Tom's Cabin*. Polk consecrated the cornerstone of the first building at Sewanee on October 9, 1860, a little under four years before his path would fatally intersect that of the First Alabama Cavalry, U.S.A. on the road to Atlanta. By that time he would have established in eastern Tennessee another of those islands that I refer to as tiny kingdoms. If Will Percy was leaving the "most Southern place on earth" in the Delta, he was arriving at the most Confederate place in the twentieth-century South.

It was a small college, in wooded mountains, its students drawn from the impoverished Episcopal gentry of the South, its boarding houses and dormitories presided over by widows of bishops and Confederate generals. Great Southern names were thick— Kirby-Smith . . . Polk . . . Gorgas . . . The only things it wasn't rich in were worldly goods, sociology, and science. A place to be hopelessly sentimental about and to unfit one for anything except the good life . . .

Until I came to Sewanee I had been utterly without friends of my own age. . . . Probably because of my size and age and length of trousers I was plentifully adopted. It is a long time now; some of them have gone the journey . . . a few have won through to autumn. But then the springtime was on them and they taught me and tended me in the greenwoods as the Centaurs did Achilles— I don't know how I ever recovered to draw my own bow. Percy Huger, noble and beautiful like a sleepy St. Bernard; Elliott Cage, full of dance-steps and song-snatches, tender and protective, and sad beneath; Paul Ellerbe, who first read me Dover Beach, thereby disclosing the rosy mountain-ranges of the Victorians; Harold Abrams, dark and romantic with his violin, quoting the Rubaiyat and discoursing Shaw; Parson Masterson, jostling with religion, unexpected and quaint; Sinkler Manning, a knight who met a knight's death at Montfaucon; Arthur Gray, full of iridescence, discovering new paths and views in the woods; Huger Jervey, brilliant and bumptious then, brilliant and wise now, and so human; all wastrel creditors who never collected. Peace to them, and endless gratitude. Here I suddenly found myself a social being, among young creatures of charm and humor, more experienced than I, but friendly and fascinating.

I never read that passage without admiring this bold announcement— to a society whose rigid sexual views Percy well understood—of a sensual education in a world of men who did not miss women. But it is deeply imprinted with a belittling conceit of the tiny kingdoms sprinkled across the map of Confederate mourning from Richmond to New Orleans, a solipsistic attitude of self-congratulation and self-pity. For our purposes, a key period began in 1932, when Shelby Foote entered fully into this gauzy world in the company of Will Percy, missionary from the Greenville province, and Walker Percy, born and wounded into fiction by the lost paradise of Mountain Brook. On April 2, 1932, what Greenville gossips called the curse of the Percys seemed to descend over Mattie Sue Phinizy Percy, mother of the three boys. The car in which she was driving veered off a bridge into Deer Creek and sank. The nine-year-old Phinizy who was in the car with her struggled free, but she refused to leave and seemed to be trying to hold him inside to drown with her. By horrible coincidence, the middle son, Roy, drove past the scene of the accident, and Will, who had just arrived, tried in vain to keep him away from the crowd of onlookers. But Phin saw the wet body lying on the bridge and moaned, "It's my mother, my mother . . ."

Uncle Will made heroic efforts to comfort Phin, reading him to sleep at night and taking him to New York for psychiatric evaluation, while sending Walker and Roy on a guided tour of the West. When Walker and Shelby finished high school in 1933, Will came up with a plan to keep them from "helling around the Delta," as Foote remembered it. A chaperoned house party for the young men and their dates was set for Brinkwood. It was a summer of romantic intrigue and excursions to the caves and waterfalls Walker would use years later in *The Second Coming*. Most importantly, it plunged the two aspiring writers into the heart of the Nashville literary establishment, many of whom vacationed in cottages at the Assembly, a tony Chautauqua-like summer retreat for wealthy, intellectually inclined southerners. In various combinations throughout the 1930s and 1940s they had access to the rising generation of grand masters of southern literature: Allen Tate, Caroline Gordon, Andrew Nelson Lytle, Robert Penn Warren, Robert Lowell, Jean Stafford, Peter Taylor. They were within the reputational circle of virtually everyone, it seemed, except the spiritual founder of Vanderbilt's Agrarian movement and the nation's preeminent Dunningite, Walter Lynwood Fleming.

Fleming died in Nashville in early August 1932, not long after the Brink-wood house party wound down.

Not that they would have found much to argue with him about. Walker and Foote were ardent Confederate partisans. Walker was a com-mitted segregationist, although Foote's belief in apartheid was wavering. Walker was so much the conservative that he rebelled against his adop-tive father's belief in FDR. The two were conjoined, however, as enthu-siasts for *Gone with the Wind* by Margaret Mitchell, whom Walker would greatly surpass as a literary artist. Surprisingly, I've not been able to document when Shelby Foote met Andrew Lytle during those long-ago summers at Sewanee. We do know they were together and jointly hon-ored at a book festival in Nashville in 1990, five years before Lytle be-came the last of the Agrarians to pass away. But they are joined forever in Civil War history, since Foote echoed Lytle's assessment of Nathan Bed-ford Forrest as the ultimate southern warrior, and went even further, putting him on the same footing as Lincoln.

That was the essence of the most wrongheaded claim that Ken Burns allowed Foote to make in editing his landmark documentary. As for what Foote might have known about the subjects of this book, the Alabama Unionists who spent months stationed in Foote's adopted hometown and burial place, we have to rely on what I've pieced together. In that regard, we know that a turning point was reached in early 1986 in a phone call between Robert Penn Warren, one of the last surviving Agrar-ians, and Ken Burns. They had met and bonded during the filming of Burns's biographical film about Huey Long, the prototype for Louisi-ana governor Willie Stark in Warren's definitive southern political novel, *All the King's Men*. Burns, then a little-known filmmaker, idolized War-ren. As Burns recalled, "He said in his wonderful Kentucky accent, 'Thinkin' about the Civil War. Thinking about, if you're gonna do it right, you have to interview Shelby Foote right away.' And that was enough for these wet-behind-the-ears novices to say, 'Okay.' So the very first frame of film exposed for the Civil War series—roll one through eight—was the first interview with Shelby Foote."

As it happened, Warren and Foote were not close. Foote, given his prickly attitude toward academic writers, felt that Warren's novels "stink too much of the lamp." But they were founding members of the Fellowship of Southern Writers, then being formed. (Walker Percy was a charter member, too.) Still having not read Foote at the time, all Burns knew was that "when Red Warren tells you what to do, you do it." At first glance, the exchange seemed nothing more than another example of the knock-on effect so common in the Deep South's tiny kingdoms. But it was not a good day for Chris Sheats.

36

THE MOUNTAIN KING

WALTER LYNWOOD FLEMING looms like forgotten royalty over higher education in the South. The Agrarian conservatives, Fugitive poets, and Confederate memorializers influenced by him at Vanderbilt founded the most important conservative intellectual movement in the twentieth-century South. His history and English PhD students set the tone at Deep South liberal arts colleges like my own, their glorification of southern gentility outstripping the influence of the more liberal Chapel Hill crowd, at least in the deepest Deep South. His scholarly legacy exists in thousands of footnotes because his 1905 pro-Klan magnum opus, *Civil War and Reconstruction in Alabama,* endured as a foundational work in national historiography, even though a few Civil War scholars began targeting him in the last decade or so—more than a century after the book came out. "Reading Fleming today provides a cold bath of retrograde racial assumptions," concluded one critic, Michael W. Fitzgerald, a professor of history at St. Olaf's College. "Fleming was the Dunning student most inclined to espouse the Klan with vigor and to celebrate its accomplishments."

Sarah Woolfolk Wiggins, a University of Alabama professor whom I interviewed shortly before her death in 2020 and herself a much-cited Reconstruction scholar, provided the explanation most frequently offered by academic historians for the astonishing longevity of Fleming's "first and most significant book": "Fleming had the courage to tackle a survey of the entire Civil War and Reconstruction period in Alabama, a feat none of the rest of us had the nerve to attempt." Despite the kind sound of her assessment, Professor Wiggins was not an apologist for the bigots in the Alabama history department. She gave me a withering critique of her longtime colleague William Stanley Hoole as a dishonest Confederate partisan and a take-no-prisoners faculty infighter.

When I survey Fleming's record as an influential force in southern graduate studies and a generational mentor, "connivance" rather than "courage" is the word that comes to mind. W. E. B. DuBois dismissed his writings as "pure propaganda." Yet Fleming has a permanent place in southern literature and American intellectual history as the dedicatee of *I'll Take My Stand,* the Agrarian manifesto published in 1930. Although he died only two years later, the book's display of the combative conservative talents of his Vanderbilt English and history departments helped nail down Fleming's standing as a rival in grooming influential scholars to Howard W. Odum (1884–1954), the University of North Carolina sociologist who exercised similar influence over graduate education in the social sciences at southern universities. Odum eventually became better known because he outlived Fleming and because Ralph McGill and other liberal southern journalists promoted his work. Even so, *I'll Take My Stand* has served ever since as a rallying point for southerners opposed to federal civil rights enforcement and social welfare programs, notwithstanding the fact that the most talented of its authors, Robert Penn Warren, renounced its racial paternalism and Confederate evangelism long before his death at eighty-four in 1989. Fleming's influence over southern pedagogy as dean of graduate studies at Vanderbilt during the takeoff of the Southern Renaissance was so formative that relatively little attention has been paid to his reactionary activism in his native state. Of greatest importance in my inquiry was his role as ally and mutual enabler of Thomas McAdory Owen in making the Alabama archives into a fortress of Rebel nostalgia for most of the twentieth century.

In fact, though, Fleming remains more of a problem for Vanderbilt and Louisiana State University than for the ADAH, which took its first steps toward modernization when Edwin Bridges took over as its first fully professional director in 1982. Vanderbilt has pretty much ignored the tainted nature of Fleming's legacy. The capsule history of Vanderbilt University on its website makes no mention of Fleming or the Agrarian/Fugitive role in the blossoming of traditionalism on the campus in the decades leading up to and following Fleming's death in 1932. LSU had a more delicate problem when it came to distancing itself from Fleming. Its annual Walter L. Fleming Lecture, established in 1936, is too important an event on the national academic awards circuit to discontinue. So it has stiff-armed Fleming, firmly but oh so delicately. The description of the series on the LSU website acknowledges that the "lectures have helped revise many of the interpretations held by historians in the 1930s, including those of Professor Fleming, on the evils of the Reconstruction era. Not without irony, then, the lectures named in his memory have come to testify to the changing nature of the southern past and southern history." As lustration statements go, that's about as tentative and obtuse as they come. Probably the Fleming Lectures are too important to LSU and the American Historical Association to either rename them or give Fleming the full rhetorical flogging his work deserves.

Being chosen to deliver the Fleming Lecture is one of the top honors for any university-based historian. Honorees have included leading names in the profession, such as Eric Foner, chief dismantler of Dunningite theory, and David Levering Lewis, who wrote of W. E. B. DuBois's confrontation with Dunning. Bad history is not easy to live with; witness the struggle of *The New York Times* to deal with the 1932 Pulitzer awarded to its Moscow bureau chief Walter C. Duranty, the Stalin apologist who covered up the Ukrainian famine engineered by the Soviet dictator. It was decided that removing his portrait from the "Hall of Pulitzers" in the old *Times* building on West 43rd Street would, in itself, amount to a cover-up. So my late colleague Al Siegal, longtime "Corrections" maven at the paper, added this legend to Duranty's portrait: "Subsequent accounts have discredited this reporting."

On the whole, Fleming has fared better, largely because his death at fifty-eight in 1932 has allowed time for his sarcastic comments on Black capability in *Civil War and Reconstruction in Alabama* to slip quietly beneath the waves of accountability. Not until 2017 did Fitzgerald's *Reconstruction in Alabama: From Civil War to Redemption in the Cotton South* appear as a specific, targeted repudiation to Fleming's scholarship. Revisionists in other Confederate states had updated racist accounts of Reconstruction, but for over a century "Fleming's book remain[ed] a starting point for scholars, despite its dated premises and factual inaccuracies." Correcting its formative influence, Fitzgerald concluded, required further study that somehow didn't happen, perhaps because of Alabama's lack of important battles and because of the importance of the Fleming Lectures as a brand name in academic honors. *Civil War and Reconstruction in Alabama* "established [Fleming] as one of the exemplars of the Dunning School," enabling him to make Vanderbilt into a kind of imperial force among southern graduate schools. Fleming's comments such as "The negro was as wax in the hands of a stronger race" became institutionalized in Alabama and account for its continuing pattern of racial gerrymandering and its poll ranking as America's most conservative state. My friend Tennant McWilliams, an authority on the University of Alabama system, described the ripple effect: "For some seventy-five years following *Civil War and Reconstruction in Alabama,* carefully controlled textbook adoptions permitted Fleming's views to dominate the teaching of economics, race, and civics in Alabama's pre-collegiate education. His influences also enjoyed iconic currency in higher education." Part of his legacy is that Zone of Exemption around the racism of southerners with the right kind of genealogical or literary credentials. Their views are excused as representing the conventional prejudices of their times, with the implication that they can be exempted from personal culpability. The failing was societal, not personal, and therefore deserved an asterisk from biographers. That overlooks the fact that Fleming and his mentor Dunning made white supremacy what a Fleming biographer called "the steel frame" of their analysis. Fleming never disavowed his "scientific racism" or denied that it was not in keeping with more enlightened opinion even while he was establishing that Arcadian realm of Confederate excuse-making encircling Nashville and Sewanee. He is a key connective figure in perpetuating the enduring brand of southern elitism so artfully recorded in Walker Percy's novels and so blatantly on display in Trump's capture of American politics.

This seems to me an apt time to explain why I have avoided the standard caveat about southern writers and intellectuals of the Civil War and Lost Cause eras—that their primitive, outdated views should not be held against them. This entire line of argument is a dodge around the fact that in slavery times—and in my own generation—privileged white southerners knew that racial bigotry was contrary to American and Judeo-Christian ideals. Thus, the theory that racist politicians, segregationist civic leaders, and biased scholars should be cut some slack because they reflected the conventional morality of their era is disingenuous. The religious literature of the Confederate states, both before and after the war, is shot through with rationalizations that betray a guilty knowledge about the falsity of slavery and Jim Crow. This accounts for the constant cherry-picking in the historical record—and the daily news—by southern conservatives for biblical snippets, constitutional phraseology, and sociological tidbits to justify mistreatment of Black people historically and in regard to the continuing systemic racism of today's majority culture.

I recall that back in the Birmingham of the 1940s and 1950s, adults had a standard defensive response for the innocent queries of children who wanted to really, really know why Black people had to be confined to shacks and tumble-down schools in neighborhoods with dirt roads and outdoor toilets. Someday things might not have to be that way, we children of segregation were told, but as for the present, "you can't legislate morality." That is to say that even segregationists always knew that the system was morally wrong for refusing to treat all God's children equally. The whole skein of lies came unwound when Dr. King's movement showed that it was unnecessary to worry about legislating white morality because Congress and the federal government could very easily legislate behavior in the public square. Reviewers of Fleming's work were quick to recognize the defensive tone in his condemnation of northern historians as a "tell" about the guilty knowledge of a southern gentry that had always known it was out of step with the national conscience. The same trait is on display in the book of the spiritual leader of the Vanderbilt/Sewanee enclave, *Lanterns on the Levee,* which is a lyrically written, unremittingly tendentious, painfully prolonged rationalization of the indefensible. The Zone of Exemption was a necessary invention because the plantation South knew it was wrong from the get-go. The same goes for their twentieth-century apologists. The idea that dead southerners deserve a dispensation because they were following community opinion may appeal—as a matter of theoretical fairness—to Yankee scholars, but since the days when William Lowndes Yancey was taunting hissing audiences in Manhattan and Boston, the white South had known it was defying humane principles. That's why the southern Episcopal bishops founded the University of the South, and that's why Walter Lynwood Fleming hit Manhattan swinging his fists in 1900.

At twenty-six, Fleming must have abashed wet-behind-the-ears Ivy League classmates as much as his "not-too-much-reconstructed" conduct amused Dunning. Fleming had been hardened by the time he spent before college picking cotton alongside his father's Black sharecroppers and by two years of service after college as an army lieutenant in the Spanish-American War. In terms of preparation for Eastern academia, his rough edges may have been sanded down, a little, by his Auburn mentor, George Petrie, who took his PhD at Johns Hopkins before it had been displaced as the leading school for Civil War studies. I came to the full amplitude of Fleming's Alabama inferiority complex through a close reading of his letters at the ADAH and the New York Public Library.

In New York, Fleming immediately and unapologetically recognized his out-of-stepness with national standards. "There is a Jap in one of my history classes & a big black n—— in the Int. Law class," he wrote Petrie. "There are several Negroes in the university." He went on to defame the women at Barnard as "not as good" as Auburn coeds. "They are the driest looking lot the sun has ever shone upon," he added. "They are so ugly they ought to study well, too." The match between the elegant Dunning, with his Hapsburg goatee, and this lank-jawed Alabamian who sometimes threatened fisticuffs in seminar arguments, could hardly have been predicted. They came out of different worlds—the leafy suburbs of New Jersey and the dusty roads of Auburn—with a kind of imperious self-confidence. Dunning, for his part, did not care about the ideological or ethical positions his protegés adopted as long as they met his standards in defending their views in their work. Also expected was a general agreement on a common assumption. According to Dunning authority John David Smith, the Old Chief's acolytes all had to swallow his theory that "considered Reconstruction a conspiracy by vindictive and power-hungry northern Republicans determined to have white Southerners, who genuinely accepted military defeat and emancipation, 'pay' for their apostasy." And that part came naturally to Fleming, one of those droll-looking Alabamians always more interested in a chance to fight than a fighting chance. When the facts did not fit this narrative, Fleming happily ignored or twisted them, which cemented his alliance with both Petrie and, more importantly for his doctoral studies, with Thomas McAdory Owen at the Alabama Department of Archives and History.

Professor Petrie, dean of the Auburn graduate school and by some accounts the first Alabamian to earn a PhD, introduced Owen and Fleming by letter just after the department moved into its original quarters in the state capitol in 1901. First in Montgomery and then while Fleming was in New York, Bankhead fed him documents for his dissertation and collected illustrations for the book version that followed in 1905. In some respects, Fleming was a cutting-edge scholar. He was one of the first to rely heavily on newspaper clippings, helping break the academic addiction to official documents. He was also a pioneer in the use of oral history, conducting personal interviews with some key players, including Union general Wager Swayne, the head of the Freedman's Bureau in Alabama, interviewing him twice (though he left out of his work anything they said that didn't fit with his views). He even talked Union general Frederick Crayton Ainsworth, the famously crusty Vermonter who was the chief custodian of the Civil War archives at the War Department in Washington, D.C., into giving him access to records from which other southerners were de facto barred. But when it came to the Klan in particular and repressive white behavior in general, Fleming was dishonest, ignoring twelve volumes of congressional testimony about KKK abuses in Alabama over the self-serving accounts of two interviewees who influenced him greatly—Ryland Randolph, the gun-slinging Klan chieftain from Tuscaloosa, and John Witherspoon DuBose, Owen's designated shaper of the ADAH war holdings into a testimonial to Confederate courage and inconsequential accomplishments. Both are thanked in the foreword to *Civil War and Reconstruction in Alabama*. As recorded earlier, Fleming referred to Owen's extensive private collection of documents that were being withheld from the official files in the capitol building. We can only guess what letters, diaries, and military accounts went up in flames when the Bankhead residence burned in 1906, shortly after the *Times* reviewed Fleming's new book as "An Alabamian's View of the Contest."

Fleming and Owen corresponded regularly between 1901 and 1912, and the surviving letters, loosely stored in undifferentiated folders at the Alabama archives, were invaluable, and not only for what I deduced about the winnowing of Unionist history in Alabama. The correspondence reminded me of what I had concluded about the mutability of evidence as a professional journalist and in decades as a sporadic but persistent recreational historian: What is believed is as important as what can be documented. In that respect, Fleming arrived in New York ready for the big time—parochial, to be sure, but in a way that made him able to rely on force of personality until he developed the charm that was his hallmark among the mannered aspiring esthetes of the Agrarian and Fugitive set at Vanderbilt. He came into Columbia as the pure essence of Alabama, whip-smart, angry, and hungry. New Yorkers tended to be shocked by the degree to which the ambition and intelligence of expatriate southerners defied the regional stereotype of lassitude. Already an astute faculty politician, Fleming had allied himself with two of his

state's best-connected intellectuals, Petrie and Owen. (A footnote in
Owen's biography notes that he regularly corresponded with about fifty
of the nation's top historians and librarians.) Fleming would soon add
the Confederacy's most prominent national apologist, Dunning, to his
list of boosters. Another graduate of Petrie's "Oasis" who became a famous historian, Frank Lawrence Owsley Sr., summed up the ambition of
these New South hustlers who would ride Old South values to academic
success both in the Ivy League and at Fleming's mountain redoubt, the
Vanderbilt/Sewanee Axis. Owsley took his PhD at Chicago, but his values were Dunningite to the core. Fleming would lure him to Vandy, then
dispatch him to Tuscaloosa as the spiritual leader of the history department's Confederate corps. Lytle might have been speaking for the entire
Vanderbilt/Sewanee claque when he said to his fellow Agrarian Allen
Tate: "The purpose of my life is to undermine by 'careful' and 'detached,' 'well-documented,' 'objective' writing, the entire Northern myth
from 1820 to 1876." Tate's monumental poem, "Ode to the Confederate
Dead," captured the Zeitgeist of Fleming's world of yesterday on the
high ground of Tennessee. In terms of its influence on white America—
not just its way of thinking but its attitude toward the Other—this group
must not be underestimated. Fleming was made to stand on Dunning's
shoulders. "Seminar discussions with Northerners were heated to the
point of potential fisticuffs, and Dunning too noted that his student
wasn't 'any too much reconstructed himself,'" according to Michael
Fitzgerald. In a department that fostered belief in John W. Burgess's
"Teutonic white supremacy," Fleming emerged as a vociferous warrior
for the white tribe, and he did not need Dunning's example to trump
facts with fiction. Fleming had barely arrived in Manhattan before he
was writing Owen and Alabama governor William Jelks for a copy of the
most racist document in Alabama—perhaps, indeed, in American—
history: the 1901 state constitution, which effectively outlawed Black
voting. (It remains in force today, guaranteeing control of state government by the corporations that succeeded plantation owners as the
oligarchs of Alabama.) "I have some rather rampant Republican ac-

quaintances to whom I want to show it. Most of them seem to think that it disfranchises at once & forever all negroes whether educated, or property owners, or not." Not so, Fleming would crow in his mendacious book. Fully 2 percent of Black males would be able to vote in Alabama. It was a view he never repudiated, even when he stood atop the pyramid of graduate education in the South.

37

Last Answer, Last Question

By 2018, after six decades of snooping in the neglected crevices of the hill country past, I still had two unanswered questions. Had Chris Sheats ever told his story to a trained historian? Why was the First Alabama Cavalry, U.S.A. still unknown to most Americans? Donald Dodd's search for the "Henderson letter" inspired me to return to the hushed study rooms of the Alabama Department of Archives and History full of optimism about new discoveries on the Free State of Winston, Chris Sheats, Colonel Spencer, and the First Alabama Cavalry, U.S.A. After all, I had never been inside its dazzling white walls without gaining at least a tidbit of knowledge. Now I knew more about where to dig and had the time to do it. Alas, there were no entries in the archives' newly digitized catalogue for any of my prime targets.

If there was to be a smoking gun as to the conspiracy to erase the First Alabama, I'd be hard-pressed to find it. But there was a consolation prize, an unindexed folder of correspondence between Thomas McAdory Owen and Walter Lynwood Fleming in those determinative years when Owen was setting up the boundaries against outsider viewpoints and Fleming was bouncing back and forth between Montgomery and New York collecting incriminating evidence about the evils of carpetbaggers, scalawags, and Black Republican voters. Their correspondence depicted a symbiotic determination to fence out critical analysis of the Confederate era in Alabama's official records and historical texts. They exchanged letters regularly for the first decade of the twentieth century, and the mood-capturing epistolary capstone was penned on June 12, 1907, by Tom Owen. He had just read an essay by the ambitious Fleming in *The Dial,* a respected review published sporadically across the course of nine decades ending in 1929. In a tone of friendly correction, Owen pointed out two errors in the piece. One was that he had left out the *t* in the surname of Confederate general Joseph E. Johnston. The other was in the use of the term "ex-Confederate." "In my humble judgment the prefix 'ex' ought never to be used anywhere, certainly not in connection with anything Confederate." It seemed not to have occurred to Owen that *Dial* copy editors could be at fault, but both men surely knew they were on the same page as to what needed to be inserted in and left out of the Civil War canon. They conspired intimately about how Owen could use his influence with the legislature to purchase copies of Fleming's book for Alabama schools. Owen wanted to know how much he could discount the $5.00 cover price. Fleming inquired repeatedly about Colonel DuBose and Ryland Randolph, his two principal sources on Klan violence. Was it possible, Fleming wanted to know, that Randolph could supply a secret copy of Klan precepts?

The correspondence showed both men had a grasp of Unionist leaders in the state. They were working together to secure photographs of them for Fleming's book. Owen had located a usable if rather unsatisfactory portrait of Jeremiah Clemens. Fleming reported that he would send to Owen's collection an excellent steel engraving of Colonel Spencer that he had located at the War Department. And after Fleming gained access to Ainsworth's War Department archives, Owen wrote to him on March 5, 1902, to say, "I congratulate you on your successful attack upon the archives of the War Department." He signed himself, "Your friend."

With repeated references to the twelve volumes of congressional testimony on the Klan, Fleming showed he was well familiar with evidence given by and about Chris Sheats, though it would be fulsomely misrepresented in his book. By requesting Owen's correspondence, I found a folder of incoming letters in Fleming's flowery handwriting and typewritten transcriptions of the director's dictated replies that amounted to a diary of their research strategies. One dated January 7, 1903, started out as a routine update on their successful campaign to lure Dunning to Montgomery, but then what I read made my jaw drop:

> *Dear Mr. Fleming:*
> *I am indebted to you for several favors, with sundry notices*
> *concerning the recent meeting of the American Historical*
> *Association. I thank you for your attention. I am delighted that*
> *the association will come to New Orleans for its next meeting, and*
> *you may depend upon it that we will have several representatives*
> *from Alabama.*
>
> *I shall use your queries in the coming number of the Gulf*
> *States Historical Magazine. It may interest you to know that Mr.*
> *C. C. Sheats is living in Decatur. You will find a sketch of him in*
> *"Northern Alabama Illustrated."*
>
> *I have been very closely engaged for weeks now on my Official*
> *publications, hence have been unable to do very little general*
> *work. The State Legislature convenes next week, and I expect it to*
> *treat the Department kindly. If I can serve you further at any*
> *time command me.*

The letter was signed "Yours faithfully."

Discovering this document was one of the most exciting moments in a lifetime of investigative reporting and public-records research. It meant that somewhere in the ADAH files or in Fleming's correspondence at the New York Public Library there might be proof that the historian had traveled to Decatur and interviewed Sheats. If he had done so and still libeled and shortchanged him in *Civil War and Reconstruction in Alabama,* that would be my smoking gun of belligerent intent and collusion by Fleming and probably his enablers, Thomas and Marie Owen, to exclude information they knew to exist. And what if Fleming had left notes of what Sheats actually said about his life and career?

The timing for such a meeting with Sheats was perfect. I knew from elsewhere in the correspondence that Fleming had spent the summer of 1903 in Auburn and Montgomery. Writing from his alma mater at Auburn on Columbia letterhead, he asked for Owen's help on citations and for Colonel DuBose to critique some of his chapters. He also wanted help in getting from the Wisconsin archives some documents relating to activities in Alabama of the Knights of the White Camellia, a smaller terrorist group that claimed to have a more elite membership than the Klan. Fleming apologized for missing Owen in a drop-by visit to the archives, but that showed that north Alabama was still on his research radar. He asked Owen about securing for him the White Camellia document from Wisconsin archives. Knights of the White Camellia was a white supremacists terrorist organization that claimed to have an upper-class membership. "Do you suppose they would make a copy of [the Wisconsin document] for the Dept Archives & History for a reasonable amount. I should be willing to pay something to get the use of the thing. . . . The KK seem to have held forth in North Ala & the Camellia in Central and So. Ala."

I can't show, however, that Fleming's curiosity drew him north that summer to talk to Sheats at Decatur, which is 175 miles from Montgomery and was easily reachable by train. We know that Owen had no qualms about asking Alabama railroad executives for free passes for relatives and friends, so transportation would likely have been no problem for Fleming. We can also surmise that Sheats, who would live for another seventeen months after Fleming learned of his whereabouts, would hardly have been in a position to dodge a visit, and he was not hiding out. Indeed, he was known statewide in his last years by the unearned honorific "Colonel," probably because of his Grant administration appointments in Denmark and the port of Mobile, his service in Congress, his election as mayor of Decatur, and his financially successful law practice in that city. He married a younger woman and lived grandly for a time in a mansion there.

His press coverage was mixed but generally friendly in tone, even to the point of hometown exaggeration. The *Decatur Weekly News* even contended, on scant evidence, that he "was one time slated as a nominee for vice president, but by some mysterious manipulation of the wise workers in the national convention he was sidetracked and Chester A. Arthur was nominated." That claim was erroneous, as was another report that he had once been elected governor of Alabama but was "counted out" by corrupt ballot officials. But the point stands that he was not an easy man to ignore or a difficult one to find in his last months.

In a display of political agility, Sheats was on friendly terms with two Confederate heroes. In 1896, he endorsed for reelection to Congress the same "Fighting Joe" Wheeler whose troops had pursued Sheats across north Alabama when he was lying out in the caves and recruiting the initial volunteers for the First Alabama. When Sheats fell on hard times in his last years another famous Rebel general, U.S. senator Edmund W. Pettus (1821–1907), a "fearless and dogged fighter" against Sherman in the Atlanta campaign, came to his aid. He was also Grand Dragon of the terrorist group that assaulted Sheats in 1868, and his success as a Klan organizer led to his election to the Senate in 1896. According to *Generals in Gray*, he was "the last of the Confederate brigadiers to sit in the upper house." In that role, he was able to secure a federal pension for his old adversary, and he had the political clout to withstand grumpy coverage in the Republican-leaning Moulton, Alabama, *Advertiser* of March 27, 1902.

> Christopher Columbus Sheets [*sic*] has been put on the pension list, and now draws a salary of $30.00 per month. Senator Pettus, in making the arrangement, said, "The beneficiary is a very old man, and was late a recruiting officer of the U.S. army in the civil war." [The pension] is news to us, and we regard it as an injustice to the brave federal soldiers who are now receiving only about $10.00 per month.

Sheats' s death was statewide news. It ran in thirty-six-point type in a two-column headline in *The Birmingham News:*

SUDDEN DEATH OF COL SHEATS;
NOTED CHARACTER IN ALABAMA

(The "noted character" language made the Jasper *Mountain Eagle* obituary and was picked up repeatedly in other dailies.)

Col. C. C. Sheats was found dead in bed at his home in Decatur last Thursday morning. He had been in bad health for some time and has been unable to walk for several months. Col. Sheats was a noted character of Alabama.

He was one of the members of the cesession [*sic*] convention who voted against Alabama going out of the Union. He was raised in Winston county and at one time was United States minister to Denmark. He was, shortly after the war, elected governor of the state but was counted out.

Formally [*sic*] he owned valuable property in Decatur, but died a pauper in a hovel on Bank street. One of the handsomest residences in the city was his, but he willed it to his wife, who recently died, and who obtained a divorce from him some time ago.

Audacity and doggedness were among Fleming's traits as an academic politician, and in a way, one had to admire his effort—successful in the long term—to use a book published only a few months after Sheats's death to make sure the old Unionist would be not only gone but forgotten in later decades, culminating in his omission from Shelby Foote's narrative history of the Civil War. Old foes like Wheeler and Pettus might coddle Sheats, but that was not Fleming's style. It will be recalled that Fleming described how a single incident of Klan intimidation left Sheats "a changed man," implying that he was too scared to play a prominent role as a Scalawag leader in Reconstruction—a complete misrepresentation of the last thirty-six years of Sheats's career, which was ending as Fleming published his enduring book of Lost Cause propaganda.

But not even Fleming's dominance at Vanderbilt could escape the long, ironic reach of Alabama connectivity. In 2019, his university hired the African American author Caroline Randall Williams as its writer-in-residence. In a *New York Times* op-ed, she revealed that Senator Pettus was her great-great-grandfather, noting that "the black people I come from were owned and raped by the white people I come from." In June 2020, MSNBC reported her call for the Edmund Pettus Bridge in Selma to be renamed for Congressman John W. Lewis, the civil rights leader beaten there by Alabama troopers on March 9, 1965. In a statement she said, "We name things after honorable Americans to commemorate their legacies. That bridge is named after a treasonous American who cultivated and prospered from systems of degradation and oppression before and after the Civil War. We need to rename the bridge because we need to honor an American hero, a man who made that bridge a place worth remembering. John Lewis secured that bridge's place on the right side of history."

Not all accounts can be settled so categorically. Witness Ken Burns's reliance on Shelby Foote's vision of postbellum reality.

38

THE CUTTING ROOM FLOOR

THE USUALLY EBULLIENT Ken Burns was clearly feeling beat up when I called him on August 19, 2019, to ask a question that had never been put to him. Why had the First Alabama Cavalry, U.S.A. not made it into his Civil War documentary? The omission seemed especially odd to me since the militarily inconsequential Free State of Jones, a county in Shelby Foote's native Mississippi, had been accorded pride of place among southern Unionists.

Burns's initial sensitivity to my inquiries seemed understandable. The 2015 rerelease of Burns's documentary by PBS—intended as a twenty-fifth-anniversary celebration of triumphant television storytelling—had instead unleashed a tidal wave of revisionist commentary, some of it focusing on the disproportionate airtime (some eighty-nine sound bites) granted to Foote's reminiscences. The lordly-looking Mississippi novelist/historian had provided a charismatic anchor to a version of the Civil War that has since come to be seen as overly kind to the Confederacy. "He was oral bourbon," said one grateful southerner. The historian Michael Beschloss may have sensed a put-down of Lincoln in Foote's description of him as "unfettered by any need for being or not being a gentleman."

Burns felt he had been falsely accused of "antiquated Lost Cause views." He protested published accounts that suggested he had been "seduced by a racist Southerner who charmed me with his accent." But despite this reversal in critical attention, Burns was forthcoming in our conversation as to the question of the First Alabama.

Had he ever heard of the regiment? He answered unequivocally, "No, and I would have put it in significantly" if that had been the case. To confirm Burns's account, I conferred with the two co-authors who had done most of the screenwriting for the documentary. They had impressive resumes. One was Ken Burns's brother Ric, himself an accomplished filmmaker who had visited me at *The New York Times* in connection with his documentary about Eugene O'Neill. The other was Geoffrey C. Ward, a former editor of *American Heritage* magazine and winner of the National Book Critics Circle Award for his 1989 biography of Franklin D. Roosevelt. Both responded with genial surprise when I told them about the First Alabama. "For heaven's sake," Ric Burns exclaimed. "I never knew any of this." Ward, winner of seven Emmy Awards for historical scripts, could afford to be self-deprecating. He laughed when I asked why they had left the First Alabama out of both the broadcast and print versions of the work he did with the Burns brothers. "Just pure ignorance," he said. "You know, I mean, I knew there were Unionist southerners, vaguely. That would be my answer. And it's my ignorance. It's not even Ken's because he relies on me for a lot of this stuff."

The consistent response from this trio raised two tantalizing and essential questions. Did Shelby Foote know about the existence of the First Alabama? If so, did he purposely keep Burns's team in the dark about this gem of a sideshow drama? "Absolutely not," Burns told me on the second question.

But I still wondered: Was his confidence in the wily Mississippian misplaced?

To try to sort out the matter, I turned to a University of the South graduate who is now the leading historian in the Nashville/Sewanee Axis, Jon Meacham. No one has better current credentials in that world. As a literature student in Sewanee's class of 1991, he was tapped to drive the last Fugitive, the aging Andrew Lytle, to dine with old friends in Nashville. Meacham's grandfather had roomed with Lytle at Vanderbilt in the 1920s (those southern connections again). After he won a Pulitzer in 2009 for his biography of Andrew Jackson and emerged as a leading critic of the Trump presidency on MSNBC's cutting-edge Washington news show *Morning Joe,* Vanderbilt named him the Carolyn T. and Robert M. Rogers Chair in American Presidency. Meacham has the kind of prestige once enjoyed on that campus by Walter L. Fleming, but their takes on southern history could hardly be more different.

Jon and I were somewhat connected, too. He had chosen my article "Grady's Gift" for his 2001 anthology of civil rights journalism, *Voices in Our Blood: America's Best of the Civil Rights Movement.* Although twenty-six years apart in age, we had traveled similar paths to the Eastern media world. While I was executive editor of *The New York Times,* he became the youngest-ever editor in chief of *Newsweek.* Jon, a devout Episcopalian, and I, a social-gospel Methodist in college, were greatly influenced by the civil rights movement, and individually, each of us had a sense of wonder about growing up in an unusually hybridized Deep South way. I straddled the worlds of segregated Birmingham and the vestigial Unionist hill country. Jon was reared near the Lookout Mountain battlefield and lived eight hundred yards from Braxton Bragg's headquarters. But he roamed a park that had monuments to Illinois and Wisconsin troops and General Sherman. His own experience at Sewanee "was more Trollope than Lost Cause," but the Confederate ambiance was still strong at this favorite college of the plantation gentry. "It was tough up there. The War was still being romanticized. The Kappa Alpha fraternity still had the portrait of Lee in the house," he told me. "For a boy from Chattanooga who grew up on Missionary Ridge I am amazed all the time—particularly in this climate, as I think back—that I wasn't more caught up with that."

Would southerners who escaped the dark and weighty part of our regional legacy have been better equipped than Ken Burns to cope with Shelby Foote's gray-ghost theatricality? I could tell the filmmaker sensed that many of his newly emerged critics believed his noble project to in-

form the American public about our defining national trauma had been
compromised by a guileful old Confederate apologist. For my part, I am
sympathetic about what happened to Burns and his brother when they
set up their cameras in Foote's study in Memphis in April 1986. As earnest northerners who had grown up on the liberal University of Michigan campus, they were not prepared culturally, in my view, for the
exculpatory subtexts of a performance that had been decades in preparation and echoed in all those long, bourbon-soaked rehearsals atop the
mountain at Sewanee with master spinners associated with Andrew
Lytle, Allen Tate, Will Percy, and the most prominent Alabamian among
the Agrarians, Frank Lawrence Owsley Sr.

Meacham and Burns mutually admire each other, so I put the same
question to both. Had Shelby Foote hijacked Burns's project? Meacham
responded energetically, "Oh yeah, oh yeah. I mean, most people remember it because of him. I think Ken had television gold in front of
him. [It] was right there."

If so, Burns and Foote paid a steep price in slings and arrows. Burns
is still regarded as the premier documentary auteur of his generation.
The initial run of *The Civil War* brought critical accolades, praise from
a southern president, and a record public television audience of forty
million. It also made a national celebrity of Shelby Foote. It was almost
as if no one was listening to the subtext of the Delta honey-dripper. The
message had filtered through from Foote's three-part narrative history of
the Civil War. "Really, what the trilogy is, it is the world according to
Jefferson Davis," Meacham said, and this piercing observation came
from the scholar who edited a promotional monograph for Random
House awarding Foote the title of the "American Homer." It's an essay
collection that is balanced by some telling criticisms of Foote's soft focus
on Rebel morality, including the comment that there is nothing in the
three books "a white Southern readership would find objectionable."
Still, the overall flavor of *American Homer: Reflections of Shelby Foote
and His Classic "The Civil War: A Narrative"* is laudatory. It begins
with Meacham's introductory observation that Burns's "epic film" grew
from an "enormously influential collaboration" between the filmmaker

and Foote. "By the time of Foote's death in Memphis in 2005, he was one of the most iconic American writers," Meacham wrote. Jay Tolson, editor of Foote's correspondence with Walker Percy, said he had overshadowed the less favored narrators in the program to become a "bardic figure." That was a huge payoff for a middling novelist who could never throw off Faulkner's influence.

Those chickens started coming home to roost after 2015 when PBS aired a celebratory silver-anniversary rebroadcast of the entire series. The Black Lives Matter movement had started in 2013. Then came the murder of George Floyd following a gusher of pro-Confederate, anti-Black statements from President Trump. Reappraisals flowed from a new generation of scholars and journalists. The debunking efforts had actually started earlier among heavyweight scholars like Eric Foner, who had doubts about the project dating back to November 1986, when Burns invited a blue-ribbon panel of twenty-four historians to Washington, D.C., to discuss his project. No one who attended forgot how heated it became, in part because Marxist historians urged a radical corrective to the Dunning tradition. Burns's most eminent ally, C. Vann Woodward of Yale, then nearing eighty, helped calm the meeting with an emotional give-the-young-man-a-chance plea to the prickly commentators from the history-teaching establishment. I found the meeting noteworthy for another reason: No one seems to have brought up the subject of southern Unionism. What better demonstration could there be that the First Alabama Cavalry had been written out of the historical mainstream?

Eric Foner, irritated that he was listed as a consultant on the entire project simply because he had attended the 1986 meeting with Woodward and others, contributed to a debunking essay collection entitled *Ken Burns's The Civil War: Historians Respond* by Robert Brent Toplin. Foner summed up his criticism by saying, "Faced with a choice between historical illumination or nostalgia, Burns consistently opts for nostalgia." James M. Lundberg, a historian at the University of Notre Dame, addressed Burns directly in a 2011 *Slate* article, "Thanks a Lot, Ken Burns." Wrote Lundberg, "Because of you, my Civil War lecture is always packed—with students raised on your sentimental, romantic, deeply misleading portrait of the conflict."

But that was mild compared to the critical assault during the Trump years. A *Washington Post* headline, "Re-watching 'The Civil War' During the Breonna Taylor and George Floyd Protests," captured the spirit of major editorial and op-ed pages and the revisionist reviews. "While still giving credit where it's due," the article said, "scholars have spent three decades trying to undo the damage of 'The Civil War,' writing op-ed after op-ed, and even whole books of criticism, charging large sections of it are misleading and inaccurate." The fact that Burns's work garnered forty filmmaking and broadcast awards after its original five-night telecast seemed not to matter once the critics got Burns's treatment of Foote in their sights. Professor Lundberg weighed in again, telling the *Post*, "You really get the feeling that Burns, for all his incredible gifts as a filmmaker, he really kind of fell in love with Shelby Foote."

Some of the criticisms seemed over the top to me, but it's obvious the work had not aged well. "Seeing Shelby on that program now is difficult, because so much has changed in the last thirty years," Jon Meacham told me in 2020. In a related conversation a year later, he added, "You could not make that film today."

Foote's approach in his trilogy infused the film because he was given so much airtime. He focused on battlefield heroics and large personalities. The work was "light on politics," serving the venerable Lost Cause tactic of drawing the curtain of states' rights over the sins of slavery. "When it comes to writing the war trilogy," Meacham said, "if you want to put those books in a time capsule to say this is how most southern and border state white people viewed the Civil War, you could do no better."

A number of critics shared my surprise that Burns aired Foote's observation that Nathan Bedford Forrest ranked with Lincoln as a genius. Harvard history professor Annette Gordon-Reed noted "Foote's admiration (love?) for the notorious" villain of the Fort Pillow Massacre. When I raised the subject with Burns during our conversation, he said he was a "storyteller" and suggested that reining in Foote would have amounted to a kind of censorship: "This is part of the tyranny of a specific historiography which is that it then does not permit any other perspective to obtain." Burns pointed out to me that the film had described Fort Pillow as an atrocity, and he suggested that the Forrest-Lincoln passage could be seen as depicting an almost childlike awe on Foote's part. It certainly captured what Meacham called "the performative Foote." That aptly describes the clip. Here was a professional southerner acting out his stereotype with gleeful flourishes.

> Bedford Forrest's granddaughter lived here in Memphis. She recently died. I got to know her and she even let me swing the general's sword around my head once, which was a great treat. I had thought a long time and I had called her and said, "I think that the war produced two authentic geniuses. One of them was your grandfather and the other was Abraham Lincoln." And there was silence at the other end of the phone and she said, "Well, you know, in our family we never thought much of Mr. Lincoln." She didn't like me coupling her grandfather with Abraham Lincoln all those years later. Southerners are very strange about the war.

"No, no, no!" Burns said when I asked if he agreed with Foote's controversial comparison of Lincoln and Forrest as the two great geniuses of the war. I wanted to know if the comment caused his radar to flare up during the interview. He replied, "No. That's just Shelby." Burns made a fair comparison between his profession and mine at a time when the news media allows for the repeated reporting of crazy comments and verifiable lies. "History and journalism share many genetic similarities. We listen and we put stuff in." It's a circular debate, but I have to say that allowing the film's star to portray the Confederacy's most sociopathic general as an admirable military figure seems inconsistent with the concept of corrective archaeology. It is consistent, however, with the "Wizard of the Saddle" image established as a Lost Cause trope by no less a figure than Meacham's mentor Andrew Lytle, with his worshipful biography *Bedford Forrest and His Critter Company*. We don't know exactly how much Foote and Lytle interacted. They appeared together at a literary event in 1990, but by that time Foote's interviews were in the can and awaiting broadcast. We also know that Percy's literary salon at Brink-wood was minutes away from Lytle's log cabin home in the Monteagle Assembly, a compound of summer homes for elite Episcopalians. It's a high-gloss environment, and as *American Homer* puts it, "the Percy salon fundamentally shaped Foote" and his decision to become a writer.

Provocatively, Andrew Lytle was one of the few Agrarians who knew anything about the Free State of Winston. Another was the abovemen-tioned Frank Lawrence Owsley Sr., the fellow Agrarian who was as militant a Confederate cheerleader as Lytle and went on to cement the pro-Confederate hegemony in the University of Alabama history de-partment. My hillbilly guru, Donald Dodd, was one of the few trained historians to follow this bouncing ball of connectivity. In describing the remoteness of Winston County in his Civil War book, Dodd quoted a passage from Lytle's 1936 novel *The Long Night,* about a disenchanted Confederate named Pleasant McIvor. Sickened by the carnage in Ten-nessee, he has decided to desert and also to abandon his quest for re-venge against the men who killed his father in the Black Belt before the war. Lytle imagined the ruminations of this Alabamian about the ideal hideout, and the novel ends with a lyrical invocation of the county's dra-matic landscape.

> Far to the south the hills of Winston rose close and stubborn out of the lowlands. The hills of Winston. It was no long journey to a man who knew the way, who had lost every other way. There he would go. There, in the secret coves, far away from the world and vengeance, a deserter might hide forever.

Although Lytle always presented himself as a man of Tennessee, I learned from his autobiography, *A Wake for the Living,* that his Nelson relatives had founded Murfreesboro, Tennessee. He was born there, but during Andrew's boyhood his father bought two thousand acres near Guntersville, Alabama, and allowed his son to name the new plantation. "I named the place Cornsilk. No place have I loved as much," Lytle wrote. Then came an event that probably fed the intense hatred that he and the other conservatives felt for the federal government—the "Leviathan," as one of them called it. "During the Depression the TVA drowned the place under waters," Lytle wrote. "Since that time I have felt in exile."

Late in my research, I learned that, like me, Lytle was a straddler of southern cultures, but he had taken a very different ideological turn. He had absorbed his reverence for the Confederacy as an adolescent at the Sewanee Military Academy. (William Alexander Percy's parents had sent him there in hopes of curing his effeminacy. Percy became a passionate fan of *I'll Take My Stand* and in 1932 received a copy autographed by six of the twelve southerners who wrote it, probably including Lytle.) But Lytle also became a student of the obdurate Scots-Irish clans of Alabama and lower Appalachia. The mix was reflected in his Monteagle home, which hosted Sunday afternoon drinking sessions and toasts to the Confederacy to which invitations were coveted. The large cabin has peeled logs on the outside, but it was furnished plantation style, with oil portraits and on the sideboard silver goblets for the W. L. Weller bourbon. As an aspiring writer, he had composed most of *The Long Night* at Cornsilk. Studying maps, I discovered that Cornsilk was only sixty miles from my grandparents' farm at Arley. This meant that he spent much of his youth in Unionist country. Cornsilk was in Marshall County. Only one county, Cullman, stood between it and Winston. All three sent men to the First Alabama Cavalry.

The provenance of *The Long Night* touched on Winston, too. Donald Dodd's footnotes tipped me off that there was a tie between Lytle and Owsley in regard to Winston lore. Pleasant McIvor was based on the uncle of Frank Lawrence Owsley Sr., the most passionate Yankee-hater among the Agrarians. ("The purpose of my life," he wrote to a colleague in 1932, "is to undermine . . . the entire Northern myth from 1820 to 1876.") In 1935, he told Lytle the story of his uncle Dink's pilgrimage to Winston, and Lytle quickly converted that account into the novel written one county over from Winston. Owsley's own story helps us understand how the Dunning influence infiltrated the South. He left my alma mater, Birmingham-Southern College, in 1920 for Vanderbilt, where he was hired by Walter L. Fleming, Dunning's most powerful emissary to the Deep South. In 1949, the University of Alabama scored a coup by stealing this Agrarian author to start its new graduate program for the training of PhDs in the style Fleming had absorbed at Columbia and installed at Vanderbilt. In the 1920s, Owsley had taken his doctorate under a Jeffersonian liberal, William E. Dodd, at the University of Chicago, but he was alienated by Dodd's criticism of plantation economics and the slave-owning class. He rejected Dodd's skepticism about the Confederacy with an Alabama ferocity that resembled Fleming's, and he became a brother-in-arms to the Dunningites.

Lytle had not only come of age amid Alabama's strongest Unionist counties, he had absorbed the essence of Winston exceptionalism. *The Long Night* opens with Pleasant McIvor's visit to a long-lost uncle who lived in a Winston pocket canyon that "had the air of a feudal retreat an outlaw might well defend indefinitely." In Lytle's telling, the guide who had agreed to take him there, but abandoned him partway, mirrored the contempt of plantation masters for Free Staters. He pointed out the trail to the uncle's hideaway and said, "If you stumble off the way, ask a fox or a crow to set you right. Them's the only smart critters you'll run into up thar."

Once Donald Dodd's footnotes put me on the trail of this vociferous pair, I became determined to find out what Shelby Foote might have learned from Lytle and Owsley on "The Mountain," the literary world at Sewanee in which they were so prominent. Their overlapping influences made me believe that Foote probably had been exposed to the lore of Alabama Unionism in general and the First Alabama in particular. But the testimony of the Burns brothers and Ward had convinced me that whatever Foote had learned on the subject, he had withheld it from them. As Civil War experts, they would have been too steeped in the subject matter to have forgotten such a piquant detail if Foote had mentioned it. But I had no evidence, such as a "smoking letter," to close the case as to what Foote knew and when he knew it.

Instead I found a "smoking book." In 1969, John Carr, a literature student at Hollins College, taped an interview with Foote. He included the transcription in *Kite-Flying and Other Irrational Acts: Conversations with Twelve Southern Writers,* a collection he edited for LSU Press. As the author of an oral history, I perceived Carr as a well-prepared interviewer with a saucy touch. Like Foote, he grew up in the Delta, and in introducing Foote, he told readers that "one of the things you have to understand about the Delta is its enthusiastic and malicious parochialism." I was impressed that he got Foote to acknowledge that Forrest had had no strategic impact on the war's outcome. Foote said of "the various victories he won, none . . . was of any value whatsoever except that they were victories." Seemingly out of the blue, Carr told Foote that in preparing for the interview, he had discovered there were Union troops from the two Mississippi counties closest to the Battle of Shiloh, which Foote had researched for a novel.

"What did you find out about dissident Southerners?" Carr asked.

"I found a whole belt of dissident Southerners right along the lower reaches of the Appalachians," Foote responded. "It comes down through the end of Tennessee down into northern Alabama and peters out in northern Mississippi. There were a lot of Union-loyal Alabamians, for instance, along that range of hills, and they rode with Streight on his raid through there."

So there it was at last. The words "rode with Streight" proved Foote had to have known about the First Alabama Cavalry, U.S.A. Their presence on Streight's Raid was their claim to fame even before Sherman adopted them as his guides and camp companions. In regard to the raid, the First appears in the *Official Records,* which Foote claimed was his main source. At first, finding this interview filled me with a happy feeling of discovery. Of course Foote had had to know about these Alabamians who were organized between the two towns where he spent most of his life and within a few miles of the battles he knew best, Shiloh in 1863 and Brice's Cross Roads on June 10, 1864. The latter was one of the Forrest "victories" Foote researched. At one time he was going to write an entire book about it. Surely he had to have known that the First Alabama Cavalry was involved in screening actions in the months leading up to that battle. Also, in studying the battle as closely as he did, Foote had surely discovered that freed slaves from Alabama in the First Alabama Infantry Africa Descent had put a blemish on Forrest's "victory." The Black soldiers disrupted his hero's pursuit of the fleeing Union forces back toward Memphis. *Alabamians in Blue* reported that this unit of the U.S. Colored Troops earned "unanimous praise in preventing the retreat from becoming a rout."

In closing the loop on Foote and the Alabamians he ignored, I had to admit that I had originally developed a theory of the case that was unfair to Ken Burns. I had started out believing that Foote must have talked Burns out of including the First Alabama in the film. It would have been consistent with Foote's Mississippi chauvinism. If he had to describe "disloyal" southerners, at least they could be from his own state. I also knew that Foote was one of those southerners who could, as the saying goes, talk a dog off a meat wagon. Now, armed with my research, I have a different theory of the case. Foote did know about the patriots of the Alabama hills. But he didn't convey that knowledge for a very specific reason. He realized that if he told Burns about the First Alabama, they would not wind up on the cutting room floor of Burns's studio. So he simply did not share what he had learned about Sherman's Alabamians, who were closing in on Atlanta while the "genius" Forrest engaged in his meaningless exploits in Mississippi.

In the long view, Ken Burns's trust in Foote arose from what my historian classmate Tennant McWilliams calls the "interpersonal connectivity that makes history fascinating." Burns was sent to Foote by Robert Penn Warren, the best of the Agrarian writers and the first to reject Lost Cause racism. Also, Foote had known William Faulkner, the utmost star in the Old South constellation, since he and Walker Percy had showed up uninvited at Rowan Oak as eighteen-year-olds and were welcomed. Later Foote and Faulkner would cruise Greenville together, sharing a bottle of whiskey. Foote was a regular at the Percys' summer salon at Sewanee. No one in his generation had better literary connections, but in fact, the bard of Oxford had a cautious reaction to Foote. He saw Foote's imitation of Faulknerian rhetoric as the major obstacle to the younger man becoming a great writer. He "told friends he would like Foote better if he sounded less like Faulkner."

Ken Burns's susceptibility to Foote's credentials and his spin is understandable. Arriving in Memphis when he was thirty-three years old, Burns had just released his film on Huey Long and knew about the Kingfish's undereducated populist South, the poor folks' Dixie. But what he encountered on Foote's side of the Mississippi River was the gauzier, highly burnished version of southern history that came to dominate his film—the privileged white folks' view of the Confederacy's doomed courage. In that version, the First Alabama Cavalry had always been on the cutting room floor, thanks to the minions of Jubal Early, the Owens, and their friend William Archibald Dunning.

A man as gregarious as Foote couldn't help but reveal himself some of the time. In the end, my habit of searching footnotes and bibliographies for books or articles I might have missed paid off. Foote had come clean in interviews collected in *Conversations with Shelby Foote,* a 1989 publication from the University Press of Mississippi. The questions were mostly softballs, but Foote seemed compelled to ponder the new bestselling life that Ken Burns had made possible. He had even called Burns to thank the filmmaker for making him a millionaire.

He believed there was a "chasm" between the uplanders despised by William Alexander Percy and the high-toned plantation class of the Delta. "As far as my Civil War is concerned there are serious gaps in it," he said in 1973. "I left things out on purpose." For example, he said, he had ignored the shaky finances of the Confederate government because they were "not important to MY story of the war." Clearly, he believed disloyal Alabamians were similarly dismissible. He added that "professional historians are going to be able to point out shortcomings" in his work but that "it doesn't bother me."

But the gap about the First Alabama did bother me. I had been put on the trail of its untold story under the shade of an elm tree in the backyard of a grandmother born only six years after the war ended. I could not have put together the entire story without the active and growing school of Civil War scholars who are younger than I by a generation or more. I stand on the shoulders of Grandma Raines and on theirs as well. Their work shows that truth can eventually leak out of the seams of "accepted" history. It also shows the long reach of omissions, distortions, and subterfuges like those nurtured in the Alabama Department of Archives and History. We are still not out of the long shadow of the Dunning School and *Gone with the Wind,* as the wannabe neo-Confederate from New York City showed us while he was president.

All these complications proceed from a singular fact about Civil War historiography, and it seems fitting to have it stated by the man who made Shelby Foote a millionaire and offered him, whether earned or not, an exculpatory elegy as well. "In most of history," Ken Burns said, "the story of the past is written by the victors but Southerners wrote our history—Southerners like Shelby who felt the tragedy of it all, the blood and the sacrifice and the human toll from Ford's Theatre to Grant's tent to Forrest's Critter Company. That was his story, and ours."

39

FORGOTTEN, BUT NOT GONE

OVER TIME, I have learned to think of the Alabama archives as being like the box of chocolates described by Forrest Gump's indomitable mother, the sage of Greenbow, Alabama. You never know what you are going to pull out. When I made a fact-checking visit to Montgomery on February 11, 2022, Steve Murray, the ADAH director, gave me the newly completed initial folder listings for the collected papers of Tom Owen and Miss Marie. There were thirty-eight boxes for him and twenty-four boxes for her. The effort to codify the papers began with Murray's predecessor, Ed Bridges, when he inherited "the sea" in the attic of the ADAH in 1982. Murray, who succeeded Bridges in 2012, had just completed the task of organizing the papers by topic.

Before the arrival of these two trained professionals, the collection was a midden heap of paper and artifacts. Prior to their regimes, the ADAH had been run by a series of gossipy amateurs with good political connections—a description that fit the Owens, whose footprints endure in the director's office, literally. The original carpet installed by Tom Owen more than a century ago is still in place in the high-ceilinged, paneled office, and Murray showed me the bare spots where they had slid their feet under their desks, which were across from each other.

Returning from the printer that had just spit out the newly constructed listings, Murray said, "No one has ever been through their papers." Although curators were now reading those documents systematically, Murray's words dampened my hopes of someone finding a "smoking gun" letter or notes that would show that Fleming had blown off Owen's suggestion about finding Chris Sheats or, alternatively, that he had visited the old patriot and left some record. No matter how biased, anything Fleming wrote would have been an invaluable addition to Alabama's documentary cache. But the task of reading this material page by page will take years. There is as yet no alphabetical listing of all the individual correspondence in the dozens of boxes devoted to the Owens' personal and official letters. Similarly, H. A. M. Henderson's spy report on Chris Sheats's speech at Looney's Tavern—the eyewitness account that eluded Don Dodd—could be tucked in there, waiting for some future scholar to get lucky.

On the last visits that my grandson Jasper and I made to the ADAH, Tom and/or Marie, those arch-censors of Alabama's story, reached across the years to remind us that they might still surprise us. We experienced an odd piece of luck in the research room just down the corridor, the room featuring a portrait of Marie Bankhead Owen looking like Queen Victoria. Steve Murray had crafted for the portrait a new plaque that serves as a symbolic end to her reign of error and exclusion. It says: "Marie Bankhead Owen was an anti-suffragist and legislative chair of a group opposed to ratification of the 19th Amendment. Owen believed that the right to vote should be governed by state law because federal protection would lead to increased voting by African Americans." In a sense, though, her crusade for a changeless Alabama has not ended in the white-domed capitol visible from her old office. In her day, legislators there had trembled at news that the "Tiger Woman" was coming across the street to do battle against the Nineteenth and Fifteenth Amendments. As I write, their successors are supporting the Republican Party's nationwide crusade to limit minority voting and signing up by the dozen to outlaw the teaching of critical race theory in Alabama educational institutions. With an outspokenness rare in Montgomery in any century, Steve Murray has warned that the legislation would cripple the teaching of history in Alabama's schools from kindergarten through the twelfth grade by making teachers liable for "offending" anyone's racial views.

In early February 2022, Jasper arrived in Montgomery after the end of Friday classes at the University of South Alabama, and we prepared to devote the next day to a final search for archival tidbits. In 2018 I had lucked into the Owen-Fleming correspondence but failed to find anything useful on Chris Sheats, Colonel George Spencer, the First Alabama Cavalry, U.S.A., or even Confederate general Philip Dale Roddey, the "Defender of North Alabama." I wanted Jasper to use his superior computer skills to search for something I might have missed or to reveal any updating of the catalogue. He joined me at the archives the next morning, where his assignment was to revisit the catalogue searches I had made in 2018. He punched in "First Alabama Cavalry" rather than "First Alabama Cavalry, U.S.A.," as I had done on previous visits; Steve Murray felt that probably accounted for his getting forty-seven hits where I recalled getting none. Of those hits, one seemed of particular interest to Jasper, and he called me over to look at it.

The title was "Consolidated morning reports of Alabama Cavalry Regiment, 1st, 1863–1865." It was attributed to the Alabama Adjutant's General Office, which was absorbed into the Confederate hierarchy, but down in the body of the text were these words: "Spencer, George E.; Confederate States of America. Army. Alabama Cavalry Regiment, 1st, Rome (Ga.)." Were there two George Spencers? Why would Rome, where Sherman had rallied the Alabama Union regiment, be singled out, as well as Huntsville, where it was first organized? I also spotted the name of Ozro J. Dodds, an Ohio politician known to have served with the First Alabama Union Cavalry.

We asked for the documents, which arrived bundled in a sleeve of white linen fastened by Velcro snaps. The presentation bespoke meticulous preservation practices. The curator who put it on the table in front of Jasper said she knew that he was interested in Union outfits, but this was a Confederate army unit. Nonetheless, we unfolded the ledger to find a "Consolidated Morning Report" of a roll call from Corinth, Mississippi, of Union troops "commanded by Colonel George E. Spencer." There were page after page of these printed forms, where the names of Colonel Spencer and other Union officers had been written in with a flowing penmanship of near calligraphic quality. The form was not very different from the roll call grids I had handled a hundred years later as a U.S. Army reserve clerk in the Alabama National Guard. Across the years, what millions of soldiers called "the army way" had remained remarkably consistent.

About this time another staff member showed me a listing for four equipment ledgers that also bore a First Alabama designation. We ordered up the first, which was also wrapped in a sleeve of white linen. This turned out to be a ledger that had a navy blue cardboard cover with a red binding along the spine. The cover page read "Clothing [Account] Book Costs . . . circa 1862–1865." The penmanship was less flowing but unambiguously clear. This was volume one of the clothing and equipment issue for the "U.S. First Regiment of Cavalry/Alabama Volunteers." It was alphabetized, and I quickly looked up the name of a Winston County soldier I remembered because I knew some of his kin, one James Cagle. He was enrolled in Company A, the first of the three companies to enter federal service.

I reported my findings a few days later to a stunned Steve Murray. These were the sort of original documents more commonly associated with the National Archives and the *Official Records* collection in Washington, D.C. How had these records wound up in the Alabama archives listed by registrars who apparently didn't realize they were not part of the Confederate records? As this book is going to press, I am researching that question and trying to determine if they are one of a kind, as I suspect, or if other copies exist elsewhere. Frankly, the entries look so labor-intensive as to make me doubt that a new regiment in the field had the stenographic resources to generate more than an original document.

I even have a theory of the case that accords with Steve Murray's speculation that Thomas McAdory Owen may have hand-carried the records from Washington. He was known for wanting to collect regimental histories of every Alabama Confederate unit. Perhaps these were swept up in his net—or, despite his own statements to the contrary, perhaps he was interested in Union troops as well. In any event, we know that from 1894 to 1897, Owen served as chief clerk in Washington for the division of post office inspectors. He became a protegé of Dr. Ainsworth B. Spofford, the librarian of Congress. Wendell Holmes Stephenson, author of *Southern History in the Making,* states in a chapter entitled "Thomas M. Owen: Pioneer Archivist" that "the clerkship in the Post Office Department became a means to an end, for Owen's leisure time was spent in the Library of Congress searching for materials on his section of the South and discussing historical sources with Spofford and other scholars who frequented the library." The experience convinced Owen to abandon his legal career and draft the 1901 legislation that created the nation's first state-funded archive. While still in Washington, Stephenson reported, Owen used the Library of Congress to compile a 472-page bibliography of Alabama based on "publications of learned societies, maps of Alabama and official documents." I believe that the provenance of those First Alabama documents may eventually emerge from the midden, perhaps proving that Spofford helped Owen liberate them from federal custody.

Both Steve Murray, the archives director, and Haley Aaron, the ADAH registrar, were surprised by our discovery, but the provenance records shed little light on the acquisition. In the early decades of the century, there was sporadic record keeping as to the flow of documents into and out of the collection. It seems a stroke of luck that Owen did not divert this incriminating evidence of dissent into what Fleming called the "large private collection" lost when his house burned. The Union roster seems exactly the kind of documentation of Confederate "disloyalty" he would not have wanted in the public collection.

Early in 2022, I had Jasper spend a week searching for correspondence between Owen and Spofford between 1901 and 1905, but he found nothing. Murray confirmed to me that even at this late date, no ADAH curator has been through all the hundreds of thousands of pages of letters and records left behind by Tom and Marie, so for many documents there's no way of reconstructing a paper trail or even establishing if one exists. Registrar Haley Aaron identified 1990 as the first year that the regimental roster was entered in the archive's computerized catalogue, but whoever made the entry mistakenly thought the First Alabama Union Cavalry was under the command of the state militia and the Alabama adjutant general rather than the United States Army, Sherman, and Lincoln. Only spotting the name "George E. Spencer" in the contents paragraph short-circuited the error. In this case, I believe the mislabeling really was an accident.

In one essential respect, the records in Montgomery are definitive, proving how and when the Alabama boys who helped Sherman burn Atlanta got into the Union army. For the first time, genealogists will have an original list of enlistees in the first three companies, clearing up some ambiguities in the roster published during the Civil War centennial by William Stanley Hoole and his Confederate Press in Tuscaloosa. The survival of these Union records in what was, by design, a Lost Cause repository, with its thousands of unexamined files, raises my hope that someone someday may unearth the spying report on the Looney's Tavern rally penned by H. A. M. Henderson, the Confederate lieutenant who wound up preaching at the funeral of Ulysses S. Grant's mother.

That hope lingers as a realistic possibility because of the enduring truth of what I sensed so long ago amid the smokestacks of Birmingham and the hills and hollows of Winston County. When you start digging in Alabama, there's no telling what you'll uncover—especially if it was buried in Miss Marie's shiny alabaster building.

A C K N O W L E D G M E N T S

Most obviously, I am indebted to my family members who kept alive the frail threads of memory that connected our ancestors to the First Alabama Cavalry and the Free State legacy. Among the living, I thank my sister, Mary Jo Raines Dean, our cousin, Eudalia Raines Hicks, and Anne Gautney Raines, the wife of our late cousin Charles Howell Raines. For help in tracing the Winston County lineage of our Walker relatives, I am grateful to my cousins Martha Sue Walker Freeman, Jeanne Lee Walker Terpo, Norman Jerome Walker, Charles Ray Walker, and the late John Dennis Walker. My debt to Gradystein Williams Hutchinson for her memories of my family is equally profound.

The other group to which I owe unstinting homage is the new generation of twenty-first-century historians who, through their books and dissertations, have gathered into coherent form the saga of patriotic sacrifice that was neglected by the American history establishment throughout the previous century. To those already mentioned I add the names of those who blazed the trail even earlier, a group that includes the redoubtable Free State scholar Donald Dodd and university historians including Carl N. Degler, Thomas G. Dyer, and John C. Inscoe and Robert C. Kenzer for their essay collection, *Enemies of the Country: New Perspective on Unionists in the Civil War*. I am especially indebted to the Stanford University historian Terry L. Seip, whose indispensable monograph on George E. Spencer provided a career overview nowhere else available.

At the Alabama Department of Archives and History I owe my

thanks to the two directors who brought it into modern times, Edwin C. Bridges and Steve Murray. I send special thanks to the emeritus professor Allen W. Jones of Auburn University for sharing his memories of the Marie Bankhead Owen regime. I have also benefited greatly from the writings and advice of two distinguished Alabama-born historians, J. Mills Thornton and Tennant S. McWilliams. For interviews and conversations that deepened my understanding of historiographic processes, I am grateful to Ken Burns, Ric Burns, Geoffrey F. Ward, Eric Foner, Christopher Lyle McIlwain, and Christopher R. Rein. I am grateful to W. Steven Harrell, author of a historical novel about the First Alabama, who generously shared his careful research and documents. I also corresponded with Don Umphrey, who used his knowledge of Winston County in a historical novel. I corresponded and visited with Ricky Butch Walker, who has written about the Native American and Civil War history of the Tennessee Valley. I benefited from these natives of Winston County who shared their insights: Hobson Manasco, the late Probate Judge Lecil Gray, and the late Judge Frank M. Johnson. I am appreciative of the writings of two longtime friends from the newspaper world: the late Wane Greenhaw, who shared his knowledge of the north Alabama roots of Big Jim Folsom's progressive populism, and Jack Bass, whose biography of the civil rights pioneer Judge Frank M. Johnson explored how Johnson's Winston County upbringing and Unionist family heritage influenced his watershed court rulings. I am forever grateful for several personal conversations with Judge Johnson that helped me understand Winston County's reverence for the Constitution. I was also assisted by Treva Hood and the staff of the Winston County Archive in Double Springs, Alabama.

I owe a special word of gratitude to Nic Stanton-Roark, archivist of the Robert A. Nicholson Library of Anderson University. His diligent search of Church of God archives for documents about my family's involvement with that denomination enabled me to reconstruct the career of my great-uncle, the Rev. W. S. Best. In the matter of family history, I also owe a debt of gratitude to two skillful geneaologists, Melissa Folsom Boyen and Judy Culbreth, for sharing their time and expertise. I am grateful to the photographer Peter Gonze for his expert copying of vintage photographs. For research assistance at the Alabama Department of Archives and History, I thank its director, Steve Murray, as well as Scotty Kirkland, Hayley Richards, Ken Barr, Robby Elmore, Courtney Pinkard, and the staff of the Research Room. I also thank Kelsey Berryhill of the State Archives of Iowa and Bill Short of the Barret Library at Rhodes College.

I have been since age twenty-one a newspaperman, and as I complete this long investigative journey, I must thank my colleagues at the *Birmingham Post-Herald, The Tuscaloosa News, The Birmingham News, The Atlanta Constitution, The St. Petersburg Times,* and *The New York Times.* Through them I learned the collecting skills that made this book possible. That is to say, this is a reporter's book, not a scholarly work of original research like that done by professional historians. For over six decades, I have monitored the work of others, collected documents, harvested tidbits, stowed them away, and used the synthesizing techniques of old-school journalists to create a fresh mosaic from facts that have been buried, misinterpreted, or ignored.

I thank my agent, Rob McQuilkin, for encouraging me to polish my original proposal and to Tim Duggan who started the process at Crown that was then so skillfully completed by executive editor Paul Whitlatch. Paul's storytelling advice, line editing, and flawless taste have been invaluable. I am greatly indebted to his associate Katie Berry for her efficient coaching. I knew that I would have to hire a research assistant to finish the book on time, and I decided to give my grandson Jasper Raines, a history major at the University of South Alabama, a crack at the job. He has proved to be a whiz at tracking down hard-to-find books and finding gems of information in the Alabama Department of Archives and History, and I express my appreciation for his diligence. Most deeply appreciated of all is my brilliant wife, Krystyna Stachowiak Raines. At every stage of this project, I have benefited from her support, enthusiasm, editing skill, and her tactful, patient advice.

NOTES

ix **Alabama regiments enrolled under the true flag** *New-York Daily Tribune,* as reprinted in the *Sacramento Daily Union,* December 28, 1864.

Introduction

xix **"the forgotten men of the Civil War"** Richard Nelson Current, *Lincoln's Loyalists* (Boston: Northeastern University Press, 1992), 5. See also Margaret Storey, *Loyalty and Loss: Alabama's Unionists in the Civil War and Reconstruction* (Baton Rouge, LA: Louisiana State University Press, 2004). I am indebted to Professor Storey, of DePaul University, for focusing my interest in Winston County, which had developed over several decades, and showing me that the bits of family lore I had inherited fit into a broad, documentable, and largely ignored patriotic movement centered in the Alabama hill country. She is rightly recognized as providing a foundational work that inspired this century's wave of new scholarship about the growing field of southern Unionism. Her *Loyalty and Loss* demonstrated that the neglected records of the Southern Claims Commission were a treasure house of information about white southerners who had opposed secession. She followed the trail blazed by Richard Nelson Current, whose *Lincoln's Loyalists* was hailed as opening a new field of study and then mostly ignored. In the last twenty years, this developing theater of Civil War scholarship produced a rush of books and dissertations that illuminated the informational tunnel I had been groping along since childhood. These fresh-eyed writers provided the documentation I have drawn upon in assembling a full portrait of the military importance of the First Alabama Cavalry, U.S.A. As an alumnus of the University of Alabama, I'm proud that several of the most authoritative recent books came from the university's press, long a wellspring of Lost Cause argumentation. These include two detailed studies of special importance for readers wanting an overview: Christopher Lyle McIlwain, *Civil War Alabama* (Tuscaloosa, AL: The University of Alabama Press, 2016), and Christopher M. Rein, *Alabamians in Blue: Freedmen, Unionists, and the Civil War in the Cotton State* (Baton Rouge, LA: Louisiana State University Press, 2019). I will cite other additive books and graduate-school studies at pertinent points in the narrative.

xx **"white supremacist historiography"** Columbia University and Slavery, https://columbiaandslavery.columbia.edu/seminars/hist-3518.html.

xxi **The remarkable success of this academic cover-up** I would be remiss if I did not cite the fulsome misrepresentations about slaves and mountain Unionists in

Walter L. Fleming, *Civil War and Reconstruction in Alabama* (New York: The Columbia University Press, 1905) and Wesley S. Thompson, *Tories of the Hills* (Winfield, AL: Christopher Pub. House, 1953) for arousing my reporter's curiosity to know what really happened. As for convincing me that something too important to be ignored had taken place in my ancestral counties, I should also cite the importance of my belated discovery in General Sherman's *Memoirs* that he was joined on the March to the Sea by a "small company of irregular Alabama cavalry." For the role of Columbia University and William Archibald Dunning, see John David Smith and J. Vincent Lowery, eds., *The Dunning School: Historians, Race, and the Meaning of Reconstruction* (Lexington, KY: University Press of Kentucky, 2013).

xxi **"my bad old man"** Major General Jubal A. Early's remarkable gift for influencing southern and then national opinion has been abundantly studied. I depended particularly on Charles C. Osborne, *Jubal: The Life and Times of General Jubal A. Early, C S A, Defender of the Lost Cause* (Chapel Hill, NC: Algonquin Books, 1992), Benjamin Franklin Cooling III, *Jubal Early: Robert E. Lee's "Bad Old Man"* (New York: Rowman & Littlefield Publishers, 2014), and Millard K. Bushong, *Old Jube: A Biography of General Jubal A. Early* (Shippensburg, PA: Carr Publishing Company, 1955).

xxii **Thomas McAdory Owen (1866–1920) and his widow, Marie Bankhead Owen** For an introduction to this remarkable couple's impact on Alabama's politics, culture, educational system, race relations, and delusional self-image, see Kari Frederickson, *Deep South Dynasty: The Bankheads of Alabama* (Tuscaloosa, AL: The University of Alabama Press, 2022), 58–63.

Maps

xxiii **Alabama in 1860: Union Volunteers by County** The late Donald Dodd, the first professionally trained historian to study Winston County, told me that he compared roster and census records to arrive at the hard count of 239 Winstonians in the First Alabama Union Cavalry. The industrious amateur historian Glenda McWhirter Todd used a similar approach to arrive at the figure of 229. (Legibility issues probably account for the difference.) A census review by an Eastern Michigan University graduate student listed 92 First Alabama volunteers for Walker County, but my research showed that he missed eight of my collateral kin in the politically influential Barton family, as well as their neighbor, my great-great uncle Israel Abbott, who died at eighteen while serving and is buried in the national military cemetery at Chattanooga, Tennessee. Donald Dodd told me he regretted bowing to local pressure to impose a false equivalency on Winston's Unionist and Confederate histories. He composed the historical marker about the "Dual Destiny" represented by a Civil War statue erected outside the Winston County courthouse in 1987. The marker stands in front of a statue of a soldier who has an American flag over one shoulder and a Rebel battle flag over the other. Dodd included the fact that in addition to its 239 Union veterans, Winston provided 112 men for the Confederate forces, mainly as a sop to a newly organized group of Confederate reenactors in the county. But he knew that many of these Winston Confederates were drafted under threat of death or prison. There was little equivalency in public opinion on the issue of leaving the Union. Anti-Secessionists carried a county election for the 1861 state convention by a five to one margin, and in the first call for Confederate volunteers, no Winston residents stepped forward. See Donald B. Dodd, *Win-*

ston: *An Antebellum and Civil War History of a Hill County of North Alabama* (Jasper, AL: Oxmoor Press, 1972), 83, 264–268; William Stanley Hoole, *Alabama Tories: The First Alabama Cavalry, U.S.A., 1862–1865* (Tuscaloosa, AL: Confederate Publishing Company, 1960), 16–17; Glenda McWhirter Todd, *First Alabama Cavalry, U.S.A.: Homage to Patriotism* (Bowie, MD: Heritage Books, 1999), 165 and passim; Joel S. Mize, *Unionists of the Warrior Mountains of Alabama, Volume B* (Lakewood, CO: self-pub.), 7; Stephen E. Brannan, "Disaffection with the Confederacy, in Walker County, Alabama, During the Civil War," (master's thesis, Eastern Michigan University, 1981), 61–63; Scott Morris, "Free State of Winston Honors Its Dual Destiny as Confederate Monuments Fall," *Birmingham Watch: Alabama Initiative for Independent Journalism*, June 13, 2020, https://birminghamwatch.org/free-state-winston-honors-dual-destiny -confederate-monuments-fall/.

Chapter 1: What Happened to Me at Ma 'n' Ada's

4 **Miss Love's mother was an Owen** I am grateful to Judy Culbreth, a former editor of *Working Mother* and *Redbook* in New York and an expert on the genealogy of our native state, for helping me sort out the connection that brought my class special attention from Miss Marie. Her husband, Thomas McAdory Owen, and Miss Love's father, Rose Wellington Owen, were first cousins once removed. As was the habit of elite white Alabamians, the families nurtured their connections. Today both the McAdory and Owen homes near Birmingham are museums.

4 **Dr. Owen hobnobbed with the nation's top scholars** Patrick L. Tomlin, "The Archival Unconscious: Thomas McAdory Owen and the Founding of the Alabama Department of Archives and History," master's thesis, University of North Carolina at Chapel Hill, 2008. Tomlin noted that the founding of the ADAH "preceded that of the National Archives by more than three years and its influence on state archives across the nation was unparalleled."

4 **"meal ticket"** Kari Frederickson, *Deep South Dynasty: The Bankheads of Alabama* (Tuscaloosa, AL: The University of Alabama Press, 2022), 186.

6 **to condemn a bestselling book entitled *Stars Fell on Alabama*** In Montgomery, Miss Marie and the son of Captain Jones's son, Judge Walter B. Jones, worked closely on celebrating their city as the "Cradle of the Confederacy." For Judge Jones, see Harrison Salisbury, *Without Fear or Favor: The New York Times and Its Times* (New York: Times Books, 1980), 385–386. His candid discussion of Jones's racism and pedophilia were confirmed by Ray Jenkins, longtime editor of the *Montgomery Advertiser* and a Carter administration press spokesman, in an interview with *Mobile Bay Times* reporter Chip Drago, http://www.mobilebaytimes.com/digression.html. For Jones's venomous attack on *Stars Fell on Alabama,* see his "Off the Bench" column in the *Montgomery Advertiser,* July 9, 1934, 4.

6 **"one big front porch"** Kathryn Tucker Windham, *Alabama, One Big Front Porch* (Montgomery, AL: NewSouth Books, 2018).

Chapter 2: The Centrality of Gradystein Williams Hutchinson

14 **predestined by Grandma Raines's profanity** For Birmingham's distinctive geology as accounting for its growth, see Ethel Armes, *The Story of Coal and Iron in Alabama* (Birmingham, AL, 1910). For a summary of economic and political

sectionalism in Alabama, see William D. Barnard, *Dixiecrats and Democrats: Alabama Politics, 1942–1950* (Tuscaloosa, AL: The University of Alabama Press, 1974). For the Black Belt view of the political unreliability of mountain whites, see Walter L. Fleming, *Civil War and Reconstruction* (New York: The Columbia University Press, 1905), 10–14, and William Stanley Hoole, *Alabama Tories: The First Alabama Cavalry, U.S.A., 1862–1865* (Tuscaloosa, AL: Confederate Publishing Company, 1960), 5–6. For a fictional portrait of the social division between wealthy and working-class whites in the Birmingham suburb of Mountain Brook, see Walker Percy, *The Last Gentleman* (New York: Farrar, Straus and Giroux, 1966).

15 **Emmett Till** "Nation Horrified by Murder of Kidnapped Chicago Youth," *Jet,* September 22, 1955.

15 **Grady's influence on me** Howell Raines, "Grady's Gift," *New York Times Magazine,* November 30, 1991. This was the key passage in the article, which won the Pulitzer Prize for Feature Writing in 1992: "Gradystein Williams Hutchinson and I are two people who grew up in the 50's in that vanished world, two people who lived mundane, inconsequential lives while Martin Luther King Jr. and Police Commissioner T. Eugene (Bull) Connor prepared for their epic struggle. For years, Grady and I lived in my memory as child and adult. But now I realize that we were both children—one white and very young, one black and adolescent: one privileged, one poor. The connection between these two children and their city was this: Grady saw to it that although I was to live in Birmingham for the first 28 years of my life, Birmingham would not live in me."

16 **"sunset towns" or "sundown towns"** Carl Carmer, *Stars Fell on Alabama* (New York: Farrar and Rinehart, 1934), 59. In a 1920s tour of the hill country that took him to Winston County, Carmer reported seeing Alabama's most famous sundown sign: "A neatly painted sign confronted us—'Nigger, Don't Let the Sun Go Down on You in This Town.'" See also Nicholas Dawidoff, "Race in the South in the Age of Obama," *New York Times Magazine,* February 25, 2010. He maintains the signs in Cullman persisted into the 1970s, but I never saw them on my visits to the area during that period. I consulted Hubert Grissom, now an attorney in Tampa, Florida, who grew up in a politically active family in Cullman. He believes any "official" sign probably disappeared by the 1950s but may have been succeeded by "cornfield signs" painted by amateurs. In the fifties and sixties, the United Klans of America had professionally made signs showing a robed Klansman on a rearing horse erected around Tuscaloosa, Birmingham, and other towns, possibly including Cullman. While clearly intended to rattle travelers, these signs carried no warning message.

17 **"Those men would be sitting down on the storefront"** Author's interview with Gradystein Williams Hutchinson, November 2022.

17 **Unionists in north Alabama** Imani Perry, *South Toward America: A Journey Below the Mason-Dixon to Understand the Soul of a Nation* (New York: Ecco, 2022), 26–27. See also Carmer, *Stars Fell on Alabama,* for an account of how Appalachia's fragile racial accord could be disrupted when the mountain whites were inflamed by events like the infamous Scottsboro Boys trial in 1931. In that north Alabama town, nine young Black males were convicted of dubious rape charges by an all-white jury. Carl Carmer's variable Yankee radar was tricked by statements that Black Belt whites were gentler with Blacks than the hill country residents. For the influence of Andrew Jackson and his enemy, the arch-secessionist John Calhoun, see David Hackett Fischer, *Albion's Seed: Four British Folkways in America* (New York: Oxford University Press, 1989). For their

rivalry, see Jon Meacham, *American Lion: Andrew Jackson in the White House* (New York: Random House, 2008).

19 **"I am a Jeffersonian Democrat"** This was the clue that my grandfather, nominally a Republican, had been touched by what Duke historian Lawrence Goodwyn described as "the populist moment" in southern history. For how the Jeffersonian Democrats split from the regular Democrats in a populist revolt, see William Warren Rogers, Robert David Ward, Leah Rawls Atkins, and Wayne Flynt, *Alabama: The History of a Deep South State* (Tuscaloosa, AL: The University of Alabama Press, 1994), 309–316, 441–442. I am indebted to Samuel L. Webb in *Two-Party Politics in the One-Party South: Alabama's Hill Country, 1874–1920* (Tuscaloosa, AL: The University of Alabama Press, 1997), 104–112, 133–136, for his meticulous account of how Bourbon Democrats stole the 1892 and 1894 gubernatorial election from the Jeffersonian Democrats in the most infamous election frauds in Alabama history. These were formative experiences for my grandfather.

Chapter 3: Saved by Uncle Sim

21 **It has taken me decades** Charles Ewing Brown, *When the Trumpet Sounded: A History of the Church of God Reformation Movement* (Anderson, IN: The Warner Press, 1951), loc. 4173–4183. Other important works on CHOG history that I used include Merle Strege, *The Desk as Altar: The Centennial History of Anderson University* (Anderson, IN: Anderson University Press, 2016) and Gilbert W. Stafford, *Seven Doctrinal Leaders of the Church of God Reformation Movement* (Anderson, IN: Reformation Publishers, 2008). I also drew on papers about my relatives in the Charles Ewing Brown Papers at Anderson University's Library. Brown credited an autobiographical novel by the Reverend Elizabeth Ann Mitchell, *Anchored to the Rock* (Anderson, IN: Gospel Trumpet Company, 1950), as factually correct regarding attacks on CHOG members and facilities in Alabama in the late nineteenth and early twentieth centuries. For the Hartselle Incident, see Charles Ewing Brown, *When the Trumpet Sounded*. For Reverend W. S. Best as a "radical preacher," see Charles Ewing Brown Papers, "Townley Letter," 1–4.

23 **I discovered that this "Uncle John"** John Best, Confederate Pension Records for Company L, 28th AL Infantry. David Best's escape to Union forces, author's interview with W. S. Raines, circa 1989. For Hiram Raines "lying out," see Hial Abbott testimony to the Southern Claims Commission, January 25, 1872.

26 **"Late in the nineteenth century"** Brown, *When the Trumpet Sounded*, 266.

27 **Laurel, Mississippi, where the preacher died** For the Mitchells' career and the events at Penton, Brown, *When the Trumpet Sounded*, 268–269; Mitchell, *Anchored to the Rock*, 66–67. For Rev. Beatrice Sapp and "white and colored work" at Bessemer, AL, see Brown, *When the Trumpet Sounded*, 269.

Chapter 4: Reading the Stars

33 **Henry King Stanford** Henry King Stanford, *Campus Under Political Fire and Other Essays* (Columbus, GA, 1987), 23–41. This firsthand account of Bull Connor's attempt to intimidate Birmingham-Southern College and its president is essential reading as to state repression in Birmingham. It includes Stanford's dealings with *New York Times* men Harrison Salisbury and James Reston Sr. Stanford's legal adviser in the battle with Connor over BSC students' contacts

with civil rights leaders was Charles Morgan Jr., who would be run out of town for exposing Birmingham's collective guilt for the Sixteenth Street Baptist Church bombing. For his account, see *A Time to Speak: The Story of a Young American Lawyer's Struggle for His City—and Himself* (New York: Harper & Row Publishers, Inc., 1964), 61–85.

35 **For me, *Stars Fell on Alabama* was transformative** Carl Carmer, *Stars Fell on Alabama* (New York: Farrar and Rinehart, 1934). My eyes were opened by his argument that Alabama was so different from other states that it had to be studied like a foreign nation.

Chapter 5: My Rosetta Stone

42 **Winston remained "a stranded frontier"** Donald Dodd and Amy Bartlett-Dodd, *The Free State of Winston* (Charleston, SC: Arcadia Publishing, 2000), 11.

47 **my fellow Alabamian Paul M. Gaston** Paul M. Gaston, *The New South Creed: A Study in Southern Mythmaking* (Montgomery, AL: NewSouth Books, 2001) is the definitive study of how northern investors financed southern economic growth while helping entrench racist officeholders. It helped southern scholars and journalists see that this symbiosis was the opposite of a virtuous circle. For assessing how white Alabamians became racial liberals, see also Gaston's history of the Christian socialist experiment in Fairhope, Alabama, *Coming of Age in Utopia: The Odyssey of an Idea* (Montgomery, AL: NewSouth Books, 2010).

49 **"As 1892 approached"** William Warren Rogers et al., *Alabama: The History of a Deep South State* (Tuscaloosa, AL: The University of Alabama Press, 1994), 308–310.

50 **"It was generally agreed"** Samuel L. Webb and Margaret Armbrester, ed., *Alabama Governors: A Political History of the State* (Tuscaloosa, AL: The University of Alabama Press, 2001), 120.

54 **"Big Mules"** Ibid., 177. The term for the state's industrial oligarchs was coined by two-term governor Bibb Graves, the Yale-educated lawyer who was both a Klan official and the most progressive Democrat elected in the first half of the twentieth century.

54 **"Archives about unfamous"** Edward Ball, *Life of a Klansman: A Family History in White Supremacy* (New York: Farrar, Straus and Giroux, 2020), 365.

54 **"emotional archaeology"** For Burns's use of the term for unearthing feelings lurking beneath "dry facts," see https://blogs.wnpt.org/mediaupdate/2008/10/02/the-emotional-archaeology-of-ken-burns/.

Chapter 6: Chris Sheats: Phantom of the Hills

56 **Winston County abuzz with talk** Wesley S. Thompson, *Tories of the Hills* (Winfield, AL: Christopher Pub. House, 1969). I treasure the autographed first edition found in my mother's library after her death in 2002. The book still has an underground reputation among history buffs, but it is extremely hard to find even though it went through several editions.

58 **"Primary sources"** Sarah Woolfolk Wiggins, *The Scalawag in Alabama Politics, 1865–1881* (Tuscaloosa, AL: The University of Alabama Press, 1977), 3.

59 **probate judge John Bennett Weaver** John Bennett Weaver, *A Brief History of Winston County, Alabama,* Winston County, Alabama: An Historical Online Database, http://www.freestateofwinston.org/abriefhistory.htm. In addition to this foundational essay, Weaver also contributed to a centennial pamphlet, *Fact and*

Fiction of the Free State of Winston (Haleyville and Double Springs, AL, 1950). His address to the student body of Howard College (now known as Samford University) in Birmingham on December 9, 1948, can be found in the Birmingham Public Library. But his monograph *A Brief History of Winston County, Alabama* was written around the same time and is the more important document. Without it, the story of Chris Sheats and the meeting that led to the creation of the First Alabama Cavalry, U.S.A. would almost certainly have been lost.

61 **"the business proposition"** John Bennett Weaver, address to Howard College students, December 9, 1948, transcript in Birmingham Public Library.

61 **"Well, I don't know"** John Bennett Weaver, ibid.

62 **"[The delegates] were elected"** John Bennett Weaver, from a transcript in the Birmingham Public Library of his address at Howard College (now Samford University) on December 9, 1946, 9–10.

63 **the court-like transcripts** William Russell Smith, *The History and Debates of the Convention of the People of Alabama: Begun and Held in the City of Montgomery, on the Seventh Day of January, 1861: in Which Is Preserved the Speeches of the Secret Sessions and Many Valuable State Papers* (Tuscaloosa, AL: White Pfister & Co, 1861).

64 **Governor John Gill Shorter's "letter boxes"** Donald B. Dodd and Wynelle S. Dodd, *Winston: An Antebellum and Civil War History of a Hill County of North Alabama* (Jasper, AL: Annals of Northwest Alabama, 1972), 83–87, 99–101, 103–105. Donald Dodd's combing of Shorter's correspondence also represents foundational research. Without it, I could not have reconstructed the timeline of events in Winston County. My researcher and I spent a day going through files in Dodd's garage, but most of his original notes had not been preserved. For Governor Shorter's arrest of Sheats, see Dodd, *Winston*, 100–105, and Charles Rice, *Hard Times: The Civil War in Huntsville and North Alabama, 1861–1865* (Huntsville, AL: Old Huntsville, 1995), 147–149.

65 **"prize captive"** For the most complete summary of Sheats's double life as Confederate state official and Union recruiter and Bradley's attempts to gull Shorter, see Dodd, *Winston*, 100–105. For another good account of the Sheats-Bradley collusion, see also Rice, *Hard Times*, 147–151. Rice believed Sheats was first arrested by the Huntsville sheriff on Shorter's orders before being taken to Montgomery by Fennel's cavalry. Eager to get the troublemaker out of Alabama, Shorter sent him to the Confederate prison at Salisbury, North Carolina. For Bradley's cooperation with the Lincoln administration, see also Christopher Lyle McIlwain, *Civil War Alabama* (Tuscaloosa, AL: The University of Alabama Press, 2016), 35. On Sheats's career, see McIlwain, *Civil War Alabama*, 31. On Sheats's jailing as an impetus to Union recruiting and his career, see Christopher M. Rein, *Alabamians in Blue: Freedmen, Unionists, and the Civil War in the Cotton State* (Baton Rouge, LA: Louisiana State University Press, 2019), 40. For brief but fair references to Sheats and his movement by an Alabama historian, see Virginia Van der Veer Hamilton, *Alabama: A History* (New York: W. W. Norton & Company, 1977), 26–29. For similar treatment, see also Martine G. Bates, *Chris Sheats: The Man Who Refused to Secede* (Hartselle, AL: Seacoast Publishing, Inc., 2004). For fragmentary or hostile references to Sheats, see Walter L. Fleming, *Civil War and Reconstruction* (New York: The Columbia University Press, 1905), 115, 126, 365, 681; Charles Grayson Summersell, *Alabama History for Schools* (Birmingham, AL: Colonial Press, 1957), 300, 324; A. B. Moore, *History of Alabama* (Tuscaloosa, AL: Alabama Book Store, 1951), 421, 442, 484. To contrast Moore's scanty references to Sheats in *History of Ala-*

bama, see his foreword to *Tories of the Hills*, by his friend W. S. Thompson. He refers there to Sheats as Alabama's "great Tory leader" but adds the misleading promotional comment that Thompson's novel is "definitely more factual than fictional." This hopscotching across incomplete or contradictory sources illustrates the process necessary for constructing an overview of Sheats's career.

67 **Two young Free Staters** Author's interviews and conversations with Donald Dodd and Judge Frank M. Johnson Sr.; "Free Stater's Grave Found After Many Years of Frustrating Search," *Daily Northwest Alabamian*, March 20, 1962; letter to the editor from Frank M. Johnson, *Daily Northwest Alabamian*, March 26, 1962. For rich details on the politics of Winston County, I am indebted to Jack Bass, *Taming the Storm: The Life and Times of Judge Frank M. Johnson, Jr. and the South's Fight over Civil Rights* (New York, 1993). Bass documented interactions among Donald Dodd and his father, "Uncle Ben" Dodd, the Johnsons, and Judge Johnson's bodyguard, "Pert" Dodd.

68 **the legend of Chris Sheats** For examples of brief, distorted mentions of Chris Sheats, see especially Fleming, *Civil War and Reconstruction*, 115, 126, 365, and 681, the last depicting him as silenced by the Ku Klux Klan. See also Moore, *History of Alabama*, 421, 442, 484. In a satirical footnote, Moore calls him a "prominent Tory" scalawag but gives no hint that he was a popular hero and effective recruiter of Union troops. Moore, whose book was the standard Alabama reference for forty-three years, did not list the First Alabama Cavalry, U.S.A. in his index. Moore excused the theft of the 1892 gubernatorial election as a mere "manipulation of the Negro vote." That is to say, in the Black Belt, thousands of living and dead Blacks who never went to the polls were listed as voting against their own interests. While Moore's book was thoroughly dishonest, he would later adjust his opinion of Sheats to help his friend Wesley S. Thompson promote *Tories of the Hills*.

72 **"Dynamite Bob" Chambliss** Howell Raines, *My Soul Is Rested: Movement Days in the Deep South Remembered* (New York: G. P. Putnam's Sons, 1977), 167; author interview with Robert Chambliss for "The Birmingham Bombing," *New York Times Magazine*, July 24, 1983; author interview with Bob Eddy, Pratville, AL, 2021.

74 **"maintaining the fiction of"** Rein, *Alabamians in Blue*, 43.

Chapter 7: A Discovery in Atlanta

77 **the newspaper of Henry W. Grady** Paul M. Gaston, *The New South Creed: A Study in Southern Mythmaking* (Montgomery, AL: NewSouth Books, 2001), 1, 49, 87–90; David W. Blight, *Race and Reunion: The Civil War in American Memory* (Cambridge, MA: Belknap Press, 2001), 200.

78 **"It's Nice to Have You in Birmingham"** Howell Raines, *My Soul Is Rested: Movement Days in the Deep South Remembered* (New York: G. P. Putnam's Sons, 1977). For multiple citations on Townsend and Lankford's clandestine operations with the Birmingham Police Department and the FBI, see Diane McWhorter, *Carry Me Home: Birmingham, Alabama: the Climactic Battle of the Civil Rights Movement* (New York: Simon & Schuster, 2001), 205–207. For the misleading press release from the University of Alabama College of Communication and Information Sciences Hall of Fame, September 23, 2009, see https://news.ua.edu/2009/09/four-communication-information-leaders-to-be-inducted-into-ua-cis-hall-of-fame/.

79 **Smyer, a former Dixiecrat** For his background see Raines, *My Soul Is Rested,* 154–166.

80 **Rollin Osterweis observed** Rollin Osterweis, *The Myth of the Lost Cause, 1865–1900* (Hamden, CT: Archon Books, 1973), 127. I am indebted to my late *New York Times* colleague William Borders, a Yale student during Osterweis's tenure, for introducing me to this essential book and its concept of a Lost Cause "blockade" against northern ideas.

80 **"the tough fiber"** Ibid., 125.

81 **"center of the literary"** Old New York Book Shop, "About This Seller," Abe Books website, https://www.abebooks.com/old-new-york-book-shop%2c-abaa/14367/sf.

82 **William Stanley Hoole** Author's interviews with Sarah Woolfolk Wiggins, Tennant S. McWilliams, Mary Jane Foley, and Donald Dodd on Hoole's personality. For Hoole's career, see Martha Dubose Hoole, *William Stanley Hoole: Student-Teacher-Librarian-Author* (Wilmington, NC: Broadfoot Publishing Company, 2001); Elizabeth Hoole McArthur, "William Stanley Hoole, A Man of Letters," *Alabama Heritage,* Winter 2008, 36–44; W. Stanley Hoole, *According to Hoole: Collected Essays and Tales* (Tuscaloosa, AL: The University of Alabama Press, 1973). For the history of Birmingham-Southern College and the Mungers, see Donald Brown, *Forward, Ever* (Birmingham, 2005). I am indebted to the late Dr. Wiggins for a frank discussion of the difficulty of working with Dr. Hoole at the University of Alabama Press, where he insisted on books with a pro-Confederate slant. He enforced the same policy as editor of *The Alabama Review* and as a founding member of its sponsor, the Alabama Historical Association. Dr. Wiggins said that he sometimes used his role in the selection process for the University of Alabama Press to snag books for his own publishing company. In 2021 and 2022, his surviving daughter, Elizabeth Hoole McArthur, declined repeated email requests to discuss her father's professional reputation or why she and her late sister did not mention in their writings his condemnatory history of the First Alabama Cavalry, U.S.A.

84 **"In the North"** William Stanley Hoole, *Alabama Tories: The First Alabama Cavalry, U.S.A., 1862–1865* (Tuscaloosa, AL: Confederate Publishing Company, 1960), 5–6.

84 **"Destroying Angels"** Ibid., 6.

85 **"tales of suffering and misery"** Ibid., 6.

85 **Hoole's naked class rage** Ibid., 5–6. Despite his distaste for " 'mountain whites' or, to use a modern term, 'hillbillies,' " Hoole expressed pride at being the first scholar to write a monograph on the First Alabama when its existence was unknown to most Civil War historians. He can also be credited with publishing the first roster of the First Alabama Cavalry, U.S.A., which was a great help to me in advancing my research.

85 **"Altogether, in North Alabama"** Ibid., 6–7.

Chapter 8: How the First Alabama Almost Saved Atlanta from Burning

92 **"was not conspicuous"** William Stanley Hoole, *Alabama Tories: The First Alabama Cavalry, U.S.A., 1862–1865* (Tuscaloosa, AL: Confederate Publishing Company, 1960), 14–16.

92 **"weasel words"** Ibid. These passages contain the core of Hoole's argument. Having depicted the First Alabama as "not conspicuous" in battlefield accom-

plishments, Hoole claimed that it merited scholarly attention only by virtue of its "existence." That left him with the problem of circumnavigating the inconvenient fact that they were singled out by Sherman.

92 **"True enough"** Ibid.

93 **Sherman's autobiography** Sherman's comments on Old South character types shows his analytical skills in full flower. His dyspepsia about southern Unionists shows that the First Alabama had to earn his confidence. See William Tecumseh Sherman, *Memoirs* (New York: D. Appleton & Company, 1875), 309–317.

93 **"The young bloods of the South"** Sherman, *Memoirs,* 309–317. This off-the-cuff essay on Rebel society shows Sherman's social anthropology skills at full brilliance.

95 **droves of Alabama Union men** For an overview of this critical period in the formalization of north Alabama's Union sympathies, see Donald B. Dodd and Wynelle S. Dodd, *Winston: An Antebellum and Civil War History of a Hill County of North Alabama* (Jasper, AL: Annals of Northwest Alabama, 1972), 86–122; Hoole, *Alabama Tories,* 21–51; Christopher M. Rein, *Alabamians in Blue: Freedmen, Unionists, and the Civil War in the Cotton State* (Baton Rouge, LA: Louisiana State University Press, 2019), 2; Christopher Lyle McIlwain, *Civil War Alabama* (Tuscaloosa, AL: The University of Alabama Press, 2016), 107.

95 **With just the title** Wilson, *Patriotic Gore.* The quoted phrases are from an autobiographical sketch, "Northern Soldiers: William T. Sherman," 174–218.

96 **"constantly sustained by"** Edmund Wilson, *Patriotic Gore: Studies in the Literature of the American Civil War* (New York: W. W. Norton & Company, 1962), 184–185.

96 **"passion for order"** John F. Marszalek, *Sherman: A Soldier's Passion for Order* (New York: Free Press, 1994).

96 **"We are aware"** Wilson, *Patriotic Gore,* 184.

96 **"War is cruelty"** William T. Sherman, Sept. 12, 1864, letter to the mayor of Atlanta, who was protesting Sherman's order that all civilians leave the ravaged city, https://ironbrigader.com/2-13/02/09/war-cruelty-refine-it-william-t-shermans-september-1864-letter-mayor-atlanta/.

96 **"there was evidently"** Wilson, *Patriotic Gore,* 184.

96 **"orderly at hand"** Sherman, *Memoirs,* 549.

97 **"a full-court press"** Robert L. O'Connell, *Fierce Patriot: The Tangled Lives of William Tecumseh Sherman* (New York: Random House, 2014), 132.

97 **"It will be a physical impossibility"** Sherman, *Memoirs,* 519. This was a letter Sherman wrote Grant as a sales pitch for the March to the Sea. He was fending off proposals that he move his army to Virginia to help Grant conquer Richmond. In strategic terms, he was right. Leaving the transportation hubs of Atlanta and Savannah intact would have allowed Davis to continue a hopeless fight in the Deep South even after Richmond fell. The line "I can make this march, and make Georgia howl!" in this letter is one of Sherman's most famous bellicose quotes. For Sherman's reasoning regarding strategy, see *Memoirs,* 519; for Sherman's account of his three armies and the "Cavalry Division" he intended to be a small fast-moving force into which would be merged those companies of the First Alabama not assigned as his personal escort, see *Memoirs,* 386–400.

98 **"No wall tents"** Sherman, *Memoirs,* 406.

99 **"mechanized warfare"** Wilson, *Patriotic Gore,* 179.

99 **"The perpetrator of"** Ibid., 179–180.

99 **"almost scored a knockout"** O'Connell, *Fierce Patriot,* 137. Ever since, partici-

pants and historians have argued about the incident. Sherman believed for the rest of his life that if General Dodge's cavalry, including riders from the First Alabama and its commander, Colonel George E. Spencer, had not been called back, that would have been the beginning of the end of the campaign. In that case, the city of Atlanta would never have burned and the March to the Sea might have been unnecessary. For accounts that support the "knockout" interpretation and Spencer's role, see Terry L. Seip, "Of Ambition and Enterprise; the Making of Carpetbagger George E. Spencer," in Kenneth W. Noe, ed., *The Yellowhammer War; the Civil War and Reconstruction in Alabama* (Tuscaloosa, AL: The University of Alabama Press, 2013), 204. For Dodge's account, see Grenville Mellen Dodge, *Personal Recollections of President Abraham Lincoln, General Ulysses S. Grant, and General William T. Sherman* (Glendale, CA: The Arthur H. Clark Company, 1914), 146–147.

100 **"Sherman's tears"** Ezra J. Warner, *Generals in Blue: Lives of the Union Commanders* (Baton Rouge, LA: Louisiana State University Press, 1964), 308.

100 **"On May 9, Dodge proceeded to Resaca"** Stanley P. Hirshson, *Grenville M. Dodge: Soldier, Politician, Railroad Pioneer* (Bloomington, IN: Indiana University Press, 1967), 93–95.

101 **To be sure** O'Connell, *Fierce Patriot,* 107.

101 **"which Gen'l Dodge"** Hirshson, *Grenville M. Dodge,* 94–95.

101 **"sealed his historical reputation"** Seip, "Of Ambition and Enterprise," 191, 204.

101 **"I remember that"** Dodge, *Personal Recollections,* 145–146.

102 **"This enabled us"** Ibid.

102 **Johnston ridiculed Sherman's claim** Robert Underwood Johnson, ed., *Battles and Leaders of the Civil War* (Secaucus, NJ, n.d.), Volume IV, Joseph E. Johnston "Opposing Sherman's Advance to Atlanta," 260–277. Johnston always denied that he had been caught napping at Snake Creek Gap, even though he and Sherman became friends, dining companions, and political allies after the war. See Lloyd Lewis, *Sherman: Fighting Prophet* (New York: Harcourt, Brace and Company, 1932), 618. See also Craig L. Symonds, *Joseph E. Johnston: A Civil War Biography* (New York: W. W. Norton, 1992), 380–381. Participants and historians have argued ever since about whether the war could have been ended there. Not everyone agrees with Sherman's assessment that McPherson fumbled away an opportunity to end the war almost a year before Appomattox. Typically, Alabama's Lost Cause historians responded by ignoring a debate that endured for over a century among scholars and Civil War enthusiasts. Rather than put the First Alabama at the center of a pivotal event, they devoted thousands of words to pretending that Streight's Raid and Emma Sansom's Ride had anything to do with the outcome of the war. Given the serious scholarly debate over the incident, the Alabama blackout seems indefensible. The expert revisionist historian Christopher M. Rein told me this is the kind of irresolvable what-if retired generals like to argue about in print, as Sherman and his foe Joseph Johnston did until 1891, when Johnston died of pneumonia after standing in freezing rain at Sherman's funeral. I think the evidence supports Sherman's heartbroken conclusion that McPherson blew the chance of a lifetime. For varying viewpoints, see William Tecumseh Sherman, *Memoirs* (New York: D. Appleton & Company, 1875), 409–410; Stanley P. Hirshson, *Grenville M. Dodge: Soldier, Politician, Railroad Pioneer* (Bloomington, IN: Indiana University Press, 1967), 93–95; James Patrick Morgans, *Grenville Mellon Dodge in the Civil War* (Jefferson, NC, 2016).

102 **"wholly unprotected"** Col. W. P. C. Breckinridge, "The Opening of the Atlanta Campaign," in *Battles and Leaders of the Civil War, Vol. IV,* edited by Robert Underwood and Clarence Clough Buel (New York: The Century Co, 1884), 278.

102 **"if the fifteen thousand men"** Dodge, *Personal Recollections,* 146–147.

102 **"Well, Mac, you have missed the great opportunity"** O'Connell, *Fierce Patriot,* 137. See also Lewis, *Sherman: Fighting Prophet,* 357, for Sherman's remark to McPherson and how he covered for his favorite in "reports to Washington."

103 **"McPherson had startled"** Sherman, *Memoirs,* 409–410.

Chapter 9: Quoth the General

104 **Major General Will Hill Tankersley** Tony Horwitz, *Confederates in the Attic: Dispatches from the Unfinished War* (New York: Pantheon Books, 1998), 359–369; Will Hill Tankersley obituary, *Montgomery Advertiser,* November 29, 2015, https://www.legacy.com/us/obituaries/montgomeryadvertiser/name/will-tankersley-obituary?id=16503228.

105 **"Tankersley's balanced"** Horowitz, *Confederates in the Attic,* 358–359.

107 **the *Montgomery Independent*** Tom Johnson, "Kindly Bend, if You Will," *Montgomery Independent,* October 16, 1990.

108 **"Limousine Liberals"** Will Hill Tankersley, "Limousine Liberals Take Unfair Shots at Gov. Hunt," *Montgomery Advertiser,* December 9, 1990; H. Brandt Ayres, "Alabama 'Parliament' Has Had No Prime Ministers," *Montgomery Advertiser,* December 2, 1990, 3D.

109 **Scots-Irish settlers** David Hackett Fischer, *Albion's Seed: Four British Folkways in America* (New York: Oxford University Press, 1989), 659.

109 **"the archetypical back"** Ibid., 643.

110 **the tight inner circle of Winston politics** Donald Dodd, *Alabama Now and Then: A Contemporary Look* (Montgomery, AL: Advertiser Company, 1994), 165–166; author interview with Donald Dodd, April 8, 2019. As an example of the enduring cohesion of Winston families who guard its history, Donald Dodd told me that Sam L. Weaver (1925–2000), the judge's last surviving son, was Dodd's scoutmaster in the 1950s. Sam Weaver, in turn, gave his father's historical papers to Winston scholar Susan Dealey-Swearingen for her University of New Hampshire dissertation because her parents had Winston relatives. She showed up for a prearranged meeting with Sam Weaver the day after he died. His family conducted a wake in the living room while Dealey-Swearingen examined the collection in his bedroom.

110 **Wesley S. Thompson's piggybacking on Judge Weaver's work** Donald Dodd in a letter to the author dated June 17, 2020: "Local conventional wisdom is that most of Thompson's sources for *Tories of the Hills* came from Judge Weaver." He added, "The specific atrocities related by Thompson were apparently embellishmens of passed-down stories by John Bennett Weaver and others. I doubt that Thompson examined any of the papers by the three Civil War governors of Alabama—Moore, Shorter and Watts—or ever learned how to use the *Official Records of the War of the Rebellion.*" Thompson, a minister, used his Church of Christ contacts in the Auburn University administration to obtain a photocopy of Dodd's master's thesis for use in his nonfiction history of Winston County published in 1968. The timing lends credence to Dodd's account. In a rare nod to attribution, Thompson said in his foreword that he had learned in 1967 that

Dodd was working on a new history of Winston County for his master's thesis at Auburn. The distinctively Alabama connectivity doesn't end there. The late Carl Elliott, the former congressman who published Dodd's history of Winston County in 1972, told Dodd that he had refused a bid by Thompson to be listed as a co-author of Dodd's book because he knew that the minister had cribbed from the master's thesis. As a service to the general reader, I resisted the temptation to explore deeply the proprietary attitudes of Winston historians in the main text, but footnote it here as another example of how the past penetrates the present in Carmer's "strange country."

Chapter 10: Open Season in the Hill Country

113 **Hiram Raines (1829-1914) was "lying out"** Testimony of Hiram Raines to the Southern Claims Commission, January 25, 1872. Hiram testified he "was kept lying out a large portion of the time during the Rebellion." He told the commission agents who came to Jasper to gather testimony that Hiel Abbott kept a "canoe in the Sipsey River, that he has seen claimant ferrying Union men across said river" thereby "keeping [them] from being arrested & conscripted in the Rebel army." Hiram said he had heard his father-in-law threatened with hanging as "a damned old Lincolnite."

113 **As a stronghold** Joel S. Mize, *Unionists of the Warrior Mountains of Alabama* (Lakewood, CO, 2004–2005), 7.

113 **A pod of Unionists** If I have any claim to original scholarship, it may be defining the parameters of the cluster of Unionist families in northern Winston County and central Walker County. That was made possible by two remarkably detailed collections of maps and land records. They are Gregory A. Boyd, *Family Maps of Winston County, Alabama, Deluxe Edition: With Homesteads, Roads, Waterways, Towns, Cemeteries, Railroads and More* (Norman, OK, 2008) and Gregory A. Boyd, *Family Maps of Walker County, Alabama, Deluxe Edition: With Homesteads, Roads, Waterways, Towns, Cemeteries, Railroads and More* (Norman, OK, 2007). I am also indebted to Joel S. Mize for his two-volume set, *Unionists of the Warrior Mountains of Alabama.* Also essential to the genealogical aspect of this research was a four-volume set assembled by the tireless Glenda McWhirter Todd, *Unionists in the Heart of Dixie: 1st Alabama Cavalry, USA* (Westminster, MD: Heritage Books, 2012–2015). As for reconstructing the lives of my Abbott, Best, Barton, Key, and Raines ancestors and collateral kin, the publications of Robin Sterling, a collector of historical north Alabama newspapers, have been invaluable, especially *People and Things from the Walker County, Alabama Mountain Eagle (1884-1897)* (2013). I am indebted to these works collectively for giving me access to a depth of authoritative documentation without which this book could not have been created. I was more fortunate than many in the stories and family records I inherited, but these works showed me how much had been lost. As products of boutique publishing operations, they were expensive, but worth many times what I paid.

114 **Hiram's older brother, Allen Raines** My great uncle Allen Raines was a member of Company L, 28th Alabama Infantry Regiment, CSA, who died in a military hospital in Macon, Georgia, April 28, 1864.

114 **Winston resident James B. Bell** Donald B. Dodd and Wynelle S. Dodd, *Winston: An Antebellum and Civil War History of a Hill County of North Alabama* (Jasper, AL: Annals of Northwest Alabama, 1972), 78–80. See also Hugh Bailey, "Disloyalty in Early Confederate Alabama," *Journal of Alabama History* 23

(1957). This was the most anti-Confederate document preserved in the Alabama archives, and one of the few. It was sent to Governor Shorter in the hope that he would arrest Bell as a traitor. This was another case in which the governors' letter boxes reserved essential documents of the movement they wished to erase.

116 **reference to a "Mr. Raines"** John Martin Dombhart, *History of Walker County, Alabama: Its Towns and People* (1937), 74. This phrase from the Moses Barton family tree unlocked the Walker County Unionist pod for me: "Milley Barton, who married a Mr. Raines." For years, I had been looking for a man my father remembered as "old man Jimmy Raines" or "the Old Italian" because of family rumors that he spoke with an accent. The clue led me to the grave of Millia Rains, a turning point in my research. Following Dombhart's clue about Millia marrying "a Mr. Raines," I found that the husband's given name was "James"— the elusive "old man Jimmy Raines," who had been a missing link in our family tree.

117 **"The Alabama tory"** Walter L. Fleming, *Civil War and Reconstruction in Alabama* (New York: The Columbia University Press, 1905), 114.

117 **lawless "hillbillies"** William Stanley Hoole, *Alabama Tories: The First Alabama Cavalry, U.S.A., 1862–1865* (Tuscaloosa, AL: Confederate Publishing Company, 1960), 6.

118 **Forming "themselves into bands"** William Stanley Hoole, *Alabama Tories: The First Alabama Cavalry, U.S.A., 1862–1865* (Tuscaloosa, AL: Confederate Publishing Company, 1960), 6.

Chapter 11: A Revolving Spy

119 **Confederate secretary of war LeRoy Pope Walker** Daniel E. Sutherland, *A Savage Conflict: The Decisive Role of Guerrillas in the American Civil War* (Chapel Hill, NC: The University of North Carolina Press, 2009), 27.

119 **Jefferson Davis was tempted** Ibid., 54.

120 **"any citizen declaring himself in favor"** Donald B. Dodd and Wynelle S. Dodd, *Winston: An Antebellum and Civil War History of a Hill County in North Alabama* (Jasper, AL: Annals of Northwest Alabama, 1972), 82.

120 **Confederate captain H. A. M. Henderson** Ibid., 90.

122 **Goldthwaite's April 9 letter** Ibid.

125 **Goldthwaite (1809–1879) was born** Elbert W. Watson, "George Goldthwaite," last updated August 8, 2022, *Encyclopedia of Alabama,* http://encyclopedia ofalabama.org/article/h-2968.

125 **The arc of the life of H. A. M. Henderson** Peter Cozzens, "Surviving a Confederate POW Camp," HistoryNet, January 26, 2011, 2, https://www.historynet .com/surviving-a-confederate-pow-camp/.

126 **"Isn't that horrid?"** William S. Williams, *The Ohio Repository,* July 31, 1861.

127 **The newcomer Henderson married** H. A. M. Henderson obituary, *Bourbon News,* January 5, 1912.

127 **About 70 of Marengo's 24,409 slaves** Alabama Department of Archives and History, 1850 Slave Schedule for Marengo County, AL.

127 **"a relative of Jefferson Davis"** The Papers of Jefferson Davis, Rice University, https://jeffersondavis.rice.edu/about-jefferson-davis/genealogy-davis-family; see also Ancestry.com, https://www.ancestry.com/family-tree/tee/10219472/ family?cfpid=-677191633&fpid=340122060220&usePUBJs=true.

128 **Henderson's "humanity"** Cozzens, "Surviving a Confederate POW Camp."

128 **six-week search at the ADAH** Dodd interview, April 8, 2019.

129 **Brigadier General Napoleon J. T. Dana** Peter Cozzens, "Surviving a Confederate POW Camp," HistoryNet.com, https://www.historynet.com/surviving-a -confederate-pow-camp.htm, 14–15.

Chapter 12: The Tattler of the Hills

131 **"Southern Gentlemen"** D. R. Hundley, *Social Relations in Our Southern States* (New York: Henry B. Price, 1860), 7, 163.

132 **Chambersburg** For Early's demand, Jubal A. Early, *A Memoir of the Last Year of the War for Independence in the Confederate States of America, Containing an Account of the Operations of His Commands in the Years 1864 and 1865* (New Orleans: Bielock & Co., 1867), 66–70.

132 **Kaeiser bought forty acres** Gregory Alan Boyd, *Family Maps of Winston County, Alabama, Deluxe Edition: With Homesteads, Roads, Waterways, Towns, Cemeteries, Railroads and More* (Norman, OK: Arphax Publishing Company, 2008). For Scots-Irish migration and land preferences, see James G. Leyburn, *The Scotch-Irish: A Social History* (Chapel Hill, NC: The University of North Carolina Press, 1962), especially 196–200. See also James Webb, *Born Fighting: How the Scots-Irish Shaped America* (New York: Broadway Books, 2004), especially 131–173 in regard to how its culture of "preachers and warriors" filtered south from Pennsylvania to influence the South and the Confederacy. For land prices, see Donald B. Dodd and Wynelle S. Dodd, *Winston: An Antebellum and Civil War History of a Hill County in North Alabama* (Jasper, AL: Annals of Northwest Alabama, 1972), 30.

133 **"robbers and plunderers"** Daniel E. Sutherland, *A Savage Conflict: The Decisive Role of Guerrillas in the American Civil War* (Chapel Hill, NC: The University of North Carolina Press, 2009), 92.

134 **Based on his surviving letters, Dr. Andrew Kaeiser** Dodd, *Winston;* John Bennett Weaver, *A Brief History of Winston County, Alabama,* Winston County, Alabama: An Historical Online Database, http://www.freestateofwinston.org/ abriefhistory.htm; Wesley S. Thompson, *"The Free State of Winston": A History of Winston County, Alabama* (Winfield, AL, 1968); Charles Rice, *Hard Times: The Civil War in Huntsville and North Alabama, 1861–1865* (Huntsville, AL: Old Huntsville, 1995).

134 **"All persons desiring"** Dodd, *Winston,* 83.

135 **" 'First, all that want' "** John R. Phillips, *The Story of My Life* (Tuscaloosa, AL: 1923), 50.

135 **"Rebel citizens blamed"** Sutherland, *A Savage Conflict,* x.

135 **"driven from the Winston"** Dodd, *Winston,* 104.

136 **"8,000 to 10,000 deserters"** Dodd, *Winston,* 114; William Stanley Hoole, *Alabama Tories: The First Alabama Cavalry, U.S.A., 1862–1865* (Tuscaloosa, AL: Confederate Publishing Company, 1960), 6; Christopher Lyle McIlwain, *Civil War Alabama* (Tuscaloosa, AL: The University of Alabama Press, 2016), 126.

137 **Dr. P. C. Winn** For Winn's letters, see Milo Howard, "A. B. Moore Correspondence Relating to Secession," *Alabama Historical Quarterly* 23 (Fall–Winter 1961), 278–284; Dodd, *Winston,* 83–84.

138 **his wife divorced him** For Winn's legal difficulties and the rape allegation, see the Race & Slavery Petitions Project, University of North Carolina at Charlotte,

"Petition 20186029 Details," December 27, 1860, http://s-libweb2.uncg.edu/slavery/petitions/details.aspx?pid+3537.

138 **"Anyone who had"** James Dodd Manasco, *Walking Sipsey: The People, Places, and Wildlife* (Danville, AL: Lawrence County Schools' Indian Education Program, 1992), 41–42.

138 **"So Kaeiser did his civic duty"** Ibid., 41–42.

Chapter 13: In the Unionist Pod

140 **James Hiel Abbott** Larry Abbott's *The Abbott Newsletter* is a carefully researched website that has been run since 1987 by a distant cousin of mine living in Texas. Here I discovered the basic information about my direct forebears James Hiel Abbott and Jane Mills Key Abbott. To fill in missing pieces of my family tree, I relied on the expertise and generosity of two accomplished genealogists, Melissa Folsom Boyen of Honolulu, Hawaii, the daughter of former governor James E. Folsom of Alabama, and Judy Culbreth, a magazine editor and writer living in Fairhope, Alabama. I have mined *The Abbott Newsletter* for most of the details in this chapter.

141 **John Martin Dombhart's *History of Walker County*** Without this book, I would never have found James Raines and Millia Raines, my link to both the Abbott and Barton stories. Its existence represents to me the frail links of happenstance essential to reconstructing obscure histories. Congressman Carl Elliott, my Walker grandfather's political ally, met Dombhart by chance at the Jasper courthouse and decided to keep his book in print through his money-losing boutique publishing company. Although an outsider, Dombhart preserved pioneer lore and family histories that are preserved nowhere else.

144 **But Wesley Abbott** Wesley Abbott obituary, *Cullman Democrat,* October 7, 1915.

145 **bloody, ritualized slashing contests** Shearan Abbott's knife-fighting memories appeared in issues 2 (August 31, 1988) and 9 (January 17, 1992) of *The Abbott Newsletter.* For the death of Copeland Abbott and the trial of his assailants, see the Jasper *Mountain Eagle,* March 15, 1893, September 6, 1893, and September 13, 1893.

147 **"best underground railroad"** Frank Moore, *Anecdotes, Poetry and Incidents of the War: North and South, 1860–1865* (New York, 1866), 216.

147 **Hiel Abbott's involvement in smuggling would-be soldiers** Testimony of Hiel Abbott, Hiram Raines, and Jerry O'Rear about Hiel Abbott's hidden canoe and its use to transport Union recruits and soldiers, January 25, 1872, Southern Claims Commission, in *Southern Loyalists in the Civil War: The Southern Claims Commission* (Baltimore, 1994), Gary B. Mills, ed., 3.

149 **Israel Pickens Abbott** For his service record, see Glenda McWhirter Todd, *Unionists in the Heart of Dixie: 1st Alabama Cavalry, USA* (Westminster, MD: Heritage Books, 2012–2015), 47.

Chapter 14: Cotton Thieves and Draft Dodgers

153 **"Ol' Stars"** Phineas Campbell Headley, *Old Stars: The Life and Military Career of Major-General Ormsby M. Mitchel* (Boston, 1883); F. A. Mitchel, *Ormsby MacKnight Mitchel, Astronomer and General: A Biographical Narrative* (Boston, 1887); Christopher Lyle McIlwain, *Civil War Alabama* (Tuscaloosa, AL: The University of Alabama Press, 2016), 81–83.

156 **Bruce Catton** Bruce Catton, *This Hallowed Ground: A History of the Civil War* (New York: Doubleday, 1956), 145–146.

156 **"Mitchel was a voice"** Ibid., 145.

157 **fomented by Chris Sheats and Jeremiah Clemens** McIlwain, *Civil War Alabama*, 84.

157 **"for novelists, dramatists"** Catton, *This Hallowed Ground,* 146.

158 **Halleck and Buell hated Mitchel** Stephen E. Engle, *Don Carlos Buell: Most Promising of All* (Chapel Hill, 1999), 266; Ohio Civil War website, https://www .ohiocivilwarcentral.com/ormsby-macknight-mitchel/.

158 **"Your spirited operations"** Engle, *Don Carlos Buell,* 245.

158 **"a new era of generalship"** Mitchel, *Ormsby MacKnight Mitchel,* 288.

158 **"to eliminate"** Engle, *Don Carlos Buell,* 196.

159 **"the army's second most"** Ibid., 212.

159 **Mitchel's selling of cotton** Ibid., 243–246, 267. See also Stephen D. Engle, *Struggle for the Heartland: The Campaigns from Fort Henry to Corinth* (Lincoln, NE, 2001).

159 **"Such petty smuggling"** Robert Frank Futrell, "Trade with the Confederate States, 1861–1865: A Study of Government Policy," PhD dissertation, Vanderbilt University, 1950, 67–68.

161 **"temper her husband's vanity"** Sean E. Andrews, "Louisa Clark Trask Mitchel," https://queensofqueencity.com/2017/08/02/louisa-mitchel.

161 **"sale and transportation of cotton"** Mitchel, *Ormsby MacKnight Mitchel,* 328–329.

161 **Colonel Jesse Norton** William S. Williams, Ohio Repository, July 31, 1861, https://dan-masters-civil-war.blogspot.com/2018/05/a-scary-affair-at-scary-creek .html?m=1.

162 **"Col. Norton was a great favorite here"** Mary Jane Chadick, *Incidents of the War: The Civil War Journal of Mary Jane Chadick* (Silver Threads Publishing on Internet Archive, 2005), 51, 44–45.

162 **"first stopped at Louisville"** F. A. Mitchel, *Ormsby MacKnight Mitchel,* 354. The journalist Whitelaw Reid in *Ohio In the War: Her Statesmen, Her Generals, and Soldiers* (New York, 1868) made the essential point about Mitchel's coup at Huntsville: "Two years before Sherman he showed how armies might depend on single lines of railroad through great tracts of the enemy's country for supplies" (384).

163 **"you colored people"** Mitchel, *Ormsby MacKnight Mitchel,* 364.

163 **Mitchel died** Ibid., 65.

163 **"We have achieved"** "From General Mitchel's Division," *Cincinnati Daily Gazette,* April 23, 1862.

163 **"Marching south from Nashville"** Christopher M. Rein, *Alabamians in Blue: Freedmen, Unionists, and the Civil War in the Cotton State* (Baton Rouge, LA: Louisiana State University Press, 2019), 61–62.

164 **Alabama historian Charles Summersell** Charles Grayson Summersell, *Alabama History for Schools* (Birmingham, AL, 1957), 309.

164 **"His Russian ideas of the rules of war"** Walter L. Fleming, *Civil War and Reconstruction* (New York: The Columbia University Press, 1905), 63, 65.

Chapter 15: The Slave Owners' Friend

166 **Don Carlos Buell** This summary of Buell's career is based on Stephen E. Engle, *Don Carlos Buell: Most Promising of All* (Chapel Hill, NC, 1999).

169 **Brigadier General James Dada Morgan** For Morgan's appeal to Buell for troops, *OR*, Morgan to Buell, July 28, 1862, https://ehistory.osu.edu/books/official -records/023/0223; for Buell's response, see Christopher Lyle McIlwain, *Civil War Alabama* (Tuscaloosa, AL: The University of Alabama Press, 2016), 95.

170 **"Rock of Chickamauga"** William Stanley Hoole, *Alabama Tories: The First Alabama Cavalry, U.S.A., 1862–1865* (Tuscaloosa, AL: Confederate Publishing Company, 1960), 20–21.

171 **"The volunteers from Alabama"** Don Carlos Buell, "Operations in North Alabama," in *Battles and Leaders of the Civil War*, edited by Robert U. Johnson and Clarence C. Buell (New York, 1884), II:701–708; *Official Records*, 1, XVI (2), 182.

171 **"vertebrae of the Confederacy"** McIlwain, *Civil War Alabama*, 73.

171 **"not competent to criticize your views"** Engel, *Don Carlos Buell*, 136.

172 **"commendable energy"** William Tecumseh Sherman, "Papers Accompanying the Report of the General-in-Chief. Report of Lieutenant General W. T. Sherman.," November 1, 1868 (St. Louis, MO), https://freepages.rootsweb.com/ ~familyinformation/history/transcripts/sec_war_1868_rpt.pdf.

172 **Grant's letters show that he had been thinking** Ulysses S. Grant, *Personal Memoirs of U.S. Grant / Selected Letters, 1839–1865* (New York: Library of America, 1990), 1040–1042.

173 **"Battle Above the Clouds"** David Powell, *Battle Above the Clouds: Lifting the Siege of Chattanooga and the Battle of Lookout Mountain, October 16–November 24, 1863* (El Dorado Hills, CA, 2017).

173 **"surrender was never made"** Andrew Lytle, *Bedford Forrest and His Critter Company* (Nashville, TN: J. S. Sanders & Company, 1931), 276.

174 **In 1862 Lincoln finally sacked Buell** William M. Lamers, *The Edge of Glory: A Biography of General William S. Rosecrans, U.S.A.* (New York: Harcourt, Brace, 1961), 391–394.

175 **"Old Rosey"** Lamers, *Edge of Glory*.

Chapter 16: Chris Sheats in the Wilderness

177 **"Although most Southerners"** Thomas Goodrich, "Guerilla Warfare," *Encyclopedia of the Confederacy* (New York, 1993), 720.

178 **Streight's Raid** Robert L. Willett, *The Lightning Mule Brigade: Abel Streight's 1863 Raid into Alabama* (New York: Guild Press, 1999); Brandon H. Beck, *Streight's Foiled Raid on the Western & Atlantic Railroad: Emma Sansom's Courage and Nathan Bedford Forrest's Pursuit* (Charleston, SC: History Press, 2016).

178 **William Wiley Sheats** *Cullman Tribune*, August 23, 1894; obituary at https:// www.findagrave.com/memorial/11171223/william-wiley-sheats.

179 **Sheats's biographer** Martine G. Bates, *Chris Sheats: The Man Who Refused to Secede* (Hartselle, AL: Seacoast Publishing, Inc., 2004), 37.

179 **"vote against Secession"** Weaver, "A Brief History of Winston County Alabama," http://www.freestateofwinston.org/abriefhistory.htm, 4.

180 **"a great stump speaker"** T. A. Deland and A. Davis Smith, *Northern Alabama, Historical and Biographical Illustrated* (Birmingham, 1888), 327; *OR*, I, XVI (1), 785–791; Donald B. Dodd and Wynelle S. Dodd, *Winston: An Antebellum and Civil War History of a Hill County of North Alabama* (Jasper, AL: Annals of Northwest Alabama, 1972), 87–89; John Bennett Weaver, *Fact and Fiction of the Free State of Winston* (Haleyville and Double Springs, AL, 1950).

181 **P. J. Gossett** P. J. Gossett email to the author, December 31, 2021.

181 **"'Payne money' has been in circulation"** Don Dodd, *Unionism in Confederate America* (Athens, GA: University of Georgia, 1969), 88–90.

182 **"Defender of North Alabama"** Joshua Shiver, "Philip Dale Roddey," *Encyclopedia of Alabama,* last updated May 25, 2021, http://www.encyclopediaof alabama.org/article/h-4196. For the spectacular scandal that enveloped Roddey after the war, see "A Farce Ended," *New York Times,* July 22, 1874, 8, and Carlotta Frances Roddey, *A General Betrayal: The Sufferings and Trials of Carlotta Frances Roddey, Recently Indicted and Acquitted, in New York City, on the Charge of Stealing a Pair of Opera Glasses from Her Husband, Gen. P. D. Roddey, 1878* (Bellevue, WA, 2017).

182 **"I wish to say a word"** Colonel Abel D. Streight, *OR,* I, XVI (1), 789.

183 **Chris Sheats came limping into camp** Frank Moore, *The Civil War in Song and Story, 1860–1865* (New York, 1882), 215–217.

Chapter 17: A Murderous Conspiracy in the Whirling Hills

186 **semi-official Confederate murder plot** John Lucian West, "Sons of Solomon," in Charles E. Wilson, . . . *And West Is West: The Wests of Winston County, Their Kin and Kith* (Birmingham, AL, 1991), 30–44. This hard-to-find, privately published book is a key to the Curtis murders, written by a member of a related family.

187 **gave the speech that probably sealed his fate** Peter J. Gossett, "Free State Civil War Events and the Jasper Raid," http://www.freestateofwinston.org/jasperraid .htm, 3–5.

188 **"atrocious and systematic"** Daniel E. Sutherland, *A Savage Conflict: The Decisive Role of Guerrillas in the American Civil War* (Chapel Hill, NC: The University of North Carolina Press, 2009), 76.

188 **"Unionists believed that"** Daniel E. Sutherland, ed., *Guerrillas, Unionists, and Violence on the Confederate Home Front* (Fayettville, AR: The University of Arkansas Press, 1999), 12.

189 **Surviving documents leave no doubt** Christopher M. Rein, *Alabamians in Blue: Freedmen, Unionists, and the Civil War in the Cotton State* (Baton Rouge, LA: Louisiana State University Press, 2019), 70, for coordination of Shorter and Watts with the Confederate leaders in the field, including General Roddey and Capt. Dan Whatley, a terrorist "with increasing autonomy" for attacking Unionist households in Winston County; see also 98 for Shorter's attempt to have First Alabama Cavalry troops captured during Streight's Raid hanged as traitors. See Donald B. Dodd and Wynelle S. Dodd, *Winston: An Antebellum and Civil War History of a Hill County of North Alabama* (Jasper, AL: Annals of Northwest Alabama, 1972), 83–87, 98–101, and 102–105 on Shorter's correspondence about military operations against Unionists including the imprisoned Chris Sheats.

189 **a sociopathic torturer** Sue Spearman Abernathy, "'Old Stoke' Versus 'Old Stout,'" Winston County, Alabama: An Historical Online Database, http:// www.freestateofwinston.org/stokestout.htm.

189 **One of Roberts's specialties** Thompson, *The Free State of Winston,* 64–97; see also Wesley S. Thompson, *Tories of the Hills* (Winfield, AL: Christopher Pub. House, 1953), for fictionalized accounts of Roberts's torture techniques. And see Joel S. Mize, "The Agonizing Death of Henry Tucker," 1st Alabama Cavalry website, http://www.1stalabamacavalryusv.com/Roster/Stories .aspx?trooperid=2335.

190 **The first Curtis to die** West, "Sons of Solomon," 32; Dodd, *Winston*, 108; Gossett, "Free State," 5–6.

191 **The second child** West, "Sons of Solomon," 32–33; Dodd, *Winston*, 285; Gossett, "Free State," 6.

191 **About a month** West, "Sons of Solomon," 35–36; Dodd, *Winston*, 108–109; Gossett, "Free State," 6–7.

192 **James G. Curtis** Dodd, *Winston*, 107–108; West, "Sons of Solomon," 37–38.

192 **"civil war within"** Sean Michael O'Brien, *Mountain Partisans, Guerrilla Warfare in the Southern Appalachians 1861–1865* (Westport, CT: Praeger, 1999).

192 **The assassination of Tom Pink Curtis** Governor Thomas H. Watts Papers, Alabama Department of Archives and History, SG24872, Reel 20, and SG24884, Reel 4, as transcribed by Peter J. Gossett and Joann Holdbrooks.

193 **"Dear Sir; I have received information"** Watts letter to Lockhart, February 6, 1864, Watts Papers, ADAH.

194 **"Capt Whatley is not, nor ever has been"** Lockhart letter to Watts, February 9, 1864, Watts Papers, ADAH.

195 **"operated with increasing"** Rein, *Alabamians in Blue*, 70.

Chapter 18: Natural-Born Spies of the First Alabama

196 **General Buel Barton** "Gilford M. Barton," Geni, https://www.geni.com/people/Gilford-Barton/6000000009120906400t.

196 **The Barton family tree** Glenda McWhirter Todd, *Unionists in the Heart of Dixie: 1st Alabama Cavalry, USA* (Westminster, MD: Heritage Books, 2012–2015), 8–84. Five Barton brothers and three of their brothers-in-law from the Unionist pod in Walker County served in the First Alabama Cavalry. Other than the Abbotts, they are my closest familial link to the First Alabama. The five brothers are my collateral kin. They were the sons of Willis Barton (b. 1803), whose sister Millia Barton Raines (1802–1843) was my great-great-grandmother and therefore the aunt of these five First Alabama soldiers. The author's records include a voluminous genealogical file on the patriarch of this Unionist clan, Moses Barton Sr., who was the father of Willis and Millia, my great-great-uncle and great-great-grandmother, respectively. Many of these records were assembled by Peter J. Gossett for the Winston County Archive in Double Springs, Alabama. My links to the Bartons were researched by Judy Culbreth. As related earlier, Dombhart's *History of Walker County, Its Towns and Its People* (1937) was the key to my establishing these links.

197 **"Overlooked No More: 'Skipped History' Explores Forgotten Events"** Pierre-Antoine Louis, "Overlooked No More: 'Skipped History' Explores Forgotten Events," *New York Times*, July 17, 2021. For the *Times*'s review of Miles's book, see Jennifer Szalai, "In One Modest Cotton Sack, a Remarkable Story of Slavery, Suffering, Love and Survival," *New York Times*, June 9, 2021.

198 **435,080 slaves living in the state** 1860 census.

198 **"History is not the past"** Hilary Mantel, "Why I Became a Historical Novelist," *The Guardian*, June 3, 2017, www.theguardian.com/books/2017/jun/03/hilary-mantel-why-i-became-a-historical-novelist.

199 **"[A] close examination"** William Stanley Hoole, *Alabama Tories: The First Alabama Cavalry, U.S.A., 1862–1865* (Tuscaloosa, AL: Confederate Publishing Company, 1960), 14–15.

199 **"It had altogether proved"** Ibid., 32.

199 **Feis's exhaustive *Grant's Secret Service*** William B. Feis, *Grant's Secret Ser-*

vice: The Intelligence War from Belmont to Appomattox (Lincoln, NB: University of Nebraska Press, 2002).

200 **His definitive book** Edwin C. Fishel, *The Secret War for the Union: The Untold Story of Military Intelligence in the Civil War* (Boston: Mariner Books, 1996).

200 **E. D. Coe** Brent H. Ponsford, "Major-General Grenville M. Dodge's Military Intelligence Operations During the Civil War," master's thesis, Iowa State University, 1976.

201 **"network that . . . Dodge was then slowly extending"** John Bakeless, *Spies of the Confederacy* (New York, 1970), 202.

201 **"send a spy to Meridian"** Dodge, Grenville M., 1831–1916, "Biography of Major General Grenville M. Dodge from 1831 to 1871. (copy)," Council Bluffs Public Library, https://www.councilbluffslibrary.org/archive/items/show/2532.

203 **Dodge's network of spies** Ponsford, "Major-General Grenville M. Dodge's Military Intelligence Operations During the Civil War," 108.

203 **Philip Henson** George Sibley Johns, *Philip Henson, the Southern Union Spy: The Hitherto Unwritten Record of A Hero of the War of the Rebellion* (St. Louis, 1887); Harnett T. Kane, *Spies for the Blue and the Gray* (New York, 1954), 207–211; Stanley P. Hirshson, *Grenville M. Dodge: Soldier, Politician, Railroad Pioneer* (Bloomington, IN: Indiana University Press, 1967), 69, 74. For John's comments on Henson's close connection with the First Alabama: "General Dodge and his adjutant, Capt. G. E. Spencer, had a private and serious conversation with Col. Henson on the risk and importance of his position," 35.

205 **"nothing was more important"** Hirshson, *Grenville M. Dodge,* 31.

206 **Adaptability was a cardinal trait** Ibid., especially 67–69 for how he invented spying techniques that were more effective than the traditional cavalry tactic of "reconnaissance in force," thus earning Grant's confidence.

206 **At Thetford** Ibid., 9.

207 **Sam Davis** Ibid., 81–84. Dodge's regretful decision to hang Davis made the charismatic Rebel spy into an enduring Confederate folk hero.

207 **a reward from a grateful president** Ibid., especially 84–85 for Lincoln's acquiescence in sweetheart financing for the Union Pacific as a favor to Dodge that would seem corrupt by modern standards, but was typical of the age and its robber baron ethos. For the meeting in which Dodge and Lincoln shared their dream of a transcontinental railroad, see 30–31. For Dodge's pursuit of Lincoln's patronage at the White House, see 42–45. Neither man could have foreseen that Dodge, an amateur "political general," would prove himself as the "Father of U.S. Army Intelligence."

Chapter 19: The First Fights of the Fighting First

208 **"The regiment fought well"** William Warren Rogers et al., *Alabama: The History of a Deep South State* (Tuscaloosa, AL: The University of Alabama Press, 1994), 197. The statement marked a major departure from the accounts of military irrelevance or lack of impact injected into Alabama histories by Walter L. Fleming, Wesley S. Thompson, and especially William Stanley Hoole.

209 **Alabama Unionists faded from memory** Virginia Van der Veer Hamilton, *Alabama: A History* (New York, 1977), 24–30.

210 **The New York Times, in its war digest** *New York Times,* August 15, 1963.

210 **Westering Man** Bil Gilbert, *Westering Man: The Life of Joseph Walker* (Norman, OK, 1985), 20–24. Although much of his work appeared in *Sports Illustrated* and he was a Michigander, Gilbert (1927–2012) had an intuitive feel for

the impact of the Scots-Irish on the combative southern temperament. The four-page mini-essay from which these quotes are drawn is a masterpiece of historical analysis.

212 **Hurlbut wrote** Hurlbut to Grant, *OR*, 1, XXX (4), 118–119.

212 **"And I want you to understand"** Stanley P. Hirshson, *Grenville M. Dodge: Soldier, Politician, Railroad Pioneer* (Bloomington, IN: Indiana University Press, 1967), 64.

212 **In his new command, Dodge quickly added** Glenda McWhirter Todd, *First Alabama Cavalry, U.S.A.: Homage to Patriotism* (Bowie, MD: Heritage Books, 1999), "Regimental History," 9–12.

213 **Battle of Stone's River** Christopher M. Rein, *Alabamians in Blue: Freedmen, Unionists, and the Civil War in the Cotton State* (Baton Rouge, LA: Louisiana State University Press, 2019), 87; Edwin C. Bearss, "Cavalry Operations in the Battle of Stones River," *Tennessee Historical Quarterly* 19, no. 2 (June 1960), 134.

214 **"Jackass Cavalry"** "Spring, 1863, Forrest Halts Yankee Raiders," *Alabama Heritage,* April 25, 2013, https://www.alabamaheritage.com/civil-war-era/spring -1863-forrest-halts-yankee-raiders.

214 **"to cut the railroads"** Brigadier General James A. Garfield, quoted in "Colonel Streight's Raid," in *Alabama Confederate Reader,* edited by Malcolm Cook McMillan (Tuscaloosa, 1963), 186.

215 **Dr. John Allan Wyeth** "Colonel Streight's Raid," in *Alabama Confederate Reader,* 188–189.

215 **"fought six successful engagements"** Hirshson, *Grenville M. Dodge,* 73.

216 **getting high grades** For Morgan L. Smith's commendation, see Rein, *Alabamians in Blue,* 159; for Sherman on Smith, see https://theodora.com/encyclopedia/ s2/morgan_lewis_smith.html.

216 **"Colonel Cornyn, hearing"** Hoole, *Alabama Tories,* 26–29.

218 **Dodge never lost faith** Terry L. Seip, "Of Ambition and Enterprise; the Making of Carpetbagger George E. Spencer," in Kenneth W. Noe, ed., *The Yellowhammer War: The Civil War and Reconstruction in Alabama* (Tuscaloosa, AL: The University of Alabama Press, 2013), 200–201.

218 **"I have succeeded in effectually destroying"** Brigadier General Samuel W. Ferguson, CSA, report on Battle of Vincent's Crossroads, October 31, 1863, https://www.mycivilwar.com/battles/631026.html.

219 **"It looked more like an immigrant train"** "Diary of Wayland Dunn," in Todd, *First Alabama Cavalry, U.S.A.,* 108.

219 **A clue to what Dodge thought of Cornyn's leadership** For battle reports on the strain developing between Dodge and the hot-tempered Cornyn's "injudicious" actions, see Todd, *First Alabama Cavalry, U.S.A.,* 27–31, 41–48. Notably, Cornyn's report of May 16, 1863, is the only one that ever questioned the fighting ability of the First Alabama Cavalry. Significantly, in *Alabama Tories,* William Stanley Hoole made it the centerpiece of his contention that the First Alabama had made a "disastrous" military debut in its "first brief but inglorious foray." Hoole did concede that the First was ordered to make its initial charge with unloaded guns, but he implied that Dodge was being overly sympathetic and he agreed with Cornyn that the Alabamians were "half-hearted comrades," 27.

219 **Bowen pulled his pistol and shot Cornyn dead** "Corinth MS—Court Martial and Murder of Colonel Francis Cornyn 10th Missouri Cavalry," posted by

lelliott19, January 17, 2015, Civil War Talk (website), https://civilwartalk.com/threads/corinth-ms-court-martial-and-murder-of-colonel-francis-cornyn-10th-missouri-cavalry.108468/.

220 **Morgan was an honorary pallbearer** John E. Marszalek, *Sherman: A Soldier's Passion for Order* (New York: Free Press, 1993), 496.

Chapter 20: Partners: A Meeting of the Minds

221 **when Spencer "charmed" Confederate pickets** Stanley P. Hirshson, *Grenville M. Dodge: Soldier, Politician, Railroad Pioneer* (Bloomington, IN: Indiana University Press, 1967), 71, 76–77.

224 **"To ascertain what enemy I would have to meet"** Grenville M. Dodge, *The Battle of Atlanta and Other Campaigns, Addresses, Etc.* (Council Bluffs, IA: The Monarch Printing Company, 1911), 113–114.

226 **"Generally, Confederate president Jefferson Davis looked"** Philip Leigh, *Trading with the Enemy* (Yardley, PA, 2014), xiii.

226 **Major General Ben Butler** Christopher Pena, *General Butler, Beast or Patriot* (Bloomington, IN, 2003), xviii.

226 **"he had made a fortune smuggling contraband cotton"** "The Transcontinental Railroad," *American Experience*, PBS, https://www.pbs.org/wgbh/americanexperience/features/tcrr-durant/.

227 **"I am d——d tired of it"** Terry L. Seip, "Of Ambition and Enterprise; the Making of Carpetbagger George E. Spencer," in Kenneth W. Noe, ed., *The Yellowhammer War: The Civil War and Reconstruction in Alabama* (Tuscaloosa, AL: The University of Alabama Press, 2013), 195–196.

228 **"Halleck runs the machine"** Ibid., 197.

228 **an even more audacious cotton thief** Hirshson, *Grenville M. Dodge*, 128–129. For the scale of the Matamoros Cotton Ring, see James William Daddysman, "The Matamoros Trade, 1861–1865," thesis, West Virginia University, 1976, https://researchrepository.wvu.edu/etd/8705.

229 **"If we can get Smith"** For Spencer's most incriminating admissions about cotton trading, see Seip, "Of Ambition and Enterprise," in *The Yellowhammer War*, 209–210. For Sherman's suspicions of Chase's involvement in cotton corruption, see also William Tecumseh Sherman, *Memoirs* (New York: D. Appleton & Company, 1875), 244.

Chapter 21: In Praise of Amateur Historians

232 **"Several years ago"** Glenda McWhirter Todd, *First Alabama Cavalry, U.S.A.: Homage to Patriotism* (Bowie, MD: Heritage Books, 2006), v.

233 **her modest obituary** *Tullahoma News*, September 9, 2017.

234 **sixteen members of the First Alabama** 1st Alabama Cavalry (website), www.1stalabamacavalryusv.com; for Amos McKinney, "Private Amos McKinney Memorial Cemetery," Lest We Forget: African American Military History by Historian, Author, and Veteran Bennie McRae, Jr., http://lestweforget.hamptonu.edu/page.cfm?uuid=9FEC4CCF-AA31-A6C2-DC894993E0816F90.

234 **As Cash noted, Confederate soldiers** W. J. Cash, *Mind of the South* (New York: Alfred A. Knopf, 1941), 44.

236 **"Hard war" is an appropriate term** Christopher Lyle McIlwain, *Civil War Alabama* (Tuscaloosa, AL: The University of Alabama Press, 2016), 6–7.

236 **a pitiable First Alabama private** For Lincoln's comments on Johnston's death, which show how closely he followed news from the battlefields, see Stanley P. Hirshson, *Grenville M. Dodge: Soldier, Politician, Railroad Pioneer* (Bloomington, IN: Indiana University Press, 1967), 77.

237 **"The scene was solemn"** Christopher M. Rein, *Alabamians in Blue: Freedmen, Unionists, and the Civil War in the Cotton State* (Baton Rouge, LA: Louisiana State University Press, 2019), 11.

237 **"Mountain Tom" Clark** Wade Pruitt, *Bugger Saga: The Civil War Story of Guerilla and Bushwhacker Warfare in Lauderdale County, Alabama and Southern Middle Tennessee* (Columbia, TN, 1977).

238 **General Florence Cornyn—called "Carcajou"** Ibid., 85.

238 **"The loss to the Confederacy"** Ibid., 90.

239 **"One of the challenges"** Thomas Jefferson Cypert, *Tried Men and True or Union Life in Dixie,* edited and with an introduction by Margaret M. Storey (Tuscaloosa, AL: The University of Alabama Press, 2011), 11.

239 **"Perhaps the most wonderfully strange"** Ibid., 29.

240 **"Invading armies did not"** Pruitt, *Bugger Saga,* 85.

240 **Indeed, it's an intuitive leap** Ibid., 85. The works cited on the neglected war in the Alabama backcountry represent a remarkable harvest inspired by *Lincoln's Loyalists: Union Soldiers from the Confederacy,* Richard Nelson Current's breakthrough examination of southern Unionism (Boston, 1992). Because of the rhythm of doctoral studies, it often takes several decades for the full emergence of a scholarly trend. Some reviewers said in 1992 that Current had opened an untouched field of Civil War study, and that seems to be the case, judging from the flood of dissertations published by academic presses in subsequent decades. Notable works, including those already cited by Margaret L. Storey, include *Civil War Alabama* (Tuscaloosa, 2016) and *1865 Alabama* (Tuscaloosa, 2017), both by Christopher Lyle McManus Sr.; Michael W. Fitzgerald, *Reconstruction in Alabama: From Civil War to Redemption in the Cotton South* (Baton Rouge, LA: Louisiana State University Press, 2017); Christopher M. Rein, *Alabamians: Freedmen, Unionists, and the Civil War in the Cotton State* (Baton Rouge, LA: Louisiana State University Press, 2019); Clayton J. Butler, *True Blue: White Unionists in the Deep South During Civil War and Reconstruction* (Baton Rouge, 2022); Susan Deily-Swearingen, *Rebel Rebels: Race, Resistance, and Remembrance in the Free State of Winston* (Lexington, KY, 2022).

Chapter 22: Dr. Kaeiser Versus the Feudists

242 **a "semi-treasonable secret order—the 'Peace Society'"** Walter L. Fleming, *Civil War and Reconstruction* (New York: The Columbia University Press, 1905), 137–143.

243 **J. J. Giers** Ibid., 119, 147. Fleming established that Giers, a Union activist from Huntsville, began corresponding with Grant early in the war. For the best account of how he and the Peace Society eventually drew in a dejected General Roddey as a participant in peace negotiations, see Donald B. Dodd and Wynelle S. Dodd, *Winston: An Antebellum and Civil War History of a Hill County of North Alabama* (Jasper, AL: Annals of Northwest Alabama, 1972), 112–113, 117; *OR,* XLIX (1), 590–593, 659, 718.

244 **"All six [victims]"** Dodd, *Winston,* 108.

244 **Jefferson Davis's War Department** James J. Horgan, *Encyclopedia of the Confederacy* (New York, 1993), 315–316.

244 **Andrew Kaeiser** I am indebted to several remarkable documents for help in piecing together the rivalries, betrayals, and murders that figured in Kaeiser's career and last days. These include his daughter Mattie's eyewitness account of his murder, to be found at "Andrew Kaeiser," Winston County, Alabama: An Historical Online Database, http://www.freestateofwinston.org/kaeiserbio.htm; Peter J. Gossett's coverage of the Curtis and Kaeiser murders in "Free State Civil War Events and the Jasper Raid," http://www.history-sites.com/cgi-bin/ bbs62x/alcwmb/arch_config.pl?md=read;id=15627; John Lucian West, "Sons of Solomon," in Charles E. Wilson, . . . *And West Is West: The Wests of Winston County, Their Kin and Kith* (Birmingham, AL, 1991), 30-44, Donald Dodd's reconstruction of Kaeiser's correspondence with Confederate authorities and his account of the Brooks' families feudist activities is in Dodd, *Winston*, 299–300. And Jenny Brooks's connection to these events is at Rickey Butch Walker, "Jane (Aunt Jenny) Brooks Johnston Family of the Byler Road," 1995, Winston County, Alabama: An Historical Online Database, http://www.freestateof winston.org/auntjenny2.htm.

245 **"idiots of the lowest"** Christopher Lyle McIlwain, *Civil War Alabama* (Tuscaloosa, AL: The University of Alabama Press, 2016), 130.

245 **"Yahoos of North Alabama"** Ibid.

247 **"one of the most spectacular Unionist raids"** Sean Michael O'Brien, *Mountain Partisans: Guerrilla Warfare in the Southern Appalachians, 1861–1865* (Westport, CN: Praeger, 1999), 88–89.

249 **Frank Curtis's brother's 1910 account and the family lore** John Lucian West, "Sons of Solomon" in . . . *And West Is West*, 30-44.

250 **He is buried under a Union Army marker** www.findagrave.com/memorial/22051010/james-j-curtis.

250 **"The evening before he had left home"** "Outlaw Days in Old Itawamba County: Homeguard Leader, Deputy U.S. Marshal and Detective Stokley Roberts," *Itawamba History Review* (blog), June 1, 2007, https://itawambahistory .blogspot.com/2007/06/outlaw-days-in-old-itawamba-county.html.

Chapter 23: Meanwhile, Back at the War

252 **Official communications show that Grant was informed** For meetings, see Stanley P. Hirshson, *Grenville M. Dodge: Soldier, Politician, Railroad Pioneer* (Bloomington, IN: Indiana University Press, 1967); Terry L. Seip, "Of Ambition and Enterprise; the Making of Carpetbagger George E. Spencer," in Kenneth W. Noe, ed., *The Yellowhammer War: The Civil War and Reconstruction in Alabama* (Tuscaloosa, AL: The University of Alabama Press, 2013).

253 **"cut their teeth on"** Clayton J. Butler, *True Blue: White Unionists in the Deep South During the Civil War and Reconstruction* (Baton Rouge, LA: University of Louisiana Press, 2022).

253 **"villainous whelps"** Ibid., 17.

254 **"Boys got to Jayhawking"** Glenda McWhirter Todd, *First Alabama Cavalry, U.S.A.: Homage to Patriotism* (Westminster, MD: Heritage Books, 2006), 105.

254 **Hoole found that birthplaces were recorded** William Stanley Hoole, *Alabama Tories: The First Alabama Cavalry, U.S.A., 1862–1865* (Tuscaloosa, AL: Confederate Publishing Company, 1960), 16–18.

256 **"almost constantly engaged"** Todd, *First Alabama Cavalry, U.S.A.*, 25.

256 **"up a cliff so steep that it was not walking"** Ibid., 129.

257 **"Sherman was disappointed"** E. B. Long, *The Civil War Day by Day* (1864).

257 **"Sherman almost scored"** Robert L. O'Connell, *Fierce Patriot: The Tangled Lives of William Tecumseh Sherman* (New York: Random House, 2014), 137.

258 **Two decades later, Johnston was still seething** Joseph E. Johnston, "Opposing Sherman's Advance to Atlanta," in *Battles and Leaders of the Civil War, Vol. IV,* edited by Robert Underwood and Clarence Clough Buel (New York: The Century Co, 1884), 260.

258 **"General Sherman claims"** Ibid., 260–277.

258 **"One serious attack"** W. P. C. Breckinridge, "The Opening of the Atlanta Campaign," in *Battles and Leaders of the Civil War, Vol. IV,* edited by Robert Underwood and Clarence Clough Buel (New York: The Century Co, 1884), 277–281.

258 **"great fodder for the 'mem-wars'"** Christopher Rein to author, email, August 23, 2022.

259 **"General Dodge sent for the best company"** Wayland Dunn in Todd, *First Alabama Cavalry, U.S.A.,* 131.

261 **he almost immediately began plotting** Terry L. Seip, "Of Ambition and Enterprise; the Making of Carpetbagger George E. Spencer," in Kenneth W. Noe, ed., *The Yellowhammer War: The Civil War and Reconstruction in Alabama* (Tuscaloosa, AL: The University of Alabama Press, 2013), 204.

262 **"You have known for ten days"** Christopher M. Rein, *Alabamians in Blue: Freedmen, Unionists, and the Civil War in the Cotton State* (Baton Rouge, LA: Louisiana State University Press, 2019), 174.

262 **"the sick and helpless"** Hirshson, *Grenville M. Dodge,* 105.

262 **"Everywhere he took"** Ibid., 96.

263 **"It will be a physical impossibility"** Sherman, *Memoirs,* 519.

264 **"I reached Atlanta"** Ibid., 542.

264 **"For military purposes"** "The March to the Sea Historical Marker," georgiahistory.com.

264 **"Sherman left Atlanta at seven in the morning"** Burke Davis, *Sherman's March* (New York, 1980), 7–8.

265 **Chris Sheats may have been a witness** W. Steven Harrell, *The Unionist: A Novel of the Civil War* (Baltimore, MD, 2002), 425–426. For Sheats's testimony about his meeting with Snelling and their friendship after the war, see Veterans Administration, Organization Index to Pension Files of Veterans Who Served Between 1861 and 1900, RG 15, NARA, "Snelling, David R." No. 971,684.

Chapter 24: Paths of Glory and Obscurity

267 **"closed corporation"** mrlincolnandfriends.org.

267 **"Go, you God-damned inefficient political general"** Stanley P. Hirshson, *Grenville M. Dodge: Soldier, Politician, Railroad Pioneer* (Bloomington, IN: Indiana University Press, 1967), 102–103.

268 **"During the Civil War era"** Clayton J. Butler, *True Blue: White Unionists in the Deep South During the Civil War and Reconstruction* (Baton Rouge, LA: University of Louisiana Press, 2022), 5.

268 **"A common refrain of Blair's orders placed"** Ibid.

269 **"Colonel: The major-general commanding"** Terry L. Seip, "Of Ambition and Enterprise: The Making of Carpetbagger George E. Spencer," in Kenneth W. Noe, ed., *The Yellowhammer War: The Civil War and Reconstruction in Alabama* (Tuscaloosa, AL: The University of Alabama Press, 2013), 206.

270 **"went so far as to organize a detective force"** Joseph T. Glatthaar, *The March to the Sea and Beyond: Sherman's Troops in the Savannah and Carolinas Campaigns* (New York: New York University Press, 1985), 150.

270 **"Captured wagons, drawn by"** C. McKinley, "The March to the Sea: A View of the Exploit from the Defensive Side," *Philadelphia Weekly Times,* reprinted in the Carlisle, PA, *Valley Sentinel,* August 20, 1880.

270 **"I never ordered the burning of any dwelling"** Glatthaar, *The March to the Sea,* 53.

271 **"Members of the First Alabama"** Ibid., 147.

271 **"Sherman's headquarters would have done justice"** Burke Davis, *Sherman's March: The True Story of William T. Sherman's Infamous Campaign Through Georgia and the Carolinas* (New York: Random House, 1980).

271 **"With his large frame"** Horace T. Porter, *Campaigning with Grant* (New York, 1906), https://www.perseus.tufts.edu/hopper/text?doc=Perseus%3Atext%3A2001.05.0034%3Achapter%3D19.

271 **"He talked of the enemy"** Davis, *Sherman's March,* 5.

272 **"it's absolutely incredible"** William C. Carter, ed., *Conversations with Shelby Foote* (Jackson, MS: University Press of Mississippi, 1989), 110.

272 **"lean, hard army"** John E. Marszalek, *Sherman: A Soldier's Passion for Order* (New York: Free Press, 1993), 297.

272 **"stragglers . . . [who] are harder to control"** Henry Hitchcock, *Marching with Sherman: Passages from the Letters and Campaign Diaries of Henry Hitchcock, Major and Assistant Adjutant General of Volunteers, November 1864–May 1865,* edited by M. A. DeWolfe Howe (New Haven, CT: Yale University Press, 1927), 75.

273 **"I was not present at these frolics"** William Tecumseh Sherman, *Memoirs* (New York: D. Appleton & Company, 1875), 553.

273 **"Sherman's march across Georgia was the successful"** Marszalek, *Sherman,* 317.

273 **"C. C. Sheats was an unusually"** Butler, *True Blue,* 21.

274 **"The lieutenant commanding"** George Ward Nichols, "Wild Bill," *Harper's New Monthly Magazine,* February 1867.

275 **"Lieutenant Snelling, who commanded"** Sherman, *Memoirs,* 550.

277 **"constant association"** James C. Bonner, "David R. Snelling: A Story of Desertion and Defection in the Civil War," *The Georgia Review* 10, no. 3 (Fall 1956), 275–282.

277 **"All through this pine country"** Hitchcock, *Marching with Sherman,* 116.

278 **"My orderly was at hand"** Sherman, *Memoirs,* 549–550.

280 **"The First Alabama Cavalry drew its men"** Clayton Butler, "'Homemade Yankees': The First Alabama Union Cavalry," master's thesis, University of Virginia, https://libraetd.lib.virginia.edu/downloads/fq977v269?filename=1_Butler_Clayton_2019_MA.pdf, 7.

280 **This supports** Richard Nelson Current, *Lincoln's Loyalists: Union Soldiers from the Confederacy* (Boston: Northeastern University Press, 1992); Paul D. Escott, *After Secession: Jefferson Davis and the Failure of Confederate Nationalism* (Baton Rouge, LA: Louisiana State University Press, 1992).

280 **"The fact that"** Wesley S. Thompson, *"The Free State of Winston": A History of Winston County, Alabama* (Winfield, AL, 1968), 51.

Chapter 25: Uncle Billy and His Boys

282 **George Spencer visited Sherman's tent** Stanley P. Hirshson, *Grenville M. Dodge: Soldier, Politician, Railroad Pioneer* (Bloomington, IN: Indiana University Press, 1967), 108; "Sherman had treated Spencer with warmth and courtesy," 105. Spencer's guile was impressive as he cultivated Sherman and used his access to protect Dodge's interests from his rival and boasted of his manipulative bond with Sherman.

282 **"aim . . . was to whip"** Allan R. Millet and Peter Maslowski, *For the Common Defense: A Military History of the United States of America* (New York: The Free Press, 1994), 230.

282 **"I wish my friends"** William Tecumseh Sherman, *Memoirs* (New York: D. Appleton & Company, 1875), 5.

284 **"Campfire discussions"** Joseph T. Glatthaar, *The March to the Sea and Beyond: Sherman's Troops in the Savannah and Carolinas Campaigns* (New York: New York University Press, 1985), 42.

284 **"I wouldn't miss going"** Ibid., 44.

284 **as part of Blair's forward element** Terry L. Seip ("Of Ambition and Enterprise: The Making of Carpetbagger George E. Spencer," in Kenneth W. Noe, ed., *The Yellowhammer War: The Civil War and Reconstruction in Alabama* [Tuscaloosa, AL: The University of Alabama Press, 2013]) became the lead scholar in tracing the First Alabama's growing prominence as a spearpoint unit. Spencer "quickly won attention for his intelligence-gathering raids" (198); Dodge kept the First out front and "diligently reported their successes up the line to . . . Grant" (201); after their showing at Snake Creek Gap, they "led the way" and took "the advance" for Howard and Blair en route to Atlanta. "Being in front, of course, meant that Spencer's men were under orders to take control of . . . towns, ferries, bridges and railroad stations" (205). To Seip, the *Official Records* read far differently from his vantage point in the Stanford history department than it did to Hoole at the University of Alabama library or, years earlier, to Fleming at Dunning's side at Columbia.

284 **"As reported by Kilpatrick and Wheeler"** Glatthaar, *The March to the Sea*, 160.

285 **"a cavalry fight"** Ibid., 159.

285 **"I have found out"** Hirshson, *Grenville M. Dodge*, 108.

285 **"with a rock in each pocket"** Burke Davis, *Sherman's March: The True Story of William T. Sherman's Infamous Campaign Through Georgia and the Carolinas* (New York: Random House, 1980), 74.

286 **"He would only call a halt"** Michael David Kaplan, *David Frakes Day, Civil War Hero and Notorious Frontier Newspaperman* (Jefferson, NC: McFarland, 2011), 71–72.

286 **"On those occasions"** Ibid., 72.

287 **"On Nov. 24, 1864"** georgiahistory.com/ghmi_marker_updated/balls-ferry/.

287 **"The regiment's advancework"** Seip, "Of Ambition and Enterprise," 206.

287 **"I learned today from"** Henry Hitchcock, *Marching with Sherman: Passages from the Letters and Campaign Diaries of Henry Hitchcock, Major and Assistant Adjutant General of Volunteers, November 1864–May 1865*, edited by M. A. DeWolfe Howe (New Haven, CT: Yale University Press, 1927), 100.

288 **"This was not war, but murder"** Sherman, *Memoirs*, 556–557; Davis, *Sherman's March*, 95; Hitchcock, *Marching with Sherman*, 161–164.

291 **"In one case torpedoes"** Grenville M. Dodge, *The Battle of Atlanta and Other*

Campaigns, Addresses, Etc. (Council Bluffs, IA: The Monarch Printing Company, 1911), 179.

292 **"in recognition of its role"** Christopher M. Rein, *Alabamians in Blue: Freedmen, Unionists, and the Civil War in the Cotton State* (Baton Rouge, LA: Louisiana State University Press, 2019), 178.

292 **For Spencer, an annunciatory moment** Seip,"Of Ambition and Enterprise," 206. By this time, Spencer had received word that the cotton he had shipped from Tuscaloosa had reached New York, and he (and possibly Roddey) would count on $50,000. He boasted in a letter that Sherman and Blair had traveled at the rear of the First Alabama for 115 days. "[Sherman] took occasion yesterday to say to me that I had the best Cavalry Regiment he ever saw & has taken his escort from the Regiment." Even allowing for their commanders' habitual bragging, the First Alabama arrived in Savannah in the company of their Union's hero of the moment.

Chapter 26: Skedaddling Home

293 **Hiel Abbott was keeping his youngest son, Israel** Glenda McWhirter Todd, *Unionists in the Heart of Dixie: 1st Alabama Cavalry, USA* (Westminster, MD: Heritage Books, 2012–2015), 47. "He is buried in the Chattanooga National Cemetery with a Union tombstone."

294 **"Colonel Spencer alone"** Terry L. Seip, "Of Ambition and Enterprise: The Making of Carpetbagger George E. Spencer," in Kenneth W. Noe, ed., *The Yellowhammer War: The Civil War and Reconstruction in Alabama* (Tuscaloosa, AL: The University of Alabama Press, 2013), 207.

294 **"one of the most thorough"** Ibid.

297 **"In the cavalry camp"** William Stanley Hoole, *Alabama Tories: The First Alabama Cavalry, U.S.A., 1862–1865* (Tuscaloosa AL: Confederate Publishing Company, 1960), 46–47.

297 **"Only rarely in its three years"** Hoole, *Alabama Tories*, 15.

Chapter 27: Viral Tuscaloosa and the Aristocratic Fallacy

303 **It was a "civil religion"** For the "civil religion" analysis, see Charles Reagan Wilson, *Baptized in Blood: The Religion of the Lost Cause, 1865–1920* (Athens, GA: University of Georgia Press, 1980).

303 **Ryland Randolph** On Ryland Randolph's lineages and criminal life in Tuscaloosa, see Gladys J. Ward, "The Life of Ryland Randolph," master's thesis, University of Alabama, 1932; see also the obituary of Gladys J. Ward, *Montgomery Advertiser,* July 12, 2001, https://www.legacy.com/us/obituaries/montgomery advertiser/name/gladys-ward-obituary?pid=156031826. On Randolph's journalism and the impact of his famous Klan cartoon, see also G. Ward Hubbs, *Searching for Freedom After the Civil War: Klansman, Carpetbagger, Scalawag, and Freedman* (Tuscaloosa, AL: The University of Alabama Press, 2015). For Randolph as a principal source for Walter L. Fleming's pro-Klan writings, see Walter L. Fleming, *Civil War and Reconstruction* (New York: The Columbia University Press, 1905), viii, 612, 667, 668, 714. On Fleming's debt to Randolph and other conservatives, viii.

307 **"most notorious image"** Hubbs, *Searching for Freedom After the Civil War,* xiii.

307 **"The lynched images represent two educators"** "Klan Cartoon, 1868," *Ency-*

clopedia of Alabama, http://encyclopediaofalabama.org/ARTICLE/m-7128, accessed March 19, 2023.

307 **We know that the striking woodcut was carved** Fleming, *Civil War and Reconstruction,* 612–613.

308 **"turned it into the South's"** Hubbs, *Searching for Freedom After the Civil War,* xii.

309 **"thinking of writing him"** Fleming to Owen, ADAH, April 30, 1904.

309 **Finding Gladys J. Ward's master's thesis** Ward, "Life of Ryland Randolph."

309 **"No one was truer"** Ibid., 1.

310 **The verdict, which was puzzling** *New York Times,* August 6, 1868, 6.

311 **"Unfortunately, the Klan began"** Fleming, *Civil War and Reconstruction,* 668.

311 **"the head devil"** Ward, "Life of Ryland Randolph," 45.

313 **"the rule of Negrodom"** Hubbs, *Searching for Freedom After the Civil War,* 13–14.

315 **I was proud to be working for Buford Boone** E. Culpepper Clark, *The Schoolhouse Door: Segregation's Last Stand at the University of Alabama* (New York: Oxford University Press, 1993); on Buford Boone, 80, 95. Boone's front-page editorial of February 1956, "What a Price for Peace," urged admission of Autherine Lucy, a Black woman applying from Birmingham, and won a Pulitzer Prize; see *Tuscaloosa News,* February 7, 1956.

316 **Here's the evidentiary timeline** For a general chronology of civil rights violence, see Howell Raines, *My Soul Is Rested: Movement Days in the Deep South Remembered* (New York: G. P. Putnam's Sons, 1977), 7–8; for 1921 and 1934, see Carl Carmer, *Stars Fell on Alabama,* 184 and 27; for 1947 and 1948, see Spencer R. McCulloch, "Fighting Alabama Editor Stops the Klan," *St. Louis Post-Dispatch,* November 29, 1949; for 1956, see Clark, *The Schoolhouse Door,* 96; for 1963, see Diane McWhorter, *Carry Me Home: Birmingham, Alabama: the Climactic Battle of the Civil Rights Revolution;* for September 15, 1963, see Howell Raines, "The Birmingham Bombing," *New York Times Magazine,* July 23, 1983.

318 **the arch-Druid himself, Hudson Strode** For Hudson Strode and his relationship with the Jefferson Davis family, see Thomas J. Rountree, "Hudson Strode: The Legend and the Legacy," *Alabama English,* Spring 1990, 16–24; James P. Kaetz, "Hudson Strode," *The Encyclopedia of Alabama,* 2009, http://www.encyclopediaofalabama.org/face/Article.jsp?id=h-2485. I have also drawn on conversations with the late Harry Mabry (1932–2004), an Alabama broadcaster who was Strode's teaching assistant in the early 1950s.

Chapter 28: Bad Boys of Richmond

319 **In singling out Edward Alfred Pollard** Hudson Strode, *Jefferson Davis: Tragic Hero* (New York: Harcourt Brace, 1964); on Pollard's treatment of Davis, see 142, 142n, 143, 372, 525.

319 **"His hostility"** Jack P. Maddex, Jr., *The Reconstruction of Edward A. Pollard: A Rebel's Conversion to Postbellum Unionism* (Chapel Hill, NC: University of North Carolina Press, 1974), 36.

319 **"'imbecility of purpose'"** Ibid., 31.

320 **Pollard's biographer Jack P. Maddex** Maddex, *The Reconstruction of Edward A. Pollard.* I have relied on Maddex's chronology for the course of Pollard's career and political evolution.

321 **Thomas Nelson Page's** Thomas Nelson Page, *In Ole Virginia or Marse Chan and Other Stories* (New York: Charles Scribner's Sons, 1888).

323 **"He pursued"** Maddex, *The Reconstruction of Edward A. Pollard*, 4.
324 **"In the ante-revolutionary period"** Edward A. Pollard, *The Lost Cause: A New Southern History of the War of the Confederates* (New York: E. B. Treat & Co., 1867), 49–51.

Chapter 29: Lee's Bad Old Man

336 **"Old South rested on a tripod"** Rollin G. Osterweis, *Romanticism and Nationalism in the Old South* (New Haven, CT: Yale University Press, 1949), vii.
337 **"It was probably Grant"** Thomas P. Abernethy, *From Frontier to Plantation in Tennessee: A Study in Frontier Democracy* (Chapel Hill, NC: University of North Carolina Press, 1932), 219–220.
339 **"But the driving force"** Thomas L. Connelly, *The Marble Man, Robert E. Lee and His Image in American Society* (New York, 1977), 51.
339 **"perchance changing the course"** Benjamin Franklin Cooling III, *Jubal Early, Robert E. Lee's "Bad Old Man"* (New York: Rowman & Littlefield Publishers, 2014), xi.
340 **"quick and generally sound tactician"** Ibid., 161.
341 **Early and Ewell called off the attack** For varied accounts of this disputed action, see Shelby Foote, *The Civil War: A Narrative* (New York: Random House, 1986), 2, 475–481; Cooling, *Jubal Early*, 38–42; Charles C. Osborne, *Jubal: The Life and Times of General Jubal A. Early, CSA* (Chapel Hill, NC: Algonquin Books, 1992); Harry W. Pfanz, *Gettysburg: The Second Day* (Chapel Hill, NC: The University of North Carolina Press, 1987). As late as July 2, 2013, *The New York Times* was still reporting on the blame placed on Ewell and Early for what turned out to be a mistake that could have changed the outcome of Gettysburg; see Terry L. Jones, "General Ewell's Dilemma." The ensuing slanging match between Early and General James Longstreet would become a main theme of Lost Cause historiography. To escape blame, Early said Longstreet disobeyed an order by Lee to attack the same ground at daylight the next day. Pfanz concluded that Early's claim that Lee gave such a "sunrise order" was "nonsense."
343 **"This brought up"** Foote, *The Civil War*, 456–457.
343 **"Informed of what"** Ibid., 458–459.
344 **"Early's march"** Bruce Catton and James M. McPherson, *American Heritage History of the Civil War* (Rockville, MD: American Heritage Publishing, 2016), 104.
346 **Despite Lee's kindness** For the full text of Lee's sugar-coated letter of dismissal, see Osborne, *Jubal*, 391–392.

Chapter 30: Hail Columbia

347 **"the ultimate accolade for an American"** "The Original Hall of Fame," *American Heritage* 52, no. 5 (July–August 2001).
348 **Young Willie Dunning** James S. Humphreys, "William Archibald Dunning: Flawed Colossus of American Letters," in *The Dunning School: Historians, Race, and the Meaning of Reconstruction*, edited by John David Smith and J. Vincent Lowery (Lexington, KY: University Press of Kentucky, 2013), 77–106. I have drawn on Humphreys's account of Dunning's career and influence, as well as the correspondence among Dunning, Thomas McAdory Owen, and Walter L. Fleming.
349 **James Ford Rhodes** Smith and Lowery, eds., *The Dunning School*, 15–20; Rich-

ard Nelson Current, *Arguing with Historians: Essays on the Historical and the Unhistorical* (Middletown, CT: Wesleyan University Press, 1987), 79, 84, 101; William Holmes Stephenson, *The South Lives in History: Southern Historians and Their Legacy* (Baton Rouge, LA: Louisiana State University Press, 1955), 11, 59, 120.

350 **"open[ing] the door of"** David W. Blight, *Race and Reunion: The Civil War in American Memory* (Cambridge, MA: Belknap Press, 2001), 358.

350 **John W. Burgess** Shepherd W. McKinley, "John W. Burgess, Godfather of the Dunning School," in Smith and Lowery, eds., *The Dunning School*, 49–76.

352 **"It is a peculiarity of the historical profession"** Eric Foner, "Foreword," in Smith and Lowery, eds., *The Dunning School*.

353 **My discovery in 2018** Thomas McAdory Owen to William Archibald Dunning, November 4, 1901; Walter L. Fleming to Thomas McAdory Owen, Dec. 1, 1902, and March 12, 13, 1903, Alabama Department of Archives and History. Fleming attests to the closeness of the three men in his letter to Owen. "Professor Dunning has just told me that the Council has decided to take the American Historical Assn. [convention] South in 1903 to Nashville or New Orleans." He added, "Professor Dunning has worked hard for it to go South and told me to tell you that they would expect you to stir up Alabama" for support.

354 **"civil religion"** Charles Reagan Wilson, ed., *The New Encyclopedia of Southern Culture: Myth, Manners, and Memory*, Volume 4 (Chapel Hill, NC: The University of North Carolina Press, 2006), 161.

357 **"Montgomery's Guests"** "Montgomery's Guests / Party of Historians En Route to New Orleans / Mr. Owen and Local Committee Showed Them over Capitol," *Montgomery Advertiser*, December 29, 1903.

358 **Self-congratulatory letters** Wendell Holmes Stephenson, *Southern History in the Making: Pioneer Historians of the South* (Baton Rouge, LA: Louisiana State University Press, 1964). The passengers on the special train from New York included the last of the great amateur historians of southern history, James Ford Rhodes, who wrote Owen that "the History and Economic people have not yet got over talking of your speech in the moonlight on the Capitol" (Rhodes to Owen, March 10, 1904, Owen Papers). The scene worked its magic on Dunning's Columbia colleague George L. Beer, who wrote Owen that "we shall not soon, believe me, forget that moonlight night in Montgomery and the guide who made the noble old city's past so charmingly alive for us" (Beer to Owen, February 20, 1904, Owen Papers). Dunning also wrote his congratulations to Owen on March 9 and 20, and Owen responded with two letters in the same period (Owen Papers). The letters attest that the formidable team of Tom and Marie had succeeded in their plans to cast a Confederate spell over the Yankee scholars.

359 **"Scarcely any states"** Stephenson, *Southern History in the Making*, 214.

360 **"I am very sorry"** Thomas McAdory Owen to Walter L. Fleming, January 3, 1905, Alabama Department of Archives and History.

360 **"Hamilton delivered a lecture"** Stephenson, *Southern History in the Making*, 144.

Chapter 31: Tom and Marie

362 **an aspiring historian named Allen Jones** Author interview with Allen W. Jones, April 16, 2020.

364 **Edwin C. Bridges** Edwin C. Bridges email to author, December 21, 2021.

365 **Thomas Owen had been respected** Wendell Holmes Stephenson, *Southern History in the Making: Pioneer Historians of the South* (Baton Rouge, LA: Louisiana State University Press, 1964), 205–216.

365 **"a veritable attic"** Virginia Van der Veer Hamilton, *Alabama: A History* (New York: W. W. Norton & Company, 1977), 125.

365 **Brookings Institution** Kari Frederickson, *Deep South Dynasty: The Bankheads of Alabama* (Tuscaloosa, AL: The University of Alabama Press, 2022), 213.

365 **Daniel Eric Cone has described** Daniel Eric Cone, "The Cause Archived: Thomas Owen, the Alabama Archives and the Shaping of Civil War History and Memory," PhD dissertation, Auburn University, August 8, 2020, 3–7.

367 **"In the past several"** Cone, "The Cause Archived," 7.

367 **"speak in defense"** Ibid., 5.

370 **"a particular historical narrative that romanticized"** Frederickson, *Deep South Dynasty*, 3.

371 **"I hope that I conducted myself as a lady"** Frederickson, *Deep South Dynasty*, 213.

371 **"did not have the money"** Ibid., 257.

371 **"two of the best reasons"** Emily S. Adams, "Memorial to a Timeless Man," *Alabama Historical Quarterly*, Spring–Summer 1982, 11.

372 **Hopkins changed his tune** Author's interview with Steve Murray, executive director of the Alabama Department of Archives and History, 2022.

373 **The point here is not that Marie Bankhead Owen had sharp elbows** Hardy Jackson, *The WPA Guide to 1930s Alabama* (Tuscaloosa, 2000).

373 **"I very quickly got the impression"** Author's interview with Donald Dodd.

377 **Updating her late husband's multivolume history** Marie Bankhead Owen, *History of Alabama and Dictionary of Alabama Biography*, Volume 1 (New York: 1949), 520–521; for statement of her devotion to white supremacy, see Owen, *History of Alabama*, Volume 2, 361.

Chapter 32: Smoking Letters

380 **"I am the author"** Marie Bankhead Owen to James E. Folsom, "ADAH Administrative Files, 1837–2020," Marie Bankhead Owen Correspondence, Alabama Department of Archives and History, Montgomery, AL, February 3, 1947.

381 **"There were large numbers"** Marie Bankhead Owen and Walter M. Jackson, *History of Alabama for Junior High Schools* (Montgomery, AL: Dixie Book Company, Inc., 1938), 83, 90, 99. This taxpayer-financed textbook used much of the same material as her other books but gave only four sentences to the Union and did not mention the Alabamians in blue who fought against the Confederacy.

386 **could Gooder Walker be** John Bennett Weaver, *A Brief History of Winston County, Alabama,* Winston County, Alabama: An Historical Online Database, http://www.freestateofwinston.org/abriefhistory.htm.

387 **the "Auburn Oasis"** Wendell Holmes Stephenson, *Southern History in the Making: Pioneer Historians of the South* (Baton Rouge, LA: Louisiana State University Press, 1964), 132–143.

388 **The lack of follow-up on Thomas H. Lay** Glenda McWhirter Todd, *First Alabama Cavalry, U.S.A.: Homage to Patriotism* (Westminster, MD: Heritage Books, 2006), 281.

Chapter 33: A Scholarly Lynching

392 **Du Bois was the first African American** David Levering Lewis, *W. E. B. Du Bois: Biography of a Race, 1868–1919* (New York: Owl Books, 1993), 384–385. Lewis not only wrote the essential biography of Du Bois, but he offers one of the few accounts that notes the dramatic tension of the scene involving four titans of the history profession at this crossroads moment: Dunning, Du Bois, Ulrich B. Phillips, and Albert Bushnell Hart. See also Tommy Song, "William Archibald Dunning: Father of Historiographic Racism Columbia's Legacy of Academic Jim Crow," paper prepared for the class "Columbia University & Slavery," Columbia University, 2017, https://columbiaandslavery.columbia.edu/content/dam/cuandslavery/seminars/hist-3518/2017-projects/Song%202017%20-%20 William%20Archibald%20Dunning.pdf. He cut to the heart of Dunning's rope-a-dope tactic, writing: "Dunning praised Du Bois' work, but his praise was aimed at the text; the humanity of Du Bois was never admitted, rather, Dunning was probably surprised by the scholastic capabilities of the black man standing before him" (23).

396 **"all its brilliance and methodological"** John David Smith, "Introduction," in *The Dunning School: Historians, Race, and the Meaning of Reconstruction*, edited by John David Smith and J. Vincent Lowery (Lexington, KY: University Press of Kentucky, 2013), 33.

398 **"American history"** "Talk of Negroes," *New-York Tribune*, December 31, 1909.

398 **"Hart, who directed Du Bois's"** John David Smith, *Slavery, Race, and American History: Historical Conflict, Trends, and Method, 1866–1953* (London: Routledge, 2015), 26–27.

Chapter 34: Birmingham Money: The Houses of Chisholm and Percy

402 **For my purposes, the many biographers of the accomplished Percy family** I am indebted to Bertram Wyatt-Brown's *The House of Percy: Honor, Melancholy, and Imagination in a Southern Family* (New York: Oxford University Press, 1994) for the framing chronology in this chapter. As for the Alabama ethos in the Percy narrative, nobody captured it better than Walker Percy in *The Last Gentleman* and nobody evaded it more artfully than William Alexander Percy in *Lanterns on the Levee: Recollections of a Planter's Son* (New York: Alfred A. Knopf, 1941).

404 **Initially, the Zone of Exemption from blame** I was influenced through an early reading of Robert Penn Warren's *All the King's Men* (New York: Grosset & Dunlap, 1946) by the artistry with which he used capitalized phrases to capture essential qualities of the southern experience in particular and the human condition in general. My three usages in this book—the Alabama Inferiority Syndrome, the Lost Cause Highway, and the Zone of Exemption—are my attempt to capture what I've learned of my native ground through lived experience and journalistic effort. They are intended as an homage to the author of an enduring masterpiece about the populist impulse that has touched every generation of my family. For an extended discussion of *All the King's Men* as the quintessential southern political novel, see my essay in *A New Literary History of America*, edited by Greil Marcus and Werner Sollors (Cambridge, MA: The Belknap Press, 2009), 677–682.

405 **mighty Tennessee Coal, Iron and Railroad Company** For an analysis of this paradigmatic display of robber baron capitalism and corporate colonialism in

the New South, see Jeanne Strouse, *Morgan: American Financier* (New York: Random House, 1999), 582–93.

412 **"He belonged to the class"** Jay Tolson, *Pilgrim in the Ruins: A Life of Walker Percy* (Chapel Hill, 1992), 29.

416 **"Foote's retroactive allegiance"** Tony Horwitz, *Confederates in the Attic: Dispatches from the Unfinished War* (New York: Pantheon Books, 1998), 150.

417 **"I am obligated"** Shelby Foote, *The Civil War: A Narrative* (New York: Random House, 1986), 971.

418 **"What has dismayed me so much"** Horwitz, *Confederates in the Attic*, 152. Foote's dialogue with Horwitz showed that southern intellectuals can be quite canny about what prejudices they cling to despite knowing better. Compare this comment with Foote assuring Horwitz that Greenville was "an oasis of tolerance." For another perspective, see Jon Meacham, ed., *American Homer: Reflections on Shelby Foote and His Classic "The Civil War: A Narrative"* (New York: Modern Library, 2011), 7: "Foote was no liberal on issues of race, but he was more fair-minded than many of his contemporaries in the South."

Chapter 35: Three Kingdoms

420 **"I don't know how to explain it"** C. Stuart Chapman, *Shelby Foote: A Writer's Life* (Jackson, MS: University Press of Mississippi, 2003), 36.

421 **"Dionysian abandon"** William Alexander Percy, *Lanterns on the Levee: Recollections of a Planter's Son* (New York: Alfred A. Knopf, 1941), 100.

421 **"godfather"** https://wapercyfoundation.org/?page_id=28.

422 **For Will Percy** This overview of Percy's life draws on these formidable books: Benjamin E. Wise, *William Alexander Percy: The Curious Life of a Mississippi Planter and a Sexual Freethinker* (Chapel Hill, NC: The University of North Carolina Press, 2012); Bertram Wyatt-Brown, *The House of Percy: Honor, Melancholy, and Imagination in a Southern Family* (New York: Oxford University Press, 1994); John M. Barry, *Rising Tide: The Great Mississippi Flood of 1927 and How It Changed America* (New York: Simon & Schuster, 1997); J. Mills Thornton, *Politics and Power in a Slave Society: Alabama, 1800–1860* (Baton Rouge, LA: Louisiana State University Press, 1978).

422 **his classmate John Williams Walker** Hugh C. Bailey, *John Williams Walker: A Study in the Political, Social, and Cultural Life of the Old Southwest* (Tuscaloosa, AL: The University of Alabama Press, 1964), 62–64.

423 **"I may seem"** Percy, *Lanterns on the Levee*, 16.

424 **"But the basic fiber"** Ibid., 19.

424 **"I know they are responsible"** Ibid., 20.

425 **"The Union of the DeBardeleben and Percy Families"** Patrick J. Samway, *The Mississippi Quarterly* 51, no. 1 (Winter 1997–98), 22–23.

427 **"His guests were Deltan"** Walker Percy, *The Last Gentleman* (New York: Farrar, Straus and Giroux, 1966), 265.

428 **"terrible and beautiful eyes"** Walker Percy, introduction to the reissue of Percy, *Lanterns on the Levee*, viii.

429 **[The Gray Eagle's] life work** Percy, *Lanterns on the Levee*, 273–274.

430 **Knopf had nursed** Wyatt-Brown, *The House of Percy*, 279–280, for Knopf's nurturing role with William Alexander Percy, and 321, 324 for his more ambivalent attitude toward Walker Percy and his novel *The Moviegoer*. See also Fred Hobson, *Mencken: A Life* (New York: Random House, 1994) for Knopf's interactions with H. L. Mencken and W. J. Cash, and Fred Hobson, *Tell About the*

South: The Southern Rage to Explain (Baton Rouge, LA: Louisiana State University Press, 1983) for the complicated interactions among Cash, Percy, and Mencken. See especially chapter 3, "Odum, Davidson, and the Sociological Proteus," 180–243, for the struggle between Vanderbilt and the University of North Carolina for academic dominance in the South, and chapter 4, "The Meaning of Aristocracy: Wilbur Cash and William Alexander Percy," 244–307, for the two authors' differing but not contradictory views of class divisions in the South. Although a populist with radical political sympathies, Cash rather passively accepted Percy's thesis that there was an aristocratic class that was naturally superior to the yeoman farmers who made up the Confederate army.

431 **As Percy grumbled** Percy, *Lanterns on the Levee,* 278–280.

431 **Huger Jervey** Wyatt-Brown, *The House of Percy,* 280.

431 **The long *New York Times* review** Herbert Brickell, *New York Times,* March 23, 1941, 5.

432 **Polk, an Episcopal bishop** Huston Horn, *Leonidas Polk: Warrior Bishop of the Confederacy* (Lawrence, KS: University Press of Kansas, 2019), 190ff.

433 **"It was a small college"** Percy, *Lanterns on the Levee,* 93.

434 **veered off a bridge** Wyatt-Brown, *The House of Percy,* 274.

434 **Robert Penn Warren** Author interview with Ken Burns.

435 **"He said in his wonderful"** Peter Tonguette, "With *The Civil War,* Ken Burns Reinvented the Television History Documentary and Captivated Millions of Americans. Here's How He Did It," *Humanities* 36, no. 5 (September/October 2015), https://www.neh.gov/humanities/2015/septemberoctober/feature/the-civil-war-ken-burns-reinvented-the-television-history-d.

Chapter 36: The Mountain King

437 **"Reading Fleming today provides a cold bath"** Michael W. Fitzgerald, *Reconstruction in Alabama: From Civil War to Redemption in the Cotton South* (Baton Rouge, LA: Louisiana State University Press, 2017), 1; see also 2 for an explanation of why a flawed reference work persists in footnotes. "Fleming's book remains a 'starting point' for scholars, despite its dated premises and factual inaccuracies." He also noted that the scope of Fleming's book deterred competitors. "One objective of this study is simply to rectify that, to provide a reliable modern account." In his Notes, Fitzgerald notes ruefully that Fleming's work was "'often labeled one of the best' of the Dunning studies," 304. Fitzgerald also observes that Fleming's work continued to be cited after scholars understood the limitations of his views, 1.

438 **"Fleming had the courage"** Sarah Woolfolk Wiggins, *The Scalawag in Alabama Politics, 1865–1881* (Tuscaloosa, AL: The University of Alabama Press, 1977).

438 **When I survey Fleming's record** I am indebted to Fred L. Hobson of the University of North Carolina for his penetrating research on the importance of the Nashville Agrarians and Chapel Hill Regionalists as scholarly power centers for, respectively, traditional and progressive academic approaches to the South's history and economic problems. See Fred Hobson, *Serpent in Eden: H. L. Mencken and the South* (Chapel Hill, NC: University of North Carolina Press, 1974), 174–179, 215. See also Hobson's introduction to *South-Watching: Selected Essays by Gerald W. Johnson* (Chapel Hill, NC: University of North Carolina Press, 1983). I have also drawn on Hobson, *Mencken: A Life* (New York: Ran-

dom House, 1994) and Richard H. King, *A Southern Renaissance: The Cultural Awakening of the American South, 1930–1955* (New York: Oxford University Press, 1980) in assessing the impact of these educators and their institutions.

438 **"pure propaganda"** John David Smith and J. Vincent Lowery, eds., *The Dunning School: Historians, Race, and the Meaning of Reconstruction* (Lexington, KY: University Press of Kentucky, 2013), 35.

440 **"Fleming's book"** Fitzgerald, *Reconstruction in Alabama*, 2.

440 **"established [Fleming] as"** Ibid., 1.

440 **"For some seventy-five years"** Tennant McWilliams, interview with author, fall 2018.

440 **"the steel frame"** Michael W. Fitzgerald, "The Steel Frame of Walter Lynwood Fleming," in Smith and Lowery, eds., *The Dunning School*, 157–177.

442 **"There is a Jap"** Smith and Lowery, eds., *The Dunning School*, 22–23.

443 **"considered Reconstruction"** Ibid., 23.

445 **A footnote in Owen's biography** Wendell Holmes Stephenson, *Southern History in the Making: Pioneer Historians of the South* (Baton Rouge, LA: Louisiana State University Press, 1964), 212.

445 **"Seminar discussions"** Smith and Lowery, eds., *The Dunning School*, 159.

Chapter 37: Last Answer, Last Question

449 **"Sheats is living in Decatur"** Owen to Fleming, Owen papers, ADAH.

451 **"was one time slated"** *Decatur Weekly News,* August 31, 1900.

451 **"the last of the Confederate brigadiers"** Ezra J. Warner, *Generals in Gray: Lives of the Confederate Commanders* (Baton Rouge, LA: Louisiana State University Press, 1959), 239.

451 **"the pension list"** *Moulton Advertiser,* March 27, 1902.

453 **Caroline Randall Williams** Caroline Randall Williams, "You Want a Confederate Monument? My Body Is a Confederate Monument," *New York Times,* June 26, 2020.

453 **"the black people I come from"** Williams, "You Want a Confederate Monument?" June 26, 2020.

453 **"We name things after"** Caroline Randall Williams, "Descendant of Edmund Pettus: Rename the Bridge and Then 'We Get to Work,'" *The Last Word with Lawrence O'Donnell,* MSNBC, July 20, 2020, YouTube clip, https://www.youtube.com/watch?v=_9h8-CSIfDI.

Chapter 38: The Cutting Room Floor

454 **The usually ebullient Ken Burns** Author conversation with Ken Burns, August 19, 2019. The following comments on his Civil War documentary are from Jon Meacham, ed., *American Homer: Reflections on Shelby Foote and His Classic "The Civil War: A Narrative"* (New York: Random House, 2011), 12.

454 **"He was oral bourbon"** Jay Tolson, "Art, War, and Shelby Foote," in *American Homer*, 14.

454 **"unfettered by any need"** Michael Beschloss, "Foote and Lincoln," in *American Homer*, 12.

454 **Burns felt he had been falsely accused** Author telephone interview with Ken Burns, August 19, 2019; Burns to Raines email, January 4, 2023.

455 **"No, and I would have put it in"** Ibid., Burns to author email, January 4, 2023.

455 **"For heaven's sake"** Author interview with Ric Burns, December 15, 2020.

455 **"Just pure ignorance"** Author interview with Geoffrey C. Ward, December 15, 2020.

455 **Jon Meacham** Author interview with Jon Meacham, April 15, 2021.

456 **"was more Trollope than Lost Cause"** Ibid.

457 **"a white Southern readership"** Meacham, ed., *American Homer,* 57.

458 **"most iconic"** Meacham, ed., *American Homer,* 9.

458 **"bardic figure"** Tolson in *American Homer,* 14.

458 **Burns's most eminent ally** Author interview with Ken Burns, August 19, 2019. I also benefited from Eric Foner's account of the meeting.

458 **"Faced with a choice"** Eric Foner, "Ken Burns and the Romance of Reunion," in Robert Brent Toplin, ed., *Ken Burns's The Civil War: Historians Respond* (New York: Oxford University Press, 1996), 112.

458 **"Thanks a Lot, Ken Burns"** James M. Lundberg, "Thanks a Lot, Ken Burns," *Slate,* January 7, 2011, https://slate.com/culture/2011/06/ken-burns-civil-war-how-the-documentary-changed-the-way-we-think-about-the-war.html.

459 **But that was mild** Gillian Brockell, "Re-watching 'The Civil War' During the Breonna Taylor and George Floyd Protests," *Washington Post,* September 26, 2020.

459 **"You really get the feeling"** Ibid.

459 **"Seeing Shelby on that program"** Author interview with Meacham, April 15, 2021.

459 **"Foote's admiration (love?)"** Annette Gordon-Reed, "History and Memory: A Critique of the Foote Vision," in *American Homer,* 64.

460 **"Bedford Forrest's granddaughter"** *The Civil War,* episode 7, "Most Hallowed Ground: 1874," directed by Ken Burns, aired September 26, 1990.

460 **They appeared together** Eve Zibart, "The South Will Write Again," *Washington Post,* November 4, 1990.

461 **"the Percy salon"** Meacham, "An American Master," in *American Homer,* 5.

461 **Provocatively, Andrew Lytle was one of the few** For Dodd, see *Winston,* 52, 100.

461 **"Far to the south"** Andrew Lytle, *The Long Night* (Tuscaloosa, AL: The University of Alabama Press, 1988), 331. See the introduction by Frank Lawrence Owsley about how Andrew Lytle acquired the Winston County story from his father. For a brief appraisal by University of North Carolina professor George Brown Tindall, see https://www.goodreads.com/book/show/354819.

461 **Although Lytle always presented himself** Andrew Nelson Lytle, *A Wake for the Living* (Nashville, TN: J. S. Sanders & Company, 1975), 259.

461 **"I named the place Cornsilk"** Ibid., 259.

462 **The provenance of *The Long Night*** Frank L. Owsley Jr., introduction to the University of Alabama Press reissue of *The Long Night,* 2–8. Auburn University historian Frank L. Owsley Jr., whose father endowed the University of Alabama history department with Lost Cause principles, included a letter of historiographic significance that his father received from Lytle in August 1936. It proves that Winston County folklore had penetrated the Vanderbilt/Sewanee Axis, reaching two of the most prominent followers of Dunning School thought, without generating any scholarly activity.

462 **"The purpose of my life"** Carroll Van West, ed., "Frank Lawrence Owsley," in *Tennessee Encyclopedia of History and Culture* (Nashville, TN: Rutledge Hill Press, 1998), 717.

463 **the essence of Winston exceptionalism** Lytle, *The Long Night,* 15–17.

463 **Instead I found a "smoking book"** John Carr, ed., *Kite-Flying and Other Irrational Acts: Conversations with Twelve Southern Writers* (Baton Rouge, LA: Louisiana State University Press, 1972), 16.

465 **The Black soldiers disrupted his hero's pursuit** Christopher M. Rein, *Alabamians in Blue: Freedmen, Unionists, and the Civil War in the Cotton State* (Baton Rouge, LA: Louisiana State University Press, 2019), 151.

465 **"interpersonal connectivity"** Tennant McWilliams interview with author, fall 2018.

466 **"told friends he would"** Jay Tolson, "Art, War, and Shelby Foote," in *American Homer*, 14.

466 **"As far as my Civil War is concerned"** William Thomas, "Shelby Foote's Love Affair with Civil War Began in '54," *Memphis Commercial Appeal*, July 15, 1973, in William C. Carter, ed., *Conversations with Shelby Foote* (Jackson, MS: University Press of Mississippi, 1989), 110. In this 1973 interview with his hometown newspaper, he attributed his Rebel tilt to "a certain sympathy for the underdog," but he never tired of casting doubt on those enduring underdogs, "the Piedmont or mountain people" who tilted the other way. He ignored the political science aspect of their doubts about the Confederacy. They believed in the Jacksonian principle of preserving an indissoluble Union whatever the future of slavery, and while most were not abolitionists, they were not devoted to the continuation of the "peculiar institution." He repeatedly attributed their opposition to the Confederacy to their backcountry cussedness. Even in the interview where he acknowledged the existence of Alabama Unionism, he held up the less important Unionist strain in Mississippi as an example of Scotch-Irish stubbornness rather than principle: "They were not going to let the state of Mississippi carry them into something they had no interest in." He didn't tell Burns about the South's Union soldiers because he didn't respect or understand them. As a result, he underestimated their role as harbingers of that collapse of Confederate nationalism now widely accepted by professional historians as the root cause of the insurrection's failure.

467 **"In most of history"** Ken Burns, interview with author.

Chapter 39: Forgotten, but Not Gone

468 **"the sea"** Ed Bridges email to the author, December 21, 2021.

472 **Dr. Ainsworth B. Spofford** Wendell Holmes Stephenson, *Southern History in the Making: Pioneer Historians of the South* (Baton Rouge, LA: Louisiana State University Press, 1964), 206.

INDEX

ABOUT THE AUTHOR

Howell Raines is a Pulitzer Prize–winning journalist and former executive editor of *The New York Times*. He is the author of four previous books: *Whiskey Man, The One That Got Away, Fly Fishing Through the Midlife Crisis,* and *My Soul Is Rested.* Based in Pennsylvania, he was born and began his career in Alabama.

ABOUT THE TYPE

This book was set in Bulmer, a typeface designed in the late eighteenth century by the London type cutter William Martin (1757–1830). The typeface was created especially for the Shakespeare Press, directed by William Bulmer (1757–1830)—hence the font's name. Bulmer is considered to be a transitional typeface, containing characteristics of old-style and modern designs. It is recognized for its elegantly proportioned letters, with their long ascenders and descenders.